The New International Commentary
on the
Old Testament

General Editors

R. K. HARRISON
(1968–1993)

ROBERT L. HUBBARD, JR.
(1994–   )

The Book of
JUDGES

BARRY G. WEBB

WILLIAM B. EERDMANS PUBLISHING COMPANY
GRAND RAPIDS, MICHIGAN / CAMBRIDGE, U.K.

Published 2012 by
Wm. B. Eerdmans Publishing Co.
2140 Oak Industrial Drive N.E., Grand Rapids, Michigan 49505 /
P.O. Box 163, Cambridge CB3 9PU U.K.

Printed in the United States of America

18 17 16 15 14 13 12   7 6 5 4 3 2 1

Library of Congress Cataloging-in-Publication Data

Webb, Barry G.
The Book of Judges / Barry G. Webb.
pages   cm   — (The New international commentary on the Old Testament)
Includes bibliographical references and index.
ISBN 978-0-8028-2628-2 (cloth: alk. paper)
1. Bible. O.T. Judges — Commentaries.   I. Title.

BS1305.53.W43   2012
222′.3207 — dc23

2012018250

www.eerdmans.com

To my mother, Gladys Webb,
who passed away on 29 July 2009,
soon after her 100th birthday

CONTENTS

GENERAL EDITOR'S PREFACE

Long ago St. Paul wrote: "I planted, Apollos watered, but God gave the growth" (1 Cor. 3:6 NRSV). He was right: ministry indeed requires a team effort — the collective labors of many skilled hands and minds. Someone digs up the dirt and drops in seed, while others water the ground to nourish seedlings to growth. The same team effort over time has brought this commentary series to its position of prominence today. Professor E. J. Young "planted" it forty years ago, enlisting its first contributors and himself writing its first published volume. Professor R. K. Harrison "watered" it, signing on other scholars and wisely editing everyone's finished products. As General Editor, I now tend their planting, and, true to Paul's words, through four decades God has indeed graciously "[given] the growth."

Today the New International Commentary on the Old Testament enjoys a wide readership of scholars, priests, pastors, rabbis, and other serious Bible students. Thousands of readers across the religious spectrum and in countless countries consult its volumes in their ongoing preaching, teaching, and research. They warmly welcome the publication of each new volume and eagerly await its eventual transformation from an emerging "series" into a complete commentary "set." But as humanity experiences a new century of history, an era commonly called "postmodern," what kind of commentary series is NICOT? What distinguishes it from other similarly well-established series?

Its volumes aim to publish biblical scholarship of the highest quality. Each contributor writes as an expert, both in the biblical text itself and in the relevant scholarly literature, and each commentary conveys the results of wide reading and careful, mature reflection. Ultimately, its spirit is eclectic, each contributor gleaning interpretive insights from any useful source, whatever its religious or philosophical viewpoint, and integrating them into his or her interpretation of a biblical book. The series draws on recent methodological innovations in biblical scholarship, for example, canon criticism, the so-called "new literary criticism," reader-response theories, and sensitivity to gender-based and ethnic readings. NICOT volumes also aim to be irenic in tone, summarizing and critiquing influential views with fairness while defending their own. Its list of contributors includes male and female scholars from a number of Christian faith-groups. The diversity of contributors and their freedom to draw on all relevant methodologies give the entire series an exciting and enriching variety.

What truly distinguishes this series, however, is that it speaks from within that interpretive tradition known as evangelicalism. Evangelicalism is an informal movement within Protestantism that cuts across traditional denominational lines. Its heart and soul is the conviction that the Bible is God's inspired Word, written by gifted human writers, through which God calls humanity to enjoy a loving personal relationship with its Creator and Savior. True to that tradition, NICOT volumes do not treat the Old Testament as just an ancient literary artifact on a par with the *Iliad* or *Gilgamesh*. They are not literary autopsies of ancient parchment cadavers but rigorous, reverent wrestlings with wonderfully human writings through which the living God speaks his powerful Word. NICOT delicately balances "criticism" (i.e., the use of standard critical methodologies) with humble respect, admiration, and even affection for the biblical text. As an evangelical commentary, it pays particular attention to the text's literary features, theological themes, and implications for the life of faith today.

Ultimately, NICOT aims to serve women and men of faith who desire to hear God's voice afresh through the Old Testament. With gratitude to God for two marvelous gifts — the Scriptures themselves and keen-minded scholars to explain their message — I welcome readers of all kinds to savor the good fruit of this series.

ROBERT L. HUBBARD JR.

AUTHOR'S PREFACE

Commentaries are generally judged good or bad according to what the reader expects of them. I hope this one will satisfy those who want the meatiness and analytical character normally expected of a commentary that includes an original translation and notes. But I have chosen to write it in an emotionally warm, rather than cool, detached, academic way, partly because that is my natural writing style, partly because I think it is what is needed to engage properly with a dynamic, narrative work like the book of Judges, and partly because I think it is what people who buy and read NICOT commentaries will most want and appreciate. I have always felt cheated by the kind of exegetical vivisection that kills by analysis until all that's left is lifeless bits and pieces, classified and arranged, conquered rather than read. For me the text is a living thing, whose life has to be respected if it is to be understood.

In keeping with this general approach, I have not tried to achieve the kind of exhaustive thoroughness that insists on putting back into the text all the data that the author has left out. There is a perverseness about this that is not only pedantic but damaging, especially when it obscures the light and shade of the text, and its background and foreground distinctions, as though they don't matter. There is a proper place for background, of course, especially in an ancient work like Judges, where the original readers presumably had a knowledge of it that cannot be assumed for modern readers. No text exists in a vacuum, and the historical setting is often important for understanding. Nevertheless, the commentator, like the original author, must be selective and not try to say everything, even if this were possible. What I have tried to do in what follows, especially in the body of the commentary, is to concentrate on what the text itself throws into prominence, and give space to background issues only where I think they throw significant light on the foreground. Of course this has required judgments to be made which I am sure I have not always gotten right. But that is where footnotes prove useful; they provide a convenient middle ground between inclusion and exclusion, where those who want more may hopefully find it, or at least be pointed in the right direction. All translations from the Hebrew are my own, unless otherwise identified.

My labors on Judges began a long time ago. I spent most of 1982-84 in Sheffield, England, working on it for my Ph.D., which was published as a monograph in 1987 and again in 2008. Those familiar with it will recognize the echoes of it here. But they will also find much that is new. In particular, large parts of Judges that were treated only in summary fashion in the monograph have been treated here with the kind of even-handed thoroughness required for a commentary. New material has been added, and old material reworked in the light of new research that has been done since the 1980s. The result is a new and different kind of work. I have had to start again, even if building on old, proven foundations.

The commentary itself has been in the making, off and on, for twelve years. I am grateful to Eerdmans for giving me the time I needed, and trusting me to finally produce what I promised them. Thanks are also due to the Governing Board of Moore College, Sydney, for their generous provision of study leave, and to the Warden and staff of Tyndale House, Cambridge, where much of the research and writing was done. Like all commentary writers, I have benefited enormously from the labors and hard-won insights of a host of other scholars and students, some of whom I have met and been able to thank personally, but most of whom I have not. I am indebted to them all, and have hopefully acknowledged them appropriately in the bibliography and footnotes.

Alison, my wife now for forty years, has shared my excitement when I have made discoveries, and patiently endured many mealtimes when I have been brooding over knotty problems instead of talking to her. I know she forgives me, but want her to know that I do not take her love for granted.

Judges is not a nice book. It's rough and raw and confronting. Working on it has been like living with someone who always tells you the truth: it is good for you, but not pleasant. In this commentary I have tried to let Judges be what it is instead of taming it. Readers will have to judge whether or not I've succeeded.

I am an evangelical Christian, and have tried to put whatever scholarly abilities I have at God's disposal. I trust this commentary will serve, in some way, his purposes for his church and his world.

BARRY G. WEBB

PRINCIPAL ABBREVIATIONS

ABD	*Anchor Bible Dictionary,* ed. D. N. Freedman
ABR	*Australian Biblical Review*
ABRL	Anchor Bible Reference Library
ANET	*Ancient Near Eastern Texts Relating to the Old Testament, Third Edition,* ed. J. B. Pritchard
ARM	Archives royales de Mari
AV	The Authorised (King James) Version
BAR	*Biblical Archaeology Review*
BASOR	*Bulletin of the American Schools of Oriental Research*
BBB	Bonner Biblische Beiträge
BBC	*The IVP Bible Background Commentary: Old Testament,* ed. J. H. Walton, Victor H. Matthews, and Mark W. Chavalas
BDB	*A Hebrew and English Lexicon of the Old Testament,* F. Brown, S. R. Driver, and C. A. Briggs
BHS	*Biblia Hebraica Stuttgartensia*
BJRL	*Bulletin of the John Rylands Library*
BO	Berit Olam commentary series
CBQ	*Catholic Biblical Quarterly*
DCH	*Dictionary of Classical Hebrew,* ed. D. J. A. Clines
edd.	Editions
ESV	The English Standard Version
ET	*The Expository Times*
FBCS	Focus on the Bible Commentary Series
FRLANT	Forschungen zur Religion und Literatur des Alten und Neuen Testaments
GKC	*Genesius' Hebrew Grammar,* ed. E. Kautzsch, tr. A. E. Cowley
HALOT	*The Hebrew and Aramaic Lexicon of the Old Testament,*

	Study Edition, ed. L. Koehler, W. Baumgartner, and J. J. Stamm, tr. M. E. J. Richardson
HCSB	Holman Christian Standard Bible
HSM	Harvard Semitic Monographs
HThKAT	Herders Theologischer Kommentar zum Alten Testament
HUCA	*Hebrew Union College Annual*
IDB	*Interpreter's Dictionary of the Bible,* ed. G. A. Buttrick
ISBE	*The International Standard Bible Encyclopedia, Revised Edition,* ed. G. W. Bromiley
JB	Jerusalem Bible (1966)
JBL	*Journal of Biblical Literature*
JETS	*Journal of the Evangelical Theological Society*
JNES	*Journal of Near Eastern Studies*
JPSA	Jewish Publication Society of America
JPSV	Jewish Publication Society Version (1917)
JSOT	*Journal for the Study of the Old Testament*
JSOTSup	JSOT Supplement
JTS	*Journal of Theological Studies*
JTSNS	*Journal of Theological Studies, New Series*
JTSSup	JTS Supplement
KJV	King James Version
KTU	*Die Keilalphabetischen Texte aus Ugarit,* ed. M. Dietrich, O. Loretz, and J. Sanmartín
LCL	Loeb Classical Library
LXX	The Septuagint
MSS	manuscripts
MT	The Masoretic Text
NAC	The New American Commentary
NASB	The New American Standard Version
NBC	*New Bible Commentary, 21st Century Edition,* ed. D. A. Carson, R. T. France, J. A. Motyer, and G. J. Wenham
NBD	*New Bible Dictionary, Third Edition,* ed. D. R. W. Wood et al.
NCBC	New Cambridge Bible Commentary
NEB	New English Bible
NIDB	*The New International Dictionary of the Bible,* ed. J. D. Douglas and M. C. Tenney
NIV	New International Version
NIVAC	The NIV Application Commentary
NJB	New Jerusalem Bible (1985)
NJPS	New Jewish Publication Society Version (1985)
NRSV	New Revised Standard Version

NSBT	New Studies in Biblical Theology
NT	New Testament
OBA	*The Oxford Bible Atlas, Fourth Edition,* ed. A. Curtis
OT	Old Testament
OTR	Old Testament Readings
PEQ	*Palestine Exploration Quarterly*
RSV	Revised Standard Version
RTR	*Reformed Theological Review*
TBT	*The Bible Translator*
TGUOS	*Transactions of the Glasgow University Oriental Society*
TNIV	Today's New International Version
TOTC	Tyndale Old Testament Commentaries
TynB	*Tyndale Bulletin*
VT	*Vetus Testamentum*
VTSSup	Vetus Testamentum Supplement
WBC	Word Biblical Commentary
WMANT	Wissenschaftliche Monographien zum Alten und Neuen Testament
WTJ	*Westminster Theological Journal*
ZAW	*Zeitschrift für die alttestamentliche Wissenschaft*
ZPEB	*Zondervan Pictorial Encyclopedia of the Bible,* ed. M. C. Tenney

INTRODUCTION

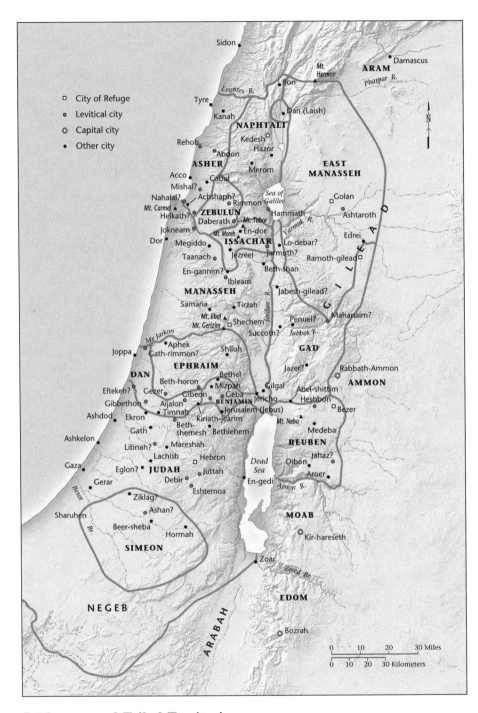

□ City of Refuge
◦ Levitical city
◎ Capital city
• Other city

Sidon

Damascus

ARAM

Mt. Hermon

Leontes R.

Ijon

Pharpar R.

Tyre

Dan (Laish)

Kanah

NAPHTALI

Rehob

Kedesh

Abdon

Hazor

ASHER

Merom

EAST MANASSEH

Acco

Cabul

Mishal?

Golan

Nahalal?

Achshaph?

Sea of Galilee

Ashtaroth

Mt. Carmel

Helkath?

ZEBULUN

Rimmon

Hammath

Daberath

Mt. Tabor

Jokneam

Mt. Moreh

En-dor

Yarmuk R.

Edrei

Dor

Megiddo

ISSACHAR

Lo-debar?

Taanach

Jezreel

Jarmuth?

Ramoth-gilead

En-gannim?

Beth-shan

Ibleam

Jabesh-gilead?

MANASSEH

Samaria

Tirzah

Penuel?

Mahanaim?

Mt. Ebal

Shechem

Mt. Gerizim

Succoth?

Jabbok R.

Me Jarkon

Aphek

Shiloh

GAD

Joppa

Gath-rimmon?

EPHRAIM

Bethel

Jazer?

Rabbath-Ammon

DAN

Beth-horon

Mizpah

Gilgal

Abel-shittim

AMMON

Eltekeh?

Gezer

Gibeon

Geba

Heshbon

Gibbethon

Aijalon

BENJAMIN

Jericho

Bezer

Ashdod

Ekron

Timnah

Jerusalem (Jebus)

Gath

Beth-shemesh

Kiriath-jearim

Mt. Nebo

Medeba

Ashkelon

Libnah?

Bethlehem

REUBEN

Lachish

Mareshah

Jahaz?

Gaza

Eglon?

JUDAH

Hebron

Dead Sea

Dibon

Gerar

Debir

Juttah

Aroer

Ziklag?

Eshtemoa

En-gedi

Arnon R.

Sharuhen

Ashan?

MOAB

Beer-sheba

Hormah

Kir-hareseth

SIMEON

Zoar

Zered Br.

Besor Br.

NEGEB

EDOM

ARABAH

Bozrah

0   10   20   30 Miles
0   10   20   30 Kilometers

GILEAD

Settlement and Tribal Territories

A commentary is a book about a book. But what is a book? The question is not as simple as it appears. There are so many different kinds of books that a generic definition is hard to produce, and to assign a different definition to each kind of book is pointless. Nevertheless, generic definitions abound, and fall into four basic categories. There are material definitions that identify a book in terms of its design and what it is made of. For example, a book is a number of leaves of paper or other material, joined down one side and bound between a front and back cover. There are functional definitions that take its material features as given and define it in terms of its purpose. In English this is normally done by prefixing a descriptive term, for example, "exercise book" (a book for doing schoolwork) or "accounts book" (a book for recording commercial transactions). Then there are definitions that identify a book by its contents, normally by a following descriptive phrase, for example, a book of stamps, vouchers, or tickets. Finally, there are literary definitions. These identify a book in terms of the genre of writing it contains: a comic book, an anthology (of poetry), or a novel. In this latter kind of definition the material properties of the thing in question become irrelevant, and we are approaching the definition of a book as a literary "work" of some kind, regardless of its material form. The Hebrew and Greek terms *sēper* and *biblos/ biblion* respectively, in both their biblical and extrabiblical usage, have a semantic range that can accommodate all these definitions.[1]

Historically, it is the material aspect of "book" that has been most changeable, and therefore least suitable as a basis for definition. The material definition above (leaves bound between covers) is technically the definition of a codex. But the codex is only one of many forms books have taken. Before the codex was the scroll, and before that there were writing boards and

---

1. Sometimes they occur with a qualifier indicating the *kind* of book or document in view, e.g., *mᵉgillat sēper, chartion bibliou* (a scroll, Jer. 36:2; Ezek. 2:9 MT and LXX).

tablets of various kinds. Before paper there were vellum, papyrus, wood, baked clay, and stone. Since the invention of movable type the form of books has remained fairly stable until quite recently, but as I write this commentary it is again undergoing radical change. New forms of books are appearing, especially virtual books of various kinds, including e-books, which tend to mimic the hard-copy form as far as possible, and online books that have never existed in anything but electronic form.

Through all these changes the notion of "book" in the literary sense has remained constant. A literary "work" is a text, a piece of writing, but it is distinguished from other pieces of writing by a number of qualities. First, its length: a book is more than a bill of sale, a list, or a brief inscription. Second, its completeness: it is not a piece of text whose length is determined by non-literary factors such as the size of a page or scroll, for example, but it has a deliberately constructed beginning and end. It is a crafted unit, or a major, clearly identifiable part of such a unit. Finally, it is distinguished by its artistic, literary quality. It is different in this respect from, say, a manual on how to operate a piece of mechanical equipment. It may surprise some readers to discover that in biblical studies scholars have not always credited Judges with being a book in this sense. The present commentary does do this, and seeks to respond to it with the kind of literary sensitivity that this requires — to serve rather than dominate it. In this sense the commentary, too, has been written as a literary work. To be sure, its literary quality will be more apparent in some parts than others; more in its treatment of the Judges narratives themselves than in the more technical parts of the introduction and footnotes. But hopefully these will not spoil the enjoyment of the reader or distract him or her from the literary quality of the book of Judges itself. Readers who do not find this material suitable to their tastes or relevant to their interests should happily ignore it.

I. JUDGES AS AN ISRAELITE CLASSIC

A. AN ANCIENT BOOK

Judges has been around for a very long time indeed. What we know as the book of Judges existed as part of the documented history of Israel from the early sixth century B.C., and the oldest material in it goes back, in oral or written form, almost to the time of the judges themselves. But attestation of it as a distinct literary unit, a "book" in its own right, begins with Philo in the first century A.D., who refers to it in this way in his treatise *On the Confusion of Tongues*. In his treatment of the tower of Babel story of Genesis 11 he compares God's scattering of the builders there to Gideon's punishment of the men of Penuel in Judges 8:8-17. Both stories involve a tower, and since for Philo they have the same allegorical significance, he can draw on the one to fill out his exposition of the other. He does this particularly with reference to the vain self-aggrandizement of the tower builders of Genesis 11:

> Having received from their father [Cain] self-love as their portion, his children desire to add to it and raise it heaven high, until Justice, who loves virtue and hates evil, comes to their aid. She razes to the ground the cities which they fortified to menace the unhappy soul, and the tower whose name is explained *in the book of Judges*. That name is in the Hebrew tongue Penuel, but in our own "turning from God." (*On the Confusion of Tongues* xxvi.128 [Colson and Whitaker, LCL; my italics])

The expression here translated *in the book of Judges* is *en tē tōn krimatōn anagraphomenē bibliō,* which, if rendered in more transparent fashion, would be "in the recorded book of *judgments.*" Philo distinguishes this from books he refers to elsewhere. For example, in his treatment of the expression "the sons of men" in Genesis 11:5, he refers to what is written *in the books of Kings:*

> I bow, too, in admiration before the mysteries revealed *in the books of Kings (en basilikais biblois)* where it does not offend us to find described as sons of God's psalmist David those who lived and flourished many generations afterwards (1 Kings xv.11; 2 Kings xviii.3), though in David's lifetime probably not even their great-grandparents had been born. (*On the Confusion of Tongues* xxix.148 [Colson and Whitaker, LCL; my italics])

The allusion, as indicated by the references in parentheses, is to the naming of David as the "father" of such worthies as Asa and Hezekiah. The method of citation used here (reference to a named book or books) is not typical of Philo's general practice.[2] His reference to the book containing the Penuel in-

---

2. In *Confusion of Tongues,* for example, the introductory quotation from Gen. 11:1-9 is introduced simply by *legei,* "he [Moses] says." The treatise contains a further 52 quotations or allusions to Pentateuchal material, only six of which are accompanied by an explicit indication of source. In each case this consists simply of "Moses" or "the lawgiver." In addition, two quotations are identified as "in the Psalms" (*en hymnois,* xi.39; xii.52); one, from Jer. 15:10, is attributed to "a chorister of the prophetic company possessed by divine inspiration" (xii.44), and one, from Zech. 6:2, is introduced as "an oracle from . . . one of the disciples of Moses" (xiv.62). No source is indicated for a quotation from Josh. 1:5 (xxxii.166). The only other scriptural references are the two using *biblois*

cident is therefore striking, and is the earliest extant reference to Judges as a distinct literary work. It had a long history prior to Philo's reference to it, but documentation of that history is all later than he.[3] The Greek (LXX) version of Judges to which Philo refers, predates him by a century or more. While it differs in numerous details from the still earlier Hebrew version reflected in the MT, it is unmistakably the same work.[4]

Josephus claims to have based his *Antiquities of the Jews* on "the sacred books" *(hai hierai bibloi)*,[5] of which he tells us elsewhere[6] there were twenty-two in all, five dealing with the period from creation to Moses and thirteen with the period from Joshua to Artaxerxes I. He does not give them individual titles, however, or indicate which of them he is utilizing at any given point. So it is not surprising that he does not refer to Judges by name. However, he does use almost its entire contents in his treatment of a quite distinct "age of judges" which he defines in the following terms:

> After Joshua's death for full eighteen years the people continued in a state of anarchy; whereafter they returned to their former polity, entrusting supreme juridical authority to him who in battle and in bravery proved himself the best; and that is why they called this period of their political life the *age of judges*. (*Antiquities* vi.84-85; Loeb translation, my italics)

He first surveys the material in 1:1–2:5, then moves directly to the outrage at Gibeah and the resulting war in chapters 19–21. He gives a brief account of the northward migration of Dan (chs. 17–18), omitting the parts of this narrative involving Micah's image. He then returns to 3:7 (ignoring 2:6–3:6) and moves systematically through the stories of the individual judges, omitting Tola (10:1-2), and concluding his account of the period with the Samson story (chs. 13–16).[7] Interestingly, he does not locate the story of Ruth in this "age of judges" but in the high priesthood of Eli,[8] implicitly bracketing it with 1 Samuel rather than Judges. For Josephus, therefore, the

---

quoted above. Philo does not use *biblos* (or *biblion*) in this way elsewhere in his works, although he did write separate commentaries on Genesis and Exodus.

3. With the possible exception of a few Hebrew fragments discovered at Qumran. 4QJdg[a] contains part of 6:3-13 and 4QJdg[b] preserves the whole of 21:12-25 and a fragment of 16:5-7.

4. See below in Section VIII (The Text) for more regarding the Greek text of Judges.

5. *Antiquities* xx.261 (my translation).

6. *Against Apion* i.38-40.

7. *Antiquities* v.120-317.

8. *Antiquities* v.318.

"age" of Judges appears to be co-terminous with what we know as the "book" of Judges.

Early references to Judges in its original Hebrew form yield much the same picture. There are only three references to it in the Mishnah,[9] but these are supplemented in the Gemara by approximately two hundred further references.[10] In line with general practice in the Talmud, most of these references are made without naming the book as their source. In a couple of cases, however, it does receive specific mention. Quotations below are from the English text of the Soncino editions.[11]

'Abodah Zarah 25a contains a discussion of the reference to the Book of Jashar in 2 Samuel 1:18, namely, "he bade them teach the children of Judah [to handle] the bow; behold, it is written in the Book of Jashar." In the course of this discussion R. Samuel b. Naḥmani is quoted as having said:

> It is the Book of Judges, which is here called the Book of Jashar, because it contains the verse, "In those days there was no king in Israel; every man did that which was Jashar ["right"] in his own eyes." And where is [Judah's skill in archery] referred to in it? "That the generations of the children of Israel might know, to teach them war"; now what kind of warfare requires teaching? Surely archery. But how do we know that this verse refers to Judah? — From the scriptural verses, "Who shall go up to the Canaanites for us first, to fight them? And Yahweh said, 'Judah shall go up.'"

The three citations in this quotation are from Judges 21:25 (the closing words of the book),[12] 3:2, and 1:1-2 (the opening words of the book), in that order.[13] Judges is reckoned to be the second book in "the Prophets": "Our Rabbis taught: the order of the Prophets is Joshua, Judges, Samuel, Kings, Jeremiah, Ezekiel, Isaiah, and the Twelve" (*Baba Bathra* 14b). Later in the same para-

9. Judg. 16:12 in *Berakoth* 9.5; Judg. 13:5 in *Nazir* 9.5; and Judg. 16:21 in *Soṭah* 1.8. See the index to H. Danby, *The Mishnah, Translated from the Hebrew with Introduction and Brief Explanatory Notes* (Oxford: Oxford University Press, 1933).

10. See the index to I. Epstein, ed., *The Babylonian Talmud . . . Translated into English with Notes, Glossary and Indices,* 18 vols. (London: Soncino, 1935-52).

11. 'Abodah Zarah is quoted from Epstein, *The Babylonian Talmud; Baba Bathra* from I. Epstein, ed., *Hebrew-English Edition of the Babylonian Talmud,* 13 vols. (London: Soncino, 1963-76); and *Sopherim* from A. Cohen, ed., *The Minor Tractates of the Talmud . . . Translated into English with Notes, Glossary and Indices,* 2 vols. (London: Soncino, 1965).

12. Cf. 17:6; 18:1; 19:1.

13. Other identifications for the Book of Jashar suggested in the discussion include "the book of Deuteronomy" (R. Eleazar) and "the book of Abraham, Isaac, and Jacob" (R. Johanan).

graph Samuel is credited with its authorship: "Samuel wrote his [own] book, and Judges, and Ruth." The tractate *Sopherim* provides an interesting insight into scribal practice involved in the transmission of the prophetic books:

> Between a book of the Prophets and another, one should not leave the same empty space as between two books of the Torah, but in each case the space must be that which has been prescribed for it. Furthermore, a book of the Prophets must begin at the top. (*Sopherim* 111.2)

This tractate is generally reckoned to date from the closure of the Babylonian Talmud proper, and by some from as late as the eighth century. But appeal is constantly made in it to what is established practice, with supporting "quotations" from distinguished rabbis from as early as the first century A.D. Whatever its date, this tractate witnesses to the manner in which the distinctions among the various books of the Prophets named in the Talmud were carefully preserved in subsequent transmission.

Such is the book that this commentary is concerned with. It is a given entity, a received object for study, not one whose existence or parameters must be postulated before interpretation can begin. The close scrutiny to which we will subject it is justified in part, at least, by the institutional endorsement which has guaranteed its preservation and brought it within the purview of serious interpretation. It has the antiquity and status of a classic.

B. A CONCEPTUAL UNIT?

While it is clear that early authors and commentators recognized Judges as a book with clearly defined limits and its own distinctive subject matter, it is not clear to what extent they recognized it as a *conceptual* unit — a literary work with its own unique message.

The descriptive title used by Philo, "the recorded book of *judgments (krimatōn)*" (my italics), appears to identify judgment as the ideological focus of the book. This is in keeping with the theme of judgment on impiety that he is developing in *On the Confusion of Tongues* at that point, and presumably the reason why he refers to it. Judgment is the allegorical meaning Philo finds in the Penuel incident of Judges 8. But whether this is for him also the theme of the whole book is impossible to determine because we do not know whether he coined the title "book of judgments" himself or inherited it from others. In contrast, the standard Greek and Hebrew titles, *kritai* and *šōpᵉṭîm* respectively, refer to the divinely energized agents of Yahweh's deliverance (the "judges"), and therefore suggest that salvation rather than judgment is the main focus.

In the Talmud, as in Philo, the message of the book as such is never discussed. The rabbis use it as a source from which texts can be extracted for use in theological discussion, but the book itself is hardly ever named as the source. It is significant only as part of a larger whole (the Prophets, the Scriptures) which is the true interpretive context for any of its parts, regardless of which "book" they come from. It is only on rare occasions, when the requirements of a particular discussion demand it, that the book as such receives any mention at all.

It is Josephus who comes closest to treating Judges as a meaningful whole. In line with his historiographical purpose he takes a more holistic approach to it, utilizing most of its contents, as we have seen. He does not use all of it, however, and his omissions significantly alter the perspective, especially in relation to particular characters. Gideon, for example, becomes "a man of moderation and a model of every virtue";[14] all mention of his involvement with the ephod cult at Ophrah is omitted. The arrangement of the contents, too, is drastically modified in Josephus's account, as we saw, the civil war of chapters 19–21 coming before the advent of the first judge, Othniel. By implication, Josephus does offer an interpretation, however forced, of the book as a whole. Nevertheless, in the *Antiquities,* as we have seen, attention is never drawn to the separate books as such, or the breaks between them. The effect is to emphasize their continuity rather than their separateness, their meaningfulness as a corpus of sacred books *(hierai bibloi)* rather than as literary units in their own right.

That the stretch of material comprising our present book of Judges is part of a larger narrative, and to that extent incomplete in itself, is almost too obvious to warrant attention. Moreover, it is theoretically possible that the distribution of this larger narrative over a series of books was occasioned by the physical constraints imposed on ancient writers by, for example, the length of ancient scrolls, so that the book divisions are simply divisions of convenience without any literary significance at all.[15] Yet, as far as I am aware, it has never seriously been proposed that the book of Judges is in fact an entirely arbitrary unit of this kind, and scholarly study of it, especially in recent years, has tended to show that the reverse is actually the case. We will return to this below; but first we turn our attention to the period of Israel's history that the book deals with (Section II) and (as far as we are able to determine it) the process by which the book came to be in the form we have it today (Section III).

14. *Antiquities* v.230 (Thackeray and Marcus, LCL).
15. See Moshe Greenberg's similar comments in relation to Exodus in his introduction to *Understanding Exodus,* The Heritage of Biblical Israel, vol. 2, part 1 (New York: Behrman, 1962), p. 2.

II. THE PERIOD OF THE JUDGES IN ISRAEL'S HISTORY

Since the main focus of this commentary is literary and theological, this section will not attempt to go into the complex historical background issues in detail. Excellent treatments are available in the standard histories of Israel, and in commentaries which are more historically oriented.[16] Matters of direct relevance to the meaning, and therefore exegesis, of particular passages will be dealt with as they come up in the commentary. But no responsible exegesis can or should proceed in a vacuum, so what we will attempt here is a general introduction to the history of the period in question and some of the more significant recent developments in the study of it.

A. DATING THE PERIOD OF THE JUDGES

The book of Judges deals with the history of Israel between the death of Joshua and the transition to the monarchy that began with Samuel. The end of this period can be established fairly securely by working backward from the reign of David (1010-970 B.C.).[17] Allowing thirty-two years for Saul's reign,[18] this brings us back to 1042 B.C. Samuel and (before him) Eli are both said to have died in old age, after very long ministries: forty years for Eli (1 Sam. 4:18), and (we presume) at least that for Samuel. So it would seem reasonable to allow about eighty years for the Eli-Samuel period as whole. Since Samuel's ministry overlapped with the first part of Saul's reign, however, the Eli-Samuel period proper was probably more like seventy years. This would give us an approximate date of 1092 B.C. for the end of the period covered by the book of Judges.

The book of Judges begins its account of the period with the death of Joshua (1:1; 2:8), but unfortunately this event is difficult to date with the same degree of confidence. Allowing for Israel's forty years of wilderness

16. See, e.g., Iain V. Provan, Philips Long, and Tremper Longman III, *A Biblical History of Israel* (London: Westminster John Knox, 2003); K. A. Kitchen, *On the Reliability of the Old Testament* (Grand Rapids/Cambridge, UK: Eerdmans, 2003); and Daniel I. Block, *Judges, Ruth,* NAC, vol. 6 (Nashville: Broadman & Holman, 1999).

17. K. A. Kitchen and T. C. Mitchell, "Chronology of the Old Testament," in *NBD,* p. 188; Kitchen, *On the Reliability of the Old Testament,* p. 83.

18. The statement in 1 Sam. 13:1 that "he [Saul] reigned over Israel for . . . two years" is incomplete, and the "forty years" of Acts 13:21 is probably a round number. After considering all the relevant evidence, Kitchen settles on thirty-two years for Saul's reign, which must be correct or very nearly so (*On the Reliability of the Old Testament,* pp. 82-83).

wandering (which may be a round number rather than a precise one) and Joshua's lifetime of 110 years (Josh. 24:29), and supposing that his commissioning by Moses was in about his thirtieth year, the starting point for the period covered by the book of Judges must be approximately 120 years after the exodus from Egypt. 1 Kings 6:1 locates the exodus at 480 years before Solomon began to build the temple in the fourth year of his reign, which is commonly accepted as 966 B.C. This gives a date for the exodus of 1446 B.C., close to the middle of the fifteenth century B.C. Admittedly 480 years, too, sounds more like a round number than a precise one, but the date it leads to is in line with what we would expect from the three hundred years that Israel is said to have resided in the lands east of the Jordan prior to Jephthah's judgeship (Judg. 11:26). While this, too, is probably approximate rather than precise, it is not as immediately open to suspicion as another multiple of forty might be. Furthermore, Israelite occupation of Transjordan for this period is unproblematic in terms of the archeological evidence,[19] and a fifteenth-century date for the exodus and conquest has been supported on broader archeological grounds by, among others, Jack, Bimson, Bimson and Livingston, Aling, and Shea.[20]

However, the majority of scholars who accept the historicity of the exodus place it, on archeological grounds, at about 1267 B.C. in the reign of Rameses II, near the middle of the thirteenth century B.C. Even such a strongly conservative scholar as Kenneth Kitchen continues to favor this date, taking the 480 years of 1 Kings 6:1 as representing twelve generations (in reality only about three hundred years), and dismissing the three hundred years of Judges 11:26 as an exaggeration by Jephthah for diplomatic advantage. It is noteworthy that Hoffmeier, after a judicious weighing of all the evidence in 1997, considered the date of the exodus still an open question,[21] and Provan, Long, and Longman in their recent history of Israel do the same, although cautiously favoring the earlier date.[22]

It would be foolish to think that we could resolve all the difficulties

---

19. Cf. Provan, Long, and Longman, *History of Israel,* p. 131. My treatment of the dating of the exodus (and therefore the judges period) in this part of the Introduction is substantially based on the treatment of the topic in this excellent recent work.

20. James W. Jack, *The Date of the Exodus in the Light of External Evidence* (Edinburgh: T&T Clark, 1925); John J. Bimson, *Redating the Exodus and Conquest,* JSOTSup (Sheffield: JSOT, 1978); John J. Bimson and David Livingston, "Redating the Exodus," *BAR* 13, no. 5 (1987): 40-53; Charles F. Aling, *Egypt and Bible History* (Grand Rapids: Baker, 1981); William Shea, "Exodus, Date of the," in *ISBE,* 3rd rev. ed., ed. G. W. Bromiley (Grand Rapids: Eerdmans, 1979-88), pp. 230-38.

21. James K. Hoffmeier, *Israel in Egypt: The Evidence for the Authenticity of the Exodus Tradition* (New York, Oxford: Oxford University Press, 1997), pp. 122-26.

22. Provan, Long, and Longman, *History of Israel,* pp. 122-26.

here, and there is no need to do so, given that nothing of great importance hangs on it for the exegesis of Judges. However, on balance I am more convinced by the arguments for the earlier date, and will assume for the purposes of this commentary that the exodus took place about 1446 B.C., giving us a date of 1326 B.C. for the beginning of the judges period. So we can think of the judges era as extending roughly from 1326 to 1092 B.C., about 234 years in all. This accords reasonably well with the total of 296 years obtained by simply totaling the data from the book of Judges itself,[23] especially in view of the uncertainties involved in round numbers such as the forty years of 3:11, 5:31, 8:28, and 13:1, the eighty of 3:30, and the twenty of 15:20 and 16:31.[24]

B. CANAAN IN THE PERIOD OF THE JUDGES

The Canaan that was Israel's immediate environment in the judges period was diverse in every way. It was ethnically diverse in that the subjugation of the region was incomplete and various people groups still resided in different parts of it. Among the peoples that the book mentions as living in Canaan at the time are Perizzites, Jebusites, Amorites, Philistines, Sidonians, Hivites, and Hittites.[25] It is not possible to identify all these peoples precisely, and some of the terms may simply be regional rather than ethnic, but the number of them testifies to the diversity of peoples and undoubtedly of cultures as well.

It was also diverse politically, with city-states with their own "kings" *(mᵉlākîm)* as perhaps the most clearly attested form of government, though no doubt the precise form of such kingship varied from one city to another. The Philistines, with their confederation of five cities in the southeast, seem to have had their own distinctive form of government by "lords" *(sarnîm,* 16:18). It was an unstable environment, with a tussle going on between Israel and some of these groups for control of certain areas; and there were periodic incursions by outside groups, such as Ammonites and Midianites. This instability was exacerbated by the fact that Egypt was in a period of weakness and

23. Assuming that Samson's 20-year judgeship fell within the 40 years of Philistine oppression of 13:1.

24. See the comments on the relevant verses in the body of the commentary. On the complexity of the data and the impossibility of precision see David L. Washburn, "The Chronology of Judges: Another Look," *Bibliotheca Sacra* 147 (1990): 414-25. Like Washburn, most scholars assume that some of the judges ruled concurrently in different regions, and that there was some overlap between them.

25. As we shall see, in Judges the word "Canaanites" is sometimes used as a general term for the pre-Israelite population, and sometimes in a more restricted sense of the pre-Israelite people of a particular area, who are distinguished by this term from others in the same area.

was unable to impose any kind of unity.[26] In part this instability was caused by competition for arable land and (perhaps) by uprisings against the feudal power of the city-state rulers.[27]

Most significantly for the book of Judges, it was also a very diverse environment religiously (see the comments at 2:11-13 on the nature of the Canaanite gods and the worship associated with them). The Israelites, who had been taken out of one polytheistic environment in Egypt and inserted (in the next generation) into another polytheistic environment in Canaan, found it difficult to survive there and remain faithful to their monotheistic faith. Their failure to do so is at the very heart of the account that Judges gives of the fortunes of Israel in the judges period.

C. ISRAEL'S INTERNAL AFFAIRS IN THE JUDGES PERIOD[28]

Little is known about Israel's way of life in the judges period apart from what can be gleaned from the Old Testament. The chief source of information is the book of Judges itself, but the books of Ruth and 1 Samuel also shed valuable light.

Israel's territory at the time was divided into tribal areas (see Josh. 13–21). Of the twelve tribes, nine and a half occupied the region between the Jordan River (including the Sea of Galilee and the Dead Sea) and the Mediterranean coast. The other two and a half occupied the plateau region east of the Jordan. Incursions by neighboring peoples such as the Midianites, Moabites, and Ammonites (to the east) and the Philistines and other so-called Sea Peoples (to the west) usually involved only part of Israel's territory, which meant that only one or two tribes were directly affected.

The essential bond between the tribes was their common history and their allegiance to Yahweh. He himself was their supreme Ruler or Judge (Judg. 11:27), and his law was their constitution. It was this covenant relationship with him which bound them together and gave them their identity as a distinct people. At least once a year a religious festival was held at which the people were reminded of their identity and of the obligations which this

26. As evident in the Amarna Letters, with their apparently futile appeals by Canaanite rulers in various parts to the Pharaoh to intervene to quell disturbances (*ANET*, pp. 483-90). These reflect conditions in either the period of Israelite settlement or the late pre-Israelite period, depending on whether one accepts the early or late date for the exodus.

27. On the possible relevance for this of the identity of the *'apiru* of the Amarna Letters see Provan, Long, and Longman, *History of Israel*, pp. 170-72.

28. The material in this section is based on my treatment of the same subject in B. G. Webb, "Judges," in *NBC*, ed. D. A. Carson, R. T. France, J. A. Motyer, and G. J. Wenham (Leicester: Inter-Varsity Press, 1994), pp. 261-62.

entailed. One such annual festival was held at Shiloh, which was centrally located and the place where the Tent of Meeting had originally been set up after Israel's arrival in Canaan (Josh. 18:1; Judg. 21:19; 1 Sam. 1:3). This most likely remained the place of the central sanctuary throughout the judges period, although the ark of the covenant was sometimes moved to other places, especially in times of crisis (Judg. 18:27). How well attended these festivals were and exactly what happened at them are not definitely known; the one explicit statement about them in Judges indicates that at least some of what took place was of questionable orthodoxy,[29] and the description of the state of affairs at Shiloh in the opening chapters of 1 Samuel confirms this impression.[30] There was a functioning priesthood (18:27), and the judge in office at the time may also have had a role in these festivals (see the comments on 2:17). Given the precedent set by Joshua (Josh. 24), it is likely that at least one of the festivals involved a covenant renewal ceremony of some kind.

For the most part, day-to-day administration of justice and oversight of community affairs was provided locally by the elders of the various clans and tribes (11:4-11; Ruth 4:1-12). But matters which could not be settled locally were brought for settlement to the judge who was in office at the time, either at some central location (4:4-5) or at certain designated towns which the judge visited regularly (1 Sam. 7:15-17). From time to time, as occasion warranted, ad hoc assemblies of representatives from the various tribes were convened to deal with matters of common concern, such as serious misconduct by one of the tribes or an enemy attack on one or more of them (10:17-18; 20:1-3). On such occasions decisive, concerted action was required to preserve the integrity of Israel. There was no standing army, so it was necessary to raise a fresh force of volunteer fighters each time a national emergency arose, and the personal charisma of an individual often played a crucial role in getting this done quickly. It seems that at least some of the judges[31] rose to office precisely because of their ability to provide inspiring leadership on such occasions (11:1-10). Others seem to have been appointed in more peaceful circumstances (12:8-15), though precisely how this was done is not known.

In practice, however, the system (if that is the correct term for it) rarely if ever worked as smoothly as this. There was in fact little effective unity among the Israelite tribes in the period of the judges. For a start, they were separated from each other by settlements of unconquered Canaanites, some of them in fortified cities commanding major trade and communication corridors (1:19, 27-36; 4:2-3). Furthermore, the gods of these people became

---

29. Judg. 21:20-21.

30. Especially 1 Sam. 2:12-17.

31. For the meaning of *šōpēṭ* (judge) in the book of Judges, see the comments on 2:16-19.

a "snare" to the Israelites, as Joshua had warned they would (2:3; Josh. 23:12-13). This inevitably led to a weakening of their loyalty to Yahweh and to one another, and resulted in spiritual and moral decline that was so serious that it threatened to destroy Israel from within. The tribes were often slow to help one another in times of crisis (5:16-17; 12:2) and even fell to fighting among themselves (8:1-3; 12:1-6; 20:1-48). Most people were concerned only for their own interests, and took advantage of the absence of central government to do as they pleased (17:6; 21:25). This inner decay threatened to destroy the very fabric of Israel, and actually constituted a far more serious threat to its survival in the judges period than any external attack.

But as always in such circumstances, there were faithful Israelites who continued to quietly pursue lives of genuine piety. The book of Judges focuses mainly on the frequent crises that Israel faced, and gives a rather turbulent impression of the period. But it also clearly indicates that there were long periods of peace and relative prosperity, in which life at the local level could settle down into a more even tenor (3:11, 30; 8:28; 10:3-5; 12:8-10). In this respect Judges is nicely complemented by the book of Ruth with its gentle, moving story of one family's affairs in Bethlehem. Here farmers struggled against the vagaries of the weather, people met and fell in love, and the elders sought to guide the affairs of the community along the tried and proven paths of covenant law and local custom; and both books testify to the fact that, whether in the turbulence of national crisis or the more quiet ebb and flow of village life, Yahweh was deeply involved and sovereignly at work in the lives of his people, preserving and disciplining them, and overruling all things for their good.

D. THE JUDGES PERIOD IN THE HISTORY WARS OF CRITICAL STUDY

In the context of the history of ancient Israel as a field of study, the judges period belongs to the more specific area of the history of Israelite settlement in Canaan. Specific issues relating to the book of Judges include its value as a historical source (is it, in part or as a whole, a record of real history?) and its relationship to the book of Joshua (is it an alternative, more realistic account of the Israelite settlement than the one given in the book of Joshua?).

Excellent summaries and reviews of recent developments in Israelite historiography are readily available, and it is not my intention to duplicate them here.[32] Suffice it to say that the increasing application of sociological

---

32. For example, Provan, Long, and Longman, *History of Israel,* pp. 3-104; V. Philips Long, "Historiography of the Old Testament," in *The Face of Old Testament*

approaches to Old Testament study and advances in the archeological study of early Iron Age Palestine in the latter part of the twentieth century have led to a widespread loss of confidence among scholars regarding the value of the Old Testament as a source for the study of the history of early Israel. The confident assertions of the Albright school in America and Y. Yadin and his followers in Israel regarding a basic congruence of the biblical picture of Israel's early history with what may be known from archeology about conditions in Palestine in the relevant period have been increasingly challenged (and discredited in the minds of many scholars) by the followers of a radically revisionist approach to the history of early Israel championed by scholars such as N. P. Lemche, Philip Davies, and Keith Whitelam. According to the latter school of thought, archeology gives virtually no support to the biblical account of the Israelite conquest and settlement of Canaan, and in fact the Old Testament account of Israel's early history is an ideologically motivated creation of the early Judaism of the postexilic period.

The same period has seen the rise of new literary approaches to the study of Old Testament texts (especially narratives) associated in America with scholars such as Robert Alter, and in Britain with the "Sheffield School" associated with David Clines. While there have been many positive results from these new approaches, they have tended to produce an artificial separation between historical study of the Old Testament (interested in the Old Testament texts only as possible sources for historical reconstruction) and literary study of the same texts (interested in them only as vehicles for the artistic exploration of themes). The popularity of the new literary approaches among evangelical scholars has had the unfortunate consequence that most of them opt out of the ongoing debate about the historicity of the Old Testament. This has meant that the critical response to the new historical minimalism has not been as robust and thorough as it could have been if the current generation of evangelical scholars had remained as engaged in the area as their forebears had been.[33]

Fortunately, however, the new minimalism has not had it all its own way. Significant challenges have continued to be mounted in the United States by scholars such as William Dever, James Hoffmeier, and V. Philips Long, and in Britain by the "Liverpool School" associated with Kenneth Kitchen and Alan Millard, and their followers. Kenneth Kitchen's recent,

---

Studies: A Survey of Contemporary Approaches, ed. D. W. Baker and B. T. Arnold (Leicester: Apollos; Grand Rapids: Baker, 1999), pp. 145-75; K. Lawson Younger Jr., "Early Israel in Recent Biblical Scholarship," in Baker and Arnold, *The Face of Old Testament Studies,* pp. 176-206.

33. I have in mind specialists in ancient Near Eastern archeology and history such as R. K. Harrison, Donald Wiseman, Alan Millard, and Kenneth Kitchen.

substantial book, *On the Reliability of the Old Testament* (2003), is encyclo-pedic in the mass of hard historical data it brings to bear on the issues (some-thing he believes his opponents fail to do). Of particular significance for the current state of the debate is the work by Provan, Long, and Longman, *A Biblical History of Israel* (also published in 2003). In a long and tightly argued first section ("History, Historiography, and the Bible") it mounts a strong cri-tique of the minimalist approaches at the level of epistemology (how we *know* things about the past) and historical method (responsible use of pri-mary sources, including texts). Its special contribution is to bring back to-gether historical and literary approaches to the study of Israel's history by re-instating "narrative history" (stories about the past) as a valid source of historical knowledge, and narrative poetics (how such narratives work as lit-erature) as essential to a correct use of them in historical study. Part 2 of the book then presents a history of Israel drawing on both textual evidence (bib-lical and extrabiblical) and relevant archeological data, in line with the prin-ciples presented in Part 1. This work has drawn praise from mainline scholars on both sides of the debate[34] and goes a long way to redressing the relative lack of participation by the current generation of evangelical scholars re-ferred to above. Of particular relevance for the task before us in this com-mentary is its treatment of Israel's settlement in the land in chapter 7.

While making full allowance for the theological agenda of Judges and its literary quality (to which we will give a lot of attention in this commen-tary), there is no reason in principle why it should not preserve, and indeed be anchored in, real historical knowledge of the period in question. Nor is it necessary, or even right, to subordinate its witness about this history to re-constructions based on the current state of archeological knowledge. Both texts and material remains deserve respect and careful analysis, and it is more likely that sound conclusions will be reached by some kind of synthesis between what these two have to tell us than by simply dismissing one in favor of the other.

If we set aside, then, the extreme negativity at the minimalist end of the spectrum, two particular issues have featured in scholarly discussion of the period referred to in the book of Judges: how does the book of Judges re-late to the various conquest/settlement models that have been proposed in critical scholarship, and does Judges present an alternate and more realistic account of Israel's arrival and settlement in the land than Joshua does?

The various alternatives that have been proposed (the conquest, peace-ful infiltration, peasant revolt, and other endogenous models that assume that Israel emerged within Canaan rather than entering it from outside) are gener-

---

34. Accompanying endorsements include, e.g., ones by Walter Brueggemann, Baruch Halpern, and William Dever.

ally well known, and good summaries are given in the recent works just referred to.[35] The conquest model, at one end of the spectrum, gives primary weight to the biblical account of Israel's entry to the land (especially the book of Joshua) and seeks corroboration from archeology. The various endogenous models, at the other end, base their conclusions on archeology alone and neither seek nor find confirmation from biblical material (which is regarded as of no historical value). Conservative scholars generally favor the conquest model associated with the work of W. Albright and his followers. However, the reality is that the whole truth does not lie at one end of the spectrum or the other, and that there is some value in most if not all of the models that have been proposed. The main problems that scholars have found with the conquest model is that the archeological evidence does not support widespread Israelite destruction of Canaanite sites in the relevant period. Such evidence as does exist does not correlate well with the thirteenth-century date of Israel's entry to the land favored by most scholars, and in any case is distributed across too wide a time span to have been caused solely by Joshua's concentrated campaigns. Furthermore, the material remains of early Iron (re)settlement of the hill country of Canaan suggest that the people involved were essentially Canaanites rather than Israelites with a distinctive new culture.

However, it now appears that some of the crucial weaknesses of the conquest model have been due as much to a failure to read Joshua and Judges carefully enough as to a failure to give sufficient weight to the archeological record. The fact is that the book of Joshua does not claim that the Israelites caused widespread destruction of cities; in fact, it explicitly denies this (Josh. 11:13).[36] Joshua speaks of cities being taken and people (especially kings) being killed, but "only three cities — Jericho, Ai, and Hazor — are said to have been burned" (Josh. 6:24; 8:28; 11:11, 13).[37] Furthermore, some areas seem to have been taken by something more like accommodation (or interpenetration) than conquest (e.g., Gibeon, Josh. 9; Shechem, Josh. 24:1, 25; Gen. 34). Finally, there is abundant evidence in the biblical record, especially in Judges, of Israelites intermarrying with Canaanites and worshiping their gods, so much so that Daniel Block can speak of "the Canaanization of Israel" in the judges period.[38] It should hardly surprise us, therefore, if in the material remains of the period Israelites are virtually indistinguishable from Canaanites. All of this suggests that the conflict between the biblical account and the archeological evidence has been greatly exaggerated, and that both

35. Provan, Long, and Longman, *History of Israel,* pp. 139-47; Younger, "Early Israel," pp. 178-91.

36. Cf. Younger, "Early Israel," p. 179.

37. Provan, Long, and Longman, *History of Israel,* p. 140.

38. Block, *Judges, Ruth,* p. 76.

need to be read and compared with one another much more carefully.[39] Wholesale dismissal of either is unwarranted.

A similar problem (and solution) appears when we consider the ways in which Israel's occupation of Canaan is described in Joshua and Judges respectively. Scholars who have rejected the conquest model, if they give credence to the biblical material at all, tend to favor Judges as an alternative and more realistic account of what happened than Joshua: a rather messy process of the meeting and mixing of various tribes and people groups. This is a picture much more compatible with the endogenous models, at the righthand end of the spectrum, which currently have the ascendancy in critical scholarship. On this view Judges covers the same historical period as Joshua, but much more realistically. It is a view that seems justified, at least in part, by the fact that there is undeniable overlap between Joshua and Judges; some material found in the former is repeated in the latter, for example, the death and burial of Joshua (Josh. 24:29-30; Judg. 2:6-9), Othniel's capture of Debir (Kiriathsepher), and Othniel's marriage to Achsah, Caleb's daughter (Josh. 15:15-20; Judg. 1:11-15). However, several things need to be borne in mind. First, such overlap is the exception rather than the rule; the vast majority of the material in Judges is quite different from that in Joshua, and, second, the way Judges opens explicitly locates the events it is about to describe as "*after* the death of Joshua" (1:1), that is, in a different period and situation. Third, there are repetition and overlap *within* the book of Judges itself, apparently for compositional and thematic purposes (1:1–2:5 and 2:6–3:6 both start from the death of Joshua and describe what happened after his death from two different and complementary perspectives). These observations provide a starting point for a much more discerning comparison of the books of Joshua and Judges as a whole than the one that simply sets them over against one another as competing and conflicting accounts of Israel's occupation of the land.

Careful observation of the content of the two books indicates that there is more than a merely artificial or narrative sequentiality between them. As noted by Kaufmann back in 1953, "At the time of Joshua's wars the *Philistines* of the Pentapolis [Ekron, Ashdod, Ashkelon, Gaza, and Gath] were not yet in the land of Canaan. Joshua fought only against the Canaanite peoples. In his days the Philistine cities were still occupied by Anakim. The Philistines appear only in Joshua 13, in the introduction to the Book of the Distribution of the Land. However, in this chapter Israel is unconditionally promised that they will *expel* the Philistines from the Shephelah. The real history of the Philistines is beyond the horizon of the Book of Joshua."[40] It is

---

39. For a recent treatment of the settlement which does this, see P. Pitkänen, "Ethnicity, Assimilation, and the Israelite Settlement," *TynB* 55, no. 2 (2004): 161-82.

40. Yehezkel Kaufmann, *The Biblical Account of the Conquest of Canaan,* 2nd

different in Judges; the first brief clash with Philistines occurs in 3:31 (Shamgar), but by the time of Samson the Philistines are firmly established in Gaza and are a major force to be reckoned with (16:21-23). This is only one of many indicators identified by Kaufmann of the genuine antiquity of the Joshua account, and the difference in time and situation between it and the book of Judges. In short, the chronological progression from Joshua to Judges is a real, not artificial one. In view of this it is best to understand the few duplications of material that occur as either the inclusion of something still future for completeness in the treatment of an aspect of the conquest settlement as a whole, or as flashbacks to provide the context for a better understanding of something in the present. We will reserve comment on particular passages for the appropriate place in the exegesis.

III. THE HISTORY OF THE BOOK'S FORMATION

In his landmark study of 1943[41] Martin Noth argued that the division of the historical complex Deuteronomy–2 Kings into "books" was a secondary development in the history of the tradition that partially obscured the more fundamental unity, literary and theological, of an original Deuteronomic History. In this original work Judges 2:6ff. was the direct continuation of Joshua 23, Joshua's speech in that chapter marking the conclusion of the "period of the conquest," and Judges 2:6-11, 14-16, 18-19 being the Deuteronomist's introduction to the "period of the judges," which was formally concluded with Samuel's farewell speech in 1 Samuel 12. Noth believed that Judges 3:7–12:15 was composed by the Deuteronomist himself by combining a collection of stories about local tribal heroes with a short list of judge figures (10:1-5; 12:7-15), Jephthah being the common factor (he occurred in both). Judges 13:1 was then followed directly by 1 Samuel 1:1ff. Thus Judges 2:6-11, 14-16, 18-19; 3:7–13:1 was the segment of this original Deuteronomic History from which the present book of Judges developed through a series of editorial revisions and expansions.

Noth argued that the "Deuteronomistically edited" passages, Joshua 24:1-28 and Judges 2:1-5, were inserted secondarily after Joshua 23 and,

---

ed. (Jerusalem: Magnes Press, Hebrew University, 1985), p. 123. The first edition was published in 1953.

41. Martin Noth, *Schriften der Königsberger Gelehrten-Gesellschaft,* Geisteswissenschaftliche Klasse 18 (Tübingen: Max Niemeyer, 1943), pp. 43-266. This book was published in English by JSOT Press, Sheffield, as *The Deuteronomistic History* in 1981 and 1991 (both translations of the 2nd German edition of 1957).

later still, and without any Deuteronomistic revision, "the mass of old traditional fragments which form the present Judges 1."[42] Finally the original introduction of chapter 2 was expanded, possibly in more than one stage, to give the present text of 2:11–3:6.[43]

Noth did not absolutely exclude the possibility that the Samson complex was part of the original Deuteronomic History but considered this unlikely on the grounds that it showed no signs of being worked on by the Deuteronomist, and that Samson's name is conspicuous by its absence in 1 Samuel 12, "a passage which clearly aims to be comprehensive."[44] Furthermore, he held that it was the Deuteronomist's usual practice to feature only one savior figure in each period of foreign rule, and that Samuel (not Samson) originally fulfilled this role in the context of the Philistine oppression announced in 13:1.

Noth offered no comment on the last five chapters of the book except that "Judges 17–21 was not part of the Dtr's [Deuteronomist's] work but was added later."[45] In a subsequent article[46] he does discuss the background and purpose of the narrative in chapters 17–18, but without reference to its context in Judges. In that article he remarks that "the entire story does not fit at all well into the Deuteronomistic conception of the period of the Judges."[47] Noting that the formula, "in those days there was no king in Israel . . . ," is fully integrated into the narrative of chapters 17–18 but merely brackets that of chapters 19–21,[48] he implies that those chapters were a secondary addition to chapters 17–18. The redactional history of the book of Judges as such was not a matter of primary concern to Noth, and his understanding of it must be gleaned from various asides in his treatment of other matters. Wolfgang Richter, however, in his *Die Bearbeitungen des "Retterbuches" in der deuteronomischen Epoche* (1964),[49] has undertaken a much more systematic analysis of the question. He works within the broad parameters of Noth's thesis, but seeks to refine certain aspects of it, particularly those which have a direct bearing on the early redactional history of Judges.

Richter believes that the "Retterbuch" (book of deliverers), Noth's

---

42. *Deuteronomistic History,* p. 8.

43. In particular, Noth held that 2:20–3:6 belonged to this final stage of redaction since it clearly presupposed the existence of 1:21, 27ff.

44. *Deuteronomistic History,* p. 52.

45. *Deuteronomistic History,* p. 121, n. 29.

46. M. Noth, "The Background of Judges 17–18," in *Israel's Prophetic Heritage: Essays in Honor of James Muilenburg,* ed. B. W. Anderson and W. Harrelson (London: SCM, 1962), pp. 68-85.

47. "Background of Judges 17–18," p. 82, n. 35.

48. "Background of Judges 17–18," p. 79.

49. BBB 21 (Bonn: Peter Hanstein).

postulated collection of stories about local tribal heroes, had undergone at least one and possibly two redactions before its incorporation into the Deuteronomistic History. The work of the successive redactors is distinguished partly on stylistic grounds and partly in terms of their differing horizons of interest.

The first reviser of the "Retterbuch," according to Richter, ignored its antimonarchical tendency and expressed his own theological concerns in the stereotyped editorial framework that he provided for the individual deliverer stories of chapters 3–8. In so doing he gave the periods of oppression a theological motivation (retribution), but was generally optimistic: Israel had known its rescuers who, under God, brought peace, each successive episode ending with "the land had rest." His use of the formula, "did what was evil in Yahweh's eyes," suggests some dependence on Deuteronomy 17:2; hence Richter's siglum Rdt$_1$ for this redactor, although no other Deuteronomic influence is discernible. Richter suggests that this edition of the Retterbuch served as a book of examples occasioned by the restoration of the people's militia under Josiah.

Richter assigns the "example story" ("ein narratives Beispielstück") of Othniel (minus the numbers in 3:8 and 11, the judge formula of 3:10, and the death notice of 3:11) to a second reviser, Rdt$_2$. The theological interests of this reviser are expressed in the amplifications he supplies to the framework pattern of his predecessor, particularly his detailing of the nature of Israel's sin (worship of foreign gods) and his reference to Yahweh's anger at this (3:7b, 8b). Thus he sharpens Rdt$_1$'s general theology of retribution into the more specific concept that worship of Yahweh brings victory while worship of other gods brings defeat, a matter greatly stressed in Josiah's reforms. Richter believes that the influence of Deuteronomy 13 as well as that of 17:2ff. is apparent here. He is cautious about identifying the hand of this second reviser, but on balance feels that it is justified, and suggests that he may have been a Calebite (cf. 3:9).

Richter's third redactor, DtrG, is the equivalent of Noth's Deuteronomist. This redactor introduces the "minor judges" and revises the whole Retterbuch in the process to give the segment of the Deuteronomistic History which, on Noth's view, was the nucleus of the present book. He paints a very dark picture of Israel, particularly emphasizing its inveterate apostasy (see, in particular, 2:7, 10-12, 14-16, 18-19, and 10:6-16), which explains the tragedy of 587 B.C. Richter apparently holds, against Noth, that the Samson complex *was* included in DtrG's composition, since he notes how the mention of the gods of the Ammonites and the Philistines in 10:6 (which he attributes to DtrG) prepares the way for both chapters 11–12 and 13–16.

Richter addresses himself only to that part of the book which, on his view, formed part of the Deuteronomistic History. The subsequent redactional expansion of this core into the present book did not receive his attention in any subsequent publication. Neither Noth nor Richter considers to what extent the book in its final form is a coherent whole, but we may deduce from Noth's comments on chapters 1 and 17–18 in particular (referred to above) that he, at least, saw the subsequent additions to the work of the Deuteronomist as detracting from the coherence of the core material.

Some later studies, however, have raised doubts about this rather negative assessment of the material that introduces and concludes the present book. Timo Veijola in particular has argued that chapters 17–21 in their present form are fully compatible with both the literary structure and theological concerns of the original Deuteronomistic History, and were in fact an integral part of it.[50] Veijola is perhaps the best-known exponent of a methodology that derives in the first instance from the work of Walter Dietrich,[51] and ultimately from that of Rudolph Smend, whose article "Das Gesetz und die Völker: Ein Beitrag zur deuteronomistischen Redaktionsgeschichte" (1971)[52] proved to be the point of departure for a new and influential approach to the study of the Deuteronomistic History as a whole. Smend believed that the Deuteronomist's introduction to the Judges period in the original Deuteronomistic History began in Judges 2:10,[53] and that in 2:17, 20-21, and 23 this original introduction had been expanded by a reviser (DtrN) whose overriding concern was with the law of Moses and the effects of its observance or nonobservance on Israel's relationships with the "nations" (gôyim) of Canaan. He also argued that this same redactor, at the same time as his revision of the introduction in chapter 2, had inserted 1:1–2:5[54] (a preexisting unit which he had not himself composed) since it was fully consistent with his own distinctive understanding of the "conquest" and was perhaps even the source of it.[55] Smend found

50. Timo Veijola, *Das Königtum in der Beurteilung der deuteronomistischen Historiographie: Eine redaktionsgeschichtliche Untersuchung,* Annales Academiae Scientiarum Fennicae, Ser. B, Tom. 198 (Helsinki: Suomalainen Tiedeakatemia, 1977), pp. 27-29.

51. In particular his *Prophetie und Geschichte: Eine redaktionsgeschichtliche Untersuchung zum deuteronomistischen Geschichtswerk,* FRLANT 108 (Göttingen: Vandenhoeck & Ruprecht, 1977).

52. In *Probleme biblischer Theologie: Gerhard von Rad zum 70. Geburtstag,* ed. H. W. Wolff (Munich: Chr. Kaiser, 1971), pp. 494-509.

53. "Das Gesetz und die Völker," in *Probleme biblischer Theologie,* p. 506. In contrast to Noth, Smend saw Judg. 2:10 as the direct continuation of Josh. 24:31 in the original Deuteronomistic History, Josh. 24 (to v. 31) being an original part of that work and Josh. 23 a later insertion by a redactor.

54. Repeating Josh. 24:28-31 (with appropriate alterations) in 2:6-9 in order to preserve, in essence, the original connection between Josh. 24:31 and Judg. 2:10ff. *Probleme biblischer Theologie,* pp. 506-7.

55. *Probleme biblischer Theologie,* pp. 508-9. Smend attributes to this reviser the

other clear examples of the work of DtrN in Joshua 1:7-9, 13:1, and chapter 23, and believed that further research would show that this redactor had effected a systematic revision of the entire Deuteronomistic History.

The further work proposed by Smend was undertaken by Dietrich,[56] resulting in the now familiar analysis in terms of *two* major revisions — one "prophetic" (DtrP) and the other "nomistic" (DtrN) — of the work of the "basic" Deuteronomist (DtrG),[57] an analysis which was accepted or even assumed in the work of an increasing number of European scholars.[58] In two monographs Veijola, whose work we have already mentioned, has analyzed the varying perspectives on the monarchy in these successive redactions. In the first, *Die ewige Dynastie* (1975),[59] he examines four groups of texts in which David and his dynasty are central,[60] and concludes that the texts attributed to DtrG idealize David and his dynasty in contrast to the more critical

---

introduction into the original Deuteronomistic History of the concept of "the remaining nations." The success of Joshua and his generation against the nations of Canaan was due to their strict adherence to "the book of the law [of Moses]" (Josh. 1:8; cf. 23:6). However, at Joshua's death there still remained some "nations" *(gôyim)* (Josh. 23:4) and land (Josh. 13:2ff.) to be conquered, and success in doing this depended on continued obedience to the law (Josh. 23:6ff.). Israel failed to exhibit such obedience (Judg. 1:1–2:5), and so the "remaining nations" were left permanently in Canaan as a punishment (Judg. 2:20-21).

56. In *Prophetie und Geschichte* (see above, n. 51).

57. Whereas Smend had worked with Joshua-Judges, Dietrich focused exclusively on Kings. Using methods similar to those of Smend, he argued that DtrG had contained very few prophetic traditions, and that most had been inserted by DtrP, either by utilizing old traditions or by composing his own material. The promise-and-fulfilment schema of Kings emphasized by von Rad was taken to be the contribution of DtrP. Thus for Dietrich the two later redactions by DtrP and DtrN were not minor ones, but included major additions, both of old traditions and of new compositions. By comparing the language and style of these three redactions with other Israelite literature, Dietrich concluded that DtrG had written around 580 B.C., DtrP about ten years later, and DtrN a further ten years later.

58. The surprisingly rapid acceptance of Dietrich's analysis was documented in 1980 by Gerald E. Gerbrandt in "Kingship according to the Deuteronomistic History" (diss., Union Theological Seminary, Virginia, 1980). Gerbrandt cites, in addition to Timo Veijola, Tryggve Mettinger, Ernst Würthwein, Helmut Hollenstein, Otto Kaiser, and Wolfgang Roth as being in fundamental agreement with Dietrich's proposals. To quote Gerbrandt, Würthwein and Hollenstein in particular "suggest that this is the direction Deuteronomistic studies will take, and Kaiser's introduction points in a similar direction" (p. 17).

59. *Die ewige Dynastie: David und die Entstehung seiner Dynastie nach der deuteronomistischen Darstellung,* Annales Academiae Scientiarum Fennicae, Ser. B, Tom. 193 (Helsinki: Suomalainen Tiedeakatemia, 1975).

60. Each cluster of passages is related to a lead text: 1 Kgs. 1–2 (ch. 2), 1 Sam. 25 (ch. 3), 1 Sam. 20:12-17, 42b (ch. 4), and 2 Sam. 21–24 (ch. 5).

and provisional attitudes displayed in DtrP and DtrN.[61] In his second mono-graph, *Das Königtum in der Beurteilung der deuteronomistischen Histori-ographie* (1977),[62] he extends his analysis to a second set of texts, this time from Judges and 1 Samuel, dealing with the emergence of kingship as an in-stitution within Israel prior to David.[63] He seeks to show that, in general, the same distinctions between the views of DtrG, DtrP, and DtrN respectively are evident in this set of texts as in the first set.[64] Judges 17–21 is one of the texts adduced in this second monograph in support of the part of his thesis relating to the basic Deuteronomist (DtrG). He argues that the "promonarchical no-tices" ("königsfreundliche Notizen") of 17:6, 18:1a, 19:1a, and 21:25 give kingship unqualified endorsement as a legitimate institution necessary for se-curing the realm against internal disorder, both cultic (17–18) and social (19–21) — a task beyond the competence (and specific brief) of the judges.[65] By following the account of the gross cultic irregularities practiced by Micah (17:1-5) with the note that "in those days there was no king in Israel; every-one did what was right in his own eyes" (17:6), the redactor implicitly subor-dinates cultic matters to kingly jurisdiction, a concept which played an essen-

61. In the concluding chapter, "Synthese und Konsequenzen," the views of the redactors are described. I quote here from the synopsis in *Old Testament Abstracts* 1, no. 2 (1978): 199: "DtrG idealizes David and his dynasty. He sees the king as both the *nāgîd* and the servant of the LORD. The monarch is exemplary in piety and justice, and his house is the legitimate and enduring dynasty. DtrP presents the king as sinful yet ready to repent. The ruler is never titled 'the servant of the LORD,' while two prophets are so designated. A future for the royal house is not envisaged. Finally, DtrN allows both place and future to David's house in as far as its members are obedient to the law. Thus history, prophecy, and law, three important constituents of the religion of ancient Israel, have together shaped the Deuteronomistic David tradition and created a multifaceted image."

62. See the reference in n. 50.

63. These, too, are each related to a lead text: Judg. 17–21 (ch. 2); 1 Sam. 7:2-17 (ch. 3); 1 Sam. 10:17–11:15 (ch. 4); 1 Sam. 8 (ch. 5); 1 Sam. 9:1–10:16 (ch. 6); 1 Sam. 12 (ch. 7); Judg. 8:22-23 and 9:7-21 (ch. 8).

64. Only the work of DtrG and DtrN is found in the texts studied. The views of these two Deuteronomists as found in these texts are characterized as follows (I quote here from the synopsis in *Old Testament Abstracts* 1, no. 2 [1978]: 200): "The basic Deuter-onomist uses traditions which in outlook are similar to his own and describes the rise and role of kingship in keeping with Deut. 17:14-20. In so far as kings came to rule according to that law they are divinely called and legitimated (as 'the Judges' had been before them). . . . The nomistic Deuteronomist, on the other hand, condemns kingship as the re-sult of the people's disobedience and as the rejection of Yahweh's kingship, the positive estimate of David notwithstanding."

65. ". . . the judge is a savior who frees the people from external enemies. Ac-cording to DtrG it is not his task to intervene against cultic or other offenses within the people of God" (p. 29). See his detailed analysis of the "promonarchical notices" on pp. 15-17.

tial role in the basic Deuteronomistic History of DtrG.[66] In particular, Veijola finds the locus of the expression, "everyone did what was right in his own eyes" (17:6; 21:25), in the cult-centralization legislation of Deuteronomy 12:8-12, which, with Smend, he attributes specifically to DtrG.[67]

He contends that chapters 17–21 have undergone extensive Deuteronomistic revision, discernible (apart from the promonarchical refrain of 17:6, 18:1, 19:1, and 21:25) in 17:5, 7b, 13; 18:1b, 19, 30, 31b; 19:1b, 30; 20:4, 27b-28a. These redactional elements are identified as Deuteronomistic partly on the basis of characteristic language and style, and partly on the basis of the social/theological concerns they evince. For example, Veijola argues that the redactionally produced characterization of the Levites in both chapters 17–18 and chapters 19–21 as unpropertied sojourners (gērîm) dependent on the hospitality and support of their fellow Israelites (17:7b; 19:1b; 20:4) reflects the Deuteronomistic legislation concerning "the Levite within your gates" of Deuteronomy 12:12; 28:19; 14:27, 29; 16:11, 14; and 26:11, 12, 13.[68] It adds depth to the picture of cultic and social disorder in the two narratives. The formula "from the day that the people of Israel came up out of Egypt until this day" (Judg. 19:30) is one of the more obvious examples of Deuteronomistic language on which he draws (cf. Deut. 9:7; 1 Sam. 8:8; 2 Sam. 7:6; 1 Kgs. 8:16; 2 Kgs. 21:15; Jer. 7:25; 11:7).[69] Finally, Veijola argues that these chapters are an integral part of a final cycle of apostasy — punishment — deliverance which conforms to the DtrG's conception of the judges period in general, and brings it to a close. After the death of the judge Samson (16:30-31), Israel again does evil in the sight of Yahweh (chs. 17–21) and suffers a humiliating defeat at the hands of the Philistines (1 Sam. 4), after which Samuel, the last judge, is raised up as a deliverer (1 Sam. 7, esp. vv. 8-15).[70]

The impact of Veijola's work is apparent in Alberto Soggin's Judges commentary of 1981. In his introduction to chapters 17–21 Soggin comments that "the arguments put forward by Veijola in favor of a Dtr edition . . . are weighty ones, which open up a new period in the study of these chapters."[71]

---

66. "With this he shows at the same time that he subordinates the cultic matters to the realm of the king, which is completely in agreement with the concept that plays an important role in the later interpretation of history in DtrG" (p. 27).

67. Veijola refers (p. 16, n. 5) to a seminar presentation in which Smend held that Deut. 12:13-28 (with "you" singular) was original, while vv. 1-12 (with "you" plural) was made up of two additions, by DtrG (vv. 8-12) and DtrN (vv. 1-7) respectively.

68. Das Königtum, pp. 17-27.

69. Das Königtum, pp. 18-19.

70. Das Königtum, pp. 28-29.

71. J. Alberto Soggin, Judges: A Commentary, Old Testament Library (Philadelphia: Westminster, 1981), p. 263.

Noth, Richter, Smend, and Veijola are all major scholars whose work may fairly be regarded as representing the main lines of development of redactional-critical study relevant to the Judges material. The work of Smend and Veijola taken together suggests that the opening and closing sections of the book are much more closely integrated, redactionally and conceptually, into its central section than was recognized by Noth and Richter. However, they continue to consider Judges 1 and 17–21 primarily in relation to the structure of the Deuteronomistic History with its periods as conceived by Noth, and only secondarily as the beginning and ending of the book of Judges. We conclude this redaction-critical survey by looking at the work of two scholars, Robert Boling and Graeme Auld, who, while still working within the broad parameters of Noth's thesis, have addressed the final form of the book much more directly.

Boling's understanding of the redactional history of Judges is summarized in the introduction to his Anchor Bible Commentary.[72] We will not repeat the details here, but simply note the substantial agreement between Boling and the major works reviewed above and indicate where Boling's own distinctive contribution lies, particularly with reference to the opening and closing segments of the book. Boling agrees with Noth that the author of the original Deuteronomic History combined stories of "saviors" with archival notes about so-called "minor judges" and contributed introductory material in chapter 2.[73] He agrees with Richter, however, that the stories of the "saviors" had already been formed into an edited cycle (which he calls "the pragmatic edition") before they came into the hands of the Deuteronomistic historian.[74] Boling's particular contribution comes in his treatment of the *later* redactional history of the book. Here his analysis is strongly determined by his acceptance of F. M. Cross's thesis that there were two major editions of the historical work identified by Noth. Cross reserved the term "Deuteronomistic" for the second edition, which he distinguished from an earlier "Deuteronomic" edition. The first, seventh-century edition was ideologically supportive of Josiah's reforms. The second, sixth-century edition transformed the earlier work into a sermon on history addressed to the Judean exiles.[75] Boling discerns a similar, two-stage redaction

---

72. Robert G. Boling, *Judges,* The Anchor Bible (New York: Doubleday, 1975), pp. 29-38.

73. *Judges,* p. 36.

74. Boling spells out the extent of his indebtedness to Richter in Robert G. Boling, "In Those Days There Was No King in Israel," in *A Light unto My Path: Old Testament Studies in Honor of Jacob M. Meyers,* ed. H. N. Bream, R. Heim, and C. Moore (Philadelphia: Temple University Press, 1974), p. 36. Cf. *Judges,* p. 36.

75. "The Structure of the Deuteronomic History," *Perspectives in Jewish Learning* 3 (1968): 9-24. Cf. Boling, *Judges,* p. 36.

of the material we now know as the book of Judges. He assigns the whole of 2:1–18:31 to a Deuteronomic edition, which thus begins with Yahweh's messenger indicting the Israelites at Bochim (= Bethel)[76] and ends with a polemic against the shrine at Dan. Centrally located between these two limits is Abimelech's disastrous reign and destruction of Shechem in chapter 9. Boling comments:

> It is difficult to avoid the conclusion that the historian has deliberately arranged his presentation so that the period of the Judges begins, centers, and ends with accounts that devalue possible competitors to the Jerusalem temple, thus endeavoring to legitimate King Josiah's policies in the late seventh century.[77]

Boling attributes chapters 1 and 19–21 to a sixth-century updating which produced "the final or Deuteronomistic edition" of the book.[78] For Boling, this did not detract from the coherence of the earlier edition, but supplemented and enhanced it. His sensitivity to the literary structure of the final product is apparent in the following comment on chapter 1:

> The final (exilic) redactor of the introduction was . . . supplementing the critical perspective of the seventh-century Deuteronomic Historian when he built into the interim between Joshua's death and Othniel's rescue of the nation (3:7-11) his prelude to the era, a little known period which he indicated unfolded from an eagerly united beginning to a scattered and indecisive conclusion. *Compare the movement within the body of the book from Othniel in the south (3:7-11) to the Danite traditions in chs. 13–16.*[79] (my italics)

Boling and Smend both see chapter 1 as part of a major revision of the Deuteronomistic History, and although Boling assigns chapter 1 and 2:1-5 to separate stages, he does agree with Smend that 1:1–2:5 is a logical unity (ch. 1 now documents the charge made in 2:1-5). However, Boling's observation about the correspondence between the schematic arrangement of chapter 1 and the plan of the central section of the book counts strongly against Smend's notion that 1:1–2:5 was added as an old, pre-formed unit. Instead, it appears to be a deliberately constructed introduction to what follows.

76. An identification made explicitly in both the A and B texts of LXX Judges. Cf. "the oak of weeping" near Bethel in Gen. 35:8.

77. *Judges,* pp. 184-85.

78. *Judges,* p. 31.

79. *Judges,* p. 64, and cf. p. 36: "to the exilic (Deuteronomistic) redactor is left the addition of the bulk of ch. 1 (in itself a configuration of some of the oldest material of the book)."

Boling's position vis-à-vis Smend receives independent corroboration in an article by Graeme Auld published in the same year as Boling's commentary.[80] Auld argues that Judges 1:1–2:5 is "a deliberately contrived introduction to the book of Judges."[81] Basing his case on an examination of the links between Judges 1 and material elsewhere in the Old Testament (especially Joshua), and an analysis of the structure and development of the passage as a whole, he concludes that it is

> a late prefatory note to the book of Judges which supplements, corrects, and explains the treatment by the Deuteronomistic History of the period of the Judges. Part of it suggests that the troubled history of the northern tribes, about which the body of the book is largely concerned, was due to the failures during their settlement in Canaan. Part of it compensates for the scanty mention of Judah in the rest of the book. . . . It is not unlikely that this new preface is contemporaneous with the division of the Deuteronomistic History into the now familiar separate books.[82]

In relation to the closing chapters of the book, Boling anticipates a major aspect of the work of Veijola in finding a link between the portrayal of the Levites in chapters 17–21 and one of the major areas of concern of Deuteronomy and the Deuteronomistic historians.[83] Chapters 17–18 depict "the easy exploitation and corruption of a promising young Levite at secondary shrines," and chapters 19–21 portray an "outrage which was touched off by a failure of Yahwist 'hospitality' toward another Levite."[84] Boling differs from Veijola in assigning chapters 19–21 to a Deuteronomistic *revision* of the basic history,[85] but is in agreement with him in proposing an exilic provenance for them.[86] Evidence for the exilic dating of chapters 19–21 is found in the

---

80. A. G. Auld, "Judges 1 and History: A Reconsideration," *VT* 25, no. 2a (1975): 261-85.

81. "Judges 1 and History," p. 265.

82. "Judges 1 and History," p. 285.

83. *Judges,* p. 35: "The disaster of 721 only heightened one of Deuteronomy's enduring concerns — to find provision for jobless rural Levites at the central Yahweh sanctuary (Deut. 18:1-8). Provision for the Levites presents, in fact, the most notable discrepancy between the Deuteronomic platform of reform and its implementation as reported in Kings and Chronicles. That discrepancy became a source of controversy that now provides an important clue to the redactional history of Judges: compare the contrasting characterizations of two Levites in chs. 17 and 19."

84. *Judges,* p. 36.

85. But he does have the support of Noth for his view that chs. 19–21 as a unit are secondary to chs. 17–18. See the discussion of Noth above.

86. For Veijola, following Dietrich, the basic Deuteronomic History itself was exilic. See the discussion of their work above.

prominence they give to Judah and Benjamin,[87] and to the old general assembly *('ēḏâ/qāhāl)*, an institution largely suppressed during the monarchy, but which blossomed again as the postmonarchical "congregation."[88] Similar arguments for the setting and function of Judges 19–21 in its final form were subsequently proposed in a major monograph by H. Jüngling.[89]

Boling's most distinctive contribution is his thesis that chapters 1 and 19–21 now provide the entire book with a "tragicomic" framework:

> In its finished form the Book of Judges begins with Israel scattered and ineffective by the close of chapter 1. It ends with a very delicate, persistent ideal — *Israel,* reunited at last in the wake of a tragic civil war — in an account that swarms with incongruities. . . .[90]

It is with this survival of "Israel" in spite of all the vicissitudes and absurdities of the judges period that the Deuteronomistic editor consoles the exiles who live in a period when, once again, there is "no king in Israel."

In reviewing Boling's *Judges,* Graeme Auld takes issue with him on points of detail. For him 1:1–2:5 and chapters 17–21 are "post-Deuteronomistic."[91] He does agree with Boling, however, in recognizing a strong affinity between the beginning and end of the book. He finds the close verbal parallels between 1:1-2 and 20:18, and the prominence both passages give to Judah, particularly striking.[92] Boling and Auld are in substantial agreement with Noth and Richter as to the earlier redactional history of Judges. What they both try to do is achieve a more precise description of the *final* stages of its redactional history. As we noted above, Boling's work in particular represents an application to Judges of F. M. Cross's work on the Deuteronomistic History — a refinement of Noth's thesis which has commanded widespread

---

87. *Judges,* p. 278.

88. R. G. Boling, "Response," *JSOT* 1 (1976): 49.

89. Hans-Winfried Jüngling, *Richter 19 — Ein Plädoyer für das Königtum: Stilistische Analyse der Tendenzerzählung, Ri. 19,1-30a; 21,25,* Analecta Biblica 84 (Rome: Biblical Institute Press, 1981). Jüngling finds the setting for the final redaction of the whole unit, 19–21, to be the exilic or postexilic period, in which it served to instruct the community (on the basis of ancient precedent) how a sinning brother is to be disciplined (excommunicated and restored) in a context where "there is no king in Israel." See esp. pp. 244-46.

90. *Judges,* pp. 37-38.

91. A. Graeme Auld, "Review of Boling's *Judges:* The Framework of Judges and the Deuteronomists," *JSOT* 1 (1976): 45.

92. "One cannot but agree with Boling, even if in different spirit, that the repetition of the oracular device and the primacy of Judah in 1:1-2 and 20:18 'is something quite out of the ordinary'" ("Boling's *Judges,*" p. 45). Compare his analysis of the literary interdependence of these two passages in "Judges 1," pp. 267-68.

acceptance, particularly in American scholarship.[93] Hence the area of agreement between Boling and Auld represents a refinement of earlier major studies. Taken together, their work suggests that the final editing of the Deuteronomistic History in effect redefined the *period* of the judges so that its limits now correspond to those of the *book of Judges,* which in its final form is a rounded literary unit. A further, distinct transitional period (from the birth of Samuel to the death of Saul) is covered in 1 Samuel before the monarchy period proper begins with David's accession to the throne in 2 Samuel.[94] My monograph of 1987[95] was a literary rather than a historical study of Judges. However, the evidence it found for the distinctiveness and coherence of the book in its own right lent support to conclusions that were already emerging from historical-critical study of Judges. Since then the flourishing of new literary-critical methods and the continued questioning and revision of Noth's thesis about an original Deuteronomistic History[96] have opened the way for reconsideration of the redactional history of Judges and its contribution to the biblical account of Israel's history in the premonarchy period. In 2003, the fresh treatment of Joshua, Judges, and 1 and 2 Samuel in Provan, Long, and Longman's *A Biblical History of Israel* was a clear sign of renewed interest in the contribution these books as such could make to the historical and theological study of the Old Testament.

The most striking manifestation of these trends to date is the recently published HThKAT Judges commentary by Walter Gross.[97] Applying traditional German-style literary-critical method, he finds ten redactional layers in Judges, from a core of ancient hero stories, through a pre-Deuteronomistic edition of them, to two Deuteronomic redactions (Dtr^R, Dtr^S), expansions by two postexilic authors and three supplementers, to completion by a final postexilic author who supplied the frame of chapters 1 and 17–21. The result is a book with a clear structure and well-defined boundaries, but with an unresolved tension between a core that has a negative view of kingship (2:6–16:31) and a frame (chs. 1 and 17–21) that sees it as a necessity if Israel is to overcome the chaos of the judges period and move forward. In its canonical

93. See R. D. Nelson, *The Double Redaction of the Deuteronomistic History,* JSOTSup 18 (Sheffield: JSOT, 1981).

94. This is a more adequate description of the literary structure of the text, in my judgment, than Veijola's proposal of a final cycle of the judges period extending from Judg. 17 to 1 Sam. 12.

95. *The Book of the Judges: An Integrated Reading,* JSOTSup 46 (Sheffield: JSOT).

96. For the latter, see the detailed review of developments from Noth's original work to the present in Trent C. Butler, *Judges,* WBC 8 (Nashville: Thomas Nelson, 2009), pp. xliii-li.

97. *Richter,* HThKAT (Freiburg im Breisgau: Herder, 2009).

context it acts as a bridge between Exodus–Joshua, which describe Israel's development as a nation before the emergence of kingship, and 1 Samuel–2 Kings, which describe its existence under the monarchy.

Gross's understanding of the unique character and function of Judges emerges from his redaction-critical analysis. It is not clear yet how his account of its formation will be received, and whether his attempt to combine final form literary-canonical criticism with historical criticism can be judged successful. Nevertheless, given his stature as a scholar and the status of the HThKAT commentary series, his work may fairly be taken as representative of the state of redactional-critical study of Judges at the beginning of the twenty-first century.

Further comment on Gross's commentary will be made in Section V. By way of summary of the ground covered here, however, it is clear that the redactional unity of the central section of Judges, dealing with the careers of Othniel to Samson, has long been recognized, and insofar as historical-critical scholars have addressed themselves to the *final* stages of the book's formation, early skepticism about it being a distinct work in its own right has effectively been answered.

IV. ITS SHAPE AND CONTENT[98]

Whatever its history, Judges as we now have it has a very clear structure. The long central section that deals with the careers of the judges themselves extends from 3:7 to 16:31. It is preceded by an introduction in two parts (1:1–2:5 and 2:6–3:6) and followed by an epilogue, also in two parts (chs. 17–18 and 19–21). The question that is asked at the beginning of the book (1:1-2) is asked again in very different circumstances at the end (20:18). So as we come to the end of the book we are invited to reflect on the point from which we set out, and on all that has happened in between.[99]

The first part of the introduction (1:1–2:5) is about the progressive deterioration in Israel's position vis-à-vis the Canaanites that followed the

---

98. This section is based on my treatment of the same topic in "Judges," in *NBC*, pp. 263-65.

99. Dennis Olson has pointed out that the two parts of the introduction deal with "social fragmentation" and "religious deterioration" respectively, and that the two parts of the conclusion deal with the same two things in reverse order, giving an ABBA frame around the book as a whole. Dennis T. Olson, "The Book of Judges," in *The New Interpreter's Bible*, ed. Leander E. Keck et al. (Nashville: Abingdon, 1998), vol. 2, p. 863. Cf. K. Lawson Younger Jr., *Judges, Ruth,* NIVAC (Grand Rapids: Zondervan, 2002), pp. 30-31.

death of Joshua (1:1). The efforts of the various tribes to possess and occupy the lands that had been allocated to them (Josh. 13–19) run into increasing difficulties as the Canaanites, particularly on the coastal plain and in key fortified cities in the north, put up very determined resistance (see esp. vv. 19, 27-28). This leads to a tense stalemate situation in which Israelites and Canaanites live side by side. The Israelites hold the upper hand but are still excluded from significant parts of the land. The tribe of Dan in particular is confined to the hills and is unable to get a secure foothold in its allotted territory near the coast (1:34). It is a situation that falls far short of the expectations with which Israel had set out, expectations grounded in the promises God had made to their ancestors (Josh. 23:1-5; cf. Gen. 12:1-3; 15:12-21; 28:13-15). This part of the introduction ends with the Israelites weeping before Yahweh at Bochim (Bethel) and being told what has gone wrong (2:1-5). The reason for their failure has not been the iron chariots or strong fortifications of the Canaanites, but their own unfaithfulness. In the territory they had succeeded in taking they had begun to compromise by allowing the altars of the Canaanites to remain standing, and because of this Yahweh had withdrawn his help from them. In addition to looking back, this key speech by Yahweh's messenger also looks forward, with the prediction that the Canaanites and their gods will become a snare to the Israelites.

The second part of the introduction (2:6–3:6) returns to the beginning (notice how Joshua reappears in 2:6) and makes this underlying spiritual problem the main focus of attention. In a few deft strokes Israel's initial decline into apostasy is sketched (2:6-10) and then the whole pattern of the ensuing judges era is laid out (2:11-19). It is presented as a period of persistent apostasy, in which Yahweh alternately judges the Israelites by handing them over to foreign oppressors, and then (when they are in great distress) has pity on them and raises up a judge to save them. At these times the Israelites temporarily give up their apostasy, but quickly return to it when the judge dies (v. 19a). In short, despite Yahweh's many attempts to retrieve them from their evil ways, the Israelites persist in them (v. 19b). This leads to another crucial speech in 2:20-22, in which Yahweh announces what he intends to do as his final response to all that has taken place. The nations which were originally left (at the time Joshua died) to test Israel's faithfulness will now be left permanently as a punishment for her unfaithfulness. This is the climax of the second part of the introduction, and to the introduction as a whole. The verses that remain (2:23–3:6) are essentially a summary of all that has gone before.

So the introduction, as well as diagnosing what went wrong and mapping out what is to follow, makes it very clear what the central issue of the book is, namely, Israel's persistent apostasy in the judges period and Yahweh's response to it. The book answers the question, "Why didn't Israel ever fully possess the land that God promised to their ancestors?" and gives the answer, "Because of the apostasy that followed the death of Joshua, and continued in spite of all Yahweh's efforts to reclaim Israel from it." Judges defends Yahweh's action in leaving the remaining nations long-term as fully justified in view of Israel's behavior. The later books of the Deuteronomistic History go on to explain and justify his later, more drastic act of evicting Israel from the land altogether.

The central section of the book (3:7–16:31) fills out the outline already given in the introduction (2:11-19) and develops a number of subthemes in the process. It records the careers of twelve judges in all: Othniel, Ehud, Shamgar, Barak, Gideon, Tola, Jair, Jephthah, Ibzan, Elon, Abdon, and Samson. Deborah and Jael both play very significant roles in the Barak episode, and Deborah is even said to have judged Israel (4:4-5), but in terms of the overall design of the book chapters 4–5 must be seen as essentially about Barak; and although the activities of Gideon's son Abimelech are recounted in some detail, he is not a judge at all in terms of the way that office has been described in the introduction.

Just as the first part of the introduction began with Judah and ended with Dan (1:1-34), so this central section begins with judge Othniel from Judah (3:7-11) and ends with judge Samson the Danite (chs. 13–16). Othniel is a model judge whose career exemplifies what a judge was meant to be and do. The following judges represent a series of variations on this basic pattern, culminating with Samson, whose behavior is so bizarre that he is barely recognizable as a judge at all. The pattern of this part of the book has frequently been described in terms of a repeating cycle of apostasy, oppression, calling on Yahweh, deliverance, peace, and renewed apostasy. There is certainly much repetition in this long central section, but there is also progressive change, so that the result is better described in terms of a downward spiral than a simple cycle. Disunity among the Israelites first appears in the Barak episode (5:16-17, 23), and grows worse under later judges. After the forty years that follow Gideon's victory (8:28) the land is never again said to enjoy rest, and by the time of Samson the Israelites no longer even cry out to Yahweh to save them. Furthermore, as these chapters run their course, the judges themselves gradually become more and more implicated in the wrongdoing of the nation as a whole. The climax is reached in Samson, whose personal waywardness and reluctance to embrace his calling perfectly epitomize the waywardness and struggle of Israel. As Israel had been set apart from other nations by God's covenant with her, so Samson is set apart from other men by his calling as a Nazirite. As Israel went after foreign gods, Samson goes after foreign women. Israel wanted to be as other nations; Samson wants to be as other men; and as Israel repeatedly called on Yahweh in its distress, so does Samson. In short, the subthemes that run through the whole central section of the book (Israel's struggle against her destiny and Yahweh's perseverance with her in judgment and grace) are finally brought to a sharp focus in the story of Samson. His personal story is also the story of Israel as a whole in the judges period.

The two stories that form the epilogue (chs. 17–21) are also located in the judges period (when "there was no king in Israel") but do not follow chronologically from what has gone before. There is also a shift of focus in them, from the sin of Israel as a whole to the sins of the individuals and communities that comprise it: everyone does what is right in his own eyes (17:6). The first story, in chapters 17–18 (Micah and his idols), is about the religious chaos of the period; the second, in chapters 19–21 (the Levite and his concubine), is about the accompanying moral chaos. Together they show that Israel was even more endangered by its own internal decay, morally and spiritually, than by any external attack. In particular, the second story shows how the very institutions which should have provided stability (the Levitical priesthood, hospitality and family life, eldership, and the assembly of tribal leaders) were all rendered ineffective, and even positively harmful, because of the moral bankruptcy of individuals. The way the book ends leaves us in no doubt that it was certainly not the quality of its leadership or its institutions that held Israel together. Israel's survival in the period of the judges was a miracle of God's grace.

The refrain that runs through the epilogue ("In those days there was no king in Israel . . . ," 17:6; 18:1; 19:1; 21:25) rings down the curtain on one period and anticipates another. Kingship, like judgeship, will have its place in Israel's ongoing history and prove useful in its time. But it, too, will fail through human sinfulness. As the Deuteronomistic History as a whole shows, no institution, however valid, holds the key to Israel's future. It is only God's ongoing commitment to his people, in spite of everything, that does this.

V. RECENT SCHOLARLY STUDY OF JUDGES

The 1970s and early 1980s saw two developments in biblical studies that had major significance for the study of Judges, as for all other biblical books. The first was the advent of canonical criticism, heralded by the publications of Brevard Childs, especially his *Biblical Theology in Crisis* (1970) and *Introduction to the Old Testament as Scripture* (1979).[100] The second was the emergence of what might be called "pure" literary criticism (the study of

---

100. *Biblical Theology in Crisis* (Philadelphia: Westminster, 1970); *Introduction to the Old Testament as Scripture* (London: SCM, 1979).

texts as literature rather than as sources for history or theology), which was popularized by the work of Robert Alter, especially in *The Art of Biblical Narrative* (1981).[101] Both were fresh ways of studying biblical texts which gave new freedom and energy to the scholarly study of them.

Canonical criticism reinstated the final (canonical) form of the text as an object of primary concern for biblical scholars. It also placed the canon back in place as the primary context in which to consider the theological contribution of each of the books to the theology of the Bible and the church. The new literary criticism was quite different from this in its motivation, having very little interest in either theology in the traditional sense or the canon as such, but complemented canonical theology in two key ways: it shared with it an interest in the final form of the text, but brought a new sophistication to the study of the literary craftsmanship exhibited by the biblical texts. The combination of the two has proved to be a potent brew which has produced some excesses (inevitable in an age of experimentation) but also many fine and insightful new explorations of how the biblical texts "work" as finished pieces, including the book of Judges. My own doctoral thesis, published in 1987, was the first attempt, as far as I am aware, to apply the new literary approach to the book as a whole. This commentary has given me the opportunity to update it where necessary, and bring its findings into connection with the theological concerns normally associated with canonical criticism; that is, to work through the book of Judges again, this time as both literature *and* Scripture. But first, let us take time to note here some of the more significant studies of Judges since 1987 which show the influence of these new approaches but move beyond them in the spirit of emerging postmodernism with its unabashed acceptance of the subjectivity involved in the reading of texts, including biblical texts.

Mieke Bal's *Death and Dissymmetry: The Politics of Coherence in the Book of Judges* (1988) is a feminist reading of Judges which is deliberately subversive, marginalizing what has been regarded as central (theology, history) and focusing on what has been marginalized by traditional (and mostly male) biblical scholarship.[102] She seeks to bring to light the roots of the gender-bound violence she finds in Judges, and argues that the murders of young women in the book are caused by "uncertainty about fatherhood" (p. 6). She summarizes her findings as follows:

> Reading the book of Judges within the margins of the traditional readings has led us to realise how deeply violence is anchored in the domes-

---

101. Robert Alter, *The Art of Biblical Narrative* (New York: Basic Books, 1981).

102. Mieke Bal, *Death and Dissymmetry: The Politics of Coherence in the Book of Judges* (Chicago and London: The University of Chicago Press, 1988).

tic domain. I conclude with the suggestion that the political violence of wars and conquests is secondary in relation to the institutional violence of the social order. This violence seems to be the inevitable consequence of a social structure that is inherently contradictory. Between the two poles of the contradiction, x and y, the young woman, the virgin daughter, has to pay with her life for the society's incapacity to solve the conflicts. (p. 231)

On such a reading it is Jephthah's daughter, rather than Jephthah or any of the other judges, who best encapsulates the angst — the intractable and deeply rooted problem — which lies at the heart of the book. Bal's work is symptomatic of the new freedom to experiment, and engages in the kind of study of biblical texts that had been impossible in the context of traditional biblical scholarship. Positively it highlights the unusually large number of women in Judges, both named (Achsah, Deborah, Jael, Delilah) and unnamed (Sisera's mother, Jephthah's daughter, the women of Thebez and Timnah, the thirty daughters of Ibzan, the Levite's concubine, and the young women of Shiloh), who are both impacted by and impact upon the male-dominated central plot. There is a sense, however, in which Bal's work is also subversive of the *new* literary criticism, in that it reads *against* the text in its finished form, deconstructing it to expose what is beneath it rather than what has been consciously crafted into it by its author(s). It is part of the ferment of a new era in the study of biblical texts, rather than (like Alter) a mainstream representative of it. But Judges, precisely because it does feature so many women, has proven to be a particularly fruitful field for feminist study, in which quality writers like Mieke Bal, J. Cheryl Exum, and Phyllis Trible have contributed many fine exegetical insights. Mieke Bal's work is representative of the significant contribution being made to contemporary Judges scholarship by such writers.[103]

As its name suggests, Lillian Klein's monograph *The Triumph of Irony in the Book of Judges,* also published in 1988, is a specialized work rather than an overall interpretation of the book.[104] She seeks to show how irony and literary structure function in the text, especially how they contribute to the particular perspective on the period of the judges that the book provides. She argues that Judges is a tour de force of irony, and that this irony is *progressive.* The exposition in chapters 1 and 2 is largely free of it. In the first

---

103. See Athalya Brenner, ed., *Judges,* The Feminist Companion to the Bible (Second Series) 4 (Sheffield: Sheffield Academic Press, 1993), and the bibliography in Victor H. Matthews, *Judges and Ruth,* NCBC (Cambridge: Cambridge University Press, 2004), pp. 25-28. For an example of contemporary postcolonial feminist work on Judges, see Katharine Doob Sakenfeld, "Whose Text Is It?" *JBL* 127, no. 1 (2008): 5-18.

104. Lillian R. Klein, *The Triumph of Irony in the Book of Judges,* JSOTSup 68 (Sheffield: Almond, 1988).

part of the central section (from Othniel to Barak), the irony is mainly at the expense of figures who are contrasted with the judges (e.g., Eglon and Sisera); from Gideon to Samson, however, irony is a key aspect of the portrayal of the judges themselves. The epilogue, chapters 17–21, is highly ironic, exposing the deep contradictions at the heart of the national psyche that bring Israel to the brink of destruction. The categories of this analysis (structure, irony, progressive development, point of view) are entirely representative of the interests and methods of the new literary criticism. Klein seeks to understand how one particular aspect of the literary craftsmanship of the text works to produce a particular (intended) effect. The presence of irony in Judges has long been recognized, of course, but Klein's contribution has been to examine it in a systematic way, using the kinds of tools which have become available to biblical scholars as part of the new literary criticism.

E. John Hamlin's commentary of 1990 is his contribution to the Eerdmans International Theological Commentary series.[105] It draws on exegetical insights from practitioners of the new literary criticism (Exum, Trible, Webb), but in terms of method is only marginally affected by it. In line with the requirements for contributions to this commentary series it is avowedly *theological* in character. It aims to respect the integrity of the Old Testament as Jewish scripture, but also to show how, for Christians, the story of God's saving purposes which it contains finds its fulfillment in Jesus Christ. In other words, it is fundamentally an exercise in applying the method of *canonical criticism*. It takes the canon as the proper context for reading Judges as Scripture, and applies this principle to the task of writing a commentary for "ministers and Christian educators" (p. viii). The "international" nature of the treatment shows in the way Hamlin relates his exposition to issues such as colonialism, nationalism, oppression, and liberation, refers to non-Western classics, and draws on the contributions of non-Western as well as Western scholars. In this sense, this commentary reads Judges in the context of the whole contemporary world.

Of particular interest is the way Hamlin sees "the land" as the key to both the canonical/theological significance of Judges and its contemporary relevance. In Judges the promised land is "the God-given arena where the gifts of freedom (space) and security (place) are constantly threatened" (p. 1). Personal and social identity, and therefore true humanity, is inseparable from "landedness"; but in biblical-theological terms the land of Canaan is a symbol of something greater that is secured for us by and in Christ. So, paradoxically, it is possible to be exiles (landless) and yet truly free, secure, and human. The preeminence given to Judah in Judges is the key to the way the

---

105. *At Risk in the Promised Land: A Commentary on the Book of Judges,* International Theological Commentary (Grand Rapids: Eerdmans, 1990).

story told there will continue and reach its climax. It is only reading Judges in the context of the entire canon as well as the contemporary world that enables us to see its full Christian significance. This is not a major piece of scholarship, but is nevertheless an interesting application of a basically canonical/theological approach to the important task of expounding Judges as Christian Scripture today.[106]

Yairah Amit's *The Book of Judges: The Art of Editing* (Hebrew 1992, English 1999) uses literary analysis to try to establish the provenance and purpose of Judges.[107] Amit sees the treatment of "leadership" and "signs" (indications of divine presence and involvement in the historical process) as guidelines for the editing process. The way they are treated is the key to understanding how the book was intended to convey a message to its readers. In terms reminiscent of both canonical criticism and new literary criticism, Amit maintains that "a presumption of unity" is necessary if the connections which exist between things in the text are to be found and properly understood (pp. 22-23). It is rather surprising, in view of this, that she ends up dismissing chapters 19–21 as "late and tendentious," and therefore limits her conclusions about the time and purpose of the book to chapters 1–18.[108] She argues that the book of Judges, redefined in this way, belongs to the period of Hezekiah in the late eighth century, between the collapse of the northern kingdom in 732-722 B.C. and the reforms of Josiah in the late seventh century. This rather radical suggestion (that the editorial production of Judges was pre-Deuteronomic) is supported by three main observations: prophecy in Judges is not yet predictive and doesn't interpret history as the fulfillment of the prophetic word as later prophecy will do; while there is harsh criticism of the northern sanctuaries of Bethel and Dan, this is not related to a strong view regarding the centralization of the cult (as in Deuteronomy); and finally, while there is strong insistence on the need for Israel to worship

106. Cf. Michael Wilcock, *The Message of Judges: Grace Abounding,* The Bible Speaks Today (Leicester: Inter-Varsity Press, 1992); Terry L. Brensinger, *Judges,* Believers' Church Bible Commentary (Scottdale: Herald, 1999); Dale Ralph Davis, *Such a Great Salvation: Expositions of the Book of Judges* (Grand Rapids: Baker, 1990).

107. Yairah Amit, *The Book of Judges: The Art of Editing,* tr. from the Hebrew by Jonathan Chipman, Biblical Interpretation Series 38 (Leiden: Brill, 1999). It was first published in Hebrew in 1992.

108. Chapters 19–21 are found to be an artificial and forced attempt to integrate a final cycle of punishment and deliverance into the rest of the book. Problems she sees include the way the statement that Judah will go first in 20:18 has no narrative realization (as it does in ch. 1), the improbability of the Israelites repeatedly assembling at Bethel in ch. 20 (when the battle zone is at Mizpah, close to Gibeah), and the way no explanation is given for the repeated defeat of the Israelites in their war against Benjamin (in contrast to the way such defeat *is* explained in the "parallel" story of the setbacks suffered at Ai in Josh. 7). See pp. 356-57.

only Yahweh, this falls short of the explicit monotheism of Deuteronomy and later works.

Whether they are sound or not, arguments and conclusions of this kind belong solidly in the realm of historical criticism rather than the new literary and canonical criticism. However, the influence of new literary criticism is apparent in two main areas. First, particular narrative episodes such as the Ehud, Gideon, and Samson stories are analyzed in terms of plot structure, characterization, viewpoint, and thematics; and second, the book of Judges is treated as an early example of narrative history — an example of how, within a particular social and historical context, "narrative served as a means of documenting history and deriving therefrom necessary lessons" (p. 382). In short, Amit's work brings narrative criticism and historical criticism together. In doing so it makes some excellent contributions to the literary analysis of particular episodes, and anticipates the full, principled reengagement of literary and historical approaches advocated and applied in the work of Provan, Long, and Longman on the history of Israel.[109] For Amit the message of Judges is that what Israel needed to do in the wake of the fall of the northern kingdom was to allow the tribe of Judah to lead it, come together around its king, and renew its covenant loyalty to God. It was a piece of narrative history which prepared the way for the Deuteronomic reforms.

Gale Yee's *Judges and Method* (2007)[110] is a collection of essays illustrating a range of new approaches to the study of biblical texts, and their application to the book of Judges. It is intended as a college course book, and Judges was chosen as a test case because its content is relatively unfamiliar to college students, and it includes a relatively high number of women characters and so lends itself well to introducing students to women's studies as a branch of biblical scholarship. The introduction helpfully distinguishes between "historical criticism," which treats Judges as a "constructed work," and "literary criticism," which treats it as a "unified work." The bulk of the book, however, is devoted to approaches which, for the most part, have developed *since* what we might call the classical period of new literary criticism (the 1970s and 1980s), with an example of each: Social Scientific Criticism (Naomi Steinberg, "Judges 9 and Issues of Kinship"), Feminist Criticism (J. Cheryl Exum, "Whose Interests Are Being Served?"), Structuralist Criticism (David Jobling, "The Text's World of Meaning"), Deconstructive Criticism (Dana Nolan Fewell, "Achsah and the (E)rased City of Writing"), Ideological Criticism (Gale Yee herself, "Judges 17–21 and the Dismembered Body"), Postcolonial Criticism (Y. Kim Uriah, "Who Is the Other in the

109. *A Biblical History of Israel.*
110. Gale A. Yee, ed., *Judges and Method: New Approaches in Biblical Studies,* 2nd ed. (Minneapolis: Fortress, 2007).

Book of Judges?"), and Cultural Criticism (David M. Gunn, "Viewing the Sacrifice of Jephthah's Daughter").[111] The need for such new*er* approaches in biblical studies is explained by reference to some inherent limitations that Yee sees in the now "older" kind of new literary criticism:

> The turn to the text [as in the new literary criticism of the 1970s and 1980s] underscores the aesthetic beauty of the biblical literature and the religious power of its rhetoric. One encounters the *text* firsthand and not simply the formative historical situations *behind the text*. Nevertheless, text-centered approaches are susceptible to certain problems in their analyses. Severing the text from its author and history could result in an ahistorical inquiry that regards the text primarily as an aesthetic object unto itself rather than a social practice intimately bound to a particular history. Privileging the text overlooks the workings of ideology in the text. It disregards the fact that ideology is *produced* by a particular author who is culturally constrained by historical time, place, gender, class, and bias, among other things. The biblical texts were not written to be objects of aesthetic beauty or contemplation, but as persuasive forces that during their own time formed opinions, made judgments, and exerted changes. Moreover, in all its historical, cultural, and linguistic constraints, the Bible continues to be a powerful standard for present-day social, as well as religious, attitudes and behavior. Readers inhabiting various social locations will nevertheless understand the biblical text differently. . . . [T]he position for the reader with respect to overlapping factors such as gender, sexuality, race, economic, class, and colonial history is of critical importance in answering the question, What does the text mean? Newer methods continue to appraise such a foundational work as the Bible in light of its powerful (mis)use in diverse social, religious, and academic communities that have traditionally overlooked such factors. (pp. 11-12)

One might respond that the need for such methods is overstated here, since the old historical criticism was well aware of many of the issues referred to, especially those related to the particulars of place and time and situation, and the ideological agenda(s) of biblical texts. It is also going too far, in my judgment, to hold that the particulars of the reader's position and outlook are "critical" for the question of meaning, especially if it means they are determi-

---

111. The first example, "Narrative Criticism" (Richard G. Bowman, "Human Purpose in Conflict with Divine Presence"), a study of God as a character in the Judges narrative, is an example of more or less "pure" new literary criticism, and is there (I think) more as a foil for what follows than as an example of the newer methods to which the book is primarily devoted.

native. This would be to deny the text its power and right to critique the reader's culture and worldview.

The three things that are genuinely new and necessary in the methods advocated in this book are a recovery (after the heady days of the 1970s and 1980s) of some of the valid concerns of the old historical criticism, a new awareness of gender-related issues and their importance for the humanity of the text, and a new emphasis on the need for self-awareness on the part of the reader about what he/she brings to the text and how this might influence his/her reading of it for good or ill. These are all issues of importance for an author such as myself, writing a commentary on a book which features an unusually large number of women and is grounded in a particular and largely alien social/historical context. The special contribution of this book is the way it raises these issues and uses Judges as a prism through which to focus them for us. In particular it highlights the following questions:

1. How is the interplay between divine and human initiative portrayed in Judges? In particular, how is God represented as a character through his interaction with human beings?
2. How do issues of kinship social structures shape the characters and influence what happens?
3. How do women feature in Judges? To what extent are they passive and active, powerless and powerful? What is the interplay between what is implicit and what is explicit in the way women are portrayed?
4. To what extent do things that lie on the surface of the text (e.g., winepresses, fords, fire) give symbolic expression to things that are deeper?
5. Do the book and the narratives it contains have one meaning or several? Are there submerged or discordant voices that need to be heard in order to appreciate the richness of the text?
6. Are there ideological agendas in Judges (or parts of it) that can be understood only in relation to what they are intended to attack or support (e.g., Josiah's reforms)?

These are all important questions, and Yee's book is helpful in sensitizing us to them.

Robert O'Connell's monograph, *The Rhetoric of the Book of Judges* (1996), is a thorough and substantial work.[112] It offers "a coherent reading of the present form of the book" (p. 1), and most of the analytical techniques it uses (study of plot structures, characterization, and literary devices such as

---

112. R. H. O'Connell, *The Rhetoric of the Book of Judges*, VTSup 63 (Leiden: E. J. Brill, 1996).

satire) place it in direct continuity with the kind of literary criticism associated, for example, with Robert Alter. But it moves beyond an appreciation of the artistry of the text to focus on purpose, and belongs (as its title indicates) in the more specialized field of *rhetorical* criticism. The essential question addressed is, What is "the ideological purpose or agenda of the Judges compiler/redactor with respect to the implied readers of the book?" (p. 1). Posing the question in this way takes us beyond consideration of the text as an aesthetic object to the writing of the book as a speech-act intended to have certain consequences. But the analysis remains essentially literary in that this purpose, and those at whom it is directed (the implied readers), are constructed from an analysis of the text itself. The conclusion, as summarized at the end of the work, is that

> the rhetorical purpose of Judges is ostensibly to endorse a divinely appointed Judahite king who, in contrast to foreign kings or non-Judahite deliverers in Israel, upholds such deuteronomic ideals as the need to expel foreigners from the land and the need to maintain intertribal loyalty to YAHWEH's cult and its regulations concerning social justice. (p. 343)

The intertribal dynamic of Judges as a whole (the promotion of Judah at the expense of Benjamin) is intended to persuade its readers to "endorse the dynasty of David over that of Saul" (p. 344).

I am not persuaded that Judges does in fact idealize Judah; indeed, Judah is shown in an increasingly negative light as the book runs its course. Nevertheless, this is an impressive piece of work, and one of the many fine insights it contributes has to do with the *theological* significance of the combination of apparently Deuteronomic and non-Deuteronomic language in the way Judges is constructed. It is generally recognized that the stories of deliverance that make up the bulk of the book have been framed by material which uses characteristically Deuteronomic language. This applies particularly to the material that introduces each episode, the occasional speeches by a prophet or Yahweh accusing Israel of unfaithfulness to the covenant, and the preview of the entire period in 2:11-19. The stories of deliverance themselves, leading to the recovery of rest in the land, contain little or no Deuteronomic language. O'Connell finds this combination of different types of material highly significant:

> As an evaluative framework, the cycle-motif portrays Israel's departure from YAHWEH in deuteronomic language, perhaps to emphasise Israel's covenant waywardness. YAHWEH's restoration of Israel to blessing in the land is expressed without deuteronomic language in terms that show YAHWEH exceeding his obligations to the covenant. (p. 343)

In theological terms we might say that the phenomenon that O'Connell has observed is the interplay between judgment and grace in Yahweh's administration of his covenant relationship with Israel in the judges period. It is an excellent example of what is gained by putting back together what more traditional historical-critical methods have tended to separate. Traditional historical criticism has enabled a scholar like O'Connell to recognize the presence of the two different kinds of material. What O'Connell has done is to address the *effect* when they are combined in the way they are in the finished form of the book. It is an example of the potential value of an approach that is eclectic in the best sense of that term.

One of the most substantial commentaries on Judges to appear in recent times is Daniel Block's contribution to the New American Commentary series, published in 1999.[113] It covers both Judges and Ruth, with 586 of its 765 pages devoted to Judges. It is based on the NIV and avoids technical language as much as possible, but is clearly the result of extensive research. The many footnotes enable those who have the tools and wish to do so to delve more deeply into the relevant scholarly literature. Block is familiar with the contribution of both historical-critical scholarship and the newer approaches we have been considering here, and makes use of their insights where appropriate. He identifies the theme of the book as a whole as "the Canaanization of Israel" in the judges period: the background to it (1:1–3:6), God's response to it (3:7–16:31), and the depths of it (chs. 17–21). He finds the key to the theology of the text in the way God is portrayed as the principal character in it: he is the "true hero" of the book, who perseveres with Israel in judgment and grace despite its waywardness, and it is this alone that accounts for Israel's survival. He finds the relevance of Judges in the parallel between Israel's situation and that of the church today. The church, like Israel, has to live out its faith in God in a pluralistic and seductive environment, where accommodation and apostasy are ever present dangers.

While this commentary owes a lot to both traditional historical criticism and the newer, more literary approaches, it is primarily an example of a canonical reading of Judges; that is, a reading of Judges within the context of the Christian Bible as a whole. It is also, in terms of its intended purpose, a reading of Judges in the context of the church and the world. It shows a thorough knowledge of the original, historical context of the book, and of the world that modern (especially Western) Christians live in. What is of particular interest to us here is how it moves from the one to the other; how it does theological exegesis *for* pastors and those they teach. Block notes that "Hebrews 11:32 [where Gideon, Barak, Samson, and Jephthah are mentioned in

---

113. Daniel I. Block, *Judges, Ruth,* NAC 6 (Nashville: Broadman & Holman, 1999).

the context of that chapter's discourse on faith] has exercised a profound and pervasive influence on the history of Christian interpretation of the Book of Judges." This had led to many holding up the major judges as "virtuous heroes, mighty men of God . . . [and] models after whom Christians should pattern their lives." In contrast, Block himself believes that "the primary significance of the book for the modern reader lies in a quite different direction," which becomes clear "when we allow the author of Judges to speak for himself." If we do this, we will see that "the Canaanization of Israel" is both "the central theme of the book of Judges" and also "the key to the relevance of this ancient composition for North American Christianity" (p. 71).

There are huge issues here that every Christian interpreter of Judges must grapple with — issues that lie in the areas of biblical theology and contextualization; and while what Block is doing is far more particular in terms of its theological commitments and pastoral purpose than Childs's canonical criticism, it does share fundamental areas of method with it. First, it focuses on the final form of the text as the primary datum for exegesis; it focuses on the canon as the primary context in which Judges must be read to access its theology; and finally, it has a strong interest in what lies in *front of* the text (in the life of the church) as well as what lies behind it (in the history of Israel). It will become apparent in what follows that, while my essential purpose is the same as Block's, the way I go about it will be different in some important ways. The main significance of Block's commentary for us here, however, is the way it illustrates the big challenges that must be faced by anyone who wants to move beyond pure academic study of the biblical text — historical, literary, or canonical — to the task of theological exegesis for the contemporary church.[114]

In contrast to Daniel Block's work, Tammi Schneider's volume of 2002 in the Berit Olam[115] series reflects a general interest in religion and women's studies without a commitment to any specific theological tradition. It is also quite self-consciously aligned with the new literary criticism. It is a *reading* of Judges; a treatment of it in that mode rather than a commentary on it in the usual sense. In the author's own words:

> The present examination is interested in how the entire book of Judges functions as a unified literary document. The focus is on the major themes which run throughout the book: the search for, as well as an ex-

114. Cf., in addition to the work of McCann referred to below, Matthews, *Judges and Ruth;* Wilcock, *The Message of Judges;* Davis, *Such a Great Salvation;* and C. Pressler, *Joshua, Judges, and Ruth,* Westminster Bible Companion (Louisville: Westminster John Knox, 2002). These are all much less substantial works than Block's, but are intended to serve the same basic purpose.

115. *Judges,* BO (Collegeville, MN: Liturgical Press, 2000).

amination and critique of, differing forms of leadership, the role of women as the barometer of how society functions, the polemic regarding the north/south tensions among the tribes of Israel as well as that related to David and Saul, and Israel's relationship to its deity. These themes are inherent in the narrative, as is made evident by the issues the book addresses, the amount of text dedicated to each topic, the terminology employed, and intertextual references tying Judges into the larger biblical corpus. The text of Judges expresses these concepts through the content, terminology, and structure of the individual narratives and also that of the book as a whole. Despite what are considered to be Deuteronomistic additions at the beginning and end of the book, Judges is a well-integrated theological narrative which builds its story and supports its thesis until its conclusion. (p. xiii)

The major conclusion of the study is completely unexceptional:

[T]he book of Judges stresses the theological message that during the period of the Judges the Israelites strayed from their deity. The deity repeatedly responded by appointing temporary leaders or judges. Each judge acted progressively worse than the predecessor had, leading Israel finally to anarchy and civil war. In the eyes of the narrator of Judges, Israel reached a point where kingship was Israel's only option, so laying the groundwork for the following books of Samuel through Kings. (p. 287)

While the approach taken yields nothing new in terms of the central message of the book, there are several significant outcomes at the level of subthemes and related issues. In regard to kingship, Schneider concludes that the evaluation of the monarchy in Judges is neither simply positive or negative, but genuinely ambivalent (p. 288). The second has to do with the role of women. In Judges women are not focused upon in their own right, but serve as foils for the evaluation of the character and actions of the leading male figures. "There is too little information in the text to evaluate the women themselves, but the impact they have on the action of the male protagonists is of crucial importance" (p. 289). Finally, Schneider concludes that the theological message of the book (which she agrees is essentially Deuteronomistic) is not only expressed in this or that redactional layer, but is inherent in the way the entire book is structured and functions (p. 287). These subsidiary conclusions are a direct consequence of the approach that has been taken and illustrate very well the special contribution that the new literary criticism can make to the study of a book like Judges: not to radically revise or overthrow the central message of the book, but to fine-tune and enrich the understanding of its meaning at other levels.

J. Clinton McCann's 2002 treatment of Judges[116] is brief (only 146 pages), and governed by a very specific purpose. As a volume in the Interpretation series, its interests are strongly theological and expositional, with a specifically Christian readership in mind. Its methodological commitments are not spelled out explicitly but are apparent from the table of contents, which features a major section on "The Book of Judges in the Context of the Canon." The consequences of this commitment to reading Judges in its canonical context show in the theological issues which, for McCann, emerge as the most significant ones for those who want to expound it as Scripture:

> The connections between the book of Judges and its canonical context . . . remind the reader that the book of Judges is one of the prophetic books. By highlighting the question: Will Israel worship and serve God alone? the book of Judges joins the other prophetic books in calling the people of God in every generation to covenant faithfulness — the worship of God alone and the pursuit of the justice, righteousness, and peace that God wills. Like the other prophetic books, the book of Judges, by way of its portrayal of the destructive consequences of idolatry and disobedience, serves as a warning. But also like the other prophetic books, the warning is grounded in the hope that the God of Israel will ultimately be faithful to even a persistently unfaithful people. (pp. 15-16)

For McCann, then, the key to reading Judges in its canonical context is the recognition that it is a prophetic book, and in particular belongs to that part of the prophetic corpus, Joshua–2 Kings, that seeks to interpret the eventual loss of the land in 587 B.C. theologically and to draw the appropriate lessons from it for those living in later (exilic and postexilic) times. Within this broad interpretive framework he identifies a number of key issues to which Judges makes a significant contribution. First, it emphasizes the conditional nature of the covenant relationships. The land is a gift, and life in the land is possible only within a faithful relationship to the one God of Israel (p. 17). Second, the Canaanites and their culture represent a pattern of existence that perpetuates injustice and ultimately produces oppressive inequalities that threaten human life (p. 19). Judges shows that violence and vengeance are the results of idolatry, and that they attract God's righteous anger against any nation that practices them — including Israel (p. 26). Third, it shows that as Israel's pattern of life moves further away from covenant faithfulness, the result is increasing injustice and moral chaos, "a primary indicator of which is the abuse of women" (p. 23). Finally, the humor of the book does not undermine the seriousness of these issues, but gives the treatment of them a sharp satirical edge that heightens the work's impact (pp. 23-24).

116. *Judges,* Interpretation (Louisville: John Knox, 2002).

Importantly, for McCann, in the context of the canon as a whole, the land, the Canaanites, and the warfare of the book all take on symbolic significance, which rules out any use of Judges to justify war over land, for example, or race. Rather, as Scripture the book functions as a prophetic call to repentance, and to a life lived free of idolatry and all its social and moral consequences. At the same time it highlights the grace and faithfulness of the covenant-keeping God, and demands that we worship and serve him alone.

Mark Zvi Brettler's 2002 contribution to the Routledge "Readings" series[117] is another relatively short book, but it represents the fruit of the author's thinking about Judges over several decades.[118] It is not an exposition of the book, but seeks to locate the task of *reading* Judges in the context of recent developments in biblical studies (especially the rise of historical minimalism) and to answer the question, "If Judges is not history, what is it?" He argues that, among other things, the evident "strangeness" of Judges (e.g., the bizarre feats of Shamgar and Samson, the portrayal of the judges as anti-heroes) argues against trying to read it as history, but evidence of careful design points toward a literary approach as more appropriate in principle and more likely to be successful. His own conclusion is that Judges is not literature which is of a particularly high order in terms of its aesthetic qualities, but a highly political work which is ideologically supportive of the Davidic monarchy.

Brettler's work is an interesting study of developments that have taken place in recent years within the broad framework of the newer literary approaches. In its earlier stages the new literary criticism generally eschewed, on principle, any interest in "authorial intention" and focused purely on the "meaning effect" created by the interaction of elements within the plane of the text itself.[119] Brettler's work, however, shows how a consideration of the text as literature can, and has in the case of Judges, led Brettler and others to come back to the issue of authorial intention in another guise — the ideology expressed in the way a piece of literature like Judges has been written. What used to be "theme" has become "ideology,"[120] and history an expression of power, the activity of victors. His work is an interesting example of how the new literary criticism and the new historical minimalism have come together to produce a reading of Judges that is not new in itself — scholars have always seen apologetic or polemic agendas at work in Old Testament texts, including Judges[121] — but new in the way it has been arrived at and executed.

---

117. *The Book of Judges,* OTR (London and New York: Routledge, 2002).

118. As seen in a series of articles and monographs by him on Judges.

119. See, e.g., David J. A. Clines, *The Theme of the Pentateuch,* 2nd ed. (Sheffield: Sheffield Academic Press, 1997). First edition 1978.

120. A secular replacement for theology?

121. See, e.g., A. E. Cundall, "Judges — An Apology for the Monarchy?" *ET* 104 (1970): 105-9.

Whether his thesis about Judges is sound or not is of course another matter, and one on which we reserve judgment at this point.

Victor Matthews' commentary (2004) is a recent addition to the New Cambridge Bible Commentary series.[122] While written for the nonspecialist, and therefore avoiding technical, academic language, it gives the reader more exposure to the fruit of recent scholarly study than most commentaries of its kind. It is also more traditional in its approach than the other works we have surveyed above, situating its treatment of the text in the context of the best available knowledge of the social and historical situation of Israel in the period in question, especially from studies of the way of life in the early Iron Age settlements of the central highlands of Canaan. The influence of the new literary criticism is evident particularly in the place given to insights from feminist studies of Judges (e.g., Bal, Exum, Trible, Brenner, Fewell, Niditch, Yee).[123] Application to contemporary life ("Bridging the Horizons") is done mainly by drawing analogies between the situations depicted in Judges and contemporary experience, rather than via the kind of biblical theology associated with canonical criticism (a serious weakness in my judgment). In short, Matthew's work in this commentary is a reminder that the newer literary and canonical approaches to biblical interpretation have not swept all before them, and that the traditional emphasis on historical background as the necessary foundation for sound exegesis is still with us, and has much to offer.[124]

Susan Niditch's Old Testament Library commentary on Judges was published in 2008.[125] The author has an interest in the oral background and social context of biblical literature expressed in her important contributions to biblical studies over three decades.[126] In the present work she brings this

---

122. *Judges and Ruth,* NCBC (Cambridge: Cambridge University Press, 2004).

123. Which may be due as much to the prominence of women characters in Judges as to any special valuing of feminist approaches to interpretation. See the relatively large number of references to the authors I have listed in the Author Index.

124. Cf. in this respect Barnabas Lindars, *Judges 1–5: A New Translation and Commentary,* ed. A. D. H. Mayes (Edinburgh: T&T Clark, 1995). This unfinished commentary, published after his death, was to have been the new International Critical Commentary on Judges. While not unaware of the newer literary criticism, it is a fairly traditional, historical-critical commentary, with a particular strength in the area of textual criticism.

125. Susan Niditch, *Judges: A Commentary,* The Old Testament Library (Louisville: Westminster John Knox, 2008).

126. For example, "The 'Sodomite' Theme in Judges 19–20: Family, Community, and Social Disintegration," *CBQ* 44, no. 3 (1982): 365-78; *Underdogs and Tricksters: A Prelude to Biblical Folklore,* New Voices in Biblical Studies (San Francisco: Harper & Row, 1987); "Samson as Culture Hero, Trickster, and Bandit: The Empowerment of the Weak," *CBQ* 52 (1990): 608-24; *Text and Tradition: The Hebrew Bible and Folklore* (Atlanta: Scholars Press, 1990); *War in the Hebrew Bible: A Study in the Ethics of Violence*

expertise to bear on the treatment of the book of Judges as whole. Her commentary is modest in scope,[127] but contains many fine insights. In particular she finds three "voices" in the book which stand in a kind of creative tension with one another (pp. 8-13). The "epic-bardic" voice is heard most clearly in the old stories themselves, which present the judges as hero-warriors and revels in their often bloody exploits with virtually no concern for morality in the modern sense. The "voice of the theologian" is Deuteronomic in style and content, and is found in the editorial framework of the judge narratives. It sees the judges as agents of Yahweh's administration of his covenant relationship with Israel, and is largely negative toward monarchy as an institution. The third voice, which Niditch calls "the voice of the humanist," is heard mainly in the outer frame of the book, chapters 1 and 17–21, and has a more detached, ironical perspective. It documents the progressive slide of Israel into religious and moral chaos, and sees the transition to the monarchy as "inevitable if not always glorious" (p. 13).

As work on the present commentary was nearing completion in 2009, two more major contributions to Judges scholarship appeared: the Word Commentary by Trent Butler and the HThKAT commentary by Walter Gross. Butler offers extensive bibliographies and a thorough review of Judges scholarship, especially in the last thirty years. He treats the whole book of Judges as a riddle, with numerous particular riddles embedded in it. The nature of judgeship itself is a riddle, as are the history of the book, its structure, and its purpose. Butler takes as his starting point for reading Judges in its context the way the book begins and ends. It deals with the question, "Who will lead?" after Joshua is dead and before Israel has a king. While it has some elements of structure, Butler does not think that this unifies it. The model provided by Othniel's judgeship is never followed. The cyclical structure of the central section progressively breaks down until, in the Samson story, it collapses completely. Joshua is a book of order and accomplishment; Judges is a book of chaos that systematically destroys everything Joshua achieved. Its broken structure mirrors the brokenness of Israel and its relationship with Yahweh. What unifies it is its sustained ironic tone and its exploration of certain themes: leadership versus chaos, obedience and the consequences of disobedience, politics (power struggles between the tribes and the pros and cons of kingship), the character of Yahweh and Israel and their troubled relationship. Like Younger, Butler notes the deterioration in the depiction of women as the narrative unfolds: "female heroes vanish from

---

(New York: Oxford University Press, 1993); *Oral World and Written Word: Ancient Israelite Literature,* Library of Ancient Israel (Louisville: Westminster John Knox, 1996).

127. Only 211 pages of introduction and commentary, including the translation. A second translation is included as an appendix.

the scene, replaced by female victims raped or kidnapped" (p. lix).[128] He follows Provan, Long, and Longman *(A Biblical History of Israel)* in accepting the basic historicity of the book, though it doesn't provide an exact chronology of the judges period. He places it in the early period of the divided monarchy when Israelites had to decide "which king to follow and which sanctuary to recognize as the true center of worship. The writer of Judges obviously places Judah first and condemns Bethel and Dan — and the entire northern kingdom with them — because of their idolatrous worship" (p. lxxiv).

We have already commented on Gross's commentary in Section III. It is noteworthy for three main reasons. First, it is the first scholarly study of Judges in German in nearly fifty years.[129] Second, it contains a fresh German translation based on the Masoretic Text and reflecting Gross's expertise in text-linguistics and especially Hebrew syntax.[130] Third, and of most interest to us here, is the way it uses a blend of redaction-critical method and literary-canonical method in its treatment of the book. Gross fully accepts the fact that the essential task of the biblical exegete is to elucidate the final, given form of the text in its canonical setting. In his own words, the modern exegete engages with the text as an *End-textleser* and a *kanonischer Leser* (an "end-text reader" and a "canonical reader," p. 79).[131] He also believes that the final form of the text may have dimensions of meaning that were not consciously intended by the authors and redactors who contributed to its formation. Each piece of material that is added by a contributor interacts with everything that is already present, producing effects that are real, intended or not (p. 79). The situation of the text in its canonical context further enriches its meaning. Nevertheless, Gross is wary of a merely ahistorical literary reading of the final form of the text on the grounds that it may miss aspects of meaning that are there, and import into it forced meanings (such as "sermonic moralizing," "psychologizing," and "aggressively feminist" readings) that are inappropriate to its character as an ancient text with a complex history (p. 81). In short,

---

128. Cf. Younger, *Judges, Ruth,* p. 37. Cited in Butler, p. lv.

129. Since Wolfgang Richter's *Die Bearbeitungen des "Retterbuches"* (1964) and *Traditionsgeschichtliche Richterbuch* (2nd ed. 1966). In some respects Gross can be considered a disciple of Richter. See Walter Gross et al., eds., *Text, Method, und Grammatik: Wolfgang Richter zum 65. Geburtstag* (St. Ottillen: EOS, 1991).

130. See, e.g., *Text, Method, und Grammatik* (1991) and "Is There Really a Compound Nominal Clause in Biblical Hebrew?" in *The Verbless Clause in Biblical Hebrew: Linguistic Approaches.* ed. Cynthia L. Miller, tr. John M. Frymire (Winona Lake, IN: Eisenbrauns, 1999), pp. 19-49.

131. The English translation here and in what follows is my own. I was assisted with the often technical and demanding German by two of my students, Klaus Hickel and Bruce Pass, but they should not be blamed for any infelicities. If these exist, they are entirely my own.

51

"end-text" reading needs appropriate controls if it is to be exegetically sound and responsible.

Gross proposes two kinds of controls and uses them in his commentary. The first is an attempt to understand the formation of the text through a careful, scholarly use of redaction criticism. By this means Gross believes that "in many cases it is possible to contrast older text forms with younger additions, redactions, reinterpretations, relecture-attempts and to survey the intended meaning of each author with a certain probability" (p. 78). Through this means the end-text reader is made aware of the kinds of issues that engaged those who contributed to the formation of the text and may still be detected to some extent in its final form, even if they are in tension with one another (as, e.g., in the negative view of kingship in the central section of Judges and the positive view of it in chapters 1 and 17–21, which frame it). This acts as a check on readings that are overly harmonistic and do not do justice to the multi-voiced nature of the text. It also provides a helpful guide to the kinds of meanings that are compatible with the nature of the text as an ancient document with a complex history, and readings that are alien to it. The second kind of control is provided by careful attention to the precise syntactical structure, narrative logic, and other literary features of the text in its final form, and any additional dimensions of meaning that are produced by the text's relationship to its literary context in the canon. This is the point at which Gross's expertise in text-linguistics comes into play, discriminating between what can plausibly be claimed to be there in the text and what cannot, between responsible exegesis of the text and forced exegesis in support of an ideology that is foreign to it.

Gross's work is open to question at a number of levels. For example, he overrates, in my judgment, the probability with which the work of the many contributors to the book and their various concerns can be distinguished from one another. This seriously weakens the capacity of the kind of redaction criticism he uses to serve as an effective control on the responsible reading of the end-text. At the other end of the interpretative process, he is so wary of readings foreign to the nature of the text that he restricts the context to be taken into account by the "canonical reader" to the account of Israel's history as a nation from Exodus to 2 Kings. This allows him to cite the presentation of the judges as men of faith in Hebrews 11:32-34 as an example of later, illegitimate moralizing of the text than as a legitimate part of its canonical meaning (p. 82). Nevertheless, Gross's scholarly thoroughness and his concern to be true to the text are very commendable, and his commentary is bound to be an important reference point for scholarly study of Judges for the foreseeable future. None of the contributions we have surveyed in this section (or others like them) has all the answers to the interpretation of such a complex work as Judges. But each has the potential to enrich in some way all subsequent readings of it, including the one in this commentary.

VI. ITS CONTRIBUTION TO OLD TESTAMENT THEOLOGY

A great deal of what has already been covered in the preceding sections is relevant to the question of Judges' contribution to Old Testament theology, and we won't repeat that here. Rather, what we will try to do is draw attention to some of the key issues that have emerged and set them in the broader context of Old Testament theology.

Judges is undeniably a theological text, first, because God (Yahweh) is present throughout. This means that we cannot read Judges without encountering him and being forced to think about who he shows himself to be by the things he says and the way he acts. Second, it is theological in that it interprets what takes place from a religious, prophetic perspective. Israel suffers because its people forsake Yahweh for other gods. They are saved because Yahweh takes pity on them in their distress. It is not theological in a systematic, abstract way but in a dynamic, highly relational way. Judges is a narrative work, and its theology is narrative theology. To access its theology we have to read it as narrative. Its theology emerges gradually as the story progresses.

At the most general level Judges contributes to Old Testament theology by providing a theological interpretation of one particular period in Israel's history. But its theology cannot be understood adequately without considering its connectedness with both what precedes it and what follows. The way it opens ("After the death of Joshua") links it to what goes before; and the way it ends ("in those days there was no king in Israel . . .") links it to what follows. Our task at this point is to consider how it functions theologically in its Old Testament narrative context.

Judges' indebtedness to Deuteronomy is universally recognized. The key speeches at 2:1-5, 6:7-10, and 10:11-14 are all cast in typical Deuteronomic language. So is the overview of the judges period as a whole in 2:11–3:6, and the editorial framework of the individual judge narratives in 3:7–16:31. There is also a clear connection with the "blessing/curse" alternatives of Moses' valedictory sermons in Deuteronomy 28–33. In Judges Israel experiences God's presence and sovereignty over its affairs as either blessing (peace in the land) or curse (oppression at the hands of enemies), very much as Moses warned it would. The stark alternatives put to Israel in Deuteronomy 30:11-20 give voice to the truth that Israel has real choices to make, and those choices will have real consequences: blessing or curse, life or death. In that sense Israel could expect to get what it deserved. But to depict this in a mechanistic way, as though everything in Judges can be understood in terms of a rigid principle of retribution and reward, would not do justice to either the book of Judges itself, or the book of Deuteronomy.

The deeper truth of Deuteronomy, and closer to its heart, is the truth that Yahweh's relationship with Israel has never been based upon Israel's desert, but on Yahweh's elective love. Israel is Yahweh's "treasured possession" *(sᵉgullâ),* not because it deserved to be, but because Yahweh chose it to be so; and the only reasons that are given are that he "loved" her and was determined to fulfill the promises (also unmerited) that he made to her forefathers (Deut. 7:6-8). Furthermore, the speech by the Yahweh messenger at the beginning of Judges (2:1-5) confirms that this principle is still in operation: Yahweh will punish Israel for her unfaithfulness; the remaining nations will be left to be a snare to Israel, to test her, and to teach her war, but there is never any suggestion in either Deuteronomy or Judges that Yahweh will ever renege on his relationship with her (2:3; 2:20–3:6). The alternating punishment and deliverance happen within this relationship, not in fundamental contradiction to it. Furthermore, the periodic change from punishment to deliverance can never be fully explained by a change in Israel's attitude to Yahweh. Repentance is absent from the overview in 2:11–3:6, and in the book as a whole it is always more apparent than real. That Israel survives the judges period at all is a miracle of divine mercy rather than something Israel herself achieves. The theology of Judges is fundamentally relational rather than mechanistic, dynamic rather than static, and raw rather than refined. It is a theology of conflict in which both parties suffer, and in which Israel survives only because Yahweh does not give up on her and simply walk away.

It is clear from the way Judges ends that Israel will have a future. After the period of the judges will come the period of the kings (21:25). And there is more than a hint in the way Judah is singled out for leadership at both the beginning of the book (1:1-2) and again at the end (20:18) that the kind of kingship that God will finally approve of and establish will arise from the tribe of Judah. In terms of Old Testament theology more generally, the legitimate place of kingship in Israel is secured in the specific mention of kings in the promises made to Abraham ("kings will come from you"; Gen. 17:6) and the provision for kingship, under certain conditions, in the book of Deuteronomy (Deut. 17:14-20). Judges participates in the theological preparation for kingship as an institution by showing both the dangers of it and the need for it given the state to which Israel's religious and moral life has come by the end of the book.

Judges also participates in the important theological theme (very prominent in the Pentateuch) of the promise under threat. As the story of Joseph presents a situation in which Israel may well have perished, cutting off any possibility that the promises made to Abraham would be fulfilled, so too does the book of Judges. As we have seen, Judges shows that not even Israel's apparently incurable unfaithfulness to God could thwart his determination that its history as a chosen nation would continue. It is an unfinished story, of course, for the situation at the end of Judges, like that at the end of the Pentateuch, falls far short of what was promised to Abraham. But the sheer miracle of Israel's existence at the end of Judges gives confidence that there will be a future; that the history of salvation will go on because God is determined that it will. In the context of Old Testament theology the book of Judges is a chapter in the history of salvation that leads to the fulfillment of the Abrahamic promises in the kingdom of David and Solomon (1 Kgs. 4:20-25).

There are many more particular aspects of the theology of Judges and its contribution to Old Testament theology that we will note as we go along. But it is well to have a grasp of the big picture in order to avoid getting lost in the detail; and for Christians, of course, that big picture necessarily includes the way that Judges relates to the fulfillment of salvation history that comes in the person and work of Jesus Christ, to which the New Testament bears witness.

VII. JUDGES AS CHRISTIAN SCRIPTURE

A. JUDGES IN NEW TESTAMENT PERSPECTIVE

It is understandable that Christians have felt some embarrassment about the book of Judges, given the theological support it gives to the violent seizure of Canaanite lands, the killing or expulsion of the former inhabitants, and the destruction of their culture. The abhorrence felt at these things is entirely understandable, and requires a response. However, the New Testament (which indubitably *is* Christian Scripture) does not give us the option of simply rejecting Judges. Instead it teaches us to read it in the light of the gospel and see its connection with us as being through Christ rather than apart from him.

The New Testament contains very few clear references to the book of Judges. There is a passing reference to the judges period as a whole in Acts 13:20, and some of the judges are named as men of faith in Hebrews 11:32. Apart from this there are only, at best, veiled allusions. For example, Mary is hailed in terms which suggest that her blessedness is comparable to that of Jael (Luke 1:42; Judg. 5:24), and there are possible allusions to Samson (esp. Judg. 13:4-5) in the birth announcements of both John the Baptist (Luke 1:15) and Jesus (Matt. 2:23).

The Hebrews reference is by far the most substantial, and gives us a convenient starting point for considering Judges from the standpoint of the New Testament as a whole:

> 32And what more shall I say? I do not have time to tell about Gideon, Barak, Samson, Jephthah, David, Samuel and the prophets, 33who through faith conquered kingdoms, administered justice, and gained what was promised. . . . (Heb. 11:32-33 NIV)

The first and most obvious thing to note is that the judges are not repudiated, but lauded along with such obviously worthy figures as Enoch, Noah, Abraham, and Moses. Furthermore, they are named here in a book which is very explicitly about the new and better covenant which has been inaugurated in Christ. In this respect the author of Hebrews reflects the perspective of the New Testament writers as a whole, who continue to see the Old Testament as Holy Scripture and a rich source both for understanding the person and work of Christ and for instruction in Christian living. The New Testament does not give us the option of simply disowning the judges as Jewish, or as belonging to a barbaric age in which mistakes were made because people had wrong ideas about God. The letter to the Hebrews does not put us in the position of being able to "judge the judges," so to speak. Quite the reverse, in fact. It locates them among the "great cloud of witnesses" by which our own performance as Christians can be evaluated.

Second, the judges appear here in a passage introduced by the theme statements of Hebrews 11:1-2: "Now faith is being sure of what we hope for and certain of what we do not see. This is what the ancients were commended for" (NIV). The two verses that refer to the judges specifically pick this up with the clause "who through faith conquered kingdoms." In other words, they are not negative examples which support the main theme of the chapter by way of contrast; they serve here, along with Abraham, Moses, and David, as examples of the faith that the whole chapter is about. It would be inappropriate, therefore, in reading the stories of the judges, simply to point out their faults and leave it at that. If we do not find "faith" in them, then, according to letter to the Hebrews, we are missing something — perhaps even missing what is most important.

Third, the judges appear in Hebrews 11 in a summary of salvation history that runs from Abel, through Abraham, Moses, David, and the prophets, to Jesus Christ (11:4–12:3). The same is true of Acts 13:20, where the period of the judges is referred to in Paul's sermon at Pisidian Antioch. In other words, the God whom we meet in the book of Judges is the same God who has acted in Christ for our salvation. What we see him doing in Judges must be understood as moving forward his saving purposes, which will eventually find their fulfillment in Christ. In Judges we are on a trajectory on which we might, with good reason, expect to see some backward reference to the promises to Abraham and the deliverance of the exodus, and some anticipations of God's future work in David and in Christ. So, in New Testament perspective, the judges not only have an illustrative function (with reference to the Christian life), but they also have a typological function (with reference to the person and work of Christ). It is interesting, in this respect, that the other allusions to Judges we noted above all occur in passages related to the birth of Christ and allude specifically to Judges 13, which has to do with the birth of Samson. This is startling, because Samson's conduct is so *unlike* that of Christ. But the New Testament allusions alert us to the fact that there is a connection between Samson and Christ that needs to be acknowledged in reading Judges as part of the Christian Bible. The same is true, to a lesser extent, of all the judges.

None of this means that the book of Judges cannot be allowed to speak for itself, or that we must whitewash the judges and turn them into paragons of virtue and models in all respects for Christian behavior. That would be to overlook the obviously flawed character of the judges and the very real differences between life under the old covenant and life under the new. In short, it would be bad exegesis, and bad exegesis cannot be a foundation for good biblical theology. In fact, reading Judges as Christian Scripture requires us to do justice, as far as we are able, to both the continuities and the discontinuities between the Old and the New Testaments; and of course this is what typology does, by its very nature. The type is always less than the antitype, or the language is meaningless. According to Paul, Adam is a type of Christ, but the difference between them is just as significant as the similarity (Rom. 5:18-19). In view, therefore, of the way the New Testament refers to Judges we may expect typology to play a significant part in our reading of it as Christian Scripture, particularly in relation to Christology. But we may also expect Judges to contribute to what the whole Bible has to say about the life of faith.

With this framework in mind, we turn now to two areas where Judges appears to be most at odds with the Christian life as the New Testament describes it: its portrayal of women, and its justification of violence.

B. WOMEN IN JUDGES

We have already noted in our survey of recent study of Judges the way the significance of women in Judges has been recognized, especially in feminist studies.[132] In general, the way women feature in Judges is in line with the

---

132. For a concise review of all the women, named and unnamed, that appear in Judges, see Susan Ackerman, *Warrior, Dancer, Seductress, Queen: Women in Judges and Biblical Israel,* ABRL (New York: Doubleday, 1998), pp. 1-4.

way they are viewed in the Bible as a whole. They are not stereotyped as either good or bad, passive or active, wise or foolish, but are shown as exhibiting the same basic traits of character and capacities for good or ill as men are. Most of the women are not named, but neither are most of the men (e.g., the men of Judah, the elders of Gilead, the Levites of chs. 17–21, and so on). Some women are portrayed as leaders and heroes who equal or outdo men (Deborah, Jael, and the woman of Thebez); some show themselves shrewd and able to manipulate men to their own advantage (Achsah, Delilah); some are pure victims of male power, insecurity, ambition, or folly (Jephthah's daughter, the young Timnite woman, the Levite's concubine, the young women of Shiloh); and one is a traitor (Delilah).[133] Some of them are presented in a way that engages our sympathy at a very profound level (Sisera's mother, Jephthah's daughter, the Levite's concubine). All of them, as we have seen, function in one way or another as foils for the evaluation of the character and behavior of the leading men.

True, the perspective of Judges is patriarchal, but in this respect there is nothing unusual about it; the whole Bible is the same. It is assumed that men will and should normally exercise leadership in the home and in the wider covenant community, especially in crisis situations such as war. This is justified in the New Testament on the basis of the relationships between the sexes established at creation, the relationship between Christ and the church, and the relationships of equality and subordination within the being of God himself (1 Tim. 2:11-15; Eph. 5:22-24; 1 Cor. 11:3). The book of Judges cannot be viewed as out of step, in this matter, with Scripture as a whole, or with a Christian worldview that is grounded in Scripture. It is also important to note that *abuse* of women (unless that is taken to include *any* form of male headship) is viewed as abhorrent in Judges, and associated with idolatry and apostasy. It is something that happens when Israel moves away from faithfulness to Yahweh and descends into moral and religious chaos. The portrayal of women in Judges as a whole has been well summarized by Susan Ackerman as follows:

> In the end . . . there is no easy categorising of Judges: it is neither a handbook of patriarchy nor a celebration of matriarchy; it can neither be condemned as a remorseless portrait of unrelenting misogyny nor be heralded as an archaic precursor of twentieth-century feminism. It paints no picture of a world of men alone, but it portrays no women's garden of paradise in-

---

133. The young Timnite woman (Samson's wife) also betrays him, but only in order to save her life and the lives of her family (14:15). She is "a wife, a woman who operates very much within a world of male hegemony. . . . She functions in the story's action primarily as an object. . . . Delilah, however, is a woman who is unmarried and . . . lives a life independent of male authority" (Ackerman, *Warrior, Dancer,* p. 233).

stead. It is, if anything, a book not of "either/or" but of "both/and," a book that both glorifies the deeds of men and embraces the tales of women. Perhaps, moreover, this multidimensionality is just as it should be, for multiple dimensions are surely a hallmark of all religious traditions, including the Israelite religious traditions from which the book of Judges springs. (Ackerman, *Warrior, Dancer,* pp. 201-2)

C. JUDGES AND VIOLENCE

The book of Judges poses in a particularly acute form the issue of divinely sanctioned violence in the Old Testament, and how Christians should respond to it. It is not an easy topic to deal with. At the time of writing, genocide was still going on in Darfur and elsewhere, and jihad as practiced by al-Qaida and others was on everyone's mind. What are Christians to say when similar things are found in their own Bibles? Our focus here is on the book of Judges and the particular problems it presents, but these inevitably raise wider issues.[134]

First, we need to note carefully the raw data that Judges presents us with. There are basically three kinds of war in Judges: wars of conquest and occupation in the introduction (1:1–3:6), wars of liberation in the main central section (3:7–16:31), and civil war in the epilogue (chs. 17–21). There are also wars of pillage and subjugation waged against Israel, and various feuds among the tribes themselves which anticipate the way Israel almost self-destructs at the end. It is clearly a very violent book. In addition to war itself there are also individual acts of particular brutality: the mutilation of Adoni-bezek in chapter 1, and the disemboweling of Eglon in chapter 3. In chapters 4 and 5 Jael kills Sisera by driving a tent peg through his head. In chapter 11 Jephthah kills and burns his daughter as a sacrifice. Samson's eyes are gouged out in chapter 16, and in chapter 19 the Levite's concubine is raped and dismembered. And this by no means exhausts the catalogue of violence. What are we to say about all this?

---

134. For all the relevant biblical data and a representative range of views on the topic, see C. S. Cowles, Eugene H. Merrill, Daniel L. Gard, and Tremper Longman III, *Show Them No Mercy: 4 Views on God and Canaanite Genocide,* Counterpoints (Grand Rapids: Zondervan, 2003); Peter Craigie, *The Problem of War in the Old Testament* (Grand Rapids: Eerdmans, 1978); J. Holloway, "The Ethical Dilemma of Holy War," *Southwestern Journal of Theology* 41, no. 1 (1998): 44-69; Millard C. Lind, *Yahweh Is a Warrior: The Theology of Warfare in Ancient Israel* (Scottdale, PA: Herald, 1980); Susan Niditch, *War in the Hebrew Bible;* Gerhard von Rad, *Holy War in Ancient Israel,* tr. Marva J. Dawn (Grand Rapids: Eerdmans, 1991 [German 1961]); John Howard Yoder, *The Original Revolution: Essays on Christian Pacifism* (Scottdale, PA: Herald, 1971).

The starting point must surely be to recognize that something already *has* been said about it. It is generally agreed that Judges was developed from a cycle of stories depicting the exploits of hero figures from Israel's heroic age in which the leading figures are virtually *defined* by their violence.[135] Ehud *is* the man who thrust a short sword into Eglon's belly; Jael *is* the woman who "nailed" Sisera to the ground, Samson *is* the man who slaughtered the Philistines with the jawbone of an ass, and so on. But these have been overwritten by someone who felt bound to *explain* these acts of violence and the situations that gave rise to them.[136] He uses the language of theology and ethics. The mutilation of Adoni-bezek was retribution for what he had done to others. The Israelites were suffering at the hands of the Moabites because they had done what was evil in the eyes of Yahweh, who punished them by letting the Moabites conquer and oppress them. Jael was able to kill Sisera because Yahweh decided to punish Barak by giving the glory that could have been his to a woman. Samson's feats were not his own, but those of Yahweh, whose Spirit rushed upon him at critical moments in order to begin the process of setting Israel free from the Philistines. But not all acts of violence are given this kind of treatment. Gideon's personal vendetta in chapter 8 and Abimelech's wars of self-aggrandizement in chapter 9 are seen as such, and no attempt is made to justify them. The barbaric behavior of the Levite (and almost everyone else) in chapters 19–21 contributes to the depiction of Israel as spiritually and morally bankrupt, and of the Levite himself as an antihero and caricature judge.

By far the greatest proportion of the warfare happens in the context of Israel's struggles to free itself from foreign powers that had a stranglehold on it and were bringing it to the brink of extinction. For the most part they were fought by bands of volunteers against enemy forces that were much larger, and much better trained and equipped. They were wars of emancipation, and those who led Israel in them are viewed as heroes and saviors. As judges they act to bring about a just or right state of affairs, and are agents of Yahweh, *the* supreme Judge (Judg. 11:27). So a large part of the violence in Judges cannot be repudiated unless we are prepared to be absolute pacifists — a position which Scripture in general (including the New Testament) does not appear to endorse. This theologizing of the source material is not only part of the creation of the book of Judges, but the first step in its progress toward its accep-

---

135. For a fine treatment of the Samson story as an example of this genre see Gregory Mobley, *The Empty Men: The Heroic Tradition in Ancient Israel,* ABRL (New York: Doubleday, 2005), pp. 171-223.

136. See Lawson G. Stone, "Judges, Book of," in *Dictionary of the Old Testament Historical Books,* ed. B. T. Arnold and H. G. M. Williamson (Leicester: Inter-Varsity Press, 2005), pp. 592-606. Stone calls this contributor "the moralist."

tance as Scripture. Judges does not simply give us raw violence, but interpreted violence. The challenge for those of us who read it as Scripture is not whether we can identify with the violence, but whether we can identify with the theology that frames and interprets it.

The coarse humor of Judges is typical of the heroic genre, but it may cause offense to modern readers, and not least to Christians. This is especially so when it is obviously intended to evoke laughter at violent acts such as Shamgar's single-handed victory over six hundred Philistines, making asses of them by goading them to death with a cattle prod (3:31), or the deadly aim of the nameless woman who drops a grinding stone from a tower and crushes Abimelech's skull (9:53), or the wily Ehud who lures the fat Eglon into position before popping his huge belly with his dagger, releasing its disgusting contents on the floor (3:21-22). It is sickening. But those of us who have never experienced the violence of war firsthand would do well to pause before running too quickly to judgment on those who take satisfaction at seeing a villain getting his just deserts. Laughter of the kind we find in Judges is sometimes the only thing that enables victims of injustice to remain sane. According to Psalm 2, God himself laughs at the foolishness of those who set themselves against him and his people (Ps. 2:4). The laughter of Judges is an invitation for us to stand with God, and see tyrants for the fools they really are.

As in all wars, innocent people suffer as well as the guilty, and it seems clear that even Judges is not without some sensitivity to this issue, as shown by the deep pathos that is generated in chapter 11 at the fate of Jephthah's daughter, and the way Sisera's mother is portrayed in chapter 5, waiting with fading hope and growing dread for a son who will never come home. There is no perfect justice in this world, as the New Testament also acknowledges;[137] but that is not a reason never to take up arms in a just cause.

Far more difficult for the modern, and especially Christian, reader is the way the opening chapters of Judges share the perspective of the whole preceding book of Joshua on the Israelite conquest and forceful occupation of Canaan. Surely there is something going on here that is at fundamental variance with Christian morality. There definitely is a problem here, and it may be that nothing can be said that will ever entirely dispel the unease we feel about it. Furthermore, any response which ignores or downplays the immense human suffering involved in order to find a tidy theological solution will be inadequate and grossly insensitive. But a response which is entirely determined by our feelings will also be inadequate. Part of the challenge of being a Christian is to bring our thoughts and feelings under the discipline of scriptural teaching. A thing is not necessarily wrong because it is presented

---

137. For example, John 16:33.

61

in an insensitive way, or because we experience a strong negative reaction to it. So, with reference to the book of Judges in particular, what are the relevant facts?

The opening chapters of the book tell us that after Joshua's death the Israelites tried to occupy all the territories that had been assigned to them, but they did not succeed in doing so completely, or to Yahweh's satisfaction (1:1–2:5). As a result they ended up immersed in Canaanite culture, with dire consequences. The rest of the book shows the progressive Canaanization of Israel,[138] despite Yahweh's repeated attempts to reclaim them from it (2:6-19). Of the battles described in 1:1–3:6, three involve the total destruction of civilian populations (1:8, 17, 25), which is said to have been authorized by Yahweh and done with his help (1:1, 22). In one case the technical, holy-war verb "totally destroy" *(ḥrm)* is used (v. 17); the other two use the more neutral expression, "put to the sword" *(nkh lpy-ḥrb)*. But the reality is the same. What are we to do with this as Christian readers? This kind of warfare has been cited, among other things, as symptomatic of the harmfulness of religion in general (Dawkins, Hitchens),[139] as grounds for rejecting the Old Testament as incompatible with the New (Marcion and his followers, old and new), and as testimony to God's commitment to the survival of Israel, and therefore as validating warfare for the same purpose today (Jewish and Christian Zionism). In short, biblical holy war has spawned hermeneutical chaos, sometimes with dire consequences. If a solution is to be found, it must be sought by considering the issue in the context of the Bible's total message. In what follows I will argue that the canon provides the controls needed for a responsible Christian reading of this material.

Fundamental to this undertaking is the recognition that Judges is one of "those canonical books of the Old and New Testament whose authority was never any doubt in the Church" (Article VI of the "Thirty-Nine Articles" of the Anglican Church). Among other things, this means that certain options are not available to us as Christian people.

First, we cannot simply view the wars of the judges period as an unfortunate episode in the history of religion, like the Crusades, from which we can draw various salutary lessons depending on how we view them. There may be similarities between the wars of Judges and the Crusades, but the former are part of the canon and the latter are not. Hence they are not subject to our judgment in the same way the Crusades are. On the contrary, we are bound as Christians to let them inform our doctrine and practice.

---

138. Cf. Block, *Judges, Ruth,* pp. 75-76.

139. Richard Dawkins, *The God Delusion* (London: Bantam, 2006), pp. 237-50; Christopher Hitchens, *God Is Not Great: How Religion Poisons Everything* (New York: Twelve, 2007), pp. 97-107.

Second, the acceptance of the Old Testament as part of the church's canon acknowledges that there is an organic relationship between Christianity and Judaism. The church has been grafted into Israel, as the New Testament affirms, not only by direct statement but by the way it is so densely referenced to the Old. As Paul put it, Abraham "is the father of us all" (Rom. 4:16 NIV). So we cannot view the wars of Judges as a purely Jewish affair — something that Jews have to own as part of their story, as Christians have to own the Crusades as part of theirs. The acceptance of the Old Testament as canon means that the wars of Judges are part of our history too.

Third, the church's rejection of Marcionism means that it is committed to the view that the Old Testament does not present us with an alternative God from the New, or a fundamentally distorted view of the character and purposes of God. It acknowledges progressive revelation (and therefore difference between the Old Testament and the New), but affirms that it is the same God that is revealed in both. Fourth, the church's acceptance of the very human, historically conditioned writings of the Old and New Testaments as Scripture acknowledges that revelation necessarily involves God accommodating himself to the limited capacities of the human recipients. However, the acceptance of *these particular texts* as Scripture rules out the extension of the accommodation principle as a strategy for avoiding the moral and theological dilemmas they pose for us. Holy war is a case in point. The relevant Scriptures insist that the obligation to utterly destroy the Canaanites and their culture was not something the Israelites were naturally inclined to do. In fact, they did not do it in many cases, even though they were commanded to do so. This command was not a case of God accommodating himself to Israel's worldview, but of overturning it. In short, acceptance of Judges as canonical rules out such strategies of avoidance. Positively it commits the Christian to listening respectfully to what the biblical text has to say about such war, with a view to learning from it. In what follows we will attempt to do this.

The introduction to Judges ends with a passage that explains why the post-Joshua generation was given the responsibility of completing the conquest and occupation of Canaan that Joshua had begun (2:20-3:6). Three reasons are given.

First, it was to *test (nissâ)* that next generation (2:22; 3:1, 4). It is the same word that is used in Genesis 22:1 for the "testing" of Abraham by requiring him to offer up Isaac. In other words, the task the post-Joshua generation was given was difficult for them, and would therefore force them to confront the basic issue of whether or not they would choose obedience to Yahweh over following their own inclinations. As the whole book of Judges shows, they failed this test.

Second, it was to *teach* that next generation warfare (3:2). This is not explained, so we are left to draw inferences from common sense and the clues we are given elsewhere. The most obvious is that this generation needed to be "taught warfare" in order to prepare them for what lay ahead. The rest of the book shows how frequent military crises were; people who had no experience of war would not have survived in such circumstances.

The third reason is given less directly, by showing us the conse-quences of Israel's failure to fully carry out the charge Joshua had given them: "They took their daughters [the daughters of the Canaanites] in mar-riage and gave their own daughters to their sons, and served their gods" (3:6 NIV). This was the danger that the command to destroy the Canaanites and their way of life was intended to protect them from, as spelled out explicitly in Deuteronomy 7:1-6 and elsewhere. It was to stop Israel from simply merg-ing into its pagan environment and ceasing to exist. In the context of the canon as a whole, the importance of this derives from the central place of Is-rael in God's long-term purposes for the world — a biblical theme which arcs right across the canon from Abraham to Christ to world mission.[140] These reasons may shock us, or at the very least leave us profoundly uneasy, but they are the ones that this part of the canon gives us.[141]

What this key passage from Judges says is clear enough, but listening to it involves more than hearing the particulars. It involves attending to it as part of Scripture as a whole and trying to understand its significance in that wider context. If the passage is listened to in this way, it contributes at least three things to a biblical view of God and the human condition. First, it tells us that culture is not morally neutral; it is simply the manifestation of what we are, and is therefore no more exempt from moral judgment than individual people are. The culture of the Canaanites was not simply a preferred way of life with no moral significance, and insofar as the Israelites were seduced by it they "did what was evil in the eyes of Yahweh" and made themselves liable to the same kind of judgment. Second, evil is something far too deep to be elimi-nated by the simple punishment of this or that particular act or person. It so corrupts the nature of men and women and their whole way of life that nothing and no one is exempt from it, and only wholesale destruction can remove it. In short, "evil is irremediable";[142] that is why radical root-and-branch judgment is necessary. Without hell there can be no heaven. The view of both the Old and New Testaments is that there were times in the past when such judgment was justified (e.g., the world of Noah's day, Sodom and Gomorrah, the Ca-

---

140. See A. J. Köstenberger and P. T. O'Brien, *Salvation to the Ends of the Earth: A Biblical Theology of Mission,* NSBT (Leicester, UK/Downers Grove, IL: Inter-Varsity Press, 2001).

141. For treatments of all the relevant biblical data see footnote 134.

142. Miroslav Volf, *Exclusion and Embrace: A Theological Exploration of Iden-tity, Otherness, and Reconciliation* (Nashville: Abingdon, 1996), pp. 27-28.

naan of Joshua's day[143]), and that the present world stands under the very real threat of similar destruction (e.g., Matt. 24:37; Luke 17:26; 1 Pet. 3:20). Third, and closely related to this, is the biblical message that not all religion is good, and that religion does not guarantee protection from divine judgment. Everyone in Judges is religious, Canaanites and Israelites alike. Even at their most reprobate, the Israelites are religious,[144] but their religion does not secure God's favor or make them proof against his judgment. They are warned in both the law of Moses and the prophets that if they do as the Canaanites do, they will suffer the same fate as the Canaanites.[145] The Bible's view is that religion, like everything else, is capable of being true or false, good or bad. The idea that all religions are equally valid, and therefore exempt from moral judgment, is contrary to the teaching of both the Old and New Testaments. The books of Joshua and Judges make this point in a particularly powerful way.

There is nothing in these implications of the Judges passage that is inconsistent with the New Testament; in fact, all are also taught there in one way or another. However, the fact that the canon does have two Testaments indicates that there are discontinuities as well as continuities. So far we have considered the continuities. But the discontinuities are equally important, and in fact indispensable for a responsible Christian reading of any part of the Old Testament, including the war material of Judges. That is what we turn to now. But first, a warning. It is important not to overdraw the contrast between the Old and New Testaments in this area. While the New Testament, and Jesus in particular, reject personal vengeance as a way of responding to wrongs, they do not rule out violence as wrong in all circumstances. According to Romans 13, the governing authorities are God's servants, established by him to commend those who do good and restrain wickedness by punishing evildoers:

> Do you want to be free from fear of the one in authority? Then do what is right and he will commend you. For he is God's servant to do you good. But if you do wrong, be afraid, for he does not *bear the sword* for nothing. He is God's servant, *an agent of wrath* to bring punishment on the wrongdoer. (vv. 3b-4 NIV; my italics)

Furthermore, John the Baptist, Jesus, and Paul all seem to regard being a soldier as an honorable profession (Luke 3:14; Matt. 8:5-13; 2 Tim. 2:4).

Nevertheless, in the New Testament the only kind of warfare that is

---

143. See Gen. 15:16.

144. "The peril of Israel was not irreligion; it was too much religion of a bad sort." G. Matheson, *Representative Men of the Bible* (1903), pp. 159-60, cited by David M. Gunn in *Judges,* Blackwell Bible Commentaries (Malden, MA: Blackwell, 2005), p. 32.

145. E.g., Deut. 28:27-28; Isa. 2:6-9; Hos. 5:8-14.

specifically Christian, and therefore commanded as part of Christian discipleship, is spiritual, and not violent in the normal sense of that term:

> The weapons we fight with are not the weapons of the world. On the contrary, they have divine power to demolish strongholds. We demolish arguments and every pretension that sets itself up against the knowledge of God, and we take captive every thought to make it obedient to Christ. (2 Cor. 10:4-5 NIV)

> Put on the full armor of God so that you can take your stand against the devil's schemes. For our struggle is not against flesh and blood, but against the rulers, against the authorities, against the powers of this dark world and against the spiritual forces of evil in the heavenly realms. (Eph. 6:11-12 NIV)

The fundamental difference from the Old Testament is the way in which the kingdom of God is manifested in the world under the new covenant: no longer in the form of a nation with political and military power, whose continued existence must be secured by the sword where necessary, but as a church which exists in the world as salt and light, and maintains itself and grows by the preaching of the gospel.[146] It is the state, not the church, which has the responsibility of wielding the sword as the agent of God's wrath, though Christian people can and should play their part in shaping public policy.

Of particular interest for our present topic is the way four of the judges, Gideon, Barak, Samson, and Jephthah, turn up in Hebrews 11:32 in a catalogue of Old Testament heroes running from Abel to the prophets and martyrs, remembered now not for their violence but for their faith, which is the theme of the whole chapter. At their best moments these judges knew their need of God. They believed that he who made the world was able to deliver on what he had promised, and could be counted on to do so, and made this rather than fear the defining principle of their lives. Fear (good and bad) is one of the subthemes of the chapter, along with conflict, suffering, and victory, and all of these find their resolution in the cross of the crucified Messiah, the perfectly faithful One, as described in the first three verses of chapter 12. The whole of chapter 11 builds to this as its climax, which provides us with the key to appropriating all that has gone before. Faith has been perfected; the war with evil has been won. On the other side of the cross the fol-

---

146. The redeployment of military language in the New Testament in a metaphorical way gives some legitimacy, in my view, to the practice of reading the war passages of the Old Testament as illustrative of principles which have relevance to the Christian life. But this should not be used as a strategy for sidestepping the basic theological and ethical problems involved in the literal warfare of the Old Testament.

lowers of Jesus find themselves in a fundamentally different situation. God has taken the sword of his wrath from them and plunged it into his own heart. They share in the victory of Christ by embracing suffering. The weapons they now carry are the word of God and prayer. They overcome evil as Jesus did, not by preserving their life but by laying it down. Wrath remains only for those who refuse to do this, and it is God's place to judge them, not ours.[147]

In the matter of warfare, then, Judges does not provide a model for Christian living, and there are serious dangers in any attempt to make it do so. Divine wrath has been focused on the cross and the last day, and the church exists in the interval between them. In the New Testament, war language is metaphorical for the struggle involved in resisting temptation and engaging in gospel ministry (Eph. 6:10-18; 2 Cor. 10:4-5), and for the final judgment of the world by God himself (Rev. 6-20). But the wars of Judges remain part of the Christian canon, and contribute to biblical teaching about faith, the character of God, the human condition, and the reality of divine judgment. The church needs to be reminded of these things again and again if it is to impact the world about it in an authentically Christian way instead of capitulating to it.[148] A church that merely plays catch-up to its ambient culture will increasingly have nothing to say to that culture, and in the end, no reason to exist. If we find Judges shocking, that may be no bad thing. It is not the task of the Christian scholar to tame the Bible, but to play his or her part in helping the church to listen to it.

VIII. THE TEXT

The *BHS,* which is based on the Leningrad Codex of A.D. 1008, represents the type of Hebrew text preserved and transmitted by the Masoretes of the fifth to tenth centuries A.D. The text of Judges in this form is relatively well preserved, as indicated by its general intelligibility and the relatively few significant variants in the critical apparatus. Apart from a few fragments found at Qumran, the main surviving witness to the original form of the text is the LXX, which, in the case of Judges, exists in two basic recensions.

The two oldest and best manuscripts of LXX Judges, in Codex Alexandrinus (A) and Vaticanus (B) respectively, differ in so many details

---

147. See Heb. 10:30-31; 12:29.

148. Cf. Volf, *Exclusion and Embrace,* p. 36: "Our coziness with the surrounding culture has made us so blind to many of its evils that, instead of calling them into question, we offer our own versions of them — in God's name and with a good conscience. Those who refuse to be party to our mimicry we brand as sectarians."

from the beginning to the end of the book that Rahlfs, in his *Septuaginta* of 1935, found it necessary to follow the precedent established by Ussher (1665)[149] and Lagarde (1891)[150] and print the two texts side by side. In Rahlfs's edition the A text is at the top of each page and the B text is at the bottom, with separate critical notes for each. The textual phenomenon exhibited in this way is unique to Judges, and has given rise to a vigorous debate, still ongoing, about the textual history of the book.

A review of the debate to 1968 is given, with appropriate bibliography, in Sidney Jellicoe's *The Septuagint and Modern Study*,[151] and developments since Rahlfs are helpfully summarized by Philip Satterthwaite in the new translation of the Septuagint recently published by Oxford University Press.[152] The details need not be repeated here. In general the tide of opinion has swung away from explanation in terms of two independent translations (favored by, among others, Grabe [1705], Lagarde [1891], Rahlfs [1935], and Kahle [1959]) toward explanation in terms of successive and more or less independent revisions of a common archetype, a hypothetical Old Greek version (favored in various forms by Pretzl [1925], Billen [1942], Cooper [1948], Soisalon–Soininen [1952], and Bodine [1980]), with A now generally regarded as representing an earlier form of the text than B.[153]

Common to all this work is the recognition that the phenomenon exhibited in Rahlfs's *Septuaginta* points to a textual history for Judges which distinguishes it from the books which precede and follow it in the LXX. In addition, the mobility of Ruth in the uncial MSS serves to underline not only *its* own separate identity but, incidentally, that of Judges as well: in B (Vati-

149. In his *Syntagma,* cited in H. B. Swete in *An Introduction to the Old Testament in Greek* (Cambridge: Cambridge University Press, 1902), p. 191. The two texts are in parallel columns: (1) "ex codice Romano" and (2) "ex codice Alexandrino."

150. P. A. de Lagarde, *Septuaginta–Studien, Teil I* (Göttingen, 1891), pp. 14-71 (Judg. 1–5 only).

151. S. Jellicoe, *The Septuagint and Modern Study* (Oxford: Clarendon, 1968), pp. 280-83.

152. P. E. Satterthwaite, "To the Reader of Judges," in *A New English Translation of the Septuagint and the Other Greek Translations Traditionally Included under That Title,* ed. Albert Pietersma and Benjamin G. Wright (New York: Oxford University Press, 2007), pp. 195-200.

153. See, e.g., Satterthwaite, "To the Reader of Judges," in *A New English Translation of the Septuagint,* pp. 195-96, and Boling, *Judges,* pp. 41-42. Others, however, maintain the primacy of B, most notably W. R. Bodine, *The Greek Text of Judges: Recensional Developments,* HSM 23 (Chico, CA: Scholars Press, 1980). Bodine concludes (p. 186) that "the latter [the B text] constitutes a part of the revision of a form of the Old Greek toward the developing Hebrew text carried out near the turn of the era and known as the *kaige* recension, while the former [the A text] represents a later form of text which is influenced primarily by Origen's fifth column."

canus) and A (Alexandrinus), Ruth occurs between Judges and 1 Samuel,[154] but in N (Basinalo) it occurs between Joshua and Judges.[155]

The differences between the A and B texts of Judges, though extensive, are mainly differences in wording that do not affect the substance of the text: both recensions begin and end at the same point, contain the same subject matter in the same order throughout, and are in agreement in this respect with the MT. Fragments of the Hebrew text of Judges found at Qumran vary from one another and do not consistently support either LXX[A] or LXX[B]. It is unclear whether the differences from the MT (e.g., the omission of vv. 7-10 in a fragment containing 6:2-13) are due to different textual traditions or accidental changes.[156] The Targum (Aramaic), Peshitta (Syriac), and Vulgate (Latin) versions generally follow the MT. Most of the LXX variants noted in the *BHS* apparatus appear to be either easier readings (and therefore suspect as likely "improvements" introduced by the LXX translators), or are suspect on other grounds. Few of them are convincing as witnesses to a different, and better, Hebrew original.

IX. THE TRANSLATION

A. GENERAL CHARACTERISTICS

Translation theory continues to be a field of vigorous and sometimes heated debate between, at the two extremes, advocates of direct or transparent translation (in which the translation mirrors, as far as possible, the precise wording of the original) and of dynamic or functional equivalence (in which the sense of the original is represented as naturally as possible in the translation, using whatever wording best achieves this).[157] Some English versions represent a more or less pure form of one or the other, while most involve some kind of compromise between the two.[158]

---

154. 1 Samuel is *Basileiōn A* in the LXX.

155. Swete, *Introduction,* pp. 201-2.

156. See the discussion in J. Trebolle Barrera, "Textual Variants in 4QJudg[a] and the Textual and Editorial History of the Book of Judges," *Revue de Qumran* 54 (1989): 229-45.

157. See Moises Silva, "Are Translators Traitors? Some Personal Reflections," in *The Challenge of Bible Translation, Communicating God's Word to the World: Essays in Honor of Ronald F. Youngblood,* ed. M. L. Strauss, G. G. Scorgie, and S. M. Voth (Grand Rapids: Zondervan, 2003), pp. 37-50. See also the other essays in this volume for the range of views on the topic.

158. See, most recently, the "optimal equivalence" approach of the Holy Bible,

A related issue, on which a similar range of views exists, concerns the validity or otherwise of using inclusive (gender-neutral) language wherever possible, rather than the gender-specific (mainly masculine) language which was accepted as normal until relatively recently. At base this is simply a particular aspect of the "direct" or "transparent" versus the "functional equivalence" issue. The use of inclusive language where no specific gender distinction is involved is simply an application of a functional equivalence approach to a particular set of terms. It ought not to be regarded as wrong simply because it is sometimes advocated for questionable reasons.[159]

The view I have taken in this commentary is that there is no one "right" method of translation. All translations are for a purpose, and no one translation is right for all purposes.[160] Since the foundational business of a commentary such as this is exegesis, and many of the users of the commentary will probably not have Hebrew, I have tried to produce a translation which makes the features of the text I refer to in the exegesis as visible as possible to the reader. This means that, in general, my translation is toward the "direct" or "transparent" end of the spectrum, even though I am not committed to this as a method of translation that is right for all purposes. Every translation is a compromise, in which something is gained and something is lost; or, perhaps more accurately, something is sacrificed in order that something else may be achieved. In this case what is sacrificed is the elegance and ease of beautifully written contemporary English. What is achieved, I hope, is a translation which makes it as easy as possible for the reader to see what is being talked about in the commentary without continuous and tedious reference to what the text "literally" says. In short, while all translation involves a degree of interpretation, I have reserved the bulk of this for the commentary that accompanies the translation rather than work it into the translation itself.

In keeping this approach I have not striven for originality. While the translation is new in the sense that it has been freshly done from the Hebrew text, it is identical at many points to existing translations, especially those at the more conservative end of the spectrum. In other words, I have not tried to be original as a conscious goal, but have tried to keep the purpose of this particular translation in mind and be guided as far as possible by that alone. Where nothing of exegetical significance is at stake I have generally used

---

Red-Letter Edition: HCSB (Nashville: Holman Bible Publishers, 2004), as explained on pp. xi-xii of the preface.

159. For a discussion of the issues see Mark L. Strauss, *Distorting Scripture? The Challenge of Bible Translation and Gender Accuracy* (Downers Grove: InterVarsity Press, 1998).

160. So Silva, "Are Translators Traitors?" in *The Challenge of Bible Translation,* p. 51. In an innovative response to this issue Susan Niditch has provided *two* complementary translations of Judges in her recent commentary (*Judges,* 2008).

gender-neutral terms such as "Israelites," "people," and "ancestors" rather than "men of Israel," "sons," "fathers," and so on. Where the persons involved are clearly male, I have used the corresponding masculine English terms. I have tried to capture the force of the demonstrative term *hinnê* in various ways according to the context, instead of the traditional "Behold!" which has long since become too archaic to be serviceable.

For reasons given in the previous section (on the text of Judges), I have generally tried to render the Masoretic Text (MT) as it stands, rather than to emend it on the basis of the LXX or other witnesses. However, I have not done this slavishly, preferring variants from other witnesses where I felt there was sufficient warrant for doing so, and even resorting to conjectural emendation on the few occasions it was necessary. I have given reasons for text-critical decisions in the notes to the translation, and alerted the reader (usually in a footnote) when there are consequences for the exegesis.

B. THE DIVINE NAME

There is admittedly something rather presumptuous about scholars (especially Christian ones) deciding to use the personal name of God (in reality their own hypothetical version of it) when those who transmitted the text to us as Holy Scripture refrained from doing so.[161] Nevertheless I have chosen to render the Tetragrammaton as Yahweh, mainly because of the intensely personal way in which God is depicted in the Judges narrative — as a character interacting with other characters and manifesting all the angst involved in being in a committed relationship with people who are again and again unfaithful to him. A descriptive title such as LORD seemed to me to throw the emphasis too much on one dimension of this relationship at the expense of others, and therefore to be much less suited to the drama involved than the personal Name. I hope that Jewish readers will forgive my impertinence.

C. THE PROBLEM OF THE LARGE NUMBERS

In war passages such as Judges 20, the English versions generally translate the Hebrew word *'elep* as "a thousand." So in 20:15-18, for example, the Benjaminites mobilize a fighting force of 26,700 men, and the rest of Israel 400,000. And there are correspondingly large numbers of casualties: 22,000 Israelites in verse 21, and 25,000 Benjaminites in verse 46. But these numbers are hugely out of proportion to the size of comparable armies for which

161. Cf. Mobley, *Empty Men*, p. xii.

we have extrabiblical evidence.[162] For example, documents from the royal archives of Mari, in what is now Syria, tell of Mari itself raising 4,000 troops, Shamsi-Adad of Assyria 10,000, and the kingdom of Eshnunna 6,000, making a total of 20,000 for their combined forces. Figures for casualties and troop movements from Babylon, in southern Mesopotamia, and Alalakh, in what is now Turkey, suggest similar-sized armies. Given that these are all significant centers, large enough to have royal archives and standing armies, the vastly larger numbers for Israel in the judges period are problematic, to say the least. Furthermore, the Amarna letters (14th cent. B.C.) indicate that Canaanite kings had only a few hundred men in their armies, and even in the great battle fought at Qadesh in 1274 between Egypt and the Hittites (both of them superpowers), the opposing armies were at most 20,000 men.[163] Even within the biblical material itself, Joshua's total fighting force seems to have been only about 40,000 (Josh. 4:13; 8:3, 11-12).[164] Even this is large by contemporary standards, but still many times smaller than the comparable figures in Judges.

Scholarly attention to the issue has generally focused on the census lists of Numbers 1 and 26, where similar numbers occur. These are lists of "men in Israel twenty years old or more and able to serve in the army" (Num. 1:3; 26:2 NIV). They present similar problems to the numbers in Judges, and could be the source on which they were based. Various solutions have been proposed, including the following: the census lists reflect the population of a later period (Dillman, Albright), they are symbolic (Barnouin), or they have been corrupted through a misunderstanding of the meaning of *'elep* in military contexts (Petrie, Mendenhall, Wenham).[165] This last option has proven the most popular, and has been adopted, for example, by Robert Boling in his 1975 Anchor Bible commentary on Judges. George Mendenhall, its chief proponent, has summarized it as follows:

1. The census lists of Numbers 1 and 26 represent an old tradition of tribal quotas committed for war on specific occasions.
2. *Eleph* originally referred to a subsection of a tribe; the term was then carried over to designate the contingent of troops under its own leader which the subsection contributed to the [Israelite] Federation.
3. The old Federation broke down in the early Monarchy if not before.

---

162. The following data is taken from G. Mendenhall, "The Census Lists of Numbers 1 and 26," *JBL* 77 (1958): 64-65, who compares the census figures with the size of armies in the relevant Mari texts.

163. Cf. Gordon J. Wenham, *Numbers: An Introduction and Commentary,* TOTC (Leicester: Inter-Varsity Press, 1981), p. 62.

164. Cf. J. N. Oswalt, "Numbers, Book of," *ZPEB* 4:465.

165. For a helpful summary, with references, see Wenham, *Numbers,* pp. 60-66.

The royal army included units of approximately a thousand men under the command of an officer appointed by the king. This system was naturally read back into the census lists of the federation period, yielding impossibly high figures.[166]

In short, the word 'elep, which originally referred to a contingent of five to fourteen men, was later misunderstood as a force of one thousand men. The mistake can be corrected if a total such as, say, "46,500 men" (Num. 1:21), is read instead as "46 contingents, 500 men," each contingent ('elep) in this case consisting of approximately eleven men. By applying the same principle to Judges, the 400,000 Israelites of 20:17 becomes 400 contingents (about 4,400 men) and so on — figures that are much more realistic for Israel in the judges period.

Unfortunately, however, there are problems for this approach in both Numbers and Judges. In Numbers it works tolerably well for the census lists of chapters 1 and 26. But it cannot be applied to the count of Levites and Israelite firstborn in 3:39-43. The totals here (22,000 and 22,273 respectively) have the same form as those in chapters 1 and 26, but are clearly intended to be taken as actual numbers, since the difference between them (273) is used as the basis for calculating the amount of redemption money needed to cover the additional number of firstborn: five times 273 = 1365 shekels (vv. 44-51).

'elep occurs thirty-five times in Judges. In 6:15 it could refer to a contingent of the kind proposed by Mendenhall.[167] But in association there with Gideon's tribe Manasseh, and his family (bêt 'ābî), it is more naturally taken as referring to Gideon's "clan," the Abiezrites (v. 34). In the four places where it refers to a number of shekels, it clearly means "a thousand" (8:26; 16:5; 17:2, 3). The remaining thirty occurrences are all in military contexts. In two of these (9:49; 16:27) it refers to a large crowd of people of both sexes, making the "contingent" proposal inapplicable. The remaining twenty-eight do all refer to numbers of fighting men, but it is doubtful whether 'elep can be rendered "contingent" in four of them, and it definitely can't be taken that way in a third. In 15:15-16 taking 'elep as a "contingent" makes Samson's feat with the jawbone of an ass more believable, but probably tames it too much given the "heaps" of bodies in verse 16 (suggesting a large number). It also makes Samson's feat less impressive than Shamgar's slaughter of six hundred with an ox goad in 3:31, where the absence of 'elep makes a corresponding reduction impossible. If 'elep is taken as a "contingent" in 20:15, the result is a large

---

166. Mendenhall, "The Census Lists," p. 66. In a fourth point Mendenhall states that "there is now no cogent reason for denying that the lists [of Num. 1 and 26] are authentic, but were misunderstood in post-Exilic times."

167. Cf. Boling, *Judges*, p. 128.

discrepancy between the number of men mustered from Gibeah (700) and the total from all the other towns of Benjamin combined — a mere 26 contingents, about 260 men. This is possible, but unlikely. A similar problem arises in 7:1-7, where instead of Gideon's fighting force being reduced from 32,000 to 300, it would be reduced from only about 320 men (32 contingents) to three hundred. Finally, despite the military context and the reference to numbers of fighting men, 'elep clearly cannot be rendered as a "contingent" in 20:10: "We will take ten men from a hundred from all the tribes of Israel, and a hundred from a thousand ('elep), and a thousand ('elep) from ten thousand, to take provisions for the people." The other approaches listed above have equally difficult problems.[168]

Given this situation, and the lack of scholarly consensus on the issue, I have chosen to translate 'elep as "a thousand" in line with the LXX and all the mainline English versions.[169] This has a number of advantages. It provides an objective platform for exegesis rather than one that has been reconstructed on questionable grounds. Second, it preserves the ratios between numbers that seem to be required by the logic of the respective narratives in which they occur. For example, Samson's victory in 15:15-16 (of which much is made) remains greater than that of Shamgar in 3:31, and Gideon's three hundred remains a tiny fraction of his original force and therefore an effective safeguard against any claim that the subsequent victory was achieved by the Israelites themselves rather than by Yahweh. Finally, it supports the presentation of the civil war in chapters 19–21, where most of the huge numbers occur, as a large-scale, climactic struggle, in which Israel's worsening disunity came to a head and almost destroyed it.

In short, no workable solution to the problem of the large numbers has so far been found, and the advantages of leaving them as they are outweigh any gains involved in changing them. They cannot be changed without upsetting their relationship to other numbers, and they serve an important rhetorical purpose that is lost if they are altered.

X. SELECT BIBLIOGRAPHY

Ackerman, James S. "Prophecy and Warfare in Early Israel: A Study of the Deborah-Barak Story." *BASOR* 220 (1975): 5-13.

Ackerman, Susan. *Warrior, Dancer, Seductress, Queen: Women in Judges and Biblical Israel.* ABRL. New York: Doubleday, 1998.

168. See the review of the major approaches in Wenham, *Numbers,* pp. 62-66.
169. The single exception is 6:15, for reasons I have given above.

Aling, Charles F. *Egypt and Bible History: From Earliest Times to 1000 B.C.* Grand Rapids: Baker, 1981.

Alonso Schökel, L. "Erzählkunst im Buche der Richter." *Biblica* 42 (1961): 148-58.

Alter, Robert. "Samson without Folklore." In *Text and Tradition: The Hebrew Bible and Folklore,* edited by Susan Niditch, pp. 47-56. Atlanta: Scholars Press, 1990.

———. *The Art of Biblical Narrative.* New York: Basic Books, 1981.

Amit, Yairah. "Hidden Polemic in the Conquest of Dan: Judges 17–18." *VT* 40, no. 1 (1990): 4-20.

———. "Judges 4: Its Contents and Form." *JSOT* 39 (1987): 89-111.

———. "The Story of Ehud (Judges 3:12-30): The Form and the Message." In *Signs and Wonders: Biblical Texts in Literary Focus,* edited by J. Cheryl Exum, pp. 97-123. Semeia Studies 18. Atlanta: Society of Biblical Literature, 1989.

———. "The Use of Analogy in the Study of the Book of Judges." In *"Wünschet Jerusalem Frieden": Collected Communications to the XIIIth Congress of the International Organisation for the Study of the Old Testament 1986,* edited by M. Augustin and K.-D. Schunck, pp. 387-94. Frankfurt: Peter Lang, 1988.

———. *The Book of Judges: The Art of Editing.* Translated by Jonathan Chipman. Biblical Interpretation Series 38. Leiden: Brill, 1999. First published in Hebrew in 1992.

Armerding, Carl E. "Judges." In *A Bible Commentary for Today,* edited by G. C. D. Howley, F. F. Bruce, and H. L. Ellison, pp. 337-68. London: Pickering and Inglis, 1979.

Arnold, Bill T., and John H. Choi. *A Guide to Biblical Hebrew Syntax.* Cambridge: Cambridge University Press, 2003.

Arnold, Patrick M. "Rimmon." In *ABD,* 5:773-74. 6 vols. New York: Doubleday, 1992.

Assis, Elie. *Self-Interest or Communal Interest: An Ideology of Leadership in the Gideon, Abimelech and Jephthah Narratives (Judg 6–12).* VTSup Series 106. Leiden: Brill, 2005.

Auld, A. Graeme. "Judges 1 and History: A Reconsideration." *VT* 25, no. 2a (1975): 261-85.

———. "Review of Boling's *Judges:* The Framework of Judges and the Deuteronomists." *JSOT* 1 (1976): 41-46.

Bal, Mieke. *Death and Dissymmetry: The Politics of Coherence in the Book of Judges.* Chicago and London: The University of Chicago Press, 1988.

Barre, Michael L. "The Meaning of *PRŠDN* in Judges 3:22." *VT* 41, no. 1 (1991): 1-11.

Barrera, J. Trebolle. "Textual Variants in 4QJudgᵃ and the Textual and Editorial History of the Book of Judges." *Revue de Qumran* 54 (1989): 229-45.

Bartlett, J. R. "The Conquest of Sihon's Kingdom: A Literary Re-examination." *JBL* 97 (1978): 347-51.

Beyerlin, W. "Geschichte und heilsgeschichtliche Traditionsbildung im Alten Testament: Ein Beitrag zur Traditionsgeschichte von Richter vi–viii." *VT* 13 (1963): 1-25.

Bimson, John J. *Redating the Exodus and Conquest.* 2nd (new format) edition. JSOTSup 5. Sheffield: Almond, 1985.

———, and David Livingston. "Redating the Exodus." *BAR* 13, no. 5 (1987): 40-53.

Blenkinsopp, J. "Ballad Style and Psalm Style in the Song of Deborah." *Biblica* 42 (1961): 61-76.

———. "Some Notes on the Saga of Samson and the Heroic Milieu." *Scripture* 11 (1959): 81-89.

———. "Structure and Style in Judges 13–16." *JBL* 82 (1963): 65-76.

Block, Daniel I. "Echo Narrative Technique in Hebrew Literature: A Study in Judges 19." *WTJ* 52, no. 2 (1990): 325-41.

———. *Judges, Ruth.* NAC 6. Nashville: Broadman & Holman, 1999.

Bluedorn, W. *Yahweh versus Baalism: A Theological Reading of the Gideon-Abimelech Narrative.* JSOTSup 329. Sheffield: Sheffield Academic Press, 2001.

Bodine, Walter Ray. *The Greek Text of Judges: Recensional Developments.* HSM 23. Chico, CA: Scholars Press, 1980.

Boling, Robert G. "And Who Is *Š-K-M?* (Judges IX 28)." *VT* 13 (1963): 479-82.

———. "In Those Days There Was No King in Israel." In *A Light unto My Path: Old Testament Studies in Honor of Jacob M. Meyers,* edited by H. N. Bream, R. Heim, and C. Moore, pp. 33-48. Philadelphia: Temple University Press, 1974.

———. "Response." *JSOT* 1 (1976): 47-52.

———. *Judges.* The Anchor Bible, Volume 6A. New York: Doubleday, 1975.

Brenner, Athalya, ed. *Judges.* The Feminist Companion to the Bible (Second Series) 4. Sheffield: Sheffield Academic Press, 1993.

Brensinger, Terry L. *Judges.* Believers' Church Bible Commentary. Scottdale: Herald, 1999.

Brettler, Marc Zvi. *The Book of Judges.* OTR. London and New York: Routledge, 2002.

———. *The Creation of History in Ancient Israel.* London and New York: Routledge, 1995.

Bright, John. *A History of Israel, Fourth Edition.* Louisville/London: Westminster John Knox, 2000.

Brown, Francis, S. R. Driver, and Charles A. Briggs. *A Hebrew and English Lexicon of the Old Testament.* Oxford: Clarendon, 1953.

Bruce, F. F. "Hebron." In *New Bible Dictionary. Second Edition,* edited by J. D. Douglas, N. Hillyer, F. F. Bruce, D. Guthrie, A. R. Millard, J. I. Packer, and D. J. Wiseman, pp. 471-72. Leicester: Inter-Varsity Press, 1982.

———. "Judges." In *The New Bible Commentary, Revised,* edited by D. Guthrie, J. A. Motyer, A. M. Stibbs, and D. J. Wiseman, pp. 252-76. Leicester: Inter-Varsity Press, 1970.

Brueggemann, Walter. "Social Criticism and Social Vision in the Deuteronomic Formula of the Judges." In *Die Botschaft und die Boten: Festschrift für Hans Walter Wolff zum 70. Geburtstag,* edited by J. Jeremias and L. Perlitt, pp. 101-14. Neukirchen-Vluyn: Neukirchener, 1981.

Buber, Martin. *The Kingship of God.* 3rd, newly enlarged edition. Translated by R. Scheimann. London: Humanities Press, 1990.

———. *The Prophetic Faith.* New York: Harper and Row, 1960.

Budde, Karl. *Das Buch der Richter.* Freiburg: Mohr, 1897.

Burney, C. F. *The Book of Judges, with Introduction and Notes.* 3rd edition. London: Rivingtons, 1930.

Butler, Trent C. *Judges.* WBC 8. Nashville: Thomas Nelson, 2009.

Carson, D. A. "Matthew." In *The Expositor's Bible Commentary,* edited by Frank E. Gaebelein and J. D. Douglas, 8:3-599. 12 vols. Grand Rapids: Zondervan/Regency, 1985-92.

Childs, Brevard S. *Biblical Theology in Crisis.* Philadelphia: Westminster, 1970.

———. *Introduction to the Old Testament as Scripture.* London: SCM, 1979.

Cohen, A., ed. *Joshua and Judges.* Revised by A. J. Rosenberg. Soncino Books of the Bible. London: Soncino, 1982.

———, tr. and ed. *The Minor Tractates of the Talmud.* 2nd ed. 2 vols. London: Soncino, 1965.

Coogan, M. D. "A Structural and Literary Analysis of the Song of Deborah." *CBQ* 40, no. 2 (1978): 143-66.

Cowles, C. S., Eugene H. Merrill, Daniel L. Gard, and Tremper Longman III. *Show Them No Mercy: 4 Views on God and Canaanite Genocide.* Counterpoints. Grand Rapids: Zondervan, 2003.

Craigie, Peter C. "A Reconsideration of Shamgar ben Anath (Judg. 3:31 and 5:6)." *JBL* 91, no. 2 (1972): 239-40.

———. *The Problem of War in the Old Testament.* Grand Rapids: Eerdmans, 1978.

Crenshaw, James L. "The Samson Saga: Filial Devotion or Erotic Attachment?" *ZAW* 86, no. 4 (1974): 470-504.

Cross, F. M. "The Structure of the Deuteronomic History." *Perspectives in Jewish Learning* 3 (1968): 9-24.

Crown, A. D. "A Reinterpretation of Judges IX in the Light of Its Humor." *Abr Nahrain* 3 (1961-62): 90-98.

Crüsemann, Frank. *Der Widerstand gegen das Königtum: Die antiköniglichen Texte des Alten Testamentes und der Kampf um den frühen israelitischen Staat.* WMANT 49. Neukirchen-Vluyn: Neukirchener, 1978.

Culley, Robert C. "Structural Analysis: Is It Done with Mirrors?" *Interpretation* 28 (1974): 165-81.

Cundall, Arthur E. "Judges — An Apology for the Monarchy?" *ET* 104 (1970): 105-9.

———. *Judges: An Introduction and Commentary.* In *Judges, Ruth: An Introduction and Commentary,* by Arthur E. Cundall and Leon Morris. TOTC. London: Tyndale, 1968.

Currie, S. D. "Biblical Studies for a Seminar on Sexuality and the Human Community, I. Judges 19–21." *Austin Seminary Bulletin* 87 (1971): 13-20.

Curtis, Adrian, ed. *Oxford Bible Atlas.* 4th ed. Oxford: Oxford University Press, 2007.

Dahlberg, B. T. "The Unity of Genesis." In *Literary Interpretations of Biblical Narratives.* Volume 2, edited by K. R. R. Gros Louis, with J. S. Ackerman, pp. 126-44. Nashville: Abingdon, 1982.

Danby, Herbert. *The Mishnah, Translated from the Hebrew with Introduction and Brief Explanatory Notes.* Oxford: Oxford University Press, 1933.

Danelius, Eva. "Shamgar Ben ʿAnath." *JNES* 22, no. 3 (1963): 191-93.

Davies, G. Henton. "Judges VIII 22-23." *VT* 13, no. 2 (1963): 151-57.

Davis, Dale Ralph. *Such a Great Salvation: Expositions of the Book of Judges.* Grand Rapids: Baker Book House, 1990.

Dawkins, Richard. *The God Delusion.* London: Bantam, 2006.

Day, J. "Asherah in the Hebrew Bible and Northwest Semitic Literature." *JBL* 105, no. 3 (1986): 385-408.

Dietrich, Walter. *Prophetie und Geschichte: Eine redaktionsgeschichtliche Untersuchung zum deuteronomistischen Geschichtswerk.* FRLANT 108. Göttingen: Vandenhoeck & Ruprecht, 1977.

Dumbrell, W. J. D. "'In those days there was no king in Israel; every man did what was right in his own eyes': The Purpose of the Book of Judges Reconsidered." *JSOT* 25 (1983): 23-33.

Echols, Charles L. *"Tell Me, O Muse": The Song of Deborah (Judges 5) in the Light of Heroic Poetry.* Library of Hebrew Bible/Old Testament Studies 487. New York: T&T Clark, 2008.

Edelman, Diana V. "Jabesh-Gilead." In *ABD,* 3:594-95. 6 vols. New York: Doubleday, 1992.

Eissfeldt, O. *Die Quellen des Richterbuches.* Leipzig: J. C. Hinrichs, 1925.

Elliger, K., and W. Rudolph, eds. *BHS.* Stuttgart: Deutsche Bibelgesellschaft, 1997.

Emerton, J. A. "The 'Second Bull' in Judges 6:25-28." In H. L. Ginsberg volume, edited by Menahem Haran et al., pp. 52-55. Eretz-Israel, Archaeological, Historical, and Geographical Studies 14. Jerusalem: Israel Exploration Society in cooperation with the Jewish Theological Seminary of America, 1978.

Epstein, I., ed. *The Babylonian Talmud; . . . Translated into English with Notes, Glossary and Indices.* 18 vols. London: Soncino, 1935-52.

——. *Hebrew-English Edition of the Babylonian Talmud.* 13 vols. London: Soncino, 1963-76.

Exum, J. Cheryl. "Aspects of Symmetry and Balance in the Samson Saga." *JSOT* 19 (1981): 3-29.

——. "Promise and Fulfilment: Narrative Art in Judges 13." *JBL* 99, no. 1 (1980): 43-59.

Fensham, F. C. "Shamgar Ben ʿAnath." *JNES* 20, no. 3 (1961): 197-98.

Fokkelman, J. P. "Structural Remarks on Judges 9 and 19." In *Shaʾarei Talmon: Studies in the Bible, Qumran and the Ancient Near East Presented to Shemaryahu Talmon,* edited by Michael Fishbane, Emanuel Tov, and Shemaryahu Talmon, pp. 33-45. Winona Lake, IN: Eisenbrauns, 1992.

Gaster, Theodor H. *Myth, Legend and Custom in the Old Testament: A Comparative Study with Chapters from Sir James G. Frazer's* Folklore in the Old Testament. Volume 2. 2 vols. New York: Harper & Row, 1969.

Gerbrandt, Gerald E. "Kingship according to the Deuteronomistic History." Th.D. diss. Union Theological Seminary, Richmond, VA, 1980.

Gevirtz, S. "Jericho and Shechem: A Religio-Literary Aspect of City Destruction." *VT* 13, no. 1 (1963): 52-62.

Ginzberg, L. *The Legends of the Jews.* 7 vols. Philadelphia: JPSA, 1909-38.

Globe, A. "The Literary Structure and Unity of the Song of Deborah." *JBL* 93, no. 4 (1974): 493-512.

Good, E. M. *Irony in the Old Testament.* 2nd ed. Bible and Literature Series. Sheffield: Almond, 1981.

Gooding, D. W. "The Composition of the Book of Judges." In *Harry M. Orlinsky Volume,* edited by B. A. Levine and A. Malamat, pp. 70-79. Eretz-Israel 16. Jerusalem: Israel Exploration Society in cooperation with Hebrew Union College/Jewish Institute of Religion, 1982.

Gray, J. *Joshua, Judges, and Ruth.* The Century Bible. New Edition. London: Nelson, 1967.

Greenstein, Edward L. "The Riddle of Samson." *Prooftexts* 1/3 (1981): 237-60.

Greus, C. H. J. de. "Richteren 1.1–2.5." *Vox Theologica* 36 (1966): 32-53.

Gros Louis, Kenneth R. R. "The Book of Judges." In *Literary Interpretations of Biblical Narratives,* edited by J. S. Ackerman, K. R. R. Gros Louis, and T. S. Warshaw, pp. 141-62. Nashville: Abingdon, 1974.

Gross, Walter. "Is There Really a Compound Nominal Clause in Biblical Hebrew?" In *The Verbless Clause in Biblical Hebrew: Linguistic Approaches,* edited by Cynthia L. Miller, translated by John M. Frymire, pp. 19-49. Winona Lake, IN: Eisenbrauns, 1999.

————. *Richter.* HThKAT. Freiburg im Breisgau: Herder, 2009.

———— et al., eds. *Text, Method, und Grammatik: Wolfgang Richter zum 65. Geburtstag.* St. Ottillen: EOS, 1991.

Grossman, David. *Lion's Honey: The Myth of Samson.* Melbourne: Text Publishing, 2006.

Gunn, David M. "Joshua and Judges." In *The Literary Guide to the Bible,* edited by Robert Alter and Frank Kermode, pp. 102-21. London: Fontana, 1989.

————. *Judges.* Blackwell Bible Commentaries. Malden, MA: Blackwell, 2005.

————. *The Story of King David: Genre and Interpretation.* JSOTSup 6. Sheffield: JSOT, 1978.

Gurewicz, S. B. "The Bearing of Judges 1:1–2:5 on the Authorship of the Book of Judges." *ABR* 7, nos. 1-4 (1959): 37-40.

Halpern, Baruch. *The First Historians: The Hebrew Bible and History.* University Park, PA: Pennsylvania State University Press, 1996.

Hamlin, E. John. *At Risk in the Promised Land: A Commentary on the Book of Judges.* International Theological Commentary. Grand Rapids: Eerdmans, 1990.

Hauser, Alan J. "Unity and Diversity in Early Israel before Samuel." *JETS* 22, no. 4 (1979): 289-303.

Hitchens, Christopher. *God Is Not Great: How Religion Poisons Everything.* New York: Twelve, 2007.

Hoffmeier, James K. *Israel in Egypt: The Evidence for the Authenticity of the Exodus Tradition.* New York and Oxford: Oxford University Press, 1997.

Holloway, J. "The Ethical Dilemma of Holy War." *Southwestern Journal of Theology* 41, no. 1 (1998): 44-69.

Honeyman, A. M. "The Salting of Shechem." *VT* 3, no. 2 (1953): 192-95.

Humphreys, C. J. "The Number of People in the Exodus from Egypt: Decoding Mathematically the Very Large Numbers in Numbers I and XXVI." *VT* 48, no. 2 (1998): 196-213.

Jack, James W. *The Date of the Exodus in the Light of External Evidence.* Edinburgh: T&T Clark, 1925.

Jones, T. H. "Jonathan." In *New Bible Dictionary, Second Edition,* edited by J. D. Douglas, N. Hillyer, F. F. Bruce, D. Guthrie, A. R. Millard, J. I. Packer, and D. J. Wiseman, p. 614. Leicester: Inter-Varsity Press, 1982.

Jüngling, Hans-Winfried. *Richter 19 — Ein Plädoyer für das Königtum: Stilistische Analyse der Tendenzerzählung, Ri. 19,1-30a; 21,25.* Analecta Biblica 84. Rome: Biblical Institute Press, 1981.

Katzenstein, H. J. "Gaza." In *ABD,* 2:912-13. 6 vols. New York: Doubleday, 1992.

Kaufmann, Yehezkel. *The Biblical Account of the Conquest of Canaan.* 2nd ed. Jerusalem: Magnes Press, Hebrew University, 1985.

————. *The Book of Judges* [Hebrew]. Jerusalem: Kiryat Sefer, 1962.

Keil, C. F., and F. Delitzsch. "The Book of Judges." In *Commentary on the Old Testament in Ten Volumes,* 2:237-464. Grand Rapids: Eerdmans, 1973.

Kitchen, Kenneth A. "Dagon." In *New Bible Dictionary. Second Edition,* edited by J. D. Douglas, N. Hillyer, F. F. Bruce, D. Guthrie, A. R. Millard, J. I. Packer, and D. J. Wiseman, pp. 258-59. Leicester: Inter-Varsity Press, 1982.

————. *On the Reliability of the Old Testament.* Grand Rapids and Cambridge: Eerdmans, 2003.

Klein, Lillian R. *The Triumph of Irony in the Book of Judges.* JSOTSup 68. Sheffield: Almond, 1988.

Köstenberger, Andreas J., and Peter T. O'Brien. *Salvation to the Ends of the Earth: A Biblical Theology of Mission.* NSBT. Leicester, UK and Downers Grove, IL: Apollos, 2001.

Kraeling, E. G. "Difficulties in the Story of Ehud." *JBL* 54 (1935): 206-7.

Landers, Solomon. "Did Jephthah Kill His Daughter?" *Bible Review* 7, no. 4 (1991): 28-31, 42.

Lapsley, Jacqueline E. *Whispering the Word: Hearing Women's Stories in the Old Testament.* Louisville: Westminster John Knox, 2005.

Layton, S. *Archaic Features of Canaanite Personal Names in the Hebrew Bible.* HSM 47. Atlanta: Scholars Press, 1990.

Leach, Edmund R. "The Legitimacy of Solomon: Some Structural Aspects of Old Testament History." *Archives Européennes de Sociologie* 7 (1966): 58-101.

Lilley, J. P. U. "Aijalon." In *New Bible Dictionary, Second Edition,* edited by J. D. Douglas, N. Hillyer, F. F. Bruce, D. Guthrie, A. R. Millard, J. I. Packer, and D. J. Wiseman, p. 23. Leicester: Inter-Varsity Press, 1982.

————. "Jabesh-Gilead." In *New Bible Dictionary, Second Edition,* edited by J. D. Douglas, N. Hillyer, F. F. Bruce, D. Guthrie, A. R. Millard, J. I. Packer, and D. J. Wiseman, p. 544. Leicester: Inter-Varsity Press, 1982.

————. "A Literary Appreciation of the Book of Judges." *TynB* 18 (1967): 94-102.

Limburg, J., "The root *byr* and the Prophetic Lawsuit Speeches." *JBL* 88, no. 9 (1969): 291-304.

Lind, Millard C. *Yahweh Is a Warrior: The Theology of Warfare in Ancient Israel.* Scottsdale, PA: Herald, 1980.

Lindars, Barnabas. "Deborah's Song: Women in the Old Testament." *BJRL* 65, no. 2 (1983): 158-75.

————. "Gideon and Kingship." *JTS* n.s. 16, no. 2 (1965): 315-26.

————. "The Israelite Tribes in Judges." In *Studies in the Historical Books of the*

Old Testament, edited by J. A. Emerton, pp. 95-112. VTSup 30. Leiden: Brill, 1979.

―――. "Jotham's Fable: A New Form-Critical Analysis." *JTS* n.s. 24, no. 2 (1973): 355-66.

―――. *Judges 1–5: A New Translation and Commentary.* Edited by A. D. H. Mayes. Edinburgh: T&T Clark, 1995.

Long, V. Philips. "Historiography of the Old Testament." In *The Face of Old Testament Studies: A Survey of Contemporary Approaches,* edited by D. W. Baker and B. T. Arnold, pp. 145-75. Leicester and Grand Rapids: Apollos/Baker, 1999.

Malamat, Abraham. "The Danite Migration and the Pan-Israelite Exodus-Conquest: A Biblical Narrative Pattern." *Biblica* 51, no. 1 (1970): 1-16.

―――. "Hazor, 'The Head of All Those Kingdoms.'" *JBL* 79, no. 1 (1960): 12-19.

―――. "The War of Gideon and Midian: A Military Approach." *PEQ* 85 (1953): 61-65.

Maly, Eugene. "The Jotham Fable — Anti-monarchical?" *CBQ* 22 (1960): 299-305.

Marcus, David. *Jephthah and His Vow.* Lubbock, TX: Texas Tech Press, 1986.

Martin, James D. *The Book of Judges.* NCBC. Cambridge: Cambridge University Press, 1975.

Matthews, Victor H. *Judges and Ruth.* NCBC. Cambridge: Cambridge University Press, 2004.

McCann, J. Clinton. *Judges.* Interpretation: A Bible Commentary for Teaching and Preaching. Louisville: John Knox, 2002.

McNutt, P. M. *The Forging of Israel: Iron Technology, Symbolism, and Tradition in Ancient Society.* JSOTSup 108. Sheffield: Almond, 1990.

Mendenhall, G. "The Census Lists of Numbers 1 and 26." *JBL* 77, no. 1 (1958): 52-66.

Milton, John. "Samson Agonistes: A Dramatic Poem." In *Milton: Poems,* edited by L. D. Lerner, pp. 261-314. London: Penguin, 1953.

Mobley, Gregory. *The Empty Men: The Heroic Tradition in Ancient Israel.* ABRL. New York: Doubleday, 2005.

Moore, George F. *A Critical and Exegetical Commentary on Judges.* 2nd ed. The International Critical Commentary. Edinburgh: T&T Clark, 1908.

Moran, W. J. "A Study of the Deuteronomic History." *Biblica* 46, no. 2 (1965): 223-28.

Murray, D. F. "Narrative Structure and Technique in the Deborah-Barak Story, Judges iv.4-22." In *Studies in the Historical Books of the Old Testament,* edited by J. A. Emerton, pp. 155-89. VTSup 30. Leiden: Brill, 1979.

Nathhorst, Bertel. *Formal or Structural Studies of Traditional Tales: The Usefulness of Some Methodological Proposals Advanced by Vladimir Propp,*

Alan Dundes, Claude Levi-Strauss, and Edmund Leach. Translated by Donald Burton. Stockholm: Almqvist & Wiksell, 1969.

Nelson, Richard D. *The Double Redaction of the Deuteronomistic History.* JSOTSup 18. Sheffield: JSOT, 1981.

Niditch, Susan. "Samson as Culture Hero, Trickster, and Bandit: The Empowerment of the Weak." *CBQ* 52 (1990): 608-24.

———. "The 'Sodomite' Theme in Judges 19–20: Family, Community, and Social Disintegration." *CBQ* 44, no. 3 (1982): 365-78.

———. *Judges: A Commentary.* The Old Testament Library. Louisville: Westminster John Knox, 2008.

———. *War in the Hebrew Bible: A Study in the Ethics of Violence.* New York: Oxford University Press, 1993.

Noth, Martin. "The Background of Judges 17–18." In *Israel's Prophetic Heritage: Essays in Honor of James Muilenburg,* edited by B. W. Anderson and W. Harrelson, pp. 68-85. London: SCM, 1962.

———. *The Deuteronomistic History.* JSOTSup 15. Sheffield: JSOT, 1981. Translation of Martin Noth's *Überlieferungsgeschichtliche Studien,* pp. 1-110. 2nd ed. Max Niemeyer, 1957. First German edition, 1943.

O'Connell, R. H. *The Rhetoric of the Book of Judges.* VTSup 63. Leiden: E. J. Brill, 1996.

Ogden, Graham S. "Jotham's Fable, Its Structure and Function in Judges 9." *The Bible Translator* 46, no. 3 (1995): 301-8.

Olson, Dennis T. "The Book of Judges." In *The New Interpreter's Bible: General Articles and Introduction, Commentary, and Reflections for Each Book of the Bible, Including the Apocryphal/Deuterocanonical Books,* edited by Leander E. Keck et al., 2:723-888. 12 vols. Nashville: Abingdon, 1994-98.

Pitkänen, P. "Ethnicity, Assimilation and the Israelite Settlement." *TynB* 55, no. 2 (2004): 161-82.

Polzin, R. M. *Moses and the Deuteronomist: A Literary Study of the Deuteronomic History, Part One: Deuteronomy, Joshua, Judges.* New York: Seabury, 1980.

Pressler, Carolyn. *Joshua, Judges, and Ruth.* Westminster Bible Companion. Louisville: Westminster John Knox, 2002.

———. *The View of Women Found in the Deuteronomic Family Laws.* Beihefte zur Zeitschrift für die alttestamentliche Wissenschaft 216. Berlin: de Gruyter, 1991.

Provan, Iain W., V. Philips Long, and Tremper Longman. *A Biblical History of Israel.* Louisville: Westminster John Knox, 2003.

Rad, Gerhard von. *Holy War in Ancient Israel,* translated and edited by Marva J. Dawn. Grand Rapids: Eerdmans, 1991. First published in German in 1961.

Radday, Yehuda T. "Chiasm in Joshua, Judges, and Others." *Linguistica Biblica* 27/28 (1973): 6-13.

Richter, Wolfgang. "Zu den Richtern Israels." *ZAW* 77 (1965): 40-72.

―――. "Die Überlieferungen um Jephtah, Ri 10,7–12,6." *Biblica* 47 (1966): 485-556.

―――. *Die Bearbeitungen des "Retterbuches" in der deuteronomischen Epoche.* BBB 21. Bonn: Peter Hanstein, 1964.

―――. *Die sogenannten vorprophetischen Berufungsberichte.* Göttingen: Vandenhoeck & Ruprecht, 1970.

―――. *Traditionsgeschichtliche Untersuchungen zum Richterbuch.* 2nd ed. BBB 18. Bonn: Peter Hanstein, 1966.

Rösel, Hartmut N. "Jephtah und das Problem der Richter." *Biblica* 61 (1980): 251-55.

Rowbottom, David. "The Rhetorical Function of Poetry within Narrative Texts of the Old Testament: A Case Study of the Song of Deborah." Unpublished Honours Project, Moore College, 2005.

Sakenfeld, Katharine Doob. "Whose Text Is It?" *JBL* 127, no. 1 (2008): 5-18.

Satterthwaite, Philip E. "Narrative Artistry in the Composition of Judges XX 29ff." *VT* 42, no. 1 (1992): 80-89.

―――. "To the Reader of Judges." In *A New English Translation of the Septuagint and the Other Greek Translations Traditionally Included under That Title,* edited by Albert Pietersma and Benjamin G. Wright, pp. 195-200. New York: Oxford University Press, 2007.

Schneider, Tammi. *Judges.* Berit Olam: Studies in Hebrew Narrative and Poetry. Collegeville, MN: Liturgical Press, 2000.

Selms, Adrianus van. "Judge Shamgar." *VT* 14, no. 3 (1964): 294-309.

Seow, C. L. *A Grammar for Biblical Hebrew: Revised Edition.* Nashville: Abingdon, 1995.

Seters, John van. "The Conquest of Sihon's Kingdom: A Literary Examination." *JBL* 91 (1972): 182-97.

―――. "Once Again — The Conquest of Sihon's Kingdom." *JBL* 99 (1980): 117-19.

―――. *In Search of History: Historiography in the Ancient World and the Origins of Biblical History.* New Haven: Yale University Press, 1983.

Shea, William. "Exodus, Date of the." In *ISBE,* 2:230-38. 4 vols. 3rd revised edition. Grand Rapids: Eerdmans, 1979-88.

Silva, Moises. "Are Translators Traitors? Some Personal Reflections." In *The Challenge of Bible Translation, Communicating God's Word to the World: Essays in Honor of Ronald F. Youngblood,* edited by M. L. Strauss, G. G. Scorgie, and S. M. Voth, pp. 37-50. Grand Rapids: Zondervan, 2003.

Simpson, C. A. *Composition of the Book of Judges.* Oxford: Basil Blackwell, 1957.

Smend, Rudolph. "Das Gesetz und die Völker: Ein Beitrag zur deuteronomistischen Redaktionsgeschichte." In *Probleme biblischer Theologie: Gerhard von Rad zum 70. Geburtstag,* edited by H. W. Wolff, pp. 494-509. Munich: Chr. Kaiser, 1971.

Soggin, J. Alberto. *Judges: A Commentary.* Old Testament Library. Philadelphia: Westminster, 1981.

Stager, Lawrence E. "Archaeology, Ecology and Social History: Background Themes to the Song of Deborah." In *Congress Volume, Jerusalem, 1986,* edited by J. A. Emerton, pp. 221-34. Leiden: Brill, 1988.

————. "The Song of Deborah: Why Some Tribes Answered the Call and Others Did Not." *BAR* 15, no. 1 (1989): 51-64.

Steinberg, Naomi. "Social-Scientific Criticism: Judges 9 and Issues of Kinship." In *Judges and Method: New Approaches in Biblical Studies,* 2nd ed., edited by Gale A. Yee, pp. 46-64. Minneapolis: Fortress, 2007.

Stone, Lawson G. "Judges, Book of." In *Dictionary of the Old Testament Historical Books,* edited by Bill T. Arnold and H. G. M. Williamson, pp. 592-606. Downers Grove, IL: InterVarsity Press, 2005.

Strauss, Mark L. *Distorting Scripture? The Challenge of Bible Translation and Gender Accuracy.* Downers Grove IL: InterVarsity Press, 1998.

Swete, H. B. *An Introduction to the Old Testament in Greek.* Cambridge: Cambridge University Press, 1902.

Taylor, John B. "Shiloh." In *New Bible Dictionary, Second Edition,* edited by J. D. Douglas, N. Hillyer, F. F. Bruce, D. Guthrie, A. R. Millard, J. I. Packer, and D. J. Wiseman, p. 1105. Leicester: Inter-Varsity Press, 1982.

Thompson, H. C. "*Shophet* and *Mishpat* in the Book of Judges." *Transactions of the Glasgow University Oriental Society* 19 (1961-62): 74-85.

Tollington, Janet. "The Ethics of Warfare and the Holy War Tradition in the Book of Judges." In *Ethical and Unethical in the Old Testament: God and Humans in Dialogue,* edited by Katharine Dell, pp. 71-87. New York and London: T&T Clark, 2010.

Trible, Phyllis. "A Meditation in Mourning: The Sacrifice of the Daughter of Jephthah." *Union Seminary Quarterly Review* 36 Supplementary (1981): 59-73.

————. *Texts of Terror: Literary-Feminist Readings of Biblical Narratives.* Overtures to Biblical Theology 13. Philadelphia: Fortress, 1984.

Vaux, Roland de. "Sur l'Origine Kenite ou Midianite du Yahvisme." *Eretz Israel* 9 (1969): 28-32.

————. *The Early History of Israel, to the Period of the Judges.* Translated by D. Smith. London: Darton, Longman and Todd. 1978. First published in French, 1971.

Veijola, Timo. *Die ewige Dynastie: David und die Entstehung seiner Dynastie nach der deuteronomistischen Darstellung.* Annales Academiae Scientiarum Fennicae, Ser. B, Tom. 193. Helsinki: Suomalainen Tiedeakatemia, 1975.

———. *Das Königtum in der Beurteilung der deuteronomistischen Histori- ographie: Eine redaktionsgeschichtliche Untersuchung.* Annales Aca- demiae Scientiarum Fennicae, Ser. B, Tom. 198. Helsinki: Suomalainen Tiedeakatemia, 1977.

Vickery, J. B. "In Strange Ways: The Story of Samson." In *Images of Man and God: Old Testament Short Stories in Literary Focus,* edited by B. O. Long, pp. 58-73. Sheffield: Almond, 1981.

Volf, Miroslav. *Exclusion and Embrace: A Theological Exploration of Identity, Otherness, and Reconciliation.* Nashville: Abingdon, 1996.

Wallis, G. "Eine Parallele zu Richter 19:29ff. und 1 Sam. 11:5ff. aus dem Briefarchiv von Mari." *ZAW* 64, no. 1 (1952): 57-61.

Walton, John H., Victor Harold Matthews, and Mark W. Chavalas, eds. *The IVP Bible Background Commentary: Old Testament.* Downers Grove, IL: InterVarsity Press, 2000.

Washburn, David L. "The Chronology of Judges: Another Look." *Bibliotheca Sacra* 147, no. 588 (1990): 414-25.

Webb, Barry G. "The Theme of the Jephthah Story." *RTR* 45, no. 2 (1986): 34- 43.

———. "Judges." In *NBC,* edited by D. A. Carson, R. T. France, J. A. Motyer, and G. J. Wenham, pp. 261-86. Leicester: Inter-Varsity Press, 1994.

Weddle, F. "Mahaneh-Dan." In *ISBE,* edited by Geoffrey W. Bromiley et al., 3:223. 4 vols. Grand Rapids: Eerdmans, 1979-88.

Weiser, Artur. "Das Deboralied: Eine gattungs- und traditionsgeschichtliche Studie." *ZAW* 71, nos. 1-4 (1959): 67-97.

Wenham, Gordon J. *Numbers: An Introduction and Commentary.* TOTC. Leicester: Inter-Varsity Press, 1981.

Wenham, John W. "Large Numbers in the Old Testament." *TynB* 18 (1967): 19- 53.

Westermann, Claus. *Basic Forms of Prophetic Speech.* Translated by H. C. White. Foreword by Gene M. Tucker. New reprint. Cambridge: Lutterworth, 1991. Originally published, Philadelphia: Westminster, 1967.

Wilcock, Michael. *The Message of Judges: Grace Abounding.* The Bible Speaks Today. Leicester: Inter-Varsity Press, 1992.

Wüst, M. "Die Einschaltungen in die Jiftachgeschichten, Ri 11.13-26." *Biblica* 56 (1975): 464-79.

Yee, Gale A. *Judges and Method: New Approaches in Biblical Studies.* 2nd ed. Minneapolis: Fortress, 2007.

Yoder, John Howard. *The Original Revolution: Essays on Christian Pacifism.* Scottdale, PA: Herald, 1971.

Younger, K. Lawson, Jr. "Early Israel in Recent Biblical Scholarship." In *The*

Face of Old Testament Studies: A Survey of Contemporary Approaches, edited by D. W. Baker and B. T. Arnold, pp. 176-206. Leicester and Grand Rapids: Apollos/Baker, 1999.

―――. *Judges and Ruth.* NIVAC. Grand Rapids: Zondervan, 2002.

TEXT AND COMMENTARY

I. INTRODUCTION (1:1–3:6)

A. AFTER JOSHUA: MILITARY DECLINE (1:1–2:5)

As explained above,[1] 1:1–2:5 is the first of two passages which together form a two-part introduction to the book. It tells how the Israelites fared as they tried to complete the conquest of Canaan by occupying the areas that had been allotted to them by Joshua (Josh. 13–19). Like the biblical accounts of the careers of Saul, Solomon and Uzziah, it begins well and ends badly. It begins with Israel as a whole seeking direction from Yahweh (1:1-2), and ends with them weeping before him (2:1-5).[2] The intervening verses recount the activities, successes, and failures of the individual tribes, beginning with Judah and Simeon in 1:9, and ending with Dan in 1:34. The fortunes of the southern tribes led by Judah are described first (vv. 3-17), then those of the northern tribes led by the two Joseph tribes, Ephraim and Manasseh (vv. 22-35). Each of these major sections has a short appendix (see p. 92). Of particular interest is the strategic repetition of the verb *ʿālâ,* "to go up," in 1:1–2:5 as a whole. In 1:1-2 the Israelites ask, "Who will *go up?*" The account of the fortunes of the southern tribes begins when Judah "goes up" in verse 4. The corresponding section dealing with the northern tribes begins when Joseph "goes up" in verse 22, and the conclusion is reached when the angel of Yahweh "goes up" in 2:1. This is partly a simple matter of topography — a movement up into the central hill country.[3] There

---

1. In Section IV of the Introduction.

2. The chapter division after 1:36 mistakenly locates 2:1-5 with what follows rather than with what precedes it. While v. 3 clearly does anticipate what is to come, the primary function of 2:1-5 as a whole is to bring closure (as we will see) to the first major part of the introduction to the book.

3. On the probable point of departure for the upward movements (and therefore the place where the inquiry of 1:1-2 is made), see my comments below on 1:16.

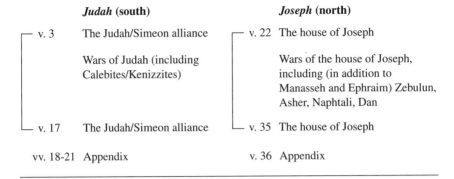

Judah (south)		**Joseph (north)**	
v. 3	The Judah/Simeon alliance	v. 22	The house of Joseph
	Wars of Judah (including Calebites/Kenizzites)		Wars of the house of Joseph, including (in addition to Manasseh and Ephraim) Zebulun, Asher, Naphtali, Dan
v. 17	The Judah/Simeon alliance	v. 35	The house of Joseph
vv. 18-21	Appendix	v. 36	Appendix

is a subsequent "going down" (v. 9). But the "going up" has more significance than this. The repetition of *'ālâ* unifies the passage as a whole, helps to delineate its parts, and shows us that the end comes in 2:1-5 rather than at the end of chapter 1. When the angel of Yahweh "goes up" in 2:1 a climax is reached. All that has gone before is reviewed and evaluated, and this evaluation produces the weeping of 2:4. While there have been successes in chapter 1, overall it has been a chronicle of failure.

1. The Israelites Inquire of Yahweh (1:1-2)

> *Every limit is a beginning as well as an ending.*
>
> George Eliot[4]

1 *After the death of Joshua,[5] the Israelites asked Yahweh, "Who will go up to the Canaanites for us first, to fight them?"*
2 *Yahweh replied, "Judah[6] will go up; hear this[7] — I have given the land into his hand."*

1 *After the death of Joshua* links what follows to what has preceded it. It tells us that the death of Joshua did not end Israel's story; something followed it, and the book of Judges will tell us what it was. But the same words also separate what follows from what has gone before. The death of Joshua was a

---

4. The opening sentence of the finale in George Eliot's *Middlemarch*.

5. The note in the *BHS* apparatus, "perhaps originally Moses," reflects the view of some scholars that what begins here is a second, more realistic account of the conquest. But this has no hard textual evidence to support it. See the discussion in Section II of the Introduction.

6. That is, the tribe of Judah.

7. Hebrew *hinnê*, represented by "Behold" in older English versions.

boundary event, dividing Israel's time into a "before" and an "after," as Jesus was later to divide the world's time into B.C. and A.D. Moses personally commissioned Joshua as his successor (Deut. 31:1-8). The "book of the law," which was the charter for Joshua's life, was the revelation God had given to Israel through Moses (Josh. 1:1-9). Joshua led Israel across the Jordan as Moses had led them through the Red Sea. In other words, Joshua's ministry had been a continuation and completion of Moses' ministry, as the ministry of the apostles would the continuation and completion of Jesus' ministry (Josh. 4:14, 23-24). The death of Joshua was the end of an era. Israel's life would go on, but would never be quite the same again.

The first difference Israel had to confront as they went forward was one of leadership. After Moses there had been Joshua, but after Joshua there was no one in particular. Who would lead them now? There was no longer anyone who was obviously chosen by God as Moses and Joshua had been; certainly no one with the same commanding profile and character. So the question asked at the beginning of the book is a natural one in the circumstances: Who will lead us now that Joshua is dead? The good news is that while Joshua himself was dead, the impact of his life lived on. He left behind him a united Israel who knew that even with Moses and Joshua gone they were not leaderless, for Yahweh was their supreme leader now as he had always been. It was a lesson they had learned from Moses and Joshua themselves, and learned well. These men had always pointed beyond themselves to Yahweh, and taught the Israelites that it was he, above all, that they must obey. So it is to him that they turn as the book of Judges opens. It is a promising start to this next chapter of Israel's life. After Joshua's death the Israelites *asked* Yahweh something. What a disarmingly simple way this is of telling us how the Israelites understood themselves to be related to God! They could ask him questions and expect that he would hear and answer them. They were on speaking terms with him. So, of course, had Moses and Joshua been, and Abraham, Isaac, and Jacob. It was the way it had always been from the beginning of Israel's history, and of history itself. Of course it was God, not they, who had begun the conversation. It was his initiative that had made it possible. But it was a real conversation, based on real revelation and real grace. They had met and come to know the God who draws people into relationship with himself by speaking to them, and allowing them to speak to him. All parts of the conversation were not of the same importance. What God had said to Adam, Moses, and Abraham was foundational to everything else. Nor did he speak to everyone in the same way, or with the same directness and intimacy; not even to all his chosen prophets. Since Moses no prophet had arisen whom Yahweh knew "face to face" as he knew Moses (Deut. 34:10). But the conversation did go on, and it remained at the very center of Israel's life with God. Judges begins with the resumption of this conversation: the Israelites *asked* Yahweh something, and he *replied.* As we shall see, dialogues (conversations) are at the core of the Judges narrative as a whole, and play a key role in the development of its themes — especially dialogues between the two principal characters, Yahweh and Israel.

We are not told how the "asking" was done, and in terms of how the story works it is probably not important for us to know. It is the fact of the asking rather than the manner that matters. But if we are curious and want to know, we will have to work with the clues we have been given in the story so far (Genesis to Joshua), and in the book of Judges itself. In this connection it is noteworthy that Judges closes (or nearly so) with the Israelites inquiring of Yahweh again, and this time more details are provided. In chapter 20 they ask the same question as in 1:1, this time at Bethel, and it seems that the place is significant: "they *went up to Bethel;* and the Israelites asked God . . ." (v. 18). They do so again in verses 27-28, again at Bethel, and this time we are told why they went there: "The ark of the covenant of God was there in those days, and Phinehas, the son of Eleazar, the son of Aaron, was ministering before it." It appears that Bethel itself is not the primary thing, but the presence there of the ark and the high priest *at that time.* In 1:1 we are at a different time, before Bethel was conquered and occupied (1:22-26). But it is reasonable to assume that the other conditions for proper inquiry were already in place. The law of Moses indicates that, as well as a duly appointed priest, the Urim and Thummim were normally involved in seeking direction from God (Exod. 28:29-30; Lev. 8:8). The high priest carried these two stones in the breastpiece which he wore over his heart, and somehow used them to "make decisions" for the Israelites; that is, to determine what God wanted them to do (Exod. 28:30 NIV). According to Numbers 27:18-21, this is the way in which Joshua himself had been given instructions concerning Israel's movements and encampments in the wilderness.[8] However, it would be hazardous to assume that anything was completely normal in the period of the judges, including the manner of "asking God" about things. Fortunately the next verse throws a little more light on the issue.

2 The nature of Yahweh's response given here (a whole complex sentence rather than a simple "yes" or "no") suggests that in this case something more was involved than the simple use of the oracular stones — most likely the delivery of a spoken oracle by the priest himself, or (as elsewhere in Judges) by a prophet, or by the mysterious "messenger of Yahweh."[9] The substance of the question presupposes that part of the Joshua narrative which

8. Contrast the immediacy of Moses' direct, "face-to-face" communication with God (Deut. 34:10).

9. 2:1-3; 4:4-7; 6:7-12; 10:11-14. See the comments at 2:1 on the identity of this messenger, and why I have chosen to translate the expression *mal'ak-Yahweh* in this way.

refers to the "remaining nations" and Yahweh's promise to dispossess them; that is, Joshua's farewell address in Joshua 23 (esp. vv. 4-5). After the death of their great military leader the Israelites (still full of enthusiasm to continue the struggle) seek guidance directly from Yahweh concerning the further conduct of the war. Their inquiry envisages a series of campaigns by individual tribes or groups of tribes. But the concept of a united Israel is also present. Whoever goes *first* will also go for *us*, that is, for Israel as a whole. It will be the first symbolic blow which will open the next phase in the struggle between Israel and the Canaanites. In his reply Yahweh gives this honor to *Judah*. The tribe is here referred to by the name of its ancestor. The tribe of Simeon is referred to in the same way in the next verse.

The force of the statement, "I *have* given[10] the land . . . ," is probably, "I have decided to give it";[11] that is, the divine decision has already been made, and therefore the outcome is certain. Furthermore, given the symbolic nature of what Judah is about to do, the *land* in question is best taken here as the whole land of Canaan as promised to Israel. The effect of this brief exchange, and particularly the promise of victory at the end of the verse, is to suggest that the struggle for full possession of Canaan is about to enter its last phase, and will soon be brought to a successful conclusion. That the tribe of Judah is designated as *first* would have surprised no one familiar with Israel's past. Nor will it surprise anyone now who has read up to this point in Israel's story from its patriarchal beginnings. In Jacob's blessing of his sons in Genesis 49, Judah is singled out for leadership in the most emphatic terms:

> The scepter will not depart from Judah,
>> nor the ruler's staff from between his feet,
> until he comes to whom it belongs
>> and the obedience of the nations is his. (v. 10, NIV)

Rather strangely in view of such a pronouncement, none of the outstanding leaders of Israel since then (Joseph, Moses, Joshua) had arisen from Judah. It is as though through all the intervening years the prophecy about Judah had been biding its time. Against this background the announcement of 1:2 is like a declaration of arrival: Judah's time has come, or at least it has begun to come, like the first rays of a rising sun. The full glory of Judah's destiny (at least in the Old Testament) will not be seen until the reign of David, but the period of the judges will see the beginning of it. Judah is destined to rule, not just its own tribal allotment, but the whole (promised) land of Canaan. It "has been given" into Judah's hand by divine resolve. This pronouncement in

---

10. The Hebrew *qatal* (perfect). Alternatively, the *qatal* could here be performative: "I *hereby* give" (as in the NRSV). But the effect is the same.

11. So Lindars, *Judges 1–5,* p. 7.

verse 2 is pregnant with import. A lot will unfold from it. What follows immediately will be only the first stage.

To summarize, the way the book of Judges opens is full of optimism and promise. Sadly, as we will see, the expectation it creates will not be realized until well after the story of the judges has been told. A dark shadow falls between.

2. The Successes and Failures of the Southern Tribes (1:3-21)

a. The Battle for Jerusalem (1:3-8)

Jerusalem itself does not come into view until near the end of this unit (vv. 7b-8), but everything before leads up to it. The passage ends with Jerusalem in flames.

> 3 *Judah said to Simeon his brother, "Go up with me into my allotted territory and let us fight the Canaanites! And I likewise will go up with you into your allotted territory." So Simeon went with him.*
>
> 4 *Judah went up, and Yahweh gave the Canaanites and Perizzites into their hand. They struck them down in Bezek — ten thousand men.*
>
> 5 *They found Adoni-bezek[12] in Bezek, and fought against him, and struck down the Canaanites and Perizzites.*
>
> 6 *Adoni-bezek fled, but they pursued him and seized him, and cut off his thumbs and his big toes.*
>
> 7 *Adoni-bezek said, "Seventy kings with their thumbs and big toes cut off used to forage under my table. God has paid me back[13] — he has done to me what I did to others"; and they brought him to Jerusalem, and he died there.*
>
> 8 *Then the men of Judah fought against Jerusalem, and took it; they struck down its inhabitants with the edge of the sword, and the city itself they sent up in flames.*

12. In line with all the major English versions I have rendered *ʾᵃdōnî bezeq* as a personal name, like *ʾᵃdōnî-ṣedeq,* the name of the king of Jerusalem, in Josh. 10:1-4. Boling (*Judges,* p. 90), following S. Layton, *Archaic Features of Canaanite Personal Names in the Hebrew Bible,* HSM 47 (Atlanta: Scholars Press, 1990), p. 117, treats it as a title, "Lord of Bezek." The reason is that in personal names of this type, the second part is normally the name of a god, and Bezek is not the name of any known god. Given the connection with Jerusalem in both passages, it's tempting to think that "Adoni-bezek" is a corruption of the name "Adoni-zedek," but if so, this must be *another* king of Jerusalem of that name, since the previous one was killed by Joshua according to Josh. 10:26. More likely, as suggested by Lindars (*Judges 1–5,* p. 15), Adoni-bezek is a corruption of a personal name of this general type under the influence of the place name Bezek.

13. Note how "repayment" also features in Gideon, Abimelech, and Samson.

3 Now the focus shifts from the land as a whole to the particular parts of it that had been assigned to the various tribes, and from Judah acting symbolically for all Israel to Judah addressing the practicalities involved in taking secure possession of its own *allotment (gôrāl)*. In recognition of Judah's importance, its allotment is mentioned first in the book of Joshua, and an entire chapter is devoted to it (Josh. 15). According to the details given there, it covered the entire southern part of Canaan, from the Dead Sea to the Mediterranean coast, and from Jerusalem to the southern desert.

Here in Judges 1:3 the tribe of *Judah* is again referred to under the name of its eponymous ancestor, and now its *brother* tribe *Simeon* is referred to in the same way. The categories are personal and fraternal, and these opening words of the unit set the agreement between the two tribes here in the context of the tradition, reflected in Genesis 29:31-35, that they were descended from full-blooded brothers. In this sense the alliance is a natural one. Judah's actual words, however, express a much more immediate and practical concern. They take for granted the situation described in Joshua 13–19, according to which Joshua allocated land to the various tribes by lot *(gôrāl),* and especially Joshua 19:1-9, where Simeon's allotted territory is described as falling within that of Judah. In these circumstances the advantages of Judah's proposal are obvious. If Judah's words evince a keen eye for the practicalities of the situation, they do not betray any lack of enthusiasm for the task. The parts of verse 3 are arranged concentrically around the exhortation, *let us fight the Canaanites!*

> A *Judah said to Simeon his brother,*
>   B *"Go up with me into my allotted territory*
>   C *and let us fight the Canaanites!*
>   B′ *And I likewise will go up with you into your allotted territory."*
> A′ *So Simeon went with him.*

Kinship ties were very important in the period of the judges, at times causing tension by being stronger in the minds of some groups than their solidarity with Israel as a whole (e.g., 12:4). Expulsion from the family because of being "the son of another woman" (in Jephthah's case a prostitute) was a way of disinheriting someone, which could lead to deep and lingering resentments, and even fratricide (8:31; 9:1-5). Here, however, true brotherliness is expressed in the way Judah goes about exercising the leadership that has been assigned to it. Judah does not act alone, but seeks the cooperation and support of *Simeon his brother.* After v. 17, where the Judah-Simeon pact is referred to again, Simeon disappears and plays no further part in the book. This is perhaps a reflection of the eventual absorption of the tribe of Simeon into Judah; a kind of "conquest" of Simeon by its stronger brother.[14] But there is no suggestion that this is Judah's intention here. Cooperation was a lesson the Israelite tribes had been taught by Moses and Joshua (Deut. 32:1-27; Josh. 22:1-9), and the present passage is one of the indications that their influence lived on. One of the great legacies of Moses and Joshua was a united Israel. That unity was to come under increasing strain, however, as the judges period ran its course.

4-8 It is not clear whether the plural in v. 4b *(into their hand),* and the plural verbs which follow, refer distributively to (the men of) Judah (v. 4a), or to the allies, Simeon and Judah. The fact that Judah is the only subject specified *(Judah went up)* suggests the former. Given the context, we must assume Simeon to be actively involved, but the primary focus is on Judah, and will remain so.

The victory at Bezek is described in verses 4-7 according to a traditional pattern clearly attested elsewhere in the Former Prophets, especially in the books of Samuel (1 Sam. 4:10; 4:17; 2 Sam. 2:17; 18:6-7). The elements are as follows:

1. a brief statement that the battle was joined
2. a brief mention of the outcome (typically in terms of the flight/defeat of one side)
3. a mention of casualties (typically large) suffered by the defeated side
4. an account of the death of a person or persons of importance on the defeated side[15]

In the present passage the wording of elements 1 and 2 links the victory firmly with the oracle of verse 2: Judah "goes up," and the enemy is "given" into his hand. Element 3 is entirely typical. Element 4 is much more elaborate than the typical instances cited above: three whole verses (5-7) are devoted to the description of the capture, mutilation, and death of Adoni-bezek.

Given the global way the term *Canaanites* has been used in the opening verse of the book, the expression *the Canaanites and Perizzites* in verse 4 is probably best understood as a hendiadys (a single idea expressed by means of two words linked by "and") — Perizzite Canaanites (cf. African Americans). *Canaanites* is the general term (the pre-Israelite inhabitants of Canaan); *Perizzites* is the specific one (those who lived in and around *Bezek*). According to Genesis 13:7, Perizzites were already living in Canaan in Abra-

---

14. Simeon is not named in the blessing of Moses in Deut. 33.

15. D. M. Gunn, *The Story of King David: Genre and Interpretation,* JSOTSup 6 (Sheffield: JSOT, 1978), pp. 51-54, 56-62. Gunn identifies the pattern in the instances I have cited above from 1 and 2 Samuel, and accounts for it in terms of an originally oral mode of composition. The application to the present text is entirely my own.

ham's time, probably (as here) in the central hill country to the north of Jerusalem. When Abraham and Lot encounter Perizzites in Genesis 13, they are in the vicinity of Bethel and Ai (v. 3), from which they could view "the whole land" (v. 10). Bezek was almost certainly in the same general area, though its exact location is unknown.[16] It appears, though, that in this first campaign Judah and Simeon had moved up into the hill country at the very center of the land before moving south, first to Jerusalem (v. 8), then to the southern highlands (v. 9), then the Negev (the lowlands of the central south, vv. 9, 15), and finally the coastal plain (v. 18). It was an ambitious and (as it turned out) impressive operation that covered the same basic territory as the first phase of Joshua's conquest in Joshua 8–10.

The expression *struck them down* (*wayyakkûm*, v. 4) indicates the infliction of a decisive defeat. The semantic range of *nāḵâ* (to strike) is wide, even in specifically military contexts (see BDB, p. 645). When used unqualified in listing casualties, as here, it appears to mean "to put out of action" (by killing or severely wounding). When used, again unqualified, as a general statement of the outcome of a battle (as in v. 10), it certainly means to defeat but not necessarily "to annihilate" (see 2 Kgs. 13:25; Gen. 14:5-7, 17).

The size of the enemy force, *ten thousand men*,[17] is impressive, and underscores the significance of the victory. It could be that the Adoni-bezek of this pericope was charged with the defense of Jerusalem and therefore led a force drawn from a relatively wide area, not just from Bezek itself.[18] The number of his conquered enemies in verse 7 implies widespread influence. This would explain (at least at one level) why so much is made of his defeat (the battle with Adoni-bezek was the battle for Jerusalem), and why he is taken to Jerusalem and dies there. It would also shed further light on why Judah sought assistance from Simeon for this campaign: given the size and strategic importance of Jerusalem, engagement with a major enemy force could be expected. It is likely, therefore, that we are meant to take the *ten thousand* of verse 4 as a round number for major casualties inflicted on a large enemy force.

The course of the conflict as described in verses 4-7 is as follows: Judah and Simeon "find" Adoni-bezek in Bezek, and it is here that the first battle is fought. With his forces decisively defeated, Adoni-bezek flees, as Sisera later flees in 4:15 after the battle at the Kishon. But he is pursued, captured, and punished by having his thumbs and big toes cut off (v. 6), and then

---

16. The only other reference to a Bezek in the Old Testament is in 1 Sam. 11:8, but as a mustering point for action at Ramoth-gilead this is far too north to be the Bezek in view here. See the discussion in Butler, *Judges,* p. 21.

17. See Section IX.C of the Introduction: "The Problem of the Large Numbers."

18. Cf. the forces of Sisera of Harosheth-ha-goyim in 4:1-2.

taken to Jerusalem, where he dies (v. 7). With Adoni-bezek gone, Jerusalem holds out for a time, but it is eventually (and now perhaps inevitably) taken and burned by the men of Judah, and its inhabitants killed (v. 8).

So much for the grim, basic facts. But in these verses there is more than mere reportage. The direct speech attributed to Adoni-bezek in verse 7 opens up a quite definite perspective on the whole episode which is clearly of considerable importance for how we are meant to understand it. The enemy general is condemned out of his own mouth as a sadistic tyrant who has been treated exactly as he deserved (strict retributive justice), and his punishment is attributed directly to God. In keeping with the limitations of his understanding, Adoni-bezek speaks only of God ($^{e}l\bar{o}h\hat{\imath}m$), not Yahweh. In terms of its function in the narrative, this brief speech offers us an apology (in the technical sense) for what is an undeniably gruesome punishment. But it does more than this. Adoni-bezek is the first Canaanite we meet in Judges, and as a leader he is more than a random individual. He represents the kind of Canaanite regimes that God is overthrowing through the Israelites, who (we are to understand) are the agents of his just judgment. This narrative cameo opens a window onto Canaanite culture as embodied in its leaders — a culture ripe for judgment, a culture whose day of reckoning has come (see Gen. 15:16).

Of course this leaves many questions unanswered. For example, what about the slaughter of Jerusalem's inhabitants, many of whom were presumably the victims rather than perpetrators of the kind of thing Adoni-bezek represents? No matter how urgent such questions may be for us, we must bear in mind that we haven't yet heard all that Judges has to say on this topic; some other very significant perspectives on the conquest will be offered in chapters 2 and 3, and all these have to be read against the background already provided in Genesis to Joshua. This is a very sensitive and complex issue, and no one passage can say all that needs to be said about it.[19] The present passage is a good example of how the prologue to Judges introduces themes that will be taken up and developed in subsequent chapters.

In verse 8 the eponymous singular, "Judah," is replaced by the distributive, *men* (literally "sons") *of Judah,* and this kind of terminology becomes the norm for the rest of the chapter. Even the collective term for the northern tribes is "house ($b\hat{e}\underline{t}$) of Joseph" rather than simply "Joseph." In all cases, however, the underlying idea is solidarity: the solidarity of the present Israelites with their ancestors and/or with one another. Their allotted territories are various, as are their fortunes, but they are nevertheless "brothers." members of the one nation referred to in verse 1 as "the Israelites" ($b^{e}n\hat{e}$ $yi\acute{s}r\bar{a}\,\bar{e}l$).

---

19. See the discussion of this issue in Section VIII.C of the Introduction.

b. Battles in the Southern Hills, the Negeb, and the Shephelah (1:9-17)

9   *After that the men of Judah went down to fight against the Canaanites who lived in the hill country, the Negeb, and the Shephelah.*

10   *Judah advanced against the Canaanites who lived in Hebron (the name of Hebron was formerly Kiriath-arba), and struck down Sheshai, Ahiman, and Talmai.*

11   *From there he [Judah] advanced[20] against those who lived in Debir (the name of Debir was formerly Kiriath-sepher).*

12   *Caleb said, "Whoever strikes Kiriath-sepher and takes it — I will give him Achsah my daughter as his wife."*

13   *Then Othniel son of Kenaz, Caleb's younger brother, took it, so Caleb gave him Achsah, his daughter, as his wife.*

14   *When she came, she urged him[21] to ask her father for a field,[22] and got down off her ass.[23] Caleb said to her, "What do you want?"*

15   *She replied, "Give me a present; since you have given me the land of*

---

20. The LXX has "went up" *(anebēsan),* probably to agree with Josh. 15:15. The subject of the verb is *yᵉhûḏâ* (Judah), as in v. 10a. The intervening *wayyakkû* (v. 10c) also has the same subject despite its plural form (LXX^A has the singular here also). Comparison with Josh. 15:15 in which Caleb is the subject has led to the suggestion that v. 20 of Judges 1 should be between vv. 10 and 11: C. H. J. de Greus, "Richteren 1.1–2.5," *Vox Theologica* 36 (1966): 37; J. Van Seters, *In Search of History: Historiography in the Ancient World and the Origins of Biblical History* (New Haven and London: Yale University Press, 1983), p. 339. But this is to ignore the fact that it is quite explicitly *Judah's* progress that is being traced schematically in vv. 9-19. See my further comments below on v. 20.

21. The LXX has "he urged her," which produces a smoother reading; Achsah then gets down off her donkey to do as Othniel has urged her to do. But as the smoother reading it must be suspect as an "improvement" introduced by the LXX, especially since there is no hard textual evidence to support it, and the parallel in Josh. 15:18 has the same hard reading as this one. Neither reading is very flattering to Othniel, who is either passive (MT), or asks Achsah to do what he is apparently reluctant to do himself (LXX).

22. Reading "field," without the article, with *BHS* apparatus and the LXX. The article has probably arisen by dittography.

23. The precise meaning of the verb, *wattiṣnaḥ,* is uncertain. It occurs only here and in 4:21, where it has to do with Jael's tent peg "going down" through Sisera's temple into the ground. The context here in 1:14 makes the translation *got down* a natural one, though the sequence of the two actions, "she urged him to ask . . ." and "she got down off her ass," is puzzling. The reverse (she got down . . . and urged him) would be more natural. In any case, however, the dismounting makes sense as an act of respect for her father before asking something of him. As indicated in the *BHS* apparatus, the LXX has here, "she murmured and cried from off her ass," which is of no real help. For a full discussion of the issues see Lindars, *Judges 1–5,* pp. 29-31.

the Negeb, give me also springs[24] of water." So Caleb gave her upper springs and lower springs.

16 *Now the descendants of the Kenite,[25] Moses' father-in-law, having gone up[26] from the city of palm trees with the men of Judah into the wilderness of Judah, which is in the Negeb of Arad, went and settled there with the people.*

17 *Then Judah went with Simeon his brother and struck down the Canaanites who were living in Zephath, and totally destroyed them, and called the name of the city Hormah.*

9 The second phase of Judah's campaign begins with the "going down" of verse 9. The *hill country* referred to here consists of the hills of the central range running directly south from Jerusalem. The *Negeb* is the dry plain south of these hills, and the *Shephelah* is the lower hill country between the central highlands and the coastal plain. Verse 9 is a summary of what follows in verses 10-18.

10 The account of this phase of the campaign opens with another victory, this one at *Hebron,* about 19 miles (30 km.) south-southwest of Jerusalem.[27] The name *Kiriath-arba* means "city of Arba." This and the three names at the end of this verse connect the victory reported here with a specific Hebron tradition that the reader is assumed to be familiar with, according to which *Sheshai, Ahiman,* and *Talmai* were the sons of Anak, whose father was Arba, *"the* great man[28] among the Anakim" (Josh. 14:15; cf. Josh. 15:14; 21:11; Num. 13:22). Thus the parenthesis in the middle of the verse *(the name of Hebron was formerly Kiriath-arba)* provides the link between the general statement which precedes it *(Judah advanced against the Canaanites who lived in Hebron)* and the particular one that follows it *(and struck down Sheshai, Ahiman, and Talmai).*

The tradition in question adds time depth to the three names at the end of the verse, which here evidently signify not individuals but families of Anakim whose association with Hebron was believed to reach way back to the Mosaic period and beyond (Num. 13:22).[29] The presence of people in

---

24. Or "reservoirs"; elsewhere the word *gullâ* means a bowl (Zech. 4:2-3; Eccl. 12:6) or the bowl-shaped top of a pillar (1 Kgs. 7:41). BDB, p. 165.

25. Reading *haqqênî* with the *BHS* apparatus. Cf. 4:11.

26. With HCSB I take the *qatal* (perfect) verb here, in the syntactical construction X + *qatal,* as indicating action which is antecedent to that of the two *wayyiqtols* that follow.

27. At 2,800 feet above sea level, Hebron is actually higher than Jerusalem, which is at 2,500 feet. The presentation in terms of two major movements, "up" and "down" respectively, is schematic rather than strictly literal.

28. This is the force of the Hebrew, *hā'āḏām haggāḏôl.*

29. According to Josh. 11:21-22 Joshua "eradicated" *(wayyakrēṯ)* the Anakim

Hebron still using these names is testimony to the tenacity with which the Canaanites (here of the Anakim kind) clung to their land and traditions, despite repeated attempts by the Israelites to dislodge them. Although this is a victory, it has embedded in it hints of a problem (the continued presence of Canaanites in "conquered" territories) which will gradually emerge into full view as the chapter proceeds.[30]

11-15 *Debir* is now generally identified with Khirbet Rabud, roughly 7.5 miles (12 km.) south-southwest of Hebron.[31] The previous name of Debir *(Kiriath-sepher)* means "book city" or something similar, suggesting that it had been a center of learning or perhaps administration.[32] With Judah's advance there the text moves again into a more expansive literary style. Individual characters[33] are singled out for our attention — *Caleb, Othniel,* and *Achsah* — and they achieve a degree of personal identity through their actions and (in the case of Caleb and Achsah) through their speech. Caleb acts here in his traditional role as a "leader" *(nāśî')* of Judah (Num. 13:1-2, 6; 34:18; cf. Josh. 14:6).[34] Othniel, of the same clan as Caleb, and linked in close family ties with him (v. 13a),[35] is also a distinguished Judahite, so the victory at Debir is both their personal triumph and, at the same time, yet another success for Judah.

---

from Hebron and the surrounding hills, though some survived in Gaza, Gath, and Ashdod. The reappearance of Anakim at Hebron after the withdrawal of Joshua is plausible from a narrative point of view, but unexplained. More problematic is the claim in Josh. 11:21 that Joshua "utterly destroyed" *(heḥᵉrîm)* Hebron and its inhabitants, since Sheshai, Ahiman, and Talmai are specifically Hebronite Anakim in the tradition (Num. 13:22). We are evidently meant to understand that the names *Sheshai, Ahiman,* and *Talmai* are being used here, like *Judah,* of people groups (here Anakim clans) rather than individual persons.

30. The same tradition provides "depth" in another sense, of course, by making us aware of what is in front of the text — the time between the events themselves (when Hebron was called *Kiriath-arba*) and the time of the writer. Cf. the similar note concerning *Debir,* formerly *Kiriath-sepher* ("Book City") in v. 11.

31. Lindars, *Judges 1–5,* p. 26.

32. The Hebrew word *sēper* means "document, book." LXX[A] has *Polis grammatōn.* For a full discussion of the possible meanings of the name see Lindars, *Judges 1–5,* pp. 26-27.

33. In contrast to the way the names "Judah," "Simeon," and even "Sheshai," "Ahiman," and "Talmai" are used in the preceding verses.

34. The progression from "men of Judah" to "Caleb" in Josh. 14:6 is the same as that from "Judah" to "Caleb" as leading representative of Judah in the present passage.

35. They are both Kenizzites, members of the "Kenaz" clan. The expression *son of Kenaz, Caleb's younger brother,* is as ambiguous in the Hebrew as it is in English. Othniel is either Caleb's younger brother (LXX[A]) or his nephew (LXX[B]). The intricate genealogical data of 1 Chron. 4:13-15 appears to represent an independent tradition, and is even more difficult to interpret.

Verses 11-15 are another embedded mini-narrative with its own characters and plot, like the one about Adoni-bezek in verses 4-7. A drama is enacted here on a different plane from that being played out in verses 3-19 as a whole. The plot concerns a father, a daughter, and an aspiring suitor. The issues are essentially personal and domestic. The successful military action, so important in the larger narrative, is reported with extreme brevity: *Othniel . . . took it (Debir)*. Within the mini-narrative itself the taking of Debir is of interest primarily because of the way it affects the relationships between Caleb, Othniel, and Achsah.[36] From the moment of her entry (v. 14a), Achsah ceases to be an object acted upon by the two men. She seizes the opportunity to get something which neither her father nor her husband has considered.[37] Her father has already given *the land of the Negeb* as her dowry (v. 15c). Achsah greatly enhances its value by negotiating successfully for water rights, something of great importance given the predominantly dry nature of the area.

All three characters in this vignette will assume greater significance in the larger narrative which is yet to unfold. Othniel will appear as the first judge (3:7-11). In the light of 2:7 Caleb will serve as a notable example of "the elders who outlived Joshua," in whose days Israel still served Yahweh. On the other hand, his promise to give Achsah to whoever would take Debir for him (v. 12)[38] will find a grotesque and tragic parallel in Jephthah's vow (11:30-31). Achsah's practical shrewdness and resourcefulness in seizing the initiative from Caleb and Othniel, the two dominant males of the story, introduces a motif which will recur at crucial points in 3:6–16:31, particularly in 4:17-22 (Jael), 9:53-54 (the "certain woman" of Thebez), and 16:14-21 (Delilah). Othniel's marriage to Achsah also assumes greater significance in view of the developments described in 3:6. Unlike the marriages of many of his fellow Israelites, Othniel's is not tainted by covenant unfaithfulness.

The entire account of the taking of Hebron and Debir in verses 10-15 repeats, with only minor variation, the account of the same events in Joshua 15:13-19, and is one of the more conspicuous instances of overlap between the two books. As a story about occupation of previously allotted territory it appears to belong chronologically here in Judges, and to have been included in Joshua for thematic reasons.[39]

---

36. Cf. Jephthah's victory in 11:32-34 and its implications for the outcome of his vow.

37. Cf. Josh. 14:12. Achsah shows the same enterprising spirit as her father!

38. A particular point is made of the fact that Othniel is *younger* than Caleb (v. 13). The aging Caleb depends on younger men for the most demanding aspects of his military operations, though this is not always made explicit (v. 20).

39. The initial conquest of the two cities in the context of Joshua's southern campaign is recorded in Josh. 10:36-39, after which the Israelites withdraw to their camp in Gilgal (Josh. 10:43). See also my comments above (including footnotes) on v. 10.

16-17   From the hill country Judah now moves down into the *Negeb* (or more precisely the *Negeb of Arad*).[40] This move has been anticipated by the program of verse 9 *(hill country, the Negeb, and the Shephelah)* and by Caleb's granting of *the land of the Negeb* to his daughter in verse 15 — confirming the southward direction of Judah's progress. As the Judahites continue their advance into the Negeb, the focus of the narrative shifts from Kenizzites (Othniel's clan, vv. 11-15) to Kenites (v. 16).[41]

Verse 16 has a number of textual uncertainties,[42] with the result that some details remain obscure. Some things are clear, however. The opening words, *the descendants of the Kenite, Moses' father-in-law,* set the present report against the background given in Numbers 10:29-32. There Moses prevailed upon Hobab,[43] a leading member of this same clan,[44] to accompany Israel as a guide, promising that "as Yahweh does good with us, so we will do good for you" (v. 32). Judges 1:16 reports the fulfillment of this promise by showing how the Kenites benefited from Judah's penetration into the Negeb: they enter the Negeb with Judah (v. 16a) and settle there (v. 16b). The very different consequences for the *Canaanites* in the area are reported in the next verse.[45]

One particular uncertainty in the text calls for special comment at this point, however, since it foreshadows an important development which will

---

40. *Arad* is 30 mi. (43 km.) south of Bethlehem and 17 mi. (23 km.) west of the lower reaches of the Dead Sea. The MT's *bᵉnegeḇ ᵃrāḏ (in the Negeb of Arad)* is not entirely free of suspicion. The LXX reads *epi katabaseōs Arad, "at the descent* of Arad." In any case the proper name *Arad* (and *Zephath/Hormah* in the next verse) identifies the wilderness in question as the southern wilderness rather than the one that borders the northern end of the Dead Sea. Furthermore, the anticipatory use of *negeb* in v. 9 strengthens the case for retaining it here in v. 16. Cf. C. F. Burney, *The Book of Judges: With Introduction and Notes,* 3rd ed. (London: Rivingtons, 1930), pp. 15-17.

41. It is possible that a catchword principle has played some part in the inclusion of the Kenite note at this point, even though *qᵉnaz* (v. 13) and *qênî* (v. 16) are not identical.

42. See the standard commentaries on, in particular, *bᵉnê qênî, miḏbar yᵉhûḏâ, negeḇ ᵃrāḏ* (see my note on this above), and *hā'ām.* On *hā'ām* see my further comments below.

43. The text does not explicitly say that Hobab eventually agreed, but this is implied by the way the journey begins directly after Moses has had the last word (vv. 32-33).

44. "Hobab, the son of Reuel, the Midianite, Moses' *ḥōṭēn*" (v. 29). The tradition has "Jethro" and "Reuel" variants (Exod. 2:16, 18; 3:1; 18:1). It also has "Midianite" and "Kenite" variants (Num. 10:29; Judg. 1:16), but it is clearly the same clan that features in all of them; *ḥōṭēn mōšeh* establishes the continuity. In all probability the Kenites were Midianites by political affiliation: Boling, *Judges,* p. 57; R. de Vaux, "Sur l'origine Kenite ou Midianite du Yahvisme," *Eretz Israel* 9 (1969): 29.

45. In this respect vv. 16 and 17 are a contrasting pair, both dealing with Judah's move into the Negeb.

take place in the ensuing narrative. What are we to make of the vague *hā'ām (the people)* at the end of v. 16? Most scholars emend it to *hā'ᵃmālēqî* (the Amalekites), following Budde and Moore (cf. 1 Sam. 15:6).[46] Budde also considered *'ammô* (his [Hobab's] people) possible,[47] in which case the Kenites who have accompanied Israel/Judah are reunited with fellow Kenites who have already settled in the Negeb.[48] Kaufmann suggests *hā'ām 'ᵃrād* (the people of Arad): "[the Kenizzites] have got for themselves a new heritage on the border of the wilderness."[49] Whether *hā'ām* is left to stand or one of the suggested emendations is adopted, the text leaves us in uncertainty about what form the relationship between Israel and the Kenites will assume in the future. The Kenizzites of verses 11-15 were shown as thoroughly integrated into Judah, southern Israel's leading tribe. Those in verse 16, however, have a more tenuous connection with Judah, and their long-term loyalties remain in doubt. We are hereby prepared for the ambivalent role Kenites will play when they reappear in chapter 4 (vv. 11, 17ff.).

The statement that the Kenites had *gone up from the city of palm trees with the men of Judah* identifies, by implication, the point from which the Judahites themselves went up in verse 4a as Jericho, the city of palms (Deut. 34:3).[50] A retracing of Judah's steps in Judges 1 leads us northward and eastward to the same general locality, and 2:1 provides further confirmation, im-

---

46. Karl Budde, *Das Buch der Richter* (Freiburg: Mohr, 1897), p. 9; George F. Moore, *A Critical and Exegetical Commentary on Judges,* 2nd ed., The International Critical Commentary (Edinburgh: T. & T. Clark, 1908), pp. 32, 34-35; and, more recently, J. Alberto Soggin, *Judges: A Commentary,* Old Testament Library (Philadelphia: Westminster, 1981), p. 19. This reading is attested in Moore's "N" group of the LXX, MT, and the Sahardic. However, the loss of the "missing" letters in the MT cannot be explained in terms of any commonly attested scribal error. It appears more likely to me that *'ᵃmālēqî* was itself an early emendation made under the influence of 1 Sam. 15:6 and/or Num. 24:20-22.

47. A *waw* having been lost by haplography, and the article then supplied in compensation. *Richter,* p. 9.

48. Cf. Hobab's reluctant words in Num. 10:30: "I will go to my own land and to my people."

49. Y. Kaufmann, *The Book of Judges* [Hebrew] (Jerusalem: Kiryat Sefer, 1962), p. 82 (my translation).

50. It is similarly identified, outside the Deuteronomic History, in 2 Chron. 28:15. It may be referred to simply as "City of Palms" here in Judg. 1:16 (without using the name Jericho at all) to avoid an apparent contradiction with the account of the destruction of Jericho in Josh. 6. See also the comments on 3:12. While an original reference to the Tamar (palm [city]) of Ezek. 47:19 and 1 Kgs. 9:18 is sometimes alleged (and hence an entry of the Kenites from further south), it is generally recognized that the reference in the final form of the text is to Jericho. J. D. Martin, *The Book of Judges,* NCBC (Cambridge: Cambridge University Press, 1975), pp. 22-23; Boling, *Judges,* p. 57.

plying that Gilgal, near Jericho,[51] was the site at which the Israelites had assembled to ask direction from Yahweh back in 1:1.

References to *Zephath* in the time of Moses and Joshua imply that it was in the lowlands adjacent to the Negeb.[52] The present passage seems to locate it between the Negeb itself (v. 16) and the coastal plain to the west (v. 18), and therefore at the southern end of the Shephelah.[53] The fact that *Zephath* of verse 17 is not mentioned anywhere else in the Old Testament by this name is mute testimony to the fact that its population was *totally destroyed* (the new name, *Hormah*, means "destruction").[54] While there is reference in a couple of places to people living there subsequently,[55] what remained (under its new name) was probably only a shadow of its former self. The eradication of the Canaanite population of Zephath brings Judah's subjugation of the Negeb/Shephelah to a point of decisive closure. The reappearance of Simeon suggests that the larger unit that opened in verse 3 is also coming to a close. Interestingly, whereas there Simeon went with Judah, here it is the other way around: Judah goes with Simeon. Block suggests that this may indicate greater zeal on Simeon's part for carrying out the mandate Israel had been given.[56] Another reason, not necessarily in conflict with this, is that Zephath was in the territory specifically allocated to Simeon (Josh. 19:4).[57] At the very least the mention here of both Judah and Simeon (as in the battle for Jerusalem) is an added indication of the scale of this battle, and that the alliance between the two tribes played some part in the decisive outcome. Zephath was no pushover!

c. The Judah Appendix (1:18-21)

18 *Judah took*[58] *Gaza and its territory, Ashkelon and its territory, and Ekron and its territory.*

19 *Yahweh was with Judah, and he took possession of the hill country,*

---

51. The associations with the conquest and the *mal'ak Yahweh* (messenger of Yahweh) make it clear that it is the Gilgal of Josh. 5:10-15 which is intended — against Kaufmann, who thinks the *mal'ak Yahweh* is a prophet, and identifies the Gilgal of 2:1 with "the Gilgal which is close to Bethel" in 2 Kgs. 2:1-2. Kaufmann, *Judges,* p. 82.

52. Num. 14:45; 21:3; Deut. 1:44; Josh. 12:14; 15:30; 19:4.

53. *OBA* locates it about 6 mi. (10 km.) west of the probable site of Arad.

54. *Hormah* is a play on *ḥerem,* the total destruction entailed in holy war.

55. 1 Sam. 30:30; 1 Chron. 4:30.

56. Block, *Judges, Ruth,* p. 98.

57. Referred to there as Hormah.

58. Both LXX[A] and LXX[B] have the negative: "did *not* take possession of Gaza. . . ." This accords better with the next verse, but is probably a harmonizing emendation. Auld, "Judges 1 and History," p. 272.

but he was not able[59] to dispossess those who lived on the plain, because they had chariots of iron.

20 *They gave Hebron to Caleb, as Moses had said, and he drove out from there the three sons of Anak.*

21 *But as for the Jebusites who were living in Jerusalem — the men of Benjamin did not drive them out, so the Jebusites have lived with the Benjaminites in Jerusalem to this day.*

Verses 18-21 continue the account of Judah's fortunes. But they stand outside the frame formed by the references to the Judah-Simeon alliance in verses 3 and 17. They also fall beyond the threefold schema for Judah's "downward" progression in v. 9. At the same time, however, they occur before the movement that begins in verse 22: "The house of Joseph went up. . . ." So formally they are a kind of appendix to the preceding passage. In keeping with its function as an appendix, its content is rather untidy. It consists of a number of things that need to be said for completeness, but which come (on the whole) by way of qualifications of the positive picture of Judah's progress in the preceding passage.

18-19 This first item contains some new material, but functions mainly as a summary of Judah's achievements. Two notes on their efforts to occupy the coastal plain (v. 18 and v. 19b) frame a central statement about their success in the hill country (v. 19a). The retrospective reference to Yahweh in verse 19a *(Yahweh was with Judah)* is the counterpart of the oracle of verse 2, giving the following symmetrical arrangement of major compositional elements in verses 2-19:

A	*Prospect:* Yahweh's promise to give Judah victory		v. 2
B	The Judah-Simeon alliance		v. 3
X	Judah's successful campaign	up	vv. 4-8
		down	vv. 9-16
B′	The Judah-Simeon alliance		v. 17
A′	*Retrospect:* Yahweh was with Judah		vv. 18-19

But the qualifications in verses 18 and 19b are very significant. They are the first disquieting admission[60] that everything did not go according to plan: Ju-

---

59. Restoring *yākelû* (was not able) with the *BHS* apparatus and the major versions. This is in any case implied by the explanation which follows.

60. The position of v. 19b near the end of vv. 2-19 is significant. Like an admission reluctantly made, it is held over until all the possibilities for positive comment have been exhausted.

dah *took* Gaza, Ashkelon, and Ekron and their environs, but *he was not able to dispossess* the inhabitants of the plain *because they had chariots of iron*.[61] That is, despite initial successes there, Judah was not able to consolidate its hold on the lowlands, where the Canaanite[62] inhabitants remained dominant. We are left to wonder why iron chariots should have proven so decisive if *Yahweh* was indeed *with Judah* as verse 19a says he was. It is not a circumstance we could have anticipated. According to the oracle of verse 2, Yahweh has delivered *hāʾāreṣ* (the land) into Judah's hand. Compare Joshua's words to the northern tribes in Joshua 17:18: "you shall dispossess the Canaanite, *even though he has chariots of iron and is strong*" (my emphasis). Furthermore, the Deborah-Barak story of chapters 4 and 5 will demonstrate how ineffective iron chariots are against Yahweh. So there is something profoundly unsatisfying about the simple juxtaposition of the two statements in verse 19. It is not so much explanation-without-remainder[63] as paradox, and we are left to wonder what, precisely, it signifies. It is the beginning of a much more mixed picture of Israel's military fortunes that will be revealed in the rest of the book.

20-21 Two further notes complete the appendix to this part of the introduction. Like verses 18 and 19 they are a pair, the first positive and the second negative. But this pair deals with two distinct locations *(Hebron* and *Jerusalem),* and two distinct protagonists *(Caleb* and the *Benjaminites).* Both are supplementary notes to the victories reported in verses 3-7, the first at Jerusalem in the upward phase of Judah's progress (v. 8), and the second at Hebron in the downward phase (v. 10). The supplementary notes reverse the order: first Hebron (v. 20), then Jerusalem (v. 21). *As Moses had said . . .* (v. 20b) explicitly connects the note of verse 20 with the tradition according to which Hebron was promised to Caleb as his special inheritance (Josh. 14:6-15, esp. v. 9). The second note (v. 21) assumes that Jerusalem was in the

---

61. Iron chariots (probably wooden chariots fortified with iron) were new in the region. They gave Judah's enemies the advantage on the coastal plain, but not in the hills, where they were much less effective. It used to be thought that it was the Philistines who introduced iron chariots to Palestine, but this has now been discredited. For a detailed treatment of the issue see P. M. McNutt, *The Forging of Israel: Iron Technology, Symbolism, and Tradition in Ancient Society,* JSOTSup 108 (Sheffield: Almond, 1990). Here it is probably Amorites rather than Philistines who have them (see vv. 34-35).

62. I use the term "Canaanite" here in the general sense of 1:1. The precise identity of the Canaanites in this region is not indicated in the present passage. The Danites are hard pressed by the Amorites here in chapter 1 (vv. 34-36), not by the Philistines, as they will be in the Samson story. Cf. Kaufmann, *Conquest of Canaan,* pp. 98-99.

63. The Targum adds, "after they had sinned." One anonymous Greek author writes, "They were unable, not because of powerlessness, but because of laziness." Moore, *Judges,* p. 38.

territory allocated to Benjamin, as in Joshua 18:28 (cf. Josh. 15:8, where Judah's northern border passes just south of Jerusalem).[64] Both notes are concerned with the attempted occupation *(yrš)* of these sites after the victories reported in verses 8 and 10.

They are a contrasting pair. The contrast is emphasized in the underlying Hebrew text by the inverted syntax of verse 21a and the repetition of *yrš:*

> A   B
> v. 20b he [Caleb] drove out *(yrš)* from there [Hebron]
>   C
> the three sons of Anak
>   C′
> v. 21a but the Jebusites, the inhabitants of Jerusalem,
>   B′   A′
> [them] they did not drive out *(yrš)* — the Benjaminites

Whereas Caleb follows up Judah's successful strike against Hebron by driving out *(yrš)* its Anakite inhabitants (v. 20b), the Benjaminites fail to do the same to the Jebusite inhabitants of Jerusalem (v. 21a). The contrast made by the juxtaposition of these two notes sets the failure of the Benjaminites in a particularly bad light. A comparison with the corresponding negative note in the first half of the appendix adds further weight to the indictment: while the Judahites *were not able* to drive out those who lived on the coastal plain (v. 19b), the Benjaminites *did not* drive out the inhabitants of Jerusalem (v. 21a). Worse still, *the Jebusites have lived with the Benjaminites in Jerusalem to this day* (v. 21b, my emphasis).[65] It is the

64. A circumstance which makes Judah's attack on it understandable. A fortified Canaanite city on its northern border would be a serious threat to its own security. The oracle of 2:1 did not limit the promise of victory over the Canaanites to Judah's own allotted territory (note *hāʾāreṣ* [the land] in v. 2b, and cf. 3:10-11; 5:31; 8:28; 2:1, 2), though the distribution of the land (presupposed in the narrative) makes it natural that Judah's efforts should be concentrated there. Besides the attack on Jerusalem on its northern border, Judah is shown to extend its activity also (by agreement) into Simeon's territory on its southern flank. Kaufmann unnecessarily limits the meaning of *hāʾāreṣ* in v. 2b by saying that it must be understood here as referring to *Judah's* land. He is right, however, in the light of v. 1b (*"Who will go up . . . first?"*), to comment that Judah's victory is intended to be "a sign and banner for the whole land." Kaufmann, *Judges,* p. 72.

65. This note views the coexistence of Benjaminites as continuing to the present time and not just as a past state of affairs. The parallel in Josh. 15:63 also has *to this day,* but has Judahites instead of Benjaminites and apparently refers to the continued presence of Jebusites in Jerusalem after David had established himself there (2 Sam. 5:6ff.; 24:17-18). Judges 1:21 could be taken to reflect a "present" prior to this. So, by implication, Martin, who comments, "This difference [Judahites instead of Benjaminites in Josh. 15:63] is no

harbinger of a much more serious state of affairs which will emerge in the
second half of the chapter.

3. The Successes and Failures of the Northern Tribes (1:22-36)

At verse 22 we have passed beyond the limits of the "Judah" section and
stand at the beginning of a new unit. This is signaled by the introduction of
the expression "the house of Joseph (*bêt-yôsēp*)." It is used twice in quick
succession (vv. 22, 23) and then dropped until it reappears in verse 35. These
references frame the intervening material, which deals with the wars of the
northern tribes.[66] Verse 36 stands outside this frame as an appendix. As noted
above, this "Joseph" section as a whole is parallel to the "Judah" section of
verses 3-21. The expression "The house of Joseph, too, went up" in verse 22
alludes back to "Judah went up" in verse 4, and so draws attention to the parallel between the two at the very beginning of this new section.

a. The Victory at Bethel (1:22-26)

22 *The house of Joseph, too, went up — to Bethel, and Yahweh was with
them.*

23 *The house of Joseph secretly investigated Bethel (the name of the city
was formerly Luz).*

24 *Those who were keeping watch saw a man leaving the city, and they
said to him, "Show us the way into the city, and we will deal faithfully
with you."*

25 *So he showed them the way into the city, and they struck the city with
the edge of the sword; but the man and all his family they let go.*

26 *The man went to the land of the Hittites and built a city, and called it
Luz. That is its name to this day.*

---

doubt due to the fact that at a later historical period Jerusalem became the capital of Judah"
(Martin, *Judges,* p. 26). But there is no need to ascribe the two versions of the note to two
historical periods like this (with the implication of a very early date for Judg. 1:21). If David
did not expel the Jebusite inhabitants of Jerusalem, presumably he did not expel its
Benjaminite inhabitants either. Judges 1:21 may simply indicate that the continued association of Benjaminites with Jebusites in Jerusalem was viewed as a scandal by the more zeal-
ous Judahites of a later time. Both Josh. 15:63 and Judg. 1:21 seek to absolve Judah of responsibility for this continued intercourse with Canaanites — in the nation's capital, no less!

66. Cf. Auld, *Judges 1,* p. 267: "the mention of Josephites in both 22[ff.] and 35
suggests that for one compiler at least all the northern tribes could be conveniently sub-
sumed under this name — just as Qenites and Qenizzites are casually mentioned in the
first part of the chapter alongside Judah and Simeon." The same usage of "Judah" and
"house of Joseph" occurs in Josh. 18:5; cf. 2 Sam. 19:20; 1 Kgs. 11:28.

A good starting point for our consideration of this significant passage is to ask how it functions in the context of the chapter as a whole. Here verse 22 provides us with our clue, especially by its use of the verb *'ālâ (went up)* and the words *gam-hēm (they too,* i.e., the house of Joseph). We are invited by these syntactical links, and by the way Judges 1 as a whole is structured, to compare the Bethel campaign of verses 22-26 with the Bezek-Jerusalem campaign of verses 4-7. Both result in victory. In verse 4 Judah's victory is attributed directly to God's intervention: "Yahweh gave the Canaanites and Perizzites into their hand." The corresponding statement in verse 22 *(Yahweh was with them)* creates an *expectation* of victory here too, but does not explicitly connect Yahweh and victory in the way that verse 4 does. The focus in verses 22-26 is rather on the human *strategy* used to take Bethel (spies, an informer, an agreement, and a secret entrance), which gives the attackers the advantage of surprise. In both stories one Canaanite in particular is singled out for close attention, Adoni-bezek in the first, and the unnamed informer in the second, but the way they feature in the two narratives is completely different. Adoni-bezek is shown as wholly within the power of the Judahites: they find him, fight against him, pursue him, seize him, mutilate him, and take him to Jerusalem. He survives the attack on Bezek only long enough to acknowledge the justice of what he has suffered; then he dies. A quite different relationship, however, develops between the Josephites and the informer here in verses 22-26: they see him, speak to him, make an agreement with him, he helps them, they release him and all his family, and he builds a new city. But the most radical difference between the two stories is the pledge, in the second, to deal faithfully *(ḥesed)* with a Canaanite.

To return briefly to the statement *Yahweh was with them* in v. 22, it is noteworthy that, unlike the similar expression in verse 19a in the Judah section, this is not a summary remark at the end. It is not brought forward at the conclusion as an explanation for why things turned out the way they did: "so, you see, *Yahweh was with them.*"[67] Rather, all it does is raise *expectations* of another Bezek-type victory. We have to read on to find out whether or not these expectations are realized.

22 The fact that Joseph was the father of Ephraim and Manasseh, the ancestors of the two largest northern tribes (Gen. 41:50-52), makes his name a suitable shorthand term for the northern tribes as a whole. The expression *house (bêt)* of Joseph is a metaphorical way of alluding to the solidarity of the northern tribes with one another.[68] That the same expression oc-

---

67. As in Josh. 6:27.
68. Cf. the reference to the Judean exiles as a "rebellious house (community)" in Ezek. 2:5.

curs again in a summary way in verse 35 indicates that it includes (as well as Ephraim and Manasseh) Zebulun, Asher, Naphtali, and Dan.[69]

Bethel (which means "The House of God") is normally identified with Tell Beitin, in the central hill country, 12 miles (19 km.) north of Jerusalem. Given its commanding position, its capture was of great strategic significance. It also had considerable sentimental and religious significance. Bethel had Israelite connections reaching back to patriarchal times (see Gen. 12:8-9 and the excursus below on the Jacob/Bethel traditions), so in that sense the taking of Bethel was a reclaiming, by the Israelites, of a place which they may have felt was rightly theirs already. Bethel will feature in 2:1-5 under the name "Bochim" (weeping), and reappear toward the end of Judges as an apparent sanctuary site[70] where the Israelites gather to worship and inquire of God (20:18, 26-27; 21:2-3). In later times, of course, it acquired much more negative connotations as one of the places where Jeroboam I erected his golden calves after the break with Judah (1 Kgs. 12:25-33). In effect, Bethel became the northern counterpart of Jerusalem.

Besides being the beginning of a new structural unit, verse 22 is also the beginning of a new *movement* in the narrative. The "Judah" and "Joseph" passages are linked by a narrative chronology which is schematically linear: Judah *first* (v. 2), then Joseph. In the first part of the chapter the momentum begins with Judah "going up," is sustained through verses 4-19a, checked in verse 19b, momentarily recovered in verse 20, and lost again in verse 21.[71] If the Judah section is considered a "movement," it falters and finally stops in the appendix of verses 18-21. At verse 22, however, the momentum is resumed: *The house of Joseph . . . went up.* The narrative begins to surge forward, and our expectations are at once raised again by verse 22b, *and Yahweh was with them* (echoing v. 19a).[72] Like the Judah section, the Joseph section begins with a notable victory.

---

69. The reason why Dan is included among the northern tribes will emerge later, especially in v. 34 and ch. 18. See further on this below.

70. Shiloh was another (21:19).

71. Note the disjunctive syntax in vv. 19b and 21a, in contrast to the flow of narrative verb-forms in vv. 3-19a, interrupted only by the peaceful interlude of v. 16.

72. The MT of v. 22b is supported by LXX[B] but not by LXX[AL] and OL, which read "Judah" instead of "Yahweh." Their combined witness is weighty and cannot be dismissed out of hand. In favor of the MT is the clear literary structure of the chapter in which "Judah" and "Joseph" are dealt with in parallel sections. Budde holds that an original *yᵉhôšuaʿ* (Joshua) was changed first to *yᵉhûḍâ* (Judah) and finally to "Yahweh" when the separate Judah section (vv. 1-21) was added (Richter, *Die Bearbeitungen des "Retterbuches,"* p. 11). However that may be, the MT is perfectly intelligible as it stands and is arguably the intended "finished" form of the text. There is no compelling reason to emend it (cf. Moore, *Judges,* pp. 41-42).

There is also a change of style in verses 22ff. The summary reporting of verses 16-21 gives way again to a more expansive narrative style. Traditional motifs appear (the sending out of spies, leniency to an informer, the secret entrance to the city), together with direct speech (v. 24b) and a simple plot. In terms of plot this Bethel passage is another complete, if simple, story in its own right — another mini-narrative. Only the word *too (gam)* of verse 22a *(Joseph, too, went up)* explicitly connects it to the larger narrative of which it is a part.

23-26   In view of the way verse 22 ends *(Yahweh was with them)*, we expect the conquest of the city to be the climax of the story. It is this to which our expectations, and hence our interest, are initially directed. Before this climax is reached, however, a complication is introduced, which means that the story cannot end with this victory; if it is achieved, it will lead to something else. An agreement is made with a man who is seen leaving the city:

> *"Show us the way into the city,*
> *and we will deal faithfully (ḥeseḏ) with you"* (v. 24bc)

Thus a new focus of interest is established, and the plot now consists of two strands which cannot be resolved simultaneously. The first strand reaches its resolution in the destruction of Bethel (v. 25a);[73] the second in the discharge of the *ḥeseḏ* obligation (v. 25b). But at this point the plot takes a surprising turn: the discharge of the *ḥeseḏ* obligation leads to the building of a "new Luz" (v. 26). Only in retrospect do we see the anticipatory function of the note in verse 23: *the name of the city [Bethel] was formerly Luz.*

The victory is reported briefly as follows:

v. 22a   The house of Joseph goes up to Bethel
v. 22b   Yahweh is with them
v. 25b   They strike the city with the edge of the sword

The direct speech, the traditional motifs (spies, informer, secret entrance) and the unexpected twists of the story (and hence the dramatic interest of the story) are all located in the *second* strand of the plot. It is this strand that makes verses 22-26 what they are, a story rather than a mere victory report. We conclude, therefore, that the true climax of the story, and therefore its unique contribution to this part of the introduction to the book, is to be found by following this "strand two" of the plot to its resolution (v. 25c, the release of the informer) and its surprising consequence (v. 26). This is a story about

---

73. See the comment on v. 25 below regarding the nature of this destruction.

114

an agreement made with a Canaanite, and not only, or even essentially, about the conquest of a Canaanite city.[74]

The released informer builds a city and names it Luz. He raises up a new Luz as a memorial to the city he betrayed. Is it an act of penance, or of defiance, or simple nostalgia? The text does not tell us. What is clear is that the informer has not become an Israelite. He remains a "Luzite," and therefore a Canaanite, at heart. Precisely what, in geographical terms, is signified by *the land of the Hittites* in verse 26 is not certain.[75] Clearly the man retires to a safe distance — beyond the limits of Israelite settlement. But he does not go away into oblivion. He (re)builds something that is within the sphere of awareness, and contact,[76] of future generations of Israelites: *Luz. . . . That is its name to this day* (v. 26). It is not just a man and his family that survive to flourish again, but Canaanite culture in a very tangible form — a city.

25   The expression, *they struck the city,* is ambiguous; did they destroy the city itself, or only its inhabitants? The latter is more likely for several reasons: the verb *nkh* (to strike [down]) is used both in Joshua,[77] and here in Judges 1 (v. 8), of the killing of people; "striking the city" here is contrasted here with the sparing of one particular person; and the destruction of Jerusalem in 1:8 (sending it up in flames) is described as something additional to, and different from, striking it with the sword.

Excursus 1: Judges 1:22-26 in the Light of the Jacob/Bethel Traditions

The conquest of Bethel in Judges 1 takes on additional significance when read against the background of the Jacob/Bethel tradition(s) attested in Genesis 28 and 35 (cf. 48:3). A number of details in the present text evoke this background: *The house of Joseph went up (wayya`ªlû) to Bethel* (cf. Gen. 35:1); "the name of the city was formerly Luz" (cf. Gen. 28:19; 35:6-7; 48:3); "he built a city and called its name Luz" (cf. and contrast Gen. 28:18-19; 34:5). When read against

---

74. Cf. S. B. Gurewicz, "The Bearing of Judges 1–2:5 on the Authorship of the Book of Judges," *ABR* 7 (1959): 37-40. On p. 37 he observes that the capture of Bethel is given prominence in the second half of the chapter "probably because of the action of the man who showed them the way into the city."

75. The inclusive sense in which "the land of the Hittites" is used in Josh. 1:4 is clearly not applicable here. Almost certainly the reference is to the location of the seven city-states in Syria which perpetuated the name "Hittite" for several centuries after the fall of the empire. Cf. the references to "the kings of the Hittites" in 1 Kgs. 10:29; 2 Kgs. 7:6. The MT of 2 Sam. 24:6 should probably be emended to read (with LXX[L]), "Kedesh, in the land of the Hittites" (see *BHS*).

76. Israel had commercial and military links with "the kings of the Hittites" during the monarchy period. See the references in the previous footnote.

77. For example, Josh. 10:28, 30, 32, 35, 37; 11:10, 11.

this background, the Bethel of Judges 1 appears as a place that Yahweh has already claimed as a site sacred to himself by a theophany (Gen. 28), and a place that Jacob has already claimed for Yahweh by raising a pillar there (Gen. 28), building an altar (Gen. 35), calling it Bethel, and burying his dead there (Gen. 35:8). Luz has already been exposed, leached, purged of its Canaanite identity.[78] Canaanite Luz has no right to exist; all that remains is for its physical "remains" to be obliterated. This is what we expect to happen when the Joseph tribes go up to Bethel in 1:22 — Yahweh with them. What in effect happens, though, is that Luz is not obliterated but "moved."[79] The building and naming of the new Luz in verse 26 is an ironic inversion of Jacob's symbolic building and naming of Bethel in Genesis 28 and 35. The relationship between "Bethel" and "Luz" (Israelite and Canaanite culture) is not decisively resolved in Judges 1 (see 2:1-5!).

Excursus 2: Judges 1:22-26 and the Taking
of Jericho in Joshua 2 and 6[80]

The narrative of verses 22-26 has some fairly obvious resemblances to the story of the capture of Jericho in Joshua 2 and 6. I have given priority to the comparison between verses 22-26 (Bethel) and verses 4-7 (Bezek/Jerusalem) since this "parallel" is in the immediate context, and arises directly out of the literary structure of Judges 1. The "Jericho parallel" cannot be passed over without comment, however, first because it is so striking (at least superficially) and because the capture of Jericho is a highlight of the Joshua story which is presupposed in Judges 1. The relevant points of similarity and difference may be summarized as follows:

78. So J. P. Fokkelman in his very perceptive stylistic and structural analysis of Gen. 28:10-22 in *Narrative Art in Genesis: Specimens of Stylistic and Structural Analysis* (Amsterdam: Van Gorcum, 1975), ch. 2, esp. p. 69.

79. Of course, this is not to call into question the archeological evidence that "Bethel [i.e., Luz] is known to have been destroyed in the latter half of the thirteenth century by a terrific conflagration that left a layer of ash and debris several feet in depth" (J. Bright, *A History of Israel, Fourth Edition* [Louisville/London: Westminster John Knox, 2000], p. 131). The observation I make here is a purely literary one. Archeology knows nothing, so far, of "new Luz," but our narrative does!

80. It is more customary to compare 1:22-26 with the battle for Ai in Josh. 7–8 and to suggest that both narratives refer to the taking of Bethel (e.g., J. Bright, *History of Israel*, p. 131). The reasons are partly archeological (Ai was destroyed in the third millennium and not reoccupied until after the Israelite conquest) and partly literary-critical — the mention of Bethel with Ai at a number of points in Josh. 7–8 (7:2; 8:9, 12, 17; cf. 12:9). Spies are used in both stories, but otherwise (in terms of plot structure and motifs) there is no resemblance between them. Within Joshua it is the Jericho story which offers the most parallels to the Bethel story of Judges 1.

Bethel (Judg. 1)		*Jericho* (Josh. 2, 6)	
1. Yahweh is with them	v. 22b	1. (see 11. below)	
2. They reconnoiter Bethel	v. 23a	2. Joshua sends out spies	2:1a
3. The sentries meet a man	v. 24a	3. The spies meet a harlot	2:1b
4. —		4. The harlot helps the spies	2:3-6
5. A *ḥeseḏ* agreement is made with the man	v. 24b	5. A *ḥeseḏ* agreement is made with the harlot	2:8-14
6. The man helps the attackers	v. 25a	6. The harlot continues to help the spies	2:15-21
7. The city is taken — directly through the help of the man and indirectly through the help of Yahweh	v. 25ab	7. The city is taken — directly through the help of Yahweh and indirectly through the help of the harlot.	6:1-21
8. The man and all his family are spared	v. 25c	8. The harlot and all her family are spared	6:22-25
9. The man goes to "the land of the Hittites"	v. 26a	9. The harlot lives "in the midst of Israel"	6:25
10. The man builds a new Luz	26b	10. "Cursed be the man before Yahweh who rises up and builds this city of Jericho"	6:26
11. (See 1. above)		11. Yahweh was with Joshua	6:27

Both stories involve a *ḥeseḏ* agreement with a collaborator (element 5). In the Jericho story the collaborator cooperates spontaneously and at great personal risk to herself (2:1-7). She then declares herself to be a believer in Yahweh as supreme God and asks for a pledge of *ḥeseḏ* ("swear to me by Yahweh"). She subsequently lives in the midst of Israel as one who has renounced her former Canaanite religion (6:25).[81] In the Bethel story the agreement is proposed by the attackers, and it is the pledge of *ḥeseḏ* which induces the man to cooperate.[82] He shows that he is still a Canaanite by building a new Luz (here the contrast with Josh. 6:26 is quite striking). In the Jericho story the Rahab strand of the plot, while prominent, is nevertheless secondary to that which deals with the spectacular victory described in 6:1-21. This is achieved by a divinely revealed strategy and divine power. The statement that "Yahweh was with Joshua" comes as a

81. Note the company she keeps in Heb. 11:31 and Jas. 2:25!

82. It could be argued that the pledge of *ḥeseḏ* in Joshua 2 likewise induces Rahab to cooperate (by maintaining her silence). At least that is how the spies seem to view it (2:14, 20). But this reflects the nervousness of the spies, or perhaps an attempt to preserve their dignity (by seeming to be in charge) rather than the realities of the situation. Rahab has already committed herself irrevocably to Israel's cause; she would have nothing to gain by revealing her act of treason to the authorities.

summary statement at the end of the story and gives implicit endorsement to all that has taken place.

The victory at Bethel is in some ways similar to that achieved at Jericho, but with some disquieting variations and shifts of emphasis. The comparison raises again the same questions about verses 22-26 as emerged from the comparison with the Bezek/Jerusalem episode of verses 4-7.

b. The Subsequent Deterioration in the Fortunes of the Northern Tribes (1:27-35)

After the account of the united assault on Bethel there now follows a series of reports on the successes and failures of the northern tribes taken individually: first the two Joseph tribes proper, Manasseh (vv. 27-28) and Ephraim (v. 29), then the Galilean tribes, Zebulun, Asher, and Naphtali (vv. 30-33),[83] and finally Dan (vv. 34-35).[84]

27 *Manasseh did not drive out the people of Beth-shean and its villages, nor Taanach and its villages, nor the inhabitants of Dor and its villages, nor the inhabitants of Ibleam and its villages, nor the inhabitants of Megiddo and its villages, for the Canaanites were determined to remain in this area.*

28 *When Israel became strong, it set the Canaanites to work as forced labor, but certainly did not drive them out.*

29 *Ephraim did not drive out the Canaanites who were living in Gezer, so the Canaanites lived in their midst in Gezer.*

30 *Zebulun did not drive out the inhabitants of Kitron, nor the inhabitants of Nahalol, so the Canaanites lived in their midst and became forced labor.*

31 *Asher did not drive out the inhabitants of Acco, nor the inhabitants of Sidon, nor those of Ahlab, Achzib, Helbah, Aphik, or Rehob.*

32 *The Asherites lived among the Canaanites, the inhabitants of the land, because they had not driven them out.*

33 *Naphtali did not drive out the inhabitants of Beth-shemesh, nor the inhabitants of Beth Anath; they lived among the Canaanites, the inhabitants of the land, who became forced labor for them.*

34 *The Amorites pressed the people of Dan back into the hill country, for they did not allow them to come down to the plain.*

83. Between the Joseph tribes in the narrower sense and the Galilean tribes lies the line of unconquered Canaanite cities listed in v. 27.

84. See the comment on vv. 34-35 for why Dan is included here.

35 *The Amorites were determined to live in Har-heres, Aijalon, and Shaalbim, but the hand of the house of Joseph was heavy on them, and they became forced labor for them.*

The momentum that was regained in verses 22-26 is immediately lost again. No further taking of cities or killing or expulsion of Canaanites is reported; only arrangements by which Israelites and Canaanites come to coexist. The note about Manasseh in verses 27-28 begins and ends with the same statement: Manasseh *did not drive out (lō'-hôrîš)* the Canaanites in the cities listed. In verse 28b this is reinforced by the infinitive: *certainly did not drive them out (hôrêš lō hôrîšô).*[85] The explanation, in verse 27b, is cast in the most general terms: *for the Canaanites were determined (wayyô'el) to remain in this area.* What appears to be envisaged is a stalemate in which the Canaanites make a determined stand and their assailants lack either the ability or the will (or both) to dislodge them (cf. v. 35, where the same verb is used).[86] A compromise arrangement eventually emerges: the Canaanites remain in possession of their cities but have to provide forced (servant or slave) labor *(mas)*[87] for Israel. See further below.

The formula, *They did not drive out (lō'-hôrîš),* which is used of Manasseh in verse 27, recurs in connection with Ephraim (v. 29), Zebulun (v. 30), Asher (v. 31), and Naphtali (v. 33). In the climactic report concerning Dan it is replaced by *The Amorites pressed the people of Dan back (wayyilḥᵃṣû,* v. 34). The Danites were repelled from the coastal plain and confined to the hills (v. 34; cf. v. 19b). The introduction of the verb *lḥṣ,* "to press (back)," is ominous, and in fact turns out to be a foretaste of things to come (cf. 2:18; 4:3; 6:9; 10:12, where the same Hebrew word is used). In the note concerning Ephraim (v. 29b), *did not drive out (lō'-hôrîš)* is combined with another expression which draws attention specifically to the coexistence of Ephraimites and Canaanites in the same locality: *so the Canaanites lived in their midst (bᵉqirbô) in Gezer.* This second expression, too, is repeated in subsequent reports, with portentous variations as follows:[88]

___

85. Cf. Moore, *Judges,* p. 47; Burney, *Judges,* p. 25, The weaker sense, "did not completely dispossess them," would require *lō' hôrîs hôrîšû;* cf. Amos 9:8.

86. The semantic range of the Hiphil of *y'l* is wide, including, in its OT usage, "to be willing, to be pleased, to decide, to undertake, to determine" (BDB, pp. 383-84). It occurs again in Judg. 17:11 in the context of an amicable agreement. The context of hostility in ch. 1, however, makes the stronger sense the probable one. Cf. Moore, *Judges,* p. 47.

87. The full expression *mas-'ōḇēḏ* occurs in Josh. 16:10 (cf. 17:13, which is parallel to Judg. 1:28, and Gen 49:15).

88. Using the generalization "Israelites" for "house of Joseph," Manasseh, etc., and "Canaanites" for all non-Israelites.

v. 30b   the Canaanites live *in the midst of (bᵉqirbô)* Zebulun

vv. 32a, 33b   Asher and Naphtali live *in the midst of (bᵉqirbô)* the
                  Canaanites, *the inhabitants of the land*

This is part of a carefully articulated double progression spanning verses 22-34 as follows:

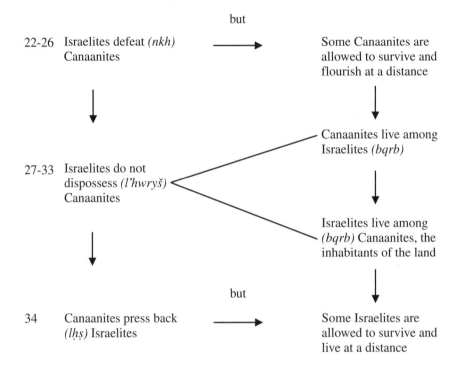

After the Bethel episode of verses 22-26 the notices are simply juxtaposed (note the disjunctive syntax). The "progression" has no chronological (narrative) sequentiality; it is purely compositional and thematic. It draws attention in a striking way to the *vulnerability* of the northern tribes to counterpressure from the Canaanites; some tribes (those later in the list) more so than others.

But here we must return and pick up another thread, beginning with the reference to *forced labor (mas)* in verse 28. The compositional pattern we have just observed (focusing on the vulnerability of the tribes) is punctuated at certain points by comments in which this vulnerability in relation to the Canaanites is said to have been reversed. There are four references in all to Canaanites being forced into virtual slavery *(mas),* the first and last being fuller than the intervening two:

v. 28   Israel becomes strong *(ḥāzaq)*
         and sets the Canaanites to work as *forced labor (mas)*
v. 30   they [the Canaanites] become *forced labor (mas)*
v. 33   the inhabitants of Beth-shemesh and Beth-anath become
         forced labor (mas)
v. 35   the hand of the house of Joseph becomes heavy *(wattikbad)* on
         them [the Amorites], and they become *forced labor (mas)*

In verse 28 the imposition of the forced labor in Manasseh's territory is not attributed to Manasseh itself but to *Israel,* and then only after a period of consolidation *(when Israel became strong).* A similar process is envisaged in verse 35, where it is *the house of Joseph* which subjugates certain Amorite cities within Dan's allotted territory. While a process involving the passage of time is indicated, it is all in the past from the point of view of the narrator.

This past time in which the events of Judges 1 are set is framed by the death of Joshua in 1:1 and the indictment of Israel in 2:1-5. Only twice is clear reference made to a later period, in both cases by means of the formula *to this day* in verses 21 and 26. No such breaking of the time frame occurs in connection with the *forced labor (mas)* in verses 27-35.[89] It is often assumed that verse 28 refers to the pressing of Canaanites into service in the early monarchy, for which the same technical term *mas* is used (1 Kgs. 9:15-21, esp. vv. 20-21).[90] The wording of verse 28 *(when Israel became strong)* certainly admits of such an interpretation, but the same can hardly be said of verse 35,[91] nor verse 33. Nor do the expressions *house of Joseph* and *Israel* necessarily involve any reference to the kingdom period, especially in view of the way they have been used earlier in the chapter *(house of Joseph* in vv. 22, 23, and *Israel* in v. 1).[92] The use of forced labor in the monarchy period in fact lies beyond the horizon of the present narrative.[93] What is envisaged,

89. Contrast 1 Kgs. 9:21, where "to this day" *is* used in connection with the continued conscription of Canaanites as forced labor, but the earlier time in view there is the time of Solomon, not (as here) the period of the judges.

90. So Budde *(Richter,* p. 12); Moore, *Judges,* p. 45; J. Gray, *Joshua, Judges, and Ruth,* The Century Bible, New Edition (London: Nelson, 1967), p. 154; Martin, *Judges,* p. 27.

91. Cf. Kaufmann, *The Conquest of Canaan,* p. 83.

92. Admittedly it is *bᵉnê yiśrā'ēl* (Israelites) rather than simply *yiśrā'ēl* (Israel) in 1:1. But cf. the use of *yiśrā'ēl* in 2:7, 10, 14, 22, and throughout the book generally.

93. So Kaufmann, *The Conquest of Canaan,* pp. 83-84. The corvée system of the early monarchy was different in both conception and effect. It included both Israelites and Canaanites and was remembered as a decisive ground for the secession of the northern tribes (1 Kgs. 12:1-4). My argument here has to do essentially with what is being *depicted* in the references to forced labor in Judg. 1, and is independent of the historicity or other-

rather, is joint action to achieve what was beyond the capacity of the several tribes acting independently, namely, to ensure that where Israelites and Canaanites lived in close proximity, hegemony lay with the Israelites. The Deborah-Barak story, however, will show how fragile this solution to the vulnerability of the northern tribes was.

It can now be seen that the Bethel story of verses 22-26 anticipates the developments which take place in verses 22-35 as a whole. As we have seen, it doesn't focus on the victory itself, but on the *arrangement* worked out between the Josephites and the informer, whereby Israel gains the advantage but the Canaanite (in this case a single man) is allowed to exist and perpetuate his own culture, albeit at a distance. The remainder of the Joseph section shows the vulnerability to which the northern tribes were exposed by their repeated failure to dispossess certain Canaanites within their borders, and the arrangement that finally emerged as a means of coping with this situation. In other words, verses 27-35 show the full consequences of a policy of accommodation that begins with the anecdote of verses 22-26.[94]

27 According to the book of Joshua, the tribe of Manasseh received two territories, one east of the Jordan, allotted to it by Moses (Josh. 13:29-31), and the other west of the Jordan, given to it by Joshua (Josh. 17:1-11). Only the latter is in view here in Judges 1. According to Joshua 22:9, the eastern half of the tribe of Manasseh had already gone back across the Jordan and settled in its territory there. Interestingly, though, according to Joshua 17:11 all the towns mentioned here in Judges 1:27 belonged to a special category; they were assigned to Manasseh, but actually lay within the territory of the tribes of Issachar and Asher, to Manasseh's north. Why Manasseh's border was not drawn further north so as to include them in a straightforward fashion is something of a mystery.[95] It is easy to understand, however, why Manasseh, as a more numerous and powerful tribe than its northern neighbors, was assigned the task of conquering and occupying these particular cities: Beth-shean, Taanach, Dor, Ibleam, and Megiddo. *Ibleam, Taanach,* and *Megiddo* lay in a line, overlooking the wide and fertile Jezreel Valley, which runs the entire width of northern Canaan from the Jordan to the Mediterranean coast. *Beth-shean* guarded its entrance at the eastern end. The fifth, *Dor,* lay close to the western end, but a few miles south, on the coast itself, where

---

wise of the passage. However, cf. Boling (*Judges,* pp. 60-61): ". . . the kings of the tenth century must have had some precedent, and it would have been remarkable if the Israelites, many of whom had been recruited from the ranks of forced labourers, did not make use of the same system when faced with the problems of geographical expansion." The corvée system is well attested as a Canaanite institution in the Ras Shamra texts (references in Gray, *Joshua,* p. 154). Solomon appears to have merely adapted it to his own purposes.

94. Cf. Boling, *Judges,* p. 65.

95. 1 Chron. 7:29 locates them right on the border.

it served both as a port city and a staging post on an important trade route that ran north-south along the narrow coastal plain. In other words, they were all strategic, and most (possibly all) of them were heavily fortified. Whoever held these towns could effectively cut northern Israel in two and maintain a stranglehold on agricultural and trading activity over a wide area. They were too important to leave unchallenged, and too strong to be dealt with by Asher and Issachar. Furthermore, as border towns four of them posed a direct threat to Manasseh itself, as well as to its northern neighbors. It is possible that, as with Bethel, the "Joseph" tribes as a whole participated in the attempt to take them, but it is *Manasseh* in particular, as the one to whom they had been directly assigned, that is charged here with the failure to expel the Canaanites from them.

28   Whether or not the attempt to take the cities of verse 27 had been a shared effort, reference to *Israel* here does seem to indicate that the solution that was eventually found and put into effect was not the work of Manasseh alone, but of the tribal confederacy as a whole.[96] As explained above, however, this does not entail a reference to the much later imposition of forced labor in the time of Solomon.

29   The territory allotted to Ephraim lay immediately south of Manasseh's, and like it extended from the Jordan River to the coastal plain (Josh. 16:5-9). *Gezer* is mentioned in Joshua 21:21 as one of the cities in Ephraim's territory that was set aside for the Levites. But taking it proved very difficult. It lay approximately 19 miles (30 km.) west-northwest of Jerusalem, in the lower hills overlooking the coastal plain. It was another city of great strategic significance, like those in verse 27, and the Egyptians had maintained a presence there since the mid-fifteenth century. At the time of Joshua's campaigns its king had tried to support Lachish. He was unsuccessful, as it turned out, and his army was virtually wiped out; but the city itself did not fall. In the time of David it seems to have been controlled by the Philistines, probably with Egyptian support (2 Sam. 5:25), and eventually it passed into Israelite hands as a marriage dowry during the time of Solomon, who showed his awareness of its strategic importance by rebuilding its defenses (1 Kgs. 9:15-17).[97]

It seems likely from Judges 1:29 that the Ephraimites, finding Gezer in a weakened state after the defeat of its army by Joshua, were able to enter the city and establish a strong presence there; but they either could not or simply did not expel its Canaanite inhabitants, who continued to live there *in their midst*. Given this situation, plus the generally chaotic nature of the times, it is little surprise that the ideal of Gezer and other cities being set

96. Cf. the use of the expression *Israelites* (sons of *Israel*) in v. 1.
97. See G. G. Garner and J. Woodhead, "Gezer," in *NBD,* pp. 407-9.

aside for the Levites was not realized in the judges period, and perhaps never.[98] This also helps explain the unsettled condition of the Levites that features in Judges 17–21.

30 Zebulun's territory was in the central north, between Asher's allotment on the west (along the Mediterranean coast) and Issachar and Napthali's to the east (along the Jordan River and the Sea of Galilee) (Josh. 19:10-16).[99] Uncertainty surrounds the identity and location of both *Nahalol* and *Kitron.* Nahalol, with the slightly different vocalization, Nahalal, occurs among the towns of Zebulun in Joshua 19:15. Albright identified Nahalol as *Tel en-Naḥl,* near modern Haifa, but this would put it south of the River Kishon and outside Zebulun's territory. Most likely it is near the modern Nahalal, 5.5 miles (9 km.) west of Nazareth, in central Zebulun. Kitron may be the same as the Kattath also listed in Joshua 19:15, but the location of Kattath, too, is unknown. In general, the present passage indicates the continued presence of Canaanites in these two towns, but with the balance of power shifting, and eventually settling, with the Israelites.

31-32 The identity and location of some of the towns mentioned here *(Ahlab, Helbah, Aphik,* and *Rehob)* are either unknown or uncertain. The others *(Acco, Achzib,* and *Sidon)* are strung out along the northern Mediterranean coast toward and into modern Lebanon, and confirm the general description of Asher's territory in Joshua 19:24-31. Possession of such a string of port cities would have given the Israelites direct access to the seaborne trade that the Phoenicians later exploited to the full. It seems from the present passage, however, that in the period of the judges the Israelites had to settle for a presence there, without the dominance they were able to achieve further inland: "The Asherites lived among the Canaanites, the inhabitants of the land, because they had not driven them out" (v. 31). The picture that is emerging as the passage runs its course is that in the north the Israelites were denied control of all the most desirable parts of the land: the most strategic mountaintop sites, the fertile valleys, and the coastal plain with its port cities.

33 Naphtali's allotted territory as described in Joshua 19:32-39 was

98. According to 1 Chron. 6:67 Gezer was given to the Levites in the time of David, but this may have been simply a confirmation of their right to it, as in Josh. 21:21. As we have already seen, Gezer remained under Egyptian control until the time of Solomon. For this and other reasons most scholars see the legislation about the Levitical cities as an ideal that was never realized. See the article, "Levitical Cities," in *NIDB,* pp. 116-17.

99. There is some uncertainty about Zebulun's western border (with Asher). In the description of its borders in Josh. 19:10-16, Zebulun's territory does not extend to the sea, but it does have contact with the sea in the blessings of both Jacob (Gen. 49:13) and Moses. In the latter both Zebulun and Issachar "will feast on the abundance of the seas" (Deut. 33:19 NIV), though this does not necessitate direct contact with the Mediterranean coast.

to the east and north of Zebulun's. Its northern half bordered directly on Asher's territory, and on the south it had a common border with Issachar. The present brief report of Naphtali's fortunes focuses on two cities, *Beth-shemesh* and *Beth-Anath,* probably because what happened there was decisive for Naphtali's fortunes as a whole. Their names, "House/temple of the sun" and "House/temple of Anath," hint at their deeper significance for what was happening in Judges 1 — not just a military clash for control of land, but a clash between two mutually incompatible religious cultures: the worship of Yahweh versus the worship of natural phenomena such as the sun *(šemeš),* or gods such as Anath (the Canaanite goddess of war).[100] Furthermore, given the terms in which Israel's monotheistic faith had been spelled out at Sinai, no accommodation was possible without compromising the very heart of Israel's covenant faith. But according to verse 33, accommodation did take place. Finding the Canaanites in these cities too entrenched to expel, the Israelites *lived among* them *(the people of the land)* and eventually got the mastery of them: the Canaanites of these cities *became forced labor for them.* Unfortunately, as the rest of the book shows, the Israelites were in turn mastered by the Canaanite gods. So this brief report of Naphtali's fortunes is a kind of microcosm of what happened to Israel as a whole following Joshua's death.

The Beth-shemesh here is clearly not the same as the town of the same name in Dan's territory in the south referred to in Joshua 19:41 as Ir-shemesh (city of the sun).[101] The presence of two known towns with "sun" names is mute testimony to how widespread sun worship had been in Canaan at one time, probably reflecting Egyptian influence.[102] Since the northern Beth-shemesh is mentioned in Joshua with reference to the allotments of both Naphtali and Issachar (Josh. 19:22 and 38), it must have been on or very close to their common border, probably overlooking the Jordan Valley close to the southern end of the Sea of Galilee.[103] This would make it another place of great strategic significance. The location of Beth-Anath is unknown. However, references to it in the annals of Seti I and Rameses II suggest that it was probably at the opposite end of Naphtali's territory in northwest Galilee, in the mountains about 15.5 miles (25 km.) east-southeast of Tyre.[104]

34-35 In view of the broad south-north schema of this section, and of chapter 2 as a whole, the location of Dan in the final position is unexpected

---

100. See on 3:31.

101. Cf. Josh. 15:10; 1 Sam. 6:9-19.

102. Cf. Heliopolis (sun city) in the Nile Delta, and see, e.g., Jer. 43:13. As early as the 14th century B.C., Amenophis IV (= Akhenaten) had promoted the worship of the sun to the virtual exclusion of all other gods, and in the pre-Israelite period Egypt exercised significant, if waning, imperial power in Syria-Palestine.

103. *OBA* locates it 5 mi. (8 km.) southwest of the Sea of Galilee.

104. See A. R. Millard, "Beth-Anath," in *NBD,* p. 130, and the map in *OBA,* p. 72.

since its tribal allotment, along with Benjamin's, was roughly midway between northern and southern Israel: south of Ephraim's territory and northwest of Judah's (Josh. 19:40-46). However, its inclusion here is understandable on two grounds: first, it anticipates the northward migration of Dan in chapter 18, by which Dan ends up in the extreme north; and second, it makes sense thematically, since Dan's situation of being *pressed . . . back* into the hill country (v. 34) marks the end point of the progressive deterioration of Israel's fortunes which has been traced through the whole second part of the chapter. The final position of Dan here also corresponds, as we have seen, to the final position of Samson the Danite in the lineup of the judges in chapters 3–16.

The term *Amorites* here refers to the Canaanite population of the southern coastal plain.[105] By the time of Samson, they will have been displaced by the Philistines, who established a strong presence in the area and finally extinguished any hopes Dan may have still had of living there (13:1). *Har-heres* (Mountain of the Sun) is otherwise unknown, but it is probably an alternative name for the Ir-shemesh (City of the Sun) of Joshua 19:41.[106] *Aijalon,* another of the towns mentioned here, also has associations with the sun, as reflected in the famous lines:

"O sun, stand still over Gibeon,
    O moon, in the Valley of Aijalon."
So the sun stood still,
    and the moon stopped,
    till the nation avenged itself on its enemies. (Josh. 10:12-13 NIV)

Israel had won a famous victory in this area in the days of Joshua. But now Joshua is dead, and the situation Israel finds itself in could not be more different. *Har-heres, Aijalon,* and *Shaalbim* are all in the Shephelah, and lie roughly in a line from south to north, approximately 22 miles (35 km.) in from the coast. As Amorite strongholds, they indicate how far back from the coastal plain the Danites had been forced.[107]

As we have already seen, the reference to *the house of Joseph* at the end of verse 35 effectively closes a bracket around verses 22-35 as whole. It also supplies the one positive note in an otherwise bleak situation by indicating that Dan's failure was redressed to some extent by a combined effort by

---

105. See "Canaan in the Period of the Judges," in Section II.B of the Introduction.

106. As suggested by the *BHS* apparatus. Cf. Lindars, *Judges 1–5,* p. 71. The term *ḥeres* is a rare synonym for *šemeš,* "sun" (Job 9:7). As we saw above (on v. 33), *Ir-shemesh* is also an alternative name for *Beth-shemesh* (House or Temple of the Sun).

107. The impressive ruins of Beth-shemesh (Har-heres) can still be seen today on a hilltop overlooking the valley of Sorek and the coastal plain, 17.5 mi. (28 km.) west-southwest of Jerusalem.

the northern tribes in general, possibly led or represented by Ephraim (whose territory lay immediately north of Dan's). Exactly what took place we cannot be sure, but it is likely that what this note refers to is the response of the more powerful tribe of Ephraim to Dan's withdrawal as described in chapter 18. Rather than allow the Amorites to move in and occupy the whole of Dan's territory, some kind of holding operation was mounted by the northern tribes to move in and establish a line of control, eventually subjecting the Amorites, at least in the hill country, to Israelite rule.

c. The Amorite Appendix (1:36)

36 *The border of the Amorites was from the ascent of Akrabbim, from Sela and upward.*

36 The obvious semantic link between this note and the Joseph section it is appended to is *the Amorites*.[108] As we have seen, the Amorites are mentioned twice in verses 34 and 35, which conclude the Joseph section. But there is a difference in how the term is now used. The geographical place names *Akrabbim* and *Sela* locate the *border* referred to in verse 36 in the southern part of Canaan, but not near the coastal plain as we might have expected from the previous two verses. In verse 36 *Amorites* no longer refers to the Canaanites of the coastal strip, but either to Canaanites in general (as in Josh. 24:8; cf. Gen. 48:22) or to those living in the hills bordering the eastern Negeb, near Edom (as in Deut. 1:44).[109] A consideration of the narrative function of the note may help us decide between these two possibilities.

The note seems to be anachronistic in its context. Hasn't Judah effectively disinherited the Amorites/Canaanites in the south (vv. 9, 16)? Wouldn't it be more appropriate now to call this southern boundary, if there still is one, the border of Judah (the tribe) or the Israelites?[110] No, because by the time we have reached this point in the chapter, the focus has shifted away from the more or less successful occupation and settlement of conquered territory. Verse 36 is telling us that when the whole process of conquest and settlement has run its course, the only border of any significance is the border of *the*

108. The expression is not entirely free of lexical uncertainty. LXX[AL] has "the border of the Amorite, the Edomite," and cf. S[h]. Note the explicit reference to Edom in the parallel in Num. 34:3. The term *hā'ᵉmōrî* (the Amorite) could have displaced *hā'ᵉḏōmî* (the Edomite) by a simple scribal error. But since *hā'ᵉmōrî* provides the raison d'être for the inclusion of the note in its present context, the change (if there was one) was deliberate, or the error (if there was one) must have preceded the inclusion of the note here. The same border is referred to whichever term is used; only the point of view changes.

109. Cf. Josh. 15:1-4; Num. 34:1-5, and see *OBA*, pp. 72, 79.

110. As anticipated in Josh. 15:1-2 and Num. 34:1-3 respectively.

Amorites.[111] In other words, the Amorites/Canaanites are still "the inhabitants of the land," and far from driving them out, Israel lives "among them" (as we saw in vv. 32 and 33).

So this note provides a final sardonic comment on the chapter as a whole. In terms of structure it is parallel to the "Judah" appendix of verses 18-21. But it can hardly be called the "Joseph" appendix since it contains no reference to the northern tribes, nor indeed to any part of Israel at all — a silence that speaks volumes about Israel's failure to realize the high expectations with which the chapter began.

4. Israel Accused of Disobedience (2:1-5)

As we have already seen, 2:1-5 is the climax of the first major part of the introduction to the book. The basic shape of this whole extended passage is as follows:

A^1	1:1-2	The assembled Israelites ask Yahweh, "Who will *go up* . . . ?"
B^1	1:3-21	Judah *goes up*
B^2	1:22-26	Joseph *goes up*
A^2	2:1-5	The messenger of Yahweh *goes up* and confronts the assembled Israelites

In the assembly of A^1, which opens the passage, the activity of B^1 and B^2 is anticipated. In the assembly of A^2, which closes the passage, the activity of B^1 and B^2 is reviewed and evaluated.

But 2:1-5 also acts as a transition to what follows. It is the first of a series of three confrontations between Yahweh and Israel which extend into the very center of the book:

2:1-5	The messenger of Yahweh confronts Israel
6:7-10	A prophet sent by Yahweh confronts Israel
10:10-16	Yahweh himself confronts Israel[112]

There are also other, more immediate ways in which it anticipates what follows, which we will come to in due course.

---

111. A similar effect is produced in 21:12 when Shiloh is said to be "in the land of Canaan."

112. After the specification of means ("messenger" and "prophet" in 2:1-5 and 6:7-10 respectively), the bald "*Yahweh* said" of 10:11 contributes to the sense of climax that is achieved in the angry confrontation which takes place there.

128

1 *The messenger of Yahweh[113] went up from Gilgal to Bochim,[114] and said, "I brought you up from Egypt, and brought you into the land about which I had sworn to your fathers. I said, 'I will never break my covenant with you.*

2 *As for you, you will not make a covenant with the inhabitants of this land; their altars you will break down.' But you have not listened to my voice. What is this you have done?*

3 *I also said, 'I will not drive them out from before you; they will become thorns in your sides,[115] and their gods will become a snare to you.' "*

4 *While the messenger of Yahweh was speaking these words to all the Israelites, the people lifted up their voices and wept.*

5 *So they called the name of that place Bochim, and sacrificed there to Yahweh.*

1a The title *the messenger of Yahweh (mal'ak-Yahweh)* brings us to a thorny and much discussed exegetical issue. It is translated "the *angel* of Yahweh" in most English versions. I have chosen the more general translation, *messenger,* here because the identity of the messenger is problematic, and because the text itself does not draw attention to the question of his identity (in contrast to 6:22; 13:6, 16-22). Only the *function* of the messenger is important; he is the means by which Yahweh on this occasion addresses his words of indictment to Israel. Targum Jonathan and the medieval Jewish commentators understand the messenger to be a prophet, a view still advocated by some[116] (cf. Hag. 1:13; 2 Chron. 36:15-16). Certainly the messenger behaves like a prophet here, addressing the assembled Israelites in the form of a covenant lawsuit.[117] In many other places the *mal'ak-Yahweh* speaks pri-

---

113. See the exegetical comments on v. 1 for my choice of this translation for *mal'ak-Yahweh.*

114. On the occurrence of the article on the proper names *Gilgal* (circle) and *Bochim* (weeping), see GKC, #125d. The article suggests that the *meaning* of these names was remembered and was of some significance.

115. This assumes, with the NIV, NASB, and AV, that the MT's *l^eṣiddîm* (sides) is defective for *liṣnînim b^eṣiddêkem* (thorns in your sides); cf. Num. 33:55. See the discussion in Block, *Judges, Ruth,* p. 116.

116. For example, Kaufmann, *Judges,* p. 92. Boling renders it "Yahweh's envoy" (*Judges,* p. 53). *Midrash Leviticus Rabbah* (1:1) takes the messenger of Judg. 2:1 as a prophet rather than an angel on the grounds that he "went up" from Gilgal to Bochim rather than "came down" from above. Gunn, *Judges,* p. 18.

117. Furthermore, the MT has a gap after *wayyō'mer,* "and he said," in 2:1, and LXX[B] has "Thus says Yahweh" in this position. With reference to 2:1-5 in general Boling suggests that "an old story of one incident involving Yahweh's heavenly envoy has here absorbed something of the character of the prophetic lawsuit" (*Judges,* p. 62). However, if

vately to individuals, does not use the speech forms of classical prophecy (e.g., Gen. 16:7-11; 22:11-15; Exod. 3:2; Num. 22:22), and has more the character of a heavenly visitor. In such passages, including Judges 6:11-22; 13:3-21, "angel" is a more justifiable translation. However, in this commentary I have chosen to use *the messenger of Yahweh* throughout, and to let the text itself reveal more of his identity if and where it chooses to do so.

The name *Bochim* (weeping) of verse 1 is anachronistic in terms of the narrative's own chronology, for the weeping in question does not begin until verse 4b, and the naming of the place as Bochim does not happen until verse 5. However, the introduction of the name in verse 1 contributes significantly to the design of the unit. It anticipates its explanation in verse 5, and these two verses function as a frame around the passage. The real identity of the place is not given, but it is in all probability Bethel.[118] The taking of Bethel in 1:22-26 would have made it available for such a meeting. It was a place with a tradition of encounter with God going right back to patriarchal times (Gen. 28:10-22; 35:1-15), and there is repeated reference to the Israelites meeting Yahweh there later in the book of Judges itself (20:18, 26, 31; 21:2). There is even weeping there in 20:26 that echoes the weeping here in 2:4. It is as though the book turns full circle by the end; Israel will finally find itself at Bethel, the place of weeping, again.

Gilgal is simply dropped into the narrative in verse 1 without comment. But it is a name pregnant with connotations in a narrative which presupposes, as this one does, our familiarity with the exploits of Joshua and his generation (1:1; cf. 2:6-10). Gilgal, near Jericho, is the point from which the *messenger* "goes up," and so (as we have already noted) is most likely the point from which all the other "goings up" of chapter 1 have originated.[119] Also, Joshua's encounter with the mysterious "commander of the army of Yahweh" before the assault on Jericho happened "near Jericho" according to Joshua 5:13, and probably at Gilgal, since that is where the Israelites are camped in the immediately preceding verses (5:1-12). If that is so, then two encounters with an emissary of Yahweh, by Joshua and the Israelites respectively, frame the entire account of the conquest in Joshua 6–Judges 1, and the

---

a messenger of Yahweh (a prophet) were in view, normal grammatical usage would require *mal'ak l^eYahweh* rather than simply *mal'ak-Yahweh*. Also "*a* prophet" and "*the* messenger of Yahweh" are clearly distinguished from one another in Judg. 6:7-10 and 11-24 respectively.

118. Yairah Amit, "Hidden Polemic in the Conquest of Dan: Judges XVII–XVIII," *VT* 40, no. 1 (1990): 4-20, argues that the substitution of the name "Bochim" for Bethel is part of a hidden polemic against Bethel, the northern sanctuary established by Jeroboam I, and that chs. 17–18 contain a similar polemic: "Judges begins and ends with two hidden polemics against Beth-el" (p. 19, n. 32).

119. See my comments on 1:16.

"going up" of the messenger from Gilgal to Bethel indicates that the time for review and assessment has come. The same ironic twist is given to the expression "go up" *(wayya'al)* here as the expression "Come" *(hāḇâ)* has in Genesis 11:7. There, after the repeated use of this word by the builders of the tower of Babel (*"Come,* let us make bricks. . . . *Come,* let us make ourselves a city. . . ."), Yahweh declares, *"Come,* let us go down. . . ." It is the climactic, defining moment in that narrative, when Yahweh comes to pass judgment on all that the builders have done.[120] So here, Yahweh, in the person of his *messenger,* "goes up" to give his verdict on all the "goings up" of the Israelites in chapter 1.[121] The recurring use of *'ālâ,* "to go up," in chapter 1 raised expectations high; but to what an unexpected end those expectations have now come: Israel weeping under the stinging rebuke of Yahweh's messenger! Or, to put the same issue in slightly different terms, what a mess Israel has got itself into "after the death of Joshua"!

1b-5 The speech of the messenger makes specific connections with chapter 1. The charge brought against the Israelites is that they have disregarded Yahweh's prohibition against making any agreement with *the inhabitants of this land,* and his command to *break down* their altars (v. 2).[122] We have been prepared for the use of *yôšᵉḇê hā'āreṣ* (the inhabitants of the land) by its two occurrences in the Joseph section of chapter 1 (vv. 32a and 33b). There it was used in connection with the coexistence at close quarters of Israelites and remaining Canaanites, and the emergence of forced labor as a solution to the problems this coexistence posed for Israel. The messenger's speech makes it clear that this "solution" is totally unacceptable to Yahweh.

The whole process of coming to terms with these Canaanites is denounced as the making of a *covenant (bᵉrît)* with them (v. 1b) — a covenant which is incompatible with Yahweh's own *covenant* with Israel (v. 2a). Particularly offensive to Yahweh is the fact that Canaanite altars have been left standing, not only in areas where Israel has come to terms with the Canaanites, but also, as will appear later, in areas they fully occupied.[123] Yahweh's covenant, which he said he would never break, is the oath he *swore* to their fathers (ancestors) — to give the land to their descendants (v. 1).[124] The driving out of the Canaanites *before* Israel is viewed in the speech as an activity

---

120. Fokkelman, *Narrative Art in Genesis,* p. 14. The translation is Fokkelman's.

121. It is possible that 2:1 contains an allusion to the transference of the ark from Gilgal to Bethel, where it is said to be located in 20:26-27. But the focus of the narrative is on the indictment of Israel by Yahweh at Bethel, not the movement of the ark and the establishment of a new worship center there.

122. Cf. Exod. 23:32 and 34:13 respectively.

123. For example, in Ophrah (6:25-32). Cf. J. P. U. Lilley, "A Literary Appreciation of the Book of Judges," *TynB* 18 (1967): 97.

124. Cf. Lev. 26:42-44; Exod. 3:16-17.

of Yahweh; the reasons why he chose to do it gradually rather than all at once are taken up in 2:21–3:4, which we will come to in due course. But it is noteworthy that it is not failure to expel all the Canaanites that Israel is charged with in verse 2, but with "making a *covenant*" with them.[125] The implication is that the process of driving out the Canaanites would have been completed in due course (by God himself) if the Israelites had fulfilled their obligation not to make a covenant with them. Now their disobedience has placed the completion of the conquest in jeopardy, for Yahweh *also said* something else (v. 3): *"I will not drive them out from before you; they will become thorns in your sides. . . ."*

Everything in verses 1-3, however, is about things that have already been said and done (or not done) up to this point. There is no announcement here of what Yahweh will now do in response to Israel's unfaithfulness, only the implication that the Canaanite gods will become a *snare* to them as Yahweh has already said they would. In other words, the speech of the messenger in verses 1-3 is entirely one of indictment. The corresponding announcement of judgment (in the form of the specific action Yahweh will now take) does not come until verses 20-22, after the judges period as a whole has been previewed in verses 6-19. For now all we have is Israel's response to the indictment they have heard: *While the messenger of Yahweh was speaking, . . . the people lifted up their voices and wept, . . . and sacrificed there to Yahweh* (vv. 4-5). These signs of contrition provide some grounds for hope. Perhaps Israel will henceforth be faithful to Yahweh and come into full possession of the land he swore to give them after all? But what follows in 2:6-19 shows that this hope is illusory: Israel's contrition evaporates, and they sink into an apostasy from which even Yahweh himself seems powerless to retrieve them. And this, sadly, leads to and justifies the judgment which is finally announced in verses 20-22.

Excursus 3: Bethel as a Sanctuary in Judges

In Judges 20:27-28 the ark of the covenant is in Bethel, with Phineas, son of Eleazar, son of Aaron, ministering before it. That is, "Bochim," by virtue of the encounter with God that happens there, again becomes *bêt 'ēl* (Bethel, house of God, sanctuary), as it was in patriarchal times.[126] The burden of the messenger's speech in 2:1-5 is that Israel has come to terms with the Canaanites, a process that began at Bethel according to 1:22-26. Because of this the newly established (or re-

---

125. Cf. again Lilley, "A Literary Appreciation of Judges," p. 97.

126. Cf. Gen. 28:17-19, and my comments in Excursus 1, "Judges 1:22-26 in the Light of the Jacob/Bethel Traditions."

established) sanctuary becomes a place of weeping rather than of celebration. In 20:26 it is to Bethel that the Israelites go up to weep again, as we have seen, and to sacrifice to Yahweh. The implied identification of Bochim with Bethel is made explicit in the LXX.[127] Cf. the "oak of weeping" at Bethel in Gen. 35:8.

B. AFTER JOSHUA: A RELIGIOUS DECLINE (2:6–3:6)

As we saw in the introduction, 2:6–3:6 as a whole is the second part of the introduction to the book. It takes another look at what happened after the death of Joshua, this time focusing on Israel's religious affairs. In broad outline it can be summarized as follows:

2:6-10   Preface: from Joshua to "another generation"

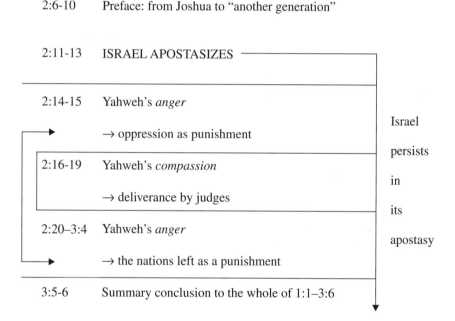

2:11-13	ISRAEL APOSTASIZES	
2:14-15	Yahweh's *anger*	
	→ oppression as punishment	Israel
2:16-19	Yahweh's *compassion*	persists
	→ deliverance by judges	in
2:20–3:4	Yahweh's *anger*	its
	→ the nations left as a punishment	apostasy
3:5-6	Summary conclusion to the whole of 1:1–3:6	

1. From Joshua to "Another Generation" (2:6-10)

> 6 *Joshua dismissed the people, and the Israelites went each to his inheritance to take possession of the land.*

127. Both A and B recensions have "from Gilgal to the [place of] weeping, and to Bethel, and to the house of Israel. . . ." Comparison with Josh. 18:1, however, has suggested to some that the Bochim referred to in the MT of Judg. 2:1 must have been in the vicinity of Shiloh (for references see Moore, *Judges,* p. 58). But the alleged parallel with Josh. 18:1 is extremely tenuous. Cf. Kaufmann, *Judges,* p. 92.

7 *The people served Yahweh all the days of Joshua, and all the days of the elders who outlived Joshua, who had seen all the great work that Yahweh had done for Israel.*

8 *Then Joshua, son of Nun, the servant of Yahweh, died, a hundred and ten years old,*

9 *and they buried him within the border of his inheritance, in Timnath-heres in Mount Ephraim, to the north of Mount Gaash.*

10 *Likewise that whole generation were gathered to their fathers, and there arose after them another generation that did not know Yahweh, or the work that he had done for Israel.*

The opening verse of this unit raises the question of the text's coherence in an acute form. Formally (in terms of the syntax) the narrative flows on from verse 5 without disturbance: *wayyiqrᵉʾû . . . wayyizbᵉḥû . . . wayᵉšallaḥ . . . wayyēlᵉkû* (and they called . . . and they sacrificed . . . and he dismissed . . . and they went). The Israelites are dismissed — presumably from Bochim where they were gathered in verses 2-5. But a moment's reflection on the *content* of verse 6 makes clear that this cannot be the case. A major temporal disjunction has occurred at this point, because it is *Joshua* who dismisses them! The content demands that we read this as a flashback to an earlier assembly (see further below) even though the formal indicators of a flashback are absent (cf. 3:7).[1] It could simply be a case of defective syntax, for which various kinds of diachronic explanation are possible.[2] On the other hand (and this is generally overlooked),[3] there is an important sense in which 2:6ff. *does* in fact follow on from 2:1-5: the apostasy which is the principal subject matter of 2:6–3:6 both follows and is derived from the gradual coming to terms with the Canaanites that happens in 1:1–2:5. This consequence is anticipated, as we saw above, in the ominous words of the messenger in 2:3: "their gods will become a snare to you." While the content of 2:6 makes clear that a major temporal break has taken place, the syntax reflects the more fundamental continuity of thought.[4]

---

1. Contrast the disjunctive syntax at 1:16 and 11:1, which in each case *does* clearly mark what follows as a flashback.

2. Either vv. 6-10 were the original continuation of Josh. 23 (Noth, *Deuteronomistic History,* p. 94), or the author has quoted from Josh. 24:28-29 without emending the syntax (cf. Kaufmann, *Judges,* p. 94).

3. Most commentators simply treat 2:6ff. as a "second," "deuteronomic," or "proper" introduction to the book/period, separating it from what precedes by a major sectional heading (so Soggin, *Judges,* p. 36; Gray, *Judges,* p. 255; Moore, *Judges,* p. 62; Martin, *Judges,* p. 32).

4. Cf. C. F. Keil and F. Delitzsch, "The Book of Judges," in *Commentary on the Old Testament in Ten Volumes,* vol. 2, tr. J. Martin (Grand Rapids: Eerdmans, 1973), p. 267.

But then why the flashback at all? Why not proceed directly from 2:1-5 to the announcement of Israel's apostasy in 2:11? The period between Joshua and the assembly at Bochim has already been surveyed in chapter 1. So what narrative purpose does the reprise 2:6-10 serve?

The survey of chapter 1 was concerned primarily with the military and political aspects of the period in question, and only secondarily with the religious dimension; with Israel's relationships with the Canaanites rather than its relationship with Yahweh. Yahweh's accusation that they have "made a covenant" with the people of the land (2:2) comes as no surprise after 1:22-36, but the focus is shifted by the messenger's speech in 2:1-5 to the religious implications of this. The charge concerning not "breaking down their altars" (2:2) further sharpens this new religious focus, but it is quite unexpected after chapter 1, since there has been no mention at all there about these shrines. In chapter 1 we see the period unfolding from the perspective of the Israelites themselves; in 2:1-5 we see it for the first time from Yahweh's perspective. In 2:6-10 the *whole* period is then reviewed from this new perspective. The religious question (Israel's relationship with Yahweh) is now the focus of attention, and it is the military and political aspects of the period which are passed over in silence. A three-phase analysis is presented:

1 The days of Joshua, the "servant of Yahweh"	Yahweh did a "great work" for Israel	The Israelites "served" Yahweh
2 The days of the elders (e.g., Caleb) who outlived Joshua	They had seen "Yahweh's great work" that he had done for Israel	The Israelites "served" Yahweh
3 The time when another generation arose	They did not know "the work" that he had done for Israel	They did not know Yahweh.

The first intimations of the "arising" of this "other generation" are to be found, on reflection, in chapter 1, but its full manifestation does not come until the outright apostasy of 2:11ff. Verses 9-10 as a whole serve as a preface to the shocking announcement that is made there: "the Israelites did what was evil . . . they abandoned Yahweh." It offers us an explanation of how this came about: the Israelites of this generation, unlike their forebears, did not have firsthand experience of the *great work* that Yahweh had done for Israel under Joshua. At the same time it recognizes, in fact underlines, the evil character of the apostasy by setting it against the background of what Yahweh had done for Israel, and the faithfulness of Joshua himself and his generation.

A similar contrast is implicit between the startling transition made in verse 6 from the assembly at Bochim that has just been addressed by Yahweh's messenger, and the earlier assembly at Shechem that was addressed by Joshua (Josh. 24:1). Judges 2:6-9 is almost an exact duplication of Joshua 24:28-30.[5] Before dismissing them from that assembly, Joshua had challenged the Israelites to choose between Yahweh and other gods (v. 15), and confirmed their choice to serve only Yahweh by making a $b^e r \hat{\imath} t$ (covenant) with them (v. 25; cf. Judg. 2:1).

Certain of the leading motifs and concepts of 2:6-10 recur as the larger unit that it introduces (2:6–3:6) draws to a close. The death of Joshua is referred to once more in the divine speech of 2:20-22, and the contrast is again drawn between the faithfulness of Joshua and his generation and the unfaithfulness of the Israelites of the judges period. Further, the connection made in 2:10 between "knowing" Yahweh and "knowing" the great work he had done for Israel is recycled in 3:1-2 in a new form: it is the Israelites who have "not known" war (v. 2), and in particular "the wars of Canaan" (v. 1), who fail the test of loyalty to Yahweh. There the verb $y\bar{a}da\'$ (to know) acquires fresh dimensions of meaning through its assimilation to the new "test" motif, and becomes a key word in 3:1-6 as a whole (see below). So 2:6-10 serves as a preface, not just to verses 11-19, but also to the whole of 2:6–3:6.

6 The concept of the land as an *inheritance (naḥ^alâ)* entails the idea of a gift or legacy, something received because of the hard work and goodwill of another person. The reason for viewing Canaan in this way here lies in Yahweh's solemnly sworn promise to Israel's ancestors to give this land to their descendants (2:1; cf. Exod. 32:13), and the battles already fought by Joshua and his generation to secure it for those who would follow them. The dividing up of the land among the various tribes by Moses and Joshua was a tangible expression of the fact that the promised inheritance had been received, and in doing this Moses and Joshua had acted as executors of the divine will. Each tribe's allotment was understood to be its share of this inheritance (Josh. 13:6-7). Here in Judges 2:6, as in the law of Moses, the idea of the inheritance is taken further: the people go *each to his inheritance.*[6] It is doubtful whether this was ever understood in purely personal terms, as it is

5. Kaufmann (*Judges,* p. 94) thinks that the changes made in the text of Judg. 2 indicate that an earlier dismissal from the camp at Gilgal is in view, after which, at the end of his life, Joshua reassembled the Israelites at Shechem (Josh. 24:1). This makes good sense of *the people served Yahweh all the days of Joshua* in v. 7. But the almost identical expression (Israel served Yahweh all the days of Joshua) occurs in Josh. 24:31, where it is clearly the Shechem assembly that is in view, and the similarities between the two passages are so extensive that the attempt to make them refer to different occasions is forced and unconvincing.

6. Cf. Num. 26:52-56.

today, since to be expelled from your family or clan was to lose your share in the inheritance (Judg. 11:1-3). Nevertheless, there was a sense in which the idea of sharing in the land as Israel's inheritance did extend, in some cases, right down to each particular member of a family, clan, or tribe (see v. 9). The reference here to *each* going to *his inheritance, to take possession of the land* carries with it the overtones of gift and privilege normally associated with inheritance. But against the backdrop of Joshua's exhortations before he died (Josh. 23:1–24:27), which are clearly in view here, it also carries overtones of responsibility. Each tribe, clan, and person must play their part in taking hold of what has been given, and honoring the giver.

7 "Serving Yahweh" is shorthand here for a way of life that properly honors Yahweh, who had given Israel the land. Centrally, of course, it involved worshiping him alone, as the law of Moses taught them to do in the Shema and the first commandment (Deut. 6:4; Exod. 20:3; Deut. 5:7). But it included more than this. At the beginning of his leadership Joshua had had the "book of the law" placed in his hands by Moses and been told that he was to be careful to obey all that was written in it (Josh. 1:7-8), and it was Joshua's faithful service to Yahweh that had brought Israel, under his leadership, into the land. At the end of the book of Joshua, Joshua is called "the servant of Yahweh" as a kind of epitaph, a way of summing up his entire life and character (Josh. 24:29), and this is repeated in Judges 2:8. The same is said of Moses at the end of Deuteronomy (Deut. 34:5). "Serving Yahweh," then, is the way of covenant obedience exemplified by these two leaders, who set the pattern that Israel was to follow. According to Judges 2:7, it was also the pattern of the Joshua generation, including those, like Caleb, who outlived him. Yahweh's great *work* that that generation "saw" was his giving of the land to Israel by the instrumentality of Joshua, his servant.

8 Joshua's age when he died, *a hundred and ten years,* is noted here as a mark of respect, and as evidence of Yahweh's approval of him. The same is done for Moses at the end of Deuteronomy, where not only the length of his life is noted (in his case a hundred and twenty years), but the extraordinary vitality he had to the very end of it: "his eyes were not weak nor his strength gone." In the world of the Old Testament such longevity and vitality are viewed as the divine seal of approval on a righteous life:

> Gray hair is a crown of splendor;
> > it is attained by a righteous life. (Prov. 16:31 NIV)

> The righteous will flourish like a palm tree,
> > they will grow like a cedar of Lebanon;
> planted in the house of the LORD,
> > they will flourish in the courts of our God.

They will still bear fruit in old age,
    they will stay fresh and green. (Ps. 92:12-14 NIV)

The references to Moses' and Joshua's long and blessed lives not only honor them and set a standard of "service to Yahweh" for others to follow, but implicitly hold promise of similar blessing for those who do so.

9 The statement that Joshua was buried within the border of *his inheritance* is an allusion to Joshua 19:49-50, which tells how the Israelites of his generation, as a way of honoring him, had given him a portion of land in the territory of Ephraim (the tribe he belonged to) as his personal inheritance. It also tells how Joshua, when he was free to do so, "built up the town and settled there" (NIV). In this way too, Joshua had been an example to the rest of Israel; Joshua himself had "gone to his inheritance" and "taken possession" of it, as he later told all his fellow Israelites to do (Judg. 2:6).

Timnath-heres is suspect on the grounds that its existence is otherwise unknown, and that the parallel passage in Joshua 24:30 has *Timnath-serah.* This is also the name given to it in Joshua 19:50. *Timnath-heres* could be an alternative name for the place, or (more likely) a simple scribal error.[7] *Timnath-serah* (Kh. Tibnah) is located in the central hill country, about 10 miles (16 km.) northwest of Bethel.[8] *Mount Gaash,* to the south of it, is mentioned in connection with Hiddai, one of David's choice warriors (2 Sam. 23:30), but it is otherwise unknown.

10 The generation that "arises" in this verse is not just *another* one in time, but also in character: the Israelites of this generation do not *know (yāḏaʿ)* Yahweh. This is a very ominous development, like the coming to power in Egypt long before of a new king who did not "know" Joseph. Later this same king boasted that he did not "know" Yahweh and would not obey him (Exod. 5:2). In both cases "not knowing" involves more than lacking information; it is a refusal to accept the obligations entailed in a relationship. The new Pharaoh did not show respect for Joseph's people (and their God), as his father had done. The post-Joshua generation did not follow the pattern of service to Yahweh that Joshua had set for them.

Being "gathered to one's fathers" is a euphemism for death in the Old Testament. It doesn't necessarily imply conscious existence after death. It does, however, suggest a solidarity (being at one) with the fathers that is not broken by death. Here it stands in contrast to the *break* of solidarity involved in the arising of "another" generation. Joshua's generation had been at one with the Moses generation, in life and in death. But the solidarity is now bro-

---

7. The two names have the same three letters in the original, consonantal text; only the order of the letters is different.

8. *OBA,* p. 85.

ken; the new generation is not at one with the Joshua generation. The previous generation had served Yahweh; the new generation will not.

The way the two expressions "not knowing *Yahweh*" and "not knowing the *work (ma*ᵃ*śeh)* he had done" are set side by side in the last part of the verse suggests a close relationship between them, but without making the nature of the relationship clear. Did they just happen at the same time, for example, or did one *cause* the other to happen? The first four verses of chapter 3, which complete the introduction to the book, will shed more light on this issue. However, given the way in which the revelation of God's name (Yahweh) is associated with the exodus (a "work" of Yahweh if ever there was one) in the book of Exodus, it is reasonable to assume that there is a causal connection between the two things mentioned here in Judges 2:10. The new generation did not know *Yahweh* because it did not know the *work* (the crossing of the Jordan and the conquest) God did for Israel in the days of Joshua. The problem with this, of course, is that if this is the case, then *no* post-Joshua generation would be able to "know" Yahweh since none could "know" the exodus and conquest as the Joshua generation did, because it was a once-for-all set of events. This problem is well recognized in Deuteronomy, where parents are commanded to be diligent to instruct their children in the law and to tell them of the great works of Yahweh by which he had called Israel into existence (Deut. 6:20-25). It could be, therefore, that the Joshua generation unintentionally contributed to what happened after their passing by failing to be as diligent as they might have been in teaching their children. But that is hardly where the passage before us lays the blame. Given the shortness of the time involved, and the overlap of the generations represented by "the elders [such as Caleb] who outlived Joshua" (v. 6), the new generation could hardly plead ignorance. Rather, as the following verses will make clear, their "not knowing" was a choice caused much more by the enticements of Canaanite culture and their own willfulness than by any failure of their parents.

2. The Downward Spiral (2:11-19)

11 *Then the Israelites did what was evil in the eyes of Yahweh, and served the Baals.*

12 *They abandoned Yahweh, the God of their fathers, who had brought them out of the land of Egypt, and went after other gods — from the gods of the peoples who were around them — and prostrated themselves to them; so they provoked Yahweh to anger.*

13 *They abandoned Yahweh and served Baal, and the Ashtaroths.*

14 *So Yahweh became angry with Israel, and gave them into the hand of plunderers who plundered them, and sold them into the hand of their*

enemies round about, and they were no longer able to stand before their enemies.

15 *Whenever they went out, the hand of Yahweh was against them for evil,[9] as Yahweh had said, and as Yahweh had sworn to them, and they were in dire straits.[10]*

16 *So Yahweh raised up judges, and saved them from the hand of those who were plundering them.*

17 *But even to their judges they did not listen, but played the harlot after other gods and bowed down to them; they quickly turned aside from the way in which their fathers had walked (listening to the commands of Yahweh); they [themselves] did not do this.*

18 *Whenever Yahweh raised up judges for them, Yahweh was with the judge and saved them from the hand of their enemies all the days of the judge, for Yahweh was moved to pity by their groaning because of those who were oppressing them and harassing them.*

19 *But whenever the judge died, they turned back and acted more corruptly than their fathers by going after other gods, serving and bowing down to them; they did not drop any of their deeds or their stubborn[11] way of life.*

11-13 Here the gods whose altars were referred to in the speech of 2:1-5 come directly into view, and the prophecy of verse 3b begins to be fulfilled. This unit is composed as indicated on p. 141. B¹ and B² frame a detailed exposition of A. In B¹ the *evil (hāraʿ)* that they did is first defined positively (they *served the Baals*), and then negatively *(they abandoned Yahweh)*. In B² the same two things are said in reverse order. C and D describe, respectively, the God the Israelites *abandoned* and the gods they *served*. Two expressions are used in each case. The description of *Yahweh* in C draws upon the two most fundamental historico-religious credal confessions: he is the God of patriarchal promise and of exodus deliverance. The twofold description of *the Baals* in D draws attention to their foreignness; they are *other gods,* worshiped by *the peoples who were around them.* The two expressions which frame element D *(went after* and *prostrated themselves)* express Israel's devotion to these gods, and give more specific content to the *served* of

9. Or "disaster." The sense of *rāʾâ* is not moral here, but I have translated it as *evil* to preserve the play on *hāraʿ* in v. 11: the punishment fits the crime.

10. The LXX has "and he afflicted them," taking "Yahweh" as the subject and apparently reading the verb as a Hiphil rather than (as it is pointed) a Qal. The following *lāhem* is compatible with both readings (BDB, p. 864), but the parallel in Judg. 10:9 favors the former one, as do the English versions in general.

11. Literally their "*hard (qāšâ)* way," but I have avoided the word "hard" because of the quite different meaning it has in the English idiom "*hard*-hearted" (harsh, unforgiving).

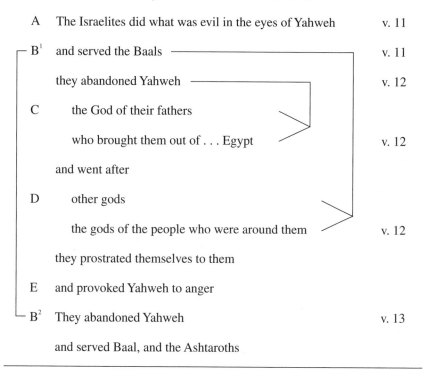

A   The Israelites did what was evil in the eyes of Yahweh   v. 11

B¹   and served the Baals   v. 11

     they abandoned Yahweh   v. 12

C   the God of their fathers

         who brought them out of . . . Egypt   v. 12

     and went after

D   other gods

         the gods of the people who were around them   v. 12

     they prostrated themselves to them

E   and provoked Yahweh to anger

B²   They abandoned Yahweh   v. 13

     and served Baal, and the Ashtaroths

B¹ and B². The succession of verbs *(served, abandoned, went after, prostrated themselves, abandoned, served)* emphasize the radical nature of the apostasy. Element E does not properly belong to this exposition but anticipates the subject matter of verses 14-15 and so helps to unify the larger composition.

The way Israel's apostasy is spoken about in these verses makes very clear the fundamental tension (and temptation) that the Israelites experienced after their arrival in Canaan. They had recently been removed from one pluralistic environment in Egypt (v. 12) and been inserted into another in Canaan. Between these two defining moments in their history they had received the law at Sinai with its uncompromising first commandment: "I am Yahweh your God, who brought you out of the land of slavery. You shall have no other gods in my presence"[12] (Exod. 20:2-3). The first requirement of the covenant Yahweh had made with them was that they worship no other gods but him. On the plains of Moab this basic commandment had been re-expressed positively in terms of Yahweh's "oneness": "Yahweh our God, Yahweh is *one.*" Other translations are possible, but whichever is preferred the use of the numeral *one* (*'eḥād*) remains the key to the underlying logic of

12. Hebrew *'al-pānāy.* Cf. Exod. 33:19; 34:6.

this key confession,[13] and this "oneness" of Yahweh is to be understood in relation to the plurality of the gods worshiped by other peoples, especially the Canaanites.

It is noteworthy in this respect that in the Old Testament the term *ba'al* (Baal) is frequently used in the plural and with the article (*the* Baals) as here in verse 11, or with some specifying term attached (e.g., Baal-berith, Baal-gad, Baal-hamon, Baal-hanan, Baal-hazor, Baal-peor, Baal-perazim, and so on). In other words, it is treated as a common noun. Even where it occurs in the singular (Baal), this is usually shorthand for *the* Baal worshiped in a particular place (e.g., Baal-Melqart, the god of Tyre).[14] In contrast to this, "Yahweh" is always used as a personal name, never with the article, never in the plural, and never with a qualifier comparable to those used with "Baal."[15] In other words, according to the biblical writers the Canaanites, in contrast to Israel, worshiped many different "Baals." Moreover, it is likely that this was fully in accord with the understanding of the Canaanites themselves.[16] They worshiped many gods; Israel worshiped and believed in only one. To worship

13. The following four possibilities are listed by M. Weinfeld (*Deuteronomy 1–11,* The Anchor Bible [New York: Doubleday, 1993], p. 337):

1. YAHWEH is our God, YAHWEH is one.
2. YAHWEH is our God, YAHWEH alone.
3. YAHWEH our God is one YAHWEH.
4. YAHWEH our God, YAHWEH is one.

Although it suits the context well, the second, the "Lord is our God, Yahweh alone," is extremely unlikely on two grounds: first, this would arguably be the only occurrence of *'eḥād,* meaning "alone," in the Hebrew Bible. Second, the expressions "God" (*'elōhîm*) and "Yahweh" (Yahweh) are juxtaposed 313 times in Deuteronomy, and in every other instance they are in apposition (Yahweh our God), and do not constitute a statement (Yahweh *is* our God). It is unlikely that the Shema, which is effectively a summary, would depart from the uniform usage elsewhere in the book. So alternative 2 must be rejected. All the others affirm, either directly or indirectly, the "oneness" of Yahweh, however this is best understood. Weinfeld himself opts for the third alternative.

14. As in 1 Kgs. 18:21; note that the plural (the Baals) occurs in v. 18. The Baal being worshiped at this time was just the latest in a whole series of such gods that had been worshiped by Ahab's family. In v. 13 of the present passage the singular *Baal* is shorthand for "the Baals" of v. 11, as the pairing with *the Ashtaroths* and the structure of the passage make clear.

15. The qualifiers used with Yahweh are either descriptive of his attributes (e.g., Yahweh of Hosts, Yahweh your healer), or of his special relationship with Israel (Yahweh our God).

16. The "Baal" of the mythical pantheon, a leading character in the Canaanite epic of creation, was presumably thought of as lying behind all the other "Baals" in some way. It does seem clear, however, that each of the local Baals had his own identity and devotees. It was the Baals (plural) that the Canaanites worshiped rather than Baal himself.

any others, or combine them with the worship of Yahweh, was apostasy; it was to do *what was evil (hārā')* in the eyes of Yahweh (v. 11) and provoke him to *anger* (v. 12).

The *Ashtaroths* (Hebrew *'aštārôt*) of verse 13 were the female counterparts and consorts of the Baals. The strong appeal that these male and female gods had for the Israelites had to do with their association with agriculture, and especially with the *fertility* of land and livestock which was essential to successful farming. The Canaanites, "the inhabitants of the land" (1:32-33), were practiced at working the land and attributed their success to the worship of these gods. The new generation of Israelites, who had known only desert life, had no such skills, but their survival now depended on adapting to their new situation as quickly as possible. What else could they do but learn from their Canaanite neighbors? It was the way of "common sense" and "necessity." It was not the way of Yahweh, however; it was the triumph of pragmatics over principle, and a failure to trust the God who had proven himself capable of meeting their needs in the wilderness, and would surely have done so again in the land he had given them if only they had trusted him to do so. But they did not; they abandoned him and *went after other gods — from the gods of the peoples who were around them* (v. 12). They *served Baal, and the Ashtaroths* (v. 13).

14-15   Israel's apostasy kindles Yahweh's *anger* (v. 14a). The balance of this unit describes the way in which this anger was expressed, and the consequences it had for Israel.

A   [He] gave them into the hand of plunderers
B   who plundered them
A′   and sold them into the hand of their enemies round about
B′   and they were no longer able to stand before their enemies

Within the parallel structure there is cumulative meaning.[17] In AB the focus is on the kind of depredation to which the Israelites were subjected (cf. 6:1-6); in A′B′ it shifts to their powerlessness to resist it, and it is this latter thought that is elaborated upon in the following verse:

15a   Whenever they went out
   b   the hand of Yahweh was against them for evil *(lᵉrā'â)*
   c   as Yahweh had said
   d   and as Yahweh had sworn to them
   e   and they were in dire straits

17. Cf. Richter, *Die Bearbeitungen des "Retterbuches,"* p. 34.

Considerable pains are taken here to depict Yahweh's angry response as controlled and fully justified. The $l^e r\bar{a}'\hat{a}$ (for evil)[18] of line b plays nicely on the $h\bar{a}ra'$ (what was evil) of verse 11a: the punishment fits the crime! With less subtlety the parallel in lines c and d doubly stresses that the punishment was entirely in keeping with warnings previously given.[19] Line e draws the verse to a close by neatly summarizing the consequences of the anger: Israel was *in dire straits!*

16-19   The subject of verses 14-15 was Yahweh's anger expressed in his punishing Israel at the hands of "plunderers" and "enemies." The contrasting subject of verses 16-19 is Yahweh's compassion expressed in his saving them *from* "plunderers" and "enemies" (vv. 16 and 18 respectively). As in verses 14-15, repetition and elaboration are used. The unit consists of two parts, with the second subordinated to the first by the temporal clause at the beginning of verse 18:

> vv. 16-17 Yahweh raised up judges
> vv. 18-19 *whenever* Yahweh raised up judges . . .

The statement that *Yahweh raised up judges* (v. 16) follows directly after the statement that Israel was in dire straits (v. 15). The implication is that the raising up of judges was an emergency measure which Yahweh took from time to time in order to save Israel in dire circumstances. The implied motivation in verse 16 is his compassion, and this is made explicit in verse 18: *for Yahweh was moved to pity (nāḥēm) by their groaning because of those who were oppressing them and harassing them.* The statement, "The Israelites cried out *(wayyiz'ªqû)* to Yahweh," does not occur here — a striking omission in view of its repeated and conspicuous occurrence in similar circumstances in subsequent chapters (3:9, 15; 4:3; 6:6; 10:10).[20] We will return to this in our treatment of the central part of the book.

The closest possible connection is made in both parts of this unit between Yahweh's "raising up" of the judge and his "saving" Israel by him (vv. 16 and 18). In this role the judges were successful, liberating Israel from foreign oppression *all the days of the judge* (v. 18). However, a different role, in which the judges were less successful, is implied in verse 17a: "the Israelites *did not listen (lō' šāmē'û) to their judges.*" By implication the judges, as well

---

18. Or "for disaster." See the note on the translation.

19. The terminology indicates clearly that it is warnings such as those of Deut. 31:29 and 28:25 that are in view.

20. *Groaning (na'ªqātām, v. 18) cannot simply be equated with "crying out* to Yahweh" here, especially in view of the precise formula used elsewhere in the book for the latter. Cf. the distinction between "groaning" and "crying out" in Exod. 2:23; they are not the same thing. Cf. also the "groanings" *(na'ªqôt)* of the slain in Ezek. 30:24.

as being saviors, were also proclaimers.[21] What they proclaimed is implied by what follows. The way of the fathers — faithful Israelites of the past such as Joshua and the elders who had outlived him (2:6-9) — had been to listen to the commands *(miṣwōt)* of Yahweh (v. 17b). But this is precisely what those who followed them did not do. The judges proclaimed these same *miṣwōt* to subsequent generations, but they were unable to stem the tide of Israel's apostasy.

In verses 16-17, then, the Israelites of the judges era as a whole are contrasted with *their fathers* as a whole. In verses 18-19, however, a different perspective is introduced and *fathers ('ābôt)* undergoes a shift in meaning: each particular generation in the judges era itself is now compared with the generation (their *fathers*) that immediately preceded it (v. 19b). Both parts of this unit (vv. 16-17 and vv. 18-19 respectively) imply that there were periods of recovery, but neither draws attention to them. Rather, they emphasize the persistent and worsening nature of the apostasy which characterized the era as a whole. In verse 17b we are told that the Israelites of the judges period *quickly (mahēr)* turned aside from the way of their fathers. Although the language is not entirely perspicuous, it seems to envisage apostasy setting in very soon after the passing of the Joshua generation. Verses 18-19, in keeping with their focus on successive generations within the judges period, locate the time of "turning back" *(šûb) after* the death of each judge (v. 19b).[22] But here the turning back of each generation is to a *worse* state of apostasy than that of the one before it: *they turned back and acted more corruptly than their fathers.* As the judges period unfolds, Israel is described as spiraling downward into worse and worse apostasy. The closing line of the passage provides the final summary comment on the subject: *they did not drop any of their deeds or their stubborn way of life* (v. 19b).

3. The Outcome (2:20–3:6)

a. Yahweh's Verdict (2:20-22 + 23)

Verse 20 opens with the same words as verse 14: *So Yahweh became angry with Israel.* In other words, the subject of the divine anger is resumed here. But there is a difference. Verse 20 is not simply a return to where we were in verse 14, but the beginning of a new narrative movement. The previous pas-

---

21. Cf. Richter, *Die Bearbeitungen des "Retterbuches,"* p. 34 (with reference to v. 17: "The verse sees the judges (singular) as teacher, instructor, whom one listens to, because they show the way the fathers went, which is obeying the laws of Yahweh. Then the judges would appear to be a Dtr preacher."

22. In the case of Gideon the slide back into apostasy began even *before* his death (8:22-35).

sage showed Yahweh alternately punishing and rescuing Israel — to no effect; Israel did not desist from "its stubborn way of life" (v. 19). Now Yahweh's patience has been exhausted, and his anger flares up again. The anger expressed in what follows is his response to Israel's conduct throughout the judges period as a whole. We have reached a climactic point in the narrative; what will Yahweh do in view of the situation he is now faced with? The answer to this critical question (Israel's future hangs on it) is given in a divine speech (vv. 20-22). The balance of the unit, 2:23–3:6, underlines the climactic nature of this speech by reviewing the background to it and the justification for the judgment that is announced in it.[23]

20 *So Yahweh became angry with Israel, and said, "Because this nation has transgressed my covenant which I commanded their fathers, and have not listened to my voice,*

21 *I, for my part, will not continue to drive out people before them, that is, any of the nations which Joshua left when he died,*

22 *in order to test Israel by them*[24] *— [to see] whether they would observe the way of Yahweh by walking in it*[25] *as their fathers did, or not."*

20-22 There is nothing here of the indeterminacy we found in the speech of the messenger in 2:1-3 (What would Yahweh do?). In contrast, this speech consists of a very clear "announcement of judgment"[26] in two parts:

the crime (accusation)   v. 20b
the punishment   vv. 21-22

Yahweh no longer speaks *to* the Israelites (as in 2:1-3), but *about* them. By referring to them as *this nation* (*haggôy hazzeh*, v. 20a), he implicitly associates them with *the nations* (*haggôyim*) whose gods they have embraced (v. 21a). He is angry, but tight-lipped. A firm rein is kept on his responses by

23. Contrary to Boling (*Judges,* p. 74) the speech continues to the end of v. 22. The change of subject in v. 23a marks the transition back to indirect speech. The commentary on the speech begins at that point and continues to the end of 3:6.

24. In terms of the syntax, it is *Joshua* here who left certain nations *to test Israel by them.* The allusion seems to be Joshua's speeches to Israel in Josh. 13:1 and 23:1-5, where he speaks of land and (Canaanite) nations that still remained. By leaving his work of conquest incomplete, he effectively set Israel a test of their faithfulness to Yahweh. This is clear from the way he exhorts and warns them in Josh. 23 and 24.

25. Reading the singular, *bāh,* with the versions.

26. Cf. C. Westermann, *Basic Forms of Prophetic Speech,* tr. H. C. White (Cambridge: Lutterworth, 1991), pp. 169-98.

the legal form of the speech. There is nothing comparable here to the exclamatory question of verse 2: "What is this you have done?" Although Israel is not addressed, the form of the speech (an announcement) implies an audience of some kind. Perhaps it is meant for the ears of the heavenly court where Yahweh presides as judge (cf. 11:27).[27] Certainly Yahweh has distanced himself from Israel and adopted the measured tone appropriate to the handing down of a considered judgment.

The judgment is handed down here in the context of Yahweh's covenant considered as a treaty. The wording of verse 20b, "*my covenant (b^{e}rîtî) which I commanded their fathers*," implies that the obligations of the weaker party are determined and imposed by the stronger party, as in a suzerainty treaty.[28] Yahweh is the judge because he is the suzerain (great king/overlord). In the speech of the messenger, Yahweh referred to his ("my") covenant (b^{e}rîtî, v. 1). There he struggled with the dilemma posed by the tension between his covenant considered as a *promise* which he had sworn never to break, and as a treaty or contract that required a certain response from Israel. Now he confronts that dilemma head-on by invoking the covenant purely as a *treaty*. The logical structure of the speech is indicated by the *ya'an ^{a}šer (because)* near the beginning of verse 20 and the *gam-^{a}nî (I, for my part)* at the beginning of verse 21:

> "*Because this nation* has transgressed my covenant,
> *I, for my part*, will not continue to drive out . . . the nations."

In view of Israel's failure to meet its obligations, Yahweh puts the promise aspect of the covenant into abeyance.[29] But the *I, for my part* tacitly acknowledges that in doing this he *technically* breaks his own covenant;[30] his justification for doing so is Israel's prior breaking of it. So, the covenant as contract is broken because of Israel's apostasy, but the covenant as promise still stands. What is needed for its fulfillment is an Israel which does not fail to keep its obligations. In New Testament terms, this fulfillment comes in Jesus the Messiah, who is everything that Israel should have been but was not: the perfectly obedient "Israel."

In terms of the preview we are given in 2:11-22, however, the judges

---

27. Cf. 1 Kgs. 22:19-22.

28. A treaty between a great (imperial) king and the ruler of a small, subject state.

29. I choose this expression advisedly. The language of the speech stops short of an explicit repudiation of the promise. Contrast 1 Sam. 2:30: "I promised that your house . . . would minister before me for ever; but now Yahweh declares, 'Far be it from me. . . .'"

30. Cf. Kaufmann, *Judges*, p. 98: "Because Israel broke the covenant law of Yahweh, Yahweh will break his covenant promise to give them the whole land of Canaan" (my translation).

period ends with the relationship between Yahweh and Israel in a state of deadlock. The remaining Canaanites will now be left indefinitely as a punishment for Israel's apostasy, but no solution to the problem of this apostasy is yet in sight. What remains, though, before the introduction to the book comes to an end, is some amplification, by way of explanation, of the judgment that has just been announced. Verse 23 acts as a bridge into what follows in 3:1-6:

> 23 *Yahweh left these nations with the intention of not driving them out quickly. He did not give them into the hand of Joshua.*

23 In verses 21-22 it was *Joshua* who left the nations (unspecified) as a test of Israel's faithfulness.[31] The allusion is clearly to his speeches in the closing chapters of the book of Joshua, where he speaks of "the nations" that "remained" in various parts of Canaan at the end of his life (Josh. 23:4), and challenges the Israelites to prove their faithfulness to Yahweh by completing the work of conquest that he had begun (Josh. 24:6-13, 14-24). But now in verse 23 the focus is shifted to the deeper truth that it was *Yahweh* who left these nations; Joshua was simply his agent. Yahweh did not allow Joshua to make a full end of them, but left some to be driven out more slowly (as we see in Judg. 1) by the Israelite tribes in a series of campaigns over a period of time. The gradualness of it was in accord with Yahweh's purpose. The opening verses of the next chapter specify who these "remaining nations" were.

b. Appendix: The Remaining Nations (3:1-6)

> 1 *Now these are the nations which Yahweh left in order, by them, to test Israel — all who had not known all the wars of Canaan —*
> 2 *only that the Israelites should know, by teaching them warfare — only those who had not formerly known it:*[32]
> 3 *the five lords of the Philistines, and all the Canaanites (Sidonians and Hivites) living in the mountainous area of Lebanon, from Mount Baal Hermon to the approach to Hamath.*

31. See the footnote on my translation at that point.

32. The plural suffix on *yᵉdā'ûm* (had not known *them*) is puzzling. What does it refer to? As Lindars points out, the suggestion of *BHS* that it is an enclitic *mem* is unlikely at the end of a sentence and before a hard guttural (*Judges 1–5*, p. 114). If it is a suffix, it must refer either to *milḥāmâ* (warfare, v. 2), or *milḥᵃmôt* (wars [of Canaan], v. 1). Given its plural form, Lindars is probably right that it must refer to *milḥᵃmôt*, despite the difference of gender (cf. GKC #135 [o]). But given that nothing is really at stake exegetically, I have taken it as referring back to *milḥᵃmôt* via *milḥāmâ*, which is closer to it: "those who had not formally known *it* [*warfare*, i.e., the *wars* of Canaan]."

4 *They were left in order to test Israel by them, to know whether they would listen to Yahweh's commandments which he had commanded their fathers by the hand of Moses.*

5 *But the Israelites lived among the Canaanites (the Hittites, the Amorites, the Perizzites, the Hivites and the Jebusites).*

6 *They took their daughters for themselves as wives, and their own daughters they gave to their sons, and they served their gods.*

1-6   We are already familiar from chapter 1 with appendices as part of the way the introduction to the book has been composed. The first part of the introduction had two appendices (1:18-21 and 1:36 respectively). Now we come to a rather longer one that completes Part 2 of the introduction, and therefore the introduction as a whole. We have also noticed how appendices, by their very nature, are somewhat untidy; they are a way of adding material which needs to be there for the sake of completeness, but has not been easy to accommodate within the more tightly written body of the composition. Something of that untidiness is apparent in the broken syntax (which I have deliberately allowed to show in the translation) of this particular appendix.

However, 3:1-6 is not quite as untidy as it may appear at first sight. It is unified by the theme of the remaining nations' being a test for Israel. This theme is elaborated on here in some detail. Furthermore, if we include 2:23 as the transition which effectively leads into the appendix, it shows the following symmetrical structure:

A   *Recapitulation:* How it came about that there were   2:23
     nations left when Joshua died. They were left by
     Yahweh, who did not drive them out quickly by
     giving them into the hand of Joshua.

B   *Who the remaining nations were.* "These are the   v. 1a
     nations that Yahweh left to test Israel."

C   *Parenthesis on the test itself.*

     a   The *subjects* of the test: those Israelites who had   v. 1b
         not known *(yd')* the wars of Canaan.

     x   The *purpose* of the test: so that they might know   v. 2a
         (yd') — to teach them war.

     a' The *subjects* of the test: those who had not known   v. 2b
         (yd') them previously.

B'   *Who the remaining nations were* (the list anticipated in   v. 3
     B is now given).

A'   *Recapitulation:* These nations were left to test Israel,   v. 4

so that Yahweh would know *(yd')* whether they would keep his commands.

D   *Conclusion:* the *result* of the test: The Israelites lived   vv. 5-6
among the Canaanites, intermarried with them, and
served their gods. (That is, Israel failed the test, as
implied by the closing words of Yahweh's speech
back in 2:20-22.)

The concentric structure of 2:23–3:4 gives surface unity to a passage which is highly repetitious and, on first reading at least, not very coherent. It also serves to draw attention to the parenthesis (C), which in fact contains the central subject matter of the whole piece. The passage as a whole is about the *test* rather than the remaining nations as such. The repetition of the keyword *yd'* (to know) further helps to unify the passage, and to establish links between apparently disparate elements. Thus, for example, the *war* which the Israelites were to *know* by being taught it (Cx) was the war which earlier generations had *known* (Ca), that is, the *wars of Canaan,* or holy war. Further, the two objects of the test in Cx and A^1 are complementary: Yahweh would *know* whether they would keep his commands by giving them the opportunity to *know* holy war. The conclusion (D) confirms what is implied by the closing words of Yahweh's earlier speech: Israel failed the test, which is why the remaining nations were left indefinitely as a punishment.

Element D, however, has a more independent status within the whole passage than the other parts do. It stands outside the concentric structure of 2:23–3:4 and does not contain any of the three keywords *nsh* (to test), *yd'* (to know), or *gwym* (nations). It does contain a list of Canaanite peoples (v. 5) but in a much more standardized form than that of verse 3.[33] But this relative separateness of verses 5-6 enables them to serve a double function. In addition to drawing out the implications of 2:23–3:4 and relating this back to Yahweh's speech of 2:20-22, they provide a summary conclusion to the whole introduction to the book.

As we have seen, this introduction has two major parts: 1:1–2:5 deals with the way in which conquest gave way to coexistence as Israel came to terms with the Canaanites; and 2:6–3:6 deals with the apostasy which followed and was a consequence of this accommodation. The final two verses of the introduction now summarize these two developments as follows:

v. 5   The Israelites lived among the Canaanites   Part 1 (1:1–2:5)
[v. 6a   and intermarried with them]
v. 6b   and served their gods   Part 2 (2:6–3:6)

33. See comments below, on v. 5.

Intermarriage (in v. 6a) is entirely understandable as either a middle term between the other two (explaining how "living among" Canaanites turned into "serving their gods"), or as an aspect of the first. But the specific mention of intermarriage here is unexpected since there has been no reference to it anywhere in 1:1–3:4. What *has* been mentioned, however, is the marriage of Othniel, whose career as the first judge is about to be reported (3:7-11). In view of this, the mention of intermarriage with the Canaanites in verse 6a is best understood as a contrastive background for the presentation of Othniel as a model judge in verses 7-11.

The list of nations in verse 5 *(the Canaanites, the Hittites, the Amorites, the Perizzites, the Hivites, and the Jebusites)* is the standard one used in Deuteronomy as a comprehensive list of the people whose land the Israelites were to occupy (Deut. 7:1). The only one missing here is "Girgashites," which may have been left out accidentally.[34] Such accidental omission is likely because the names all have similar endings, and because in Deuteronomy 7:1 they together comprise the "seven" nations of Canaan, a number which is hardly accidental, and would be unlikely to change in a passage like this which appears to allude to the earlier one. However, the order is different here, with *the Canaanites* brought forward so that it stands at the head of the list.[35] It is also the only name which is not connected by the conjunction "and" (Hebrew *waw*) to the next one. Furthermore this separateness of the first name is reinforced in the MT by the use of a strong disjunctive accent *(athnach)*. For all these reasons it is best to see *the Canaanites* here as a general term for the pre-Israelite inhabitants of the land, and the names that follow as specifying particular subgroups of Canaanites living in different places (the Jebusites in Jerusalem, and so on; cf. v. 3).[36] This supports the idea that the number seven (if that was originally the number here, as in Deuteronomy) is symbolic rather than literally descriptive. The implication is that wherever the Israelites went in Canaan, they failed the test that Yahweh had given them (2:22) by leaving these nations in the land.

Excursus 4: The Lists of Nations in 3:3 and 3:5 and the Arrival of the Philistines

The nations listed in 3:3 differ from those mentioned in chapter 1. The *Philistines* appear here in 3:3 for the first time in Judges, reflecting a time later than 1:34 which still has Amorites (local Canaanites) living in the coastal area

---

34. So Boling, *Judges,* p. 78.
35. In Deut. 7:1 it is in the central (4th) position.
36. For the other names on the list see any standard Bible dictionary.

that later became Philistine territory. Likewise 1:18, which refers to Gaza, Ashkelon, and Ekron, knows nothing of a Philistine presence there.

The Philistines were not native to Canaan, and their arrival had serious consequences for Canaanites and Israelites alike. The relevant historical data has recently been summarized by Daniel Block as follows:

> The name *pelištîm* identifies one of several groups of Sea Peoples who swept into Palestine from Anatolia and the Mediterranean in the twelfth to eleventh centuries B.C., leaving in their wake a trail of ruins. Biblical tradition traces their origins to Crete. It seems their original goal was to settle in Egypt, but Rameses III was able to defeat them in about 1190 B.C. He settled the vanquished forces in the coastal towns of southern Canaan, but in the mid-twelfth century the Philistines succeeded in driving out their Egyptian overlords, forming the Philistine Pentapolis, a federation of five major city-states: Ashdod, Ashkelon, Ekron, Gath, Gaza. The identification of their rulers here [in 3:3] as *serānîm* [*lords*] suggests these cities had distinctively Philistine political structures, different from both the tribal structures of Israel and the city-states of the Canaanites.[37]

Generally speaking, the Philistines established cooperative relationships with the Canaanites but clashed with the Israelites, whom they probably (and correctly) saw as competitive invaders.[38] The major clashes in Judges occur in relation to Shamgar (3:31) and Samson (chs. 13–16).

The *Sidonians and Hivites* were Canaanite peoples living in Phoenicia at the opposite (northern) end of Canaan from the Philistines, the Sidonians mainly in the coastal areas and the Hivites in the Lebanon hills.[39]

Summary: 1:1–3:6 as the Introduction to the Book

Before proceeding we pause here to reflect on the entire introduction of the book and draw out some of the main things that have emerged from our exposition of it.

a. Part 1 (1:1–2:5)

The account of the wars waged against the Canaanites by the various Israelite tribes in chapter 1 begins with the exploits of Judah and ends with the prob-

---

37. Block, *Judges, Ruth,* pp. 137-38. Detailed references are given in Block's footnotes.

38. The Israelites and Philistines arrived in Canaan at roughly the same time: the Israelites from the east and the Philistines from the west.

39. Gen. 10:17, 19; 1 Chron. 1:13-15. See "Hivites," *ABD* 3:234.

lems encountered by Dan. The central part of the book (3:7–16:31) begins with the career of the Judahite judge Othniel and ends with that of Samson the Danite. In general the south-north sequence of the tribes in chapter 1 corresponds to the south-north sequence of the judges in 3:7–16:31. The sequel to the difficulties experienced by the Danites at the end of chapter 1 is found in the account of their northward migration described in chapter 18.

Certain elements of chapter 1 assume greater significance as the book unfolds. The question that is asked in 1:1 is echoed by the question which the men of Gilead (by implication) ask in different circumstances in the middle of the book (10:17-18). More significantly, it appears again in almost exactly the same form, and receives the same reply, in 20:18, where it is asked in the context of a civil war which is tearing Israel to pieces. Its occurrence in all three major parts of the book has a unifying effect upon the whole and helps keep the reader alert to the progressive deterioration in Israel's situation in the period that the book deals with.

The vignette of 1:11-15 in which Othniel features as a hero anticipates his reappearance in 3:7-11 as the first judge. The note about the Kenites in 1:16 prepares us for the ambivalent role they play when they reappear in the Deborah-Barak story of chapter 4 (esp. in vv. 11 and 17ff.). The failure of the Israelites to dislodge the Canaanites near the Jezreel Plain, especially those of Taanach and Megiddo (1:27), is the background to the fierce battle that is fought there in chapter 4 and celebrated in chapter 5.

The mini-narratives which punctuate the summary reportage of chapter 1 also contain motifs which recur at significant points in the rest of the book:

1:4-7	The story of Adoni-bezek	Negative portrayal of (Canaanite) kingship	Cushan-rishathaim, Eglon, Jabin, (Gideon, Abimelech)
		Retribution	Abimelech
1:11-15	The story of Achsah	The woman with initiative who exercises power over men	Deborah, Jael, the "certain woman" who kills Abimelech,[40] Delilah
1:22-26	The account of the capture of Bethel	Conquest by devious means	Ehud, Jael, (Gideon), Delilah, (Samson), the conquest of Gibeah

40. Jephthah's daughter provides an ironic inversion of this motif; she "brings low" a male hero in his hour of triumph (11:35) without knowing that she does so.

The full significance of these recurring motifs will become apparent only in retrospect, but it is clear even at this stage that they form a network of connections that is part of the fabric of the larger composition.[41]

We have also seen that the confrontation between Yahweh and Israel which takes place in 2:1-5 is the first of a series of such confrontations which extend from this point to the very heart of the book (2:1-5 → 6:7-10 → 10:10-16). They dramatize Yahweh's increasing frustration and anger at Israel's persistent apostasy despite all his interventions on its behalf. The climax that is reached at 2:20-22 belongs chronologically at the end of this series but is disclosed in advance as part of the preview of the period as a whole.

b. Part 2 (2:6–3:6)

1:1–2:5 was full of the names of particular tribes, persons, events, and places. Even where similar *kinds* of events were reported (as in 1:27-33), each particular one was reported separately, with the detail appropriate to it.

A different kind of narration comes into play in 2:6–3:6. After the opening few verses about the death and burial of Joshua, particulars are lost to view and replaced by generalizations: Israel, plunderers, enemies, judges, generations, nations. Events of the same kind are grouped together: "Yahweh raised up judges . . . ," "whenever Israel went out to fight . . . ," "when the judge died . . . ," and so on. Particular nations are named (3:3, 5) but only in lists, unconnected to specific events.

This difference in the mode of narration reflects a corresponding difference in the way the two major parts of the introduction function in relation to what follows. The events recorded in 1:1–2:5 all take place prior to the onset of apostasy and the advent of the first judge. The relevant details are contained in 1:1–2:5 itself, which serves as a narrative prelude to what follows. The developments described in 2:6–3:6, on the other hand, coincide in time with those narrated in the body of the book.[42] The details are contained, not in 2:6–3:6 itself, but in what follows. Part 2 of the introduction is a narrative abstract, an outline of the plot. It reduces suspense (after reading it we already "know" the story), but it does not hinder our ability to appreciate the detailed presentation of character, situation, and theme in the fully presented narrative that follows. Indeed, it enhances it, as when one is given a summary

---

41. Cf. the observations made by K. R. R. Gros Louis in "The Book of Judges," in *Literary Interpretations of Biblical Narratives,* ed. J. S. Ackerman, K. R. R. Gros Louis, and T. S. Warshaw (Nashville: Abingdon, 1974), pp. 141-62.

42. The only exception is, again, the opening short section about the death and burial of Joshua.

of the plot of a complex drama before it is presented on the stage. Furthermore, suspense is not eliminated from individual episodes, where it often plays a significant role.

But clearly 2:6–3:6 is *more* than an outline of what follows. It contains one crucial element, the judgment speech of 2:20-22, which is not paralleled in the rest of the book. Also, it is not presented with the authorial detachment of a mere plot summary, and here we touch upon other ways in which the narrative mode of 2:6–3:6 differs from that of 1:1–2:5.

In 1:1–2:5 the narrator does not comment directly on the rightness or wrongness of the actions of the characters. The only evaluation of behavior is in the reported speeches of Adoni-bezek in 1:7 and Yahweh's messenger in 2:1-5. In both cases one character in the story comments on the behavior of other characters in the story. Neither speaks directly as the narrator. It is otherwise in 2:6–3:6. The only human individual who is named is Joshua. He is an ideal figure (*the* servant of Yahweh, 2:8), a foil for the Israelites of the judges era, who are characterized *en masse* as religiously wanton (*zānû*, 2:18), corrupt (*hištîtô*, 2:19), and stubborn (*qāšâ*, 2:19). These are the narrator's own evaluative terms, and reveal his ideological perspective directly. Again, in 1:1–2:5 all the characters, including Yahweh, are portrayed entirely from without. Our only access to their state of mind is through their reported behavior, including, in some cases, their speech. In 2:6–3:6, by contrast, Yahweh's state of mind (though only his) *is* described directly: he becomes angry with the Israelites (v. 14), is moved to pity by their groanings (v. 18), and becomes angry again (v. 20). This description of the ebb and flow of Yahweh's emotions draws our attention (in an admittedly unsubtle manner) to the depth of his personal attachment to Israel, and the reluctance with which he finally takes the decision announced in 2:20-22. It has the effect of making that decision more understandable, and therefore acceptable, to the reader. The narrator's explicit condemnation of the Israelites serves the same end. The same concern to justify God's action (of judgment) is expressed in another way, as we have seen, in 2:23–3:6.

In short, 2:6–3:6 is much more manipulative of the reader's responses than 1:1–2:5. It provides orientation to what follows, not just at the level of plot but also at the level of theme.

c. 1:1–3:6 as a Whole and the Theme of the Book

We have seen that 1:1–3:6 with its two parts is a coherent literary whole that serves as an introduction to the rest of the book in various ways.

It contains an exposition of the initial complication (Israel comes to terms with the Canaanites) out of which the basic conflicts of the ensuing narrative emerge, as outlined in 2:6–3:6. Israel is ensnared by the gods of the remaining Canaanites. This brings Israel into conflict with Yahweh and, via his intervention, with surrounding peoples. As a result Yahweh is torn between his pity for Israel and his anger at her apostasy. According to 2:6–3:6, all these conflicts grow more intense as the judges period runs its course, and at the end no solution to them is in sight. In particular Israel, more addicted to other gods than ever, continues to eke out a precarious existence in a land which it has never fully possessed and in which it is subject to continual harassment by surrounding peoples. Here the ideological perspective of 2:6–3:6 comes to the fore and provides us with at least a provisional understanding of the theme of the book as a whole. This state of affairs is interpreted as Yahweh's reluctant but just judgment on Israel (2:20-22). Israel has not come into secure possession of the land sworn to the fathers because of its persistent apostasy despite all Yahweh's exertions on its behalf. The nonfulfillment of the promise to give Israel the whole land is acknowledged, but Yahweh is absolved of any blame in relation to it.[43]

In the following chapters we will see that the thematic developments which take place in the rest of the book are in keeping with the conception of the judges period that has been presented in 1:1–3:6.

II. CAREERS OF THE JUDGES (3:7–16:31)

We first met the damning statement, "The Israelites did what was evil *(hāra‛)* in the eyes of Yahweh," in 2:11, where it introduced the overview of the judges period as a whole in 2:11-19, and we discussed its meaning in our treatment of that important passage. Within 3:7–16:31 it introduces the career of Othniel as the first savior-judge at 3:7, and that of Gideon at 6:1. In a slightly modified form, "The Israelites *continued* to do what was evil . . ." (my emphasis), it introduces the careers of Ehud, Barak, Jephthah, and Samson at 3:12, 4:1, 10:6, and 13:1 respectively. The Abimelech narrative of chapter 9 is not introduced in this way, although circumstances that would justify its use (the worship of other gods) are clearly present (8:33-34). Instead, a lengthy transitional piece (8:29–9:5) firmly joins the stories of Gideon and his son Abimelech together: the latter doesn't simply *follow* the former, but develops out of it. The statement that Israel did what was evil does not occur at all in chapters 17–21. Its main structural function is to divide the

43. Cf. Radday, who characterizes the book of Judges as, among other things, "a vindication of the God of Israel, who did not fulfil his promise of a swift conquest." Yehuda T. Radday, "Chiasm in Joshua, Judges, and Others," *Linguistica Biblica* 27/28 (1973): 11.

main body of the book, 3:7–16:31, into six major narrative episodes featuring Othniel, Ehud, Barak, Gideon, Jephthah, and Samson respectively.[1]

A number of other figures who, like these, are said to have saved and/or judged Israel are referred to in brief summary notices, introduced as follows:

3:31	After him was Shamgar . . .

10:1	After Abimelech, Tola arose
10:3	After him, Jair the Gileadite arose

12:8	After him, Ibzan . . . judged
12:11	After him Elon . . . judged
12:13	After him Abdon . . . judged

There is more variation here than in the formula that opens the major episodes. These notices are distributed over three separate locations in 3:7–16:31, with a variation in the introductory formula at each location as indicated above.[2] What all the opening lines have in common is the word 'aḥⁿrāyw, "after him," a proper name standing instead of the suffix in only one case (that of Abimelech). This consistent use of 'aḥⁿrāyw, together with the extreme brevity of the notices and the fact that they all stand at the end of a major narrative episode, marks them as supplements to the stories they follow.[3]

Taking these two formulas as markers of where units and subunits begin, we may represent the compositional shape of 3:7–16:31 as shown on page 158. The "eight years" of 3:8 introduces a chronological scheme which is carried right through to the "twenty years" of 16:31, but not into chapters 17–21.[4] In addition, as we have seen, the two introductory formulas themselves contain temporal indicators, namely, "again did (evil)" and "after him." That is, Judges 3:7–16:31 is not simply an anthology of judge stories and summary notices, but a long and complex narrative. It has an episodic structure with an underlying linear ground plan.[5] It opens with a brief account of the career of the first judge, Othniel.

1. Here I differ from Gooding, who counts 8:33 as a further occurrence of the formula. D. W. Gooding, "The Composition of the Book of Judges," in *H. M. Orlinsky Volume,* ed. B. A. Levine and A. Malamat, Eretz-Israel 16 (Jerusalem: Israel Exploration Society, 1982), pp. 70-79.

2. Incidentally, their frequency follows an arithmetic progression: first one, then two, then three.

3. Cf. Gooding, "The Composition of Judges," p. 79, and the appendices to the "Judah" and "Joseph" sections of ch. 1.

4. See the comments on 3:11.

5. Cf. in both respects the Jephthah narrative of 10:6–12:7.

A	The Israelites did what was evil . . .	Othniel		3:7-11
B	The Israelites again did what was evil . . .	Ehud		3:12-30
	and after him	Shamgar	3:31	
C	The Israelites again did what was evil . . .	Barak		4:1–5:31
D	The Israelites again did what was evil . . .	Gideon and Abimelech		6:1–10:5
	and after Abimelech	Tola	10:1-5	
	and after him	Jair		
E	The Israelites again did what was evil . . .	Jephthah		10:6–12:15
	and after him	Ibzan	12:8-15	
	and after him	Elon		
	and after him	Abdon		
F	The Israelites again did what was evil . . .	Samson		13:1–16:31

A. OTHNIEL (3:7-11)

7 *The Israelites did what was evil in the eyes of Yahweh; they forgot Yahweh their God, and served the Baals and the Asheroths.*[6]

8 *So Yahweh became angry with Israel, and sold them into the hand of Cushan-rishathaim, king of Aram-naharaim, and the Israelites served Cushan-rishathaim for eight years.*

9 *Then the Israelites cried out to Yahweh, and Yahweh raised up a savior for the Israelites and saved them — Othniel, son of Kenaz, Caleb's younger brother.*

---

6. *Asheroths* (*ʾᵃšērôṯ*) is synonymous with *Ashtaroths* (*ʿaštārôṯ*) in 2:13, and some texts and versions have *Ashtaroths* here as well. For the meaning see the comments on Canaanite religion at 2:11-13.

10 *The Spirit of Yahweh came upon him, and he judged Israel and went out to battle, and Yahweh gave Cushan-rishathaim, king of Aram-naharaim, into his hand, and his hand prevailed over Cushan-rishathaim.*

11 *Then the land had peace for forty years, till Othniel son of Kenaz died.*

After the sweeping survey of the entire judges period in 2:6–3:6, we are returned in 3:7 to the same time and circumstance as in 2:11: Israel's first lapse into outright apostasy. We also find here the same kind of unmarked flashback as we met at 2:6. There is nothing in the syntax to indicate that a time shift has occurred, but the content leaves us in no doubt that it has: verse 7 recapitulates 2:11-13, and verse 8 repeats the opening words of 2:14 exactly. But now, as we begin the story yet again, so to speak, we have a particular judge, a particular enemy, and a certain amount of chronological data. But the narrative data is minimal. A victory is reported, but not one concrete detail of the struggle is given. There is no dialogue, no reported speech of any kind, no dramatization of events, no scenic description.

7-8 In these opening two verses, those who choose to "serve" (*'bd*) foreign gods (v. 7) are made to serve (*'bd*) a foreign tyrant (v. 8) — a nice case of "poetic justice" (cf. 1:7). *Cushan-rishathaim* has been variously identified as a Babylonian Cassite (cf. Gen. 10:8), a Nubian, an Edomite, an Asiatic usurper in Egypt (Malamat), a Midianite (cf. Num. 12:1; Hab. 3:7), a chieftain of a tribe related to the Midianites who had migrated north and settled in Syria (Kaufmann), a surviving chieftain of the southern Judean hills (Boling), and, more recently, an Aramean adventurer from the great west bend of the upper Euphrates (Kitchen).[7] But no consensus exists.[8] The fact is that the identity of the tyrant remains hidden from us. The name Cushan-rithathaim is probably an intentional corruption of his true name into "Cushan-of-double-wickedness" or the like[9] — a variant of the name that is encouraged by the way it rhymes with *Aram-naharaim* (Aram-of-the-two-rivers) in verse 8, where it first appears. It is a chilling name which encapsulates a certain perception of the man; in his name we see him through the eyes of his victims, who have suffered at his hands for *eight years* (v. 8).

But the name also serves a compositional function with wider thematic implications. It is used twice in quick succession in verse 8, and then twice

7. *Reliability of the Old Testament,* pp. 211-12.

8. See the standard commentaries. The Edomite hypothesis commands widest support (read *ᵉdōm* [Edom] for *ᵃram* [Aram] and delete *-nahᵃrāyim* as a gloss).

9. *rišᵉātayim* (-rishathaim) is the dual of the adjective *rišᵉâ* (wicked). What father or mother would actually give her child such a name?

again in verse 10, forming a frame around the intervening account of Othniel's exploits.[10] In both halves of this frame the tyrant is called a *melek̲ (king).*[11] Cushan-rishathaim, like Othniel, is the embodiment of an institution, and the clash between them is a clash between judgeship and kingship. Both institutions are instrumental here in Yahweh's rule over Israel: kingship in punishment, and judgeship in deliverance. The relationship between Yahweh and these two institutions will be explored further in subsequent episodes.[12]

9-11 The account of Othniel's career as the first savior-judge is firmly anchored in its literary context by the extensive reemployment of terminology and formulas introduced in 2:11-19. This is the first clue to its significance. All the key elements of judgeship as presented in chapter 2 are seen in Othniel's career here. He is "raised up"[13] by Yahweh, who uses him to "save" the Israelites, who enjoy the salvation he has won for them until he "dies." The "saving" of verse 9 is achieved by the "judging" and "going out to battle" of verse 10. "Judging" here should probably be taken to involve an element of proclamation as implied in 2:17 (cf. Samuel's judging of Israel in the context of the Philistine crisis in 1 Sam. 7).

But there are also new elements here. The Israelites "cry out" *(wayyiz'ᵃqû)* to Yahweh, and when they do, his *Spirit* "comes upon" Othniel. This may be functionally equivalent to the statement in 2:18 that Yahweh was "with" the judge, but it is far more dynamic and involves reference to Yahweh's Spirit for the first time in the book. Both of these new elements (the cry to Yahweh and empowerment by the Spirit) will recur in subsequent episodes.[14] But unlike these later occurrences, there are no complicating details here in 3:7-11. The cry meets with an immediate response. Yahweh, his anger apparently assuaged, becomes assiduously active on Israel's behalf, "raising up" (v. 9b), "coming upon" (v. 10a), and "giving" (v. 10b) — all of which are summarized in the repetition of *yš'* (to save) in verse 9b: *Yahweh raised up a savior . . . and saved them. . . .* Here, it seems, is an institution (rule by divinely called and empowered savior-judges) which holds the key

---

10. Cf. Boling, *Judges,* pp. 80-81.

11. Cf. the portrayal of Canaanite kingship in 1:7.

12. Martin Buber has claimed that the first twelve chapters of Judges contain a series of seven antimonarchical stories, and that the thesis of these chapters is spelled out explicitly in 8:23: "I will not rule over you, and my son will not rule over you — Yahweh will rule over you." *The Kingship of God,* 3rd, newly enlarged ed., tr. R. Scheimann (London: Humanities Press, 1990), pp. 66-77.

13. For an example of the process involved in the raising up of a deliverer, see 4:4-7 (though of course the particulars varied from case to case).

14. The cry in 3:15; 4:3; 6:6-7; 10:10; cf. 15:18; 16:28. The Spirit: in 6:34; 11:29; 13:25; 14:6, 19; 15:14; cf. 9:23.

to Israel's survival. Subsequent episodes, however, will show how the institution was weakened by the shortcomings of the key persons involved.

A further connection with the literary context is made in verse 9b by Othniel's being identified in precisely the same terms as in 1:13: *Othniel son of Kenaz, Caleb's younger brother.*[15] We are left in no doubt that Othniel the savior-judge is the same Othniel who displayed his prowess and won Achsah as his wife in 1:12-15. Like his father-in-law Caleb, Othniel is a survivor from earlier battles, though not necessarily an old man as Caleb was, since he was presumably a young man in 1:12-15 and the lapse of time since then need not have been great.[16] There his feats were his own; here he is supernaturally empowered, making him a charismatic leader in the strong sense, not just a daring and inspiring one. But there are also other things we already know about him that take on added significance here. The introduction ended in 3:6 by telling us that the Israelites intermarried with the Canaanites. Not so Othniel. *His* wife is a true Israelite if ever there was one; a daughter of the illustrious Caleb, no less! Furthermore, there is an appropriateness, in view of the declaration in 1:2 that "Judah" should go first and the creditable performance of Judah in chapter 1, that the first judge should be one whose Judahite connections have been so firmly established. Altogether we feel we know why Yahweh acted as he did in choosing Othniel. But we are in for a surprise. The confidence we feel at this point (even the workings of the divine mind are within our grasp!) is going to be subverted in subsequent episodes. Things will turn out to be not quite as straightforward as the introduction and the Othniel episode have led us to believe.

The *forty years* in verse 11 is the first of a series of such round numbers which span the whole central section of the book. They are all multiples of twenty (20, 40, or 80 years), and appear to be the work of an editor who constructed a more wide-ranging chronological scheme extending as far as the 480 years of 1 Kings 6:1. He apparently used round numbers where the relevant archival data was unavailable. Outside Judges, however, the relevant chronological references are scattered and unsystematic, and no explanation of how the figure of 480 years was arrived at is free of serious difficulties. If a lucid scheme on this scale ever existed, it belonged to an earlier form of the Deuteronomistic History than we now have.[17]

---

15. On the ambiguity involved, see the comments on 1:13.

16. Contrast Roland de Vaux, who comments, from a tradition-critical perspective, that "this Othniel . . . [whom we know from 1:12-15] did not belong to the period of the judges, but to that of the settlement of the tribes" (*The Early History of Israel, to the Period of the Judges,* tr. D. Smith [London: Darton, Longman and Todd, 1978], pp. 66-77). On the possible implication of longevity in the *forty years* of v. 11 see the comment below on that verse.

17. See Richter, *Die Bearbeitungen des "Retterbuches,"* pp. 132-42 (with copious

B. EHUD (3:12-30)

This is a story of much greater complexity and subtlety than the previous one. Yairah Amit has analyzed it into a series of eight episodes, all of them, except the first and last, involving trickery of some kind:[1]

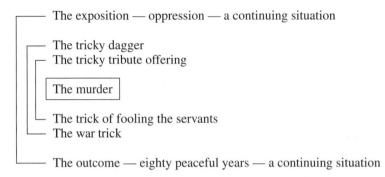

The exposition — oppression — a continuing situation

The tricky dagger
The tricky tribute offering

The murder

The trick of fooling the servants
The war trick

The outcome — eighty peaceful years — a continuing situation

The structure emphasizes the important role that deception plays in turning the opening situation of unbearable oppression into the final one of long-lasting peace.[2] What it does not show, but the story itself will make clear, is the way all the human activity involved was providentially directed by Yahweh. From this perspective the opening situation is one of deserved judgment, and the final situation one of divinely given deliverance. We will also see from the following analysis how the "trickery" element of the story is an aspect of its humor, and how this humor is one of the distinguishing features of the Ehud narrative and contributes significantly to how it makes its distinctive contribution to the book.

> 12 *The Israelites again did*[3] *what was evil in the eyes of Yahweh, and Yahweh strengthened Eglon, king of Moab, against Israel, because they had done what was evil in Yahweh's eyes.*

references to the relevant literature), and Part II.A of the Introduction: "Dating the Period of the Judges."

1. Yairah Amit, "The Story of Ehud (Judges 3:12-30): The Form and the Message," in *Signs and Wonders: Biblical Texts in Literary Focus,* ed. J. Cheryl Exum, Semeia Studies 18 (The Society of Biblical Literature, 1989), p. 103.

2. Cf. Amit, "Ehud," p. 103.

3. Or "The Israelites continued to do . . ." (cf. 4:1; 6:1; 10:6; 13:1). Boling thinks that only the latter alternative is justifiable since "only with the addition of the particle [*'ôḏ*] does the verb [the Hiphil of *ysp*] mean 'to do again'" (*Judges,* p. 85). Cf. R. M. Polzin, *Moses and the Deuteronomist: A Literary Study of the Deuteronomic History, Part One: Deuteronomy, Joshua, Judges* (New York: Seabury, 1980), p. 177. Within Judges the

13 *He enlisted the support of the Ammonites and the Amalekites, and went and struck down Israel, and they took possession of the City of Palms.*

14 *So the Israelites served Eglon, king of Moab, for eighteen years.*

15 *Then the Israelites cried out to Yahweh, and Yahweh raised up a deliverer for them — Ehud son of Gera, the Benjaminite,[4] a left-handed man.[5] By his hand the Israelites sent tribute to Eglon, king of Moab.*

16 *But Ehud made for himself a two-edged dagger, a cubit in length, and secured it under his clothes on his right thigh.*

17 *Then he brought the tribute to Eglon, the king of Moab. Now Eglon was a very fat man.*

18 *When he had finished presenting the tribute, he sent away the people who had carried it.*

19 *But he himself turned back from the sculptured stones which were near Gilgal, and said, "It is a secret message I have for you, O king." "Silence!" he [Eglon] said, and all who had been waiting on him went out.*

20 *Then Ehud approached him as he was sitting in his cool upper room alone. Ehud said, "I have a message from God for you." So he rose from his throne.[6]*

Hiphil of *ysp* is used with *ʿôḏ* in 9:37, "Gaal again spoke . . ."; 11:14, "Jephthah sent messengers again"; and 20:28, "Shall we go out again to battle"; and without *ʿôḏ* at 2:21, "I will not continue to drive out . . ." (cf. 10:13). But contrast 20:22, "The Israelites again formed the battle line . . ." (no *ʿôḏ*), and 20:23, "Shall we again draw near for battle . . . ?" (no *ʿôḏ*). In 10:13 the similarity to 2:21 (no *ʿôḏ*) makes the "I will not continue to deliver you" more probable than "I will not deliver you again," although it is not possible to be dogmatic. Similarly, against Boling and Polzin, dogmatism is not possible in 3:12 and parallels. Questions of distinctively "deuteronomic usage" are not strictly relevant to our purposes here, but I note in passing that a similar inconsistency appears in the book of Deuteronomy itself (cf. Deut. 18:16 and 28:68, which use *ʿôḏ*, with Deut 13:11 [Heb. 12], which does not). No use of the Hiphil of *ysp* comparable to that in Judg. 3:12 and parallels appears in the Deuteronomic formulas of the books of Kings.

4. Or "the son of Jemini." See Amit, "Ehud," p. 106. The MT here has the unusual expression *ben-hayᵉmînî* rather than the normal *mibbenyᵉmînî*, "from [the tribe of] Benjamin." Amit comments that "this separation [of *ben* from *yᵉmînî*] creates the foundation for the repetition of *yᵉmînî* in a new combination, *yaḏ-yᵉmînô* (his right hand)" (p. 106). This stylistic point is an astute one. Nevertheless, *ben-hayᵉmînî* should be understood as a stylistic variant (for whatever reason) of *habbenyᵉmînî* (the Benjaminite), and translated as such.

5. Literally, "a man restricted in his right hand" (*ʾîš ʾiṭṭēr yaḏ-yᵉmînô*). See the discussion in Soggin, *Judges,* p. 10, and the exegetical comments (below) on this verse.

6. Taking *hakkissēʾ* as an example of the possessive use of the article. Bill T. Arnold and John H. Choi, *A Guide to Biblical Hebrew Syntax* (Cambridge: Cambridge University Press, 2003), p. 32.

21 *Then Ehud put out his left hand, took the dagger from his right thigh, and thrust it into his belly.*

22 *The handle went in as well, after the blade; the fat closed over the blade (for he did not draw the dagger out of his belly), and the dirt came out.*[7]

23 *Then Ehud went out to the vestibule,[8] closed the doors of the upper room after him,[9] and locked[10] them.*

24 *After he had gone out, Eglon's servants came and saw to their surprise that the doors of the cool upper room were locked. They said, "He is no doubt using the toilet[11] in the cool closet."*

25 *They waited nervously until they were ashamed to do so any longer. It was clear that no one was going to open the doors of the upper room, so they took the key and opened them, and there was their lord, fallen to the ground, dead.*

26 *Now Ehud had escaped while they dilly-dallied;[12] he had gone past the sculptured stones and escaped to Seirah.*

27 *When he got there, he blew the trumpet on Mount Ephraim, and his fellow Israelites went down from the mountain with him leading them.*

28 *He said to them, "Follow me, for Yahweh has given your enemies the Moabites into your hands." So they went down after him and took control of the fords of the Jordan.*

29 *They struck down of the Moabites at that time about ten thousand men — all of them stout, substantial men — not one of them escaped.*

---

7. The word translated *dirt (parš^{e}dōnā)* occurs only here in the Hebrew Bible, and is of uncertain meaning. With most English versions (e.g., KJV, NRSV, ESV) I take it to be related to *pereš* (feces, excrement), which is supported by the Targum and the Vulgate. For a recent detailed discussion of the options see Lindars, *Judges 1–5,* pp. 146-48, and for a persuasive (in my judgment) presentation of the argument for the reading I have adopted see M. L. Barre, "The Meaning of *parš^{e}dōnāh* in Judges 3:22," *VT* 41, no. 1 (1991): 1-11.

8. The *BHS* note says that *hammisd^{e}rônâ* is a "doubtful/uncertain" hapax legomenon, and that the LXX has "(into) the porch." Cf. Lindars, *Judges 1–5,* p. 148: "*to the verandah* is the commonly accepted meaning of *hammisd^{e}rônâ,* assuming derivation from the root *sdr* (Mishnaic, Aramaic, Syriac) denoting a row or rank, and so here a colonnade or porch."

9. Keil and Delitzsch ("Judges," p. 298) read this as "not behind himself, but literally round him, i.e., Eglon; cf. Gen. vii. 16; 2 Kings iv. 4." Ehud locked Eglon in.

10. Following *BHS,* which suggests that this should perhaps ("as has been proposed") be the *wayyiktol* form *wayyinol.*

11. Literally, "covering his feet" *(mēšîk . . . 'et-raglāyw).* Cf. 1 Sam. 24:3 (Heb. 4).

12. I owe this translation to Mobley (*Empty Men,* p. 84). The underlying Hebrew word, *hitmahm^{e}hām,* involves a rare reduplication of the syllable *mh,* as in *mâ(h),* "What?" and therefore suggests delay caused by confused talk, "What? What?" A similar form occurs in Gen. 19:16, again in the context of a foolish delay.

30 *So Moab was subdued that day under the hand of Israel, and the land had rest for eighty years.*

The same basic sequence of events unfolds in this episode as in the previous one: apostasy, subjugation, appeal, the raising up of a deliverer, peace. But instead of the shadowy Cushan-rishathaim we have now the very corporeal presence of the fat Eglon, and instead of the "knight" Othniel we have the devious left-handed assassin, Ehud. The "service" *('bd)* of a tyrant (v. 14; cf. v. 8) now takes the specific form of conveying tribute to him, and this provides Ehud with the opportunity to take a daring personal initiative which effectively decides the issue *before* he rallies the Israelites and engages the Moabites on the field of battle. So within the predictable framework outlined in 2:11-19 and illustrated by the preceding Othniel episode, a highly entertaining narrative unfolds, which moves through two climaxes to the resolution, which is finally reached in verse 30.[13]

The most striking feature of the style of the story is its satirical quality. The principal target, of course, is the tyrant Eglon. We are repeatedly reminded that he is a king. Four times we are given his full title *'eglôn melek mô'āb* (*Eglon, king of Moab,* vv. 12, 14, 15, 17) before Ehud addresses him, climactically, as *hammelek (O king)* in v. 19.[14] The details of his subjugation of Israel in verses 13-14 give no hint of the satire that is to follow: he gathers allies, goes and strikes down Israel, occupies *the City of Palms* (Jericho), and maintains his hold over Israel for eighteen years. He is apparently no mean hand in military matters. Certainly the Israelites have no answer for him; that is why they cry out to Yahweh (v. 15).

But from the moment the one-to-one relationship between Ehud and Eglon (protagonist versus antagonist) is established, Eglon begins to look very foolish indeed. His obesity is presented in the most grotesque terms (his fat belly swallows up Ehud's dagger, handle and all, v. 22). By fattening himself on the tribute *(minḥâ)* he has extorted from Israel (it was probably agricultural produce),[15] Eglon has turned himself into a large, slow-moving target and a helpless sacrificial animal.[16] His obesity symbolizes his greed and

---

13. For a complete stylistic analysis of the story see L. Alonso Schökel, "Erzählkunst im Buche der Richter," *Biblica* 42 (1961): 148-58.

14. This form of address is not inevitable in the situation. Consider the more customary and polite use of *'ǎdōnāy* (my lord) in 1 Sam. 24:8; 26:17; 29:8; 2 Sam. 4:8; 13:33, etc.

15. As in the use of *minḥâ* for a cereal offering in Lev. 2:1 etc. The use of a cadre of bearers suggests its bulk. Cf. C. E. Armerding, "Judges," in *A Bible Commentary for Today,* ed. G. C. D. Howley, F. F. Bruce, and H. L. Ellison (London: Pickering and Inglis, 1979), p. 346.

16. "The adjective 'fat' also fits the association of a fatted animal" (Amit, "Ehud,"

his vulnerability to Ehud's sharp blade (v. 21). Much is made, too, of his gull-ibility. He is easily deceived by Ehud, so much so that he dismisses his own bodyguard (v. 19) and rises from his throne to receive the *dᵉḇar-ᵉlôhîm* *(message from God)* that Ehud offers him, totally deceived about its real nature (v. 20). The narrator has developed dramatic irony at Eglon's expense. Ehud's words, *two-edged* like his dagger, have a totally different meaning for us and for Ehud than they do for Eglon.[17] As Amit has noted, "The fact that the king rises is very important, given the lack of proportion between the tiny dagger and the fat king. With the king's belly stretched, Ehud [can] use his double-edged dagger to its full advantage."[18] It is a moment of exquisite high tension. And now suddenly everything is in slow motion, with precise detailing of each thing that happens — *left hand . . . dagger . . . right thigh . . . thrust . . . belly . . . handle . . . blade . . . fat . . . dirt* (vv. 20-21). So much for Eglon; Ehud's mastery of him is total.

But the satire does not end here. It is continued beyond the murder episode to the comic one that follows (vv. 24-25), in which Eglon's servants belatedly discover their master's corpse. "The courtiers' erroneous assumption that their bulky monarch is taking his leisurely time over the chamber pot is a touch of scatological humor at the expense of both king and followers";[19] they are as gullible as their master, and equally helpless against Ehud's cunning.

His troops fare no better. In full flight, trying desperately to make their escape across the Jordan, they are cut off there by the Israelites, who have rallied behind Ehud. Not one of them escapes, and the way they are described in verse 29 contains one final satirical thrust. They are all of them *stout (šāmēn)* and *substantial men (ʾîš ḥāyil)*. The term *šāmēn*, like *ʾîš ḥāyil*, can be read in more than one sense. Like *bārîʾ*, which is applied to Eglon in verse 17 *(Now Eglon was a very fat man),* it is used elsewhere in the Old Testament as an antonym of *rāzāh,* "lean,"[20] and in this context is capable of the same kind of *double entendre* as the word "stout" in English.[21] These stout

---

p. 110). Amit argues that other terms as well, used in this episode, have overtones of a sacrificial ritual. Cf. M. Z. Brettler, *The Creation of History in Ancient Israel* (London: Routledge, 1995), p. 81: "While pretending to bring tribute/offering to Eglon, it is actually Eglon, 'the calf', who becomes the offering."

17. E. M. Good, *Irony in the Old Testament,* 2nd ed. (Sheffield: Almond, 1981), pp. 33-34.

18. "Ehud," p. 113.

19. Alter, *The Art of Biblical Narrative,* p. 40.

20. For *bārî* as an antonym of *rāzāh* see Ezek. 34:20. For the corresponding use of *šāmēn* see Num. 13:20.

21. Boling (*Judges,* p. 85) renders *šāmēn* as "plump." Alter (*Art of Biblical Narrative,* p. 49) renders it by "lusty" but notes that it can also mean "fat." Soggin (*Judges,*

warriors are *subdued . . . under the hand of Israel* (v. 30) as their portly master has already been laid low under Ehud's hand.[22] In other words, "Ehud's assassination of Eglon . . . is not only connected causally with the subsequent Moabite defeat; it is also a kind of emblematic prefiguration of it."[23] The point is not that Eglon, his courtiers, and his troops were all blundering incompetents (witness the past eighteen years!) but that they were no match for a savior raised up by Yahweh. Eglon has served his purpose (v. 12); now he is removed with such ease that it is laughable. And inasmuch as our attention is specifically drawn to his office, the satirical portrayal of the man Eglon also involves an implicit critique of kingship as an institution.[24]

Equally as striking as this satirical tone of the story is the absolutely central role that deception plays in it.[25] There is something deceptive about the very physical constitution of the protagonist. He has a physical abnormality[26] which appears to fit him for one role (conveyor of tribute),[27] but actually fits him for a quite different role (assassin). Ehud destroys Eglon by means of a weapon purposely made for concealment, and hence deception (v. 16).[28] After

---

p. 49) renders it more traditionally as "able-bodied." LXX[A] has *machētas* (warlike), LXX[B] has *liparos* (well-oiled, fat).

22. V. 30 contains the final occurrence of the keyword *yad* (hand), a further connection between the murder of Eglon and the slaughter of his troops:

v. 15   Ehud is restricted in his right *yad.*
v. 17   The Israelites send tribute by his *yad.*
v. 21   Ehud reaches with his left *yad.*
v. 28   Yahweh gives Moab into Israel's *yad.*
v. 30   So Moab is laid low under the *yad* of Israel.

The stock expressions of vv. 28 and 30 are nuanced by their narrative context. Cf. Alonso Schökel, "Erzählkunst," pp. 149ff.

23. Alter, *Art of Biblical Narrative,* pp. 40-41.

24. Cf. 1:4-7 and 3:7-11, and see the table in the summary at the end of the treatment of 1:1–3:6.

25. Cf. Robert C. Culley, "Structural Analysis: Is It Done with Mirrors?" *Interpretation* 28 (1974): 165-81. Culley includes the story of Ehud and that of Jael (4:17-24) in an analysis of plot structure in six "deception stories" taken from the Old Testament.

26. Left-handedness; probably in this case because of a deformity of his right hand (see the notes on the translation of v. 15).

27. The repetition of *yad* (hand) in v. 15b (literally, "a man restricted in his right *hand,* and the Israelites sent tribute by his *hand*") suggests that his suitability for the task consisted precisely in his physical deformity: the choice of Ehud could not be construed by Eglon as a provocation, because Ehud appeared to be harmless.

28. "The dagger or short sword *(hereb)* is . . . short enough to hide under his clothing, long enough to do Eglon's [*sic*] business without the killer having to be unduly close to his victim, and double-edged to ensure the lethalness of one quick thrust" (Alter, *Art of Biblical Narrative,* p. 39).

its manufacture it is doubly concealed. First it is concealed physically on Ehud's person (v. 16); then it is concealed verbally by the deliberately misleading expressions *d^{e}bar-sēter* (secret word/thing) and *d^{e}bar-'^{e}lōhîm* (word/thing from God) in verses 19 and 20 respectively. Ehud compounds this deception by turning back from the *sculptured stones* (idols)[29] near Gilgal (v. 19), thereby adding plausibility to the suggestion that the "secret thing" is in fact an oracle *(d^{e}bar-'^{e}lōhîm)*.[30] Deception is crucial to the success of the murder, and also to the escape. The locked doors (v. 23) deceive the courtiers into the crucial confusion and delay that allow Ehud to make good his flight (v. 26). The only straightforward piece of action in the whole story is the military action in verses 27-29, but that is possible only because of the whole series of skillfully executed deceptions which have gone before. Ehud appears to have deceived even his fellow Israelites. The contrast between the final words of verse 15 *(by his hand the Israelites sent tribute)* and the opening words of verse 16 *(But Ehud made for himself a two-edged dagger)* implies that the assassination was entirely his own idea. Only when Ehud blew the trumpet in the hill country of Ephraim (v. 27) do the Israelites recognize Ehud as their *môšîa'* ("deliverer," v. 15).

The grotesquely comic character of the story makes moral judgments irrelevant. We are clearly meant to identify with the protagonist and enjoy the sheer virtuosity of this performance. It is a classic example of the underdog coming out on top, a scenario with universal comic appeal. But for all that, the entertainment is given an ideological twist by the statement in verse 15 that Ehud was raised up by *Yahweh,* and by Ehud's own rousing summons in verse 28, *Follow me, for Yahweh has given your enemies . . . into your hands.* The perfect tense here (*has* given) is nuanced by its narrative context. It is not simply an instance of the common use of the past tense to assure the troops that victory is as good as won,[31] but a reference to the very tangible grounds for such assurance in this particular case: the Moabite king himself has already been given into the hand of Ehud[32] and lies dead in his chamber. Ehud now stands unveiled as Yahweh's chosen savior.[33] He has been *raised up*

29. See the comments below on v. 19.

30. Cf. E. G. Kraeling, "Difficulties in the Story of Ehud," *JBL* 54 (1935): 206-7. The assumption that Eglon knew all about Ehud's movements, although we are not told this, is reasonable in view of the compressed narrative style. Whatever their precise identity, the *p^{e}sîlîm* mark the limits of Eglon's effective control; once Ehud passes the *p^{e}sîlîm* in v. 26 he has completed his escape and can openly muster the Israelite militia. The double mention of the *p^{e}sîlîm* in vv. 19 and 26 respectively forms a literary bracket around Ehud's private mission.

31. The so-called "prophetic perfect" (GKC, #106 n; cf. Isa. 53:2-9).

32. See the note above on the final occurrence of the keyword *yad* (hand) in v. 30.

33. In addition, LXX^A and LXX^B specify, in v. 30, that he "judged." The lack of

(v. 15), and his deceptions have been providentially directed and guaranteed by Yahweh. Ehud himself may not have been aware of it, but we readers have been privy to this divine secret from the beginning. But there is something inscrutable about Yahweh's ways here, even for us. That he chose to use *Ehud the Benjaminite*[34] is clear, but the reasons why he did so are hidden from us. We can't explain his choice of Ehud with the same confidence that we could his choice of Othniel. Why not another proven hero with impeccable credentials? Why a devious assassin? And why a Benjaminite, in view of what has been said about them in 1:21? Only on the purely formal plane — Benjamin after Judah, as in chapter 1 — is there any perceivable appropriateness in the choice.

In short, while the same broad parameters apply (Yahweh punishes the Israelites for apostasy, but saves them when they appeal to him), his activity assumes a new character here. It is secretive, deceptive, and less accessible to human perception and explanation than it was in the Othniel episode.

12-13   The double occurrence of the statement that the Israelites *did/ had done what was evil in the eyes of Yahweh* in verse 12 stresses the fact that the oppression the Israelites suffered at the hands of Eglon was thoroughly deserved; it was not just a cruel twist of fate. Notice how divine and human initiative operate together in the disciplining of Israel: "*Yahweh* strengthened Eglon king of Moab against Israel, and *he* [*Eglon*] enlisted the support of the Ammonites and the Amalekites."[35]

Like the Moabites, the *Ammonites* were related to the Israelites through Lot, Abraham's nephew (Gen. 19:36-38). They had once occupied the land between the Arnon and Jabbok Rivers, east of the Jordan and north of Moab; but it was already disputed territory (between the Ammonites and the Amorites) before the Israelites arrived, and continued to be disputed territory (between the Ammonites and the Israelites) in the period of the judges. If, as Numbers 21:21-24 seems to indicate, the Ammonites had been forced back from the Jordan into the more arid land farther east, they may well have seen an alliance with Eglon as an opportunity to recover access to this rich arable land again. Their appearance as allies of the Moabites here anticipates their reappearance in their own right in the Jephthah story of chapters 10–12. The *Amalekites* were a nomadic people of the southern Negeb and the Sinai

---

this in the MT is attributed by Boling to haplography (*Judges,* p. 87). In any case, if the episode is read in the light of 2:16-19, Ehud must be regarded not simply as a savior, but a savior-judge.

34. The use of the definite article in *ben-hayᵉmînî* (the Benjaminite) suggests that he is presented as typical — the Benjaminite par excellence. Compare the 700 Benjaminites of 20:16, likewise "restricted in their right hands." Cf. Boling, *Judges,* p. 86.

35. So Amit, "Ehud," p. 105.

desert with whom Israel had clashed in the days of Moses (Exod. 17:8; Num. 14:43, 45). Given this background, it is not surprising that Eglon found them, too, ready allies; there were old scores to settle, and a possible share in the agricultural spoil that would result. The Amalekites will appear again in a similar predatory role in the Gideon narrative (Judg. 6:3, 33). Eglon was clever enough to exploit the greed and opportunism of his neighbors for his own advantage.

Of course Eglon was unaware of how his actions served God's purpose of disciplining Israel. As we saw above, Eglon is often unaware of what is really going on! The name *Eglon (ʿeglôn)* is the diminutive form of "bull," that is, "little bull" or "bull calf."[36] Unlike the name Cushan-rishathaim in the previous episode, Eglon may well have been the Moabite king's actual name from birth.[37] But it is the kind of name that readily lends itself to satirical exploitation: will the fatted calf be killed, as in Jesus' parable of the prodigal son? Will Ehud make a meal of him?

The descriptive phrase *the City of Palms* clearly alludes to Jericho (see 1:16 and my comments there), though the city itself was probably unoccupied at the time in which the story is set. It was destroyed in the time of Joshua (Josh. 6), and, according to 1 Kings 16:34, it was not rebuilt until the time of Ahab. F. F. Bruce suggests that what is indicated is a temporary occupation of the oasis at ʿAin es-Sultan.[38] Control of the lower Jordan is what was at stake; the Israelites have been forced back and confined to the hills (v. 27). The mention of *palms,* and the references to Eglon's "fatness" (v. 17) and his "cool upper chamber" (v. 20), open up for us "the vast differences between the lives of the Moabites and the conquered Israelites — inside versus outside, cool versus hot, fatness versus barrenness, palms versus hills."[39]

The Moabite "strike" *(wayyak)* against Israel here in verse 13 is finally answered by the Israelite "counterstrike" *(wayyakkû)* against Moab in verse 29.[40]

14 As verse 15 will indicate, Israel's "service" (ʿbd) to Eglon involved the payment of tribute. There were probably other impositions, too, that are not mentioned.

15 The "cry" *(zʿq)* of this verse is an indication of the distress that the "service" to Eglon in verse 14 caused. The Israelites cry to Yahweh for deliverance as their ancestors cried out *(zʿq)* to God in Egypt (Exod. 2:23).

---

36. *HALOT,* 2:784-85.

37. It also occurs as the name of a Canaanite city in Josh. 10:3, 34; 15:39.

38. F. F. Bruce, "Judges," in *The New Bible Commentary Revised,* ed. D. Guthrie, J. A. Motyer, A. M. Stibbs, and D. J. Wiseman (Leicester: Inter-Varsity Press, 1970), p. 260.

39. Gros Louis, "The Book of Judges," p. 147.

40. Cf. Mobley, *Empty Men,* pp. 87-88.

They may not have been in literal slavery in Ehud's day, but the payment of tribute may have caused real economic hardship and, given the nature of the tribute (see below), probably hunger as well.

As in verses 12-13, we again see double causation at work: *Yahweh raised up a deliverer* (divine initiative), and *by his hand the Israelites sent a tribute payment to Eglon* (human instrumentality). The Israelites chose Ehud to deliver tribute, but God had already chosen him to deliver Israel.[41] *Gera*, his father's name, connects Ehud with the tribe of Benjamin (Gen. 46:21; cf. 2 Sam. 16:5; 19:16 [Heb. 17], 18 [Heb. 19]; 1 Kgs. 2:8).[42] So, less obviously, does his left-handedness. The expression, *a left-handed man ('îš 'iṭṭēr yad-yᵉmînô)*, is literally, "a man bound or impotent [in] his right hand." The same expression is used elsewhere with reference to warriors of the tribe of Benjamin who were famously and deadly accurate in wielding weapons with their left hands, thereby surprising and gaining advantage over their enemies (Judg. 20:16; cf. 1 Chron. 12:2). The use of the expression here hints at the role Ehud will play. The very thing that to Eglon's untrained eye may represent the impotence of his Israelite subjects actually hints at Ehud's potential as a savior.

The word translated *tribute* here *(minḥâ)* is more commonly used in the Old Testament of an offering made to God, especially a grain offering (e.g., Gen. 4:3, 4, 5; Exod. 30:9; Lev. 7:37; Isa. 66:20).[43] In view of this it is possible that the savage satire of the story reflects, in part at least, "Israel's revulsion towards the act of paying tribute to foreign powers. . . . [This was] not only economically and socially onerous, but for Israelites, blasphemous, since [Yahweh] alone was their sovereign, and the *minḥâ*, in its sacerdotal sense of 'offering,' belonged only to [Yahweh]."[44]

16 Ehud makes a dagger that is *a cubit (gōmeḏ) in length*. The term *gōmeḏ* occurs only here in the Old Testament. It probably refers to a shorter unit of length (from elbow to knuckles) than the standard cubit (*'ammâ*, from the elbow to the fingertips).[45] It was big enough to do its grisly work (see vv. 21-22), but small enough to be strapped to Ehud's thigh without impeding his movement, or in other ways revealing its presence.

17 Ehud literally "brings the tribute near" to Eglon, that is, "presents" it to him, as one might "present" an offering to God. The verb form

41. Amit, "Ehud," p. 106.

42. See also "Ehud" and "Gera" in 1 Chron. 7:10; 8:3, 5, 6, 7. Cf. Amit, "Ehud," p. 106.

43. BDB, p. 585.

44. Mobley, *Empty Men,* p. 85. Mobley acknowledges his indebtedness to Gary Anderson's *Sacrifices and Offerings in Ancient Israel: Studies in Their Social and Political Importance* (Atlanta: Scholars Press, 1987).

45. *HALOT,* 1:196; 61-62.

used here,[46] and again in verse 18 *(when he had finished presenting the tribute),* has the same kind of religious overtones as the term *minḥâ* (tribute/offering) itself did in verse 15. It is most often used in the Old Testament of presenting an offering to God by laying it on the altar as a sacrifice.[47] The sacrificial language suggests that the offering of tribute to Eglon had sacrilegious overtones for Israelites, which in turn colors the killing of Eglon which is about to take place, making it like the ritual slaughter of a sacrificial animal.

With reference to the statement here that Eglon was *a very fat [bārî]* *man,* Gregory Mobley cautions that "it is all too easy to project modern bodily conceptions onto Eglon." He notes that the word *bārî'* is used of human beings in only one other place in the Old Testament, "in a description of the young Jewish heroes in the book of Daniel who eschew the ritually unclean cuisine of a foreign court and, nonetheless, develop into living testaments to kosher eating and righteous living."[48] Needless to say, however, it can hardly be intended to have such positive connotations in its present context. The reference to Eglon's fatness here is, among other things, preparation for the grotesque description in verses 21-22 of what happens when Ehud stabs him.

18 The narrative is very compressed at this point. Since Ehud is the subject of the first part of the verse *(when he had finished presenting the tribute),* he is also the subject of the second part *(he sent away the people who had carried it).* He would hardly be in a position to do this while he was in the presence of Eglon, so it must have been after he and his attendants had left the royal complex and traveled to the point where he himself turned back alone (v. 19).

19 The *sculptured stones (pᵉsîlîm)* of this verse are referred to again in verse 26 (see the comments there). The fact that Ehud turns back from these stones and tells Eglon that he has a "message from God" for him (v. 20) suggests that these stones had some religious significance for Eglon, and that Ehud was aware of this. In every other place in the Old Testament where it occurs, *pᵉsîlîm* refers to idols,[49] and the singular *(pesel)* is used of Micah's idol in 17:4. In all probability, then, the *sculptured stones* were located at a sacred site (shrine) of some kind, possibly an Israelite one, as suggested by the proximity to *Gilgal* (cf. Josh. 4:20). The presence of idols there is not surprising considering Israel's apostasy referred to back in verse 12. More sig-

---

46. The Hiphil of *qrb.*

47. It is used in this sense, with *minḥâ,* in, e.g., Lev. 2:8, 6:14 (Heb. 7); 7:12; 23:16; Num. 5:25; 6:16; and 15:9. BDB, p. 898.

48. *Empty Men,* p. 77. The LXX translates *bārî'* as *asteios* (handsome).

49. For example, Deut. 7:25; Isa. 21:9; Jer. 8:19; Hos. 11:2.

nificantly, Ehud's returning from these stones may well have been deliberately intended to deceive Eglon into thinking that he had returned with an oracle.[50] Ehud turns back alone because there is something which only he can do. In the context of the whole Bible we might think of the "aloneness" of the one who treads the winepress of God's wrath in Isaiah 63:3, and (if we dare mention Jesus in the same breath as Ehud) the aloneness of God's Messiah in the desert and the garden (Luke 4:1-2; 22:41).

Again the narrative moves swiftly, from Ehud's "turning back" to his arrival, once more, at the audience chamber of the palace complex, where Eglon still sits with his officials about him. To accomplish his mission Ehud must first get Eglon to dismiss these officials, which he does by telling the king that he has a _secret_ message (*d^ebar-sēter*) for him. The delivery of a *secret* message requires a private audience with the king, something that Eglon (his curiosity aroused) is ready to give. So he now dismisses *his* servants just as Ehud has done in verse 18. In Eglon's case no explicit dismissal is required; just the single word *"Silence (hās)."* But his attendants need no more; they go at once, leaving the two antagonists alone.

20   The private audience takes place in a *cool upper room* specifically designed for such meetings. Baruch Halpern, in a reconstruction of Eglon's palace based on comparative data, suggests that it was within the main audience chamber, but raised up on wooden joists and separated by a screen from the larger room. Since it was closer to the upper windows, it had better light and ventilation than the main chamber (an important consideration in a warm climate), making it a more pleasant setting for private meetings.[51] In Eglon's case, however, the screen must have been substantial, and lockable (v. 23).

Ehud now has Eglon alone and vulnerable. His next task is to make him stand up, so that he can stab him effectively with his short dagger. Eglon's concept of God was no doubt different from Ehud's, but if we are right in thinking that the *p^esîlîm* to which Ehud has gone and returned were idols, there was no need for Eglon to be dismissive of Ehud's claim to have *a message from God.* At any rate, Eglon seems to take Ehud's claim to be the bearer of a divine message with respect, and shows it by standing up to receive it. He is now perfectly positioned for Ehud's dagger. Unknowingly he presents himself to Ehud like a sacrificial animal to its slaughterer.

21-22   What happens now happens quickly, but as we have already observed, it is described in slow motion, almost like a series of stills rather

---

50. Cf. Amit, "Ehud," p. 112: "We may assume that the visit to the sculptured stones made Eglon willing to listen to Ehud's secret."

51. Baruch Halpern, *The First Historians: The Hebrew Bible and History* (University Park, PA: Pennsylvania State University Press, 1996), pp. 46-58, esp. p. 51.

than as one blurred action. Here is what everything has been building toward. We are at the structural center of the narrative; from this point the second half unfolds like a mirror image of the first, until the initial "strike" against Israel by the Moabites (v. 13) is fully answered by the counterstrike against the Moabites by Israel in verse 29. The slaughter of Eglon himself is the hinge on which the entire narrative turns. It is a heroic act, like David's slaughter of Goliath, which turns the tide and guarantees that it is only a matter of time until the enemy forces as a whole are overthrown. Samson's triumph over Dagon in chapter 16 has a similar significance.

23 While the meaning of *hammisd^eron* is not definitely known, Halpern is probably right that it refers to the vestibule at the front of the palace, a place where visitors waited before being admitted to the main audience hall.[52] After killing Eglon, Ehud leaves the small upper room and passes through the large audience hall out into the vestibule, and from there away from the palace complex entirely. His locking of the doors of the upper room after him delays the discovery of the murder, giving Ehud the time he needs to make good his escape.

24 Eglon appears to have had a *cool closet* attached to his private meeting room. The thought that he was using the toilet in this closet may have been prompted by the undoubted smell caused by the release of excrement caused by the stabbing (v. 22). Even this may have been a part of Ehud's careful planning, suggesting he had a very thorough knowledge of the layout of Eglon's palace. Was he perhaps assisted by an informer, as the Josephites were in 1:23? His possession of keys to the upper room points in the same direction. But with the typical economy of Hebrew narrative, all this is left to our imagination; only the essentials are given.

25 Eglon's servants, too, have a key to the private meeting room, but they are reluctant to use it for fear of breaking court etiquette and incurring Eglon's wrath. It is exactly the kind of confusion and indecision Ehud had counted on. The double use of *hinnê* ("behold" in older English translations) marks their two-stage transition from confused paralysis to action, and from ignorance to knowledge: *It was clear that no one was going to open the door,* and when they had done so themselves and gone in, there was *their lord* — fallen, dead. Barak has a similar moment of truth in chapter 4 when he discovers the dead Sisera in Jael's private tent (4:22). For him the discovery is partly good and partly bad, but for Eglon's servants it is an unmitigated disaster; without Eglon they are nothing.

26 See the comments on verse 19 above regarding the *sculptured stones.* The mention of them again here closes a bracket around the central section of the story, where Ehud performs his lone mission. Apart from their

---

52. Halpern, *First Historians,* p. 55.

likely religious significance, they probably also mark "the border outside the town where Moabite territory ends and Israelite territory begins."[53] It is only when Ehud has *gone past* them that he can be said to have *escaped*. They mark the point of entry to and exit from "the dangerous space between enemy lines" where Ehud has been operating.[54] The location of the *Seirah* to which Ehud escaped is unknown, but it must have been in the central hill country (see v. 27) and is therefore not to be confused with the Edomite Mount Seir in the south.[55]

27 More information about the location of Seirah is provided here, since it is when he has arrived *there* (at Seirah) that he blows the trumpet on *Mount Ephraim* (the hill country of Ephraim). It seems that Ehud has positioned himself outside the relatively small allotment of Benjamin, at the highest and most central point in the whole region, in order to make clear that his trumpet blast is a rallying call to the whole of Israel. It is also a very deliberate public presentation of himself to Israel as their deliverer/savior in the present crisis — the one Yahweh has given to them in answer to their cry of verse 15. He may have known himself to be this from the start (though we have no way of knowing this), but it was tactically important for him to appear as nothing more than a tribute bearer until he had struck the decisive blow. Now it was time to go public, and his trumpet blast was his way of doing so. Word must have spread quickly; the text shows us only the result, and it is unequivocal: *his fellow Israelites went down . . . with him leading them.* It is an example of how at least some of the people named in chapters 3–16 became judges.

28 The way the action now unfolds, from the central hills down toward the Jordan Valley, indicates that the Moabites are already in flight from Israelite territory. Ehud sees this as confirmation that *Yahweh has given* them into Israel's hands, and spurs his followers on by telling them so. Ehud has escaped, but there is no escape now for his enemies: the seizure of the Jordan fords effectively shuts Eglon's followers in, just as Eglon himself had been shut in back in v. 23.[56] There is no mention of the allies of verse 13 (the Ammonites and Amalekites); in the moment of crisis they are nowhere to be seen. It is one more indication of the hopeless position in which the Moabites now find themselves.

29 See the comments above on the way the Moabite warriors are described here. *Stout, substantial men (ʾîš ḥāyil)* they may be, but there is nothing warrior-like about them now. The series of reverses that bring the narra-

53. Mobley, *Empty Men,* p. 79.
54. Mobley, *Empty Men,* p. 79. Mobley himself translates *pᵉsîlîm* as "monoliths."
55. Lindars, *Judges 1–5,* p. 153.
56. So Mobley, *Empty Men,* p. 93.

tive to a close is here completed by the "striking down" of the Moabites to a man; not one escapes. Given the roundness of the number, and the fact that (in contrast to the Gideon narrative) nothing is made in this episode about the huge size of the enemy force, it may be legitimate to render the "ten *ʾᵃlāpîm*" as "ten contingents" (about 250 men) rather than *ten thousand*.[57] But given the fact that the conflict has been widened by Ehud's recruitment drive into a showdown between Moab and the Israelites as a whole, *ten thousand* is probably the intended meaning. It was a huge, overwhelming victory.

30   The word *yad* (hand) has occurred again and again through this narrative and had many changes wrung on it, from Ehud being a *ben-hayᵉmînî* (son of the right hand [region/the south]), but restricted in his right hand, to the Israelites sending tribute by his hand, to Ehud strapping the sword on the right hand (side) of his body, to drawing it from there, to Yahweh giving Moab into Israel's hands.[58] Now *yad* occurs for the last time, as a way of expressing the outcome of it all: *Moab was subdued that day under the hand of Israel.*

The resultant period of rest *(eighty years)* is a round number for approximately two generations,[59] and is part of the broad chronological scheme of this central part of the book; it is the kind of round number the author used when specific chronological data was unavailable.[60] But the length of this particular interval of peace is rather surprising compared with the more modest forty- or twenty-year periods indicated elsewhere (e.g., 3:11; 5:31; 8:28; 15:20; 16:31). Given that the note about Shamgar that immediately follows has no separate period of peace indicated, it could be that the *eighty years* here serves for both Ehud and Shamgar. That is, the long period of peace which followed the subjugation of Moab was threatened only once, and Shamgar successfully repelled that threat. This possibility is strengthened by the fact that the episode which follows the note about Shamgar refers back to Ehud rather than Shamgar as the one whose death signaled the end of the period of peace (4:1).

C. SHAMGAR (3:31)

31   *After him [Ehud] was Shamgar, son of Anath, who struck down six hundred Philistine men with an ox goad, and he, too, saved Israel.*

57. See Section IX.C of the Introduction regarding the translation possibilities of the word *ʾelep*.
58. Mobley, *Empty Men*, p. 78.
59. So, e.g., Block, *Judges*, p. 171, and Burney, *Judges*, p. 75.
60. See the comments on 3:11, and in Section II.A of the Introduction.

31 This brief note about Shamgar is marked by the same grotesque, satirical quality as the Ehud story to which it is attached. Again the enemy is not only defeated, but made to look utterly ridiculous by the single-handed virtuoso performance of a savior who is a most unlikely hero. Again our attention is drawn specifically to the weapon he used.[1] This time it is improvised rather than purpose-made, and marks its bearer even more clearly as a makeshift warrior. Like Ehud, Shamgar is a man who is apparently fitted for one role (someone who drives oxen) but fulfills a quite different one (a savior).[2] But just as his weapon is much less subtle than Ehud's, so is his method. He overcomes an enemy force of six hundred by a feat of superhuman strength and dexterity, goading them to death like so many oxen that have displeased him (cf. Samson's feat in 15:15).

Shamgar is the son of *Anath,* which is the name of a female Canaanite god. He may have been the son of a woman named after this god, or may himself have been a devotee of the god. Narrative poems on clay tablets from Ras Shamra in Syria, the site of the ancient city of Ugarit, tell about Anath (or Anat) as a goddess of war worshiped by the people who lived there in the centuries immediately before Israel's arrival in Canaan. In Ugarit literature Anath is "female, but not a fertility goddess; she is not male, but she is a warrior."[3] Her activities are described in the poems in particularly gruesome and bloodthirsty terms. Bronze arrowheads from early Iron Age Palestine, and inscribed with names of the type, "X, son of Anath," seem to indicate the existence of a warrior class associated with Anath as their patron deity.[4] Shamgar displays something of the violent character of Anath and her devotees, but his improvised weapon (an *ox goad*) suggests that he was an amateur rather than a professional, making his feat even more remarkable than it would otherwise be.

The passing reference to the *Philistines* in 3:3 has prepared the way for their appearance here as active enemies of Israel. For their origins and time of arrival in Canaan see the excursus after 3:1-6. No details are given about them in the present note except how many of them Shamgar clashed with. The number *six hundred* is commonly used of an organized force under a commander,[5] and if that is the case here, it makes Shamgar's feat all the

---

1. The ancient versions do not agree in their rendering of the hapax *malmad.* Some render it "goad," others "plow head" or "plow beam." "Goad" still commends itself to most scholars. See the discussion in A. van Selms, "Judge Shamgar," *VT* 14, no. 1 (1964): 306. He draws attention to the use of the word in the Mishnah, e.g., *Sanhedrin* 10.28: "called *malmēd* because it teaches [the ox]."

2. Cf. Saul in 1 Sam. 11:4-8.

3. Mobley, *Empty Men,* pp. 22-23.

4. The relevant evidence is given by Mobley in *Empty Men,* pp. 27-30.

5. For example, 1 Sam. 13:15; 14:2; 27:2; 2 Sam. 15:18. Cf. Van Selms, "Judge

more remarkable. The Philistines may have been making an exploratory probe into territory they were unfamiliar with, giving Shamgar the advantage of surprise, or even ambush. But such natural factors, even if they contributed to Shamgar's victory, fall far short of being able to explain it, and another order of explanation is in fact implied by the way the note is related to its context. It is connected to the story of Ehud, not only by the *we'aḥⁱrāyw (after him)* at the beginning, but also by the *gam-hû' (he, too)* near the end: *he, too, saved Israel.* The implication is that Shamgar was another deliverer like Ehud, and therefore an agent of Yahweh. And confirmation is supplied in 10:11, which alludes back to this note: "When the . . . Philistines . . . oppressed you . . . didn't I [Yahweh] save you from their hands?" Nevertheless, Shamgar's family and tribal connections are not given as Ehud's were,[6] and what *is* given (his name) only adds to the mystery surrounding his person, leaving open the possibility that he was not a worshiper of Yahweh, and perhaps not even Israelite.[7]

Thus, by means of a more extreme example, this note adds to the impression created by the Ehud story itself, that while Yahweh does save Israel from its enemies, his chosen means of doing so may not be easy to predict or explain. This issue will be taken up again in the Deborah-Barak episode that follows, in which "the days of Shamgar ben Anath" are explicitly recalled (5:6).

D. DEBORAH AND BARAK (4:1–5:31)

In contrast to the one-verse report of Shamgar's contribution to Israel's survival in the south (against the Philistines) we now have a much longer account of battle against the Canaanites and their allies in the north for control of the strategic Jezreel Valley.[1] Furthermore, and this is unique in Judges, this

---

Shamgar," p. 305, and the six hundred warriors sent by the tribe of Dan to conquer Laish in 18:11.

6. Contrast, too, the details regularly given in the other short notices of 10:1-5 and 12:8-15.

7. The most thorough discussion is by Van Selms in "Judge Shamgar." But see also F. C. Fensham, "Shamgar ben Anath," *JNES* 20, no. 3 (1961): 197-98; E. Danelius, "Shamgar ben 'Anath," *JNES* 22, no. 3 (1963): 191-93, and P. C. Craigie, "A Reconsideration of Shamgar ben Anath (Judg. 3:31 and 5:6)," *JBL* 91, no. 2 (1972): 239-40.

1. Also known as the Valley/Plain of Esdraelon (the Greek equivalent of Jezreel). Strictly speaking, the Jezreel Valley proper is only the more limited plain sloping down from the town of Jezreel itself to the Jordan Valley at the southern end of the Sea of Galilee. But the term is also used (as here) to include the adjacent plain to the northwest, extending toward the Mediterranean coast.

time we have two accounts of the crucial events: the first a prose narrative (ch. 4), and the second a poem (ch. 5), or, to put the matter more simply, a story and a song.

1. The Story (4:1-24)

As in the Ehud episode, the oppressor is a foreign king; this time *Jabin, king of Canaan, who ruled in Hazor,*[2] but the way the story opens prepares us for the fact that Jabin himself will remain a shadowy background figure. The prologue (vv. 1-3) immediately shifts the focus to his army commander, Sisera.[3]

The two pieces of information we are given about Sisera here — that he is based in *Harosheth-haggoyim,* and has *nine hundred iron chariots* at his disposal (vv. 2, 3) — will be alluded to again in the body of the narrative, where they are directly relevant to the unfolding action (vv. 13, 16). Although Jabin falls into the background, we are reminded of his existence twice in the narrative (vv. 7, 17), and then he is brought pointedly into view again with the threefold repetition of his name and title in the closing lines:

> God subdued *Jabin, king of Canaan,* that day before the Israelites.
> The hand of the Israelites pressed harder and harder against *Jabin, king of Canaan,*
> until they cut off *Jabin, king of Canaan.*[4]

What seems to be envisaged is that with the destruction of his army at the Kishon and the death of his commander, Jabin was isolated in Hazor and

2. For a discussion of the relevant historical questions see Abraham Malamat, "Hazor, 'The Head of All Those Kingdoms,'" *JBL* 79, no. 1 (1960): 12-19. The hegemony accorded to Hazor here recalls the earlier greatness of the city in the Mari period (cf. Josh. 11:10). In the Amarna letters the ruler of Hazor, unlike most other rulers, is called "king" *(šarrum)* and, uniquely, refers to *himself* as a king in a letter to the Pharaoh (El-Amarna 227, 1.3). Judges 4 seems to envisage a situation in which Hazor retains a nominal headship (a vestige of its former greatness) while effective power lies with an alliance between Canaanites and Sea Peoples centered on the Jezreel Valley.

3. The chapter is generally considered a conflation of two separate battle accounts, one featuring Jabin as the enemy leader, and the other Sisera (J. S. Ackerman, "Prophecy and Warfare in Early Israel: A Study of the Deborah-Barak Story," *BASOR* 220 [1975]: 7), but it makes good sense read as a unity. Ackerman confines his own study to vv. 4-22.

4. Note the wordplay, "God subdued *(wayyaknaʿ)* . . . Jabin, king of Canaan *(melek-kᵉnāʿan),*" also noted by J. Blenkinsopp in "Ballad Style and Psalm Style in the Song of Deborah," *Biblica* 42 (1961): 64, n. 4. Buber refers to the "almost paean-like . . . threefold repetition of the contrast of the sons of Israel with the representative of heathen monarchism, grown to symbolic greatness" (*Kingship of God,* p. 70).

eventually overcome by the Israelites, who thus finally established their supremacy over the Canaanites in the north.[5]

a. The Prologue (4:1-3)

1 *The Israelites again did what was evil in Yahweh's eyes when Ehud had died.*

2 *So Yahweh sold them into the hand of Jabin, king of Canaan, who ruled in Hazor. His army commander was Sisera, who was based in Harosheth-haggoyim.*

3 *The Israelites cried out to Yahweh, because he had nine hundred iron chariots and he had oppressed the Israelites severely for twenty years.*

1 The circumstantial clause, *when Ehud had died,* passes over Shamgar's achievement in silence. This is normally explained in terms of 3:31 being a later addition. But if so, the reference back to Ehud in 4:1 could hardly have escaped the notice of the final editor. It is more likely that the text is in its present form for a purpose. In fact the words, *when Ehud had died,* are entirely in keeping with our comment earlier about the unusually long period of peace in 3:30, namely, that this was essentially the consequence of Ehud's decisive defeat of the Moabites, and that Shamgar simply repelled a temporary threat to it at one point.

2 *Hazor* was a fortified city in the territory of Naphtali, approximately 10 miles (15 km.) north of the Sea of Galilee, close to what is now the Israel-Lebanon border. It was at one time the most powerful city in northern Canaan, and its impressive ruins can still be seen today. *Jabin* was probably a royal title (like "Pharaoh" for the kings of Egypt). Joshua had defeated another "Jabin" at Hazor almost one hundred years earlier (Josh. 11:1-11).[6] Verses 23-24 probably refer to the final destruction of a resurgent Hazor in the thirteenth century, as attested (on at least one reading of the data) by the archeological remains there.[7]

---

5. The Canaanites in the far north (represented by Jabin, king of Hazor), like the Israelites in the far south (Judah), do not participate directly in the battle, though according to 4:13 the fighting subsequently spreads northward. On the possibility that the twelfth-century settlement at Hazor was a consequence of the battle at the Kishon see B. Lindars, "The Israelite Tribes in Judges," in *Studies in the Historical Books of the Old Testament,* ed. J. A. Emerton, VTSup 30 (Leiden: Brill, 1979), p. 109.

6. Kitchen (*The Reliability of the Old Testament,* pp. 206, 208) calls the Jabin of the book of Judges "Jabin II."

7. Bimson, *Redating the Exodus,* pp. 185-200. For alternative views on the history of Hazor and the relationship between the present passage and Joshua 11, see the standard commentaries, and histories of Israel.

The name *Sisera* is non-Semitic, possibly Illyrian, and therefore Sisera was most likely a prominent member of the so-called Sea People who arrived in Canaan from the region around the Adriatic in the early Iron Age. The Philistines probably arrived as part of the same influx of people from this general area, as we have seen.[8] He had established himself in *Harosheth-haggoyim* (Harosheth of the nations), much as the Philistines had established themselves in Ashkelon and other coastal cities in the south. The location of Harosheth-haggoyim is uncertain, but as a staging post for chariotry it was presumably on level ground rather than in the hills, and the details about the battle given later suggest that it was at the western (Mount Carmel) end of the Jezreel Valley.[9] Sisera's alliance with Jabin placed the tribes north of the Kishon in a squeeze between the two, on their north and south respectively. Sisera was someone who could not be ignored.

3   Sisera's *nine hundred iron chariots* were an impressive force. Iron chariots were the latest military hardware, and gave the enemy a virtually unassailable superiority on the low, flat land of the coastal plain and the broad Jezreel Valley.[10] They have already been given as the reason why Judah and Dan were unable to dislodge the Canaanites from the plains in the southwest (1:19, 34-35). Here they are given as the reason why Jabin and Sisera were able to oppress Israel for twenty years. The position of the Israelites seemed hopeless, which is why they *cried out to Yahweh*. It was a cry of desperation.

b. The Liberation of Israel and the Undoing of Sisera (4:4-24)

4 *Now Deborah was a prophetess, the wife of Lappidoth. She was judging Israel at that time.*

5 *She used to sit under the palm of Deborah between Ramah and Bethel in Mount Ephraim, and the Israelites went up to her for judgment.*

6 *She sent and called Barak, son of Abinoam, from Kedesh-naphtali, and said to him, "Hasn't Yahweh, the God of Israel, commanded you? Go and draw toward Mount Tabor, taking with you ten thousand men from the men of Naphtali and the men of Zebulun;*

7 *and I will draw to you at the River Kishon Sisera the commander of Jabin's army with his chariots and all his men, and I will give them into your hand."*

8. See Excursus 4, immediately after the treatment of 3:1-6.

9. See W. Osborne, "Harosheth," in *NBD*, p. 445, and Block, *Judges, Ruth,* p. 190, who places it further east on "the fertile alluvial plain between Taanach and Megiddo."

10. See the note on 1:19 regarding the introduction of this technology to Palestine (cf. 1:34-35).

8 *Barak said to her, "If you go with me, I will go, but if you will not go with me, I will not go."*

9 *She said to him, "I will go with you, but there will be no glory for you as you follow this course of action, for it will be into the hand of a woman that Yahweh will sell Sisera." Then Deborah arose and went with Barak to Kedesh.*

10 *Barak summoned Zebulun and Naphtali to Kedesh, and there went up after him ten thousand men; and Deborah went up with him.*

11 *Now Heber the Kenite was separate from the Kenite clan, the people of Hobab, the father-in-law of Moses. He pitched his tent as far away as the oak of Zaanannim,[11] which was near Kedesh.*

12 *Sisera was informed that Barak, son of Abinoam, had gone up Mount Tabor.*

13 *So Sisera summoned all his chariotry — nine hundred iron chariots — and all the people who were with him, to come from Harosheth-haggoyim to the River Kishon.*

14 *Then Deborah said to Barak, "Arise, for this is the day when Yahweh has given Sisera into your hand. Hasn't Yahweh gone out before you?" So Barak went down from Mount Tabor, with ten thousand men after him.*

15 *And Yahweh threw Sisera and all his chariotry and all his troops into disarray by the edge of the sword before Barak; and Sisera got down from his chariot and fled on foot.*

16 *Meanwhile Barak had pursued the chariots and troops as far as Harosheth-haggoyim; and all Sisera's troops fell at the edge of the sword — not even one remained.*

17 *Now Sisera had fled on foot to the tent of Jael, the wife of Heber the Kenite, for there was peace between Jabin, king of Hazor, and the house of Heber the Kenite.*

18 *Jael went out to meet Sisera, and said to him, "Turn aside, my lord. Turn aside to me. Do not fear." So he turned aside to her, to her tent, and she covered him with a rug.*

19 *He said to her, "Please give me a little water to drink, for I am thirsty." So she opened a flask of milk and gave it to him, and covered him.*

20 *He said to her, "Stand at the entrance to the tent, and if a man comes and asks you, 'Is there a man here?' say 'No.'"*

21 *Then Jael, the wife of Heber, took a tent peg, put the hammer in her hand, came to him stealthily, and drove the peg into his temple, and it went down into the ground. He was asleep with exhaustion, and he died.*

22 *Just then, as Barak came by in pursuit of Sisera, Jael went out to meet*

11. Reading $b^e\dot{s}a^{\,'a}nann\hat{i}m$, as in Josh. 19:33.

him. She said to him, "Come, so I can show you the man you are seeking." So he went into her tent, and there was Sisera, lying dead, with the tent peg in his temple.

23 *So God subdued Jabin, king of Canaan, that day before the Israelites.*

24 *The hand of the Israelites pressed harder and harder against Jabin, king of Canaan, until they cut off Jabin, king of Canaan.*

The body of the narrative, telling how the Israelites were liberated, opens in verses 4-5 with what D. F. Murray has aptly described as a "tableau,"[12] in which Deborah sits under her palm tree in the hill country of Ephraim, *judging* Israel (cf. Moses in Exod. 18:13-16). This scene introduces the character who will set the story in motion, and provides us with certain information about her. She is *a prophetess,* and hence the agent by which Yahweh's word will enter the story to summon Barak to fulfill his role as a savior.[13] Hence for the first time "judging" and "saving" are clearly distinguished from one another. While the two functions may be combined in one person, judges are not necessarily saviors, and saviors are not necessarily judges. However, Deborah does play a crucial role in the saving of Israel, in two senses: by settling disputes (*the Israelites went up to her for judgment*) she saves it from trouble within, and by commissioning Barak to deal with Jabin and Sisera she saves it from trouble from without.

Mount Ephraim (the central hill country) is the topographical link by which we pass from the southern setting of the Othniel and Ehud episodes to the northern setting of this and subsequent ones.[14] It was in this region that Ehud sounded his trumpet, and from here that he led his volunteers south to engage the enemy at the fords of the Jordan (3:27). From this same locality Deborah now sends northward to summon Barak to a battle to be fought at the Kishon. In terms of the schema of chapter 1 this is the first major episode which, with regard to both its setting and the Israelite tribes principally involved, falls within the sphere of the "house of Joseph" (note the reference to Bethel in v. 5; cf. 1:22). It is the failure of the northern tribes to dislodge the Canaanites from key fortified cities as described in 1:27-33 which provides the demographic/political background to the conflict which comes to a head here, the catalyst probably being an influx of Sea Peoples, as suggested by the name Sisera.

12. "Narrative Structure and Technique in the Deborah-Barak Story, Judges iv.4-22," in *Studies in the Historical Books of the Old Testament,* ed. J. A. Emerton, VTSup 30 (Leiden: Brill, 1979), p. 163.

13. The term does not occur in the text, but this is certainly Barak's role.

14. The Samson story is set in the south, but as in chapter 1 Dan is schematically associated with the northern tribes in anticipation of its eventual location in the north (chs. 17–18).

The initial focus on a woman is quite surprising in view of the complete absence of women in the Othniel and Ehud episodes. The fact that she holds a position of authority and takes the initiative in relation to the prospective male hero is the first intimation of a thematic development that will give this particular episode its unique character.

Deborah charges Barak solemnly in the name of Yahweh (vv. 6-7). But Barak responds by imposing a condition:

> *"If you go with me, I will go,*
> *but if you will not go with me, I will not go."*

Deborah is clearly taken aback, as her rejoinder in verse 9 shows. Saving Israel by force of arms is man's work. Barak has already received his orders and has been assured of victory. She will go with him if he insists, but he will have a price to pay:

> *"I will go with you,*
> *but there will be no glory for you as you follow this course of action,*
> *for it will be into the hand of a woman that Yahweh will sell Sisera."*

On the face of it this need mean no more than that the victory will redound to Deborah's credit rather than to Barak's. But a complication arises when Sisera escapes from the scene of battle (v. 17). The story cannot reach its dénouement now until Sisera is accounted for. That dénouement is reached with the ironic juxtaposition of victor and vanquished in the tent of Jael, the woman who has in effect conquered them both: Sisera by depriving him of his life, and Barak by depriving him of the honor that should have been his as the chosen deliverer. Murray, following Alonso Schökel,[15] has drawn attention to the compact irony of Sisera's last words:

> *"Stand at the entrance to the tent,*
> *and if a man ('îš) comes and asks you,*
> *'Is there a man ('îš) here?'*
> *say, 'No ('āyin).'"*

The 'îš who comes to the door of the tent is, of course, Barak, and the 'îš within is Sisera, who is dead by the time Barak arrives. To quote Murray,

> the confrontation is not now of two leaders at the head of vast armies, but of two men in the presence of a woman; and one word put with dreadful irony into the mouth of Sisera, who has so cravenly abandoned

15. Murray, "The Deborah-Barak Story," p. 183; Alonso Schökel, "Erzählkunst," p. 166.

184

his position of leadership, adumbrates the impending fate of them both: *'āyin* [nothing, no one].[16]

This ultimate convergence in the destinies of the two men has been foreshadowed obliquely in the course of the narrative to this point by a whole series of wordplays and syntactical parallels which have been identified by Murray; we will not repeat the details here. Suffice it to say that the final tableau in the tent of Jael balances the initial tableau under the palm of Deborah.

(1) Links with the Ehud and Shamgar Episodes

Here we anticipate what follows by including the song of chapter 5 as part of the Deborah-Barak episode. We have already noted some links between this episode as a whole and the Ehud-Shamgar complex that precedes it. Further connections with the Ehud narrative in particular may now be observed. Both narratives feature a murder scene followed by a discovery scene as follows:

	The Ehud Episode	*The Deborah-Barak Episode*
Murder scene	Ehud murders Eglon	Jael murders Sisera
Discovery scene	The courtiers discover the dead Eglon	Barak discovers the dead Sisera

In the Ehud narrative the murder takes place before the battle; in the Deborah-Barak story it follows it. But in both it is the high point of dramatic interest. Jael's murder of Sisera is told in the same vivid style as Ehud's murder of Eglon: each separate movement is described precisely (cf. 4:21 with 3:20-22). The verb *tqʻ* occurs at the height of the action in both episodes: Ehud thrusts *(tqʻ)* his dagger into Eglon's belly; Jael drives *(tqʻ)* her tent peg into Sisera's temple.[17]

Likewise, Barak's discovery of the dead Sisera has specific verbal echoes of the courtiers' discovery of the dead Eglon. Alonso Schökel has noted the frequent use of *hinnê* ("behold" in older English versions) in both, and that both the victims are found "fallen" *(nōpēl)* and "dead" *(mēt)*.[18] This similarity of style and situation in adjacent episodes invites us to read the second in the light of the first and to compare the roles played by the characters in the respective narratives.

---

16. "The Deborah-Barak Story," p. 183.

17. Compare the way in which, within the Ehud narrative, this same verb links Ehud's private initiative with its national consequences: he thrusts *(tqʻ)* his dagger into Eglon, and then blows *(tqʻ)* his trumpet on Mount Ephraim.

18. "Erzählkunst," p. 166.

185

Deborah's charge to Barak in verses 6-7 indicates that he is destined for a role comparable to that of Othniel in 3:7-11. He does win a notable victory, but his insistence that Deborah accompany him already detracts from his heroic stature. Subsequently he is reduced to playing a role analogous to Eglon's courtiers, who were held up to such ridicule in 3:24-25. He arrives too late, only to find that the man he is seeking is dead. Paradoxically that death is a defeat for himself as well; the honor that should have been his has been taken away and given to a woman (v. 9). He can only stand and stare. It is his punishment for trying to manipulate Deborah, Yahweh's prophet.[19] It is also a foretaste of the far greater evil that Jephthah will bring upon himself by trying to manipulate Yahweh directly.[20]

(2) The Surprising Jael

It is Jael who finally emerges as the real hero of the story. But she is not an orthodox hero of the Othniel kind, as Barak was supposed to be. She is more like the maverick heroes, Ehud and Shamgar. Like Ehud, Jael is a lone assassin, who accomplishes her ends by deception. Like him she dispatches her victim when they are alone in a private place (hers in this case, rather than her victim's). Like Shamgar she is a makeshift fighter who uses an improvised weapon. And if Shamgar was *probably* not an Israelite, Jael is *certainly* not; she is a member of a Kenite splinter group which is at peace with Jabin, Israel's archenemy (4:11, 17)! Her action is morally ambiguous, but her courage and the sheer brilliance of her performance are sufficient to silence criticism on that score (5:24).[21] The crowning aspect of her unorthodoxy is her gender: Yahweh sells Sisera into the hands of a *woman*.

19. His reasons for doing so are not indicated in the narrative. Barak's hesitation is further spelled out in the LXX: "for I never know the day Yahweh's angel will give me success" (my translation), suggesting that he desires her presence as a source of oracular inquiry (cf. Boling, *Judges*, p. 96; Ackerman, "Prophecy and Warfare," p. 9). But Deborah's reply clearly indicates that *she* considers his conditional response to Yahweh's command improper, and the narrative as a whole supports this view. The word of Yahweh should have been enough for him. It is not just a matter of manliness but of trust and readiness to obey.

20. Just as the vow and its fulfillment is the axis along which the tension is developed and resolved in the Jephthah story, so the bargain struck in vv. 9-10 (Deborah will go with Barak, but there will be a price to pay) is the axis along which tension is developed and resolved here.

21. Cf. Barnabas Lindars, who shows how Jael became the model for Judith, whose story in turn influenced the retelling of the Jael episode in Pseudo-Philo's *Biblical Antiquities* ("Deborah's Song: Women in the Old Testament," *BJRL* 65, no. 2 [1983]: 173-74).

(3) Irony and the Reader

In the Deborah-Barak episode Yahweh's providential activity assumes an even more mystifying character than it did in the Ehud story, and this time mystification is of the very essence of the story's narrative art. In the Ehud story we the readers were apprised of Yahweh's secret designs quite early, so that when Eglon fails to perceive the true nature of the "oracle" *(dᵉbar-ᵉlōhîm)* that Ehud brought to him, the irony was entirely at *his* expense. In the Deborah-Barak episode, however, we find out belatedly that we ourselves have been misled. Our discovery of the true identity of the "woman" is delayed as long as possible, so that the irony this time is nicely turned against us, the readers.[22] The effect is to enhance the impact, when it comes, of the revelation that Yahweh's choice has fallen, not merely on a woman, nor even on an Israelite prophetess (as we were led to expect), but upon Jael, *the wife of Heber the Kenite!*

(4) Conclusions

As in the Ehud narrative, the basic subject matter (how Israel was freed from oppression) has been given a forceful thematic shape in which the principal dramatic interest lies in how Yahweh, in the course of rescuing Israel, took the honor of victory away from a man who showed himself unworthy of it, and gave it to a woman.

At the same time the Deborah-Barak story participates in developments that happen as the book as a whole unfolds. It complements the preceding Ehud narrative by depicting Yahweh as achieving his providential designs by means which completely overturn human expectations. By showing how Barak was disciplined for manipulating Deborah, Yahweh's prophet, it raises in a preliminary way an issue (negotiation versus true religion) that will assume greater significance in the confrontations between Yahweh and Israel in 6:7-10 and 10:10-16, and become the central theme of the Jephthah narrative.

Finally, in common with the Othniel and Ehud narratives, it depicts kingship as an oppressive foreign institution, used by Yahweh at his discretion to discipline Israel, but essentially alien to it. In general, however, this theme, like Jabin himself, remains marginal here in contrast to the more central way it has featured in previous episodes.[23] It will spring into prominence again in the Gideon-Abimelech narrative of chapters 6-9.

4 *Deborah* (honey bee) is the wife of *Lappidoth* (torches),[24] but in

22. Cf. Polzin, *Moses and the Deuteronomist,* p. 163.
23. See, however, the conspicuous mention of kings at 5:19.
24. As in Judg. 7:16, where the masculine form of the same word is used.

contrast to the names of some other people we have met, such as Cushan-rishathaim and Eglon, these names are not exploited in any way in the narrative that follows. However, they do serve to anchor the narrative in the real world, where marriage and kinship are important sources of identity and well-being. That is, Deborah, despite her extraordinary gifting and calling, is a real, "normal" person (someone's wife). Lappidoth, unlike (say) Caleb, the father of Achsah and father-in-law of Othniel, is otherwise unknown, and so does not contribute anything to Deborah's status or fame, as far as we can tell; these are grounded elsewhere, as the rest of the verse indicates.

Deborah was a *prophetess* ('iššâ nᵉḇî'â), and in that sense was unusual, since it was the exception rather than the rule in Old Testament times for a woman to be a prophet, at least in Israel. Like male prophets, the women were of mixed character and legitimacy. On the positive side we know of Miriam the prophetess, the sister of Aaron, who led the other women in praising Yahweh for bringing them safely through the sea to freedom after their escape from Egypt (Exod. 15:20), or Huldah the prophetess, who played a key role in Josiah's reforms (2 Kgs. 22:14-20//2 Chron. 34:22-28), and Isaiah's wife, the prophetess who bore him children, who became key members of his band of disciples and signs of the twin themes (salvation and judgment) of his ministry to Zion (Isa. 7:3; 8:3, 16-18). On the negative side we know of Nodiah, who opposed Nehemiah (Neh. 6:14). In the New Testament we know of the aged Anna, the prophetess *(prophētis)* who saw the true significance of the birth of Jesus and spoke of him to all who were looking for the redemption of Jerusalem (Luke 2:36-38), the four daughters of Philip the evangelist, who exercised a prophetic ministry (Acts 21:8-9), and Jezebel, the false prophet in the church at Thyatira, who was leading people astray and causing them to sin (Rev. 2:20-21). It also seems that the gift of prophecy was present in the New Testament churches from Pentecost onward, and was exercised by both men and women, as had been foretold by the prophet Joel (Joel 2:28-29; Acts 2:16-18; 1 Cor. 14:29-33). So while it is unusual for Deborah to be a prophetess, it is not without precedent; nor is it out of keeping with the general direction in which things develop as salvation history runs its course to fulfillment in Christ and beyond. Here in Judges 4 Deborah acts as a war prophet, calling and commissioning Barak to lead men in battle, giving a promise of victory, and issuing the order to attack when the time is right (vv. 6-7, 14). It is a very important role.

More unusual is the statement that she was *judging (šōpᵉṭâ)* Israel, for to judge in the sense that she was doing it was to be the effective ruler of the nation as a whole — an office not held by any other woman in the Old Testament, and with no parallel in the New. Her judging is described as similar to that of Samuel, though he (later) went on a circuit, judging Israel in various places, while Deborah remained in one place, and the Israelites *went* up to her (v. 5; cf. 1 Sam. 7:15-16).[25] As Samuel appointed Saul and David as kings, Deborah appointed Barak as deliverer, but, like Samuel, she does not herself lead Israel in battle. Both places mentioned in connection with her in verse 5 (Ramah and Bethel) later come to be associated with Samuel (1 Sam. 7:15-17). In many ways, therefore, Deborah's "judging" of Israel anticipates that of Samuel; she is a kind of female counterpart of the Samuel who is to come.

There is also a sense in which she was like Moses. It is unlikely that every single issue requiring settlement was brought to her. In fact, the book of Ruth shows us otherwise; community elders played a significant role in settling matters of a more routine kind at the local level (Ruth 4:1-12). As with Moses, Deborah probably acted as a final court of appeal for the settlement of more difficult issues (Exod. 18:24-26). So her activity in judging Israel has noble precedent; but the doing of it by a woman is extraordinary. In one sense, therefore, we might say that Deborah's exercise of judgeship was an indication of how irregular things became in the judges period. But there is no hint in the narrative or elsewhere in Scripture that her exercise of such a role was contrary to God's purposes, or a breach of his declared will in the way that the irregular worship practices of the period were. On the contrary, as we will see in the song of chapter 5, Deborah's arising as "a mother in Israel" brought stability and good order to what was previously a chaotic situation (5:6-9). In this sense, too, she "saves" Israel, just as Tola will do in 10:1 after the mayhem caused by Abimelech. For all that, however, the story is centered much more on Barak and Jael than on Deborah. After setting the plot in motion, so to speak, Deborah takes a back seat, coming forward only once (in v. 14), to spur Barak on at a critical moment.

5 This verse takes us on from the bald statement in verse 4 that Deborah was judging Israel, to a description of how she used to do it. The picture of Deborah "sitting" *(yôšebet)* under her palm tree may strike us as quaint, but it is hardly meant to be a caricature of her as a kind of lightweight, comical figure. It is somewhat like the picture we have in 1 Samuel 14:2, of Saul, Israel's first king "sitting" *(yôšēb)* on the outskirts of Gibeah, under a pomegranate tree, holding a council of war with six hundred of his men. It was how Saul ruled in the unsettled situation before the establishment of a proper royal court in Jerusalem under David. Similarly, here in Judges 4, Deborah's "sitting" is probably meant to be understood in the formal sense of presiding, in her case as a judge. And the location is appropriate for at least two reasons. First, its centrality. In terms of the distribution of the tribes from north to south, *Mount Ephraim,* the central hill country, was a logical place for an all-Israel leader to be based. Second, it provided an implied connection

25. See 1 Sam. 7:15-17.

between the present Israel and its patriarchal past. Deborah's palm was *between Ramah and Bethel;* in other words, just south of Bethel.[26] This means that it was very close to the spot where another Deborah had been buried: Deborah, Rebekah's nurse, who was laid to rest under "the oak south of Bethel" (Gen. 35:8 HCSB).[27] The present Deborah does not displace Rebekah's Deborah by commandeering her tree,[28] but locates herself close to her, also under a tree (in this case a *palm*) that would henceforth always be associated with her. We can only guess why she chose a palm tree, but given the association of palms with the fertile Jordan Valley in 1:16 and 3:13, and with oases in the story of Israel's epic journey through the wilderness (e.g., Exod. 15:27; Num. 33:9), the palm may have symbolized the fruitfulness and blessing that Israel longed for, or it may have just been suitable for any of a hundred other reasons. In any case, the picture of Deborah under her palm tree became a sign of hope for Israel in an otherwise bleak and threatening environment. That's why *the Israelites went up to her for judgment.*

6-7 However, in the circumstances that had arisen Israel needed more help than Deborah's own kind of judging could provide. So she sets the story in motion by sending for Barak and commissioning him as the divinely chosen deliverer — the man for the hour. *Barak* means "lightning," which, intentionally or not, was a very suitable name for a warrior in the Canaanite environment in which Israel found itself. In Canaanite mythology Baal was pictured as riding on the storm clouds, wielding a club (thunder) in one hand and a spear (lightning) in the other, doing battle with Yam, the chaos monster of the sea.[29] It was quite a name for Barak to live up to. The comparison with Baal is interesting in view of the fact that Yahweh, in whose name Barak is commissioned here, is described in storm imagery in the song that follows (5:4-5), where what turns the tide in the battle with Sisera is a divinely sent cloudburst that turns the Kishon into a torrent that sweeps the enemy away (5:19-21). Barak's destiny is to be the agent of Yahweh, the true "rider on the clouds" (Ps. 68:4). More mundanely, Barak is the *son of Abinoam* ("father of pleasantness"),[30] which has no particular significance except that it contrasts nicely with Barak's own name, suggesting that his background has not prepared him for being a warrior. Barak will need divine aid, which is exactly what Deborah promises he will be given (v. 7).

The fact that Deborah is able to summon Barak from *Kedesh-naphtali*

---

26. Ramah is just 5 mi. (8 km.) south-southwest of Bethel.

27. Cf. the same geographical use of *mittaḥat lᵉ* (south of) in 1 Kgs. 4:12 and 1 Sam. 7:11.

28. The actual tree would in any case be long dead, I presume.

29. *ANET,* pp. 130-31.

30. Or, "my father is pleasantness"; cf. the name Naomi (pleasant), the opposite of Mara (bitter) in Ruth 1:20.

is an indication of the extent of her authority, for the town in question is some 17 miles (27 km.) north of the Sea of Galilee, at the extreme northern limits of Israelite settlement. It is called Kedesh-naphtali here to distinguish it from Kadesh-barnea in the extreme south. It also (incidentally) lets us know that Barak is from the tribe of Naphtali. But Deborah addresses him in the name of "*Yahweh, the God of Israel*," indicating both the source of her authority and the scale of the battle that is looming. While the northern tribes such as Naphtali are the most directly affected, the security and survival of Israel as a whole are at stake in the war Barak is to engage in. He is to begin by recruiting a force of 10,000 men[31] from Naphtali and its southern neighbor Zebulun, and *draw* (them) toward *Mount Tabor,* which is on the Naphtali-Issachar border at the head of a valley leading down into the contested Jezreel Plain. This will (by implication) draw Issachar into the war zone, and position Barak and his men well for an engagement at the River Kishon, just 9 miles (14.5 km.) to the southwest. He is promised that, at the same time, Yahweh will *draw* (same word) *Sisera,* with his chariotry and infantry, into a place at the Kishon that will give Barak and his men maximum tactical advantage, and *give them* into Barak's hand. So the battle plan has already been worked out, and Barak is assured of victory if he will do exactly as Yahweh has *commanded* him through Deborah (v. 6). As in the battle of Jericho, the real commander of Yahweh's army (in this case Barak's men) is Yahweh himself; Barak is just his deputy.[32]

8-9 Barak's equivocation in these verses is critical for the portrayal of his character and for the way the plot develops from here on. See my comments in the interpretation of the narrative as a whole given above. On *Kedesh* see v. 10.

10 The *Kedesh* of this verse can hardly be the *Kedesh-naphtali* from which Barak was called, as that is far too remote to be a feasible mustering point for Barak's men prior to the battle. It is far more likely to be the Kedesh listed as one of the towns of Issachar in 1 Chronicles 6:72, which, given Issachar's small holding, would put it in the right general vicinity.[33] Its exact location is unknown, but it is probably to be identified with Khirbet Qadisa "on the high ground west of the southern end of the Sea of Galilee," 12 miles (19 km.) from Mount Tabor.[34]

11 As indicated by the disjunctive syntax,[35] this verse does not carry the narrative forward to the next thing that happened, but gives us some nec-

---

31. Or ten "contingents" (about 250 men). See the discussion of the problem of the large numbers of the book of Judges in Section IX.C of the Introduction.

32. See Josh. 5:14.

33. See Josh. 19:17-22, where the "Kishion" of v. 20 may be another name for Kedesh (*OBA*, p. 133).

34. So Gray, *Judges,* pp. 269-71.

35. The subject first, followed by a *qatal* (perfect) verb.

essary background. The general topic it deals with, the *Kenite* clan, is not new; we have already heard something of the Kenites back in 1:16. The note about them there was teasingly brief, incidental to the central topic of that chapter, and left us in some uncertainty about what shape the relationship between the Kenites and Israel might take in the future.[36] Now the Kenites appear again, and we are given some new information about them that is critical to what follows.

What we are told here is that a splinter group from this clan, headed by someone called *Heber,* had left the main group in the south and moved north into the same area, around Kedesh, to which Barak has just come.[37] The expression *pitched his tent (wayyēṭ 'oh°lô)* drops into our consciousness the word 'tent' *('ōhel),* which prepares us for the role that a tent will soon play in the murder of Sisera (v. 17); and it will be the tent of a member of precisely this Kenite breakaway group. It is part of the careful construction of the plot, so that no distracting aside will be needed when we arrive at the tense dramatic moment which is to be the true climax of the story.

The *oak of Zaanannim* is referred to in Joshua 19:33 as a boundary marker on the edge of the tribe of Naphtali's allotment, and serves here to confirm the general location of the Kedesh (near the southern end of the Sea of Galilee) which is in view at this point in the narrative. It also (though we don't know it at this point) associates the second principal female character of the story, like the first, with a tree: Jael's oak versus Deborah's palm.

12-13 Sisera, whose intelligence gatherers have apparently been at work, hears that Barak and his men have *gone up* Mount Tabor (from Kedesh, where they had assembled in v. 10), and summons his entire force, including his *nine hundred iron chariots,* from their base in *Harosheth-haggoyim* to *the River Kishon* to confront them, not knowing, of course, that he is being "drawn" there by Yahweh (v. 7).

14-15 Deborah has accompanied Barak as she said she would (vv. 9, 10). Seeing that the first part of her prophecy has already been fulfilled, she now intervenes at the critical moment to spur Barak into action by reminding him of the promise of victory, and announcing that Yahweh has already *gone out before* him (a technical expression for military leadership). This time Barak does not hesitate, but immediately issues a lightning (!) strike[38] before Sisera's forces can get properly set.

---

36. See the comments on 1:16.

37. Gray (*Judges,* p. 218) has suggested that this Kedesh is different from that in v. 9, and is Abu Kudeis, on the edge of the Jezreel/Esdraelon Plain between Megiddo and Taanach. The occurrence of the name *Kedesh* in successive verses (10 and 11) without qualification makes it unlikely that they are different places; but even if Gray is right, Heber's family have still moved into the general area where the battle will take place.

38. I owe this pun to Lindars, *Judges 1–5,* p. 194.

The result is a rout, due in part perhaps to the fact that they have been taken by surprise. But this will hardly do as the real explanation, since Sisera already knew that Barak's forces were waiting for him; he just didn't expect an attack so soon. The only explanation that the text gives us, however, is theological: *Yahweh threw [them] into disarray* (as in holy war) before Barak's men (v. 15), concrete evidence that, as Deborah had said, he had already *gone out before* them (v. 14). There is more to it than this, however, as the song in the next chapter will reveal. Yahweh rendered Sisera's impressive chariots useless by unleashing a great storm upon them (5:20-21). It is a repeat, in essence, of the overthrow of Pharaoh's chariots and riders in the Red Sea (Exod. 5:4-5). But there is an important difference here that will give this story its very distinctive quality: *Sisera got down from his chariot and fled on foot.*

16-17 Apparently unaware of this complication, Barak *had pursued the chariots and troops* as they tried to escape back to their base at Harosheth-haggoyim; but *Sisera had fled on foot to the tent of Jael.* The disjunctive syntax, which I have tried to capture by the double use of the English pluperfect (*had* pursued . . . *had* fled) indicates that verses 16-17, like verse 11, are an aside. They give us the background information we need to understand what is about to happen, and why. Barak, caught up in the frenzy of the rout, has run the wrong way! Barak has gone west toward Harosheth-haggoyim; but Sisera has escaped the stampede and gone in the opposite direction, toward the east, probably because he knows that the Kenites (as v. 17 now tells us) are allies of Jabin and may therefore be expected to provide sanctuary for him. Barak went west, which has temporarily put him off screen. The real action with which the story is now concerned is going to happen on the trajectory Sisera is creating by his flight eastward.

18-22 With the conjunctive syntax at the beginning of verse 18[39] the main thread of the story is resumed. We are about to witness the next thing to happen, which will prove to be the real climax of the narrative. Alliteration gives Jael's invitation to Sisera an almost musical quality: *sûrâ ʾaḏōnî sûrâ ʾēlay ʾal-tîrāʾ* (*"Turn aside, my lord. Turn aside to me. Do not fear . . ."*).[40] Jael is like a siren, singing her victim aside to his destruction. Like Rahab the harlot, seeing the turn that events have taken, Jael breaks solidarity with her clan and casts in her lot with Israel. We have already noted the crucial significance of this episode in our survey of the narrative above.

23-24 With the death of Sisera the story is in effect at an end. Deborah's prediction that Yahweh would sell Sisera into the hand of a woman has been fulfilled, and with his greatest ally and his army gone, Jabin is nothing.

---

39. The *wayyiqtol* (or "converted" imperfect), *wattēṣēʾ*, "she [Jael] went out."
40. Cf. Yairah Amit, "Judges 4: Its Content and Form," *JSOT* 39 (1987): 98, n. 35.

His eventual subjugation by Israel follows as a matter of course, as the subjugation of Moab had followed the slaughter of Eglon. In that sense, verses 23-24 are anticlimactic. But they do provide a satisfying end to the story by rounding out its symmetry and providing an opportunity for one of the background notes of the book to be sounded once again. What began with Jabin's subjugation of Israel (vv. 1-2) ends with Israel's subjugation of Jabin (vv. 23-24); so equilibrium is restored. But we do not get, as we expect at this point, the statement that "the land had rest for X years." That is held over, as we've already seen, to the end of the next chapter, because the victory that has just been achieved with God's help is so significant, and the outcome so complete and satisfying, that celebration is called for — and how can that be done better than with a song, as in chapter 5?

Finally, it is surely significant that this part of the Deborah-Barak story ends by emphasizing, by threefold repetition, that it was *Jabin, king of Canaan,* whose oppressive rule had been brought to an end. One lesson that should have been engraved on Israel's national consciousness by this story in particular was that kingship, especially of the Canaanite kind, was something they should never have wanted to have. Unfortunately, however, as the Gideon-Abimelech episode will show, they were somehow still drawn to it with a kind of suicidal fascination.

2. The Song (5:1-31)

1 *Deborah and Barak son of Abinoam sang on that day:*

I

2 *"When locks fly free in Israel,*[41]
when people freely offer themselves —
bless Yahweh.

---

41. The first line of this verse is obscure, and neither of the LXX readings inspires much confidence. LXX^A's *en tō arxasthai archēgous en Israēl* ("When princes rule in Israel") takes *biprōaʿ pᵉrāʿôt* as related to Arabic *faraʾa,* "to excel, be a leader," and Ugaritic *prʿt,* "princess." LXX^B's *Apekalypthē apokalymma en Israēl* (a revelation was made in Israel) appears to take *prʿ* (unbind) in the sense of "disclose, reveal"; but this does not provide a parallel of any kind with the second line. Symmachus, apparently trying to harmonize LXX^B with the MT, reads *en tō anakalypsthē kephalas* (when heads are uncovered). For the full range of options see Lindars, *Judges 1–5,* pp. 225-27, and Niditch, *Judges,* pp. 70-71. The translation above takes *biprōaʿ pᵉrāʿôt* as derived from *prʿ,* "to unbind (hair), uncover, let loose" (BDB, p. 828). Cf. Ackerman, *Warrior, Dancer,* p. 32, n. 15, who cites the NRSV ("when locks were long in Israel"), and notes that similar translations are found in the JPSV (1917), NJPS (1985), JB (1966), and the NJB (1985). Cf. also, most recently, Gross, *Richter,* p. 291. See the exegetical comments on this verse.

3 *Listen, kings;*
pay attention, rulers;
I, even I, will sing to Yahweh,
I will make melody to the God of Israel.
4 *Yahweh, when you went forth from Seir,*
when you marched from the territory of Edom,
the earth shook, and the heavens dropped water.
5 *The mountains flowed before Yahweh,*
even Sinai before Yahweh, the God of Israel.
6 *In the days of Shamgar son of Anath,*
in the days of Jael,
the ways became impassable,[42]
and those who traversed the paths
went by the byways.
7 *The villagers*[43] *had their life interrupted;*
they ceased their activities in Israel
until I,[44] *Deborah, arose,*
arose a mother in Israel.
8 *Israel chose new gods;*[45]

---

42. Or, "caravans ceased," reading *'ōreḥôt* (caravans) instead of *'ᵒrāhôt* (ways, paths). See the *BHS* apparatus.

43. *pᵉrāzôn*, which occurs again in v. 11, is a rare word whose meaning is uncertain. A full account of the various views and their respective merits is given in Lindars, *Judges 1–5*, pp. 237-38. Here in v. 7 it is the subject of a plural verb, and therefore is evidently a collective singular. Lawrence E. Stager, "Archaeology, Ecology and Social History: Background Themes to the Song of Deborah," in *Congress Volume, Jerusalem, 1986*, ed. J. A. Emerton (Leiden: Brill, 1988), p. 225, argues that *pᵉrāzôn* is related to the *pᵉrāzôt* (unwalled villages) of Ezek. 38:11. Lindars finally opts for "villagers," citing Stager's study.

44. The end of the perfect verb form *šaqqamtî* is ambiguous, and could be an archaic second feminine, "until *you* arose." See C. L. Seow, *A Grammar for Biblical Hebrew: Revised Edition* (Nashville: Abingdon, 1995), p. 145. The LXX has the third person, *exanestē*. For a very full discussion of the issues see Charles L. Echols, *"Tell Me, O Muse": The Song of Deborah (Judges 5) in the Light of Heroic Poetry,* Library of Hebrew Bible/ Old Testament Studies 487 (Edinburgh and New York: T&T Clark, 2008), pp. 204-6. Echols himself favors reading the ending as second feminine singular. However, given the fact that Deborah is said to be one of the singers in 5:1, there is nothing unexpected about a first person verb here, and recourse to reading the ending in a way that is rare in biblical Hebrew is unwarranted. References to Deborah in the second and third person in vv. 12 and 15 respectively are also understandable, given that Deborah is not the *only* singer.

45. Verse 8 is obscure (possibly corrupt), and no solution is without problems. With most English versions I take the verb *yibhar* to be a *yaqtul* (preterite), with "Israel," from the previous verse, as its subject. For a discussion of all the textual difficulties and translation possibilities see Lindars, *Judges 1–5*, pp. 239-41.

then war[46] was at the gates;
a shield (if one were seen) and a spear
among forty thousand in Israel.

II

9 *"My heart is for the commanders of Israel,*
   for the volunteers among the people.
   Bless Yahweh!
10 *You who ride on white donkeys,*
   who sit on saddles of carpet,
   who walk on the way — consider.
11 *Louder than the noise of those who divide the spoil*
   between the watering troughs —
   there let them recount the righteous deeds of Yahweh,
   the righteous deeds of the villagers in Israel.
   Then they went down to the gates — the people of Yahweh.
12 *Awake, awake, Deborah!*
   Awake, awake, utter a song!
   Arise, Barak, take captive your captives,
   son of Abinoam.
13 *Then the survivors went down to the nobles;*
   the people of Yahweh went down for me against the mighty.

III

14 *"Some [went down][47] from Ephraim,*
   whose root was in Amalek.[48]
   After him,[49] Benjamin was among his[50] people;
   from Machir went down commanders,[51]

---

46. Taking *lāhem*, which occurs only here, as equivalent to *milḥāmâ*.

47. Assuming that the implied verb is the one used in the second half of the verse, and in v. 13.

48. The MT's *šārᵉsām baʿᵃmāleq* is puzzling, and is widely regarded as corrupt. Various emendations have been proposed (see Lindars, *Judges 1–5*, pp. 252-53). However, there is no scholarly consensus, and none of the proposals has strong textual or versional support. For the possible significance of the expression as it stands see the exegetical comments on v. 14.

49. That is, "after Ephraim," reading *'aḥᵃrāyw* as recommended in the *BHS* apparatus.

50. That is, "among *Yahweh's* people," reading *baʿᵃmāmāyw* with *BHS*, instead of the MT's *baʿᵃmāmêka* (among *your* people).

51. Taking *mᵉḥōqᵉqîm* (legislators) in a military sense (Boling, *Judges*, p. 103).

and from Zebulun those who hold the ruler's staff.[52]

15 *The captains*[53] *in Issachar were with Deborah,*
and Issachar, true to Barak,
into the valley was sent at his heels.
Among the divisions of Reuben
great were the deliberations[54] *of heart.*

16 *Why did you remain among the sheepfolds*
to hear the bleating of the flocks?
As for the divisions of Reuben —
great were the searchings[55] *of heart.*

17 *Gilead remained beyond the Jordan,*
and Dan — why did he stay with the ships?
Asher dwelt on the seacoast,
and on its beachheads he remained.

18 *Zebulun were a people who despised their lives enough to die,*
and Naphtali were upon the heights of the field.

IV

19 *"Then came kings, they fought;*
then fought the kings of Canaan.
At Taanach, by the waters of Megiddo,
plundered silver they did not take.

20 *From heaven fought the stars,*
from their courses they fought with Sisera.

21 *The River Kishon swept them away;*
march on, my soul, with strength!

22 *Then beat the horses' hooves,*
from the galloping, galloping of his stallions.[56]

---

52. With Boling I take *sōpēr* as related to Akkadian *šapāru*, "to rule." Cf. Matitiahu Tsevat, "Some Biblical Notes," *HUCA* 24 (1952-53): 107 (cited by Boling).

53. Reading *wᵉśārê*, with *BHS* and the versions, instead of MT's *wᵉśāray*.

54. *BHS* suggests reading *ḥiqrê* (searchings), as in v. 16b, instead of MT's *ḥiqᵉqê* (literally, "statutes"). But this is not the only difference between vv. 15b and 16b, suggesting that the variation is deliberate. MT should be retained as the harder reading. Cf. Gross, *Richter*, p. 292.

55. It is possible (as suggested by *BHS*) that v. 16b originated through an accidental duplication of v. 15b. But if so, it must have replaced what was already there, since the preceding expression, *As for the divisions of Reuben,* needs something to complete it. Furthermore the "duplication" is not exact *(liplaggôt rᵉʾûbēn* instead of *biplaggôt rᵉʾûbēn,* and *ḥiqrē-lēb* instead of *ḥiqᵉqê-lēb),* suggesting that something other than accidental duplication is involved. See the exegetical comments.

56. Literally, "his mighty ones/warriors *(ʾabbîrāyw).*" But cf. Jer. 8:16, where *ʾabbîrāyw* is parallel to *sûsāyw* (his horses).

23 *'Curse Meroz,' says*[57] *the messenger of Yahweh,*
 curse indeed its inhabitants,
 for they did not come to the help of Yahweh,
 to the help of Yahweh against the mighty.

V

24 *"Most blessed among women is Jael,*
 the wife of Heber the Kenite;
 of tent-dwelling women most blessed.

25 *He asked for water, she gave him milk;*
 in a lordly bowl she brought him curds.

26 *Her hand reached for the tent peg,*
 her right hand for the workman's hammer.
 She struck Sisera, she smote his head,
 she shattered, she pierced his temple.

27 *Between her feet he sank, he fell, he lay;*[58]
 where he sank, there he fell — destroyed.

28 *Through the window she looked, she cried out —*
 The mother of Sisera — through the lattice:
 'Why has his chariot been so long coming?
 Why have the hoofbeats of his chariots tarried?'

29 *Her wisest princesses answer;*
 indeed, she keeps saying to herself,

30 *'Aren't they locating and sharing out the spoils —*
 a woman or two[59] *for each of the leading men?*
 Spoil of dyed garments for Sisera,
 spoil of dyed garments, variously colored,
 dyed cloth, with colored embroidery on both sides,
 suitable for the necks of queens?'[60]

31a *Thus may all your enemies perish, Yahweh,*

---

57. Taking the verb *'āmar* as a perfect of "instantaneous occurrence" (Seow, *Biblical Hebrew*, p. 148) as in the prophetic messenger formula, "Thus says (*'āmar*) Yahweh." Cf. *kî yā'aṣṭî*, "So I *advise* you" (2 Sam. 17:11).

58. Omitting the repeated words, *bên raglêhā kāra' nāpāl*, as a dittography.

59. Literally, "a womb or two."

60. Reading *šēgāl* (queen), as a collective (queens) instead of *šālāl* (plunder); cf. *BHS*. The mistaken writing of *šālāl* as *šēgāl* is understandable in view of the similarity of the two words in the consonantal text, and the threefold use of *šālāl* in the preceding lines. For other possible emendments see Lindars, *Judges 1–5*, p. 286, and Boling, *Judges*, p. 115.

*but may those who love you[61] be like the sun
going forth in its strength."*

31b *Then the land had rest for forty years.*

In the book of Judges as we have it, the song of chapter 5 appears as *part* of the Deborah-Barak narrative. The *bayyôm hahû' (on that day)* of 5:1 picks up the *bayyôm hahû'* of 4:23, locating the performance of the song in the immediate aftermath of the victory which it celebrates (cf. Exod. 15:1). As we have already noted, the prose narrative of chapter 4 is not formally concluded until the song is complete (see 5:31b and cf. 3:11, 30).

Furthermore, the song assumes the reader's familiarity with the events which have just been narrated. The well-known facts are alluded to obliquely rather than presented in detail. Deborah is cryptically referred to as *a mother in Israel* (5:7; cf. 4:4-6); Sisera first appears, without explanation, in 5:20 (cf. 4:2-3), and so on. At other points, however, the song takes up elements from the story and elaborates them, giving them a dramatic force they lack in chapter 4. For example, Deborah's brief rhetorical question in 4:14, "Hasn't Yahweh *gone out (yṣ')* before you?" finds its counterpart here in the majestic picture of Yahweh *going out (yṣ')* from Seir as the divine warrior (vv. 4-5),[62] and the summary treatment of the battle in 4:15 finds its poetic parallel in the dramatic episode of 5:19-22: kings–stars–river–pounding hooves. One episode, Sisera's mother waiting in vain (5:28-30), has no antecedent at all in the preceding narrative, but greatly enhances the effectiveness of the song, as we shall see.

a. The Structure of the Song

Many attempts have been made to find a clear metrical and/or strophic pattern in the song,[63] but the task has proven to be a very difficult one. The diffi-

---

61. Reading, with *BHS*, Syriac, Vulgate, and some Hebrew MSS, *'ōhᵃḇêḵā* (those who love you) instead of MT's *'ōhᵃḇāyw* (those who love him), as seems to be required by the context.

62. Cf. Blenkinsopp, "Ballad Style and Psalm Style," p. 64, who thinks that Deborah's call to battle in 4:14 "may have provided grounds for a revisor to fill out and transpose into a more explicitly religious key the accompanying ballad."

63. For a recent review of the various attempts at analysis into stanzas see Echols, *"Tell Me, O Muse,"* pp. 70-72. Echols himself does not find any of them compelling. Blenkinsopp, "Ballad Style and Psalm Style," and Barnabas Lindars, "Deborah's Song: Women in the Old Testament," *BJRL* 65, no. 2 (1983): 158-75, both believe that an original war ballad has been adapted for liturgical use by the addition of hymnic elements which have obscured its clear stanzaic structure. The hymnic elements are identified and set aside to prepare the way for a literary analysis of the "original" ballad.

culty arises partly because the composition is of mixed genre (part ballad, part hymn),[64] partly because the text is obscure at many points (perhaps due, in part at least, to disturbance suffered in transmission), and partly because the mode of composition of such early Hebrew verse is still not sufficiently well understood.

In what is arguably the most thorough stylistic and structural analysis of the song in its finished form so far produced, M. D. Coogan[65] has discerned five stanzas, the first and last being divided into two strophes each, as follows:

$$
\begin{array}{lll}
\text{I} & \left[\begin{array}{l} \text{A} \\ \text{B} \end{array}\right. & \begin{array}{l} \text{vv. 2-5} \\ \text{vv. 6-8} \end{array} \\
\text{II} & & \text{vv. 9-13} \\
\text{III} & & \text{vv. 14-18} \\
\text{IV} & & \text{vv. 19-23} \\
\text{V} & \left[\begin{array}{l} \text{A} \\ \text{B} \end{array}\right. & \begin{array}{l} \text{vv. 24-27} \\ \text{vv. 28-30} \end{array}
\end{array}
$$

This analysis does not quite cover the song in its final form since Coogan follows J. M. Myers, W. Richter, and others in dismissing verse 31 from consideration on the grounds that it is "a liturgical gloss and hence not part of the original song."[66] Criteria used to identify the limits of the stanzas include shifts in subject and, in some cases, in meter as well, boundary-marking inclusions, and extended compositional patterns which are repeated. We will not repeat the details here.

In most cases the shifts of episode or subject matter between strophes or stanzas are clear. This is especially so in the second half of the song where III deals with the varying responses of the tribes, IV with the battle, VA with the murder of Sisera by Jael, and VB with Sisera's mother waiting in vain for her son's return. In the first stanza the first strophe (vv. 2-5) is more heteroge-

---

64. See the previous note. But contrast A. Globe, "The Literary Structure and Unity of the Song of Deborah," *JBL* 93, no. 4 (1974): 493-512, who argues that ancient Near Eastern practice in the second millennium suggests that this "mixture" of styles was in fact the rule, not the exception, and that the song in substantially its present form is from about 1200 B.C.

65. "A Structural and Literary Analysis of the Song of Deborah," *CBQ* 40, no. 2 (1978): 143-66. For a critique, see Echols, *"Tell Me, O Muse,"* pp. 70-71.

66. Page 144, n. 4. This is the only point at which Googan shows any interest in the original as distinct from the final form of the song. Did the verse prove an embarrassment to his neat stanzaic analysis?

neous in content than Coogan appears to recognize. It consists of a prelude to the song in two parts (vv. 2 and 3 respectively) and a section that deals with the coming of Yahweh as divine warrior (vv. 4-5). Stanza II is the part of the song with the most semantic and textual uncertainties and (the evidence adduced by Coogan notwithstanding)[67] would scarcely be identifiable as a stanza were it not for the fact that it is of similar length to stanzas already identified, and is preceded and followed by units that are clearly distinct from it. Its content is perhaps best summed up as a call to participate in the battle.[68] The response of the tribes follows in Stanza III, as we have noted.

The table on page 202 correlates my own content analysis of the song with Coogan's formal (stanzaic) analysis.

b. The Thematic Development of the Song

As well as being obviously different in genre, it is clear that, while the same basic subject is covered in the song as in the preceding narrative (how Israel was

---

67. Coogan (pp. 152-53) points to an inclusive (framing) use of *'ām* (people) in vv. 9 and 13, and to a similarity of compositional structure between vv. 9-13 and vv. 2-8 (Stanza I). But *'ām* is a very common word, occurring elsewhere in the song in vv. 2, 11, 14, and 18, and the parallel structure to which he points is not at all obvious and, by his own admission, "not entirely symmetrical."

68. Not literally, of course, since the battle itself is past; it is being relived imaginatively in the song. The singing of the song is a liturgical reenactment of the battle and the events associated with it. As noted by Ackerman, "Prophecy and Warfare," p. 9, some scholars (e.g., Burney, Weiser, Boling) "interpret [this] verse as calls to Deborah and Barak to begin the victory celebration — to strike up the victory song and to parade those taken captive. Verses 13-18 then follow, describing the victory march of the tribes, with flashbacks concerning their behavior in battle." Ackerman herself (p. 10) argues that v. 12 recalls an oracular song (promising victory) that Deborah sang on the day of the battle itself. The speaker, as in v. 23, is the *mal'ak Yahweh* (messenger of Yahweh). A thoroughgoing liturgical interpretation was proposed by A. Weiser in "Das Deboralied: Eine gattungs- und traditionsgeschichtliche Studie," *ZAW* 71, nos. 1-4 (1959): 67-97, in which he argued that the song was composed for a cultic ceremony at a later date. In this way he was able to explain why it mentions many tribes who are not referred to in chapter 4 in connection with the battle itself. But the fact that the list of tribes in 5:14-18 does not correspond to later lists of the twelve tribes (as, e.g., in Ezek. 48 and 1 Chron. 2–7) strongly favors the traditional view that it refers to those who actually took part in the battle or failed to do so, and this certainly is the sense required by the present literary context. The difference from chapter 4 must remain an anomaly or be explained in some other way, as, e.g., by Ackerman (p. 7): "Why are only the northern tribes mentioned in the summons to Barak? Because the tribes south of the Esdraelon [Jezreel] valley, among whom Deborah now lived, apparently respected her authority and were ready for battle (cf. Judg. 5:14). The problem was in mustering the tribes north of the Esdraelon, and Barak was commanded to do that."

Content		Stanzas
A Prelude to the song		
(1) Preliminary ascriptions of praise to Yahweh for what is about to be recounted	v. 2	
(2) A call to hear the song	v. 3	IA
B The coming of Yahweh the divine warrior	vv. 4-5	
C Conditions prevailing before the battle	vv. 6-8	IB
D A call to participate in the battle	vv. 9-13	II
E The response of the tribes	vv. 14-18	III
F The battle itself	vv. 19-23	IV
G The death of Sisera	vv. 24-27	VA
H His mother waits in vain	vv. 28-30	VB
I Concluding invocation of Yahweh	v. 31a	

freed from the predicament described in 4:1-3), it has been handled quite differently. After the preliminaries in verses 2-3, the focus falls, not on Deborah, but on Yahweh, who comes on the scene from the south with terrible majesty as Israel's champion. The preliminaries have in fact prepared the way for his advent in this capacity by drawing attention very pointedly to the special bond between *Yahweh* and *Israel.* These keywords occur as follows in vv. 2-3:

> v. 2   Israel — Yahweh
> v. 3a   Yahweh
> v. 3b   Yahweh — Israel

Both A (vv. 2-3) and B (vv. 4-5) end with the same words: "Yahweh, the God of Israel."[69] In the prose narrative Yahweh's "going forth" to fight for Israel

---

69. M. Buber, *The Prophetic Faith* (New York: Harper and Row, 1960), p. 9, called attention to the repetition of "Israel" and "Yahweh" in the entire poem. "Israel" occurs eight times, all in Stanzas I (six times) and II (twice). At the end of v. 8 and the beginning of v. 9 it is used as a catchword to link these two stanzas together. "Yahweh" occurs ten times in Stanzas I and II, but only three times in the rest of the song (Coogan, "The Song of Deborah," p. 156). Cf. Blenkinsopp, "Ballad Style and Psalm Style," p. 76.

occurs on the day of battle, well into the narrative (4:14); here in the song it is given special prominence by being placed, out of chronological sequence, at the very outset. The time-shift that follows in verse 6a takes us back to the situation before the advent of Deborah, and from there developments are traced up to the battle itself, which occurs in its proper chronological position at verses 19-23. But well before the battle, verses 4-5 already focus our attention on Yahweh, whose *righteous deeds (ṣidqôt)*[70] are to be the chief burden of the song (v. 11). Furthermore, the storm imagery used in the theophany of verses 4-5 prepares the way for the participation of cosmic elements in the song's description of the battle in verses 19-21.[71]

The advent of Yahweh is paralleled, in the second strophe of the first stanza, by the advent of Deborah, implicitly drawing a parallel between the two: the power of Yahweh, mythically described in the theophany, is historically revealed, first of all, in the arising of Deborah as *a mother in Israel.*[72] Here are the seeds of a potentially fruitful thematic development, but strangely, in view of the preceding narrative, this parallel between the action of Yahweh and the activity of a woman remains muted. Little is said about Deborah in chapter 5, as we have already observed. There is no mention of her summons to Barak, or his dialogue with her, or any reference to the prediction, so central to the narrative of chapter 4, that Yahweh will sell Sisera into the hand of a woman.

In the next stanza[73] Deborah appears in the company of Barak (Deborah sings while Barak leads the troops into battle, v. 11), but the dramatic interest remains centered on the forthcoming battle itself, not the role that a woman will play in it. The third stanza, with its list of tribes, builds up expectancy that there is to be a truly great battle, such as the theophany of verses 4-5 foreshadowed.[74] At the same time it reveals a lack of unity among the tribes — an issue that will assume growing importance in the remainder of the book (see 8:1-3; 12:1-6; 15:9-13, the Samson episode in general, and, climactically, the civil war of ch. 20). Verse 18, dealing with Zebulun and Naphtali *(people who despised their lives enough to die . . . upon the heights of the field)* provides the transition to the battle, and inci-

---

70. Or "victories" (so NEB; Boling, *Judges,* p. 102); cf. Soggin, *Judges,* p. 82 ("glorious achievements"), and see the discussion of the word in Gray, *Joshua, Judges, and Ruth,* p. 283.

71. Cf. Coogan, "The Song of Deborah," p. 161.

72. Cf. Coogan, "The Song of Deborah," p. 154.

73. The second stanza opens with an exclamation of praise which is practically the same in form and content to that which opened the first (cf. v. 9 with v. 2). Cf. Blenkinsopp, "Ballad Style and Psalm Style," p. 66.

74. Cf. Lindars, "Deborah's Song," pp. 169-70. A similar effect is produced on a much larger scale by the long review of the troops in bk. 2 of Homer's *Iliad.*

dentally confirms that these were the tribes most directly concerned, as in the prose narrative.[75]

The description of the battle in the fourth stanza fully realizes the expectations built up in the preceding ones.[76] The opening two lines, with their climactic parallelism *(kings . . . the kings of Canaan),*[77] impress on us the scale of the conflict. The fighting itself takes on cosmic dimensions: the stars fight from the heavens, and on earth the River Kishon responds by becoming a torrent and overwhelming the enemy.[78] The description of the battle ends with the pounding *dahᵃrôṯ dahᵃrôṯ (galloping, galloping)* of the horse hooves of the defeated chariotry trying to escape.[79] The style is impressionistic and allusive. We are left to conclude that the stars have acted under Yahweh's orders, and that their action took the form of a colossal storm;[80] but we have been prepared for this by the storm imagery of verses 4-5, as we noted earlier. The human element in the victory is so completely eclipsed by the intervention of the heavenly powers that Barak and his forces are not even mentioned in the description of the battle!

But there is one heroic deed on the human plane which, even in this context, cannot be overlooked. The cursing of Meroz[81] in verse 23 serves as a foil to what immediately follows (the first strophe of the last stanza) in which Jael, by contrast, is blessed (v. 24).[82] The killing of Sisera is dwelt upon with savage delight, as in the prose narrative, and here the vividness of style, if anything, surpasses that of the previous account. But this time Barak makes no appearance. Unlike the corresponding episode in chapter 4, this one is not concerned with how the honor of slaying the enemy leader was taken away from Barak and given to a woman, but solely with the fate that Sisera suf-

---

75. Cf. Lindars, "Deborah's Song," p. 170. Zebulun has also been mentioned in v. 14, a further indication of the limits of the stanza. For the *heights* on the field of battle that gave strategic value, see Boling, *Judges,* p. 113.

76. Cf. Lindars, "Deborah's Song," p. 170.

77. Probably a reference to Sisera and his allies, the local kings of the neighboring city-states (Gray, *Judges,* p. 289). Kings as such are not mentioned in the description of the battle in the prose narrative (4:14-16), but Sisera is linked with Canaanite kingship as general of "Jabin, king of Canaan."

78. Cf. Exod. 15:3-11.

79. Cf. Blenkinsopp, "Ballad Style and Psalm Style," p. 73.

80. Cf. Lindars, "Deborah's Song," p. 170. The stars are considered the source of rain in Canaanite mythology, as noted by Blenkinsopp in "Ballad Style and Psalm Style," p. 73, citing *'Anat* 2.41.

81. A town whose location is unknown but which was presumably close enough to the Jezreel Valley to have been expected to respond to Barak's summons. See Block, *Judges,* p. 238.

82. Cf. "Deborah's Song," p. 171. Unlike the inhabitants of Meroz, Jael *did* "come to the help of Yahweh against the mighty" (v. 23).

fered. Nothing is allowed to distract our attention from the spectacle with which the episode concludes: Sisera lying *destroyed (šādûd)* at the feet of Jael (v. 27). To die thus at the hand of a woman is the ultimate humiliation; Abimelech will later commit suicide rather than be exposed to the shame of it (9:54)! Jael is *most blessed among women* for her part in bringing Sisera to such an end. This strophe completes the action that was begun in the battle, but since there is no oracle carrying us forward to it and no mystery to be solved, it does not have the same quality of dénouement as the corresponding episode in the prose narrative.

In the second strophe of this last stanza the scene changes from Jael's tent to Sisera's stately home, where his mother watches anxiously from the window. The inaction (waiting) of this episode is the counterpoint of the action (murder) of the previous one. The tone is subdued. The waiting mother's two questions "convey with wonderful psychological insight her state of nervousness and impatience,"[83] and the answers given by her maids without any real conviction only thinly veil an unspoken dread. *We* know that Sisera will never return. The bereaved mother-figure, the psychological realism, and the heavy irony are powerful generators of pathos.[84] Nevertheless, it is clear that the author finds the episode deeply satisfying, and that this is meant to be our response to it also, as the final invocation of verse 31a confirms: *Thus may all your enemies perish, Yahweh!* This second strophe, like the first, shows how completely Yahweh's enemies have been undone. It also heightens the joy of victory by showing the fate that the Israelites, especially their women, would have suffered if Sisera had won (v. 30); and it effects an artistic closure to the whole song by providing, in the mother of Sisera, a negative counterpart to Deborah, the mother in Israel.

c. Conclusions

Unlike the narrative of chapter 4, the song is not concerned with how Yahweh took the honor of victory away from Barak and gave it to a woman. It pays tribute to those individuals and tribes who "came to the help of Yahweh," and rebukes those who did not. But its chief burden is "the righteous deeds of Yahweh" himself, who went forth as Israel's champion and

83. Blenkinsopp, "Ballad Style and Psalm Style," p. 75.
84. Both Coogan and Lindars refer to the equally ironical ending of the ballad of *Sir Patrick Spens:*

> O lang, lang may the ladies stand
> Wi thair gold kems in thair hair
> Waiting for thair ain dier lords,
> For they'll se thame na mair.

overwhelmed the enemy by unleashing the powers of heaven against them. The climax of the song is the battle itself, and the two strophes in the final stanza show how completely the enemy was defeated.[85] Only when the song is completed is the entire Deborah-Barak episode closed with the now familiar formula of rest for the land (v. 31b).

So the Deborah-Barak story as we have it in these two chapters concludes with a victory hymn in praise of Yahweh and his loyal supporters, but especially of Yahweh himself. The Gideon episode which immediately follows will end very differently — a striking example of the progressive decline outlined programmatically in 2:11-19. At the beginning of the Gideon episode Yahweh will have to dispatch a prophet to remind the Israelites, so soon apostate again, of his many interventions on their behalf (6:8-9).

1 As we have seen, this verse links the song to the preceding story. It identifies the singers as *Deborah* and *Barak,* so the voices we hear in the song will be theirs unless we discover strong evidence of other voices (such as a chorus, e.g., as in a Greek drama, or of the Israelites following the lead of the two principal singers and joining in as well). The circumstances in which the song is sung and the way it is introduced are both markedly reminiscent of the Exodus 15 — the song that was sung by "Moses and the Israelites" after being rescued by divine intervention from the vastly superior forces of the Pharaoh with his horse-drawn chariots (Exod. 15:1). The *day* which gives rise to the song is a day of salvation, like the day of the crossing of the Red Sea — a reminder that there is both a foundational, "once-for-all-ness" about God's saving of his people and an ongoing "here-and-now-ness." The God who saved Israel from Egypt went on saving them. The salvation we participate in under the new covenant has the same double aspect.[86]

2 The general theme of this verse is clear, namely, the willingness of people to offer themselves, in this case for battle. When this happens, as here, it is a cause for celebration, and in particular for praising God,[87] because it is evidence of the powerful impact he has had on the lives of his people. The first line of the verse, however, is obscure, and has been variously understood.[88] Our best clue to its meaning lies in the frequency of parallelism in the poetry of the song in general, and its presence in the first two lines of this particular verse. Both lines begin with the same construction: the preposition b^e joined directly with the infinitive of a verb — a normal construction for a temporal

---

85. Cf. the similar conclusion reached by Lindars in "Deborah's Song," esp. pp. 160 and 175. But Lindars' observations are made with reference to the hypothetical original (ballad) form of the song, not its finished form.

86. Eph. 2:5; 1 Cor. 1:18; 2 Cor. 2:15.

87. "Blessing" *(brk)* is synonymous with "praising" *(hll)* when it is done by a lesser person to a greater (Block, *Judges,* p. 221).

88. See the notes to the translation.

(time) clause in Hebrew, followed by a noun specifying the doer of the action. In the second line it is *'ām*, "people," who offer themselves freely. The two lines converge in the final phrase, *b^eyiśrā'ēl*, "in Israel," which qualifies both of them. So in terms of how the verse is constructed, *biprōa'* in the first line, whatever it means, is likely to be closely related in meaning to *b^ehitnaddēḇ* (offer themselves freely), and *p^erā'ôt* (the doer of the action) is likely to be closely related in meaning to *'ām* (people). In the first part of the line *p^erōa'* is the infinitive of the verb *pr'*, and *p^erā'ôt* is the plural of the corresponding noun. Unfortunately this root is not a common one, but its usage suggests that it has to do with either the unbinding, uncovering, or freeing of hair (as in Lev. 10:6; 21:10) or the freeing of people from restraint of some kind (as in Exod. 32:25). The translation most favored in the mainline English versions ("the leaders/princes took the lead," NIV, RSV, ESV) provides a neat parallel with the second line, but it does not do sufficient justice to the attested meanings of *pr'*.[89] My own translation, *When locks fly free*, takes it as an allusion to the practice (as in Samson) of allowing the hair to grow long as an outward sign of dedication to Yahweh. That is, what the second line expresses literally (the people offered themselves willingly) the first line expresses metaphorically (like Nazirites, the people voluntarily set aside their normal way of life and dedicated themselves to Yahweh to serve as warriors).[90]

3   Verse 2 ended with a call to praise Yahweh, presumably addressed by the singers (Deborah and Barak) to their fellow Israelites. This kind of call is common in the Psalter, where it appears to be a normal part of congregational worship.[91] Verse 3 follows this with an address to the leaders of the nations in general *(kings, rulers)* to learn from what Israel has just experienced. Here the language is didactic: *Listen . . . pay attention.* It is the language of a teacher addressing his or her pupils, and is commonly found in the Wisdom literature of the Old Testament, especially the book of Proverbs.[92] The first person voice, *I will sing . . . I will make melody*, is presumably that of Deborah or Barak. The verse as a whole makes the point that the joyful worship of the people of God is something that the world should take note of, for it is a witness to the worthiness of Yahweh, and a challenge to them to give him his due by joining in.

4-5   What the narrative had stated very prosaically (Yahweh "went forth" to battle before his people), these verses now describe in powerful metaphorical terms. He "marches" from Mount *Sinai* in the far south (v. 5),

---

89. It appears to rely more on the "parallel" in v. 9 than on the wording of v. 2 itself.

90. Cf. Deut. 32:42 and the discussion in Niditch, *Judges,* pp. 70-71.

91. For example, Pss. 33:2; 68:26; 105:45; 106:1, 48.

92. For example, Prov. 4:1, 10, 20; 7:24.

treading on the heights of *Seir* in the land of *Edom* as he comes (v. 4),[93] caus-ing the earth to shake, the heavens to drop their water, and the earth, too, to release its water (presumably by breaking its surface, releasing the under-ground streams) so that the mountains appear to liquefy (flow) at his pres-ence. This powerful poetry draws on the historical memory of the exodus, when Yahweh as the divine warrior manifested his presence by making wind and water change their normal behavior for the sake of his people, and Sinai, where his presence was manifested on the mountain in cloud and fire and earthquake.[94] The same kind of language is used in the Psalter either to recall God's saving works in the past (Ps. 68:7-10) or his present awesome majesty as ruler of the entire earth (Ps. 97:1-6). It would later be taken up by the prophets to speak of his final coming on the last day to judge the world (Amos 9:5-6; Isa. 2:19; Zech. 14:1-5). Here in Judges 5 it gives powerful po-etic expression to the belief that the storm which broke over Sisera and his army and threw them into panic and retreat was no merely natural event, or amazing stroke of luck; it was unleashed by Yahweh, as he had divided the Sea at the exodus and shaken Mount Sinai by descending on it. This same Yahweh had come to their rescue again.

6-7 These verses allude back to 3:31, but set *the days of Shamgar son of Anath* in a much more somber light than that short note did. They recall the situation before the victory achieved by Deborah and Barak, when the Canaanites and their allies who occupied the fortified cities in the Jezreel Val-ley were able to interrupt the flow of trade and communication between north and south, so vital for the well-being of the Israelite tribes. The *villagers* re-ferred to in verse 7,[95] isolated in the highland areas, were in particularly des-perate circumstances and apparently lacked a leader able to mobilize them ef-fectively. In the days of Shamgar son of Anath the Israelites were barely able to survive. Shamgar may have "saved" them by repelling an incursion into the (southern) highlands, but it would take more than this to free them; only a suc-cessful engagement with the enemy on the lowlands could do that, and this be-came a possibility only through the leadership eventually given by Deborah.

How Deborah *arose* (came to leadership) is not indicated.[96] The fact

---

93. *Seir* is an alternative name for *Edom.*

94. Exod. 15:3-11; 19:16-19.

95. See the note on this word in the translation.

96. Cf. the "arising" of Tola in 10:1. Ackerman (*Warrior, Dancer,* pp. 38-44) has argued that the expressions "arose," "mother in Israel," and "awake" in vv. 7 and 12 all point to Deborah as a military figure who actually led the troops into battle along with Barak, and that it is only in chapter 4, which is later, that Deborah is assigned a nonmilitary role. However this may be (and her argument from chapter 5 is quite plausible, in my judg-ment), the present form of the text requires chapter 5 to be read in the light of chapter 4, in which a clear demarcation is drawn between the roles of Deborah and Barak respectively.

that she calls on Barak to take the lead in battle makes it unlikely that she had risen to prominence in the same way that Othniel, Ehud, and Shamgar had done. Somehow she had commended herself (perhaps by her wisdom and personal resilience) as someone who could heal some of the internal conflicts and grievances that had arisen under the stressfulness of the times. Perhaps it happened slowly, without any formal recognition, that her influence spread and became more and more recognized. At any rate, it seems that Israel needed some "mothering" before it would be ready for a fight, and Deborah emerged as the person able to provide it. In the second part of verse 7, Deborah looks back to that time and boldly declares that things changed when she arose. Her reference to herself in the first person, *Until I arose . . . ,* may strike us as immodest, but, if so, there is probably no need for us to try to exonerate her; after all, why should she be wholly good while nearly everyone else in Judges is not? In any case it's possible that there is more exhilaration than boasting in her words; even she herself, looking back, is amazed at her rise, and the changes that it brought.

8   There are a number of textual uncertainties in this verse,[97] but given the translation I have made, it is both a flashback and a bridge to what follows. It recalls the root cause of Israel's problems — apostasy: *Israel chose new gods* (cf. 4:1) — and its helplessness in the face of the crisis that this eventually led to: war imminent (at the very gates of the cities), and virtually no weapons to fight with.[98] This prepares us for what is to come by hinting at the daunting prospect faced by the volunteers, and why those who chose to step forward deserved the highest praise.

9   The second stanza opens by taking up the topic of the "volunteers" directly, and making this the central focus of this part of the song. The first person voice *(My heart is for . . .)* may refer to Deborah (continuing from Stanza 1), though this cannot be known for certain. What is clear is the high esteem he/she has for the *commanders (hôqᵉqîm),*[99] who led by personal example. The *people ('ām)* are most naturally seen as a wider group, presumably men (the volunteer militia), so that the parallelism of the first two lines is not one of identity but of unity: the response of the leaders was matched by a corresponding response from the people. The exclamation of praise in the last line is the same as in verse 1, but there is an additional reason for praise here: the unity between leaders and people.

10   In its basic subject matter this verse is very similar to verse 9. Again we have two classes of people: those who *ride on white donkeys,* and

---

97. See the notes to the translation.

98. As reflected in Shamgar's use of an ox goad (3:31).

99. Literally, "[people who issue] *decrees*" or, in a military context, "[give] *commands.*" See *mᵉḥōqᵉqîm* in v. 14, and cf. *haḥōqᵉqîm* in Isa. 10:1.

those who *walk on the way.* But the categories are not quite the same: not so much leaders and people now, as the rich and "others." While the riders are clearly rich (they sit on *saddles of carpet*), it does not follow, without some corresponding but opposite detail, that those who *walk on the way* are poor; they are just "ordinary." Nor is it necessarily the case that the author of the song saw anything wrong with the opulence of the rich. But the closing exhortation, *Consider (śîḥû),* hints at something both groups might do wrong, namely, simply get on with their lives as though nothing notable has happened. In effect, it is a call to join in the song. What has happened makes it inappropriate for anyone, rich or ordinary, to merely go on riding or walking, sitting on carpeted saddles, or treading the roadways.

11   This verse presents a strikingly different picture from the preceding one. Here people are not acting as though nothing has happened. On the contrary, as they divide up the spoil between *the watering places* (traditional meeting points), they recount *the righteous deeds of Yahweh,* and of the *villagers* (common people) who participated in the battle with him. The last line, placed in quotation marks in most English versions (e.g., NIV, ESV, NRSV), is probably a quotation of what they are saying or singing. What is causing the excitement is not just, or even primarily, the spoil, but the way common people like themselves had responded *then,* when the call to battle came. The reference to *gates* here alludes back to verse 8 *(war was at the gates),* making it clear that what is in view is eagerness to engage the enemy. It could be, as Boling has suggested,[100] that the link with the previous verse is the exhortation, *Consider,* with which that verse closed. What those in verse 10 should consider is the righteous deeds of Yahweh and his people that those in verse 11 are talking about.

12   It has become clear by this point that in the literary version of the song as we have it, Deborah and Barak are not the only singers. In verse 11 we have heard others "recounting" (perhaps in song) the righteous deeds of Yahweh and his people. Now it seems that these common people address Deborah and Barak, the two principals, in antiphonal fashion, urging them on to more exuberant praise and action. Deborah is urged to strike up the song again, as though one round or part of it is complete and the next should be started by her again. Barak is urged not to stop either, but to capitalize on his victory by taking more captives. The enthusiasm of the singers seems to know no bounds.

13   The second stanza ends here with a single voice *(me),* which is most likely either Deborah or Barak since they have just been addressed. But the content of the verse strongly suggests that it is Barak. The opening *then* echoes that of verse 11 (*Then they went down to the gates*), and what follows

100. Boling, *Judges,* pp. 102, 110.

210

takes us back to that same moment, when the volunteers went down with Barak to engage the enemy (4:14). The present verse focuses on the contrast between those who went down and those they went down to face. The volunteers who went down with Barak were mere *survivors* (of the years of deprivation),[101] while those they faced as their enemies were *nobles* and *the mighty*. But (and this was the secret of their success) they were also *the people of Yahweh,* who had responded to his call and gone down with his promise (4:14). If Barak is the speaker/singer here, this is one of his finest moments, for he deflects the credit for the victory from himself and returns it to the people, and to Yahweh.

14 As the third stanza opens, the exuberant tone fades away and darker things begin to emerge. A distinction between indifference and enthusiastic participation has already been hinted at in verses 10 and 11. But now that issue is sharpened into explicit division. The roll call of those who did and did not participate begins with Ephraim, the southernmost of the northern tribes. It was in Ephraim's territory that Deborah, the initiator of the resistance, had been based before hostilities began (4:5). So we expect Ephraim to come first and receive creditable mention. What we get is a rather cryptic statement about the Ephraimites which is at best ambivalent and at worst entirely (and sarcastically) negative. The meaning depends largely on how we take the opening phrase, *minnî 'eprayim.* If the *minnî* is partitive, it could mean "*some* [a few] Ephraimites." If it is originative, what we would then have is a blanket statement: "Those who are from/of Ephraim" (i.e., the Ephraimites in general). Since, however, verses 14 and 15 in general deal with tribes that did participate, it seems best to take this opening statement as positive: "*Some [went down] from Ephraim.*" What follows, though, can hardly be anything other than negative: literally, "their root [was] in Amalek." Overall the force of the line seems to be that while volunteers did come from Ephraim, they displayed some "Amalekite" characteristics; that is, they were hostile, quarrelsome. At this stage in the book such a mixed report on the Ephraimites is very puzzling, but the negative aspect of it will be confirmed by the way the Ephraimites behave in both the Gideon and Jephthah episodes, which follow (8:1-3; 12:1).

Benjamin, Machir (a leading clan within the Transjordan Manassites),[102] and *Zebulun* all receive positive mention as participants, the last two for the way their leaders in particular came to the fray (cf. v. 9).

15a The theme of "willing leaders" continues here with a tribute to

---

101. Taking *śārîḏ* as a collective like *'ām,* with which it is parallel.

102. Machir was a grandson of Joseph and son of Manasseh (Gen. 50:23). He was the father of Gilead, the ancestor of the Gileadites of Transjordan (Num. 26:29). Gilead is assigned to Machir in Josh. 17:1-3. E. J. Young, "Machir," in *NBD,* p. 712.

the *captains*[103] in the tribe of Issachar, who were *with* Deborah. There is no necessary inference that Deborah took an active part in the battle; rather, these leaders were *with* her in the sense that they were supportive of her, responsive to her call. It is Barak who, in the next line, leads the charge into battle, with *Issachar* (both leaders and men) at his heels. The general impression is that this tribe, especially, distinguished itself by the wholehearted support it gave to Deborah and Barak — which makes the contrast with Reuben, in the second part of the verse, particularly damning. This is the point at which the tone of the poem changes.

15b-16   Now the language of unity and loyalty gives way to expressions of division and irresolution. Instead of simply *Reuben,* we have *the divisions (pᵉlaggôt)* of Reuben, and no reference to leaders. *Divisions* nicely captures both the basic meaning and the connotations of *pᵉlaggôt* in this context. With minor variations of spelling it is used elsewhere of "streams" (as distinct from rivers; Isa. 32:2; Ps. 46:5; Job 20:17), and for the various "divisions" of Levites (each group having its distinct responsibilities; 2 Chron. 35:5). Here in Judges 5:15 the usage suggests that something more like "factions" is in view. The *deliberations* among them are literally "decrees" or "statutes"; that is, rulings that this or that was the right course of action.[104] The adjective *great* indicates the intensity or earnestness of the deliberations, and what follows in verse 16 makes clear that they had to do with how to respond to Deborah and Barak's summons to battle. The near repetition of verse 15b in verse 16b, with the change from *ḥiqᵉqê (deliberations)* to *ḥiqrê (searchings),*[105] suggests that the deliberations were protracted and involved some issues of conscience. But the outcome, it seems, was negative. The Reubenite clans decided to stay at home, with the sheep (v. 16a)! The decision is understandable in view of the great difference in the proximity of the respective tribes to the place of conflict. Issachar's territory was directly adjacent to the Jezreel Valley, and it was therefore one of the tribes most directly affected. Reuben's territory, on the other hand, was in southern Transjordan, east of the northern end of the Dead Sea. In a sense it could afford to stay uninvolved in a way that Issachar could not. But that was not how Deborah and Barak and their supporters saw it! Their question, *Why?* (v. 16a) is reproachful, and expresses the disappointment and very likely the anger they felt at Reuben's behavior.

---

103. See the note on the translation.

104. See the textual note to the translation. The word is *ḥqq,* which most commonly means the ruling or decree of an authoritative figure (a judge, priest, king). See *BDB,* p. 394, which gives many references. It is a very common word in the legal material of the Pentateuch.

105. See the textual note to the translation.

17   Three more tribes are reproached in this verse. The name *Gilead* is puzzling because it is the name of a region rather than a tribe. Gilead was the center and north of Transjordan, spanning the old tribal allotments of Gad and the half-tribe of Manasseh (the part east of the Jordan). It seems to refer here to the tribe of Gad, plus the rest of the eastern Manassites (those not covered by Machir).[106] The name Gilead is used in a similar way in the Jephthah episode of chapters 10 to 12.

The reference to *Dan* "staying" *(yāgûr) with the ships* is also puzzling, since Dan did not have direct access to the seacoast, either in its original allotment in the south (1:34) or its later location in the north (ch. 18). It did have access to the inland waterways of the upper reaches of the Jordan around Lake Huleh; but the term *ships (ᵃnîôt)* normally refers to oceangoing vessels.[107] The verb *yāgûr* (from *gwr,* "to be a resident alien") probably reflects the time after the Danites were forced to leave their own territory in the south (1:34) and before they were fully recognized as permanent residents in the north (ch. 18). We can only guess what their involvement with ships was, but it may have been through some kind of arrangement with the Phoenicians (as clients or hired workers).[108] At any rate, it seems that it took priority, for them, over the war effort. The same, apparently, was true for the Asherites, who lived right on the coast (v. 17b).

18   At the end of Stanza III the song reverts to the positive, briefly describing the heroism shown by the tribes of Zebulun (whose area bordered the middle part of the Jezreel Valley), and Naphtali (to the north of Zebulun, and Barak's own tribe, 4:6). The Zebulunites were willing to sacrifice their lives for the cause,[109] and Naphtali distinguished itself by playing a key role in taking the most strategic points in the battle zone — *the heights of the field.*[110]

19   After dragging its heels somewhat in the previous stanza (bad news producing a bit of a limp), the song starts to romp along again here. This rousing stanza is about the battle itself, and especially how Yahweh overthrew the enemy. The first two lines of verse 19 are a chiasm (AB:B′A′), with the *kings* of the first line expanded into *the kings of Canaan* in the sec-

---

106. Num. 32:39-40. See v. 14 and the note there on Machir. Cf. the articles on Gilead and Machir in *ZPEB,* vols. 2 and 4 respectively.

107. For example, Jon. 1:3; Isa. 23:1.

108. So Lawrence E. Stager, "The Song of Deborah: Why Some Tribes Answered the Call and Others Did Not," *BAR* 15, no. 1 (1989): 63-64, except that Stager thinks their involvement with ships may have been while they were still in the south.

109. Cf. Paul in Acts 20:24.

110. Like most battlegrounds, the Jezreel "Valley" or "Plain" *('ēmeq)* was not featureless and flat, but had some key, higher areas which gave a strategic advantage to whoever occupied them. Boling, *Judges,* p. 113.

ond. The plural, *kings,* is unexpected, since only one king, Jabin, was referred to in the preceding narrative (4:2, 17, 23-24), and there was no indication that he was personally involved in the battle. But chapter 4 has already hinted at the larger significance of Jabin by referring to him repeatedly as *king of Canaan,* recalling Joshua 11:10, where Hazor (Jabin's city) is referred to as "the head of all these [Canaanite] kingdoms." As we have seen, the Jabin of Deborah and Barak's time was nowhere nearly as powerful as his predecessor had been,[111] but the name apparently still had symbolic significance for them. Jabin was not just a "king" but epitomized "kingship" — especially of the Canaanite kind. The way this is expressed in the poetry of the song is through the transformation of the battle between Barak and Sisera into a great final showdown between heaven and earth, between Yahweh and *the kings of Canaan.*

For *Taanach* and *Megiddo,* see the comments on 1:27. They are about halfway between the Jordan and the Mediterranean coast, overlooking the upper reaches of the River Kishon, where it flows down into the Jezreel Valley (or the Plain of Megiddo, as this central section of it was called). It was here that the decisive part of the battle was fought. The *waters of Megiddo* are either the Kishon itself, or one of the streams that flow into it as it descends through the mountain passes. The "taking" of *plundered silver* is the poetic equivalent of what is described more prosaically in verse 30. Stripping defeated enemies of anything of value was normal practice, except in Israel, where the plunder of a God-given victory was presented to Yahweh as its rightful owner.[112] Israel's enemies took no plunder in the present case because they were defeated, as the following verses describe.

20-22 As we noted earlier, these three verses elaborate on the more matter-of-fact statement of 4:15 that Yahweh "threw Sisera and all his chariotry and all his troops into disarray" before Barak. The means, as these verses disclose, was by suddenly turning the Kishon into a raging torrent that swept them all away. In verse 20 Yahweh (given 4:15 there is no need to mention him explicitly) deploys *the stars* against Sisera. The Canaanites thought of the stars as heavenly powers that controlled the weather.[113] Here they are pictured as a heavenly army[114] which fight against Sisera by a flash flood, presumably by means of a huge downpour in the mountain catchment area of the Kishon. As the water rushes down from the hills through the

---

111. See the comments (including footnotes) on 4:2.

112. Either by destroying it (in the case of people and animals) or by placing it in the temple treasury (in the case of silver and other valuables). Josh. 6:21, 24.

113. Blenkinsopp, "Song of Deborah," p. 73.

114. Cf. Deut. 4:19 (NIV), where the sun, moon, and stars are called "all the host [army] of heaven."

mountain passes, it is concentrated into a powerful torrent that catches Sisera's men by surprise and instantly nullifies their technical advantage by rendering their impressive chariots useless. It is the equivalent of the avalanche of water that did the same thing to Pharaoh's horses and riders in the Red Sea. There is no need to assume that a miraculous kind of selectivity was involved (the water "picking out" only Sisera's men and harmlessly bypassing Barak's). Since Yahweh "went out before" Barak (4:14), the water had probably already done its work before Barak and his men reached the valley floor; all they had to do was complete the rout. We have already noted the brilliant way the rhythm and sound of the stampeding horses is captured in the *dahᵃrôṯ dahᵃrôṯ* of verse 22.

The closing line of verse 21, *"march on, my soul, with strength,"* is a parenthesis; not part of the main fabric of the song as the surrounding material is. But it is not to be dismissed too easily as a mere addition, a kind of intrusive extra that is best ignored,[115] for it opens a window for us into the heart of the singer — probably Barak. As far as its form is concerned, it is self-exhortation, similar to the "Bless Yahweh, O my soul" of Psalm 103:1, and an indication of the strong encouragement the singer feels as he recalls these marvelous events. He draws strength from them, and by self-exhortation keeps himself on guard against the creeping indifference that, with the passing of time, can make them appear familiar and ordinary. It was this danger that Jesus sought to protect us against by instituting the Lord's Supper.

23   This last verse comes as a surprise after the very positive, triumphant tone of Stanza 4 in general. It is probably for this reason that *BHS* suggests that it has somehow been displaced from its "proper" position after verse 17, where it would complete, in an emphatic fashion, a section dealing with the failure of some of the tribes to respond to Deborah and Barak's summons. But this suggestion has no hard (textual) evidence to support it, and would unbalance the structure of the song by making Stanza 4 too short.[116] It is also a lazy man's solution, which cries "mistake" too quickly. Barnabas Lindars, who does not do this, makes two pertinent observations. First, verse 23 occurs in the context of the defeat and rout of Sisera's forces (vv. 19-22), and may therefore refer to a failure of a particular, well-situated town and its people to help the rest of Barak's forces by cutting off the fugitives (as in the seizing of the fords of the Jordan in 3:28 and 7:24). Second, the curse of this verse acts as a negative backdrop to the blessing of Jael which follows. Jael

---

115. *BHS* effectively does this by bracketing it out as "probably an addition."

116. In the poem as it stands the middle three stanzas all have five verses, while the opening and closing stanzas are longer (seven and eight verses respectively, or eight and eight if the title in v. 1 is counted as part of the whole).

did exactly what the people of *Meroz* failed to do.[117] The identity of Meroz has been much discussed, without any consensus being reached. The expression *yōšᵉbeyhā (its inhabitants)* suggests that it is a place (probably a town) rather than, say, a clan, but its location is unknown.[118]

The form of the curse against Meroz is also an enigma. It is similar to a prophetic judgment oracle, but instead of the normal messenger formula, "Thus says Yahweh," it has " *'Curse Meroz,' says <u>the messenger of Yahweh.</u>*"[119] It is also like a formal curse statement in a treaty document, but instead of the normal passive participle, "*Cursed* [be] he who does/does not do X" (e.g., Deut. 27:15-19), it has the imperative, " '<u>*Curse Meroz . . .*</u>' " What it appears to be is a poetic adaptation of these normal prophetic and legal forms of speech to suit the specific requirements of the song. In the context of Judges the *messenger of Yahweh* is most naturally taken as the same messenger as appeared in 2:1 and will appear again in 13:3-19.[120] He appears here as joining in the song, telling the singers to *curse Meroz* for its failure to be loyal to the cause of Yahweh and his people. It is also not clear what the "cursing" of the people of Meroz entailed. Given the fact that it is not cast in legal form, and that no specific judgment is pronounced, it is probably best seen as a particularly strong statement of disapproval, and in effect a prayer that Yahweh himself would punish them as he sees fit.[121]

24-27 The final stanza, which begins in verse 24, is concerned with the death of Sisera, and consists of two contrasting scenes: the first in the tent of Jael (vv. 24-27), where he is killed, and the second in his home (vv. 28-30), where his mother waits in vain for his return. Verses 24-27 repeat the content of 4:17-22, but without any reference to Barak. We have already commented at some length on the significance of this episode in its two

---

117. Lindars, *Judges 1–5*, p. 272. Cundall's conjecture that it "may be the modern Khirbet Maurus, 7 miles south of Kedesh-naphtali" lacks hard evidence to support it, and is not compatible with Lindars's plausible suggestion (above) that Meroz failed to cut off fugitives from the battle. Arthur E. Cundall, "Judges: An Introduction and Commentary," in *Judges, Ruth: An Introduction and Commentary,* by Arthur E. Cundall and Leon Morris (London: Tyndale, 1968), p. 100.

118. For a summary of the suggestions that have been made, see Lindars, *Judges 1–5*, p. 273.

119. Lindars's deletion of *mal'ak* on metrical grounds yields a straightforward interpretation of the verse as a judgment oracle pronounced by Deborah, the prophetess of 4:4 (although Lindars himself stops short of identifying her as the speaker) (*Judges 1–5*, p. 273). But such an emendation of the text needs to be justified on text-critical grounds.

120. See the exegetical comments in these two places.

121. As in the cursing of enemies in the Psalms; cf. Jer. 48:10. In ch. 8 Gideon personally punishes the people of Succoth and Penuel for refusing to give him support when he asked for it (8:16-17). Whether any similar action was taken against Meroz (or any of the tribes mentioned in 5:15-17) we simply don't know.

forms (in the story and the song respectively) and will not repeat the details here. In contrast to Meroz, Jael is *most blessed among women* because of the vital role she played in the destruction of Israel's archenemy.

28-30   Again, we have commented above on the significance of this closing episode of the song, and will not repeat here what has already been said. But a couple of further observations may be made. First, it is an episode heavy with irony; we know what Sisera's mother and her maids-in-waiting do not (that Sisera is dead), though clearly they fear it. The scene they paint with words in order to try to protect themselves from despair is not the reality we have just seen, and the contrast is what makes this poetic treatment of the utter ruin of Israel's enemies so effective. Unlike Deborah and Jael, Sisera's mother is a woman without a name and without power. The best she can hope for is that her son will return with a gift for her from the spoils of war; but she will not have the gift because she will not have her son. She is totally dependent on Sisera, and without him she is nothing. Second, there is strong pathos in the episode, since the aftermath of the battle is now seen from this woman's perspective, and who could not feel for a mother who has lost her son? But at the same time the episode is alienating, especially for us as modern readers. For what Sisera's mother and her attendants hope for is that their men are dividing up the plunder, including women (v. 30a). Moreover the expression I have translated as *a woman or two* is literally "a womb or two" *(raḥam raḥᵃmātayim).* So these women are doubly dehumanized; they are not only property to be divided up by men like bits of cloth, but they are also "wombs," valued only for their erotic and reproductive potential. The fact that it is other women who see this as normal, and something they hope is happening, is as telling a comment on Canaanite culture as the vignette about Adoni-bezek in 1:4-7. Finally, this last episode of the song is in effect a dramatic enactment of the statement back in verse 19: "plunder . . . they did not take"; and because the men took no plunder, the women have no hope. All is lost; Israel's enemies are utterly undone.

31a   This closing prayer raises the particular events just described, and celebrated in the song, to the level of a paradigm which the singers hope will always be reflected in God's future dealings with them: May what happened to Sisera and his allies at the Kishon happen to all God's *enemies,* and may *those who love (Yahweh)* like the singers themselves, go from strength to strength, like the rising sun. There are some very bold theological assumptions here. The first is that Israel's enemies, like Sisera and Jabin, are also God's enemies. The singers do not seem to imagine that they themselves could ever become God's enemies, which is rather ironical, to say the least, in view of the way the Deborah-Barak episode as a whole began back in 4:1, with the Israelites doing evil in Yahweh's eyes. Things are not quite as black and white as the singers, in their present high state of celebration, seem to envisage. In fact, it will only be forty years, according to the closing line of this verse and the opening words of chapter 6, before Israel will effectively have become Yahweh's "enemies" again, and find him fighting against *them* by handing them over to new oppressors.

Furthermore, given Israel's record so far, and what will unfold in the rest of the book, Israel can hardly be described as "those who *love ('āhab)* Yahweh." In the ten commandments, *'āhab,* like *ḥesed,* is equivalent to being faithful to covenant obligations, especially by not worshiping anything or anyone other than Yahweh himself:

> "You shall not make for yourself an idol in the form of anything in heaven above or on the earth beneath or in the waters below. You shall not bow down to them or worship them; for I, the LORD your God, am a jealous God, punishing the children for the sin of the fathers to the third and fourth generation of those who hate me, but showing love *(ḥesed)* to a thousand [generations] of those who love *('āhab)* me and keep my commandments. (Exod. 20:4-6 NIV)

Love *('āhab)* is the heartfelt covenant faithfulness that Yahweh requires in response to his own faithful love *(ḥesed)*. The Shema of Deuteronomy makes the same point even more powerfully:

> Hear, O Israel: the LORD our God, the LORD is one. Love *('āhab)* the LORD your God with all your heart and with all your soul and with all your strength. These commandments that I give you today are to be upon your hearts. . . .

To love God is to keep his commandments, especially the commandment not to worship anyone or anything else. There is therefore a rather sad irony in the prayer of Judges 5:31. It is not that the singers do not love God at this heady moment, but that Judges as a whole makes the sharp distinction they make here between themselves and God's enemies a rather hollow one. It is the kind of gap between what is said in "church" and what is done out of it that the prophets will later highlight as Israel's perennial problem, and the cause of the exile.

There is also irony in the reference to the *sun* in this verse. As we have already noted, the sun had been worshiped as a god by at least some of the pre-Israelite inhabitants of Canaan.[122] At their best, as here, the Israelites saw the sun, impressive though it is, as a part of the created world.[123] Their monotheism emptied it of pagan significance and made it available for use in poetry

---

122. See the comments at 1:33 on *Beth-shemesh* (house/temple of the sun).
123. Gen. 1:16; Ps. 8:3.

and song in perfectly appropriate ways.[124] At its worst, though, Israel was drawn to it again as an object of worship, and effectively became God's enemies again.[125] In Judges, Samson, whose name *(šimšôn)* is related to the word "sun" *(šemeš)*,[126] shows us that being strong like the sun, even if the strength is God-given, does not necessarily make a person immune to the allurements of Canaanite culture.

None of this means that we must take an essentially cynical view of the prayer of v. 31a. As a response to what the Israelites have just experienced at the Kishon it expresses genuine awe of Yahweh, and an intention to stand with him, not with his enemies. It may be Israel's finest moment in the book of Judges; it is certainly one of them. The only problem is that it did not issue in a lasting change for the better.

31b   What the events recalled in the story and the song did produce, however, was another intermission, so to speak, in Israel's downward spiral: *the land had rest for forty years.* See my earlier comments on this closure to the entire Deborah-Barak episode.

E. GIDEON AND ABIMELECH (6:1–9:57)

1. The Career of Gideon (6:1–8:28)

In the Gideon episode the struggle between Israel and its enemies again centers on the Plain of Jezreel (6:33), making this episode the natural sequel of the previous one. Barak's victory over the Canaanite chariot forces opened the broad, fertile plain to Israelite settlement and the cultivation of crops (6:3a); but now a different kind of enemy appears in the same region, and a new struggle for control of it ensues.[1]

God's response to Israel's appeal on this occasion is initially a stern rebuff delivered by a prophet (6:6-10). It is clear from this that the problem of Israel's apostasy remains unresolved, and as the story unfolds, it becomes apparent that this issue is of fundamental concern to the narrator. However,

---

124. For example, Ps. 19:4-5.

125. 2 Kgs. 23:11; Ezek. 8:16.

126. It has the same three root consonants, and the ending indicates that it is a diminutive, "little sun," or the like. Cf. Eglon, "little bull," in 3:14.

1. Cf. Abraham Malamat, "The War of Gideon and Midian: A Military Approach," *PEQ* 85 (1953): 61, who argues that the breach made in the Canaanite defense system under Deborah and Barak actually opened the way for foreign invasions. The Israelites had not yet attained the high material level nor the advanced political organization that would have enabled them to take the place of the Canaanites in defending the northern part of the country.

with the coming of Yahweh's messenger to commission Gideon in 6:11, it is clear that Yahweh has resolved to rescue Israel yet again. The body of the narrative, dealing with how Israel was freed from Midianite domination, extends from 6:11 to 8:28, where it is formally concluded, as in previous episodes, by the statement that the enemy was subdued before the Israelites and the land had rest (cf. 3:10b-11; 3:30; 4:23; 5:31).

This long section consists of two narrative movements. After the enlistment of Gideon in 6:11-24 there follows a series of incidents which build the sense of mounting tension by anticipating the inevitable clash between Gideon and the enemy, but delaying its arrival. The climax is reached at the end of chapter 7 with the successful surprise attack on the Midianite camp, the rout of the enemy, and the slaughter of their two commanders (7:19-25). A brief epilogue follows (8:1-3) in which Gideon successfully averts the threat of civil war by quelling intertribal jealousies which have been stirred up in the course of the campaign. At this point, with the external threat removed and internal harmony restored, we appear to have reached the end of the story.

But then quite unexpectedly it is resumed in 8:4 from the point at which Gideon and his men have crossed the Jordan, and a whole new narrative movement starts to emerge.[2] Once again a series of incidents builds the suspense; again it is Gideon and his three hundred who take the encamped enemy by surprise; again the enemy is panicked, routed, and pursued, and again two Midianite leaders are captured and executed, at which point it seems that the climax of this second movement has been reached. But this time the two leaders are kings (*mᵉlāḵîm*, 8:5, 12) rather than commanders (*śārîm*, 7:25), and they are captured and slain by Gideon himself. Gideon's personal success so elevates him in the estimation of his fellow Israelites that they offer him dynastic rule (8:22). With this Gideon has reached the peak of his power and influence, and this rather than his victory over the kings becomes the true climax of the second movement and, retrospectively, of the story as a whole, as implied by the terms in which the offer is made: "Rule over us, both you and your son and your grandson, *for you have saved us from the hand of Midian*" (8:22, my emphasis). As in the first movement, a brief epilogue follows the climax and brings the movement to a close. This relates how, ironically, Gideon himself proceeds to make an ephod, which becomes a *snare* not only to himself and his family but to *all Israel* (8:27),

---

2. Gideon had already crossed the Jordan according to 7:25. But 8:1-3 is nevertheless, in terms of plot structure, the completion of the action which had taken place west of the Jordan, not part of the new developments which now take place east of it. Hence the resumption from the crossing of the Jordan in 8:4. The LXX avoids the difficulty by rendering *mē'ēḇer layyardēn* in 7:25 as "*from* beyond the Jordan."

leading to the establishment of an all-Israel cult in Ophrah, the very place where Gideon had begun his career by tearing down the idolatrous Baal-altar (6:25-32). Nevertheless, *the land had rest for forty years* (8:28), and with this formula the story of Gideon's career is effectively at an end. The next four verses (8:29-32) relate the birth and naming of Abimelech and the death and burial of Gideon. They serve as a bridge to the account of Abimelech's career which follows.

To summarize, then, the body of the narrative begins and ends at Ophrah *('oprâ)* and consists of two distinct movements, the second of which begins at the point at which Gideon and his men cross *('ābar)* the Jordan. We may represent this as follows:

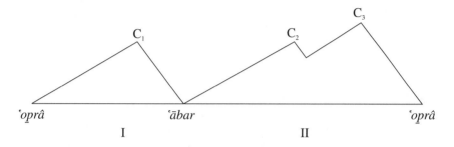

This analysis of the broad structure of the narrative provides the basis for the more detailed exegetical treatment which follows.

a. Yet Again — Apostasy, Oppression, and a Cry for Help (6:1-6)

1 *The Israelites did what was evil in the eyes of Yahweh, and Yahweh gave them into the hand of Midian for seven years.*
2 *The hand of Midian prevailed over Israel. Because of Midian the Israelites made for themselves the dens which are in the mountains, and the caves and the strongholds.*
3 *If Israel sowed, then up would come the Easterners (Midian and Amalek);[3] up they would come up against him.[4]*
4 *They would encamp against them and lay waste the produce of the land as far as the approach to Gaza, and would not leave any sustenance in Israel — no sheep, oxen, or donkeys.*

---

3. With Boling (*Judges*, pp. 124-25) I take *b^enê-qeḏem* (sons of the east) here as a summarizing appositive: "Midian and Amalek, that is, the Easterners." Cf. 8:10c, 11a.

4. *BHS* suggests that *we'alû 'ālāyw* is an addition (with the implication that it should be omitted). But the repetition may be deliberate, to emphasize the certainty and frequency of the raids at harvesttime.

5 *For they and their cattle would come up with their tents; they would come in like a huge locust plague; they and their camels were too many to count, and they would come into the land to lay it waste.*

6 *So Israel was brought very low before Midian, and the Israelites cried out to Yahweh.*

1 The now familiar words, *The Israelites did what was evil in the eyes of Yahweh,* mark the beginning of another major episode.[5] But here they stand in abrupt contrast to the high praises of Yahweh that have been sung in the previous chapter, and confront us in a particularly striking way with the fickleness of the Israelites, who cannot long resist the allurements of other gods no matter how much Yahweh exerts himself on their behalf. As we shall see, the problem of apostasy is explored much more fully in this episode than in previous ones.

2-6 This time the Israelites are punished by being subjected to the depredations of hordes of *Easterners* (v. 3). According to Genesis 25:1-6, Midian, the ancestor of the Midianites, was the son of Keturah, one of Abraham's concubines. Like Abraham's other sons by his concubines, he was sent away to the East (beyond the Jordan) to separate him from Isaac, whom Abraham had designated his sole heir. The Midianites are later found inhabiting the marginal lands on the edge of the desert to the east and south of Moab and Edom.[6] The Amalekites, too, were mainly desert dwellers. According to Genesis 36:12 and 16, their ancestor Amalek was a son of Eliphaz and a grandson of Esau. References to the Amalekites from the time of the exodus and later locate them mainly in the southern Negeb (in the extreme south of Palestine), though for a time they seem to have gained a foothold in the central highlands as well (Judg. 12:15).[7] They have already appeared in Judges as allies of Eglon, king of Moab (3:13).[8] In the Pentateuch *Midian* and *Amalek* both feature as enemies of Israel, and victory over them is closely connected with the figure of Moses (Exod. 17:8-16; Deut. 25:17-19; Num. 31). The reappearance of these ancient enemies here prepares the way for the Mosaic role in which Gideon will be cast in 6:11–8:3.

The plight of the Israelites is described here much more fully than in previous episodes. The pitiful decline in their lifestyle is conveyed by piling

---

5. However, while 4:1 states that the Israelites *again* did what was evil, 6:1 simply says that they *did* what was evil. According to Midrash Song of Songs Rabbah (4:3), this difference is not without significance. It asserts that in 6:1 the Israelites were effectively doing what was evil for the first time since "the song [of ch. 5] had wiped out all that went before."

6. See K. A. Kitchen, "Midianites," in *NBD,* p. 764.

7. See J. A. Thompson, "Amalek, Amalekites," in *NBD,* pp. 27-28.

8. See my comments on them there.

detail on detail: they live in dens and caves like animals; their produce is destroyed, and their livestock is carried off by the enemy (v. 4b). *Sheep, oxen* and *donkeys* represent, collectively, the sum total of economically valuable animals, and were therefore special objects of destruction by enemies (1 Sam. 15:3; 22:19; Josh. 6:21), or of coveting and theft (Exod. 20:17; 22:4, 9-10 [Heb. 3, 8-9). We may take it, therefore, that the reference to the destruction or theft of these three types of animals in verse 4 indicates the utter destruction of Israel's economic base. The entire land is laid waste, and with it Israel's means of sustenance. According to two well-attested Old Testament traditions, represented in Judges by 1:18 and 1:19 respectively, Israel had some successes in the "Gaza strip" but never established effective control there, even in the golden age of Joshua (Josh. 11:22; cf. 10:41 and Gen. 10:19). *As far as the approach to Gaza* must therefore be taken to mean "until one passes beyond the limits of Israelite settlement." From the Jezreel Valley as the point of entry, the raiders penetrated deeply into the highlands as well.

The enemy is as numerous as a *huge locust plague* (v. 5a) and has a tactical advantage in its possession of *camels [which] were too many to count* (v. 5c). The sequence of iterative verb forms in verses 3-5 captures stylistically the wave after wave of pillage and destruction. The whole is summarized in verse 6a: *Israel was brought very low before Midian*. Although the lexical connections are slight, the situation is reminiscent of that projected in the curses of Deuteronomy 28: Israel will be brought very low (Deut. 28:43); a nation of strong (*ʿaz*) countenance (cf. Judg. 6:2, *wattāʿāz*) will eat the fruit of Israel's cattle, and leave (*yašʾîr;* cf. Judg. 6:4) neither corn, wine, or oil, nor increase of oxen, flocks, and sheep, until Israel is destroyed (Deut. 28:50-51). Here in Judges 6 covenant unfaithfulness has brought covenant curse. In their desperation the Israelites appeal, as usual, to Yahweh, and this becomes the point of transition to the next major unit in the narrative, verses 7-10.[9]

b. Israel's Cry Rebuffed by a Prophet (6:7-10)

This unit is regarded as suspect by many scholars because it is missing from a fragment of Judges (6:2-13) found at Qumran.[10] However, it is certainly part of the canonical book as preserved in the major texts and versions. It is also, as we have seen, the second of three speeches accusing Israel of covenant unfaithfulness, extending from 2:1-5 to 10:11-14.

7 *When the Israelites cried out to Yahweh because of Midian,*

8 *Yahweh sent to the Israelites a man who was a prophet, and he said to*

9. Note how v. 7 repeats, in reverse order, the substance of v. 6.

10. See the discussion of the text of Judges in Part VIII of the Introduction.

> *them, "Thus says Yahweh, God of Israel, 'I am the One who brought*
> *you up from Egypt, and brought you out of the house of slaves.*
>
> 9 *I saved you from the hand of Egypt, and from the hand of all your op-*
> *pressors; I drove them out from before you, and gave you their land.*
>
> 10 *And I said to you, "I am Yahweh your God. You must not fear the gods*
> *of the Amorites in whose land you dwell." But you did not listen to my*
> *voice.'"*

7-10   When the Israelites cry out to Yahweh in their distress, he immediately sends a prophet (*ʾîš nābîʾ*, 6:8a), who appears at precisely the same
point in this episode as Deborah the prophetess (*ʾiššâ neḇîʾâ*, 4:4) had appeared in the previous one.[11] But the function of this prophet contrasts
sharply with that of Deborah. He does not come to set in motion the process
of deliverance, but to accuse the Israelites of covenant infidelity and tell them
(by implication) that they have forfeited all right to deliverance (6:10b).

"Crying out" *(ṣʿq/zʿq)* to Yahweh is an activity with ancient precedent
in Israelite tradition: The fathers had cried out to Yahweh in their desperate
circumstances in Egypt, and Yahweh sent them a savior in the form of Moses
(Exod. 2:23–3:12; *zʿq* is used in 2:23 as in Judg. 6:6). The appeal to Yahweh is
also part of the pattern established in the preceding episodes, but the response
it receives here is different, and wholly unexpected. Yahweh's frustration begins to show for the first time. The effect of the prophet's speech is to caution
Israel against the presumption that their appeal to Yahweh will always get a
favorable response, and to warn us, the readers, against drawing any simple
equation between calling on Yahweh and repentance. This confronting speech
by the prophet makes it clear that appealing to Yahweh is not a device by
which Israel can automatically secure its future. To call on Yahweh is to invoke a relationship, but the relationship (acknowledged in the speech) is one
that lays certain obligations upon Israel, obligations she has not fulfilled
(v. 10). The speech ends on this note of accusation. It is not clear whether or
not Yahweh will help the Israelites, or what they will do if he doesn't. Israel's
future as a nation in covenant with Yahweh hangs in the balance.

The prophet who makes a brief appearance here is anonymous, as in
1 Kings 20:13. The fact that he is *sent* to the Israelites (v. 8) does not necessarily imply that he is not one of them. The word "sent" *(šlḥ)* is a technical
term for commissioning a prophet as a messenger, and simply means that he

---

11. Both *ʾîš nābîʾ* (a man, a prophet) and *ʾiššâ neḇîʾâ* (a woman, a prophetess) are
unique in the Old Testament. The only expression which offers any comparison to *ʾîš nābîʾ* is
hannaʿar hannābî (the young man, the prophet) in 2 Kgs. 9:4, but this is used resumptively
to distinguish Elisha's apprentice (mentioned earlier) from the prophet himself, and not absolutely, as *ʾîš nābîʾ* is used here in Judg. 6:8. In every other instance where a prophetess is
mentioned, the expression used is simply *neḇîʾâ* (prophetess) without *ʾiššâ* (woman).

has been summoned into God's presence and given a message to deliver.[12] Such prophetic ministry by people "raised up" *(hēqîm)*[13] by God from time to time from among the Israelites is anticipated in Deuteronomy 18:18-22 as part of his normal, ongoing relationship with them. But the appearance of a prophet with a message of accusation, as here, indicates that the relationship has reached a point of crisis. The prophet begins his speech, appropriately, with the messenger formula, *Thus says Yahweh.* The absence of this formula in the speeches by the *mal'ak-Yahweh* (messenger of Yahweh) in verse 11 below, and at 2:1, 5:23, and 13:3, is noteworthy, and hints that the messenger on those occasions is not simply a prophet as the *'îš nābî'* of this passage is.[14] The common element, however, is the delivery of a message from Yahweh, Israel's supreme ruler, and the delivery of such a word is a serious matter.

The first two statements of the speech (vv. 8b, 9a) recall the foundational "saving" of Israel at the time of the exodus;[15] the next two (v. 9b) cover all the subsequent "savings" Israel had experienced at Yahweh's hand from then to the present time. The designation of those who had been dispossessed of their land before Israel (presumably the Canaanites) as *oppressors* is a little surprising, given that it is mainly people from outside Canaan, like the Israelites themselves, who oppress Israel in Judges. However, it could be that the language here is influenced by the preceding Deborah-Barak episode, in which "Jabin, king of Canaan," features in precisely this role. At any rate, whether or not the language is precise, the statements concerned are clearly meant to include all the Yahweh-given victories over their enemies that Israel had experienced since the exodus, every one of which had increased even further its moral obligation to be faithful to him.

For the *Amorites* (v. 10) as an alternative name for Canaanites, see the comments on 1:34-36. The general direction of the speech has been clear from the outset. Its opening statement, about Yahweh being the one who brought the Israelites up out of Egypt, already echoed the opening statement of the Ten Commandments (Exod. 20:2; Deut. 5:6). It now concludes by referring in a summary way to the first two of those commandments, which explicitly forbade worship of other gods. The expression "*you must not fear* [the gods of the Amorites]" captures in a single word the essence of all that the second commandment forbade; making (setting up) an idol, bowing down, worshiping.[16] The accusation itself, left emphatically until last, is that

12. Jer. 23:21.

13. "Raised up" is functionally equivalent to "sent."

14. See comments on *mal'ak-Yahweh* in the relevant passages.

15. The expression *house of slaves (bêt 'ªbādîm)* refers to Egypt as a whole as one huge slave barrack.

16. Cf. Deut. 5:29. To "fear" Yahweh is to keep his commandments; to "fear" other gods is to disregard those commandments.

the Israelites have *not listened* to what God said to them at Sinai. Their response to the grace God had shown in saving them has been to willfully disregard the very first, foundational commandments he gave them. In effect they have repudiated the covenant Yahweh made with them; by what right can they now expect him to help them?

c. Gideon's Career, Part 1: The Expulsion of the Midianites from Israelite Territory West of the Jordan (6:11–8:3)

(1) The Commissioning of Gideon as the Chosen Deliverer (6:11-24)

11 *Then the messenger of Yahweh came and sat under the oak which was in Ophrah, which belonged to Joash the Abiezrite, while Gideon his son was threshing wheat at the winepress to hide it from the Midianites.*

12 *The messenger of Yahweh appeared to him and said to him, "Yahweh is with you, mighty warrior."*[17]

13 *But Gideon replied, "Please, my Lord, if Yahweh is with us, why has all this happened to us, and where are all his wonders that our fathers told us about, saying, 'Wasn't it from Egypt that Yahweh brought us up?' But now Yahweh has abandoned us and given us into the hand of Midian."*

14 *Then Yahweh turned to him and said, "Go in this your strength and save Israel from the hand of Midian. Have I not sent you?"*

15 *Gideon said to him, "Please, my Lord, by what means will I save Israel? Look, my clan is the most feeble in Manasseh, and I am the least in my father's house."*

16 *But Yahweh said to him, "Surely I will be with you, and you will smite Midian as though it were just one man."*

17 *Then Gideon said, "If indeed I have found favor in your eyes, perform a sign for me that it is you who is speaking with me.*

18 *Please don't leave until I return to you and bring you my offering and place it before you." He replied, "I will stay until you return."*

19 *When Gideon had gone inside, he prepared one of the young goats, and made unleavened loaves from an ephah of flour; the meat he put*

---

17. The phrase I have translated as *mighty warrior* is *gibbôr heḥāyil*. I take the article on *heḥāyil* as vocative, as in *hammelek* (O King; 3:19). The term *gibbôr*, from *gābar* (to be strong, mighty), is regularly used in military contexts as "warrior, fighter" (cf. 5:13). *ḥāyil* (strength) may refer either to Gideon's strength as a warrior, or to his wealth (economic strength; e.g., Ruth 4:11), and therefore his ability to equip himself for war. Boling translates *gibbôr heḥāyil* here as "aristocrat," and *gibbôrîm* in 5:13 as "knights" (*Judges,* pp. 102, 111, 128).

in the basket, and the broth he put in the pot. Then he brought them out to him under the oak, and presented them to him.

20 *Then the messenger of God said to him, "Take the flesh and the unleavened loaves, and put them on this rock, and the broth — pour it out." So he did so.*

21 *Then the messenger of Yahweh stretched out the tip of the staff that was in his hand and touched the flesh and the unleavened loaves, and fire went up from the rock and devoured the flesh and the unleavened loaves, and the messenger of Yahweh withdrew from his sight.*

22 *Then Gideon saw that it was the messenger of Yahweh, and Gideon said, "Ahh, my Lord Yahweh, for[18] I have seen the messenger of Yahweh face to face!"*

23 *But Yahweh said to him, "Shalom, don't fear, you are not going to die."*

24 *So Gideon built here an altar to Yahweh, and called it Yahweh Shalom; it is there to this day in Ophrah of the Abiezrite.*

Gideon's commissioning follows the classical paradigm established by the call and commissioning of Moses in Exodus 3.[19] Gideon receives his commission in similar circumstances to Moses: in hiding from the enemy, working for his father Joash, the clan head and priest of a pagan shrine (cf. Jethro, Moses' father-in-law, whose flocks Moses is tending when Yahweh's messenger appears to him; Exod. 3:1). He receives the same word of authorization, *šᵉlaḥtîḵā,* "I have sent you" (Judg. 6:14; Exod. 3:12). Like Moses, he protests that he is inadequate for the task (Judg. 6:15; Exod. 3:11) and receives the same assurance of divine aid, *kî 'ehyeh 'immāḵ,* "Surely I will be with you,"[20] and, again like Moses, is given a *sign ('ôt)* to reassure him (Judg.

18. *kî-'al-kēn,* as in Gen. 18:5; 19:8; 33:10; 38:26; Num. 10:31, etc. *BDB,* p. 475.

19. The five essential elements of the paradigm have been listed by W. Richter as the noting of the affliction, the commission, the objection, the promise of strength, and the sign. Richter finds these five elements in both the alleged E and J strands of Exod. 3ff., in Judg. 6:11-17, and in 1 Sam. 9:1–10:16 (*Die sogenannten vorprophetischen Berufungsberichte* [Göttingen: Vandenhoeck & Ruprecht, 1970], esp. pp. 138-39). Cf. also W. Beyerlin, who argues that the historical data of an original story about the clan of Abiezer (still discernible in 8:4-21) have been worked over by a later narrator in such a way as to transform them into a typical example of salvation history based squarely on the exodus traditions: Gideon is a new Moses; Yahweh saves Israel in holy war; Yahweh alone is Israel's king ("Geschichte und heilsgeschichtliche Traditionsbildung im Alten Testament: Ein Beitrag zur Traditionsgeschichte von Richter vi–viii," *VT* 13 [1963]: 1-25). For a critical review of Beyerlin's article see Barnabas Lindars, "Gideon and Kingship," *JTS,* n.s. 16 (1965): 315-26.

20. This is a key expression in Exod. 3, involving a transparent wordplay on the divine name *Yahweh* that is about to be revealed (Exod. 3:14).

6:17; Exod. 3:12). In both cases the sign is accompanied by a fire theophany which induces fear in the one who is called (Judg. 6:22; Exod. 3:6). In Exodus 3 this proof of the divine presence is given unsolicited at the outset; in Judges 6 it is withheld until the end, so that the recognition of the messenger becomes the climax of the episode:

> *"Ahh, my Lord Yahweh,*
> *for I have seen the messenger of Yahweh face to face!"* (v. 22)

But Gideon is told not to fear; it is not Yahweh's intention to slay him (v. 23). Gideon has been commissioned, not by a prophet (as Barak was), but by Yahweh in person,[21] and Yahweh and Gideon will be in almost constant dialogue with each other in the sequence of events leading up to the battle (6:25, 36, 39; 7:2, 4, 7, 9). Again we are reminded of Moses, who received his commission directly from Yahweh, and whom Yahweh knew "face to face" (Deut. 34:10). This comparatively long account of Gideon's recruitment is without parallel in the preceding episodes, and serves to establish a distinct perspective on him at the outset of the narrative. We will return to this in due course.

11 The *messenger of Yahweh* here makes his third appearance in the book. He appeared in 2:1 to charge Israel with unfaithfulness, and in 5:23 to curse Meroz for failing to help in the war against Sisera. So his coming so far has been associated with bad news rather than good. But his "sitting" under the *oak* in Ophrah suggests that this time it may be the beginning of something positive. Deborah's sitting under her palm tree in 4:5 was the prelude to the summoning of Barak; here the similar action of the messenger is the prelude to the commissioning of Gideon. The messenger has taken his seat to judge Israel in a positive sense, by starting the process of deliverance.

The exact location of *Ophrah* is unknown, but verse 15 implies that it was in the territory of Manasseh, and therefore somewhere in the central hill country between Ephraim's territory and the Jezreel Valley.[22] *The oak* which was located there (note the definite article) was apparently well known and may have had a similar function locally to what Deborah's palm did for Israel as a whole. As subsequent events will show, *Joash,* who is said to have owned the oak, was a man of some influence in his clan (v. 25). He is *the* Abiezrite (note the definite article again), which further underlines his importance; he was probably the leading man of the Abiezrite clan, and the oak may have been the place where he sat to settle disputes. If so, the way the messenger comes and sits there indicates that Joash's clan is about to come

---

21. The *messenger of Yahweh* here is in effect Yahweh himself in manifestation, as a comparison of vv. 11, 12, 21, 22, and 23 with vv. 14 and 16 makes clear.

22. It is evidently different from the Ophrah listed as one of the towns of Benjamin in Josh. 18:23.

under a new authority, and Gideon will have to face the difficult choice of whom to obey: his father, or the messenger.

As we first meet Gideon here, he is completely unaware of the awesome responsibility that is about to be thrust upon him. He is *threshing wheat* at the *winepress,* so as to *hide it* from the Midianites. The winepress (literally the *gat,* the stone trough where the grapes were trod[23]) was hardly the normal place for such an activity, and therefore a good location for secrecy. Gideon is showing resourcefulness, though probably no more than the Israelites in general had done to survive in the circumstances (v. 2).

12 The identity of the messenger of Yahweh will turn out to be an important issue in this passage (see vv. 21-22). The first hint that he is divine occurs here in verse 12 with the verb *appeared (wayyērā᾽),* because this expression is used regularly in the Pentateuch of theophanies — manifestations of God in human or other material forms (e.g., fire, cloud, light [glory]).[24] But at first Gideon himself seems unaware that he is having an encounter with God. In fact, the messenger indirectly conceals his identity from Gideon by referring to God *(Yahweh)* in the third person. His announcement that Yahweh is *with* Gideon is ambiguous, but is probably not intended to refer primarily to physical presence (in the form of the messenger) but to Gideon's chosenness, and God's intention to support him in the task he is about to be given. The designation of Gideon himself as *the mighty warrior (gibbôr heḥāyil,* note the definite article) confirms his chosenness and indicates the nature of his task: Gideon, the thresher of wheat, will be a "thresher" of men, separating them into chosen and rejected,[25] victors and vanquished (cf. Isa. 41:14-16).[26]

13 As we noted earlier, appealing to Yahweh for deliverance from intolerable oppression echoes not only the appeals in the preceding episodes, but also the cry of the Israelites in Exodus 2:23-24.[27] This long-range precedent was implicitly acknowledged in the opening words of the prophet in 6:8b:

"I am the One who brought you up from Egypt,
and brought you out of the house of slaves."

Here in verse 13 Gideon rather cheekily picks up these words and turns them into a challenge:

---

23. Mobley, *Empty Men,* p. 133.

24. For example, Gen. 12:7; 17:1; 18:1; Exod. 3:2; Lev. 9:23; Num. 14:10; Deut. 31:15.

25. Judg. 7:1-8.

26. Cf. also Luke 1:16-17.

27. The appeal there, of course, is to Elohim (God); the personal name Yahweh is not revealed until Exod. 3.

"Wasn't it from Egypt that Yahweh brought us up?
But now Yahweh has abandoned us. . . ."

But this is really to misrepresent what the messenger has said. He has not said that Yahweh is with Israel in general, but with Gideon himself, as demonstrated by the fact that Yahweh's messenger has come to him. Furthermore, Gideon's charge that Yahweh had *abandoned* Israel and given them into the hand of Midian is also a distortion of the facts. Yahweh had certainly given the Israelites into the hand of Midian (v. 2), but not because he had *abandoned* them. On the contrary, it was because they had "done what was evil in his eyes" — a crucial fact that Gideon fails to mention. In effect, it was Israel that had abandoned Yahweh, not he them (2:12-13).[28] Finally, Gideon seeks to bolster his complaint by contrasting Yahweh's "abandonment" of Israel now with the "wonders" he had done for them at the time of the exodus — which the *fathers* (ancestors) had told the present generation about. But Gideon doesn't seem to realize that by speaking this way he is actually admitting that he and his contemporaries are without excuse. The fathers had faithfully passed on the knowledge of Yahweh's saving deeds to the following generation. If Gideon's generation did not "know" Yahweh (2:10), it was because of willfulness on their part rather than any failure of their fathers.[29]

Paradoxically Gideon's complaint is answered by his own commissioning. Here is proof, if proof is needed, that Yahweh has not abandoned Israel. But it is clear that Gideon was not an exemplary man of faith when he was called to save Israel. If God was *with* him, as the messenger has said, the reason must lie in God himself rather than in Gideon. Gideon himself was no more deserving of deliverance than anyone else.

14 The narrator now discloses directly to us that it is indeed Yahweh himself who has appeared to Gideon (*Yahweh turned to him),*[30] even though Gideon himself still seems to be unaware of it.[31] The fact that Yahweh *turns* to Gideon shows that he has not been put off by what Gideon has been saying. On the contrary, he confirms his decision to use him by formally commissioning (sending) him to *save* Israel. The expression *this your strength* is ambiguous. It may refer to the strength of character Gideon has just shown by challenging what the messenger said to him: he may be wrong, but he is not weak. More likely, however, Yahweh simply ignores what Gideon has

---

28. The word used for "abandon" in the overview of 2:11-19 is *ʿāzab* (as in Deut. 31:16); Gideon's own term is *nāṭaš,* but the effect is the same: blame is deflected from Israel and attributed to Yahweh.

29. See the comments on 2:10.

30. The LXX has "*messenger* [ἄγγελος] of Yahweh," as in vv. 11-12, but this has almost no support among copies of the Hebrew text.

31. Gideon is having a similar experience to Joshua in Josh. 5:13-15.

said and continues from where he (as the messenger) left off in verse 12. The important thing is not how Gideon himself thinks or feels, but what God has declared him to be: a *mighty warrior* (v. 12). His *strength* lies in his being chosen by God, and in God's promise to be *with* him.

15-16   Gideon's ignorance of the messenger's identity is indicated by the way he addresses him simply as *my Lord* (*ʾᵃdōnāy*) — the normal way of addressing a man of superior social position. As often in Old Testament call narratives, the one who is called pleads his inadequacy for the task.[32] God may see him as a mighty warrior, but Gideon knows that his clan, the Abiezrites (v. 11), is one of the *feeblest* (or poorest, *dal*) in the tribe of Manasseh, and that he himself is the *least* (*ṣāʿîr*) — probably because the youngest son[33] — in his father's household. As subsequent events will show, this self-estimation is not entirely accurate; verse 27 will speak of ten of Gideon's servants! Nevertheless it is probably an accurate expression of how Gideon felt, faced with the nature of the task God had given him. It may also have been a conventionally polite way of declining an offer or order from a person of superior rank. But the superior person in this case will not take No for an answer! The promised "presence" of God, in the sense of divine enablement, makes all pleas of inadequacy irrelevant (v. 16). The statement, *"Surely I will be with you (kî ʾehyeh ʿimmāk)"* is exactly the same as was spoken to Moses in Exodus 3:12, where it was soon followed by the self-disclosure of Yahweh as the great I AM (*ʾehyeh*, Exod. 3:14). Here it is an unsubtle way of forcing into Gideon's consciousness the awareness that he is having an encounter with God himself, and is being given a commission he cannot refuse.

17   Now at last Gideon begins to speak as someone who has a dawning awareness that he is being addressed by God. Instead of protesting, he speaks now of being privileged, of having found *favor (hēn)*, as Noah, Abraham, and Moses had done (Gen. 6:8; 18:3; Exod. 33:12). It is not an unambiguous admission that the messenger is God, for the same expression can be used with reference to simply finding favor with a human being (Gen. 32:5; 33:8, 10; Num. 11:15; 32:5). It does, however, indicate the direction in which Gideon's consciousness is moving, albeit cautiously. After all, there is a lot at stake here for Gideon. Hence his request for a sign: *perform a sign for me that it is you who is speaking to me.* His working hypothesis now is that his visitor is indeed Yahweh, but he needs to be sure. We will see that this kind of caution is typical of Gideon.

18   Graciously accommodating himself to Gideon's need, Yahweh agrees to wait until Gideon returns with an offering *(minḥâ)* to present to

---

32. For example, Exod. 3:11; Isa. 6:5; Jer. 1:6.
33. The opposite of *bᵉkōr,* "firstborn" (Gen. 43:33).

him. Exactly how this relates to Gideon's request for a sign is not clear, since the same term *minḥâ* has occurred in the Ehud episode for tribute offered to Eglon. That is, the presentation of a *minḥâ* (offering, gift) is not necessarily an act of worship.[34] But it is probably for this very reason that Gideon has chosen it as a sign. His visitor may receive Gideon's *minḥâ* as a man receiving a gift, or as God receiving an offering, and Gideon will know by this whether he is human or divine.

19 The gift/offering that Gideon prepares is a very large one, and must have occupied him for a long time. A *young goat* alone is more than a meal for a single visitor, and an *ephah* of flour (about 22 liters) is "entirely disproportionate, especially in the circumstances";[35] it would have made a huge amount of bread. The details about how Gideon arranged all the food is evidence of the extreme care taken. Finally, the mention of the *oak* where the messenger had sat back in verse 11 is a subtle reminder of the passing of time and the patience that the visitor is displaying.

20-21 The extravagance of the offering is an implicit invitation to the visitor to treat it as something more than a meal, and this is precisely what he does. As soon as Gideon returns with it, the visitor abandons his passivity and takes charge of proceedings. He commands that the meat and bread be placed on *this rock* (perhaps the rock on which the visitor has been sitting); at his command it is transformed into an altar. Gideon is instructed to lay the meat and bread on it, and to pour out the broth[36] over them as a libation. The visitor then provides the needed fire by touching the offering with the tip of his staff. Then, as the offering is consumed, he withdraws from Gideon's sight — the reverse of his "appearing" back in verses 11-12.

The miraculous fire of verse 21 introduces a motif (fire) which will recur throughout the Gideon and Abimelech stories (6:26; 7:16, 20; 9:15, 20, 49). The aetiological note in verse 24 about Gideon building an altar to *Yahweh Shalom . . . in Ophrah of the Abiezrite* serves a double function. With verse 11 *(Ophrah, which belonged to Joash the Abiezrite)* it forms a bracket around the account of Gideon's call. At the same time it effects the transition to the next episode (vv. 25-32) by anticipating the issue to be resolved there, namely, the rivalry between Yahweh and Baal as symbolized by the juxtaposition of their two altars.

22-23 Gideon has been given the sign *('ôt)* he sought (v. 17), and is no longer in any doubt that the *messenger* is *Yahweh* himself. It is something he had already, and increasingly, entertained as a possibility, but now that he has "seen" it (by means of the sign) he is mortally afraid, as his guttural cry

---

34. See, e.g., Gen. 33:10; 43:11; 1 Sam. 10:27.
35. Moore, *Judges,* p. 187.
36. The water in which the meat had been boiled.

(Ahh)[37] shows. Gideon apparently believes, as Exodus 33:20 reports Yahweh as saying, that no one can "see" him and live. But it does not seem to have occurred to Gideon until this moment that if that is indeed true, then he has been in mortal peril ever since the messenger appeared to him. Or has he? May not the *messenger* of Yahweh be God making himself safely "see-able," God veiled in a human form? At any rate, the danger of "seeing" has now been removed by the withdrawal of the divine messenger (v. 21). Gideon sees him no longer. Nevertheless, communication continues. Yahweh speaks to him, and what he says is mightily reassuring. *Shalom,* the first word Gideon hears, contains all that follows even before it is said; it banishes fear and preserves his life.[38]

24 In gratitude for what he has received, Gideon replaces the makeshift stone altar of verse 20 with a more permanent,[39] purpose-built one, and gives it a name that encapsulates in two words all that he has experienced: *Yahweh* (who has appeared to him) and *Shalom* (the life-giving word that has been spoken to him). It seems that the call to be a deliverer that had been the primary anxiety-inducing thing in verses 11-16 has been eclipsed by a greater reality. It will come into play again in what follows, but for the present all that fills Gideon's consciousness is the fact that he has met God, and been given his peace. There is no greater good. All he wants to do at this moment is worship.

The closing reference to *Ophrah of the Abiezrite* echoes the same words in verse 11 and closes a bracket around the whole intervening passage. At the same time it reminds us that Gideon has not been removed from the world by his encounter with God. The realities of life in Ophrah are still there, and Gideon will have to face them. But he will face them far richer for the experience he has had.

(2) Gideon Challenges and Defeats Baal (6:25-32)

25 *That night Yahweh said to him, "Take a bull (your father's ox), and a second bull (the one seven years old),*[40] *and pull down your father's Baal altar, and cut down the Asherah which is beside it.*

37. Cf. Jephthah in 11:35.
38. As in the priestly blessing of Num. 6:22-27 *šālôm* is the sum total of well-being entailed in being in covenant relationship with God. Cf. the climactic *šālôm* of Esth. 10:3.
39. The narrator notes that it is still there, *to this day.*
40. The broken syntax of vv. 25-26 (reflected in my translation) and the reference to a *second* bull (implying there are two, while only one is used) have led most scholars to suppose that the text has suffered in transmission, and various suggestions have made about what the original may have been. All of these are conjectural and have problems of

26 *Then build an altar for Yahweh your God on the top of this strong point in the defenses, and take the second bull and offer it up as a burnt offering using the pieces of the Asherah which you have cut up.*

27 *So Gideon took ten men from among his servants, and did as Yahweh had commanded him. Because he was too afraid of his father's house and the men of the town to do it by day, he did it at night.*

28 *When the men of the town got up in the morning, they were surprised to see that the altar of Baal had been torn down, and the Asherah beside it had been cut down, and the second bull had been offered on the altar that had been built.*

29 *They said to one another, "Who has done this thing?" They made urgent inquiries and were told, "Gideon, the son of Joash, has done it."*

30 *Then the men of the town said to Joash, "Bring out your son that he may die, for he has torn down the altar of Baal and cut down the Asherah which was beside it."*

31 *But Joash replied to all who stood against him, "Are you going to contend for Baal as though you could save him? Whoever contends for him will be put to death by tomorrow morning. If he is God, let him contend for himself, since someone has torn down his altar."*

32 *So on that day they called Gideon Jerubbaal, saying, "Let Baal contend with him, since he has torn down his altar."*

---

their own. For the issues involved see J. A. Emerton, "The 'Second Bull' in Judges 6:25-28," in *H. L. Ginsberg Volume,* ed. Menahem Haran et al. (Jerusalem: Israel Exploration Society in cooperation with the Jewish Theological Seminary of America, 1978), pp. 52-55, and W. Bluedorn, *Yahweh versus Baalism: A Theological Reading of the Gideon-Abimelech Narrative,* JSOTSup 329 (Sheffield: Sheffield Academic Press, 2001). Emerton thinks that the word *haššēnî* has been wrongly pointed as "the second" in the MT, and is in fact a cognate of words based on similar roots in Syriac, Arabic, and (possibly) Ugaritic, meaning "highest" in rank. Hence Gideon is not commanded to take the "second" bull, but the "finest" one, the one most suitable for a sacrifice to Yahweh. Bluedorn argues that *haššēnî* should be taken as derived from *šnh* (shining) or *šny* (full grown), and be vocalized *haššānî*, "a full-grown or fattened animal, perhaps at an age where it may be sacrificed." However, emendations based on alleged cognates with similar but not identical roots in other languages are always precarious, especially where (as here) there is no instance of the word in question having the proposed sense in Hebrew. The LXX's *ton siteuton* ("the fattened [calf/ox]") probably reflects the difficulty the translators had making sense of the text as we have it in the MT rather than the translation of a different original. The possibility of reading *haššēnî* as epexegetical, "take the bull, your father's ox, *that is,* the second one," is ruled out by v. 26, where the same expression, *haššēnî,* cannot have this meaning. It seems best, therefore, to take the MT as it stands, and understand that Gideon is told to take two bulls (cf. ESV, HCSB). See the exegetical comments on these two verses.

25-26 What Gideon has just done he has done impulsively, as his own personal response to the revelation he has received. But probably without realizing it, he has created a situation which can't remain unresolved, for there are now two altars in Ophrah, to two rival gods: his own God, *Yahweh,* who has just appeared to him, and his father's god, *Baal* (the particular one worshiped in Ophrah under his father's patronage).[41] This state of things in Ophrah is symptomatic of Israel's situation in general; the real problem is not the relationship between Israel and Midian, but the relationship between Israel and Yahweh, which has been compromised by the worship of other gods. At heart Israel's problem is a spiritual one, and therefore the "saving" of Israel (v. 14) must begin with reclaiming her from apostasy. There can be no shalom (wholeness, covenant blessing) for Israel (v. 24) as long as she remains divided in her religious loyalties.[42] So Gideon is not allowed to enjoy for very long the shalom of a merely private and personal religious experience (v. 23); he is told at once, *that night,* to begin to act out its radical, transforming consequences for his own family and community. He has to start where it is hardest — at home.

Gideon is told to take two bulls,[43] demolish his father's *Baal altar* and *Asherah,* replace them with an altar for Yahweh, and offer the *second bull* on it as a burnt offering, using the destroyed Asherah as firewood (vv. 25-26). The first bull, an *ox,* is a draught animal normally used for heavy work; the second, a prime young bull *seven years old,* is a stud animal (ideal for breeding purposes). The fact that this second bull is specified for the burnt offering suggests that it has been chosen specifically for this purpose, and that the heavy work of demolition and reconstruction is to be done mainly or solely with the first bull.

The altar to be demolished is typically Canaanite: a raised stone platform for sacrificial rites (which has to be *pulled* down), with a wooden *Asherah* beside it (which has to be *cut* down). Asherah was the female counterpart of Baal, and was represented by a carved wooden image with female features.[44] Most disturbingly for Gideon, however, is the fact that the entire complex is his *father's.* His father's name, *Joash* (v. 11), is thoroughly Israelite, and probably involves a play of some kind on the name Yahweh.[45] His altar, however, represents the kind of syncretism that had become common in

41. See the comments on Canaanite religion at 2:11-13.

42. Cf. Joshua's challenge to Israel in Josh. 24:15, and Elijah's similar challenge in 1 Kgs. 18:21.

43. For the textual-critical issues see the note on the translation of vv. 25-26.

44. See J. Day, "Asherah in the Hebrew Bible and Northwest Semitic Literature," *JBL* 105, no. 3 (1986): 385-408.

45. For example, "Yahweh has given." D. W. Baker, "Joash, Jehoash," in *NBD,* p. 588.

the Judges period: the worship of Yahweh in Canaanite fashion, effectively as an Israelite Baal. But this was clearly unacceptable to Yahweh, who had appeared to Gideon. The problem for Gideon was that to destroy his father's altar was to risk a breach with him that might never be healed, and could well mean banishment and disinheritance.[46]

The new altar that Gideon is told to build cannot be the same as that in verse 24, which seems to be more a commemorative monument than an altar in the full, cultic sense.[47] The new altar is to be in a different, very prominent place *(on the top of this strong point in the defenses),* and symbolically dedicated at once with a sacrifice that indicates its intended purpose, namely, to replace the former Baal altar as the place of worship for the community. Using the pieces of the Asherah as firewood was more than a calculated insult to Baal; it was a powerful statement that Baal worship of any kind had been brought to a complete end in Ophrah.

27 Given the nature of the task, it is hardly surprising that Gideon was too *afraid* to do it by day; the fact that he did it at all is greatly to his credit. Doing it by night also maximized his chances of getting it done before anyone could intervene to stop him. The fact that he could command the services of *ten men from among his servants* shows clearly that the messenger's description of him as *mighty* (v. 12) was more accurate, at least in terms of wealth and influence, than Gideon had been prepared to admit.

28-32 In the morning Joash finds himself having to choose between *the men of the town* (its leading citizens) and his son. At a more fundamental level he has to choose between Baal and Yahweh, syncretism and covenant obedience, polytheism and monotheism: he cannot have both. Gideon's courageous act has left him no middle ground. It is a breath-taking moment and a critical turning point in the story. But as soon as Joash speaks, it is clear what his decision is, and that the crisis is past. Joash, the erstwhile patron of a heretical cult, morphs before our eyes into a proto-Elijah, challenging his fellow citizens to avenge Baal themselves and be executed as murderers, or risk having him exposed as powerless by doing nothing (v. 31). No one moves, and Gideon is reborn as *Jerubbaal,* a revolutionary hero and living testimony to Baal's impotence. In the present context the name Jerubbaal is clearly intended to be taken as jussive, "Let Baal contend";[48] it is capable, though, of another meaning — "Baal will contend" (the indicative). This meaning is in no one's mind at the moment, and if it is a hidden prophecy, it is one that seems unlikely ever to be fulfilled. But as

---

46. Cf. the treatment of Jephthah in 11:1-2.

47. Cf. the altar built by the Transjordan tribes in Josh. 22:9-34.

48. *y*^{e}*rubba'al* is a play on the threefold use of the verb *rîb,* "to contend/fight back," in v. 31.

the rest of the story will show, there is more to Gideon and his new name than is evident at this stage.

(3) Gideon Emerges as a Man of War (6:33-35)

33 *Now the Easterners (all Midian and Amalek) had assembled together, crossed over, and camped in the Valley of Jezreel.*

34 *But when the Spirit of Yahweh clothed Gideon, he blew the trumpet, and all the Abiezrites gathered behind him.*

35 *And when he sent messengers throughout all Manasseh, they too gathered behind him; and when he sent messengers throughout Asher and Zebulun and Naphtali, they too came up to meet the others.*

33 As in verse 3, I take *Midian* and *Amalek* as constituent parts of the invading force that is described more generally as *ûḇᵉnê-qeḏem,* "[that is] *the Easterners.*" In verse 3 it was the repeated, seasonal incursions of the raiders that was described (they *used to* come up). Here it is a particular incursion that is in view, and the disjunctive syntax[49] indicates that verse 33 is a flashback: *Now the Easterners . . . had crossed over* (the Jordan)." While the events at Ophrah described in verses 11-32 were taking place, another raid by the predatory Easterners had begun. This time, however, they will find that the Israelites have a new leader and won't be as easy to rob of their produce as they have been for the last seven years.

We have also noted earlier the location of the *Valley of Jezreel.* It contained some of the best arable land west of the Jordan, and was strategically important for trade, communication, and defense. It was here that Barak had fought Sisera. Now another struggle has begun for control of the same area. The invaders *crossed over* the Jordan and *camped* in the Jezreel Valley, probably at the eastern end, close to their crossing point.[50] More details are given about their location in 7:1, though whether this refers to their initial place of encampment or a subsequent one is not clear.

34-35 Now Gideon's career begins to follow the "textbook" pattern exhibited in the Othniel episode of 3:7-11. There the Spirit (of Yahweh) "came upon" *(wattᵉhî ʿālāyw)* the chosen deliverer; here the Spirit "clothes" *(lāḇᵉšâ)* Gideon.[51] But the effect is the same: the deliverer is empowered by the Spirit to do what he has been chosen to do. The effect is immediate in

---

49. The subject first, before the verb.

50. Cf. Israel's crossing of the Jordan and encampment at Gilgal (near Jericho) in Josh. 4:18-19.

51. That is "puts him on" (like a garment); "takes possession of him" (NRSV). Cf. David's experience in 1 Sam. 16:13.

both cases. Othniel "judged Israel and went out to war" (3:10); Gideon "blows the trumpet" to summon his compatriots to war (v. 34). If, as I suggested with Othniel, to "judge Israel" before battle is to call the Israelites back to covenant faithfulness,[52] in a sense Gideon has already done that by his victory over Baal in Ophrah. In itself this was only a local affair, but news of it probably spread quickly (by Gideon's *messengers* if not before) and did a lot to establish his credibility as a divinely chosen leader (as the assassination of Eglon had done for Ehud). At any rate, the way the response to Gideon's summons is described suggests that the news of what he had already done had an electrifying and rapidly widening effect on the Israelites: beginning with the Abiezrites (his own clan), then the Manassites (his own tribe), and finally other tribes further north (Asher, Zebulun, and Naphtali). All these tribes were located more or less adjacent to the Jezreel Valley, to the south and north of it respectively, and were therefore those most directly affected by the new invasion by the marauders.

But just when events have started to move at lightning speed, they slow down again as Gideon's earlier diffidence catches up with him and makes him hesitate.

(4) Gideon Uses a Fleece to Seek Reassurance from Yahweh (6:36-40)

36 *Then Gideon said to God, "If you are about to save Israel by my hand as you have spoken —*

37 *Look, I am placing the woolen fleece on the threshing floor; if there will be dew on the fleece alone, but on the surrounding earth dryness, then I will know that you will save Israel by my hand as you have spoken."*

38 *And that is what happened. Gideon got up early the next day and wrung out the fleece, that is, squeezed dew from the fleece — a full bowl of water.*

39 *Then Gideon said to God, "Please don't become angry with me, that I may speak just once more. Please let me test only once more with the fleece. Let dryness be on the fleece alone, and on all the ground let there be dew."*

40 *And God did so that night; it came about that dryness was on the fleece alone, but on all the earth was dew.*

36-40 This passage about the fleece does not show Gideon in a good light. Twice, in verses 36 and 37 respectively, he acknowledges that Yahweh has

---

52. See on 3:10, and cf. how Samuel prepares Israel for holy war in 1 Sam. 7:5-11.

spoken (promised) that he will save Israel by his hand, but this is not sufficient for him; faced now with imminent prospect of battle, he needs confirmation that the promise still holds and can be relied upon. But in his dramatic
encounter with the messenger of Yahweh Gideon has already been given far
more to assure him than any previous deliverer. Furthermore, flanked as it is
by Barak's equivocation in the preceding episode and Jephthah's vow in the
next (both also on the eve of battle), Gideon's fleece test is hardly exemplary.
It certainly doesn't show him at his best, and the common practice of taking
it as a model for seeking and obtaining divine guidance is highly questionable, to say the least.

What it does show is, first of all, that being "clothed with the Spirit"
as Gideon was does not obliterate someone's personality and make one immune to the normal weaknesses entailed in being a fallen human being. In
spite of his encounter with God and possession by the Spirit, Gideon still
struggles to believe and act unhesitatingly upon what he knows God has said.
Second, this episode shows us again the amazing grace of God in making allowance for Gideon's imperfection. As the apologetic tone of his language
shows *("Please don't become angry . . ."),* Gideon knows that there is a certain impertinence to what he is doing, and that he should not need the sign he
is asking for. God knows it too, but not one word of reproach is spoken;[53]
God simply gives him what he asks for. A similar patience was displayed by
the divine messenger, as we have seen, in the call episode of verses 11-24,
and it will be seen again in 7:9-11. In these parts of the narrative Gideon's
imperfections serve only to magnify the grace of God; it is Yahweh's conduct, rather than Gideon's, which is exemplary.

With regard to the particulars of the sign and why Gideon requires a
second test before he is satisfied, Robert Boling's comments are apposite:

> With the physical properties of fleece lying exposed overnight on bare
> rock, the differentials of condensation and evaporation necessary to
> give rise to the story are entirely understandable; fishermen living on
> one of the streamless and springless Desert Islands have obtained suffi-
> cient water for their livelihood by spreading out fleece in the evening
> and wringing dew from them in the morning (S. Tolkwosky, *Journal of
> the Palestine Oriental Society,* 3 [1923]: 197-99). The true miracle is
> the reverse of the process, and that's what young Gideon . . . required.[54]

In other words, he asks for the lesser sign first, and then, realizing that it is in-
conclusive and that he should have asked for something harder, goes ahead
and does so.

53. Contrast Deborah's response to Barak in 4:9.
54. Boling, *Judges,* p. 141.

(5) Yahweh Reduces Gideon's Fighting Force
to Three Hundred (7:1-8)

1 *Jerubbaal (that is, Gideon) and all the people who were with him got
up early and camped by the spring of Harod. The camp of Midian was
to his north, this side of the hill of Moreh,[55] in the valley.*

2 *Then Yahweh said to Gideon, "The people who are with you are too
many for me to give Midian into their hand, lest Israel affront me by
boasting, 'My own hand has saved me.'"*

3 *So please call out so that all the people can hear, "Whoever is fearful
and trembling, let him go back and leave Mount Gilead." Then 22,000
of the people went back, but 10,000 were left.*

4 *Yahweh said to Gideon, "There are still too many people. Take them
down to the water so that I can sift[56] them for you there. Then whoever
I tell you, 'This one will go with you,' he will go with you, but whoever
I say to you, 'This one will not go with you,' he will not go with you."*

5 *So he took the people down to the water, and Yahweh said to Gideon,
"All who lap from the water with their tongues as a dog laps, set
apart by themselves, and likewise those who kneel down to drink."*

6 *And it turned out that the number of those who lapped with their
tongues[57] was three hundred men; all the rest of the people knelt down
to drink the water with their hands [raised] to their mouths.*

7 *Yahweh said to Gideon, "It is with the three hundred who lapped that
I will save you by giving Midian into your hand, but all the rest of the
people should go, each to his own place."*

8 *So they took the provisions of the rejected people in their hands, and
their trumpets, and Gideon sent away all these men of Israel, all of
them to their tents, but he retained the three hundred; and the camp of
Midian was below him in the valley.*

55. The text reads literally, "north of him, from the hill of Moreh." This may be
corrupt, as suggested by *BHS* and Moore (*Judges*, p. 199). But if so, there is no consensus
about what the original was. My translation takes the *min* of *miggib'at* as locative *(this
side of).* Cf. *mē'ēḇer hayyardēn*, "this side of the Jordan" (Num. 32:19), and *mimm^eḵā*,
"this side of you" (1 Sam. 20:21).

56. The verb *ṣārap* which is used here is a metallurgical term that normally refers
to the refining of ore by removing its impurities. In 17:4 the corresponding participle
(ṣôrēp) means "a goldsmith."

57. The text as it stands is confusing, and almost certainly corrupt. With *BHS* I
read *bilšônô (with their tongues)* here, and move *b^eyāḏām 'el-pîhem (with their hands
[raised] to their mouths)* to the end of the verse. Boling (*Judges*, p. 145) gives a plausible
explanation of how the present confusion in the MT arose as a result of common scribal
errors such as homoeoteleuton and haplography.

1   The double naming of Gideon here may stem from a blending of two originally separate Gideon traditions, one in which he was called Gideon and another in which he was called Jerubbaal. However, at times (as here) the use of the two names seems to have a deeper significance than this. *Gideon* is the name used throughout the whole of 6:33–8:28 apart from this one place, where we are pointedly reminded of the name *Jerubbaal.* In view of the circumstances in which Gideon was given this name (his victory over Baal), its brief reappearance here hints that another victory is about to take place, as indeed it is. In both cases Gideon acts as Yahweh's instrument to save Israel: from apostasy and oppression respectively.

The experiment with the fleece took place over two successive nights and mornings (6:36-40). On the day after this, Gideon, apparently now satisfied that Yahweh will indeed give him victory, gets up early with his men and moves them into position overlooking the Jezreel Valley. The *spring of Harod* is "a copious and beautiful spring at the foot of Mount Gilboa," at the eastern end of the Jezreel Valley.[58] Camped there, Gideon's men had a commanding view northward across the valley from the southern side. The *hill of Moreh* was about 8 miles (13 km.) northwest of them, to the south of Mount Tabor,[59] where Barak and his men had poised themselves to strike (4:6, 14). The situation of the Midianite camp is described as seen through Gideon's eyes: *to his north, this side of the hill of Moreh, in the valley.* The repetition of this description in verse 8 marks off verses 1-8 as a unit.

2   Just as the battle appears set to begin, there is another interruption; but this time it is Yahweh who is not happy to proceed. His concern, though, is very different from Gideon's. The victory itself is not in question; what is in doubt is how Israel will interpret the victory if Gideon is allowed to proceed with the full contingent of men that have answered his call: they are *too many.* Israel might think that the victory is their doing instead of God's. Gideon doesn't demur, though we can imagine his surprise. Even the encouragement he has derived from the show of support from his fellows is to be taken from him. Only a very radical trust in God alone will take him forward now.

3-7   The number of Gideon's men is reduced in two stages from 32,000[60] to three hundred. The site from which the fearful are dismissed, *Mount Gilead (har haggil'ād),* is problematic since the only Gilead known in the Old Testament is east of the Jordan, well away from the setting of this scene given in verse 1. Various solutions have been proposed, the most likely being that *har haggil'ād* here is an accidental miswriting of *har haggilbōaʻ,*

---

58. A. E. Cundall, "Harod," in *NBD,* p. 445.

59. R. A. H. Gunner and F. F. Bruce, "Moreh," in *NBD,* p. 783.

60. On the problem of the large numbers here and elsewhere in Judges see Section IX.C of the Introduction.

Mount Gilboa,[61] which fits the context perfectly, since the spring of Harod (v. 1) is right next to Mount Gilboa. The fact that the fearful and *trembling* (*ḥārēḏ*) are sent back from a site near the spring of Harod (*ḥᵃrōḏ*) is either exquisitely coincidental, or it was this very event which gave rise to this name for the spring, and this was known at the time the story was written. In any case, the verbal echo serves to underline fearfulness/trembling as an important motif. Gideon himself was fearful back in 6:22-23, and manifestly still lacking confidence in 6:36-39. By now being told to dismiss the *fearful,* Gideon is forced to distinguish himself from them, and from his own past. However, it must have sorely tested his resolve to see two-thirds of his men walk away, only to be told that the remaining one-third were still too many (vv. 3-4)!

The *water* where the three hundred were singled out (vv. 4, 5) was presumably the stream that issued from the spring of Harod (v. 1). The description of the way they were chosen in verses 5-6 is puzzling, almost certainly because the text has suffered some disturbance in transmission.[62] The original distinction, as indicated in my translation, must have been between those who knelt and scooped the water to their mouths, and those (the three hundred) who put their faces to the water and lapped like dogs. But if so, the reason why the "lappers" were chosen rather than the "kneelers and scoopers" remains something of a teaser.[63] It may have been because, by giving themselves wholly to drinking rather than staying partly on guard, they showed less fear. After all, fearfulness was the criterion for the culling that had already taken place. Or they may have been chosen for the completely opposite reason: that by showing no awareness of the need to stay on guard against enemy attack they indicated that they lacked the kind of alertness required to be a successful fighter. This apparently absurd explanation draws some plausibility from the reason given for the further reduction of size of the volunteer force: lest the Israelites boast that their own hand has given them victory (v. 2). The less naturally able Gideon's men were, the greater glory would go to God for the victory he would give them. A third possibility is that the method by which the three hundred were chosen had no inherent significance at all, any more than, say, the method (the fleece) by which Gideon sought assurance of victory. It was just a convenient and quick way of establishing two groups to choose between, rather than having to do it man by man, and the three hundred were chosen simply because they were the smaller group.[64] The fact is that we sim-

---

61. *DCH* 2:356. For other proposals see Block, *Judges, Ruth,* p. 276, n. 589. Block's own preferred option "associates *gil'ad* with the modern name of the spring [of Harod], Ain Galud, the latter word of which is cognate to Akkadian *galadu/galtu,* 'to be afraid.'"

62. See the footnotes to the translation of vv. 5-6.

63. See the discussion in Soggin, *Judges,* pp. 136-37.

64. So Martin, *Judges,* p. 94.

ply don't know why those who lapped were preferred over those who kneeled and scooped with their hands. What we do know is that Gideon's force was reduced to a mere three hundred to exclude any possibility that the coming victory could be interpreted as their own achievement (vv. 2, 4). Subsequent events will show just how important this issue is.

8   As it stands, the MT of this verse, too, is obscure and possibly corrupt. Literally it reads, "They took provisions, the people, in their hands, and their trumpets, and all the men of Israel he sent, each to their tents, but the three hundred he took hold of, and the camp of Midian was below him in the valley." In view of the instructions Gideon has just received in verse 7, we can take it that he is the one who does the "sending away" of some and the "taking hold" (retaining) of others (the three hundred). We can also take it as given that although they are called "all the men of Israel," those who are sent away must be all except the three hundred. The problem relates to the opening clause of the verse: Who "takes" the provisions from whom? As the text stands (although the syntax is unusual),[65] the people (those who have not been chosen) take their own provisions with them to their tents. However, if the words "provisions, the people" are emended slightly to read "the provisions *of* the people,"[66] then it is the three hundred who take the provisions from the others, who thus leave them behind when they are dismissed.[67] Either reading is possible. The latter has the weakness of requiring an emendation of the text; the former provides no explanation for the strange syntax, and no explanation for how Gideon is later able to furnish each of his remaining three hundred men with a trumpet (v. 16). We can assume, I think, that it would be normal for only some members of an armed force to carry trumpets,[68] but that those left by the 9,700 would be sufficient for all of the remaining three hundred to have one each. On balance I have thought it best to take the second of the two options and have translated the verse accordingly.

The last part of the verse *(the camp of Midian was below him in the valley)* provides closure to this part of the story by recalling the similar statement in verse 1. It also refocuses our attention on the coming battle and suggests that it is imminent. Once more we see the Midianite *camp* as Gideon sees it *(below him),* which provides the transition to what follows. It also captures deftly the loneliness of a leader. Gideon has three hundred with him, but the burden of leadership is his alone.

---

65. The object before the subject.

66. Reading the construct of "provisions" *(ṣᵉdat)* rather than the absolute *(ṣēdâ),* as recommended in *BHS.*

67. So Block, *Judges, Ruth,* pp. 274, 277.

68. See, e.g., Josh. 6:13.

(6) Yahweh Reassures Gideon by Means of a Dream (7:9-15)

9 *During that night Yahweh said to him, "Arise and go down into the camp, for I have given them into your hand.*

10 *But if you are afraid to go down, go down to the camp with Purah, your assistant,*

11 *and hear what they are speaking about. Then your hands will be strong, and you will go down into the camp, for I have given it into your hand."*

12 *Now all the Easterners (the Midianites and the Amalekites)[69] were lying in the valley, as numerous as locusts, with innumerable camels; they were as numerous as grains of sand on the seashore.*

13 *When Gideon arrived, he was surprised to hear a man telling his friend about a dream. He said, "I had a dream, and saw a loaf of barley bread rolling into the camp of Midian. It came to the tent and struck it, and it fell; it rolled it over — upside down — and the tent fell."*

14 *His friend replied, "This can be nothing other than the sword of Gideon, son of Joash, the man of Israel; God has given into his hand Midian and all its camp."*

15 *Now when Gideon heard the account of the dream and its interpretation, he worshiped; then he returned to the Israelite camp and said, "Arise, for Yahweh has given the Midianite camp into your hands."*

9-11 Despite the resolution he had shown in doing what he had been told to do, the *night* after he had sent most of his fighting force away must have been a very anxious one for Gideon, especially with the battle likely to happen the next day. In 6:36-40 he had taken the initiative in seeking a sign to assure him of victory; here, on this most critical night, he is graciously given one without having to ask for it. Furthermore, the words *if you are afraid* are ironical, and indicate that Gideon is not yet free of his past in spite of the symbolic stand he had taken against it by dismissing the "fearful" back in verse 3. Fearfulness, for most people, is not a weakness that can be conquered once and for all, but something that must be resisted and overcome again and again. Nor is it something that afflicts lesser mortals only; the permission given to Gideon to take *Purah,* his *assistant,*[70] with him is reminiscent of the permission Moses was given to take Aaron (Exod. 4:10-17). It is a reminder that the one indispensable requirement for a leader of God's people is not fearlessness, but obedience. On reflection, the dismissal of the fearful back in

---

69. See the notes to the translation of this same description of the enemy forces in 6:3 and 6:33.

70. Literally, his "young man" *(na'ar).*

verse 3 may have been another example of divine considerateness rather than
an indictment of fearfulness as such; in a situation where most were not required, the fearful were allowed to leave first. At any rate, while Gideon was
troubled by fearfulness, he was not paralyzed by it now any more than when
he had been told to destroy his father's altar; he went down to the enemy
camp as he was instructed to do (v. 13), and he received the "strengthening"
he was promised (v. 11).

12   In deliberate sharp contrast to the smallness of Gideon's band of
three hundred, this verse lays enormous stress on the vast number of the enemy forces: *all the Easterners,* not just the Midianites, but their Amalekite allies as well, as in 6:3 and 6:33. Then come the metaphors. As Gregory Mobley
has so nicely expressed it, the enemy is of "entomological" proportions, blan-
keting the valley like a plague of locusts, their camels innumerable.[71] Like a
foul counterfeit of the progeny promised to Abraham, they are uncountable
(cf. Gen. 22:17; 32:12). The language is poetic and hyperbolic, put the point is
perfectly clear: if there is to be a victory at all, it will have to be God-given. No
other kind of victory is possible for three hundred against so many.

13-14   With the stealth of spies, Gideon and his assistant enter the
enemy camp under cover of darkness and creep to within earshot of two men
discussing a dream that one of them has had. The dream symbolism reinforces, for Gideon and the reader, that what verse 12 has shown is clearly
needed (a miraculous victory) will indeed be given: Yahweh will achieve a
great victory with the most unpromising material. A *loaf of barley bread* —
unimpressive, perhaps even moldy[72] — comes tumbling out of nowhere
(down the hill?), hits *the tent,* overturns it, and makes it collapse. In the context in which it occurs the dream hardly needs interpretation: it is the projec-
tion of a strange, inexplicable dread that has come upon the enemy. It seems
that their own spies have been out, gathering the kind of intelligence that often makes the crucial difference to a battle. They have heard of *Gideon, son
of Joash, the* [well-known] *man of Israel.* But given their overwhelmingly superior numbers, they have nothing more to fear from him than from a barley
loaf, do they? Yet for some reason they do fear him, and in the dream their
fears rise up and confront them. It foretells disaster: *God has given* Midian
and its whole camp (symbolized by *the tent*) into Gideon's hand (v. 14).
There is indeed going to be the miraculous, God-given victory that is needed,
and that God has promised (v. 11).

The strange dread which has manifested itself in the dream is like the
"great fear" that came upon the citizens of Jericho before it fell to Joshua

---

71. Mobley, *Empty Men,* p. 132.

72. Boling (*Judges,* p. 146) renders ṣᵉlôl [ṣᵉlîl] leḥem śᵉʿōrîm by "moldy barley
bread," relating ṣᵉlôl to Aramaic ṣalla (to become dry, cracked, putrid).

(Josh. 2:9). It is a supernatural, divinely induced fear, and the knowledge that it has already begun to take hold of the enemy is the perfect antidote to Gideon's own fear (v. 10). It is all the proof he needs, now, that the impossible is about to happen again as it has in the past. The long drought since the time of "wonders" (6:13) is finally coming to an end. The God of the exodus has turned his face toward his people again.

15 Gideon's first response to hearing the dream and its interpretation is to worship, as he had done in 6:19-24. In a sense, even though it has come through a conversation between his enemies, this experience has been just as much an encounter with God as Gideon's commissioning by the divine messenger had been, and inspires him with just as much awe. Other urgent and necessary things must be done, but a man who has had an encounter with God knows that worship is the indispensable starting point for everything else.

The unit that began with Gideon going down to the enemy camp ends with his returning from it. It ends with Gideon telling everyone (v. 15) what Yahweh has told him personally at the outset (v. 9). But Gideon now speaks with the boldness of a man whose fears are gone. The time for action has come, and with a cry similar to Deborah's in 4:14, Gideon calls on his men to ready themselves for battle: *"Arise, for Yahweh has given the Midianite camp into your hands."*

(7) Gideon and His Three Hundred Rout the Midianites (7:16-25)

16 *He divided the three hundred men into three contingents, and put trumpets in the hands of all of them, and empty jars, with torches inside the jars.*

17 *He said to them, "Watch me, and do as I do. Look, when I come to the edge of the camp, then what I do you must do.*

18 *I will blow the trumpet — I and all who are with me — and you too will blow the trumpets around the whole camp, and say, 'For Yahweh and for Gideon.'"*

19 *So Gideon came, and the hundred men who were with him, to the edge of the camp at the beginning of the middle watch, when they had just set up the sentries. They blew the trumpets and smashed the jars that were in their hands.*

20 *Then the three contingents blew their trumpets and smashed their jars. They grasped the torches with their left hands, and with their right hands the trumpets, so they could blow them, and cried, "A sword for Yahweh and for Gideon!"*

21 *Each man stood in his place around the camp, and the whole camp ran; they shouted and fled.*

22 *The three hundred men blew the trumpets, and Yahweh set the sword of each man against his neighbor throughout the whole camp. The camp fled as far as Beth-shittah, toward Zererah, as far as the edge of Abel-meholah, near Tabbath.*

23 *The men of Israel were called out from Naphtali, from Asher, and from all Manasseh, and they chased after the Midianites.*

24 *Gideon had sent messengers throughout Mount Ephraim, saying, "Come down to intercept the Midianites, and seize the fords they are heading for, as far as Beth-barah and the Jordan. So all the men of Ephraim were called out, and seized the fords as far as Beth-barah and the Jordan.*

25 *They captured the two Midianite generals, Oreb and Zeeb. They slew Oreb at the rock of Oreb, and Zeeb they slew at the winepress of Zeeb. Then they pursued Midian, and the heads of Oreb and Zeeb they brought to Gideon beyond[73] the Jordan.*

16-18   The strategy Gideon employs in the attack is not a revealed one as far as we can tell from the details of the narrative, but one devised by Gideon himself. The only thing that has been revealed to him, by the overheard conversation in the Midianite camp, is the nervousness of the enemy. The plan that Gideon now puts into effect is clearly intended to exploit this nervousness to the full and give Israel the maximum advantage that can be gained from it. The intention seems to be to give the impression that Gideon commands a much bigger force than he actually does, and has the enemy camp completely surrounded. This will deny the enemy any obviously right place to launch a counterattack, or any one clear direction in which to flee. By attacking at night, Gideon can also make maximum use of the initial confusion caused by the sudden waking of the sleeping enemy. It is a clever plan, and shows Gideon to be surprisingly resourceful. Nevertheless, given the overwhelming size of the enemy force compared with Gideon's three hundred, it would have had no chance of success without the uncanny fear that Yahweh has already instilled in the Midianites. Gideon is simply making the most of what God has already given him, or, in other words, defeating an enemy that has already been "given into his hands" (v. 14).

As explained earlier, the required number of *trumpets* has been made available by utilizing what those who were dismissed in verse 8 were made to

73. In contrast to most English versions, the NIV renders *mēʿēber* "*by* the Jordan," presumably to avoid the apparent contradiction between this verse and 8:4. If Gideon "crosses" the Jordan there, how can he already be "beyond" it here? But *mēʿēber* is not attested with the sense "by/near" elsewhere. A better solution is to recognize 8:4 as a flashback. See the comments there.

leave behind. The same can be assumed for the *jars* and *torches*. These are strange pieces of equipment indeed to be armed with, and the willingness of Gideon's men to go into battle encumbered with them expresses a radical trust in God and in Gideon as his chosen leader. If God does not deliver on the assurances he has given, they will be even less able to defend themselves than they would normally be (e.g., with shields).

After dividing the men into *three contingents* (v. 16), Gideon keeps one of the contingents with him. When Gideon and his contingent *(I and all who are with me)* blow their trumpets, it will be the sign for the men in the other two contingents to do the same (v. 18). The cry, *"For Yahweh and for Gideon,"* expresses "the heart of Israelite social structure in the judges period. The declaration of war asserts the unity of Yahweh's action and his people's destiny, as in the stories of Ehud (3:28) and Deborah (5:8-9)."[74]

19-22a Gideon's operation was timed to perfection. It is not clear from the scant data we have what system of "watches" (periods of guard duty) was used at the time, or whether the Israelites and the Midianites used the same system. Exodus 14:24 and 1 Samuel 11:11 refer to the "morning watch" *('ašmōret habbōqer)*. Mark 13:35 implies that in Roman times there were four watches: evening, midnight, cockcrow, and morning, and the rabbis debated whether there were three watches or four *(Berakoth* 3a-b).[75] Here in Judges 7, the expression *the middle watch (hā'ašmōret hattîkônâ)* suggests that the Midianites were using a three-watch system,[76] in which case Gideon and his leading contingent of one hundred arrived on the outskirts of the Midianite camp at the beginning *(rō'š)* of the midnight shift, when those going off-duty were tired and distracted, and their replacements were not yet properly settled.

Everything goes according to plan. The only minor discrepancy between the plan itself and its execution is the additional word *sword* in the shout of Gideon's men: *"A sword for Yahweh and for Gideon!"* (v. 20; cf. v. 18). This may be due to a minor textual error in either verse 20 itself or in verse 18,[77] or more likely a slight variation introduced by the author for thematic reasons (see below), rather than any irregularity in the execution of the plan itself. In any case, a strong contrast is drawn between the discipline shown by Gideon's men *(each man stood in his place,* v. 21), and the completely opposite behavior of the startled Midianites (they all *ran, shouted, fled,* and in their confusion began to fight one another, vv. 21-22). In verse 22a this self-destructive panic is explicitly said to be Yahweh's doing, using

---

74. Boling, *Judges,* p. 147.

75. So Boling *(Judges,* p. 147), who acknowledges his indebtedness to Freedman.

76. As in Jubilees 49:10 and 12.

77. See the notes in the *BHS* textual apparatus.

a play on the word *sword: Yahweh set the* <u>sword</u> *of each man against his neighbor.* In verse 20, where it appeared unexpectedly, *sword* was probably metaphorical for "battle," whereas in verse 22 it is literal. The "swords" that Yahweh used to destroy his enemies in this "battle" were those of the Midianites themselves; which is another way of saying that, although the human tactics were brilliant, the victory was God-given. Gideon's men did not even have to fight, just do as they had been told (with the trumpets, jars, and torches), then "stand in their places" around the camp (v. 21).[78] But with the tide turned and the enemy fleeing in disarray, it was time for the Israelites to capitalize on the victory in a more conventional way, as described in verses 22b-25.

22b-24   None of the places mentioned here have so far been located with certainty, but the sites that have been suggested all lie south of Beth-shean, at the eastern end of the Jezreel Valley, and just east or west of the Jordan.[79] In any case, verse 24 makes it clear that the direction of flight of the Midianites and their allies is to the south-east, to and across the Jordan River, whence they had come.[80]

There is nothing novel or particularly creative about Gideon's tactics now; he calls for reinforcements and orders them to intercept the fleeing Midianites at the *fords of the Jordan* (vv. 23-24), just as Ehud had done (3:28). Those who answer the call, for the most part, are from the same tribes as had already responded to his first call: *Naphtali, Asher, and all Manasseh* (cf. 6:35).[81] The rapidity with which they respond suggests that the 22,000 of verse 3 and the 9,700 of verse 8 had not dispersed completely, and that many of them were still relatively close at hand.[82] Any shortfall was made up by sending messengers to call up volunteers from *Ephraim* as well (v. 24). While all participate in the general pursuit of the enemy, it is the *Ephraimites* in particular who are ordered to *seize (lākad) the fords* they are heading for, probably because their territory, further south, lay closest to the fords in question. The fords are *seized* as Gideon had ordered (v. 24), but apparently not in time to prevent at least some of the Midianites escaping, since the pursuit of them continues, beyond the Jordan, in verse 25 and the following chapter.

78. Cf. Exod. 14:13, "Take your stand and see the salvation of Yahweh."
79. See *OBA,* p. 84, and the relevant entries in *ABD* and *NBD.*
80. See comments on 6:2-6.
81. Zebulun is strangely absent, though nothing is made of this. The expression *all Manasseh (kol-mᵉnaššeh)* here, as in 6:35, probably means simply Manassites other than Gideon's own clan rather than both main parts of the tribe of Manasseh, east and west of the Jordan respectively.
82. The 9,700 of v. 8 had merely been sent "to their tents," and so in effect made reservists.

25 Despite the limited success in cutting off the fleeing enemies, this part of the narrative is brought to a point of significant closure here with the report of the capture *(lākad)* and execution of *the two Midianite generals (śārîm),*[83] *Oreb* (Raven) *and Zeeb* (Wolf). The place-names, *rock of Oreb* and *winepress of Zeeb,* are clearly used anachronistically, since it was the events that gave rise to the names. But the use of the place-names by the narrator, reflecting the situation in his own day, is testimony to the importance of the moment: it left its mark on the landscape, and Isaiah's mention of it in the eighth century shows that it also left its mark on the national consciousness for generations to come (Isa. 10:26).

In terms of the formal shape of the narrative, what began at one winepress (6:11) ends at another (7:25). The marauders have been forced out of the land as juice is pressed out of grapes. Gideon has "saved Israel from the hand of Midian" as he was commissioned to do (6:14), and here the story might have ended. But it is not to be. Gideon himself has apparently already crossed the Jordan, and the Ephraimites follow suit, bringing the *heads of Oreb and Zeeb* with them. The frame of the narrative has been broken, and unforeseen complications begin to arise.

(8) Gideon Appeases the Ephraimites (8:1-3)

1 *The men of Ephraim said to him, "What is this that you have done to us, not to call us when you went to fight Midian?" and they contended strongly with him.*
2 *But he replied, "What have I just done compared with you? Aren't the gleanings of Ephraim better than the vintage of Abiezer?*
3 *It is into your hand that God has given the generals of Midian, Oreb and Zeeb. So what have I been able to do compared with you?" Then their feeling against him abated when he said this.*

1-3 As we noted earlier in our overview of the structure of the story, the chapter division after 7:25 is misleading. The first three verses of chapter 8 are an epilogue to what has gone before rather than the beginning of the next major movement. That comes in 8:4, which reverts to the point at which Gideon had crossed the Jordan (on which see further below).

The Ephraimites are angry because they were not included in the initial call-up. As the description of that call-up in 6:34-35 shows, they are apparently right; they were not summoned until the crucial nighttime attack on the Midianite camp was over and the enemy was in headlong flight toward

---

83. The word itself is nonspecific, but in this military context the *śārîm* are probably "captains," "generals," or the like.

the Jordan (7:24). It is not clear whether this was an oversight on Gideon's part, a deliberate snub, or a decision made for strategic purposes. Because of their location (to the south of Manasseh, on the flank of the retreating enemy) they were ideally situated to make just the kind of contribution that Gideon did eventually call on them to make. But they have clearly interpreted it as a snub, and their extreme sensitivity to it (they *contended strongly* with Gideon) reflects a rivalry between Ephraim and Manasseh, the two leading tribes of northern Israel, which went right back to the time of their father Joseph[84] and, like dry tinder, needed only a spark to ignite it.[85]

This confrontation is a dangerous moment. The fact that the Ephraimites have just captured and killed Oreb and Zeeb demonstrates their capability. It would be risky for Gideon to respond with force, and in any case he has more urgent business to attend to (the escaping Midianites). So he decides on diplomacy rather than further confrontation. His soothing words, whether he realizes it or not, take up the motif of the winepress and extend it by means of a double metaphor: *gleanings* (what is gathered after harvest) and *vintage* (the grape harvest itself). It is also a paradox: in this case, Gideon says, the *gleanings* are greater than the *vintage,* because to capture and execute key enemy leaders is a more glorious achievement than merely to begin the rout of the enemy in general.[86] Whether this is actually the case or not is beside the point; it is a carefully constructed conceit, intended to placate the Ephraimites by massaging their inflated egos. And it works (v. 3)! The "grape harvest" imagery confirms the fundamental connection of 8:1-3 with what has preceded it in chapters 6 and 7. Gideon was called at a winepress to give up threshing wheat (6:11, 14) to go and harvest "grapes." Both the "vintage" and the "gleaning" of that harvest are now complete.[87] The complication involving the Ephraimites has been contained. In terms of our earlier analysis of the broad structure of the narrative, 8:3 is the end of the first major movement. The fact that Gideon is "beyond the Jordan" is the only hint that there is to be a sequel.

In this first movement Gideon is a reluctant conscript who distrusts his own competence and relies wholly on God. In short, he is a model of Mo-

---

84. Gen. 48:10-14.

85. See also 5:14 and the comments there. There will be more trouble with the Ephraimites in 12:1-6. Boling (*Judges,* p. 151) notes that the Ephraimites "characteristically . . . arrive uninvited (12:1) or unexpected (5:14) in the book of Judges."

86. Cf. the way the "glory" goes to Jael rather than Barak in ch. 4, because she is the one who kills the enemy leader. In the phrase *the vintage of Abiezer,* the term *Abiezer* is probably a metaphor for Gideon himself (the son of "Joash the Abiezrite," 6:11). The confrontation is between Ephraimites and Gideon rather than the Ephraimites and the Abiezrite clan.

87. Moore, *Judges,* p. 174.

saic piety. He is commissioned by Yahweh and invested with Yahweh's Spirit (6:34). The war he engages in is holy war in which the victory is not his personal achievement but a divine gift. A rather different Gideon, however, appears in the second movement, which begins in 8:4.

d. Gideon's Career, Part 2: His Pursuit of the Midianites in Transjordan and Its Consequences (8:4-28)

(1) Gideon's Pursuit, Capture, and Execution of Zebah and Zalmunna (8:4-21)

4 *Gideon had come*[88] *to the Jordan and crossed it*[89] *with the three hundred men who were with him, weary but pursuing.*

5 *He said to the men of Succoth, "Please give loaves of bread to the people who are following me, for they are weary, and I am pursuing Zebah and Zalmunna, the kings of Midian."*

6 *But the rulers of Succoth replied, "Do you already have the hands of Zebah and Zalmunna in your hand,*[90] *that we should give your army bread?"*

7 *Gideon said, "Because you have responded like this, when Yahweh gives Zebah and Zalmunna into my hand I will flail your flesh with desert thorns and with briers.*[91]

8 *He went up from there to Penuel and said the same thing to them, and the men of Penuel answered him in the same way the men of Succoth had done.*

9 *So Gideon threatened them as well; he said, "When I return in peace, I will tear down this tower."*

10 *Now Zebah and Zalmunna were in Karkor, and their army was with them — about 15,000 men — all who were left of the entire army of the sons of the east; the fallen were 120,000 sword-bearing men.*

11 *Gideon went up by the way of the Bedouin, to the east of Nobah and Jogbehah, and struck the enemy camp, which was undefended.*[92]

---

88. On the rendering of this as a flashback, see the exegetical comments on this verse.

89. Reading *wayyabrēhû*, with the LXX and *BHS* apparatus, instead of the anomalous *'ōbēr hû* of the MT.

90. The Hebrew uses two different words for "hand": with their hands *(kap)* in your hand *(yād)*. The ESV preserves the wordplay. Most English versions have "with their hands in your possession," or something similar.

91. Cf. Boling, *Judges*, p. 153.

92. Literally, "secure" *(betah)*, but that the intended sense is "undefended" (secure only in thought) is confirmed by the double use of the same word in 18:7 with reference to Laish, which was easy prey for the Danites for exactly the same reason.

12 *Zebah and Zalmunna fled, but Gideon pursued them and captured the two Midianite kings, Zebah and Zalmunna, and routed their entire army.*

13 *Then Gideon, the son of Joash, returned from the battle, from the direction of the Heres Pass.*[93]

14 *He captured a youth of the men of Succoth and asked him, and he wrote down for him the names of the leaders of Succoth, and the elders — seventy-seven men.*

15 *He came to the men of Succoth and said, "Look, here are Zebah and Zalmunna, about whom you derided me, saying, 'Are the hands of Zebah and Zalmunna already in your hand, that we should give bread to your weary men?'"*

16 *He took the elders of the city, and used the desert thorns and briers to teach[94] the men of Succoth a lesson.*

17 *As for the tower of Penuel, he tore it down, and killed the men of the city.*

18 *Then he said to Zebah and Zalmunna, "Where are the men you killed at Tabor?" They replied, "They looked like you; each had the bearing of a royal son."*

19 *Gideon replied, "They were my brothers, my mother's sons. As Yahweh lives, if you had spared their lives, I would not kill you."*

20 *He said to Jether his firstborn, "Arise and kill them." But the young man did not draw his sword, because he was afraid, for he was still a youth.*

21 *Zebah and Zalmunna said, "You arise yourself and attack us, for strength is the measure of a man." So Gideon arose and killed Zebah and Zalmunna, and took the ornaments which were around the necks of the camels.*

4 I have translated verse 4 as a flashback *(Gideon had come to the Jordan and crossed it)* because the context makes it clear that it is one, even though there is no indication of it in the syntax of the underlying Hebrew text. Gideon was already "beyond the Jordan" in 7:25. We have had similar unmarked flashbacks in 2:6 and 3:7.

The expression *but pursuing (wᵉrōdᵉpîm)* makes clear the purpose for which Gideon has crossed the Jordan, and which he is still intent on carrying

93. Literally, "from the *ascent (milmaʿᵃlēh)* of Heres," but in retracing his steps Gideon would be coming down (into the Jabbok/Jordan Valley) rather than up as he approached Penuel (see v. 11, where he "goes up" from Penuel on his outward journey).

94. The versions have the same verb (flail) as in v. 7, but this is more likely to be a harmonizing "correction" rather than the original reading.

through despite the near exhaustion of his men. The absence of an object, however, leaves open the question of exactly whom he is pursuing. The obvious answer is: those Midianites and their allies who managed to cross the Jordan before that escape route was cut off. But verse 5 reveals that Gideon has a more particular quarry in mind. Only the *three hundred* remain with Gideon now. With the fords seized and Oreb and Zeeb captured and killed, the rest of Gideon's men, like the Ephraimites, apparently think that they have completed their brief (7:23-24). The three hundred, however, are a more disciplined, more closely knit group over whom Gideon's personal influence is stronger. They are his personal *army (ṣābā'),* and he leads them like a warlord. Where he goes, they go.

5-7 The first town Gideon and his men come to after crossing the Jordan is *Succoth* (the modern Tell Deir 'Allah). It is situated just 4.5 miles (7 km.) east of the Jordan, where the River Jabbok flows into the Jordan Valley. The word *Succoth (sukkôt)* means "shelters," and according to Genesis 33:17 the town was so named because Jacob built temporary "shelters" *(sukkôt)* there for his cattle on his way back to Canaan. In Joshua 13:27 it is listed among the towns of the tribe of Gad. So Gideon is still in Israelite territory, and might reasonably expect to be well received — even welcomed as a hero. But he receives a rude shock: when he asks the leading *men* of Succoth (its *rulers, śārîm,* v. 6) to give his weary men bread, they refuse.

We learn here, with some surprise, that the object of Gideon's pursuit is not the fleeing Midianites in general, but two particular men: *Zebah and Zalmunna,*[95] the *kings* of Midian. Why the Midianites have two kings is not explained. Perhaps, as suggested by Daniel Block, the term "Midianites" is used rather loosely here, and the two are kings of the Midianites and their Amalekite allies respectively.[96] In any case, as *kings* they are presumably of higher rank than the "generals" *(śārîm)* the Ephraimites have already disposed of (7:25), and Gideon doesn't consider the war over until they, too, are captured and executed. But the threefold mention of the two names in verses 5-7, and the intensity with which Gideon responds to the refusal of the men of Succoth to help him get them, suggests that there may be more to Gideon's pursuit of these two men than he has so far revealed.

As far as we know, the men of Succoth, unlike the Ephraimites, don't have any personal quarrel with Gideon. But they are not confident that he will succeed, and probably fear reprisals from the Midianites if he fails. The location of Succoth east of the Jordan would leave it very exposed. Let him return with the *hands (kap)* of the two kings as trophies to prove his victory;

95. *Zebah* means "sacrifice." The meaning of *Zalmunna* is uncertain. See Block, *Judges, Ruth,* p. 289, for some of the suggestions that have been made.
96. Block, *Judges, Ruth,* p. 289, n. 652.

then they will align themselves with him, not before. But Gideon is incensed at their equivocation and promises reprisals of his own. When he returns, he will *flail* their *flesh* with *desert thorns* and with *briers* (v. 7). It is violent language and no idle threat, as subsequent events will show. In the first phase of Gideon's career we saw a diffident young man gradually becoming a warrior. Now we are witnessing another transformation. The full picture of what Gideon will become this time is not yet in place, but the promise of violence against the men of Succoth is worrying; they are, after all, fellow Israelites.

8-9 *Penuel* (Telul edh-Dhahab) is a further 5.5 miles (9 km.) east, up the course of the Jabbok. The better known "Peniel" (the face of God) is a variant of the same name.[97] It is another town with deep roots in Israel's past, for it was here that Jacob had a life-changing encounter with God, and called it Peniel because of the special significance it had for him (Gen. 32:22-32 [Heb. 23-33]). But no such encounter happens in Gideon's case, which may be why the alternate spelling is preferred. In fact, God no longer seems to have any part in his actions. The same scenario unfolds here as in Succoth, except that this time Gideon promises to tear down *this tower* when he returns *in peace (bešālôm)*. This is highly ironical, of course! The *šālôm* (victory, safe-and-soundness) in which Gideon expects to return will mean anything but *šālôm* to the people of Peniel. Their *tower (migdāl)* — fortress, stronghold,[98] their town's icon — will not protect them from Gideon's wrath. One can almost hear the disdain in his voice: "*this* tower" he will tear down (v. 9).

10-12 The scene now shifts to *Karkor,* where Zebah and Zalmunna are camped (v. 11) with what's left of their army. The location of Karkor is uncertain, but the most favored identification places it in the Wadi Sirḥan, 62.5 miles (100 km.) east of the Dead Sea, deep in the heart of Midianite territory.[99] To get there from Penuel, Gideon and his men would have to travel 81.5 miles (130 km.), no small task for men who were already weary and short on supplies. Of course Gideon may not have known how far ahead of him they were; the characters in a narrative normally do not know all that the reader knows. But press on he does, following the caravan routes *(the way of the Bedouin)* out into the desert, and southward, to the east of *Nobah* and *Jogbehah.*[100]

---

97. The two forms of the name occur in adjacent verses in Gen. 32:30-31 (Heb. 31-32). In the consonantal text the difference is between *waw* and *yod* in the second position, two letters which are easily confused in the old Hebrew script.

98. *migdāl* was the normal term for a fortress-temple in Middle and Late Bronze Age Palestine (Boling, *Judges,* p. 156).

99. Cf. H. O. Thompson, "Karkor," *ABD* 6:6.

100. Again, the locations are not known with certainty, but they were probably fortress towns guarding the north-south caravan route east of the Dead Sea. Num. 32:35 lists Jogbehah as one of the towns the Israelites had captured from Sihon, king of Ammon, in the time of Moses. Cf. P. N. Franklyn, "Jogbehah," *ABD* 3:880.

Zebah and Zalmunna's 15,000 men still far outnumber Gideon's meager three hundred, but are nevertheless only a remnant compared to the 120,000 they have lost;[101] and there is a rather sardonic touch in the way the fallen are referred to here as *sword-bearing* men. The decimation of the invading force began, we remember, when Gideon's three hundred took them by surprise and Yahweh made them turn their "swords" against one another (7:22). Will it happen again? we wonder. The possibility certainly seems to be there, because Gideon again has the advantage of surprise. Zebah and Zalmunna have not expected him to have pursued them this far. Their camp is *undefended* (v. 11);[102] they think they are safely home. But they are mistaken. When Gideon attacks, the same basic thing happens as before — flight, pursuit, and capture — but with two significant differences: there is no reference to Yahweh causing things to turn out as they do, and the two enemy leaders are pursued and captured by Gideon himself (v. 12).

13-17 With his main objective achieved, it is time for Gideon to fulfill the threats he made to the leaders of Succoth and Penuel, which he does with chilling ruthlessness and apparent relish. He is probably referred to as *Gideon, the son of Joash* (v. 13), to prompt us to recall how far this "son of Joash" has come, and compare what he does now with what he did at the beginning (6:11-32). Gregory Mobley captures the contrast nicely:

> Gideon, who had once "threshed," *hbṭ,* wheat (Judg. 6:11), now "threshes," *dwsû,* the leaders of Succoth . . . [with] thorns and briers (Judg. 8:7, 16). Gideon, who had once "torn down" *(ntṣ)* the shrine of Baal at Ophrah (Judg. 6:25 [*sic*]), now "tears down" *(ntṣ* again) the fortification tower of Penuel (Judg. 8:17).[103]

Only Abimelech will surpass Gideon's brutality in punishing Israelites who have incurred his displeasure. It is the beginning of a civil war theme that will widen as the narrative of the book continues to unfold from this point.

In verse 13 the perspective changes from the objective viewpoint of the narrator to the subjective viewpoint of the people of Penuel and Succoth. We see Gideon through their anxious eyes as he returns from the battle *from the direction of the Heres Pass (milma*ʽ*alê heḥāres).*[104] The location of this pass is unknown, but assuming that Gideon retraces his steps along the route indicated in verse 11, it was probably to the east of Penuel, where the land

101. On the problem of the large numbers in Judges, see Section IX.C of the Introduction.

102. See the note on the translation at this point.

103. Mobley, *Empty Men,* p. 144. Judg. 6:25 should be Judg. 6:32, but the point is well made.

104. See the note on the translation at this point.

drops toward the Jabbok River valley, and is not to be confused with the "Mount Heres" *(har-ḥeres)* of 1:35, which was in western Palestine.

Gideon is quite thorough and precise as he approaches his grim task, capturing and questioning a young man from Succoth to obtain the names of the seventy-seven *leaders* and *elders* of the town (v. 14). The *elders (zᵉqēnê)* would have been heads of families, and therefore the senior, governing members of the community in a general sense (2:7; cf. Ruth 4:2);[105] the *leaders (śārê)* most likely had a more specialized, military role.[106] There would probably have been some overlap between them, but together they amounted to an ideal *seventy-seven.*[107] The *young man*'s knowledge of them may indicate that he was "a young official of the town council."[108] Succoth was apparently well governed. Gideon's very deliberate getting of their names may have been to make sure none escaped, or because he held these and no others responsible (and therefore took care to limit his retaliation to them). It may (arguably) be just, but it is also cold and calculating. With Zebah and Zalmunna in his hands (v. 15), Gideon will have his pound of flesh: nothing more, but also nothing less. He does to the leaders of Succoth exactly what he said he would do, only now the verb is *teach*[109] rather than *flail,* shifting the focus from the manner to the purpose of his action: to teach them never to refuse him again (v. 16). It is a severe lesson from a severe man.

In Penuel Gideon acts even more severely; not just "tearing down" the tower, as he had threatened, but also "killing" *(hrg)* the men of the city (v. 17). Given the extreme brevity of this note, it is not clear whether the word *men ('anšê)* refers here just to the elders/rulers (as in "*men* of Succoth" in v. 8), or all the adult males. In either case, Gideon's violence escalates, and continues to do so in verses 18-21.

18   In this climactic paragraph "killing" *(hrg)* becomes the central motif, with reference to it in every verse. This is not the killing that happens in the heat of battle, but the cold-blooded payback killing that happens after it, when the man who now has unchallengeable power uses it to settle old scores. Gideon has already killed the men of Penuel (v. 17); now he turns his attention to Zebah and Zalmunna.

The score Gideon has to settle with these two men is an intensely personal one: they killed his "brothers" (v. 19) — a charge they do not deny (v. 18b). *Tabor* (= Mount Tabor), as we saw in 4:6, overlooked the eastern

---

105. In v. 16 they are all called "elders."

106. See 7:25, where I have translated *śārê* as "generals"; for the use of *śārê* and *ziqnê* see 10:18 and 11:4 respectively.

107. Cf. Ezra 8:35; Exod. 24:9.

108. Block, *Judges, Ruth,* p. 292.

109. Literally, "caused them to know," the Hiphil of *ydʿ* (cf. 3:2). See the notes to the translation at this point.

end of the Jezreel Valley, and was therefore in the same general area in which the Midianites and their allies had been active. The incident Gideon refers to could have happened in any of the incursions by the Midianites and Amalekites in the past seven years (6:1-5). This is the first we have heard of it however; it is a piece of information the narrator has held back until now, and it is that very reticence that gives this particular moment the quality that it has. The personal stake that Gideon has had in the capture of these two men makes sense of so much that we have been observing, especially in this second movement. For example, the reason why the story could not end with the capture and execution of Oreb and Zeeb is that, as Boling has so shrewdly put it, "The Ephraimites had brought [Gideon] the wrong heads"![110] His brothers' blood was crying out to him from the ground, and he could not rest until he had avenged it.[111] It also explains the intensity with which he has engaged in the pursuit and reacted to any who refused to help him.

The question that Gideon puts to Zebah and Zalmunna in verse 18 *("Where are the men you killed . . . ?")* is clearly rhetorical, and more an accusation than a question in the normal sense. Both Gideon and his two captives know *where*[112] Gideon's brothers are (dead and buried), but the question taunts Zebah and Zalmunna with the pretense that they might be able to save themselves by producing them alive. The reply, in effect a counter-taunt thrown back at Gideon himself, is that his two brothers were just like Gideon himself. *Each had the bearing of a royal son,* and therefore a prize kill, so to speak. Killing them had been one of Zebah and Zalmunna's finest achievements, which they recall with pride rather than regret. It is a defiant statement, making it clear that they are not intimidated by Gideon, and heightening his pain by stressing his closeness to the two brothers they have killed. What we are seeing here is the ritual exchange of insults before a duel. Both parties are too proud to give any quarter. The only way the matter can be settled now is for one of them to kill the other, and in this case it is Gideon who holds all the cards.

Incidentally but very significantly (as we are about to see), this verse provides the first link between Gideon himself and kingship. In the eyes of the two kings of Midian, Gideon's murdered brothers *each had the bearing of a royal son.* Literally, they were like "sons of the king *(hammelek)*." It indirectly raises the issue of how king-like Gideon himself has become in his own eyes, and in the eyes of his followers.

---

110. Boling, *Judges,* p. 152.

111. See further on this below, including the rights and obligations of a *gōʾēl* (redeemer).

112. The NIV's *"What kind of* [men]?" provides an easier connection with what follows, but is not supported by the usage of *ʾēpōh* elsewhere. It regularly means "Where?" See *HALOT* 1:43; *DCH* 1:221.

19   The oath Gideon swears here produces the first reference to *Yahweh* since the second movement of the Gideon story began in 8:4. In contrast to the first movement, Yahweh has not been depicted as having any involvement in Gideon's actions (commissioning him, commanding him to do anything, assuring him of victory, or giving his enemies into his hand). Even now Yahweh does not enter the story as an active participant, but only as someone invoked by Gideon in an oath of self-justification: *As Yahweh lives,* says Gideon, *if you had spared their lives, I would not kill you.* In other words, Gideon is fully justified in doing what he is about to do; the two kings have brought it on themselves. But given Gideon's own recent actions at Succoth and Penuel and the contrast with the first movement that I have just referred to, it is difficult to see this oath as an expression of genuine piety. Since crossing the Jordan Gideon has shown himself to be much more a law unto himself than one who lives in dependence on God and does only as he is commanded to do.[113]

20   The introduction of Gideon's son *Jether* here comes soon after the link between Gideon and kingship in verse 18. It is another clue that the narrative is in transition. We will shortly hear more about Gideon and kingship, and about his sons. At the very least the fact that Jether is Gideon's *firstborn* raises the issue of succession in some sense, and the way Gideon commands Jether to *Arise and kill* Zebah and Zalmunna instead of doing it himself entails a delegation of power to him that is highly suggestive. Furthermore, within the warrior culture of the times, it would have been regarded as a bestowal of honor upon Jether rather than the imposition of an unwelcome task (cf. 4:9). It may also have been intended as a final humiliation for Zebah and Zalmunna (to be killed by someone below their rank),[114] or as training for Jether. To be a warrior as his father was, Jether would have to be able to kill; he had to be "blooded." Finally, we cannot help but wonder whether Gideon's action here betrays a lingering uneasiness he has about the deed, in spite of his oath. Was the oath, perhaps, a case of protesting too loudly, and is the delegation of the deed to Jether a covert way of Gideon distancing himself a little from it? We cannot know for sure, but the questions are natural ones.

What does seem clear is that Jether functions as a kind of foil for Gideon that reinforces some of the changes in him that we have been observing. Jether recoils from the deed, as Gideon had once recoiled; he is *afraid,* as

---

113. Cf. Block, *Judges, Ruth,* p. 295: "The oath was undoubtedly intended to impress his captives, but it is an empty exploitation of the divine name in violation of the Third Commandment (Exod. 20:7; Deut. 5:11). It was a glib reference to Yahweh to sanctify his personal vendetta."

114. Cf. 9:54, and Mobley, *Empty Men,* p. 51.

Gideon once was; and he sees himself as too young *(still a youth)* as Gideon had once protested that he was the least in his father's house (6:15). In other words, in Jether we see Gideon as he used to be, in contrast to Gideon as he now is. Our observations have been correct: Gideon has changed.

21   Zebah and Zalmunna are defiant to the end, and take advantage of Gideon's embarrassment at Jether's hesitation to taunt him one last time. *"Strength is the measure of a man."* That is, what makes a man a man is his strength *(gᵉḇûrâ),* and Gideon's delegation of the task to Jether is a sign of weakness. If he is strong, like a real man, let him prove it by killing them himself. Gideon does so. But the closing taunt of his two enemies has clearly stung him, and also left us as readers with a lingering question. What were Gideon's real motives in delegating the execution to Jether? Is he really as strong as he has appeared to be in this second movement? Does Gideon perhaps have an underlying weakness, a fatal flaw that will be his undoing?

Having killed Zebah and Zalmunna, Gideon takes the *ornaments* from around their camels' necks as war trophies. More detail about these ornaments is given in verse 26, where they take on a more sinister significance.

Excursus 5: Gideon's Pursuit of Zebah and Zalmunna and the Duty of the *gō'ēl haddām* ("redeemer/avenger of blood")

In the analysis of 8:4-21 above I have tried to indicate how a certain perspective is developed on Gideon's pursuit of Zebah and Zalmunna in the context of the Gideon narrative more generally. However, within the larger framework of the canon, there is another context that needs to be considered, namely, the Old Testament law relating to murder, and in particular the rights and duties of the "redeemer of blood" *(gō'ēl haddām).*

In the case of murder, Israelite law gave the nearest male relative the right and obligation of killing the murderer (Num. 35:12-28; Deut. 19:4-6, 11-13). To prevent abuse, however, there were safeguards to protect the innocent. Cities of refuge were established where a falsely accused person could seek sanctuary. They had the right to have their case heard by the elders, and no one was to be put to death on the evidence of only one witness (Num. 35:24, 30; Josh. 20:4). It seems that the onus was on the person who had killed without intent to take advantage of these provisions. In the open country, the *gō'ēl* does not incur any guilt for killing someone who has slain his near relative, even if it was accidental (Num. 35:19, 21).[115]

The question is whether these laws provide a context which needs to be taken into account in evaluating Gideon's pursuit and execution of the two kings in Judges 8. Historical questions such as the relative dating of the texts

---

115. For more detail see Gary S. Shogren, "Redemption," *ABD* 5:651.

are not relevant to the kind of literary/canonical reading of Judges we are doing. In the canonical ordering of the material, the laws are part of the biblical narrative which leads up to the book of Judges. In that sense they are part of the literary context in which Judges 8 is encountered and read, and must be taken into account.

There are some obvious points of apparent connection. The two men who have been slain are Gideon's blood brothers (his *mother's sons,* v. 19), so Gideon qualifies as a *gō'ēl.* The deed was deliberate, as admitted by Zebah and Zalmunna (v. 18), so there are no complications related to intent. Also, Gideon's oath, taken in the name of Yahweh (v. 19), presupposes an Israelite framework of law or custom which gives legitimacy to what he is about to do.

However, there are complicating factors of other kinds. First, the killing of Gideon's brothers happened in the context of a conflict between two nations, possibly in the early stages of Gideon's own war with Midian. The examples given in the relevant laws, however, all seem to have the normal, daily life of an Israelite community in view. They do not seem to be intended to apply to the killing that happens in war.

Second, the Israelite laws relating to warfare have holy (divinely sanctioned) war in view, and, given the lack of any explicit involvement of God in the second movement of the Gideon narrative, it is doubtful that the category of holy war can be extended into chapter 8.

Third, while Gideon's execution of the enemy kings is arguably just, even without recourse to a particular set of laws, his treatment of the citizens of Succoth and Penuel (especially the latter) is much harder to justify, and this is very significant for how he is presented in this second movement of the narrative.

Finally, and as a matter of principle, the perspective which is developed on Gideon's character and actions *within the Gideon narrative itself* is the primary one. It should not be unduly constrained by a perspective deduced from elsewhere, especially, as in this case, where the data on which it is based are of questionable relevance. In short, in Judges 8:4-21 Gideon is conducting a personal vendetta against Zebah and Zalmunna rather than acting as the agent of Yahweh's justice by fulfilling the duties of a *gō'ēl.*

(2) The Offer of Kingship and the End of Gideon's Career (8:22-28)

22 *Then the men of Israel said to Gideon, "Rule over us, you and your son and your grandson, for you have saved us from the hand of Midian."*

23 *But Gideon replied, "I will not rule over you, nor will my son rule over you; it is Yahweh who will rule over you."*

24 *Gideon said to them, "Let me ask of you one thing: let each of you*

give me an earring he has taken as spoil, especially[116] *the gold ear-rings which you have — the Ishmaelite ones."*

25 *They replied, "Certainly we will give them." Then each man spread out his cloak and threw on it the earrings he had taken as booty.*

26 *The weight of the gold earrings which he had asked of them came to 1,700 shekels of gold, without counting the crescent ornaments, pen-dants, and purple garments which had been on the Midianite kings.*

27 *Gideon made it into an ephod, and set it up in his own town, Ophrah; and all Israel played the harlot after it there, and it became a snare to Gideon and his household.*

28 *Midian was subdued before the people of Israel, and did not raise its head again, and the land had rest for forty years in the days of Gid-eon.*

22-23 While Gideon was not received well in Transjordan, it is clear from this verse that to those in the Israelite heartland west of the Jordan he has returned as a conquering hero. He has shown himself to be a strong and effective leader. The slayer of kings has *ipso facto* achieved a kingly status in the eyes of his followers, who now attribute their escape from the Midianite yoke directly to him, and make this the basis of their offer that he and his family should rule Israel in perpetuity:

> *"Rule over us (m*ᵉ*šāl-bānû), you and your son and your grandson, for you have saved us (hôša'tānû) from the hand of Midian."*

To make Gideon's family a ruling dynasty is effectively to make him a king — a major shift from the pattern of divinely chosen, charismatic judges by which Israel has been ruled to this point. Clearly, a lot is at stake. But exactly what are we to make of this offer to Gideon? Given that the promises to Abraham anticipate a time when "kings will come" from him (Gen. 17:6), and the law of Moses foreshadows a time when the Israelites will appoint over themselves a king whom "Yahweh [their] God will choose" (Deut. 17:15), the present moment is charged with high potential. Has the anticipated moment arrived, and is the offer to Gideon a bold recognition by the Israelites that the time has come to move on and embrace their God-given future?

The critical question for us as readers is how what happens here is interpreted by its narrative context. How does it appear in the light of what precedes and follows it? Clearly there has been preparation for it. The key term, "to save" (*yš'*), in the explanatory second half of the offer (*for you have saved us*), has occurred six times previously in the narrative, all in the first move-

---

116. Taking the two uses of *kî* in this verse as intensive (BDB, p. 472).

ment (6:14, 15, 36, 37; 7:2, 7). In every case the same point has been made, either directly or implicitly: it is Yahweh who saves Israel. Gideon and his fellow Israelites participate only as his weak but divinely enabled instruments. The point is made particularly pointedly in 7:2, as we have seen:

> *"The people who are with you are too many for me to give Midian into their hand, lest Israel affront me by boasting, 'My own hand has saved (yš') me.'"*

The danger was that the Israelites would misinterpret the victory as their own achievement and fail to honor the true Savior. To credit Gideon as their savior, without reference to Yahweh, is the same in principle, and only one step away from claiming the victory as their own. To his credit, Gideon recoils from the impiety of it and gives the theologically correct answer:

> *"I will not rule over you,*
> *nor will my son rule over you;*
> *it is Yahweh who will rule over you."* (8:23)

If the rationale of the offer is that the one who saves is entitled to rule, that entitlement belongs to Yahweh, not to Gideon, and even less to his son and grandson. Gideon knows this, but the irony of the situation is that the impiety from which he recoils is of his own making. From the outset of the second movement of the narrative he has acted more and more like a king, especially in his dispensing of summary justice on those who have resisted his authority. In crossing the Jordan he had already exceeded his commission and begun to move toward the kind of rule that is now offered to him.

24-27 According to Genesis 25:1-12, Midian and Ishmael were both sons of Abraham, by Keturah and Hagar respectively.[117] Hence we might expect their descendants, the Midianites and Ishmaelites, to be closely associated but distinct from one another. It seems, however, that with the passing of time the distinction between them became blurred. For example, in Genesis 37:27-36 the two terms are used interchangeably. Here in Judges 8, the reference to "the gold earrings — the *Ishmaelite* ones" seems to imply that the Ishmaelites, like the Amalekites, were among the Easterners who were confederate with the Midianites (6:3, 33). The way their *gold earrings* are singled out for special attention suggests that they were wealthy, something confirmed, incidentally, by Genesis 37:25, which portrays them as traders in spices. The total weight of the earrings, *1,700 shekels of gold* (v. 26), about forty-nine pounds or nineteen and a half kilos, adds to this impression of wealth. The mention, in the same verse, of the *ornaments* worn by the

---

117. For the Midianites, see the comments on 6:2-6.

kings of Midian and their camels, reminds us of Gideon's personal contribution to the victory and the resultant spoils.

Gideon's request for gold earrings to make an *ephod* is unnervingly like Aaron's request for similar materials to make a golden calf (Exod. 32:2-4).[118] On the other hand, it could be seen as the logical sequel to Gideon's assertion that *Yahweh* is the one who will rule. If Yahweh is to rule, he must be inquired of, and it could be with the intention of facilitating such inquiry that Gideon made an ephod and put it in Ophrah, where Yahweh had appeared to him, and where the altar he had built for Yahweh now stood.[119] A similar practice can be seen in 1 Samuel 23:6, 9 and 30:7, where David uses the ephod which was in the custody of Abiathar the priest at that time to inquire of Yahweh. Presumably the ephod in this case was the high-priestly ephod complete with its breastpiece containing the Urim and Thummim, which were "the means of making decisions for the Israelites . . . before the LORD" (Exod. 28:30 NIV). But David's use of the ephod in this way is exceptional. The Old Testament traditions generally associate the ephod with the period of Moses and Joshua rather than the period of the monarchy (see esp. Num. 27:21). The kings characteristically consulted prophets rather than the ephod. Nevertheless, the ephod which Gideon made was probably intended as a symbol of divine government according to the Mosaic ideal.

Like much else in the period of the judges, the ephod that Gideon makes is an anomaly. It is "set up" (v. 27) rather than worn and used by the high priest. Nevertheless, given the context of the offer that was made to Gideon and his response to it, the ephod was probably intended as a sign that God, not Gideon himself, was to be recognized and inquired of as the true ruler of Israel. After setting it up, Gideon retired from public life (8:29), as if to confirm that this was his intended meaning. But if it was an act of piety, it was one that went terribly wrong. The ephod becomes an object of worship rather than inquiry, and Gideon is implicated in the impiety by his manufacture of the ephod, by his "setting it up" (like an idol), and by his involvement in the irregular worship which came to be associated with it: *it became a snare to Gideon and his household* (8:27b; cf. 2:3). For the first time in the book, the slide back into apostasy begins during the judge's own lifetime, and he himself contributes to it.

28 This conventional ending, long delayed, now comes at last — but rather awkwardly, it must be said, after the events that have just been narrated. It seems too neat an ending after such a negative conclusion to Gid-

---

118. See further on this below.

119. Cf. Davies, who argues that Gideon effectively accepted the offer of kingship and "sought to show his royal position by the possession of an ephod." G. Henton Davies, "Judges VIII 22-23," *VT* 13, no. 2 (1963): 157.

eon's personal career. If Midian was *subdued* before the Israelites, and remained so, so that *the land had rest for forty years in the days of Gideon,* it was clearly a miracle of divine grace rather than an outcome that either the Israelites or Gideon himself achieved or deserved.

Summary: The Shape and Development of the Gideon Narrative in Retrospect

We have seen that there is a marked contrast in the way Gideon is portrayed in the two major movements of the narrative. In the first (6:1–8:3) he is presented as a model of Mosaic piety, diffident but obedient, mistrusting his own ability and relying totally on Yahweh, who has commissioned him and promised him victory. In the second (8:4-28), which begins when he crosses the Jordan, his declared purpose is to capture Zebah and Zalmunna, the Midianite kings (8:5), and he presses toward this goal with frenzied determination despite the hunger and weariness of his men and the refusal of the leaders of Succoth and Penuel to give him support. He expects these two kings to be given into his hand as surely as Oreb and Zeeb were (8:7), but in fact there is no indication now of any involvement by Yahweh, and the holy war motifs that were so prominent in the first movement are entirely lacking here (contrast 8:11-12 with 7:21-22). Moreover, Gideon's diffidence has completely disappeared. He now throws diplomacy to the wind, demanding support from towns on his route with threats of retribution to those who fail to comply. Gideon's personal resourcefulness, which in the first movement had been subordinated to the fulfilling of his divinely authorized mission, is now given full play, and it is clear that what he now achieves is by his own strength of character and tactical skill. His actions against Succoth and Penuel anticipate the similar but more brutal actions of his son Abimelech against Shechem and Thebez (compare, in particular, Gideon's action against the tower of Penuel, 8:17, with Abimelech's action against the tower of Shechem, 9:46-49). At length Gideon's motivation is revealed in the dialogue of 8:18-19: Zebah and Zalmunna had been responsible for the death of his brothers. It is a personal vendetta that Gideon has been prosecuting with such ruthless determination in Transjordan. Jether, Gideon's firstborn, who is unexpectedly introduced at this point (v. 20), serves as a foil for his father and points up the contrast between Gideon as he was and Gideon as he now is. The father's earlier diffidence is now mirrored in the son, who hesitates when he is told to kill the prisoners, *because he was afraid* (v. 20b). Gideon, by way of contrast, is now a man of *strength* (*gᵉbûrâ*, v. 21), and has *the bearing of a royal son* (v. 18).[120]

120. See the comments, above, on 8:18. Since the speakers are Midianite kings

Exodus motifs are less conspicuous in this second movement, but are present nonetheless, and serve to accentuate the changed perspective in which Gideon is viewed. Gideon and his followers are in the *desert* and are *weary* (8:7, 5; cf. Deut. 25:18), but no heavenly provision sustains them. The self-assertive and vindictive Gideon of this movement contrasts sharply with the meek Moses of the exodus traditions. But this does not mean that he entirely ceases to be a Moses figure. The Moses of the exodus traditions, too, overreached his authority in the desert, and according to 2 Kings 18:4 the bronze serpent that he made, like Gideon's ephod, became an idolatrous cult object to which the Israelites burned incense.

The way in which we are pointedly returned, at length, to Gideon's *own town, Ophrah,* in 8:27 is a classic example of ring composition which provides closure and invites us to read the end in the light of the beginning. At the beginning of the story Ophrah was the site of a clan cult, a family affair. At the end it has become a center where, according to 8:27, "*all Israel* played the harlot after the ephod," presumably under Gideon's patronage. So here, at Ophrah, the final irony of the story is enacted: Gideon, champion of Yahweh against Baal, presides over national apostasy. Only after his death, though, is the impiety carried to its logical conclusion: the Israelites reject Yahweh outright and make Baal-berith their god (8:33). So Gideon's challenge to Baal has been answered in full, and Gideon himself has contributed significantly to that answer. The man who started by being a "Moses" ends here by being an "Aaron," the fashioner of an idol for Israel to worship (Exod. 32:2-4).[121] The name Jerubbaal ("let Baal contend") has acquired an ironic twist, for Baal has indeed taken up his own cause! One aspect of the initial crisis (Israel's oppression by Midian) has been decisively resolved: *Midian was subdued before the people of Israel, and did not raise its head again* (8:28), but the other and more fundamental aspect of the crisis (Israel's unfaithfulness to Yahweh) has not been resolved at all, but become more acute.

2. Transition from Gideon to Abimelech (8:29-35)

29 *Jerubbaal, son of Joash, went and lived[122] in his own house.*
30 *Seventy sons were born to Gideon, for he had many wives.*

(v. 12), and Israel itself does not yet have a king, they are probably comparing Gideon's brothers (and therefore Gideon himself) to Midianite princes.

121. Cf. David M. Gunn, "Joshua and Judges," in *The Literary Guide to the Bible,* ed. Robert Alter and Frank Kermode (London: Fontana, 1989), p. 114.

122. Or, possibly, "held court" (as a king or judge). The same verb *(wayyêšeb)* was used of Deborah "sitting/presiding" under her palm tree in 4:5. See the comments on vv. 29-32.

31   *Now his concubine, who was in Shechem — she too bore to him a son, and he named him Abimelech.*

32   *Gideon, the son of Joash, died at a good old age, and was buried in the same grave as Joash his father, in Ophrah of Abiezer.*

33   *Now it came to pass when Gideon was dead, that the Israelites turned back and played the harlot after the Baals, and set up Baal-berith as their god.*

34   *The Israelites did not remember Yahweh their God, who had saved them from all their enemies round about.*

35   *Neither did they deal faithfully with the household of Jerubbaal (Gideon, that is) in return for all the good that he had done for Israel.*

29-32   The name *Jerubbaal, son of Joash,* is a cross between "Gideon, son of Joash" (who he was, 6:11, 29), and "Jerubbaal" (who he became, 6:32). Now, in the light of 8:27, the name *Jerubbaal* has acquired an ironic twist, as we have seen, and the merging of his two names into *Jerubbaal, son of Joash,* is a subtle reminder of the very "mixed" character he has turned out to be. The present unit, which provides the transition to the Abimelech narrative, further develops this double perspective in Gideon, and shows us the mixed legacy (partly good, partly bad) that he left to Israel.

Verse 29 opens the present transitional paragraph with a pun on the word *bayit*. In verse 27 the ephod became a snare to Gideon and his "household" *(bayit);* now he goes and lives in his own *house (bayit)*. As we noted, the latter statement probably means that he retired into private life[123] in keeping with his protestation that Yahweh, not he, was to rule Israel. This retirement probably took place soon after he had installed the ephod in Ophrah, while he was still relatively young (6:15), and may have lasted many years (see v. 28). It was presumably during those years that the details of his family life given in verses 30 and 31 took place, but they have been held over until now because they are significant mainly for what follows: the career of his son Abimelech. Paradoxically, however, Gideon's household as it is described in these verses looks far more like that of a ruler than of a private citizen. Indeed, it seems that his retirement was more symbolic than real.[124] He had *many wives* (cf. Deut. 17:17) by whom he sired *seventy sons* (cf. Abdon, 12:14, and Ahab, 2 Kgs. 10:1). He also had a *concubine* at Shechem who bore him *a son* named *Abimelech*. Here, in the pointed distinction between the "seventy" and the "one" (Abimelech), is the seed from

123. So Burney, *Judges,* p. 264.

124. Cf. Block (*Judges,* p. 302), who takes his going to his own house to indicate separation from his father rather than retirement as such: "Gideon ruled as Jerubbaal ben Joash from his own house."

which the fratricide of chapter 9 will grow. Like the apostasy of verse 27, this, too, is of Gideon's own making. The name Abimelech ("my father is king") is an ironic comment on the contradiction between Gideon's public pronouncements and private practice. It is also a portent: for as the ensuing narrative clearly indicates, Gideon did become a dynast, in fact if not in name, and the succession was decided in the bloody intrigues which attended Abimelech's rise to power, a son who had far fewer scruples about the acquisition and exercise of power than his father had had. For *Shechem* see the comments on 9:1.

33 The opening words of this verse, *Now . . . when Gideon was dead,* explicitly move us forward to the period in which the following narrative is set,[125] and the reference to *Baal-berith* (Covenant Baal) anticipates 9:46, where the same god is called *El-berith* (Covenant God).[126] It is highly ironic that the deity the Israelites turn to after Gideon's death should be so named, because what they do is an act of covenant unfaithfulness of the very first order. Their true "covenant God" is, of course, Yahweh, to whom they are now giving up all pretense of being faithful. Unfaithfulness, to both Yahweh and Gideon (after his death), is a theme which links the Gideon and Abimelech stories together.

34-35 These verses continue and complete the transitional function of this unit as a whole. We will return to them in our treatment of Jotham's speech in 9:7-21.

3. Abimelech's Disastrous Experiment with Kingship (9:1-57)

> *"If a man rolls a stone,*
> *it will roll back on him."*
>
> (Prov. 26:27)

In this sequel to the Gideon story two explicit statements of theme are provided by the narrator himself. They occur at 9:23-24, at a crucial point in the plot, and at 9:56-57, after the climax has been reached with the death of Abimelech. These two statements complement one another and point to retribution as the thematic key to the story as a whole: God causes the evil that Abimelech and the men of Shechem do to rebound on their own heads. The details of the narrative show this process being worked out with almost mathematical precision (see the comments on vv. 23-55).

---

125. Cf. the boundary-marking function of "after the death of Joshua" in 1:1.

126. Possibly an allusion to the covenant ceremonies performed at Shechem in Josh. 8:30-35 and 24:1-28.

In line with its focus on retribution, the narrative as a whole unfolds in three stages, as argued by Elie Assis:[127]

1. TRANSGRESSION	Abimelech becomes king after murdering his brothers	9:1-6
2. REBUKE	Jotham's fable	9:7-21
3. PUNISHMENT	Abimelech's decline and fall	9:22-57

a. Abimelech Becomes King in Shechem (9:1-6)

1 *Now Abimelech, the son of Jerubbaal, went to Shechem, to his mother's brothers, and spoke to them — the whole clan related to his maternal grandfather. He said,*

2 *"Say to all the rulers of Shechem, 'Is it better for you to have seventy men rule over you, all of them the sons of Jerubbaal, or one man?' Remember that I am of your own flesh and bones."*

3 *His mother's brothers spoke all these words about him to all the rulers of Shechem, and their hearts went out to Abimelech, for they said, "He is our brother."*

4 *So they gave him seventy shekels[128] of silver from the temple of Baal-berith, and Abimelech used it to hire worthless and reckless men, who followed him.*

5 *He came to his father's house in Ophrah and killed his brothers, the sons of Jerubbaal (seventy men) on one stone. Only Jotham, son of Jerubbaal, survived, for he had hidden himself.*

6 *Then all the rulers of Shechem came together, the whole Beth-millo, and went and made Abimelech king by the oak which had been set up — the one in Shechem.*

1 *Shechem* (Tell Balaṭa) was in the Israelite heartland, about 31 miles (50 km.) north of Jerusalem and 15.5 miles (25 km.) west of the Jordan. It was here that Abraham had first built an altar to Yahweh after arriving in Canaan (Gen. 12:6). Here, too, Joshua had called all the tribes together for a great covenant renewal ceremony at the completion of his campaigns of conquest (Josh. 24:1), and it lay at the southern end of the valley separating Gerizim and Ebal, the mountains of covenant blessing and curse respectively (Deut.

---

127. The following table is adapted from Assis's own on p. 133 of his *Self-Interest or Communal Interest: An Ideology of Leadership in the Gideon, Abimelech and Jephthah Narratives (Judg 6–12)*, VTSup 106 (Leiden: Brill, 2005).

128. The MT does not have the word "shekels," but it is presumably to be understood since the shekel is the standard monetary unit for Israel in the Old Testament.

11:29). So it was a place of huge symbolic importance. It has already emerged as a place of potential significance for the present narrative from the fact that Gideon had had a concubine there, and that Abimelech was his son by her (8:31). The sequel to the Gideon narrative here in Judges 9 is set in motion when Abimelech goes to Shechem to speak to *his mother's brothers,* and hence *the whole clan related to his maternal grandfather* of which they were now the leading male members.

Gideon was from the tribe of Manasseh (6:15), but Shechem was a city of Ephraim (Josh. 20:7; 21:21). We can only speculate why Gideon had taken a concubine there. Was it an attempt to heal the tense relationship between himself and the Ephraimites that had flared up in 8:1-3? Or, to put the same issue more positively, was it a king-like political liaison intended to symbolically unite the two largest northern tribes under his authority as the new national leader? But why then a *concubine* rather than a wife (8:30)? Was it simply a love match which he chose not to dignify as a marriage as a snub to the Ephraimites in retaliation for the hassles they had given him? Whatever the reason, it caused trouble — big trouble.

2-3 The *rulers* of Shechem are literally its "baals" *(baʿᵃlîm),* not in the religious sense here, of course, but in the secular sense of "city fathers" or "chief citizens" — those who had control of the town's affairs.[129] But *baʿal* is always a charged word in Judges, and especially in this narrative, and its use here at the outset suggests that Abimelech will be associated with *baʿᵃlîm,* in one way or another, through the whole course of his disastrous kingship. He seeks to influence the rulers of Shechem through his relatives. His message to them is that a power struggle is under way, and they are going to have to choose between him and the other sons of Jerubbaal (the *seventy* of 8:30). His own relatives in Shechem are going to have to do the same, but Abimelech puts it to them that in their case at least the choice should be clear: he alone is *their own flesh and bones* (their blood relative).[130] It was a telling argument in a society where the cohesive power of faithfulness to Yahweh and his covenant with Israel was on the wane, and tribalism, in the worst sense, was again on the rise. Abimelech's relatives do not hesitate; they immediately take up his cause, and the rulers of Shechem follow suit. They adopt him as their *brother,* too (v. 3). If there is to be a power struggle, they will stand with Abimelech (v. 3).

4-5 The rulers of Shechem immediately put their money where their mouth is by giving him *seventy shekels*[131] *of silver* to finance his bid

---

129. Cf. Josh. 24:11; Judg. 20:5; 1 Sam. 23:11-12; 2 Sam. 21:12.

130. Cf. Gen. 2:23. With the English versions in general I take the final clause v. 2 to refer to Abimelech's relatives rather than the rulers of Shechem.

131. About 0.80 kilograms, or 1.75 pounds.

for power. The source of the money, the *temple of Baal-berith* (Covenant Baal), indicates their participation in the apostasy referred to back in 8:33[132] and plays on the ironic potential of their titles: the *ba'ălîm* (lords) of Shechem are in league with *ba'al* (Baal). They even have a *temple* for him in Shechem, and draw the funds they give to Abimelech from its treasury. So Abimelech's rule is supported by both Baal and the *ba'ălîm:* it is a very Canaanite affair indeed.

The number of shekels *(seventy)* corresponds to the number of Abimelech's half-brothers (vv. 2, 5), and hints, in a particularly sinister way, at what he might do with it.[133] If it is a prophecy, it is soon fulfilled. Abimelech uses the money to hire some *worthless and reckless men,*[134] who follow him to Shechem, where (presumably with their help) he kills all seventy of his half-brothers on *one stone,* a detail that will prove to be significant later in the story. But there is a complication: one of them, *Jotham,* escapes (v. 5b).

6 Some material features of Shechem now come into view. The first, *Beth-millo* (House of Millo, or Millo-House), was probably a building of some kind, and in view of the use of the word *millô'* elsewhere, may have been fortress-like and quite substantial.[135] Furthermore, since *the whole Beth-millo* is in apposition here with *all the rulers of Shechem,* it may have been the place where the rulers normally met.[136] The second feature that comes into view is a notable tree: the *oak ('ēlôn)* which had been *set up (muṣṣāb)*[137] — *the one in Shechem.* Just how a tree could be "set up" is not clear unless it was a monument of some kind (a carved pillar representing an

---

132. It is possible that *ba'al berît* was understood as "Covenant Lord" and used in Shechem as an alternative title for Yahweh. But clearly that is not how the writer of Judges saw the situation: for him, to worship *Baal-berith* was to worship another god (8:33). See also the comments on 9:46.

133. It also enables us, as Fokkelman has noted, "to compute the value of one human life to Abimelech and his faction: exactly one piece of silver." J. P. Fokkelman, "Structural Remarks on Judges 9 and 19," in *Sha'arei Talmon: Studies in the Bible, Qumran and the Ancient Near East Presented to Shemaryahu Talmon,* ed. M. Fishbane, E. Tov, and S. Talmon (Winona Lake, IN: Eisenbrauns, 1992), p. 36.

134. Literally, men who were "empty" *(rêqîm),* without wealth or social status, and "unrestrained, lawless" *(pōḥᵃzîm).* Cf. Jephthah's associates in 11:3, and the treatment of the social phenomenon they represent in Mobley, *Empty Men,* pp. 36-38.

135. [The] *Millo* of a town is frequently associated with its walls and other defensive structures (2 Sam. 5:9; 1 Kgs. 9:15; 11:27; 2 Kgs. 12:20; 1 Chron. 11:8; 2 Chron. 32:5), and in view of its likely derivation from *ml'* (to fill), its construction probably involved considerable earthworks.

136. Cf. Boling, *Judges,* p. 171.

137. *muṣṣāb* is the Hophal participle of *nṣb* (to be fixed, determined) (BDB, p. 662).

oak),[138] or a real tree that had been established ceremonially as having a particular significance. Given the association of trees elsewhere in Judges with government (Deborah's palm, 4:5; Joash's oak, 6:11), it is likely that the ceremonial oak (real or otherwise) here marked the *Beth-millo* as a place of governmental significance. The identification of the place in such a particular way stresses the importance of what takes place there: Abimelech is made *king*.

The installation of Abimelech as king is like a rerun of the offer of kingship to his father in 8:22-23, but with some very striking and significant differences. It was "the Israelites" who had made the offer to Gideon; here it is *all the rulers of Shechem,* with no reference to Israel as a whole. It is in effect a declaration of independence, making Shechem a breakaway city-state. Gideon was offered kingship because, in the estimation of his supporters, he had "saved" Israel. Abimelech is acclaimed because he killed his brothers. What Gideon had saved, Abimelech destroys. Gideon refused the offer of kingship; Abimelech accepts it. What happens in Shechem is a tragic perversion of the stipulation in Deuteronomy 17:15 that when the time came for Israel to have a king, "he must be from among your own brothers" (NIV).

b. Jotham's Fable and Its Application (9:7-21)

7 When Jotham was told, he went and stood on the top of Mount Gerizim. He lifted his voice, called out, and said to them, "Listen to me, rulers of Shechem, that[139] God may listen to you.

8 The trees went resolutely[140] to anoint a king to rule over them. They said to the olive tree, 'Reign over us.'

9 But the olive tree replied, 'Should I stop producing my rich oil, by which gods and men are honored,[141] to go and hold sway over the trees?'

10 Then they said to the fig tree, 'Come, you reign over us.'

11 But the fig tree replied, 'Should I stop producing my sweetness, my good fruit, to go and hold sway over the trees?'

12 Then they said to the vine, 'Come, you rule over us.'

13 The wild vine replied, 'Should I stop producing my wine, which makes gods and men happy, to come and hold sway over the trees?'

138. Cf. *BHS,* which recommends emending *muṣṣāb* to *hammaṣṣēbâ,* "the [oak] pillar."

139. A purpose clause, as indicated by the use of an imperfect *(weyiqtol)* after an imperative. Seow, *Biblical Hebrew,* pp. 243-44.

140. The infinitive absolute is used intensively before the finite verb: *hālōk hālekû.*

141. Reading Piel *yekabbedû,* with nonspecific subject, as effectively passive.

14 *Then all the trees said to the bramble, 'Come, rule over us.'*

15 *The bramble replied, 'If you are truly about to anoint me to be king over you, come and take refuge in my shadow; but if not, fire will go out from the bramble and devour the cedars of Lebanon.'*

16 *Now, if you have acted faithfully and blamelessly in making Abimelech king, and if you have dealt rightly with Jerubbaal and his house, and given him what is due to him —*

17 *my father, who fought for you, and hazarded his life in front of you, and saved you from the hand of Midian;*

18 *but you have risen up against my father's house today and killed his seventy sons on one stone, and made Abimelech, the son of his servant-girl, king over the rulers of Shechem, because he is your brother —*

19 *if you have acted faithfully and blamelessly with Jerubbaal and his house this day, then rejoice in Abimelech, and let him rejoice in you.*

20 *But if not, may fire go out from Abimelech and consume the rulers of Shechem, and Beth-Millo, and may fire go out from the rulers of Shechem, and from Beth-Millo, and devour Abimelech."*

21 *Then Jotham ran and fled as quickly as he could to Beer, and stayed there, away from Abimelech his brother.*

Jotham appears on the scene in verse 7 to confront the men of Shechem with the evil they have done. He calls on them to listen, and on God to witness their response to his words. He adapts a fable to his purpose, but the main thrust of the speech lies not in the fable itself (vv. 8-15) but in his application of it to the present situation (vv. 16-21).[142]

142. Eugene Maly has argued that "the meaning of the original fable . . . was clearly not directed against kingship itself but against those who refused, for insufficient reasons, the burden of kingship" ("The Jotham Fable — Anti-monarchical?" *CBQ* 22 [1960]: 303). Barnabas Lindars has accepted Maly's proposal and suggested that the fable may have originated in a Canaanite city-state of the conquest period when local landowners were more concerned to protect their own estates than to take responsibility for territorial claims which could no longer be sustained ("Jotham's Fable — A New Form-Critical Analysis," *JTS* 24 [1973]: 365). However, the majority view is that the fable probably arose early in Israel among those who saw kingship as an intrusion with no positive function (F. Crüsemann, *Der Widerstand gegen das Königtum: Die antiköniglichen Texte des Alten Testaments und der Kampf um den frühen israelitischen Staat*, WMANT 49 [Neukirchen-Vluyn: Neukirchener, 1978], pp. 19-32). But even granting that the original intention of the fable was to denigrate kingship as an institution, it does not follow that this is how it functions in its present literary context. The speech as a whole does not attack kingship as such but the foul play associated with Abimelech's rise to power (9:19-20). The fable is used to pour scorn on Abimelech, whom Jotham never addresses directly, by contrasting his absurd pretensions with the modest refusal tendered by men better than

The central charge he brings against his hearers is that they have not dealt *truthfully and blamelessly (beʾemet ûbetāmîm)* with Jerubbaal as they were obliged to do because of the benefits he had conferred on them (9:16).[143] He rehearses Jerubbaal's past good deeds on their behalf and the benefits they had enjoyed (v. 17), charges the men of Shechem with disloyalty (v. 18), and sets before them the alternatives of blessing (v. 19) or curse (v. 20). The blessing, of course, is delivered with heavy irony;[144] it has ceased to be a real alternative because the crime is irrevocable. The detailing of the curse in verse 20 is in effect a pronouncement of judgment. The narrator shows how the words of Jotham were fulfilled in the action of God that followed (v. 23), and the concluding words of the narrative describe the retribution which was visited on the evildoers as "the curse *(qelālâ)* that Jotham, son of Jerubbaal, spoke" (9:57).

There is a very close functional parallel, therefore, between the speech of Jotham here and the speech of the prophet in the preceding Gideon narrative. The prophet brought a lawsuit against the Israelites in the name of Yahweh; Jotham brings a lawsuit against the men of Shechem in the name of Jerubbaal. In fact, in terms of its rhetorical style and purpose, Jotham's speech as a whole is much more a covenant lawsuit than a fable; the fable is just a means to an end.[145] It does not necessarily presuppose the existence of a literal treaty between Jerubbaal and the citizens of Shechem, but it is the ideal form for a speech whose central thrust is that benefits conferred entail an obligation to show loyalty to the one who conferred them. It is also an ideal rhetorical form for a speech delivered in a city which, ironically, boasted a temple to *El-berith,* "Covenant God" (9:46; cf. 8:33; 9:4; see the comments on these verses).

Whatever Jotham's motives may have been, it is clear that he has been adopted as the narrator's own *alter ego,* the character in the story who gives voice to the narrator's own interpretation of the situation. Jotham's interpre-

---

himself (such as Gideon and his other sons?), and also, via v. 15b, to prepare the way for the pronouncement of Jotham's curse in v. 20. Cf. G. S. Ogden, "Jotham's Fable, Its Structure and Function in Judges 9," *TBT* 46, no. 3 (1995): 301-8.

143. The phrase *beʾemet ûbetāmîm* occurs in v. 16 and is repeated in v. 19 for emphasis. The same combination of terms occurs elsewhere in the Old Testament only in the covenant formula of Josh. 24:14 (Boling, *Judges,* p. 174).

144. Lillian R. Klein, *The Triumph of Irony in the Book of Judges,* JSOTSup 68 (Sheffield: Almond, 1988), p. 73.

145. As a rhetorical device the fable allows the speaker who has an unpopular point to make to gain a hearing for himself by approaching his subject obliquely and in an interesting manner (see, e.g., 2 Kgs. 14:9-10). Cf. Lindars, "Jotham's Fable," p. 361, and W. Richter, *Traditionsgeschichtliche Untersuchungen zum Richterbuch,* 2nd ed., BBB 18 (Bonn: Peter Hanstein, 1966), pp. 296-99, where the sociological-political functions of the fable genre are discussed with particular reference to the fable of 2 Kgs. 14:9.

tation of the evil committed by the men of Shechem is fundamental to the thematic connection the narrator makes in 8:34-35 between the Gideon narrative itself and its sequel:

8:34 The Israelites did not remember Yahweh = The theme of the
their God, who had saved them from all   Gideon narrative
their enemies round about.

8:35 Neither did they deal faithfully *(ḥeseḏ)* = The theme of its
with the household of Jerubbaal   sequel, the
(Gideon, that is) in return for all the   Abimelech
good that he had done for Israel.   narrative

Retribution is the primary theme of the Abimelech narrative, but by interpreting the evil done by Abimelech and his followers as faithlessness the narrator has established a firm connection with the Gideon story proper.[146] The statement in 9:22 that Abimelech ruled over Israel for three years involves the whole nation in this evil, not just the men of Shechem. Abimelech's followers are called "men of Israel" in 9:55.

7 *Jotham* was the youngest of Gideon's seventy sons, and the sole survivor of the massacre carried out by Abimelech and his hired killers (v. 5). *Mount Gerizim* is "the more southerly of the two mountains which overshadow the modern town of Nablus, 2.5 miles (4 km.) NW of ancient Shechem. . . . It has been called the mount of blessing because here the blessings for obedience were pronounced in the solemn assembly of Israel described in Jos. 8:30-35. A ledge halfway to the top is popularly called 'Jotham's pulpit.'"[147] Ironically, for the rulers of Shechem it becomes a mountain of curse.

8-9 The picture of the *trees* going to anoint a tree (whether olive, fig, vine, or bramble) symbolically represents men choosing one of their own kind as king (cf. Deut. 17:15). The distinctive quality of the *olive tree* is its *rich oil* (literally, its "fat," *dešen*). The use of *ʾelōhîm* as a true plural *(gods)* here and in verse 13 hints at the non-Israelite (probably Canaanite) origin of the fable. The practice of anointing was presumably thought of as honoring *gods* as well as *men* because it was a sign that the one anointed was chosen by the god. For an Israelite example see 1 Samuel 16:1, 13.

10-11 The distinctive property of the *fig tree* is its *good fruit*. Cf. Matthew 21:19; Mark 11:13.

---

146. Cf. L. Ginzberg, *The Legends of the Jews,* 7 vols. (Philadelphia: JPSA, 1909-38), 6:201 (citing Yelammedenu in Yalkut II, 64): "The ingratitude of the Israelites who permitted Abimelech to murder the children of their benefactor Gideon was counted unto them as though they had forsaken God; ingratitude is as grave a sin as idolatry."

147. G. T. Manley and F. F. Bruce, "Gerizim," *NBD,* p. 406.

12-13   The *vine,* of course, is especially valued for the *wine* that is produced from its fruit. Given its conjunction with *men* ("people"),[148] it is likely that *ᵉlōhîm* is again being used as a true plural *(gods),* as in verse 9. If so, it is another indication of the pagan origin of the fable. The statement about wine making both *gods* and *men* happy probably refers to revelries associated with the grape harvest, which, like the Bacchanalia of Greek and Roman times, involved drinking, singing, and dancing, which were thought to delight the gods as well as the human revelers.[149] No such activities were prescribed in the law of Moses, but the reference to girls "dancing in the vineyards" at a "festival to Yahweh" at Shiloh in 21:20-21 suggests that something akin to them was practiced in Israel in the judges period.

14-15   The identity and relevant characteristics of the *bramble* (*ʾāṭād*) are much harder to determine. It is generally reckoned to be the buckthorn,[150] a thorny bush or small tree with black berries. In some varieties the berries are edible, but this is incidental rather than central to its significance for human beings, since (unlike the olive, the fig, and the vine) it is a wild rather than a cultivated plant. It is hard to know what connotations it may have had for Jotham's audience, but the safest guide to this is the things that the text specifically associates with it, namely, *shadow* and *fire.* But even these have a riddle-like quality. Providing shade (protection) for their subjects was a traditional responsibility of kings (Lam. 4:20; cf. Ps. 91:1). But given its relative smallness, how can the bramble provide much of a shadow? And why is it prone to burst into flame? Whatever the answer may be to these questions, the point is that the bramble is a dangerous plant for human beings to associate with because it is unpredictable: it can provide a shelter (shadow) of sorts, but it can also destroy. The *cedars of Lebanon* (famously tall) are probably symbolic here, as in Isaiah 2:12-13 for the proud — in this case, the proud rulers of Shechem to whom Jotham is speaking. The bramble's response to the offer of kingship is startlingly different from that of the other trees. Far from declining the offer, it responds with a demand and a threat: "Make me your king, or I will destroy you" (v. 15).

Robert Boling has noted that three expressions from verse 8 ("to anoint," "over them," and "a king" — each one word in Hebrew) are repeated here, but with the second two reversed ("anointing," "a king," "over you").[151] This brings formal closure to the fable itself; what follows is application.

16-20   The way verse 19 repeats the opening words of verse 16 be-

---

148. Contrast Ps. 104:15, "Wine that gladdens the heart of *man*" (NIV), where the singular *ᵉnôš* is used.

149. Cf. Burney, *Judges,* p. 274.

150. *HALOT* 1:37; *DCH* 1:202.

151. Boling, *Judges,* p. 173.

fore going on indicates that verses 16 and 19-20 belong together, and that verses 17-18 are a parenthesis, as indicated in the translation.

Jotham makes it clear what the central issue is by piling up adverbs *(faithfully, blamelessly, rightly),* all of which have to do with the ethical status of what the rulers of Shechem have done. The issue is not kingship as such, but whether it was right for them to make this particular man king and, in so doing, to support and participate in his slaughter of Gideon's seventy sons. Clearly for Jotham the answer is no. In other contexts, the ethical terms in verses 16 and 19 all have strong associations with a covenantal relationship between God and human beings, and the obligations that go with it.[152] These connotations are reinforced here by the connection that has been made in 8:34-35 between the way the Israelites have treated Gideon's family and the way they have treated Yahweh (see above).

Kinship, and the entitlements and obligations that go with it, are clearly important elements of Jotham's argument in these verses, as they were of Abimelech's in verses 1-2.[153] But the point of verse 18 is that kinship alone *(because he is your brother)* is not sufficient reason for supporting someone irrespective of their character or the ethical status of their actions. Abimelech had asked the rulers of Shechem to consider what was "better" *(ṭôḇ)* for them to do (v. 2); Jotham asks them to consider whether they have acted *rightly (ṭôḇâ,* v. 16b). His basic charge is that the rulers of Shechem have debased goodness into expediency, and covenant faithfulness into tribalism. Their behavior has been inexcusable, and (as the *fire* of the fable has warned) they will pay a high price for it.

21 The unit that began with Jotham's entry in verse 7 ends here with his exit. Understandably, he flees. *Beer,* which means "a well," is mentioned in Numbers 21:16 as a place where the Israelites stopped as they were skirting around Moab on their way to Canaan. It was probably located on the edge of the desert, where it served as a watering place for nomads and traders. Its main appeal for Jotham was probably its remoteness from Shechem, and therefore from Abimelech. David later sought sanctuary for his family in the same general area during the reign of Saul (1 Sam. 22:2-4).[154]

---

152. For example, Gen. 6:9; Josh. 24:14; Job 1:1; Mic. 6:8.

153. Notice how Jotham refers to Abimelech's mother as a mere *'āmâ (servant-girl),* a person of no significance as far as kinship rights are concerned. N. Steinberg, "Social-Scientific Criticism: Judges 9 and Issues of Kinship," in *Judges and Method: New Approaches in Biblical Studies,* 2nd ed., ed. G. A. Yee (Minneapolis: Fortress, 2007), p. 247, n. 13.

154. The "Beer-elim" of Isa. 15:8 may be the same place.

c. The Battle for Shechem (9:22-41)

22 *Abimelech ruled over Israel for three years.*

23 *Then God sent an evil spirit between Abimelech and the rulers of Shechem, and the rulers of Shechem dealt treacherously with Abimelech,*

24 *so that the violence he had committed against the seventy sons of Jerubbaal, and their blood, recoiled on Abimelech their brother, who had killed them, and on the rulers of Shechem themselves, who had strengthened his hands to kill his brothers.*

25 *The rulers of Shechem set for him [Abimelech] people to lie in wait on the tops of the mountains, and robbed all who passed by them on the road, and it was reported to Abimelech.[155]*

26 *Gaal, son of Ebed, came with his brothers and passed through Shechem, and the rulers of Shechem committed themselves to him.*

27 *They went out into the fields,[156] harvested their grapes, trod them, and held a praise festival. They went into the temple of their god, ate and drank, and cursed Abimelech.*

28 *Gaal, son of Ebed, said, "Who is Abimelech, and who is Shechem,[157] that we should serve him? Isn't he the son of Jerubbaal, and isn't Zebul his commanding officer? Serve the men of Hamor, the father of Shechem. Why should we serve Abimelech?*

29 *Who will give this people into my hand, that I may get rid of Abimelech?" Then he said[158] to Abimelech, "Assemble the biggest fighting force you can, and come out."*

---

155. The meaning of this verse is uncertain, as indicated by the various ways it has been rendered in the English versions and commentaries: "In opposition to him [Abimelech] these citizens of Shechem set men on the hilltops to ambush and rob everyone who passed by" (NIV); "And the leaders of Shechem put men in ambush against him on the mountain tops, and they robbed all who passed by them on that way" (ESV); "Shechem's lords placed lookouts to warn of the approach of Abimelech while they took to plundering the caravans" (Boling, *Judges*, p. 176). I have taken *wayyāśîmû lô* to be an instance of the verb *śym* (to set in place) with the *l^e* of advantage, as in Gen. 43:32; 2 Sam. 12:20; 14:7; 2 Kgs. 4:10; 6:22; cf. Josh. 8:2; Judg. 8:33; 18:31; 1 Sam. 8:5; 1 Kgs. 20:34. The implication is that the breakdown of the relationship between Abimelech and the rulers of Shechem does not happen all at once, but in stages. See the exegetical comments on this verse.

156. Taking the singular, *haśśādeh*, as a collective. Cf. v. 42.

157. See the discussion of this question in the exegesis.

158. MT *wayyō'mer*. Qumran has *wayyō'mrû* (they said), which is reflected in the Old Latin and the Vulgate. The LXX has ἐρῶ (I would say = *wā'ōmar*), the reading favored in most English translations. However, these alternatives are both easier readings, and it is difficult to explain how *wayyō'mer* could be derived from them by any of them. I have decided to stay with the MT as the harder reading, and the one most likely to be original (cf. HCSB).

30 *Zebul, the head man of the city, heard the words of Gaal, son of Ebed, and was incensed.*

31 *He sent messengers secretly[159] to Abimelech, saying, "Listen! Gaal, son of Ebed, accompanied by his brothers, are coming to Shechem, and even now are stirring up the city against you.*

32 *Now during the night, you and the people who are with you get up and set an ambush in the field.*

33 *When the sun rises in the morning, get up early and attack the city. Then when he and the people who are with him start coming out to you, do to him whatever your hand finds to do."*

34 *So Abimelech and all the people who were with him arose during the night and lay in wait against Shechem — four contingents of them.*

35 *Gaal, son of Ebed, went out and stood at the entrance of the city gate; then Abimelech and the people who were with him got up from their ambush position.*

36 *Gaal saw them and said to Zebul, "Look, people are coming down from the mountaintops." Zebul replied, "It's the shadow of the mountains you are seeing — like men."*

37 *Gaal spoke again and said, "Look! People are coming down from the highest part of the land; one contingent is coming by way of the diviners' oak."*

38 *Zebul said to him, "What now of what you said, 'Who is Abimelech, that we should serve him?' Aren't these the people you despised? Go out now and fight them!"*

39 *So Gaal went out, leading the rulers of Shechem, and fought Abimelech.*

40 *Abimelech pursued him, and he fled before him, and many fell slain, right up to the entrance to the gate.*

41 *Then Abimelech settled in Arumah, and Zebul expelled Gaal and his brothers from Shechem, so they could no longer live there.*

22 The main thread of the narrative is resumed here after the interlude of Jotham's parable. But rather than opening with an account of the events of Abimelech's reign, it moves almost at once to his downfall. All that is said of his reign is that he ruled over Israel for three years (v. 22). This is telling, in both its brevity and its wording. With his power base established in Shechem, Abimelech ruled *Israel* as a whole. Whether Israelites outside his own clan

---

159. MT's *bᵉṭormâ* is a hapax. *BHS* takes it as a corruption of the phrase *bā'rûmâ* (in Arumah), which occurs in v. 41. But this corruption is difficult to explain, and *bā'rûmâ* here would make the later explanation of Abimelech's location redundant. With Boling, Block, and others, I take *ṭormâ* to be a noun derived from *rāmâ*, "to beguile, deceive."

acknowledged him willingly or not is not said, but an answer is hinted at in the term *ruled (wayyāśar).* This verb occurs only here in Judges, but its cognate noun, *śar,* is used nine times, always in situations of confrontation and violence.[160] Moreover, it is likely that here as in 4:2, 7 (for Sisera), 5:15 (for Issachar's "captains"), and 7:25 and 8:3 (for Oreb and Zeeb), we should understand the "rule" terminology in military terms, or at least as having strong military overtones. Abimelech had been made a king by the Shechemites, but he ruled more like a warlord, and probably brought the rest of Israel to heel by threatened or actual violence. In contrast to the normal pattern in Judges, the length of his rule is given at once rather than held over to the end. Its shortness, only *three years,* suggests that it never produced the kind of stability needed for peace, and hints at the kind of violent end it came to, as described in what follows.

23-55 The sending (by God) of *an evil spirit* between Abimelech and the men of Shechem (v. 23) sets a series of events in motion that have a relentless, repeating pattern to them.[161] Abimelech's going to Shechem to incite its leaders to conspire with him against the sons of Jerubbaal (vv. 1-2) is answered by Gaal's arrival in Shechem to incite its leaders to conspire with Gaal against Abimelech (vv. 26-29).[162] The ambush *(wayye'erḇû)* set by the men of Shechem in verse 25 is answered by the ambush *(wayye'erḇû)* set by Abimelech in verse 34 on the advice of Zebul. Finally, Abimelech, who, as we are told twice, killed the sons of Jerubbaal *on one stone* (vv. 5, 18), is himself killed beside a stone which has been dropped on his head by a woman of Thebez (v. 53).[163] So, in the outworking of the plot, act answers to act, and evil to evil. The *evil spirit (rûaḥ rā'â)* sent by God to set the whole process of retribution in motion (v. 23), itself answers to the evil *(rā'â)* com-

---

160. Judg. 4:2, 7; 5:15; 7:25; 8:3, 6, 14; 9:30; 10:18.

161. Cf. R. H. O'Connell, *The Rhetoric of the Book of Judges,* VTSup 63 (Leiden: E. J. Brill, 1996), p. 168.

162. Just as Abimelech emphasized his close ties with the men of Shechem against Jerubbaal, so Gaal emphasizes his close ties with them against Abimelech. The important place that the Gaal episode plays in this symmetry of retribution is generally overlooked by those who argue that it is an interpolation which interrupts the flow of the narrative (see the standard commentaries). A. D. Crown, "A Reinterpretation of Judges IX in the Light of Its Humour," *Abr Nahrain* 3 (1961-62): 90-98, finds further ironical comparison between the two episodes in the unusual wording, *wayyāḇō'... bišḵem,* in v. 26: "Gaal and his brothers appear to be in transit and 'pass through' Shechem on their travels. They too are nothing but vain and worthless fellows: Abimelech is simply hoist with his own petard" (p. 95).

163. Cf. Ginzberg, *The Legends of the Jews,* 4:41: "But God is just. As Abimelech murdered his brothers upon one stone, so Abimelech himself met his death through a millstone," citing *Tanḥuma* B I, 103. Further, the (literally) "one woman" *('iššâ 'aḥat)* of 9:53 answers to the "one stone" *('eḇen 'eḥāt)* of 9:5, 18, etc.

mitted by Abimelech and the men of Shechem (vv. 56, 57). This evil spirit is not exorcised until the chief instigator of the evil is struck down, whereupon his followers, as if waking from a bad dream, put down their weapons and go home without completing their assault on Thebez (v. 55).

23-24   The sending of the *evil spirit* by God does not absolve Abimelech and the rulers of Shechem of responsibility for their own wrongdoing. That would completely undermine the theme of retribution that runs right through the narrative and is stated in summary form at the end (vv. 56-57). On the contrary, it is sent precisely to call Abimelech and the Shechemites to account for what they have done. Nor does it imply that God himself is tainted by evil. Rather, it shows his complete sovereignty over it: even an evil spirit is made to serve his purpose of punishing wrongdoers (cf. 1 Sam. 16:14-15; 1 Kgs. 22:22-33). The effect of sending an evil spirit in this case was to cause the pact between Abimelech and the rulers of Shechem (a pact that was evil in itself) to break down, destroying Abimelech's power base and making his position untenable. The "treachery" referred to in verse 23 is described in what follows.

25   The *mountains* in view here are probably Gerizim and Ebal, which overlook Shechem from the southwest and northwest respectively (v. 7; cf. Deut. 11:29; 27:12-13; Josh. 8:23). They would have provided excellent vantage points from which to see anyone approaching the narrow Shechem pass below.

While it is clear from the context that what this verse describes is the first stage of the breakdown of the relationship between Abimelech and the rulers of Shechem, it is not entirely clear what happened. In what sense did the rulers of Shechem set ambushes on the mountaintops *"for* Abimelech"? Was it on behalf of Abimelech as their leader? In this case the reason would presumably be to guard the approaches to Shechem, where Abimelech now ruled. Or did they set the ambushes *"for* Abimelech" as their intended victim? The English versions in general favor the latter meaning, but the syntax, in my judgment, favors the former. So, too, does the way the narrative develops: the first outright act of treachery does not occur until verse 26. In either case, however, the outcome of what the rulers did was the same. Those who were set in ambush attacked and robbed *all who passed them by,* destabilizing Abimelech's fledgling kingdom and creating a situation like the one that had existed in the terrible days of Shamgar and Jael (5:6-7a). Abimelech is informed about what is going on, but before he can take action to stop it, another more ominous development takes place (v. 26).

26   The state of disorder resulting from the behavior of the men who had been set in ambush (v. 25) provides the climate for another opportunist to make a bid for power, and the leaders of Shechem soon change sides and align themselves with him (the details are given in vv. 27-30). Their involvement, intentionally or not, in the brigandage of verse 25 has already put their loyalty to Abimelech in question. But their desertion of him for Gaal is the outright treachery foreshadowed in verse 23, and evidence that the "evil spirit" sent by Yahweh is proving effective.

Gaal, son of Ebed, appears out of nowhere, but will soon claim to be a descendant of Hamor, the founder of Shechem.[164] It may be, as Daniel Block has suggested, that he was one of the rulers of Shechem who had not supported the move to make Abimelech king, and had fled into exile.[165] His return *with his brothers* is ominous. Abimelech had killed his brothers, and so made himself dependent on the loyalty of the rulers of Shechem, who are now proving to be unreliable. Gaal brings his own supporters, who are bound to him by blood. It is probably the fact that he has not come alone that has enabled him to safely negotiate the ambushes referred to in verse 25. Gaal does not attempt to confront Abimelech directly at this stage, but "passes through" Shechem, gathering support for his cause as he goes. The showdown with Abimelech will come later.

27 Gaal has apparently appeared at grape-harvest time, which gives him and the rulers of Shechem the opportunity to meet and plan their next move under the guise of holding a religious festival. It was probably some form of the Feast of Tabernacles, which fell in Tishri, the seventh month of the sacred calendar (September-October) and is linked with the grape harvest ("the time of your wine press"; NIV) in Deuteronomy 16:13. It was a joyous festival; hence the praise, eating, and drinking associated with it here. However, irregularities are apparent. Shiloh, not Shechem, appears to have been the place where the Israelites in general gathered for the festival (21:19; cf. Josh. 18:1; 1 Sam. 1:3);[166] and while the Shiloh festival was unambiguously a festival "of Yahweh" (21:19), the conspirators at Shechem gather in *the temple of their god.* The relationship of this temple and its god to those at Shiloh is unclear, and the "cursing" that takes place there is certainly not part of the normal celebration of the festival.

28 It is clear that dissatisfaction with Abimelech has been developing for some time. But Gaal now challenges the rulers of Shechem to bring their rejection of Abimelech into the open by boldly switching their allegiance to him, Gaal, as their rightful ruler. Like Abimelech back in verse 2, "Gaal skillfully plays the ethnicity card" in his bid for power.[167] His question, *"Who is Shechem?"* probably means "Who is this supposed Shechemite?" (referring to

---

164. Cf. Gen. 33:19.
165. Block, *Judges, Ruth,* p. 325.
166. Shiloh was 12.5 mi. (20 km.) south of Shechem.
167. Block, *Judges, Ruth,* p. 326.

Abimelech).[168] If so, it neatly distills the essence of his argument. His claim to the allegiance of Shechem's rulers is that Abimelech is related to them only by his father's liaison with a concubine (8:31), while Gaal himself and his brothers are direct descendants of *Hamor,* who was the father of Shechem (Gen. 33:19), and therefore head of the clan that founded the city. For extra measure he also plays on the evident unpopularity of *Zebul,* whom Abimelech has appointed as his *commanding officer* (v. 28), and *head man of the city* (v. 30).

29-31 In general terms Gaal's rhetorical question, *"Who will give this people into my hand?"* is an appeal for response to his challenge. In particular it is a challenge for someone to make the first move, and by so doing influence the rest *(this people)* to follow his lead. Gaal is confident that with this kind of support he will be able to get rid of Abimelech. His direct challenge to Abimelech, *"Assemble the biggest force you can, and come out,"* is a piece of bravado, like a challenge to a duel, probably intended to persuade the waverers. But the fact that Zebul quickly hears of the challenge and passes the news on to Abimelech (vv. 30-31) suggests that not everyone present changed sides; some continued to support Abimelech and his men by reporting these treacherous activities to them (cf. v. 25). The drift toward an inter-clan civil war is accelerating, and may already have passed the point of no return. The fact that Zebul has to "send" the warning to Abimelech implies that Abimelech is not in Shechem (see v. 41).[169]

Zebul warns him that Gaal and his brothers, who had previously "passed through" Shechem (v. 26), are now *coming to* Shechem (v. 31),[170] and that (probably through agents provocateurs) they are already *stirring up the city* against Abimelech. In the confrontation that is to come, the battle for Shechem will be decisive.

32-33 Zebul has already shown his loyalty to Abimelech by warning him of what is taking place. Now he shows his mettle as Abimelech's "commanding officer" (v. 28) by taking charge of operations, even telling Abimelech himself what to do. His orders assume that Gaal has already entered the city, or will have done so before Abimelech is able to get there. He tells Abimelech that, rather than launch an assault on the city at once, he should prepare for a dawn raid by "setting an *ambush* in the field" (v. 32). It is the same word that was used in verse 25 for the action by the rulers of Shechem that began the breakdown in their relationship with Abimelech, and

---

168. For a different suggestion, with a good discussion of the options, see R. G. Boling, " 'And Who Is Š-K-M?' (Judges IX 28)," *VT* 13 (1963): 479-82. The LXX has *tis estin ho huios Sychem* ("Who is the son of Shechem?").

169. See the note on *secretly* in the translation of v. 31.

170. From the temple of El/Baal-berith to the city itself. See vv. 4 and 27, and the comments below on v. 46.

is part of the theme of reversal that runs through the narrative as a whole. A dawn raid involving an ambush will enable Abimelech to take advantage of the unusual light conditions at that time of day, and, by not committing all his fighters at once, to deceive Gaal about the size of the force ranged against him (v. 33). The second wave of attack (the real one) is to be reserved until Gaal and his followers come out of the city, thinking they have only a small force to contend with.[171] Their false confidence will give Abimelech the opportunity to *do to him whatever [his] hand finds to do,* that is, have them completely at his mercy and inflict total defeat on them. Zebul shows himself here to be a loyal friend and shrewd military tactician, who fully justifies the faith that Abimelech has placed in him.

34-36 More detail is given here about the "ambush" tactics that Abimelech used. Like his father Gideon, Abimelech divides his men[172] into *contingents (rā'šîm)* — in this case four — to maximize the surprise factor and confuse the enemy about the real size of his forces.[173] The strategy works perfectly. Gaal, probably suspecting an attack at first light, goes out and stands just outside the city gate. Taking this as their cue, Abimelech and his men begin to show themselves. Given the tactics being used, *Abimelech and the people who were with him* probably refers here to the particular contingent that was with Abimelech himself, and therefore the one most likely to be mistaken by Gaal for his entire force. They are immediately spotted by him, and a curious conversation ensues between Gaal and, of all people, Zebul! Contrary to expectations created earlier in the narrative (v. 28), Zebul has apparently survived the seizure of the city by Gaal and his followers, most likely by surrendering it to them without a fight, and perhaps even welcoming them as liberators. His appearance here at Gaal's side certainly suggests so. But his speech is full of guile, intended to delay as long as possible Gaal's recognition of the real situation he is facing.

Gaal thinks he sees people coming down from the mountains to the southwest or the northwest of Shechem (Mounts Gerizim and Ebal respectively; v. 25). Zebul replies that his eyes are deceiving him; all that's really there is the shifting shadows cast by the mountains in the first light of dawn (v. 36).

37 Gaal ignores Zebel's suggestion that he is only seeing shadows

171. The same tactics were used against Ai in the time of Joshua (Josh. 8:3-23), and will later be used against Gibeah (Judg. 20:29-48).

172. "The narrator never states specifically who Abimelech's supporters were, but one may surmise that they consisted, at least, of those relatives to whom he had appealed in the first instance (v. 1), as well as the retainers who had come with him from Ophrah" (Boling, *Judges,* p. 328).

173. "Four *rā'šîm*" is literally "four *heads*," i.e., four companies, each with its own leader. Cf. 7:16.

and continues to describe what is unfolding before his eyes, the exclamation, *"Look!" (hinnê),* nicely capturing his growing alarm. He sees two more groups of people approaching, from two different directions. The first is coming from *the highest part of the land (ṭabbûr hāʾāreṣ).* This expression occurs only here and in Ezekiel 38:12, and its meaning is uncertain. The translation "center of the land," or an equivalent, in most English versions follows the LXX and the Vulgate, which render *ṭabbûr hāʾāreṣ* as "the *navel* of the land" (*tou omphalou tēs gēs* and *de umbilico terrae* respectively). But this derives from the use of *ṭabbûr* for "umbilical cord" in Mishnaic Hebrew and late Aramaic, and is unlikely to be the meaning in something as early as the Abimelech narrative.[174] In biblical Hebrew the word for "navel" or "umbilical cord" is *šōr* (Ezek. 16:4; Song of Sol. 7:3[2]; Prov. 3:8). The fact that Gaal speaks of people *coming down* from the *ṭabbûr hāʾāreṣ* indicates that it is a location higher than the valley floor on which Shechem itself is situated, but not the "mountaintops" of the previous verse. What is probably on view is the nearby Shechem pass, which opens out onto the lowlands to its northwest and southeast.[175] The strategic, central location of the site may have given rise to the later use of *ṭabbûr* as "navel."

The third contingent Gaal spotted was coming from the direction of *the diviners' oak (ʾēlôn mᵉʿônᵉnîm)* which is otherwise unknown. It may have been the contemporary equivalent of the Oak of Moreh (*ʾēlôn môreh,* "teacher's oak") of Abraham's day (Gen. 12:6; cf. 35:1-4). This oak, however, is associated with a kind of occult activity (divination, fortune-telling) practiced by the Canaanites but explicitly forbidden to Israel.[176] On the other hand, its name could have been a hangover from the past, and in Abimelech's day it may simply have been a well-known landmark with no current religious significance. But given the cultic irregularities indicated elsewhere in the present narrative (vv. 4, 27) and in Judges generally, it is likely that divination was still practiced there. An oak in or close to Shechem with at least ceremonial significance has already been mentioned in verse 6 (see the comments there). But it's unlikely that this was the same oak. The present context suggests a site visible from the city, but at some distance from it.

38-39 Gaal has been given a lot to think about. Some kind of carefully planned maneuver is taking place. He has already spotted three enemy contingents approaching from different directions. How many more might

174. I am indebted here to the excellent discussion, with reference to the relevant literature, in Block, *Judges, Ruth,* pp. 328-29. Block himself takes the expression to mean "elevated ground."

175. See illustration 6 in Boling, *Judges.* Boling himself renders *ṭabbûr hāʾāreṣ* as "navel of the land," and suggests that it refers to Mount Gerizim.

176. *mᵉʿônᵉnîm* is the Poel participle of *ʿnn,* "to divine, tell fortunes." Other forms of the same word are used in the proscriptions of Deut. 18:10, 14; Lev. 19:26.

there be? Is Abimelech's intention to lay siege to Shechem? If so, should Gaal and his followers stay where they are and risk being trapped, or should he lead them out at once and try to break through the enemy lines before the encirclement is complete? Sensing his indecision and vulnerability, Zebul now casts aside his pretense. He openly taunts Gaal and urges him to do the very thing that Abimelech's tactics were intended to induce him to do: *"Go out now, and fight them!"* (cf. vv. 28 and 33).

Without further delay Gaal does so. He goes out to fight Abimelech, taking with him the rulers of Shechem and, presumably, whatever fighting force they could command. Nothing is said of Zebul at this point. He most certainly was one of Shechem's rulers — the chief one, in fact (v. 30) — but having shown his true colors by taunting Gaal, he would hardly have gone out to fight with him. More likely he and other Abimelech sympathizers remained in Shechem to hold the city for him and prepare themselves to attack any of Gaal's followers that were driven back into it. This would in effect complete the encirclement of Gaal's forces, and may well have been part of Zebul's strategy from the start.

40-41 Very few details are given of the battle itself, but the very terseness of the account is telling. There was no real contest. Gaal realized too late that he had been outmaneuvered and tried to beat a hasty retreat, only to lose most of his men in the process. Gaal himself and his brothers — the instigators of the rebellion — did make it back into Shechem, but were unable to remain there or cause any further trouble. Zebul, now in full control of the city again, drove them out, reversing their arrival there back in verse 26 and bringing closure, apparently, to the whole Gaal episode. We never hear of Gaal again.

However, the statement that Abimelech settled in *Arumah* rather than in Shechem itself is puzzling, and prevents the closure from being total. *Arumah* is generally identified as Khirbet el-'Ormeh, 5 miles (8 km.) southeast of Shechem.[177] Abimelech had already left Shechem before the final clash with Gaal, and may even have been in Arumah (see the translation notes and exegetical comments on v. 31). But Shechem was by far the most significant city in the area, and was the place where Abimelech had first made his bid for power and been made king (vv. 1-6). To withdraw from it temporarily for tactical reasons is understandable, but to *settle (wayyēšeb)* elsewhere is odd, to say the least, even if his deputy now has firm control there again.[178] It suggests that something still remains to be resolved between Abimelech and the people of Shechem. This tension sets us up for the sequel to the Gaal episode that follows.

177. See Henry O. Thompson, "Arumah," *ABD* 1:467-68.
178. Cf. David's withdrawal and return to Jerusalem in 2 Sam. 15–19 in connection with Absalom's rebellion.

d. Abimelech's Downfall (9:42-57)

42 *The next day the people went out into the fields,[179] and it was reported[180] to Abimelech.*

43 *So he took the people and divided them into three contingents, and set an ambush in the fields. He looked, and there they were! the people, coming out of the city, so he rose up against them and struck them down.*

44 *Now Abimelech and the contingent that was with him rushed forward and stood at the entrance to the gate of the city. Then the other two contingents moved quickly against all who were in the fields, and struck them down.*

45 *Abimelech fought against the city all that day, and captured it, and all the people who were in it he killed. He tore down the city and sowed the site with salt.*

46 *All the rulers of the tower of Shechem heard about it and went into the stronghold of the temple of El-berith.*

47 *Abimelech was told that they had gathered — all the rulers of the tower of Shechem.*

48 *So Abimelech went up Mount Zalmon, he and all the people who were with him. Abimelech took an axe[181] in his hand, and cut a branch off the trees. He lifted it, put it on his shoulder, and said to the people who were with him, "Hurry and do what you have seen me do."*

49 *So all the people cut, each man a branch, and followed Abimelech. They put them against the stronghold, and set the stronghold on fire. So all the people of the tower of Shechem died, about a thousand men and women.*

50 *Then Abimelech went to Thebez. He camped near[182] Thebez and captured it.*

51 *There was a strong tower inside the city, so all the men and women (the rulers of the city) fled there, closed it behind them, and went up onto the roof of the tower.*

---

179. Taking the singular, *haśśādeh,* as a collective, as in v. 27. Cf. NRSV.

180. *BHS* has the plural, *wayyaggidû,* "they [unspecified] told [it] to Abimelech." Qumran has the singular, *wygd,* which may be read either as the Hiphil, "he [unspecified] told [it] to Abimelech," or the Hophal, "it was told to Abimelech." Qumran is supported by the LXX, which has the singular — either *apēngelē* (the passive, LXX^A) or *anēngeilen* (the active, LXX^B). See the exegetical comments on this verse.

181. Reading the singular, *qardōm* (an axe), with the LXX and the English versions generally. The MT's *'et-haqqardummôṯ* (the axes) can hardly be correct. Another possibility, noted in *BHS,* is *'aḥat haqqardummôṯ* (one of the axes). Since Abimelech commands his followers to do as he does, other axes must have been available.

182. Taking the *b^e* after *wayyiḥan* as locative, as in Num. 10:31; Josh. 4:19; 1 Sam. 4:1; 13:5, 16; 2 Sam 24:5. See BDB, p. 333.

52 *Abimelech came to the tower and fought against it. He approached the entrance to the tower to set it on fire.*

53 *Then a certain woman threw an upper millstone down on Abimelech's head and crushed his skull.*

54 *Abimelech quickly called the young man who was his armor bearer, and said to him, "Draw your sword and kill me, lest people say, 'A woman killed him.'" So the young man thrust him through, and he died.*

55 *When the men of Israel saw that Abimelech was dead, they went away — each to his own place.*

56 *Thus God made the evil that Abimelech did to his brothers, by killing the seventy of them, rebound on him.*

57 *God also made all the evil of the men of Shechem rebound on their heads. The curse that Jotham, son of Jerubbaal, spoke concerning them came to pass.*

42 With the crisis apparently over, the people[183] of Shechem go out into the fields, either to see how much damage their fields have suffered (Boling), or to start working them again (Block). Either way, it is a natural and harmless thing to do, and an indication that they are tired of war and eager to resume their normal way of life. Abimelech and his supporters, however, see it quite differently. The last time the Shechemites "went out into the fields" it was to conspire with Gaal against Abimelech (v. 27), and the closing statement of verse 42 indicates that someone loyal to him suspected that mischief was afoot again: *it was reported to Abimelech.* The fact that the informer is not named adds to the sense of intrigue. Who could he be? The same unidentified person who reported Gaal's activity to Zebul back in verse 30a, or Zebul himself, who had passed that intelligence on (v. 31)? We don't know. This time the informer is completely anonymous. Furthermore, given the absence of any indication that the Shechemites on this occasion are in fact engaged in anything sinister, what we seem to be dealing with is a case of paranoia rather than sober loyalty on the part of Abimelech's supporters — another hint that the "evil spirit" of verse 23 is still at work. That paranoia is about to manifest itself more powerfully still in Abimelech himself.

43-45 In this second campaign Abimelech uses the same strategy that he had used so successfully in the first engagement: ambush and encirclement (vv. 34-40). But now he neither receives nor needs any advice from

183. Taking *hā'ām* in the ordinary, nonmilitary sense here. With Gaal driven out, and Zebul in control again, the Shechemites would have no reason to embark on another military campaign.

Zebul, and this time victory comes even more easily because his victims are unsuspecting and presumably unarmed. In contrast to the "people" (*hāʿām,* "civilians") who come out into the fields, Abimelech's *people (hāʿām)* are fighters under his command, with experience on their side. It is an uneven match, and the only possible outcome if Abimelech holds to his purpose is a massacre.

As before, Abimelech divides his men into *contingents (rāʾšîm),* three this time, and uses two of them to *set an ambush* in the fields (v. 43a). With the preparations complete, the battle itself begins. It is first described in summary form: Abimelech sees the people still coming out,[184] rises up against them, and strikes them down (v. 43b). The details follow in verses 44-45. The third contingent, led by Abimelech himself, seizes the gate of the city (v. 44a) while the people are still coming out (v. 43a), dividing them into two groups, so that those who are outside cannot get back in, and fighters cannot be sent out to defend them. The two contingents outside the city then rise from their positions, rush on the people in the fields, and slaughter them (v. 44b). Those who try to flee back into the city are caught and dispatched by the contingent at the gate. Then all three contingents move into the city, systematically kill its inhabitants (taking a whole day to do it), tear down its buildings, and sow the whole site with salt (v. 45). The operation, from beginning to end, is carried out with ruthless efficiency. It is reminiscent, in many of its details, of the campaign against Ai in the time of Joshua (Josh. 8:3-25), but now it is Shechem against Shechem, brother against brother, clan against clan — a jagged tear in the very heart of Israel.

Abimelech's act of "sowing the site with salt" (v. 45) is unparalleled in the Old Testament, and its significance is not clear. Traditionally it has been viewed as an act intended to render a site infertile, or place it under the ban *(ḥērem)* of total destruction, or to purge it of the spirits of the dead.[185] On the basis of a number of extrabiblical texts, Gervitz has strengthened support for the second of these options, arguing that "sowing a devastated city with salt was a means of purifying it in preparation for, or as a means of, consecrating it to a god, as in holy war."[186] He is almost certainly right about it being a ritual act; a literal sowing of a ruined site with salt would be absurd and impractical. But in view of Abimelech's impiety and the absence of other in-

184. The vividness and immediacy of Abimelech's perception are conveyed by the use of *hinnê* with the participle *yōṣēʾ: there they were . . . coming out.*

185. A. M. Honeyman, "The Salting of Shechem," *VT* 3, no. 2 (1953): 192-95. Honeyman himself favors the last of these three options.

186. S. Gervitz, "Jericho and Shechem: A Religio-Literary Aspect of City Destruction," *VT* 13, no. 1 (1963): 60. The lack of attestation elsewhere in the Old Testament, and the frequency of "baal" terminology in the Abimelech narrative, suggest that it is more a pagan than an Israelite practice.

dicators of holy war,[187] it can hardly have the significance here that Gervitz has proposed. The best clue to its meaning is the way salt, when used elsewhere in the Old Testament with reference to lands and cities, is associated with barrenness, perpetual ruin, and inability to support human habitation (Deut. 29:23; Job 39:6; Jer. 17:6; Zeph. 2:9). Most likely, therefore, Abimelech in effect puts a curse on Shechem.[188] By symbolically sowing the site with salt he consigns it to permanent desolation. It is a ritual enactment of the intense hatred he now has for the place and everything associated with it. But as we are about to see, even this does not exhaust his mad fury.

46 After the complete destruction of Shechem and its people in the previous verse, it is surprising to find here that *the rulers of the tower (migdal) of Shechem . . . went into the stronghold (ṣᵉrîaḥ) of the temple (bêṯ) of El-berith,* and took refuge there. It is noteworthy that these rulers do not know the full extent of destruction of the city until they "hear" about it, that is, until the news of it reaches them. The logic of the narrative requires two things: that the tower, stronghold, and temple are all part of one complex, and that this complex is somehow distinct from Shechem itself (cf. the Beth-millo of v. 6). The term *ṣᵉrîaḥ,* which is of unknown derivation, occurs elsewhere only in 1 Samuel 13:6, along with "caves," "thickets," "rocks," and "cisterns" (NIV), as places where people hide in fear from their enemies. What seems to be in view in the present passage is a temple complex with a tower for sighting and repelling enemies, and an inner hold as a place of last resort. In common parlance the whole structure could be referred to as either "the tower" (v. 46a), or "the stronghold" (v. 49). With the Beth-millo, it was probably part of an acropolis overlooking the city, but from some distance.[189] The *rulers of the tower* may have been a subset of the rulers of Shechem as a whole, with special responsibility for the defense of the tower complex, who had remained there during the destruction of the city.[190] When they hear how total the destruction has been, they realize that it will be impossible to repel Abimelech's forces, and retreat into the inner hold to await their fate.

El-berith (Covenant God) is doubtless an alternative name for *Baal-berith* (Covenant Baal), the name by which the people of Shechem referred to their deity (8:33; 9:4). While *berith* (covenant) is a central element of Israel's distinctive religion (and may allude to the covenant making at Shechem, Josh. 24:25), *El* and *Baal* are both names of Canaanite deities. This strange con-

---

187. In the absence of *ḥērem* terminology, or any indication of divine authorization, even the wholesale slaughter of v. 45 cannot be understood as an act of holy war.

188. See the comments below on v. 48.

189. Cf. the "diviner's oak" of v. 37.

190. So Block, *Judges, Ruth,* pp. 331-32. For the literature on the archeology of Shechem and its temple tower, see p. 332 of the same commentary, n. 851. For a photograph of the site after the excavations of 1962, see Boling, *Judges,* illustration 7.

junction of terms is testimony to the corrupt, syncretistic Israelite-Canaanite religion practiced by the Shechemites in Abimelech's day.[191]

47-49   Once more Abimelech is alerted to the situation by an anonymous informer (cf. v. 42, and see the comments there), and immediately springs into action again. In what follows he behaves as his father Gideon had done in 8:13-17, but with even more brutality. The word *Zalmon* *(ṣalmôn)* in verse 48 is related to the word "shadow" *(ṣēl)* in verse 36. Hence, *Mount Zalmon* is "Shadowy/Dark Mountain." It is not to be confused with the Zalmon of Psalm 68:14, which (as the context there shows) is in the region of Bashan, northeast of the Sea of Galilee. The mountain in view in the present passage must be close to Shechem. But since no mountain by that name is otherwise attested in the area, it is likely that what we are dealing with is an alternative name for either Mount Gerizim or Mount Ebal,[192] the two mountains near Shechem where the covenant blessings and curses had been pronounced in the time of Joshua (Deut. 27:12-13; Josh. 8:33). Ironically, Jotham had stood on Gerizim, the mountain of blessing, to curse the Shechemites for making Abimelech their king (vv. 7, 19-21). The message was plain: for them there would be no blessing, only curse; no Gerazim, only Ebal. So it really doesn't matter which of the two is called "Dark Mountain" here; the appropriateness of the name derives from what Abimelech is about to do on it. Knowingly or not, he climbs it to enact Jotham's curse. The sun has set on Shechem; all that remains is darkness.

The deed itself is told with dreadful matter-of-factness. Abimelech takes an axe, walks up the mountain, lops a branch off a tree, puts it on his shoulder, and tells his followers to do the same. They do so and, still following his lead, lay all the branches against the tower and set them on fire, incinerating everyone inside (vv. 48-49). In foretelling the fate of the Shechemites Jotham had spoken of trees and fire (vv. 9-20). Now, with awful accuracy, his words have been fulfilled: fire has come out of the "bramble" they chose as their king and consumed them (v. 20), and not just the rulers themselves but every last man and woman who had depended on them as their leaders. The *thousand* such men and women of verse 49b were presumably the full contingent of the tower's staff, most likely augmented by others who had managed to escape being herded back into the city itself and taken refuge in the tower with them. All alike perished. The mention of them at the very end impresses on us the full horror of what has happened: its immense dimensions and deep tragedy.

50   The location of *Thebez* is uncertain. Some identify it with modern Tübas, 9.5 miles (16 km.) northeast of Shechem. Others take it as a cor-

---

191. See also the comments on 8:33 and 9:4.
192. See the comments on vv. 25, 36.

ruption of Tirzah (Tell el-Far'ah), in the same general area but a little closer.[193] This is the first mention of it in the narrative, so why Abimelech should go on from Shechem to attack Thebez as well is something of a mystery. It may have been a satellite of Shechem,[194] or simply another convenient target for someone who was keen to further enhance his prestige and the extent of his power by adding another conquest to his accomplishments.[195] But given the paranoia he has already exhibited in his total destruction of Shechem, it is probably unnecessary to seek any rational explanation (however thin or perverse) for his attack on Thebez, for it is the nature of paranoia to subvert rationality, and of leaders who suffer from it to commit excesses that eventually bring about their own destruction. So it was with Abimelech.

But of course there is more at work here than Abimelech's insane fury. There is Jotham's curse of verse 20 which has foretold the destruction of both the rulers of Shechem and Abimelech himself, and there is the "evil spirit from God" of verse 23, which has been sent between them to bring this about. The first part of Jotham's curse has already been fulfilled, which provides strong grounds for expecting that the second part of it will be also. Only the means remains to be revealed, as it will be — with a surprising twist — in the next few verses.

At first, however, there is no sign whatever that Abimelech is doomed. On the contrary, he appears to be in total command, as implied by the extreme brevity with which the first stages of the assault are described: he *camped near Thebez and captured it.* Abimelech goes about the destruction of Thebez with the same ruthless efficiency he had displayed against Shechem, and there is no resistance to speak of. His power is total and unassailable.

51 There were almost certainly two stages to the assault on Thebez, as there had been on Shechem (the city, then the tower), but this time the account goes straight to the final stage, for that is where the significant new development takes place. The *strong tower (migdal-'ôz)* of Thebez, unlike Shechem's temple tower, is inside the city.[196] But as at Shechem, it is a mixture of commoners *(men and women, hā'ănāšîm wᵉhannāšîm)* and *rulers (ba'ălê)* who flee into it, and shut themselves in — all who have survived the initial assault on the city. But these people show more spirit than those in Shechem. Instead of retreating into the inner hold of the tower to await their fate, they go up onto its roof, presumably to watch events unfolding below and attempt some kind of defensive action.

52 Again, the terseness of the narrative mirrors Abimelech's confi-

---

193. See the summary, with references, in Block, *Judges, Ruth,* p. 333, n. 854.
194. Block, *Judges, Ruth,* p. 333.
195. Cf. Boling, *Judges,* pp. 181-82.
196. See the comments on vv. 46-47.

dence; there is no hesitancy about his actions. The general statement comes first (he comes to the tower and fights against it); then the relevant detail (he approached *the entrance to the tower* to set it on fire). This is different from the description of his assault on the Shechem tower back in verse 49: the use of fire is the same, but this time the door in particular is approached, presumably because it was made of wood and therefore the part most vulnerable to fire. However, since an attack on the door is exactly what any canny defender could have anticipated, by approaching it Abimelech has unwittingly made himself an easy target for the defenders on the wall above. He is like Eglon rising to receive Ehud's "message from God" (3:20), or Sisera falling asleep in Jael's tent (4:21). His confidence has become his undoing by snaring him into making a fatal mistake.

53-57   The person who kills Abimelech remains nameless; she is just *a certain woman* (literally, "one woman," *ʾiššâ ʾaḥat*). Her weapon, like Jael's, is unconventional, an *upper millstone:* the smaller, upper stone of a hand-operated grain grinder. It may not have been large, but it was most likely heavier than a single woman could have picked up and "thrown" *(wattašlēk)* herself. She probably had help, but it suits the narrator's purpose to mention only her, for what is being described (and relished) is Abimelech's utter humiliation. In the warrior culture of the times, to die at the hands of a worthy adversary of equal or superior rank or strength might have been counted honorable. But to be killed by an inferior enemy, a woman no less, and not even a woman of note, but just a *certain woman,* a nobody, was to be completely undone; and Abimelech knows it.[197] That is why he *quickly* (with his last breath) calls and commands his armor bearer to run him through with his sword. It is a desperate man's way of salvaging what little scrap of dignity he can from an overwhelmingly shameful end.[198]

Furthermore, as many have noted, death by a "stone" hurled by "one woman" hints that more is involved here than bad luck or a clever enemy. Abimelech, after putting himself forward as the "one man" to rule the Shechemites (9:2), had begun his bloody career by killing his seventy brothers on "one stone" (9:5), in view of which his exquisitely fitting end can hardly be anything other than divinely engineered — as confirmed in verse 56.

Finally, the "fire" motif here also links Abimelech's death to the curse pronounced on both Abimelech and the people of Shechem back in verse 20.

---

197. Block (*Judges, Ruth,* pp. 333-34) has pointed out that "[T]he man who had shamelessly played the female card to seize the throne (vv. 1-2) now shamefully falls victim to a representative of this gender. Indeed, the story of Abimelech the macho man is framed by two women: the first, who gave him life (8:31), and the second, who took it (9:53)."

198. Cf. Saul in 1 Sam. 31:4.

Fire has certainly "come out" of Abimelech and destroyed, not only the Shechemites, but (for good measure) the people of Thebez as well! But what of the second part of Jotham's curse? Can Abimelech's death at the hands of a nameless woman in Thebez be seen in any sense as a fulfillment of the prediction that "fire" would come from the Shechemites and consume Abimelech? Apparently so (v. 57), though here the connection is more tenuous. If, as seems likely, the people of Thebez were in league with the Shechemites, the nameless woman who threw the millstone from the burning tower can be seen as a surrogate for the people of Shechem, who were unable to participate personally in Abimelech's destruction.[199] Certainly the "fire" he had unleashed proved, in the end, to be his own undoing, as well as that of the Shechemites.

Thus the whole sad story ends with no winners but God, whose retributive justice has been carried out with impressive completeness (v. 56). As for the human participants, those still standing at the end simply disperse and go *each to his own place* to try to resume something like a normal existence, with nothing gained and much lost (v. 55). The reference to them as "men of *Israel*" implies that the events just recorded had ramifications far beyond Shechem and its environs (cf. 9:22 and 10:1). In contrast to the way the Deborah-Barak episode ended, there is nothing this time to celebrate. Abimelech's three-year experiment with kingship has been an unmitigated disaster.

Summary Reflections on 6:1–9:57 as a Whole

a. The theme of Israel's unfaithfulness to Yahweh is explored much more fully in the Gideon narrative than in the previous judge narratives. In the first movement (6:1–8:3) Yahweh establishes his claim to Israel's loyalty by rescuing them yet again from their enemies. In the second movement (8:4-28) Gideon raises a lone voice in defense of this claim (8:23), but the drift back into apostasy is already too strong. The Israelites credit Gideon himself with the victory, make an idol out of his ephod, and finally abandon Yahweh altogether (8:33). The way the narrative starts out from Ophrah and returns there reinforces the theme. Even while Israel was appealing to Yahweh, there was an altar to Baal at Ophrah. In the course of the narrative it is removed, only to be replaced by a shrine where all Israel plays the harlot after Gideon's ephod. The thesis advanced at the climax of the narrative (ironically by the Israelites themselves) is that the one who saves Israel should be acknowledged as its ruler. But the way the story ends shows how the Israelites did exactly the opposite of what this thesis required. The narrator has succinctly summarized

199. Block, *Judges, Ruth*, p. 334.

the theme in 8:34: *the people of Israel did not remember Yahweh their God, who had saved them.*

In the sequel (the Abimelech narrative) this theme of unfaithfulness is transposed into a lower key. Those who had acted unfaithfully toward Yahweh now act unfaithfully toward the man he had used to save them. They did not even show faithfulness *(ḥeseḏ)* to Gideon in return for all the good that *he* had done for Israel. On the contrary, they make the murderer of his sons their king. The narrator makes the connection between these two acts of unfaithfulness directly in 8:35, and indirectly in Jotham's speech of accusation (esp. 9:16-20).

b. Three striking developments in the Gideon narrative and its sequel serve as indicators of the way in which this extended narrative participates in larger developments taking place progressively through the book.

The first is the fact that here for the first time Israel's appeal to Yahweh meets with stern rebuke rather than immediate assistance. It is clear that the privilege of appealing to Yahweh is being abused and that Yahweh is beginning to lose patience with Israel. In the next major episode the appeal will meet with a much more heated response from Yahweh (10:10-14). In the Samson episode there will be no appeal from Israel at all.

The second new feature is that the slide back into apostasy is already well advanced before Gideon dies,[200] and that he himself contributes to this regression by his own actions. The narrator puts the best possible construction on Gideon's conduct (he is presented as a flawed hero rather than as a cynical double-dealer), but the evidence of his contribution to all that went wrong is not concealed.[201] The next major savior-judge, Jephthah, is more obviously flawed than Gideon. His self-interest is evident from the start, and both his vow and Israel's "repentance" are plainly manipulative, as we will see. Samson is unfaithful Israel personified, and is scarcely recognizable as a savior-judge at all.

The third new feature is the *internal* fighting which takes place under Gideon and Abimelech. Gideon is the first judge to turn the sword against his fellow Israelites (8:16-17). Abimelech is like his father, with all the con-

---

200. Cf. 2:17: "they did not listen [to their judges], but . . . *quickly* turned aside" (my emphasis). See my comments on 2:16-19.

201. Other more sinister interpretations of Gideon's conduct are possible and have been strongly argued: e.g., his refusal in 8:23 is in reality a veiled acceptance and his manufacture of the ephod a cynical use of religion for political ends, corrupting it in the process, a scenario which becomes conspicuous by its repetition in the Deuteronomic History. There is an opacity about the text that teases us and allows us to suspect that there is more going on than meets the eye. But the narrator himself maintains a more generous perspective on Gideon.

straints of covenant piety removed. The civil war that erupts under him is a harbinger of worse to come (12:1-6; 20:1-48). As we saw, after 8:28 the formula "the land had rest . . ." does not occur again.

c. The process of exact retribution in the Abimelech story is an aberration from the alternating pattern of punishment and rescue in the stories about the major judges. The separateness of these two modes of operation is accentuated by the fact that the divine name, Yahweh, is not used in connection with the retribution theme in chapter 9. After 8:34-35, in which the Israelites reject Yahweh and make Baal-berith their god, only the general term, Elohim (God), is used (9:7, 23, 56, 57). In the stories of the judges God, as Yahweh, has operated on a different principle, namely, punishment tempered by compassion, with compassion (expressed as rescue) having the final say each time.[202] The significance of a story of such thorough and exact retribution appearing at this point in the book must be sought in the context of the serious and rapid deterioration in Israel's relationship with Yahweh that the Gideon episode has drawn our attention to, and the connection made in 8:34-35 between the unfaithfulness of the Israelites toward Yahweh and their unfaithfulness toward Gideon's household.

Ironically the Israelites benefit from the retribution worked upon their bramble king. The process of retribution has the precision of a surgical operation; it brings evil to an end, so that normal life can be resumed (9:55). But the story also has a chilling aspect. The "evil spirit from God" (9:23), agent of retribution, is the dark counterpart of "the Spirit of Yahweh" (6:34), agent of deliverance. It is a reminder that God has a different principle of operation that he can invoke at his discretion, and if it can be invoked against Abimelech and the men of Shechem, why not against Israel in general, and if against unfaithfulness in one sphere, why not against unfaithfulness in another? This story of retribution sounds an ominous note in the deteriorating situation to which the Gideon episode has drawn our attention. It carries a warning that the Israelites will ignore at their peril.

d. The issue of kingship figures much more prominently in the Gideon narrative and its sequel than in previous ones. For the first time the institution of kingship is experimented with in an Israelite context, and the result is disastrous. However, neither the Gideon nor the Abimelech stories are about king-

---

202. Cf. Polzin, *Moses and the Deuteronomist,* p. 175: "Fairness and honesty (*ʾemet ûbᵉtāmîm*) (9:16, 19) may be capable of illuminating the issues of retributive justice; they are relatively useless in clearing up the mystery of what happened to Israel in the period of the judges. Not the least aspect of the mystery consisted in the realisation that, in all fairness and honesty, Israel should not have survived."

ship as such, nor is it suggested in either story that kingship itself is evil. This is particularly clear in the Abimelech story. Divine retribution is a key issue from beginning to end, but nowhere is there any hint that Abimelech's crime was that he became a king. Nor is it suggested that the crime of the men of Shechem was that they chose to have a king. The crime is quite specifically the unfaithfulness shown to the house of Gideon by the rulers of Shechem, who conspired with Abimelech to kill his sons. That kingship as such is not the issue is clear from Jotham's words in 9:19-20:

> "If you have acted faithfully and blamelessly
> with Jerubbaal and his house this day,
> then rejoice in Abimelech,
> and let him rejoice in you.
> But if not . . ."

The same is true of Gideon's refusal of the offer made to him. This must be seen in relation to the specific terms in which the offer was made (8:22). Israel's future could not be secured by creating a new institution. Only a wholehearted return to Yahweh could do that, and that was what was conspicuously lacking in the offer made to Gideon. Gideon had to refuse, not because kingship is incompatible with Israel's covenant faith, but because Yahweh, not he, should have been given the credit for the victory. As in previous episodes, kingship is seen in an unfavorable light, but it is not rejected in principle.[203]

F. TOLA AND JAIR (10:1-5)

1 After Abimelech Tola, son of Puah, son of Dodo, a man of Issachar, arose to save Israel. He was living in Shamir, on Mount Ephraim.
2 He judged Israel for twenty-three years. Then he died, and was buried in Shamir.
3 After him Jair the Gileadite arose. He judged Israel for twenty-two years.
4 He had thirty sons, who used to ride on thirty male donkeys and owned thirty towns.[1] They are called the towns of Jair to this day, and are in the land of Gilead.
5 Then Jair died, and was buried in Kamon.

---

203. Cf. G. E. Gerbrandt, "Kingship according to the Deuteronomistic History," Th.D. diss. (Union Theological Seminary, Richmond, VA, 1980), pp. 171-86.
1. Reading 'ārîm, with BHS and the versions.

1-2 The explicit reference to Abimelech here (*After* Abimelech . . .) is a feature of this particular notice unparalleled in the notices about the other so-called minor judges. It brings the career of Abimelech into sharp focus as the backdrop to the career of Tola. The statement, *Tola . . . arose to save Israel,* clearly does not mean that Tola arose to "save" Israel as Abimelech had done! That would be patently absurd in view of what has just gone before, and in any case would more naturally be expressed in other terms, as, for example, in the Shamgar notice of 3:31:

> After him [Ehud] was Shamgar . . .
> and *he, too (gam-hû'),* saved Israel (my emphasis).

By contrast, the opening words of 10:1 simply indicate that after Abimelech Israel needed saving, and that Tola arose to do this. *Shamir (šāmîr)* is otherwise unknown, but it has the same three consonants as the better-known Samaria *(šōm^erôn)*, and is perhaps the same place under an earlier name.[2] Certainly the accompanying phrase, *on Mount Ephraim,* places it in the same general locality.

Despite the use of *yš^c* (to save), no military action is attributed to Tola; nor is there mention of any external threat during his period of office (again in contrast to Shamgar). We are told that he *was living (yšb,* "sitting" or "presiding") in Shamir and *judged (špt)* Israel for twenty-two years. This use of *yšb* in conjunction with *špt* is another feature of the Tola note that distinguishes it from those of the other minor judges. The language is strongly reminiscent of that used of the early career of Deborah, who "sat/presided" under her palm tree on Mount Ephraim and judged Israel (4:4-5). She, too, is said to have "arisen" when Israel was in disarray (5:7). Such details as are given of Tola's activity, together with the explicit reference to Abimelech's career, strongly suggest that Tola saved Israel from the disastrous effects of Abimelech's rule by providing a period of stable administration.[3] He saved it from disintegration. The similarity of his story to that of Deborah suggests that, like her, Tola may have been a charismatic leader without being a military one.

3-5 The notice about *Jair the Gileadite*[4] prepares the way for the story of *Jephthah the Gileadite* which immediately follows (cf. 10:3 with 11:1). Jair arises after the crisis that Tola faced has passed. The reference to his *thirty sons* riding on *thirty donkeys* and owning *thirty towns* suggests the peacefulness of the times and the prosperity and prestige enjoyed by the

---

2. As suggested in *BBC,* p. 260.

3. Cf. Boling, *Judges,* p. 187, who holds that the syntax of the Tola notice *requires* such an interpretation.

4. See the comments on *Gilead* at 5:17.

judge.[5] It also hints at the unpreparedness of the Gileadites for the disaster about to fall on them (10:7). Jair's pampered sons will be of little use when the Ammonites invade! Then the Gileadites will search desperately for a "fighter" (10:17-18). In order to win Jephthah over, the elders of Gilead will offer to make him "head of all the inhabitants of Gilead" (11:8). The mini-portrait of Jair presented here gives some indication of what was on offer, and why Jephthah found it so attractive. But the reality would be different for Jephthah. Unlike Jair, Jephthah would have to maintain his position by force (12:1-6), and would have no family to parade his greatness; he would be rendered childless by his vow.

The location of *Kamon*, where Jair was buried (v. 5), is unknown, but it was presumably in Gilead, and Jair's hometown.[6]

G. JEPHTHAH (10:6–12:7)

Jephthah is introduced in 11:1 as *Jephthah the Gileadite . . . a mighty warrior (gibbôr ḥayil);* the notice of his death and burial at 12:7 marks his exit, and he figures prominently in all that happens in between. This segment of text contains all the information necessary for it to be comprehensible as a complete story. We do not even have to go outside it to find the situation that forms the background to it, since this is neatly summarized in 11:4: *the Ammonites made war against Israel.* However, it is clear from the literary structure of the central section of the book as a whole that the story of Jephthah actually begins several verses earlier, in 10:6, with the formula, *The Israelites again did what was evil in Yahweh's eyes* (cf. 3:12; 4:1; 13:1). As we will see, this introductory material is in fact closely integrated into what follows, and is an essential part of the Jephthah story as Judges presents it.

A network of causation, sometimes implicit, sometimes explicit, links persons and events within this larger narrative. Israel's apostasy (10:6) leads, via Yahweh's intervention (10:7), to its subjugation by Ammon (10:8-9). This has two consequences, the first religious (Israel returns to Yahweh, 10:10-16), and the second political (Jephthah rises to prominence in Gilead, 11:4-11). Israel's relationship with Ammon moves from complication, through increasing tension, to climax (11:32a), and, again through Yahweh's intervention (11:32b), to resolution (11:33). But this resolution in turn gives

---

5. The wording *wayᵉhî-lô* suggests acquisition (by birth) rather than mere possession. His success in begetting *sons* in particular is another indication of his prestige. His sons presumably ruled the towns as his appointees, binding them into a confederation which formed Jair's power base in Gilead.

6. Cf. the burial of Samson "between Zorah and Eshtaol" in 16:31 (NIV).

rise to two further complications and crises, the first domestic (Jephthah and his daughter, 11:34-40), and the second political (Jephthah and the Ephraimites, 12:1-6). The successive resolution of these two crises brings the narrative as a whole to its conclusion. So the subject matter of the story (what happened to Israel in the time of Jephthah) is constructed as a plot with several well-defined movements or episodes. In the exposition that follows we will refine this basic analysis of the plot and see how the story's themes develop as it unfolds.

1. Episode 1: Israel and Yahweh (10:6-16)

6 *The Israelites again did what was evil in Yahweh's eyes. They served the Baals and the Ashtaroths, the gods of Aram, the gods of Sidon, the gods of Moab, the gods of the Ammonites,[1] and the gods of the Philistines. They forsook Yahweh, and did not serve him.*

7 *So Yahweh became angry with Israel and sold them into the hand of the Philistines, and into the hand of the Ammonites.*

8 *They shattered and crushed the Israelites in that eighteenth year[2] — all the Israelites who were beyond the Jordan in the land of the Amorite, which is in Gilead.*

9 *The Ammonites also crossed the Jordan to fight against Judah, and against Benjamin, and against the house of Ephraim; and Israel was greatly distressed.*

10 *So the Israelites cried out to Yahweh, "We have sinned against you, for[3] we have forsaken our God and served the Baals."*

11 *Then Yahweh said to the Israelites, "Didn't I save you from the Egyptians, and from the Amorites, and from the Ammonites, and from the Philistines?*

12 *The Sidonians and the Amalekites and the Maonites oppressed you, but when you cried out to me, I saved you from their hand.*

13 *But you forsook me and served other gods. Therefore, I will not save you any more.*

14 *Go and cry to the gods you have chosen; let them save you in your time of distress."*

1. On the god(s) of the Ammonites see 11:24 and comments.

2. The syntax is anomalous, but it seems clear that "in that year" (*baššānâ hahî'*) refers to the year of the crisis detailed in vv. 8b and 9, while *š^emōneh 'eśrê šānâ* has the same form as the expressions for the unambiguous "thirteenth" and "fourteenth" years of Gen. 14:4-5 NIV. LXX[B] produces a smoother reading, but obliterates the force of "in that year" (*baššānâ hahî*) by weakening it to "at that time" (*en tō kairō ekeinō*). See Boling, *Judges*, pp. 191-92.

3. Reading *kî* instead of *w^ekî* with *BHS*, LXX, Syriac, and Vulgate.

15 *But the Israelites said to Yahweh, "We have sinned; do to us whatever seems good to you, only save us, please, this day."*

16 *Then they put away the foreign gods from among them and served Yahweh, and he became exasperated with the misery of Israel.*

6 By now Israel's relapse into idolatry has become an all-too-familiar feature of the repeating pattern of Judges. This time, however, the detailing of the gods to which the Israelites turned is unusually elaborate. The first pair, *the Baals and the Ashtaroths,* is conventional shorthand for the male and female deities of the Canaanites (see the comments on 2:11-13). But here they are supplemented by reference to the gods of the nations that were on the periphery of Israelite settlement: Aram (Syria) and Sidon to the north, Moab and Ammon to the east, and the Philistines to the southwest.[4] In general the effect is to stress the gravity and extent of Israel's waywardness: they turned to any and every god rather than Yahweh. Their propensity for doing what is offensive to him is going from bad to worse as the central part of the book runs its course.

But there is also significance in the details. *Aram* has made a brief appearance in 3:7-11 in the form of the doubly wicked Cushan, king of Aramnaharaim (Aram of the two rivers). The fact that Israel has already been punished at the hands of a king of Aram makes their fraternizing with the gods of Aram especially perverse. The same is true for her turning to the gods of Moab (see 3:12-30). *Sidon* is a possible allusion to 1:31, where it is named as a place from which the tribe of Asher did not expel the Canaanites. Israel's attraction to the gods of this place is an instance of the prediction of 2:3 being fulfilled: they became a "snare" to the Israelites. The last pair, the gods of the *Ammonites* and the *Philistines,* foreshadows what follows in the Jephthah and Samson narratives respectively, where Israel suffers at the hands of these two peoples — fit punishment for serving their gods. There may also be an allusion to their past deliverance from the Philistines in 3:31. In short, this verse underscores the perverseness of Israel and the appropriateness of God's dealings with her by alluding to both what is past and what is to come.[5]

7 In this verse we move from the offense to the punishment. The *Philistines* and *Ammonites* are picked up from verse 6 and repeated here because they are to be the instruments of punishment. The reversal of the order (from Ammonites and Philistines, to Philistines and Ammonites) appears to

---

4. The gods of the Philistines included Ashtaroth (1 Sam. 31:10), Baal-zebub, the god of Ekron (2 Kgs. 1:1-6, 16), and Dagon (Judg. 16:23).

5. Note how a play on the word "serve" (*'bd*) describes Israel's offense both positively and negatively: they "*served* the Baals and the Ashtaroths. . . . They forsook Yahweh, and did not *serve* him."

be for purely stylistic reasons. The chronological order remains Ammonites first (the Jephthah narrative) and Philistines second (the Samson narrative). Verses 6 and 7 serve as an introduction to both. The expression *sold them into the hand of* is a metaphor for handing Israel over with no automatic right of recovery, as in 3:8 and 4:2. It is an indication of the extent of Yahweh's just anger with Israel, and puts the future of his relationship with them in serious question.

8-9 The punishment is now particularized in terms of being *shattered and crushed*. The language is graphic and powerfully depicts the severity of Israel's suffering, which came to a climax in *that eighteenth year* — the eighteenth year of the Ammonite oppression.[6] Until then their presence and activities had been confined to Israelite territory east of the Jordan, referred to in verse 8 as *the land of the Amorite,* the territory north of the Arnon River that had been occupied by "Sihon, king of the Amorites," in pre-Israelite times (11:18-22; cf. Deut. 2:24).[7] *Gilead* included this region, plus the land further north (also in Transjordan; see the comments on 5:17). In the eighteenth year, however, the Ammonites *crossed the Jordan* and extended their activities into Israel's heartland, threatening its very existence as a nation. This critical situation is what is referred to in the summary statement at the end of verse 9: *Israel was greatly distressed.*

10 This verse opens a dialogue between Israel and Yahweh which continues to the end of verse 15. It is the first of several dialogues (one in each episode):

Episode	Dialogue
1. 10:6-16	Israel and Yahweh, vv. 10-15
2. 10:17–11:11	The elders and Jephthah, vv. 5-11
3. 11:12-28	Jephthah and the Ammonite king, vv. 12-28
4. 11:29-40	Jephthah and his daughter, vv. 34-38
5. 12:1-7	Jephthah and the Ephraimites, vv. 1-3

As we will see, these dialogues are crucial for the development of the distinctive theme of the story as a whole.[8]

Here in the first episode the Israelites, in their "great distress" (v. 9), admit to having done what the narrator has accused them of in verse 6: *forsaken* Yahweh and *served* the Baals. The same two verbs are used here as in

---

6. See the footnote to this expression in the translation.

7. In other contexts the term "Amorite(s)" (westerners) refers to the inhabitants of Syria-Palestine in general, including those west of the Jordan (1:34-35; cf. Gen. 48:22; Josh. 24:15).

8. B. G. Webb, "The Theme of the Jephthah Story," *RTR* 45, no. 2 (1986): 34-43.

verse 6, but in reverse order, with *the Baals* serving as a general term for all the various gods listed there.

11-14 As in 6:8-10, Israel's cry for help meets with a stern rebuke. But there are differences: there it was a prophet who delivered the rebuke; here it is *Yahweh* himself. Presumably an intermediary was involved, since this has been the case in both 2:1 and 6:8. But the lack of reference to any agent here suggests that the confrontation between Yahweh and Israel has moved to a further level of intensity, something confirmed by the content of the speech itself. The statement about previous occasions on which Yahweh has delivered Israel only to have them prove unfaithful to him again, is longer here than in chapter 6, making the rebuke more damning. Furthermore, while the speech in chapter 6 stopped at rebuke ("but you did not listen to my voice," v. 10), this one goes beyond this to outright rejection of Israel's cry for help (*I will not save you any more,* v. 13). Clearly the relationship between the two parties has reached a major point of crisis, with a complete breakdown of it looking like a very real possibility.

The catalogue of past deliverances in verses 11 and 12 (seven in all) begins with the exodus (*from the Egyptians,* as in 2:1 and 6:8). Next come those in Transjordan, as Israel approached the promised land (*the Amorites;* see Num. 21:21-31), and then those in the promised land itself. The *Ammonites* appeared in the Ehud story as allies of Eglon, king of Moab (3:13). The reference to them at this point rather than to the Moabites is almost certainly because of their significance in the current situation: Israel is oppressed by the Ammonites again because they have been unfaithful again: they never learn(!) The *Philistines* is probably an allusion to Shamgar's successful repulsion of the Philistines in 3:31. The *Sidonians* have not appeared as oppressors prior to this point in the book. However, given the location of Sidon on the northern seaboard (1:31), it is likely that "Sidonians" is used here as a collective term for the northern coalition defeated by Barak: the northern counterpart to the Philistines.[9] The *Maonites*[10] are otherwise unknown, but may be either the Midianites,[11] or the Meunites, who lived in the same desert area east of Edom and may have been closely associated with them (2 Chron. 26:7; cf. 20:1).[12] In any case, by a process of elimination, what must be in view here is the ravaging of Israel by "Easterners," as described in 6:3-5, and their defeat and expulsion

---

9. So W. J. Moran, "A Study of the Deuteronomic History," *Biblica* 46 (1965): 227; Boling, *Judges,* p. 191; Block, *Judges, Ruth,* p. 347.

10. Literally, just "Maon" (*mā'ôn*).

11. As translated in the LXX and recommended in the MT apparatus. However, it's hard to see how *mā'ôn* could have arisen as a corruption of *midyān.*

12. So Boling, *Judges,* p. 192, citing Gold, *IDB* 3:368.

by Gideon. The *Amalekites*[13] are explicitly named (along with Midian) as part of this coalition of desert tribes in 6:2.[14] The Amalekites were also, of course, the first enemy Israel faced after their escape from Egypt, and their mention here could hardly fail to recall the first great deliverance from them that Israel had experienced in the days of Joshua (Exod. 17:8-13). In short, the seven deliverances recounted in verses 11 and 12 are symbolic of all the occasions on which Yahweh had rescued Israel in the past: whenever, in fact, they had *cried out* to him (v. 12). The summary accusation in verse 13a is that every time Yahweh saved the Israelites, they forsook him and went back to serving other gods yet again.

As in a typical prophetic judgment oracle, the word *Therefore* in the middle of verse 13 marks the transition from accusation to announcement of the judgment to be carried out. It is expressed negatively first (*"I will not save you any more"*), and then positively (*"Go and cry to the gods you have chosen; let them save you . . ."*). On this note of terrible irony Yahweh's angry speech ends. He rejects Israel's "contrition" (v. 10) as hollow, and dismisses their cry for help — even before they have made it — as purely self-serving: they cry to him now only because they judge him to be useful to them in their *time of distress* (v. 14b). Their "repentance" is merely a tactical move, a contrition of convenience that will not last. They have used him like this before, and he refuses to let them do so again. He will not save them, and the gods they have chosen cannot save them. It seems that the whole history of God's relationship with Israel has come to a shuddering halt. If he does not relent, Israel has no future. All is lost.

15-16 The fact that the Israelites persist with their appeal is evidence of their utter desperation. They repeat their confession (*"We have sinned"*; cf. v. 10), and declare their willingness to accept any punishment (*"do to us whatever seems good to you"*) if only Yahweh will save them once more (*"only save us, please, this day"*); and in order to demonstrate that this time their repentance is genuine, they back it up with actions: they *put away* their foreign gods and begin to "serve" (worship) Yahweh again. Formally at least, this is a complete about-face on Israel's part that nicely removes the initial problem and brings this entire first episode of the narrative to a point of closure:

> v. 6   *They served ('bd) the Baals. . . .*
> *They forsook Yahweh,*
> *and did not serve ('bd) him.*

13. Literally, just "Amalek" (*'ᵃmālēq*).

14. Boling (*Judges*, p. 193) suggests that Midian may have been the name of "the larger desert coalition to which Maon belonged."

v. 16   *They put away the foreign gods . . .*
         and served ('bd) Yahweh.

The situation described in verse 6 is reversed in verse 16, and these two verses frame the intervening material. All this is relatively straightforward. But in fact neither the literary structure nor the resolution of the crisis in God's relationship with Israel is as neat as this suggests. The episode does not end with Israel's repentance, however that is to be viewed, but with a further, final statement about Yahweh's response to the situation as it now stands: he *became exasperated with the misery of Israel* (v. 16b).

It is generally held[15] that this implies that Yahweh now accepts Israel's repentance as genuine and relents of his earlier threat not to save them any more. Thus, for example,

> Richter   "V. 16 links up well with v. 15: the Israelites confirm their repentance by what they do" (*Die Bearbeitungen des "Retterbuches,"* p. 23, my translation).

> Boling: "Lip service would not suffice. They had to put behind them the cause of their guilt and fear (see 6:7-10) — other gods" (*Judges,* p. 193).

On this reading the scenario here is parallel in substance to that in passages such as:

> Jonah 3:10   When God saw what they did, how they turned from their evil way, God repented of the evil which he had said he would do to them; and he did not do it (RSV).

> Jeremiah 26:19   Did he [Hezekiah] not fear Yahweh and entreat the favor of Yahweh, and did not Yahweh repent of the evil which he had pronounced against them?[16]

But there are at least two problems with this reading: it does not take sufficient account of what Yahweh has just said in verses 11-14, nor of the precise terms in which his response is described in verse 16.

Yahweh's words in verses 12b-13 clearly imply that the putting away

---

15. With the comments by Richter and Boling about to be cited, cf. Soggin, *Judges,* p. 203, and Martin, *Judges,* p. 135.

16. Compare also Exod. 32:14; Jer. 18:7-8; 26:3; Joel 2:13-14; Amos 7:3-6.

of foreign gods is part of a routine with which he has become all too familiar from previous experience. His complaint is not that Israel has failed in the past to back up its cry by putting away its other gods, but that on each previous occasion, after deliverance was granted, Israel abandoned him for these gods again (v. 13a, and cf. the refrain of 3:12; 4:1; 6:1). Hence his refusal to save Israel any more (v. 13b). In short, his interjection in verses 11-14 anticipates the putting away of the foreign gods as a regular accompaniment of Israel's cry for help, and rejects both. In view of this the precise terms in which his final response is described in verse 16b requires close scrutiny.

The two key terms are the verb *became exasperated (qṣr)* and the noun *misery ('ml)*. Neither of them occurs in Jonah 3:10 or the similar texts cited above, which characteristically use instead either *nḥm* or *šwb* (to repent) with *ra'* (evil): God "repents" of "[the] evil" he had threatened to do. As far as terminology is concerned, these other passages are like one another, but unlike Judges 10:16.

The Old Testament usage of *qṣr* can be summarized briefly as follows: literally, "to cut short, to reap," and, metaphorically, "to be powerless, ineffective," but only in the stock rhetorical question, "Is Yahweh's hand/ Spirit *too short/shortened* to do X?" (Num. 11:23; Isa. 50:2; 59:1; Mic. 2:7). In all other cases it indicates frustration, loss of patience, or anger:

Numbers 21:4-5	the people *became impatient (qṣr)* on the way. And the people spoke against God and against Moses (RSV).
Job 21:4-5	Why should I not *be impatient?* Look at me, and be appalled (RSV).
Zechariah 11:8-9	But I *became impatient* with them, and they also detested me. So I said, "I will not be your shepherd. What is to die, let it die" (RSV).

Interestingly, the only other occurrence in the Old Testament is at Judges 16:16, where it refers to Samson's response to Delilah's nagging: "When she had nagged him with her words day after day, and pressured him, *he became exasperated* to the point of death." In these contexts *qṣr* expresses inability to tolerate something any longer.

The noun *'ml* is commonly used in the Old Testament to refer to toil experienced as hardship, or more generally to hardship of any kind (e.g., Gen. 41:51; Deut. 26:7; Job 3:10; 5:6, 7; 7:3; 11:16; Pss. 25:19 [Eng. 18]; 55:11 [Eng. 10]; 73:5, 16; Prov. 31:7; Isa. 53:11; Jer. 20:18). It is therefore an entirely appropriate term to sum up the condition of Israel that caused them to cry out to Yahweh: they were *greatly distressed* (vv. 8-9). It is also a completely apt term to describe Israel's desperate attempts to get Yahweh to help them.[17] In the crucial statement at the end of verse 16 it may refer to either or both of these. In either case, however, comparison with Jonah 3:10 throws the special character of our present text into sharp relief: not, "God *repented* when he saw *what they did,* how they turned from their evil way," but "Yahweh *became exasperated with their misery*" (i.e., he could not endure it any longer).

Comparison with the use of the same verb in 16:16 is particularly illuminating. There Samson becomes exasperated *and relents* — gives Delilah what she wants. But the verb *qṣr* does not of itself carry the meaning "to relent, to yield" — this is expressed (if it happens at all) by what follows. Other, quite different responses may follow the exasperation denoted by *qṣr,* as is clear from Numbers 21:4-5, Job 21:4-5, and Zechariah 11:8-9 above. In the present case, what flows from the exasperation is not specified. We may perhaps infer from the cause of it (Israel's misery) that Yahweh, like Samson, will relent. But all that is indicated is his irritation, annoyance, exasperation. Israel's fate hangs in the balance. To find out what happens we have to read on.[18]

2. Episode 2: The Gileadites and Jephthah (10:17–11:11)

17 *Then the Ammonites were called to arms, and encamped in Gilead. The Israelites came together and encamped at Mizpah.*

18 *The people who were captains of Gilead[19] said to one another, "Who is the man that will begin to fight against the Ammonites? He will be head over all the inhabitants of Gilead."*

1 *Now Jephthah the Gileadite was a mighty warrior, but he was the son of a harlot. Gilead was the father of Jephthah.*

2 *Gilead's wife bore him sons, and when his wife's sons grew up, they drove out Jephthah, and said to him, "You will not inherit in our father's house, for you are the son of another woman."*

17. So Polzin (*Moses and the Deuteronomist,* p. 177): "[Yahweh] grew annoyed with the troubled efforts of Israel."

18. Cf. Trent C. Butler, *Judges,* WBC 8 (Nashville: Thomas Nelson, 2009), p. 267.

19. The expression *hā'ām śārê gil'ād* is anomalous, and has probably arisen through the combination of variants, in this case *śārê 'ām gil'ād* (the captains of the people of Gilead, LXX^A) and *śārê gil'ād* (the captains of Gilead), which is reflected in the LXX^B. With Boling (*Judges,* p. 197) I follow LXX^A. The *'ām gil'ād* (people of Gilead) is the Gileadite militia, a subunit within the *bᵉnê yiśrā'ēl,* and the *śārîm* (captains) are their (military) leaders. Cf. Sisera, who is general *(śar)* of Jabin's army in 4:2. Similar uses of *śar* occur at Gen. 21:22; 26:26; 1 Sam. 12:9; 1 Kgs. 22:31, 32, 33. For other instances of *'ām* as "people bearing arms" see BDB, and note particularly *bā'ām* (among the people) and *'ammô* (his people) in Judg. 11:20.

3 *So Jephthah fled from his brothers and dwelt in the land of Tob. There social misfits gathered around Jephthah, and went out with him.*

4 *After some time the Ammonites fought against Israel,*

5 *and when the Ammonites fought against Israel, the elders of Gilead went to bring Jephthah from the land of Tob.*

6 *They said to Jephthah, "Come and be our leader, so that we can fight with the Ammonites."*

7 *But Jephthah said to the elders of Gilead, "Aren't you the ones[20] who hated me, and drove me out of my father's house? Why have you come to me now, when you are in trouble?"*

8 *The elders of Gilead said to Jephthah, "No![21] We have returned to you now, that you may go with us and fight with the Ammonites, and be our head over all the inhabitants of Gilead."*

9 *Then Jephthah said to the elders of Gilead, "If you bring me home again to fight the Ammonites, and Yahweh gives them over to me, I will be your head."*

10 *The elders of Gilead said to Jephthah, "Yahweh will be witness between us; we will surely do according to your word."[22]*

11 *So Jephthah went with the elders of Gilead, and the people made him head and leader over them, and Jephthah spoke all his words before Yahweh at Mizpah.*

10:17-18 As this second episode opens, we are transported to the battle zone where the Ammonites are about to launch a major new offensive, and the Israelites are taking desperate counsel with one another. The parallelism in verse 17 (AB//A′B′) mirrors stylistically the confrontation between the two sides. But the subtle difference of nuance between *were called to arms (wayyiṣṣāᶜᵃqû)* and *came together (wayyēᵊāsᵉpû)*[23] already hints at the issue which is vocalized in verse 18: Israel is without effective leadership, and therefore extremely vulnerable in the face of this new threat. The expression

---

20. Note the emphatic use of the personal pronoun *'attem* ("you," masculine plural) before the verb. See the exegetical comments on this verse.

21. Reading *lō'-kēn* with LXX instead of MT's *lākēn*, which makes no sense after Jephthah's question in the previous verse. *lākēn* probably arose through the accidental omission of the quiescent *aleph* (Boling, *Judges*, p. 198).

22. I use this rather wooden translation here because of the significance of the term "word(s)," which will become clear in the exegesis that follows.

23. The Niphal of *ṣᶜq/zᶜq* always denotes a summons to battle and implies a "caller," that is, a leader. Within Judges see 6:34, 35; 7:23, 24; 12:1; 18:22, 23. Cf. Josh. 8:16; 1 Sam. 13:4; 14:20; 2 Kgs. 3:21. The Niphal of *'sp* is less precise. It *may* be synonymous with *ṣᶜq/zᶜq*, but is not necessarily so. Cf. Judg. 6:33 with 2:10 and 16:23. The middle sense is frequent, as in Exod. 32:26; Josh. 10:5; Amos 3:9, etc.

Israelites (bᵉnê yiśrāʾēl) now assumes a more particular and limited sense than it had in Episode 1, where it was virtually synonymous with Israel as a whole (cf. 10:6-7). Now it is used of the assembled Israelite men-at-arms (v. 17) and the captains of the Gileadite contingent (v. 18) who are singled out from the larger company to be the principal actors in the episode.

In contrast to Episode 1 the direct speech here is given a specific locale, *Mizpah* (v. 17). There are three places with this name in the books of Joshua and Judges: one just north of Jerusalem in the central highlands (Josh. 13:26; 15:38; 18:26), another in the far north in the vicinity of Mount Hermon (Josh. 11:3, 8), and a third across the Jordan in Gilead (Judg. 11:29, 34). Since the Ammonites have already crossed the Jordan at least once (10:9), it is possible that the assembly in view here in 10:17 took place in the central highlands, with the captains of Gilead crossing the Jordan to attend it. However, given the fact that all the subsequent action takes place in Gilead, it is all but certain that the Mizpah in 10:17 is the place subsequently referred to as Mizpah of Gilead (11:29), which was Jephthah's hometown (11:34). If it is the same place as referred to in Genesis 31:49, it had Israelite connections reaching right back to patriarchal times, but its precise location is unknown.

What does seem clear from the makeup of the assembly, however, is that with the beginning of Ammonite raids across the Jordan, Gilead's fight for survival became the fight of all Israel. Hence the reference to the *Israelites* coming together (v. 17), even though the *captains of Gilead* are the primary actors (v. 18). Yahweh has retired into the background. In this respect the present episode contrasts markedly with the corresponding episode in the Gideon narrative. There, after a rebuke by a prophet, Yahweh's messenger appears to commission Gideon (6:11ff.). Here, after a much sterner rebuke by Yahweh himself, there is no divine intervention. This time, it seems, Israel will have to work out its own salvation.

In this second episode the human characters are presented with greater definition than in Episode 1. This is no orderly assembly called and presided over by a competent leader. The captains do not speak with one voice, and have no strategy to put forward. They do not even address their men, but speak anxiously to *one another* (v. 18).[24] The question they ask recalls the very similar question with which the book of Judges opens (1:1), but how different the circumstances! There the Israelites, united and on the offensive against the Canaanites, address the question to Yahweh. Here, leaderless and on the defensive, the captains of Gilead address it to one another, and there is little sign of any effective Israelite unity (an issue which will surface explicitly later in the narrative). The captains, as they see it, have been left to their own devices, and none of them wants the job of leading. They are prepared to offer induce-

---

24. Cf. the townsmen of Ophrah in 6:29.

ment to anyone who will do it for them (they will make him *head over all the inhabitants of Gilead*), but no one suitable is at hand. This critical leadership vacuum sets the scene for the entry of Jephthah in 11:1.

11:1-3 The momentum of the story is briefly arrested here while we are introduced to Jephthah and told a little of his personal history. The flashback to Jephthah's birth and subsequent conflict with his brothers is formally set off from the main thread of the narrative by the disjunctive, *Now Jephthah (weʸiptāḥ)* of verse 1a. He is a *Gileadite,* and *Gilead* was his *father* (v. 1). Here "Gilead" is probably a substitute for his father's actual name, which may have been unknown to the author.[25] If so, however, this lack is made the occasion for the author to stress the point he is clearly wanting to make here: Jephthah is a Gileadite through and through, and from that point of view a suitable candidate for leadership. But he was the son of a prostitute and an outcast from his clan, disinherited by his "legitimate" brothers (v. 2).[26] He flees and becomes an exile in *the land of Tob (ṭôḇ,* "good")[27] — which for Jephthah, ironically, becomes the place of alienation, rejection, and disinheritance — where other *social misfits*[28] gather around him and "go out" with him (v. 3). We are left to draw the natural conclusion — Jephthah and his men sustain themselves by plunder. But socially undesirable as he may be, Jephthah is a survivor, a seasoned fighter, and a natural leader, with men (and presumably equipment) at his disposal.

So these verses present us with a paradox: the outcast with no social status is in fact a *gibbôr ḥayil* (a man of strength/substance) in two senses: a *mighty warrior,* and a man with human and material resources at his command.[29] The early mention of his prowess in 11:1 sets him in stark contrast to

25. "[T]he land of Gilead is personified as his nameless father." Klein, *Triumph of Irony,* p. 222, n. 7.

26. The pronouncement by his brothers *("You will not inherit, . . . you are the son of another woman")* had already taught Jephthah the power of words.

27. Perhaps *et ̕T-Aiyibeh* in the remote northeast of Gilead (*OBA,* pp. 84, 219; 2 Sam. 10:6, 8). The occurrence of "good" *(ṭôḇ)* here, and again in v. 5, recalls the words of the Israelites to Yahweh in 10:15: "Do whatever is good *(ṭôḇ)* in your eyes." Is there a suggestion that Yahweh is already moving behind the scenes?

28. *ʾᵃnāšîm rêqîm,* literally, "empty men." Cf. 9:4, where the opprobrium "reckless" is added. *rêqîm* itself does not necessarily imply moral obliquity, but a lack of the qualities which command success in the leading of a regular life, especially a lack of material goods such as property and social status (Ruth 1:21). Cf. Burney, *Judges,* p. 308, and the description of the men who attached themselves to David in similar circumstances (1 Sam. 22:2). Indeed, Jephthah's early career anticipates that of David in a number of ways: his flight, his life in exile, and the circumstances of his rise to power, first over a part of Israel, then the whole.

29. Cf. 6:12, where the primary sense of *gibbôr ḥayil* is prowess in battle, with Ruth 2:1, where it refers to wealth and social status.

the *captains* of 10:17-18, and hints that the real motive for his expulsion by his brothers may have been fear of being dominated by him.[30]

4-11   We are returned to the main story line with the news, in verse 4, that the Ammonites have now launched their threatened offensive. With the ineffectiveness of the *captains* so clearly established, and with the military situation critical, the *elders of Gilead (ziqnê gil'ād)* — the local community leaders[31] — take matters into their own hands (v. 5). The words are well chosen at this point to indicate the confidence with which the elders set out: they go to *bring* (i.e., "take," *lqḥ*) Jephthah from the land of Tob.

On meeting him they come straight to the point: *"Come and be our leader (qāṣîn), so that we can fight with the Ammonites"* (v. 6). "Be our *qāṣîn*" appears to refer here specifically to taking command of the men in the field, assuming responsibility for the conduct of the war.[32] Perhaps the elders assume that the outcast will be flattered and jump at the chance of such rapid advancement. But if so, they have underestimated his shrewdness and opportunism. He is not as amenable as they expect. He angrily rejects their appeal, charging them with responsibility for his earlier expulsion (v. 7).[33] Desper-

---

30. Cf. Gray, *Judges,* p. 332.

31. For a description of how elders normally functioned in the judges period, see Ruth 4:1-12.

32. This rather than the more general meaning, "ruler" (Isa. 1:10, etc.), is warranted by the context. See Josh. 10:24 where the *qᵉṣînîm* are ranking officers within Joshua's military organization. Cf. Boling, *Judges,* p. 198. For the use of *qāṣîn* in a non-military sense see, e.g., Prov. 6:7; 25:15; Isa. 1:10; 3:7.

33. See the narrator's account of Jephthah's expulsion in v. 2. C. A. Simpson, *Composition of the Book of Judges* (Oxford: Basil Blackwell, 1957), p. 46, finds the narrator's account and Jephthah's account contradictory and assigns them to different hands. Soggin (*Judges,* pp. 206-8) finds them "clearly difficult to reconcile," and takes v. 7 as more reliable on the grounds that v. 2 is secondary, the ensuing narrative saying nothing about the restitution of Jephthah's family rights. But neither Simpson nor Soggin takes sufficient account of the quite different narrative functions of the two accounts. The first (v. 2) is the narrator's own dispassionate account of what happened. The second (v. 7) is an accusation in the form of a question, delivered with obvious passion and an eye to its effect on the elders. Its function is primarily rhetorical, and the narrator does not accept personal responsibility for it: it is what *Jephthah* said to the elders (v. 7). In terms of narrative function, therefore, the narrator's version in v. 2 has a *prima facie* stronger claim to be taken at face value. However, even at the level of basic fact the two versions are not necessarily contradictory. The elders may have adjudicated in the legal proceedings regarding inheritance rights that led to Jephthah's expulsion. If so, even though the elders deny it (v. 8a), Jephthah would be quite right to see them, as the leaders of the community, as the ones mainly responsible for what happened (Klein, *Irony,* p. 86). The fact that there is no subsequent mention of the restitution of Jephthah's family rights is not surprising in view of his appointment as *head over all the inhabitants of Gilead* (vv. 8, 11): the greater includes the lesser.

311

ate, the elders propose new terms, and this time their tone is much more deferential: *"We have returned to you now, that you may go with us and fight with the Ammonites, and be our head (rō'š) over all the inhabitants of Gilead"* (v. 8). The change from qāṣîn to rō'š, the reversed order ("be qāṣîn and fight" to "fight and be rō'š"), and the full description *(rō'š over all the inhabitants of Gilead)* all indicate that something more permanent, wide ranging, and prestigious is now on offer, namely, "tribal chief" or the like.[34] This was the offer originally proposed by the captains back in 10:18; the elders had apparently hoped to secure Jephthah's services for less, but have realized that they can't do so.

Their revised offer brings Jephthah to the point of bargaining (v. 9):

"If you ('attem) bring me ('ôṯî) home again to fight the Ammonites,
and Yahweh gives them over to me,
I ('ānōḵî) will be your (lāḵem) head (rô'š)."

This formulation of the bargain is Jephthah's own, and it is shrewd. He had used personal pronouns emphatically in his earlier rebuttal of the elders: "Didn't you *('attem) hate me ('ôṯî)?"* (v. 7). Now he uses them again, in a chiastic pattern, to make quite clear that what is involved is a transfer of power from the elders to himself. *Head (rō'š)* stands in the emphatic, final position. Further, Jephthah draws out the implications of the order, "come-fight-be head" in verse 8. This did not specifically lay down victory as a condition, but Jephthah is realistic enough to know that only victory will create the conditions in which the offer of *rô'š* will be implemented. By invoking *Yahweh,* however, he elevates victory to the status of divine endorsement of himself, and so further enhances his authority vis-à-vis the elders. So Yahweh re-enters the story obliquely, neither speaking nor being addressed, but on the lips of Jephthah as a trump card in his negotiations with the elders, and on the lips of the elders themselves (v. 10) as a silent witness of all that takes place.

The elders acquiesce completely to the terms as Jephthah has now formulated them: *"we will surely do according to your word"* (v. 10). Satisfied, Jephthah returns with them to *Mizpah,* where he is received with such enthusiasm by the *people* that they make him both *head* and *leader* on the spot (v. 11)! As in 10:17-18, the *Mizpah* in view is presumably the "Mizpah of Gilead" of 11:11, and the *people* the assembled fighting men. The immediacy and enthusiasm with which Jephthah is received is an indication of the relief that everyone feels; at last they have someone capable of taking com-

34. Cf. the heads *(rō'šîm)* of the twelve tribes in Num. 1:4-16 and 13:1-16; cf. also Deut. 1:13; 5:23 (Heb. 20). H. N. Rösel, "Jephtah und das Problem der Richter," *Biblica* 61 (1980): 251-55, draws a distinction between qāṣîn, "military commander," and rō'š, "civil governor" or the like.

mand and giving them some hope of success. But the Gileadites are as unco-ordinated in the conduct of their internal politics as they are in their conduct of the war. The captains appear to have acted without reference to the elders in 10:17-18, and vice versa in 11:4-10. Here in 11:11 the "people" act spontaneously, without reference to anyone! When the initial excitement is over, however, the proceedings are brought to a formal conclusion at *Mizpah,* where *Jephthah [speaks] all his words before Yahweh.* The exact form of the ceremony is unknown, but clearly what it amounted to was a solemn, sworn ratification of the agreement Jephthah made with the elders in verses 8-10.[35] But as Daniel Block has observed,[36] even here there are hints of irregularity: there has been no previous indication that Mizpah in Gilead was a recognized sanctuary site, and in contrast to his raising up of previous judges, Yahweh's part in Jephthah's rise is at best ambiguous. Jephthah appears to be a man-made judge rather than a divinely called one. Furthermore, according to his agreement with the elders, his appointment as "head over all the inhabitants of Gilead" was conditional on his success in defeating the Ammonites (v. 9). So his appointment to that office can be no more than provisional at this stage. He already has popular support and provisional endorsement, but in re-ality he will get what he has bargained for only if he wins the war. The question that was asked at Mizpah in 10:17-18 is answered by Jephthah's arrival here in 11:11. But everything now depends on how Jephthah will fare in the coming conflict. A great deal hangs in the balance. The stakes are very high, not just for the people Jephthah leads, but for Jephthah himself.

This brings us to the end of the second major episode of the narrative. But before we pass on, it is worth reflecting on the remarkable similarities between Episodes 1 and 2. Both episodes follow the same basic pattern, which we may represent as follows:

Episode 1	*Episode 2*
The Israelites reject Yahweh.	The Gileadites reject Jephthah.
The Israelites find themselves in a predicament they can't deal with.	The Israelites find themselves in a predicament they can't deal with.
The Israelites seek help from Yahweh, the One they rejected.	The Gileadites seek help from Jephthah, the one they rejected.
Yahweh rebuffs their appeal.	Jephthah rebuffs their appeal.

35. "There [in Mizpah] with the 'oath of office' Jephthah was sworn in and offi-cially made head *(rōʾš)* and 'commander-in-chief' *(qāṣîn)* of Gileadite Israel" (Block, *Judges, Ruth,* p. 356).

36. Block, *Judges, Ruth,* p. 356.

Episode 1	Episode 2
The Israelites "repent" of their rejection of Yahweh.	The Gileadites "repent" of their rejection of Jephthah.
—	Jephthah agrees to help them on certain conditions.
The Israelites reinstate Yahweh as the One they serve.	The Gileadites make Jephthah their leader.
Yahweh is exasperated by Israel's misery.	—

The similarities are so striking that they invite comparison and contrast by any thoughtful reader. In particular they suggest, in retrospect, that the repentance of the Israelites has the same basic character as the repentance of the Gileadites, and this is confirmed by the reactions of Yahweh and Jephthah respectively. Both of them clearly see it as a change of strategy rather than a change of heart, and respond accordingly. Jephthah sees it as an opportunity to regain his lost rights and secure a position of power in Gilead. There is no love lost between him and the elders. He knows that the game they are playing is negotiation, and he shows that he is more than a match for them in the negotiation stakes. Yahweh is no more impressed with the "repentance" of Israel than Jephthah is with the "repentance" of the Gileadites, but he has a real dilemma because he genuinely cares about them. He cannot endure their misery any longer, but knows that to save them yet again will solve nothing. That is the deep problem Yahweh faced repeatedly in the period of the Judges, and no solution is yet in sight.

To summarize, the parallel structure of the two episodes exposes the true nature of Israel's "repentance": it has no real substance. It is no more than desperate politics: a survival strategy. The contrast between the two episodes, on the other hand, highlights the vast gulf that separates Yahweh and Jephthah at the level of character and motivation, and poses questions about how the relationship between them will develop as the narrative continues to unfold.

3. Episode 3: Jephthah and the King of Ammon (11:12-28)

12 *Jephthah sent messengers to the king of the Ammonites, saying, "What is the issue between us, that you have come to me to fight against my land?"*

13 *The king of the Ammonites replied to Jephthah's messengers, "Because Israel took away my land when it came up from Egypt, from the*

Arnon to the Jabbok and to the Jordan. Now, return these territories[37] peacefully."

14 *Jephthah again sent messengers to the king of the Ammonites.*

15 *He said to him, "Thus says Jephthah, Israel took away neither the land of Moab nor the land of the Ammonites.*

16 *When they came up from Egypt, Israel traveled in the desert as far as the Sea of Reeds, and came to Kadesh.*

17 *Then Israel sent messengers to the king of Edom, saying, 'Please let me pass through your land.' But the king of Edom wouldn't listen. Israel also sent messengers to the king of Moab, but he too refused. So Israel stayed in Kedesh.*

18 *Then Israel again traveled in the wilderness, around the land of Edom and the land of Moab, and approached the land of Moab from the east. They camped on the other side of the Arnon, and did not cross the border of Moab (for the Arnon is the border of Moab).*

19 *Israel sent messengers to Sihon, king of the Amorites, king of Heshbon, and said to him, 'Please let us pass through your land on the way to our place.'*

20 *But Sihon did not trust Israel to cross his border; Sihon gathered all his troops.[38] They encamped in Jahaz, and he fought with Israel.*

21 *Yahweh, the God of Israel, gave Sihon and all his people into the hand of Israel, who struck them down. So Israel took possession of the whole land of the Amorites, and they settled in that land.*

22 *They took possession of the whole territory of the Amorites, from the Arnon to the Jabbok, and from the wilderness to the Jordan.*

23 *So Yahweh, the God of Israel, drove out the Amorites before his people Israel, but you are trying to dispossess them.*

24 *Isn't it the case that whatever your god Chemosh gives you to possess you will possess, and everything Yahweh our God gives us to possess we will possess?*

25 *Are you far superior to Balak, son of Zippor, the king of Moab? Will you really contend with Israel? Surely you will not fight against them?*

26 *Israel dwelt in Heshbon and its villages, and in Aroer and its villages — in all the towns along the bank of the Arnon — for three hundred years. Why didn't you 'liberate' these places then?*

27 *It is not I who have sinned against you, but you who have done me wrong by fighting against me.*

---

37. The suffix is feminine plural, "return *these*" — the various regions/territories that make up the "land" (feminine singular) of the previous verse.

38. Literally, "his people."

> *Let Yahweh the Judge judge today between the people of Israel and the people of Ammon."*
>
> 28 *But the king of the Ammonites did not take any notice of the words of Jephthah, which he had sent to him.*

We have seen the crucial role of dialogue in the first two episodes. In this third one dialogue features even more strongly; in fact, it expands to fill the entire episode. But this time the dialogue takes place at a distance, through diplomatic exchange by means of messengers. The formality and distance involved mirror the distance (in terms of relationship) between the two parties. Jephthah speaks for Israel, and his adversary speaks for Ammon. Their relationship is tense and adversarial. It is more a case of maneuvering for advantage than bridge building. At the end the partners to the dialogue are more at odds than they were at the beginning, and the only alternative left is war.

The extensive dialogue slows down the forward momentum of the narrative, but it also advances two story lines simultaneously. The foreground story consists of the exchange of messages and messengers between Jephthah and his adversary, leading to the impasse that is reached in verse 28. At the same time, and by this same exchange of messengers, a retrospective story is told, concerning Israel's exodus from Egypt and arrival in the territory now under dispute between Israel and the Ammonites. Furthermore, two competing versions of this background story emerge which are irreconcilable: Jephthah's and his adversary's. It is the deadlock between these two versions of the background story that produces the impasse in the surface story.

The passage as a whole is of mixed genre. At the most general level it is narrative. At the more particular level it is a disputation, and at a more particular level still it is a mixture of diplomacy and litigation. What begins as a diplomatic exchange ends as a case laid before a judge. Jephthah, who starts off as the accused, turns the tables on his adversary. By the end Jephthah is the plaintiff, his adversary is the accused, and Yahweh is the one appealed to as Judge.

A feature of the passage that has attracted a lot of discussion is the prominence given to Moab. This is surprising in the context of a dispute between Israel and Ammon, and requires explanation. Those who have approached the passage in a historical-critical mode have generally assumed that an earlier version of the passage, involving Israel and Moab, has been adapted to function as an exchange between Israel and Ammon.[39] Of course this suf-

---

39. Various forms of this basic thesis are found, e.g., in Moore, *Judges,* p. 283; O. Eissfeldt, *Die Quellen des Richterbuches* (Leipzig: J. C. Hinrichs, 1925), p. 76; Burney, *Judges,* pp. 298-305; M. Wüst, "Die Einschaltungen in die Jiftachgeschichten, Ri 11.13-26," *Biblica* 56 (1975): 464-79; W. Richter, "Die Überlieferungen um Jephtah, Ri

fers from the obvious objection that, in that case, we might have expected the adaptation to have been more thorough. In the exposition that follows I have assumed that the frequent mention of Moab is intentional, and offer an explanation which I believe does more justice to the relevant textual data.

12 By dispatching *messengers* on a diplomatic mission Jephthah begins to exercise his new authority as head and leader of the Gileadites (11:8, 11). He also follows the precedent that Moses had set in dealing with the rulers of the same general area long before him (Num. 21:21; Deut. 2:26).[40] It is unlikely, however, that he is genuinely seeking peace, since armed conflict has already begun, and he has been engaged by the Gileadites specifically to "fight" (11:5, 8). From what follows it seems more likely that his intention is to seize the moral high ground by establishing the rightness of his cause, and to buy himself sufficient time to recruit a larger fighting force. His tone is anything but conciliatory. At the outset the expression *my land* probably refers to Gilead, Jephthah's homeland, and he challenges his opponent to justify his invasion of it. His opponent is called a *king* by the narrator, and since Jephthah is effectively engaging with him as an equal, there is an implication that Jephthah himself is beginning to act like a king. This impression will be strengthened in what follows. But the Ammonite is never referred to by his personal name, possibly as a deliberate slight since Jephthah can hardly be ignorant of it.[41] Jephthah's first move is to put his opponent on the defensive, and make it clear that the Gileadites will no longer accept their subjugation by the Ammonites as either justifiable or unchallengeable. They at last have a man of steel to lead them, and they intend to take a stand.

13 The Ammonite's reply starts off by being equally uncompromising. To Jephthah's charge that the Ammonite has come to fight against "*my* land" (v. 12), his enemy counters that Israel took away "*my* land" when it came up from Egypt (v. 13, my emphasis). This broadens the debate by bringing *Israel* into the picture and introducing a historical argument. It throws the onus back on Jephthah to prove that what he has just asserted is correct. It also gives more precision to the argument by defining the disputed territory in question as the territory between the *Arnon* River in the south and the *Jabbok* in the north.

10,7–12,6," *Biblica* 47 (1966): 522-47; and Soggin, *Judges,* pp. 211-13. Against this prevailing view Boling (*Judges,* pp. 201-5) draws attention to the absence of the kind of reflective glossing that accompanies such redactional activity elsewhere in the book (e.g., 1:36), and the intelligibility of the whole in its present context.

40. A different rule was understood to apply to Israel's relationships with the "seven nations" of Canaan proper (Deut. 7:1-5). Accordingly, Joshua is not said to have opened negotiations with any of them except the Gibeonites, who tricked him into doing so (Josh. 9).

41. Contrast, e.g., the naming of Hezekiah in 2 Kgs. 18:29, 31.

At the same time, however, this very precision opens the door slightly to negotiation. By implication the western border of the disputed territory as defined by the king of Ammon is the Jordan River, where the Arnon and Jabbok respectively end their courses. This is a tacit admission that the Ammonites provoked the present crisis by trespassing on acknowledged Israelite soil when they *crossed* the Jordan back in 10:9. Jephthah is challenged to prove that he is genuinely seeking a diplomatic settlement by returning the disputed territory (Gilead) *peacefully (bᵉšālôm),* and since the *eastern* border of this territory has been left undefined, there is room for one or both parties to moderate their demands and agree on some kind of accommodation that would allow both of them to save face. Gilead could be partitioned and a new frontier established that both parties could accept. But Jephthah is in no mood for compromise, as we are about to see.

14-15 Jephthah sends messengers again, this time prefacing his words with an expression intended to leave his opponent in no doubt about the authority with which he speaks. *"Thus says Jephthah (kōh 'āmar yiptāḥ,* v. 15)" is an example of standard ambassadorial language which heads of state used in addressing each other through messengers, especially when a superior power was addressing an inferior one.[42] It was a speech form that was used by imperial powers when addressing subject states.[43] A classic example in the Old Testament is the message Sennacherib sent to Hezekiah demanding the surrender of Jerusalem:

> "Hear the word of the great king,
> the king of Assyria!
> *Thus says the king (kōh 'āmar hammelek)."* (2 Kgs. 18:28-29 NRSV)

In addition to using this somewhat intimidating, statesmanlike language, Jephthah picks up his opponent's reference to "Israel" in verse 13 and uses it himself. If Ammon wants to escalate the conflict from the Ammon-Gilead plane to the Ammon-Israel plane, so be it; Jephthah is quite prepared to speak for Israel as a whole. It shows his ambition and confidence, and his command of the "cut and thrust" of diplomatic engagement. In the war of words he is more than equal to his royal adversary.

The reference to *Moab* in verse 15 is at first sight surprising, since it is not a party to the present dispute.[44] However, Moab will be referred to frequently in what follows, and its occurrence here is the first indication of the

---

42. 1 Kgs. 20:2; 2 Kgs. 9:18-19; cf. 1 Kgs. 2:30; 2 Kgs. 19:3. The vast majority of instances of this formula in the Old Testament is by prophets acting as messengers of the divine king, Yahweh (Exod. 4:22, etc.).

43. 2 Chron. 36:23; Ezra 1:2.

44. But note the reference to "the gods of Moab" in 10:6.

direction in which Jephthah intends to take his argument. It may also have been triggered by his opponent's reference to the Arnon in verse 13, since this river was the northern border of traditional Moabite territory (Num. 21:13). More will be said about this below, especially in connection with the reference to Chemosh, the god of the Moabites, in verse 24. The general point Jephthah is making is that Israel did not wrongfully seize anyone's land, something that is borne out by the record of its dealings with all the nations in the region, not just Ammon.

16-18   Jephthah now begins to develop his argument in detail. In response to his opponent's reference to "when [Israel] came up from Egypt" (v. 13), he begins to tell his own (and Israel's) version of what happened at that time, but going into particulars only on matters pertinent to his argument. The *Sea of Reeds* (*yam-sûp*, v. 16) is the northwestern extremity of what is now the Red Sea (Exod. 13:18), in the Bitter Lakes region north of Suez along the line of the present Suez Canal.[45] *Kadesh* is short for Kadesh-barnea, on the northern fringe of the Sinai peninsula. It was here that Israel first emerged from the desert and came to the southern outskirts of the land God had promised to give them (Deut. 1:19). But things did not go well for them there. After a failed attempt to enter the land they withdrew into the Sinai desert again, only to return to Kadesh forty years later (Num. 13:1–20:1). Most of the exodus generation had passed away by then, and it was time for a new start. Jephthah passes over all this in silence, however, and picks up the story from the point where they are planning to leave Kadesh for the second time and make a second approach to the land — from the east this time, between the Arnon and Jabbok rivers, just north of the Dead Sea. This is where they first came to the territory now in dispute.

Edom lay to the south of the Dead Sea, and *Moab* to the east of it. The shortest route from Kadesh to the Arnon River would have been through these two countries. Furthermore, since the Edomites were descendants of Esau, Jacob's older brother (Gen. 35:27–36:19), and the Moabites were descendants of Lot, Abraham's nephew (Gen. 11:31; 19:36-37), it was reasonable to expect they would be willing to give the Israelites safe passage. But this turned out not to be so, making it necessary for the Israelites to take a much more indirect route, skirting *around the land of Edom and the land of Moab,* to avoid conflict with them (v. 18; cf. Deut. 2:2-23).

Jephthah's claim that Israel had *sent messengers* to the king of Edom is supported by Numbers 20:14. There is no similar corroboration of his claim that they had also sent messengers to the king of Moab, though it is entirely probable that they did so. And the repetition has an important rhetorical function, for Jephthah wants to show (among other things) that in sending

45. K. A. Kitchen, "Red Sea," *NBD,* p. 1004.

messengers to the king of Ammon he has acted as a true statesman in the tradition of Moses, and that Ammon's refusal to listen is as reprehensible as the refusal of Edom and Moab had been. After all, the Ammonites, too, had ancestral ties to Israel (Gen. 19:38).

Of particular importance, however, is his claim that on arrival Israel had camped on the *other [northern] side of the Arnon* (v. 18), and had not even entered Moabite territory, let alone misappropriated any of their land. It is curious that he should be talking so much about Moab rather than Ammon at this point,[46] but, as we will see, a probable reason for it will emerge later, especially in verses 24-25.

19-20 So far Jephthah's historical review has proceeded rapidly, in summary form only. But now the account slows down and more detail is given, because the crucial part has been reached. In verses 19-22 Jephthah speaks directly of how it was that Israel came into possession of the land between the Arnon and the Jabbok that the king of Ammon had claimed was rightfully his. When Israel arrived on the scene, this territory was not ruled by the Ammonites, but by *Sihon, king of the Amorites,* whose capital was *Heshbon* (v. 19). We have already seen that "Amorites" is a flexible term, sometimes used broadly of the pre-Israelite inhabitants of Canaan in general, and sometimes of the inhabitants of a particular area.[47] Here it is clearly used in the narrow sense, of the pre-Israelite inhabitants of the territory in dispute between Jephthah and the king of Ammon. *Heshbon* was near its center, midway between the Arnon and the Jabbok. This stretch of land lay directly across Israel's path, and so they sent *messengers* to seek safe passage through it (v. 19), as they had done for Edom and Moab. But this time their request was met, not just with refusal, or even the threat of war, but with war itself: *Sihon gathered all his troops.* They camped at *Jahaz,* 7 miles (15 km.) south of Heshbon, *and fought with Israel* (v. 20). This meant that an entirely different situation now existed. It was no longer a case of diplomacy but warfare, and at stake was no longer right of passage through the territory, but the territory itself. Sihon staked everything on being able to defeat Israel in battle, but it was a fatal miscalculation.

21-24 So far Jephthah's account has dealt with matters that were in the domain of public knowledge: Israel sought right of passage; it was refused, and a battle ensued. He could have continued in this matter-of-fact fashion by simply reporting that Israel defeated Sihon. Instead (and very significantly) he lifts matters onto a higher plane by introducing theology for the first time: Israel defeated Sihon because Yahweh, Israel's God, *gave* Sihon

---

46. Especially since Israel had also refrained from intruding into Ammonite territory according to Deut. 2:19.

47. See the commentary on 1:34-36.

and all his people into their hand (v. 21). Jephthah is not saying anything novel here; it is part of the tradition he has been appealing to all along.[48] But the movement to theological explanation at this point has particular rhetorical significance, and brings us to the heart of Jephthah's case regarding Israel's title to the territory in question.

In the world most of us live in, diplomacy is normally conducted in purely secular terms, and the introduction of theology would probably be viewed as a distraction and lead nowhere. But it was not so in Jephthah's world. On the contrary, in that world the outcome of battles was generally understood to be divinely determined, and as indicating the will of God or the gods concerning the matter in dispute — especially title to land. This understanding of how land changed hands is clearly reflected in the Old Testament itself, and in extrabiblical texts from both before and after the time of Jephthah.[49] Within this frame of thought Jephthah's claim that Yahweh, Israel's God, had given Israel title to Sihon's former territory by enabling them to defeat him in battle would have made sense to Jephthah's opponent, and could have been expected to carry some weight with him.

Much more puzzling, though, is the concession Jephthah makes to his opponent in verses 24: "Isn't it the case that whatever your god Chemosh gives you to possess you will possess, and everything Yahweh our God gives to us to possess, we will possess?" The tone of sweet reasonableness is entirely appropriate to what Jephthah is trying to do. But there are two obvious problems. First, according to the universal testimony of both biblical and extrabiblical texts, the god of the Ammonites was not *Chemosh* but Molech.[50] Chemosh was the god of Moab.[51] It could be that Jephthah is simply mistaken regarding this matter. That would hardly be surprising given the narrator's frankness about his other imperfections.[52] However, the reference to Chemosh rather than Molech needs to be considered in the context of the

---

48. As attested in Num. 21:21-34 and Deut. 2:24-36.

49. See, e.g., the biblical account of Israel's occupation of Canaan in the book of Joshua, and in *ANET,* pp. 234-38 and 287-94, the annals of Thutmose III of Egypt (15th cent. B.C.) and Sennacherib of Assyria (8th cent. B.C.).

50. See, e.g., 1 Kgs. 11:7. The name Molech, which has the same vowels as *bōšet* (shame), may be a pejorative name used by the Israelites for an original "Malcolm" or "Milcom." See the NRSV, which reflects the pointing of the name in the MT of 1 Kgs. 11:5, 33; 2 Kgs. 23:13; 1 Chron. 20:2; Jer. 49:1, 3; Zeph. 1:5.

51. See, e.g., Num. 21:29; 1 Kgs. 11:7, and the Moabite Stone (*ANET,* pp. 320-21).

52. Block (*Judges, Ruth,* p. 362) suggests that Jephthah's reference to Chemosh rather than Molech is an intentional insult, showing contempt for his adversary. But see my comments on vv. 25-26, which suggest an alternative explanation that is more likely in my opinion.

puzzling prominence given to Moab rather than Ammon in the passage as a whole, and since there is more data relevant to this in verses 25-26, we will reserve further comment on it until then.

The second problem is the way verse 24 is at odds with the very tradition that Jephthah has been drawing on with considerable accuracy in the rest of his speech. According to that tradition, it was Yahweh who gave both Israel and Ammon their respective territories (Deut. 2:19, 36). No other god played any part in it at all. It is possible that this deviation is indicative of a flaw in Jephthah's basic theology. He appeals to the orthodox tradition where it suits his purposes, but he is syncretistic at heart, and that Yahweh and Chemosh gave Israel and Ammon their respective territories is a straightforward statement of what he believes.[53] On the other hand, it is possible that it is merely something he is willing to concede for the sake of argument, as his best chance of getting his adversary to accept the legitimacy of Israel's claim to the territory in question. It is hard to choose decisively between those two options; there are aspects of Jephthah's character and motives that remain hidden. However, the fact that verse 24 occurs at the climax of a diplomatic speech, and the way Jephthah appeals to Yahweh as *the* Judge who alone will decide the issue in verse 27, favor the second alternative. Jephthah is a monotheist,[54] even though his words and actions are not always consistent with what he believes.

25-26 In these two verses Jephthah elaborates on his claim that Yahweh and Chemosh gave certain territories to Israel and Ammon respectively, and that his opponent should accept this.[55] Furthermore, it is clear from the content of verse 26 in particular that the two territories in question lie on either side of the Arnon River: Israel's to its north, and Ammon's to its south. What then are we to make of Jephthah's appeal in verse 25 to the precedent set by *Balak, son of Zippor, the king of Moab?* This is the final piece of the puzzle concerning the prominence given to Moab in Jephthah's speech as a whole, and at last gives us the key to understanding it. Jephthah's focus on the Arnon as the border implies that by the time he came to power the Ammonites had already occupied the former Moabite territory south of it, and were intent on occupying the Israelite territory to the north of it as well — in fact, were well on their way to doing so (10:8-9). That is why Jephthah can speak to the king of Ammon as the successor to the kings of Moab. It is probably also why he referred to Chemosh as "your god" back in verse 24:

---

53. Block, *Judges, Ruth,* p. 362.

54. Contra those who believe that monotheism was a late development in Israelite religion. At the very least Jephthah speaks as one who believes in the unrivaled supremacy of Yahweh (see v. 27).

55. See the comments on vv. 21-24.

not because he believed that Chemosh was Ammon's only or supreme god, but because the Ammonites now occupied the "land of Chemosh," so to speak, and therefore Chemosh was the technically correct god to refer to in the present negotiations.[56] In view of the content and purpose of the speech as a whole, this is more likely than that the reference to Chemosh was either a mistake or an intentional insult.

Balak, son of Zippor (v. 25), was the ruler of Moab when Israel first arrived in Transjordan in the time of Moses. He is recalled here and in Joshua 24:9 as the king who tried to destroy the Israelites by hiring the prophet Balaam to curse them, but was thwarted when God made Balaam bless them instead (Num. 22–24). Jephthah warns his opponent against disregarding this lesson from history.

The *three hundred years* of verse 26 is the time from Israel's arrival and settlement in the territory north of the Arnon to the present.[57] The Israelites *dwelt in Heshbon* following their defeat of the Amorite king, Sihon, who had made it his capital (see the commentary on vv. 19-20). *Aroer* was well south of Heshbon, on the north bank of the Arnon at modern ʿAraʾir, 16 miles (25 km.) east of the Dead Sea.[58] Until now the territory under dispute has been defined in terms of its geographical boundaries (v. 22). Now, with reference to the period of Israel's residence in it, it is defined in terms of its two main population centers and their satellite *villages*[59] and *towns*. Those associated with Heshbon presumably lay in the center and north, as far as the Jabbok; those associated with Aroer were in the south, along the Arnon. For most of that period Ammon lay to the east and Moab to the south; now Ammon flanked it on both these fronts. At any time during those three hundred years Ammon could have tried to wrest control of this territory from Israel, but had not done so. Jephthah's challenge, "Why not?" is unanswerable, and its implication clear. The Ammonites had not challenged Israel for control of this territory before because they had no grounds for doing so. The war they

---

56. The idea that the god of a particular place determined who ruled it is reflected, e.g., in both the Moabite Stone of approximately 830 B.C., and the Cyrus Cylinder of 536 B.C. (*ANET,* pp. 320 and 315-16 respectively). In the former, King Mesha of Moab tells how "Chemosh was angry at his land" and allowed Israel to conquer it. In the latter, Cyrus of Persia tells how Marduk, Babylon's chief god, handed the city over to him and made him "the legitimate king, king of Babylon." Cf. Boling, *Judges,* pp. 203-4, who likewise holds that Ammonite sovereignty of the former Moabite territory south of the Arnon is assumed.

57. For its significance for the date of the exodus and the chronology of the judges period, see Section II.A of the Introduction: "Dating the Period of the Judges."

58. K. A. Kitchen, "Aroer," *NBD,* p. 84; *OBA,* p. 85.

59. Literally, "daughters" (*bᵉnôt*) in line with the normal Hebrew convention of using feminine metaphors for town and cities.

have launched now is purely opportunistic; not a war of liberation, but one of naked aggression.

27 Jephthah's challenge of verse 26 has effectively brought diplomacy to an end. So now he stops talking like a diplomat and instead speaks like a litigant seeking a favorable ruling from a judge, and since *the Judge* in question is Yahweh, the categories Jephthah uses are moral and theological. Jephthah (and Israel) have not *sinned* against the Ammonites; it is they who have *sinned* and done *wrong (rāʿâ)* by making war against Jephthah and his people.[60] This, in sum, is what he has been arguing all along, but he now states in the baldest terms. And while it is ostensibly spoken to his adversary, it is not intended primarily for his ears, or aimed at securing a favorable response from him. There is no sweet reasonableness now, or concessions for the sake of argument. The time for that is over. Instead, the theological summary of his case is primarily for the ears of Yahweh, on whom Jephthah now depends utterly for a favorable outcome. His appeal to Yahweh to judge between him and his adversary *today* is in effect a declaration of war. At the same time it expresses a belief that the issue will be settled in heaven (by the decision of the divine Judge) before it is settled on earth (by trial of arms). It is neither Jephthah himself nor his adversary who will have the final say, nor Chemosh or any other god, but Yahweh. At this critical moment Jephthah's belief in the unrivaled supremacy of Yahweh shines through. It is his finest hour.[61]

28 The rejection of Jephthah's words by the Ammonite king is hardly surprising. In its enfeebled state (10:8-9) Israel was in no position to negotiate acceptable terms of peace, and Jephthah must have known this. Nevertheless, if we have been right in seeing a concession for the sake of argument in verse 24, then in true statesman-like fashion Jephthah had been willing to give peace a chance. At the very least he has shown that he is a person to be reckoned with. He has shown that he has the knowledge and skill to speak for Israel as a whole, and is capable of giving a measured response to a crisis rather than simply rushing headlong into battle. Furthermore, assuming that what we have just read is a summary of negotiations which would have taken some time to complete — at least several days — he has probably bought valuable time for himself and those whom he will lead in battle. In view of all this, the fact that his adversary has rejected his words can hardly be taken as an indication of Jephthah's ineffectiveness as a leader. On the

60. There is a certain irony in this, of course, since Israel, too, has done wrong *(hāraʿ)* in forsaking Yahweh (10:6), and their suffering at the hands of Ammon has been "right" in the sense of being a fitting punishment. But this does not absolve Ammon from moral responsibility, nor overturn the fact that, in the particular matter of the territory in question, Ammon, not Israel, has been the aggressor. Cf. Acts 2:23.

61. This episode, like the previous one, ends with Jephthah speaking all his words before Yahweh (cf. vv. 11 and 27).

contrary, if anything he has grown in stature as a leader and demonstrated again what a master he is at using words strategically to further his own interests and, in this case, those of Israel as a whole.

Two matters of theological importance deserve special mention before we pass on. First, the reference to Yahweh as *the Judge (haššōpēṭ)* in verse 27 is striking, coming as it does at the climax of the episode, and is of considerable importance for the theology of the entire book. It reminds us that what we have in Judges is much more than a collection of warrior stories from Israel's heroic age. It is fundamentally a theological work. Behind all the human judges stands Yahweh, *the* Judge, whose existence and action is the ultimate determinant of all that happens.

Second, this third episode provides us with the best explanation of why Jephthah's name appears in Hebrews 11:32 in a catalogue of Old Testament figures who were commended for their faith (vv. 1-2). In the first two episodes we saw something of Jephthah's background, and the circumstances of his rise to prominence in Gilead. We saw a hardness in him, and a shrewdness and ambition that made him appear much more like a self-made man whose character had been forged in the school of hard knocks than a man of faith. But there is more to Jephthah than we realized. He takes his leadership responsibilities seriously, and discharges them with maturity and impressive skill. Most of all, he knows that it is Yahweh who rules the world, including his own part of it, and not Jephthah himself. He realizes that he is utterly dependent on God for the victory he hopes for, and stakes all on God giving it to him. That is faith, and it may well be this moment in Jephthah's life that the writer to the Hebrews had in mind.

4. Episode 4: Jephthah and His Daughter (11:29-40)

This is the climactic episode of the Jephthah narrative. It is here that the final showdown takes place between Jephthah as Israel's leader and the Ammonites. It is also here that the we find Jephthah's infamous vow and its horrifying outcome. In fact, once it is introduced, the vow effectively takes over and dominates the rest of the episode.

The two main sections feature, respectively, the making of the vow (vv. 29-33) and its outcome (vv. 34-40), and the plot consists of two interlocking sequences as indicated on p. 326. The common element is Jephthah's victory over the Ammonites in verses 32-33, and this is what the entire narrative since the beginning of chapter 11 has been heading toward as its expected climax. But the vow of verses 30-31 begins a sequence that cannot end with the victory itself. It effectively eclipses the expected climax by subordinating it to a new climax which does not come until verses 34-37, where

A. Jephthah's	leads	his victory		
endowment	to	over		
with the	→	Ammon.		
Spirit				
B.	Jephthah's	his victory	leads	the fulfillment
	vow +	over	to	of his vow.
		Ammon	→	

Jephthah fulfills his vow by sacrificing his daughter. This event, which is described in much greater detail than the battle, becomes the main focus of interest and the real climax of the episode.

As in previous episodes, dialogue plays a crucial role and occurs, appropriately, at the climax we have just identified by our analysis of the plot: in the aftermath of the battle, when Jephthah returns home and his daughter comes out to meet him (vv. 35-38). The dialogue in Episode 3 was conducted at a distance, and couched in the formal language of diplomacy. The dialogue here in Episode 4 is intimate and personal, and painfully tragic. It is arguably the dramatic climax of the entire Jephthah narrative.

The issue of whether or not Jephthah literally sacrificed his daughter, and whether or not he should have done so, has occupied the minds of commentators from time immemorial. My own view on these issues is presented in the exegesis of the passage and the excurses that follow.

a. The Making of the Vow (11:29-33)

29 *Then the Spirit of Yahweh came upon Jephthah, and he passed through Gilead and Manasseh, and passed on through Mizpah[62] of Gilead;[63] and from Mizpah of Gilead he went on to the Ammonites.*

30 *Jephthah vowed a vow to Yahweh, "If you will indeed give the Ammonites into my hand,*

31 *then whatever comes out of the doors of my house to meet me when I*

---

62. Vocalized here as Mizpeh. The Masoretes appear to use the vocalizations "Mizpah" and "Mizpeh" interchangeably.

63. *BHS* recommends omitting *'eṭ-miṣpê gil'ād*, but this has no hard evidence to support it. The two witnesses it cites in support of the required *subsequent* adjustment of the following verb *'āḇar* (crossed over/through) to the adverbial phrase *lᵉʿēḇer* (to the other side) do not support the prior omission of *'eṭ-miṣpê gil'ād*. The only difficulty (grammatically) with the MT is the use of the object marker *'eṭ* after *'āḇar* rather than the (expected) preposition *bᵉ*. But the MT is intelligible as it stands, and the *BHS* emendation should be rejected as an unnecessary attempt to smooth it out.

return victorious from the Ammonites will be Yahweh's, and I will of-
fer it up as a burnt offering."

32 *Then Jephthah went across to the Ammonites, to fight against them,*
and Yahweh gave them into his hand.

33 *He struck them down from Aroer to the neighborhood of Minnith,*
twenty towns, and as far as Abel-keramim, with a very great slaugh-
ter. So the Ammonites were subdued before the Israelites.

29 For the whole of the previous two episodes, Yahweh has played no active role in the narrative, or at least he is not said to have done so. Jephthah
has spoken about Yahweh in 11:9 and 21-24, and "before Yahweh" in 11:11.
He has also appealed to Yahweh as "the Judge" in 11:27. But Yahweh has not
appeared to Jephthah, as he did to Gideon, nor spoken to him either directly,
as he did to Gideon, or indirectly, as he did to Barak (through Deborah). In
fact, he has not said anything at all. Nor has the narrator given us any indication of whether or not Yahweh approves of Jephthah. Jephthah has been
called and appointed by men, not (as far as we know) by God. The narrator
told us back in 10:16 that "Yahweh became exasperated with the misery of
Israel," but left the question of what might follow from this unanswered, and
Yahweh's silence and apparent inactivity since then have been striking, to
say the least, especially given the speed with which he had come to Israel's
help in similar situations previously.

All this changes now, however, with the statement that *the Spirit of
Yahweh came upon* Jephthah. It is the same expression that was used in relation to Othniel in 3:10 and Gideon in 6:34, and at last leaves us in no doubt
that God has chosen to use Jephthah, too, to deliver Israel. It also implies that
Jephthah's activity that immediately follows is a consequence of the Spirit
coming upon him, whether or not Jephthah himself is aware of it.[64] The momentum of the story had slowed right down in the previous episode while the
diplomatic exchange between Jephthah and the king of Ammon took place.
Now it picks up again. The repeated use of the verb *'ābar* creates the impression of continuous purposeful movement as Jephthah "passes through,"
"passes on," and "goes on." The places visited are Gilead, Manasseh, and
Mizpah of Gilead (Jephthah's hometown), culminating in "the Ammonites"
(i.e., the place in Gilead where they were camped, 10:17). *Manasseh* here
probably refers to East Manasseh, north of the Jabbok (Deut. 3:13; 29:8), but
it may include West Manasseh as well, on the other side of the Jordan (Josh.
13:7). If so, Jephthah's tour was quite extensive, even though of necessity it
was undertaken hastily. Its purpose is not stated, but in view of its end point it

---

64. Cf. the similar link between Spirit endowment and immediate action in 3:10
and 6:34.

was presumably connected in some way with his preparations for battle. Israel had already pledged its loyalty to Yahweh in the assembly of 10:10-16, and an army of sorts, composed of "Israelites," had already taken up a forward position at Mizpah (10:17). But prior to Jephthah's appointment morale had been very low. We may reasonably surmise that in these circumstances the aim of Jephthah's tour was to show himself as leader and call up reinforcements.

30-31 Hardly has the narrative picked up speed after the protracted negotiations of the previous episode, however, than it slows down again for further negotiations, this time in the form of a vow. It happens at the same point in this narrative as the fleece test did in the Gideon narrative (6:36-40). Like Gideon, Jephthah seeks reassurance that Yahweh will give him victory:

> v. 30 *"If you will indeed give the Ammonites into my hand,*
> v. 31 *then whatever comes out of the doors of my house to meet me when I return victorious from the Ammonites will be Yahweh's, and I will offer it up as a burnt offering."*

It is strange to find Jephthah so unsure of the outcome after his apparently confident appeal to Yahweh the Judge. But psychologically it is quite understandable. This is the first time Jephthah has addressed Yahweh directly, and dealing with God is something of a quite different order from dealing with men, however formidable they may be. The bold appeal to Yahweh in verse 27 was public, and probably intended (partly at least) to unsettle his enemy. He had to appear confident in public or there would have been no point in exchanging words with his enemy at all. The vow, though, takes us much deeper into Jephthah's psyche and shows us a man still haunted by his past. Publicly he has argued that Israel is the innocent party and expressed confidence that God's judgment will be in their favor; privately he remembers that he himself has been the innocent party in a dispute and found his rights disregarded by those who should have protected him (11:1-3, 7). The emphatic infinitive (*nāṯôn* — *"if you will indeed give"*) expresses his deep angst. Will Yahweh, after all, reject him, too? Jephthah has everything to lose if the battle goes against him, including his life (see 12:3), but also his position in his clan and tribe, and that clearly means a great deal to him. Formerly an outcast, he is now "head and leader of all the inhabitants of Gilead" (11:6, 8, 11). But if he loses the war, the whole cycle of rejection will begin again. If Yahweh rejects Jephthah now, so, too, will Jephthah's people. He will be an outcast again.

The deep irony is that *we* know that the rejection Jephthah so much fears is a phantom. Yahweh's Spirit has already come upon him; the divine Judge has already decided to save Israel by his hand. But this is information that has been given to us, the readers; Jephthah himself shows no awareness of it. Nor is this contradicted by the fact that in verse 29 he has already begun to move at the impulse of the Spirit. The last major judge narrative, that of Gideon, has illustrated two quite different kinds of activity by Yahweh in relation to his chosen instrument. On the one hand are the visual and verbal activity of Yahweh's messenger (6:11-24), and the dream report and its interpretation that he allows Gideon to overhear (7:13-14). These are addressed to Gideon's senses, and affect his behavior *indirectly,* through his consciousness. On the other hand, as a separate event, is the intervention of Yahweh's Spirit that affects his behavior *directly* at a certain point (6:34-35). Jephthah has received no visitation, as Gideon did, nor any prophetic word, as Barak did (4:6-7). His words, *"If you will indeed give the Ammonites into my hand,"* recall his own words to the elders (11:9), not a promise he has received from Yahweh. No dialogue has taken place between him and God; the only dialogue that has place as part of this enlistment has been with men. From Jephthah's point of view, Yahweh is still aloof and uncommitted. Jephthah has already become Yahweh's instrument without being aware of it (cf. Samson in 13:25–14:4). We watch from a vantage point he doesn't share as he takes extreme measures to secure divine help that *we* know has already been given to him.[65]

The vow is effectively a bribe. As the elders once offered inducement to Jephthah, so Jephthah now offers inducement to Yahweh. Jephthah is now the suppliant, but even in this role his words exhibit all the shrewdness that we have come to expect of him. The vow is quite specific in pledging a burnt offering (v. 31), but more circumspect in nominating the victim. In fact, it does not specify any particular victim at all, but only the *means* by which it will be identified. This immediately introduces a high degree of dramatic tension into the story — Who or what will the victim turn out to be? The language is ambiguous,[66] but more applicable to a human being than an animal, especially the phrase *liqrā'tî,* "to meet me."[67] The gravity of the situation,

65. Phyllis Trible, "A Meditation in Mourning: The Sacrifice of the Daughter of Jephthah," *Union Seminary Quarterly Review* 36 Supplementary (1981): 60-61, reads too much into v. 29a when she says, "Jephthah himself does not evince the assurance that the spirit of Yahweh ought to give. Rather than acting with conviction and courage, he responds with doubt and demand." No, Jephthah is not responding to Yahweh but still trying to prevail upon *Yahweh* to respond to *him.*

66. *hayyôṣē' ʾašer yēṣē'* (the coming out [person or thing] that comes out) specifies neither species (human or animal) nor gender.

67. Cf. Moore (*Judges,* p. 299), who, however, overstates the case and hence resolves the ambiguity which properly belongs to the building of suspense: "that a human victim is intended is, in fact, as plain as words can make it; the language is inapplicable to an animal, and a vow to offer the first sheep or goat that he comes across — not to mention the possibility of an unclean animal — is trivial to absurdity." Contrast Boling (*Judges,* p. 208), who, in addition to the ambiguity of the language, refers to the more or less standard plan of Iron Age houses, designed to accommodate livestock as well as family.

too, suggests that human rather than animal sacrifice is being contemplated.[68] The vow puts all the occupants of Jephthah's house at risk, but Jephthah will offer only what is forced from him. Like the elders of Gilead, he will not (metaphorically) offer *rō'š* (head) if he can get by with *qāṣîn* (leader); he is willing to take his chances. The vow is not impulsive; it is shrewd and calculating — and in this respect entirely in keeping with Jephthah's character as we have come to know it.

32-33   The opening words of verse 32a *(Jephthah went across to the Ammonites . . .)* resume the closing words of verse 19, clearly implying that the vow was an interruption to Jephthah's progress from his endowment with the Spirit to his victory in battle. It has been an irrelevancy; he would have been victorious anyway. The victory itself, remarkable though it is, receives only summary treatment (vv. 32b-33), its chief interest being that it creates the conditions under which Jephthah will have to fulfill his vow. Unfortunately the locations of *Minnith* and *Abel-keramim* are not known with any certainty.[69] However, *Aroer,* in southern Gilead, has already been mentioned in verse 26, and since the Arnon has been the border repeatedly referred to in verses 14-28 it is likely that the *twenty towns* mentioned here are the "towns along the bank of the Arnon" mentioned there. But the expression *as far as Abel-keramim* suggests that Abel-keramim was not in this immediate area, but some distance away — probably to the north. In any case, the battle was decisive and *the Ammonites were subdued* (v. 33). Jephthah got what he wanted. But now he must pay for it; his victory over the Ammonites brings him, predictably, to the door of his house.

b. The Keeping of the Vow (11:34-40)

34 *Then Jephthah came to Mizpah, to his house, and there was his daughter, coming out to meet him with timbrels and dances — only she, alone; beside her he had neither son nor daughter.*

35 *When he saw her, he tore his clothes, and said, "Ahh, my daughter, you have indeed laid me low; you have become the cause of my calamity,[70] for I have opened my mouth to Yahweh, and I cannot turn back."*

---

68. Compare the situation in which the king of Moab offers his son and heir as a burnt offering (2 Kgs. 3:26-27).

69. For suggestions see Block, *Judges, Ruth,* p. 370, and Butler, *Judges,* p. 290. Abila, near the Sea of Galilee, is too far north to be the site of ancient *Abel-keramim.* The archeological evidence for its identification with Tell el-'Umeri, 7 mi. (11 km.) southwest of Amman, is disputed.

70. I follow BDB, pp. 88-89, where *beʿōkeráy* is taken to involve the idiomatic use of *Beth essentia,* as in *beʿōzeráy* in Ps. 118:7 (not "Yahweh is among/one of my helpers," but "Yahweh is my essential/chief helper"). Cf. Burney, *Judges,* p. 321: "the supreme

36 *She replied, "My father, you have opened your mouth to Yahweh, so do to me according to what has gone forth from your mouth, now that Yahweh has avenged you on your enemies, the Ammonites."*

37 *She said to her father, "Let this thing be done for me; leave me alone for two months, so that I can go and wander*[71] *on the mountains and weep about my virginity, I and my companions."*

38 *He replied, "Go," and sent her away for two months. So she departed, she and her companions, and bewailed her virginity upon the mountains.*

39 *Then at the end of two months she returned to her father, and he did to her [according to] the vow that he had vowed. She had never had sexual intercourse with a man. So it became a custom in Israel*[72]

40 *that the daughters of Israel went year after year to commemorate the daughter of Jephthah the Gileadite, for four days each year.*

34 The opening words of this verse, *Then Jephthah came . . . to his house,* echo the words of his vow (v. 31) and evoke keen anticipation. In what follows the use of *hinnê* (the "behold" of older English versions) with the participle gives an awful immediacy to what happens. We are transported to the scene of the action and see it through Jephthah's eyes as it unfolds: *there was his daughter, coming out.*

Again the narrative is heavy with irony, this time with a particular poignancy because of the innocence of the daughter. She knows not what she does. She comes out *to meet him* (another echo of the vow) with *timbrels and dancing,* to celebrate a joyful occasion in the traditional way. She is glad because her father has returned victoriously and safely (in *šālôm,* v. 31). But unlike Miriam, who went out to celebrate Yahweh's victory at the sea (Exod.

---

cause of my trouble." On the strength of the verb *'kr* cf. Gen. 34:30; Josh. 6:18; 7:25; 1 Sam. 14:29; 1 Kgs. 18:17-18.

71. The MT's *weyāradtî,* "and *go down* upon the mountains," does not make sense. With the English versions in general I assume it is a corruption of *weradtî,* from the hollow verb *rwd,* "to roam/wander." The corruption probably arose from the accidental doubling of the initial *waw,* which was then "corrected" by writing it as a *yod.* Cf. Block, *Judges, Ruth,* p. 373, and Boling, *Judges,* p. 209.

72. Taking *wattehî* as a "neuter-feminine" as in Ps. 69:11, "It became reproaches unto me." On the use of the feminine in a neuter sense see GKC §122q. Trible ("A Meditation in Mourning," p. 66), following König, renders it as a true feminine, "She [Jephthah's daughter] became a tradition in Israel." The weakness of this view is that it involves a "special" use of *ḥōq* (a person = a tradition) without parallel in the Old Testament, while the context provides an *activity* of the kind *ḥōq* normally refers to (v. 40). In fact, the troublesome v. 39d is exegeted by v. 40, which immediately follows: "It became a custom in Israel, *that is,* the Israelite women went out year by year." For the almost certain reason for the false verse division in the MT see Burney, *Judges,* p. 325.

15:19-21), or those who will celebrate David's victories in later times (1 Sam. 18:6-7), she comes out alone, and it is her solitariness which is given terrible emphasis in v. 34: *only she, alone; beside her he had neither son nor daughter.* The words underline both the isolation of the child (she alone will be sacrificed) and the plight of the father (he has none but her; his personal *šālôm* is shattered).

35-36 When Jephthah sees her, he tears his clothes and cries out in anguish. He had risked his daughter, true, but had hoped to avoid the necessity that now confronts him. Then he was in a state of intense anxiety; now he is in the flush of victory. Face to face with her, he finds that he values her more, much more now, after the battle, than he had before. But for all that, it is not his daughter's predicament that unmakes him, but his own:[73]

> *"Ahh, my daughter, you have indeed laid me low (kr');*[74]
> *You ('at) have become the cause of my calamity ('kr)."*

He calls her *my daughter* but offers her no solace;[75] only accusation. The emphatic pronoun *'at,* and the play on the roots *kr'* and *'kr* underline both the reproach and the self-absorption that his words express. He refers to the vow only indirectly, but with pointed significance:

> *"I have opened my mouth to Yahweh,*
> *and I cannot turn back."*

It is partly an admission of responsibility *("I have opened my mouth")* and partly a denial of responsibility *("I cannot turn back").* The problem is of his own making, so at best we can give him only our qualified sympathy.

It is otherwise with his daughter, however. When she speaks, she echoes her father's words: *"My father, you have opened your mouth to Yahweh"* (v. 36). As the remainder of her speech shows, she says these words not in counter-recrimination but as a way of grasping their significance, coming to terms with them, and steadying herself for a dignified response. Her next words show that she has fully grasped the dreadful logic of the situation. Literally,

> "Do *('śh)* to me what has gone forth from your mouth,
> for Yahweh has done *('śh)* for you deliverance from your enemies."

---

73. "At the moment of recognition and disclosure Jephthah thinks [only] of himself." Phyllis Trible, *Texts of Terror: Literary-Feminist Readings of Biblical Narratives,* Overtures to Biblical Theology 13 (Philadelphia: Fortress, 1984), p. 63.

74. As Sisera was laid low by Jael (5:27). Cf. 2 Sam. 22:40, where the same verb is used of laying low enemies in battle.

75. Contrast Abraham in Gen. 22:8.

37-39a Jephthah's daughter asks only for two months to bewail her virginity with her female friends. She will find solace there (v. 37). Her father has only one word for her — *"Go"* (v. 38). It is the last word he speaks in this episode. From now on only the narrator is heard.

At the end of the two months she returns to her father, her submission complete. The time has come, and there is no word from heaven to stay Jephthah's hand.[76] So now quickly, without judgment, the narrator tells the deed. Only the narrator refers to the vow directly, by its name, but even here there is reticence: not, "he offered her up as a burnt offering," but (literally), "he did (*'śh*) to her his vow which he vowed (*niḏrô 'ᵃšer nāḏār*)." The one, of course, implies the other, and given the wording of the vow itself, we are clearly meant to understand that Jephthah literally sacrificed his daughter.[77]

39b-40 In terms of the literary structure of this fourth episode verses 39b-40 are a postscript; the climax has already been reached and passed with the closure effected by verse 39a.[78] In terms of its subject matter, however, it is closely related to what immediately precedes it. The corresponding elements are as follows:

vv. 37-39a	*vv. 39b-40*
two months	yearly, four days in the year
she went *(hlk)*	the daughters of Israel went *(hlk)*
her companions	the daughters of Israel
bewail *(bkh)*	commemorate *(tnh)*

For the most part the before (vv. 37-39a) and after (vv. 39b-40) are related as particular to general. The daughter and her companions go once, for one two-month period; the Israelite women go year by year, for four days each year.

---

76. Both Gen. 22 and Judg. 11 feature a father sacrificing his "only" *(yāḥîd)* child. In Abraham's case the obligation is divinely imposed; Jephthah incurs it through his own voluntary act (the vow).

77. For good summaries of the history of interpretation, see David Marcus, *Jephthah and His Vow* (Lubbock, TX: Texas Tech Press, 1986), pp. 8-9, and Moore, *Judges*, 304-5. The nonliteral, minority view is that Jephthah dedicated her to Yahweh as a perpetual virgin (e.g., Keil and Delitzsch, *Judges*, pp. 388-95, and more recently S. Landers, "Did Jephthah Kill His Daughter?" *Bible Review* 7, no. 4 (1991): 28-31, 42.

78. Contrast Martin, *Judges*, p. 146: "*It became a custom:* This is the point at which this section of the Jephthah narrative (11:29-40), with its emphasis on the fate of the virgin daughter, has been aiming. It is an attempt to explain by means of a legend about the sacrifice of a virgin, an annual four-day festival in Israel." Episode 4 does offer an explanation of the custom, but it is clear from its literary structure and its context in the wider Jephthah narrative that it does so only incidentally.

Before the sacrifice the daughter and her companions "weep" *(bkh);* after it the Israelite women "commemorate" it *(tnh).* Compare 5:11, where *tnh* is used of "rehearsing" the righteous deeds of Yahweh, that is, keeping the memory of them alive by repetition.[79] Though the "commemorating" of verse 40 probably involved weeping, it became something more than this: a "custom" *(ḥōq)* which honored the memory of Jephthah's daughter year after year.[80] A striking parallel is found in 2 Chronicles 35:25:

> Jeremiah composed laments for Josiah, and to this day all the men and women singers commemorate Josiah in the laments. These became a tradition *(ḥōq)* in Israel and are written in the Laments. (NIV)

The postscript of verses 39b-40 shifts the focus from the vow to the victim, and draws our sympathy even more firmly away from the father and toward the daughter. It was her virginity that she had asked leave to bewail upon the mountains. This was the bitterest thing of all for Jephthah's daughter: not to die, but to die young, unfulfilled, childless. For she, too, not just her father, was rendered childless by the vow. Cut off, with no child to succeed her, she may well have been numbered among the unremembered, among those who "have perished as though they had not lived" (Sir. 44:9 RSV).[81] Indeed, she remains nameless in the narrative. But, we are told, there *were* those who remembered: the *daughters (bᵉnôt)* of Israel went out year after year, and it was the *daughter (baṯ)* of Jephthah whose memory they honored (v. 40). Phyl-

---

79. Ugaritic usage verifies the meaning "to repeat, recite" (Weiser, "Das Deboralied," pp. 67-97).

80. Suggestions that the activity of the Israelite women in 11:40 was "really" something other than this (e.g., a fertility cult, a female rite of passage), or that it became such, generally rely on extra-biblical parallels (see, e.g., Susan Ackerman, *Warrior, Dancer,* p. 111, citing P. L. Day). These could form part of an interpretation of the Jephthah story as a literary composition only if they found confirmation in the text itself. As far as I can see, this is not the case. For a brief but helpful bibliography of relevant literature see Trible, "A Meditation in Mourning," p. 72, n. 44.

81. I owe this apposite reference to Sirach, again, to Trible ("A Meditation in Mourning," p. 65), whose sensitive analysis of 11:29-40 in particular has considerably influenced my own appreciation and understanding of this part of the Jephthah story. I have noted some of my disagreements with her above (in the relevant footnotes). The full text of Sir. 44:8-9 reads:

> "There are some who have left a name,
> so that men declare their praise.
> And there are some who have no memorial,
> who have perished as though they had not lived;
> they have become as though they had not been born,
> and so have their children after them." (RSV)

lis Trible has captured the deep pathos of these verses in a lament of her own, based on David's lament for Jonathan in 2 Samuel 1:19-27:

> The daughter of Jephthah lies slain upon thy high places.
> I weep for you, my little sister.
> Very poignant is your story to me;
>> your courage to me is wonderful,
>> surpassing the courage of men.
> How are the powerless fallen,
>> a terrible sacrifice to a faithless vow![82]

Through all of this Yahweh remains silent. In this respect there is a terrible contrast with the story of Abraham and Isaac. Genesis 22 and Judges 11 both feature a father faced with the prospect of sacrificing an "only" (*yāḥîd*) child (Gen. 22:2; Judg. 11:34). In Abraham's case the obligation is divinely imposed; Jephthah incurs the obligation through his own voluntary act (the vow). In Genesis a substitute is provided; in Judges there is none.[83] In Genesis there is a voice from heaven; in Judges the heavens are silent. And here in Judges the outcome is precisely the opposite of that in Genesis: not "descendants as the stars of heaven" (Gen. 22:17), but no descendants at all (Judg. 11:34).[84] Whether or not Jephthah should have kept his vow (see the Excursus below), he clearly *thought* he had to, and there was no voice from heaven to tell him otherwise. He was left to reap the consequences of his folly, and his daughter, like a lamb caught in a thicket, paid for it with her life. If laying his cause before Yahweh the Judge was Jephthah's greatest act of faith, his attempt to bribe him with a vow was his greatest folly.

The closing reference to "Jephthah *the Gileadite*" (v. 40) recalls the first mention of him in 11:1. It reminds us of Jephthah's origins and prepares us for a development about to take place in the final episode of the narrative.

---

82. Trible, *Texts of Terror,* p. 109. The full lament extends over several stanzas.

83. Does no substitute appear in Jephthah's case because the substitute (Jephthah had hoped to sacrifice something else) has already been imposed in the form of his daughter? Is *she* the "ram caught in the thicket" by divine providence? We simply do not know.

84. For the suggestion that the story of Jephthah's vow is a "mirror image" of the testing of Abraham I am indebted to Edmund R. Leach, "The Legitimacy of Solomon: Some Structural Aspects of Old Testament History," *Archives Européennes de Sociologie* 7 (1966): 64. The validity of the detailed comparisons made by Leach has been challenged by Bertel Nathhorst in *Formal or Structural Studies of Traditional Tales: The Usefulness of Some Methodological Proposals Advanced by Vladimir Propp, Alan Dundes, Claude Levi-Strauss and Edmund Leach,* tr. Donald Burton (Stockholm: Almqvist & Wiksell, 1969). In my own judgment the comparison is of heuristic value even though it cannot be used to establish firm conclusions. The primary context for interpreting the episode of the vow is the Jephthah narrative as a whole.

Excursus 6: Should Jephthah Have Broken His Vow?

It is clear that vows are taken very seriously in the Old Testament. The general rule is that they are voluntary, but once made must be kept (Num. 30:2 [Heb. 3]). Even a rash (thoughtless) vow must be kept, unless it is overruled in a specified time by someone who has the authority to do so (e.g., a father or husband; Num. 30:3-16). However, if someone unwittingly vows to do something *evil,* when he realizes he has done wrong he must confess it and bring a suitable animal as a sin offering, and the priest will offer it on his behalf and make atonement for him (Lev. 5:4-6).

As the exegesis of the passage has shown, Jephthah was wrong to make the vow in the first place. Not only was it unnecessary (God would have given him the victory anyway), but it was effectively a bribe, and therefore a denial of his bold, public expression of confidence in Yahweh, the (righteous) Judge in 11:27. Furthermore, since child sacrifice was a pagan rite condemned in the law of Moses (Lev. 18:21; 20:2-5), to do it — even in fulfillment of a vow — would be to commit an abomination (Jer. 32:35), and therefore incur God's judgment rather than secure his help.

So there is no question that Jephthah did wrong in making the vow, and compounded that wrong by sacrificing his daughter. But since his intention was to secure God's help, he cannot have known he was doing something that was forbidden. He certainly knew the history of Israel's arrival in Transjordan (11:15-26), believed that Yahweh was the supreme Judge, and was capable (at his best) of having faith in him (11:27). But he was also capable of making theological compromises (11:24), and (at his worst) of doubting God and resorting to pagan ways of trying to secure his favor (11:30). This should hardly surprise us given the generally confused state of Israelite religion in the period of the judges and the mixed career of the previous judge, Gideon (6:25-32; 8:27).

5. Episode 5: Jephthah and the Ephraimites (12:1-7)

1 *The Ephraimites were called to arms, and went across to Zaphon. They said to Jephthah, "Why did you go across to fight against the Ammonites without calling us to go with you? We will burn your house over you with fire!"*
2 *Jephthah replied, "I was in fierce dispute, I and my people, with the Ammonites. I called you, but you did not save me from their hand.*
3 *So when I saw that you would not save me, I took my life in my hands and crossed over to the Ammonites, and Yahweh gave them into my hand. Why then have you come up to me this day to fight against me?"*
4 *Then Jephthah gathered all the men of Gilead, and fought with Ephraim. The men of Gilead struck down Ephraim, because they had*

336

said, "You Gileadites are fugitives of Ephraim in the midst of Ephraim and Manasseh."

5 *The Gileadites captured the fords of the Jordan to prevent the Ephraimites crossing. Whenever any of the fugitives of Ephraim said, "Let me cross over," the men of Gilead would say to him, "Are you an Ephraimite?" and he would say, "No."*

6 *Then they would say to him, "Please say 'Shibboleth'; and he would say, "Sibboleth," for he would not be able to say it correctly. Then they would seize him and slaughter him at the fords of the Jordan. There fell at that time 42,000 Ephraimite men.*

7 *Jephthah judged Israel for six years. Then Jephthah the Gileadite died, and was buried in his own town[85] in Gilead.*

Episode 4 explored the private and domestic consequences that flowed from Jephthah's victory over the Ammonites. With the change of episode and the introduction of the Ephraimites in 12:1 we are returned to the public and political sphere. This fifth and final episode of the narrative will explore the political consequences that flowed from that same victory.

Success in battle has confirmed Jephthah's right to be recognized as head and leader of the Gileadites (11:9-11). But if his authority is now accepted in the eastern sector of Israel (Gilead), it is clearly not so in the west — Israel's heartland. With the external threat removed, intertribal jealousies flare up again (cf. 8:1-3). As in previous episodes, dialogue again plays a key role, in this case between Jephthah and the Ephraimites.

1 *Zaphon,* referred to in Joshua 13:25-27 as one of the "towns of Gilead," was 5 miles (7 km.) north of the Jabbok, and just 2.5 miles (4 km.) east of the Jordan.[86] The *Ephraimites* "cross" *(wayyaᶜᵃḇōr)* the Jordan and confront Jephthah there.[87] When they speak of Jephthah himself "going across" *(ᶜāḇartā)* to fight the Ammonites, they are describing his movements from their perspective as people who live in Palestine proper, west of the Jordan. The implication is that when Jephthah went on his tour of 11:29, he had not confined himself to east Manasseh, but had crossed the Jordan to visit west Manasseh as well. But then he had gone back across the Jordan to fight the Ammonites without visiting Ephraim. The Ephraimites are clearly not happy about this. They feel snubbed, and are spoiling for a fight. In fact, they

85. With the LXX and OL (Old Latin) against the MT, which has "in the towns [plural] of Gilead. Cf. the *BHS* apparatus.
86. *OBA,* p. 84. Cf. Block (*Judges, Ruth,* p. 380), who suggests that "the site is probably to be identified with Tell es-Saʿdidiye, seventeen miles SSE of Beth Shan, just across the Jordan River."
87. They cross ṣāpônâ (*to* Zaphon). "Northward" (LXX[B]), another meaning of ṣāpônâ, would seem to be topographically impossible.

behave much as the Ammonites have done; they mobilize for war and move into Gilead (v. 1; 10:17). The direction they come from is different, of course, and so is the issue they have with Jephthah. The stated grievance this time is not about land but leadership. The Ephraimites demand an explanation from Jephthah as to why he did not summon them to help in the war. They are not prepared to acknowledge any leader of Israel who acts independently of Ephraim. Ephraim's territory spanned the central hill country. They were one of Israel's leading tribes, and knew it. Their wounded sense of self-importance is focused nicely by the emphatic use of the personal pronoun before the verb, "and us *(lānû)* you did not call." Their show of arms and threat to burn Jephthah's house over his head are plainly intended to intimidate him.[88] It is a powerful challenge to Jephthah's credibility as the would-be leader of the nation.

According to 8:1-3, Gideon had faced a similar problem with the Ephraimites. But in his case the challenge was less intense. They did not mobilize specifically to confront Gideon. Indeed, they had already mobilized at his request (7:24) and had further recognized his leadership by bringing him the heads of the two Midianite princes they had captured and executed (7:25). Their complaint was that Gideon had not summoned them *earlier* (8:1). Their "contending sharply" with him *(wayᵉrîḇûn 'ittô bᵉḥāzᵉqâ)* may have involved threats, but if so, no details are given.[89] Gideon's personal circumstances, too, were different. He had not completed the war with the Midianites, at least to his own satisfaction (8:4-5), and could not risk fighting on two fronts. So he appeased them with flattery and avoided military conflict (8:2-3). Jephthah's situation is different; two months or more have elapsed since his defeat of the Ammonites (11:37-39), and he has no pressing business to distract him from the matter in hand.

2-4a Jephthah takes the same basic approach to the Ephraimites as he had to the Ammonites. He resorts to diplomacy in the first instance, rebuffing the charge they have brought against him and giving his own account of the circumstances leading up to the present confrontation (vv. 2-3a; cf. 11:15-22). He refers to Yahweh's involvement in what has happened (*Yahweh* gave the Ammonites into his hand; v. 3b; cf. 11:21),[90] and ends with a rhetorical question implying that he is in the right, and the Ephraimites are wrong to act as they have (v. 3c; cf. 11:27). The Ephraimites make no reply, so Jephthah takes to the field and wins another resounding victory (vv. 4-6; cf. 11:29-33). The summary notice of verse 7 makes the political conse-

---

88. Cf. 14:15.

89. Cf. Boling (*Judges*, p. 150): "they argued vigorously with him."

90. Of course he avoids any reference to the vow; that was a private affair and one he would rather forget.

quences clear: the tribes west of the Jordan are brought to heel and Jephthah judges *Israel* (all of it) for six years (v. 7). In times of crisis, whether external or internal, Jephthah emerges as a strong, effective leader. Something of the potential for greatness foreshadowed in the third episode is realized in this final one.

But there is another perspective on Jephthah that emerges here on closer examination. The Ephraimites take issue with him personally (v. 1). Jephthah responds by declaring his solidarity with his own tribal group: *"I was in fierce dispute, I and my people, with the Ammonites"* (v. 2, my emphasis). This at once sets the point at issue in the context of Ephraimite-Gileadite relations in general, and prepares the way for an escalation of the conflict into a full-scale intertribal war. Furthermore, the diplomacy of verses 2-3 lacks the quality of high moral seriousness that had characterized Jephthah's diplomacy with the king of Ammon. Jephthah's claim that he *did* summon the Ephraimites lacks any confirmation in the preceding narrative (v. 29). There is no solemn appeal here to Yahweh the Judge to decide the issue; Jephthah mentions him only to enhance his authority vis-à-vis the Ephraimites (v. 3; cf. his similar tactic in dealing with the elders of Gilead in 11:9). If he argues that he is in the right, it is not in this case to establish an entitlement to divine help but solely to score a psychological advantage over his opponents. Jephthah is still the same skillful practitioner with words, but he is more eager for a fight on this occasion, and more confident.

His solidarity with his own people takes concrete form in verse 4: *Jephthah gathered all the men of Gilead, and fought with Ephraim* (my emphasis). At this point Jephthah recedes into the background (he is mentioned no more in the battle report of vv. 4-6), and the broad deep-seated intertribal animosities which he has triggered come explicitly to the fore as the *real* cause of the war:

> *The men of Gilead struck down Ephraim,*
> *because they had said,*
> *"You Gileadites are fugitives of Ephraim (peliṭê 'eprayim)*
> *in the midst of Ephraim and Manasseh."* (v. 4)

4b-6 We saw that Jephthah's parley with the Ephraimites in verses 1-3 was superficially like his exchange with the Ammonites, but with significant differences. The same applies to the battle reports in 11:32-33 and 12:4-6 respectively, only here the contrasts are more striking than the similarities. This time there is no mention of divine charisma, nor does Yahweh give the victory. Indeed, as far as we know, God is not involved in any way. This battle is not represented as a holy war, but with wry humor as a rather squalid tit-for-tat tribal feud. The Gileadites respond to the taunt of the Ephraimites,

"You Gileadites are fugitives of Ephraim" (v. 4), by putting them to inglorious rout, thereby making them the real *fugitives of Ephraim* (v. 5). The pronunciation test of verses 5-6 adds a further sardonic touch to the episode. The word *shibboleth (šibbōleṯ)* can mean either "ear of corn" or "torrent, flood." But the meaning is irrelevant; all that matters is the pronunciation. It is purely an instrument for identifying Ephraimites trying to pass themselves off as Gileadites. They could not, even to save their lives, say it in the distinctive, Gileadite way.[91] The tactic of seizing the fords of the Jordan (v. 5), previously used to such effect by Israelites against Moabites (3:27-30), and by Israelites against Midianites (7:24-25), is now used by Israelites against Israelites (v. 6), with devastating consequences. The word *fell* without qualification in verse 6 probably means "were killed" rather than simply "were wounded,"[92] and their number, *42,000,* indicates slaughter on a massive scale.[93] This deadly intertribal feud under Jephthah was a major step on the downward path to the full-scale civil war of chapters 19–21.

7 It is difficult to see what else Jephthah could have done in the circumstances, and it may well be that his conduct served the interests of Israel better than any other available option. But the narrator does not allow us the luxury of any simple categorization of him as worthy or wicked. He is strong, decisive, capable, but at the same time thoroughly parochial, a *Gileadite* first and foremost (v. 7), and thoroughly enmeshed in the destructive intertribal jealousies of the period. There is no magnanimity about him; if he serves the national interest, he does so incidentally. From being a figure of almost Mosaic proportions in Episode 3, he modulates here into a tribal chieftain, drawing upon the loyalty he can command from his own people to settle old scores, consolidate his position, and extend his sphere of influence. Holy war gives way to power politics. Yahweh apparently has no further interest in him. It was only as his instrument to free Israel from the Ammonites that he had God's endorsement.

This final episode brings together two contrasting perspectives on Jephthah which have been juxtaposed earlier in the narrative: Jephthah the Gileadite (Episode 2) and Jephthah the Israelite statesman (Episode 3). The summary notice of v. 7 provides the final comment on this dual perspective:

---

91. For details see Boling, *Judges,* pp. 212-13.

92. As in Josh. 8:25; Judg. 20:46. Contrast Judg. 9:40, *wayyippᵉlû ḥᵃlālîm,* "fell wounded" (ESV and the English versions in general).

93. It exceeds the number of Ephraimite men of military age in the census lists of both Num. 1 and Num. 26 (40,500 and 32,500 respectively), and is comparable to the 50,100 Benjaminites of Judges 20:35, 46, whose slaughter almost destroyed the tribe of Benjamin completely. Cf. Block, *Judges, Ruth,* p. 384. See the note on the large numbers of Judges in Section IX.C of the Introduction.

Jephthah judged Israel for six years.
Then *Jephthah the Gileadite* died,
and was buried in his own town in Gilead (my emphasis).

Summary: The Themes of the Jephthah Narrative

We are now in a position to try to grasp the Jephthah narrative as a whole, and reflect on its meaning in the light of the foregoing analysis. In one sense all the judge narratives are the same. They are all about Israel's persistence in apostasy, and Yahweh's persistence in disciplining and saving them. But each narrative is also unique and makes its own particular contribution to the message of the book. Our purpose here is to try to identify the particular way the struggle between God and Israel is played out in the Jephthah narrative, and how this gives rise to a theme that is distinctive of this particular story.

The setting is the Ammonite oppression of Israel in the days of Jephthah. The turning point comes in the final showdown between the two sides in 11:32-33. That is where the tide turns in Israel's favor. Everything prior to that leads up to it, and everything that follows flows from it in some way. Episode 4, in which this turning point occurs, is on any reckoning the climactic episode of the narrative. In terms of Yahweh's long-awaited and decisive intervention, in terms of the profound way in which the personality of Jephthah is explored through his dealings with Yahweh on the one hand and his daughter on the other, and in terms of the dramatic intensity generated there, this episode is the heart of the entire Jephthah narrative. As we have seen, however, Jephthah's vow shifts the center of dramatic interest from the victory itself to what follows it: Jephthah's returning home and fulfilling his vow. Furthermore, what is true of this episode is also true of all the other episodes. The Israel-Ammonite conflict is the narrative thread connecting them all, but within each episode it provides the occasion, the background, for a dialogue, and it is in the dialogue that the real dramatic interest is centered. It follows that if the story has a major theme, these dialogues are likely to be the key to it.

To return to the fourth climactic episode, the dialogue there concerns Jephthah's *vow* and its implications. The vow is not referred to directly, but Jephthah and his daughter both allude to it using the same expression:

First Jephthah —
v. 35   "I have *opened my mouth* to Yahweh
           (*'ānōkî pāṣîtî-pî 'el-Yahweh*)."

then his daughter —
v. 36   "You have *opened your mouth* to Yahweh
           (*pāṣîtā 'eṯ-pîkā 'el-Yahweh*)."

The statement is striking enough in itself, involving both alliteration *(p-p)* and assonance *(î-î)*, and its repetition at this crucial point in the story throws it into special prominence. It gains thematic significance from the motif, "the word(s) of Jephthah," which links the two previous episodes. Jephthah's negotiations with the elders, his diplomatic exchange with the king of Ammon, and his vow have amply displayed Jephthah's facility with words. Jephthah, we know, is a skillful negotiator; he is *good* at opening his mouth.[94] What has precipitated the crisis with his daughter is that he has opened his mouth to *Yahweh.* That is, he has tried to conduct his relationship with God in the same way he has conducted his relationships with men. He has debased religion (a vow, an offering) into a bribe. It is the sequence of dialogues in Episodes 1-4 which gives the point its dramatic force. The same point is made by the parallel dialogues of Episodes 1 and 2: Israel, too, has debased religion (in this case, repentance) into negotiation. This is the distinctive theme of the narrative as a whole. It is about the tendency of people to turn religion into politics, into negotiation with God instead of submission to him. It shows this happening at both the personal and national levels. It shows us God's reaction to it, and how (in the case of Jephthah himself) it brought tragedy in its wake. The literary pattern of the story — five episodes, each featuring a dialogue — reinforces the theme by throwing these dialogues (the primary carriers of the theme) into prominence and into association with one another.

As for good literary works in general, however,[95] the meaning cannot be stated adequately in terms of a single theme. The story also has something to say about how Yahweh engages with Israel, and this is also part of its meaning. It portrays his involvement as deeply personal and emotional rather than merely formal or legal. It is not, in the end, governed by rigid principles of reward and punishment, justice and retribution, but is stressful and painful. Yahweh saves the Israelites under protest. He is angered by their apostasy and affronted by their "repentance,"[96] but he cannot tolerate their continued misery. He cannot simply leave them to their fate.[97] He intervenes briefly to save them from the Ammonites, but he does not intervene to relieve Jephthah's anguish, or spare his daughter. In contrast to previous episodes he is strangely silent and withdrawn — another sign of his increasingly strained relationship with his wayward people.[98]

---

94. How ironical that his name should be *yiptāḥ,* "he opens"!

95. In contrast, say, to political tracts and other types of advertising material.

96. See Dennis Olson's treatment of "shallow repentance" as a biblical theme and pastoral issue in "Judges," pp. 825-27.

97. Cf. Hos. 11:8-9; Isa. 1:4-9.

98. Contrast his explicit involvement from the very beginning in the careers of Othniel, Ehud, Barak, and Gideon (3:9-10, 15; 4:6-7; 6:11-12). Note in particular the extent of his ongoing involvement with Gideon in 6:11–7:23.

In its penetrating study of the man Jephthah, the story also has something to say about the human condition. Jephthah is a capable man — capable with words, capable in battle; he has a strong, decisive personality and is a leader of men. At his best he can exercise exemplary faith. But he has a background, a personal history, which helps us to understand his limitations even if we cannot condone them. He is insecure and self-centered. He can never fully engage with anyone's interests but his own. This is the hardness in the man and the reason he can never be truly great. It is to this insecurity and self-interest that his daughter is sacrificed; Jephthah cannot be a father. For the same reason he cannot be a Moses or a Joshua. *Jephthah the Gileadite,* head and leader of all the inhabitants of Gilead, is as high as Jephthah can rise. He may judge Israel — even save it — but he can never *care* about it as God does.

So we could go on. The meaning cannot finally be abstracted from the story. The narrative itself is the only formulation of it that contains all its aspects. The purpose of the kind of analysis offered above has been to provide a kind of map, so that readers can explore its riches more fully for themselves.

H. IBZAN, ELON, AND ABDON (12:8-15)

8 *After Jephthah, Ibzan from Bethlehem judged Israel.*
9 *He had thirty sons, sent thirty daughters away to marry outside, brought in thirty daughters from outside as wives for his sons, and judged Israel for seven years.*
10 *Then Ibzan died, and was buried in Bethlehem.*
11 *After him Elon the Zebulunite judged Israel. He judged Israel for ten years.*
12 *Then Elon the Zebulunite died, and was buried in Aijalon in the territory of Zebulun.*
13 *After him, Abdon, the son of Hillel the Pirathonite, judged Israel.*
14 *He had forty sons and thirty grandsons who rode on seventy male donkeys, and he judged Israel for eight years.*
15 *Then Abdon, the son of Hillel the Pirathonite, died, and was buried in Pirathon in the territory of Ephraim, in the hill country of the Amalekites.*

After the two Gileadites, Jair and Jephthah, the judgeship returns to the tribes west of the Jordan. The present passage completes the notices about the minor judges. As we have seen, these are distributed across chapters 3–12 in groups of one, two, and three respectively (3:31; 10:1-5; and 12:8-15).

8-10 The *Bethlehem* associated with *Ibzan* (v. 8) is taken by most scholars to be the northern Bethlehem of Joshua 19:15, on the border of the territory of Zebulun.[1] Its association with Ibzan is its only claim to fame, as far as we know. Little is known, either, about Ibzan himself. This is the only place he is mentioned, and the details about him are sparse. The statements about his judgeship are all formulaic, except those about his extraordinarily large family. This is apparently what distinguished him, or at least lingered most in the national consciousness.

He had *thirty sons* and *thirty daughters* whom he sent away to marry *outside,* and he brought in *thirty daughters from outside* as wives for his sons. This sending away and bringing in of daughters as marriage partners is done so consistently that it appears to have been a deliberate strategy by Ibzan to widen his connections and influence. Just how far the resultant family network extended is unclear: was it *outside (ḥûṣ)* his clan (NIV, NRSV, ESV), his tribe (HCSB), or even Israel? Solomon later pursued a similar policy, with (eventually) dire consequences for Israel because in his case it involved bringing in non-Israelite women who worshiped other gods. It is doubtful that Ibzan would have had the status to cast his net as wide as Solomon, and there is no hint of negative consequences as there were in Solomon's case. Nor is there any suggestion that Ibzan's family arrangements involved intermarriage with Canaanites, a practice strongly condemned elsewhere in Judges (esp. 3:5-6). The only clue is the adjacent statement that Ibzan judged *Israel,* implying that his marriage policy was a means of establishing and/or consolidating his position as judge.[2] The absence of any reference to "saving" Israel suggests that his rule was peaceful rather than turbulent, and what we are told of his family is more indicative of peace than of war, and of wealth and prosperity rather than of leanness. Any sensibilities that we may have about women being commodified for political advantage are probably irrelevant in the present context.[3]

The best clue to the significance of Ibzan for the reader of Judges is the juncture at which this brief note about him comes. Ibzan, with his *thirty daughters,* comes after Jephthah with his one daughter, his only child; "be-

---

1. So Moore, *Judges,* p. 310; Burney, *Judges,* pp. 290-34; Boling, *Judges,* pp. 215-16; and Soggin, *Judges,* p. 223. Josephus took it as the Judean Bethlehem, as did Rashi, Kimchi, and Levi ben Gershon, who identified Ibzan with Boaz, the ancestor of David. Cf. Block, *Judges, Ruth,* pp. 388-89. Its exact location is unknown, but see *OBA,* p. 84.

2. Alan J. Hauser, "Unity and Diversity in Early Israel before Samuel," *JETS* 22, no. 4 (1979): 301. But Hauser himself thinks that Ibzan was only a "leader in the region surrounding Bethlehem."

3. Contrast chs. 19–21, where the abuse of women is integral to the narrative and does feature as a moral issue. See also Section VII.B of the Introduction.

side her he had neither son nor daughter" (11:34). In literary terms Ibzan is a foil for Jephthah. After Jephthah's desolation comes Ibzan's fullness, and the contrast serves to underscore even further the extent of the loss Jephthah suffered in consequence of his vow.

11-12 Nothing is reported about *Elon* except the tribe he belonged to (he was a *Zebulunite*), the length of his judgeship *(ten years),* and the place of his burial *(Aijalon).* A similar situation exists for Aijalon as for Bethlehem. The better-known town with this name was in the south, in the territory of Dan (Josh. 19:42; 10:12). The present passage is the only reference to the northern town of the same name, in the territory of Zebulun. Its exact location is uncertain, but it is thought by some to be Khirbet el-Lon, approximately 14 miles (22.5 km.) north-northeast of the Bethlehem of verse 10.[4] Interestingly, it is very similar in Hebrew to the name Elon, the judge, and may have been named after him.[5] If so, it is an indication of the high esteem he was held in — especially in the north — but unfortunately no further information about him has survived.

13-15 *Pirathon,* the hometown of *Abdon,* was also, at a later time, the hometown of Benaiah, one of David's warriors (2 Sam. 23:30). Whether Abdon himself was a warrior we do not know. As we have seen, the expression *"judged Israel"* allows this but does not require it. According to verse 15, Pirathon was *in the territory of Ephraim* — the heartland of northern Israel — and, more particularly, in an area called *the hill country of the Amalekites.* It is generally identified as Fer'ata, 6 miles (9 km.) west-southwest of Nablus (Shechem). In pre-Israelite times the Amalekites had lived mainly in the Negeb, the desert fringe of southern Canaan. But the present passage, like 5:14, alludes to a time when there was also an Amalekite presence in the central highlands significant enough for a certain part of this region still to be named after them.[6]

A striking feature of this brief account of Abdon's judgeship is the reference to sons. Abdon himself was the *son* of Hillel (who is otherwise unknown), and himself had forty *sons* and thirty *grandsons* (vv. 13-14). The note about his sons and grandsons riding on *seventy male donkeys* (v. 14) recalls the similar ostentation of Jair and his family (10:4). In the light of this, and the career of Gideon's son Abimelech, there is a suggestion that from Gideon onward judgeship was always on the verge of turning into kingship, in which sons would succeed their fathers.[7] It is not until 1 Samuel, however,

---

4. J. P. U. Lilley, "Aijalon," *NBD,* p. 22.

5. It is identical in the underlying consonantal Hebrew text. It differs only in the pointing (pronunciation). Cf. Block, *Judges, Ruth,* pp. 389-90.

6. See the comments on 3:2-6.

7. Cf. Gooding, "The Composition of the Book of Judges," p. 79, n. 23.

that a judge actually appoints his son to succeed him, which triggers (via their corrupt behavior) the formal demand for a king (1 Sam. 8:1-5).

Since this brings us to the end of the six notices about the minor judges, it is the appropriate point for some more general reflections about their contribution to the book as a whole. In fact, we have already begun to do this with reference to Abdon's sons and grandsons. In general the interest in the numbers of sons and daughters, grandsons, donkeys, and marriages in the notes about the minor judges generally presents a striking contrast to the preoccupation with apostasy, oppression, war, and deliverance in the major episodes. To be sure, the brief note about Shamgar in 3:31 does not lose contact with these concerns, and the two notices in 10:1-5 are closely connected to the major episodes that precede and follow them, as we have seen. But in the three notices of 12:8-15 we have a longer interlude between major episodes in which contact with the major themes of the work is all but lost. It seems that the narrative is on the point of losing its way and that the story of Yahweh's struggle to reclaim Israel from apostasy and dissolution is breaking down into a mere catalogue of judges whose careers were so undistinguished that scarcely anything about them could be recalled — a chronicle of trivialities. It is as though Israel and Yahweh have wearied of the struggle, and the conflict between them has resolved itself into a kind of truce in which there is nothing of substance to report.

But there is an air of unreality about this situation, and we know Israel and Yahweh too well by this point in Judges to believe that it could last. In fact, it lasts just long enough to enhance the impact, when it comes, of the Samson episode as the climax of the series of major episodes which span the central section of the book. Here the major themes are taken up again and receive their final, climactic treatment before the epilogue of chapters 17–21.

I. SAMSON (13:1–16:31)

Long hair flowing, the original Hell's Angel,
rambling through Philistia like a one man army[1]

A Nazirite of God from birth until the day of his death[2]

Samson is a perplexing figure, and so is the account of his birth and turbulent career in the following chapters. It contains riddles, and in a sense that is what the whole story is — a riddle, an enigma, like Samson himself. Perhaps that is why it has always been so popular. The account of Samson simulta-

1. Mobley, *Empty Men,* p. 7.
2. Judg. 13:7.

neously attracts and repels us, pulls us this way and that with its strong currents of physical and emotional energy, and presents us at last with a broken man whom we cannot help but feel for, even though it is clear that he has been his own worst enemy. Samson is no cardboard cutout or plastic hero; he is too hot-blooded and raw for that. Whatever else he is, he is a real human being. His humanity calls to our own in a way that makes us identify with him even if we cannot understand or like him. In a sense, he *is* us; that is what is so disturbing about him. But of course he is also much more than this.

Samson is the last of the judges the book presents to us, and more space is given to him than to any of the others.[3] His story spans four whole chapters, and his importance is dramatically impressed on us by the fact that his birth and destiny are announced in advance. Furthermore, despite the chaotic nature of his personality and conduct, the account of his adult life which follows has all the marks of a carefully constructed narrative work. The plot is set in motion by the unsolicited appearance of Yahweh's messenger to a barren woman, the wife on Manoah the Danite (13:2-5). He makes two predictions: the barren woman will bear a son (v. 3), and this son will begin to save Israel from the hand of the Philistines (v. 5). The first is fulfilled in 13:24, *the woman gave birth to a son, and called his name Samson;* the second is fulfilled progressively in two major movements spanning chapters 14 to 16. The first begins with Samson going down to Timnah in 14:1 and climaxes in the slaughter of the Philistines at Ramath-lehi in 15:14-20. The second begins with his going to Gaza in 16:1 and climaxes in the slaughter of the Philistines and his own death in the temple of Gaza in 16:30. The references to Zorah and Eshtaol in 13:25 and 16:31 respectively form a bracket around these two movements, both of which end with a note that Samson judged Israel for twenty years (15:20 and 16:31).[4] The references to Manoah, Samson's father, in 13:2 and 16:31 frame the entire narrative.[5]

While the place of the Samson story in the alleged original form of the Deuteronomic History has been questioned,[6] it is clearly of major importance in the book of Judges, as the following analysis will show.

---

3. Only the Gideon narrative is comparable to it in length, and then only if the story of his son Abimelech is included. The narrative dealing with Gideon himself is shorter, and so is the story of Jephthah.

4. This "double ending" of the narrative is unique in Judges, and has led Boling and others to suggest that chapter 16 is secondary (see Boling, *Judges,* pp. 29-38). But see the comments on these two notes in the following exposition.

5. I am indebted for these observations about the formal design of the narrative to J. Cheryl Exum, "Aspects of Symmetry and Balance in the Samson Saga," *JSOT* 19 (1981): 3-29.

6. See the discussion of the views of Martin Noth and others in Section III of the Introduction, which deals with the history of the book's formation.

1. Introduction — The Birth of Samson and the Shape of Things to Come (13:1-25)

His mother bore nothing at first, then — everything (Rilke).[7]

1 *Again the Israelites did what was evil in the eyes of Yahweh, and Yahweh gave them into the hand of the Philistines for forty years.*

2 *There was a man from Zorah, from the clan[8] of the Danites, whose name was Manoah, and whose wife was barren and had not borne children.*

3 *The messenger of Yahweh appeared to the woman and said to her, "It is true that you are barren and have not borne children, but you will conceive and bear a son.*

4 *Now take care that you don't drink wine or strong drink, nor eat anything unclean,*

5 *for you will conceive, and will bear a son. No razor shall come upon his head, for the boy will be a Nazirite of God from birth, and he will begin to save Israel from the hand of the Philistines."*

6 *The woman came and said to her husband, "A man of God[9] came to me whose appearance was like the appearance of the messenger of God — very awesome. I did not ask him where he was from, and as for his name — he didn't tell me."*

7 *He said to me, 'You will conceive and will bear a son. So now you are not to drink wine or strong drink, nor eat anything unclean, for the boy will be a Nazirite of God from birth until the day of his death.'"*

8 *Manoah prayed to Yahweh, and said, "Please, my Lord, let the man of God whom you sent come to us again and teach us what we are to do for the boy who is to be born."*

9 *God listened to what Manoah said, and the messenger of God came again to the woman while she was sitting in the field; but Manoah her husband was not with her.*

10 *The woman quickly ran to tell her husband. She said to him, "Listen! he has appeared to me again — the man who came to me the other day!"*

---

7. R. Rilke, *Duino Elegies* (tr. E. Snow), cited by Mobley in *Empty Men,* p. 15.

8. See the comments and footnotes on "clan of Judah" in 17:7.

9. Taking the article in *ʾîš hāʾĕlōhîm* (literally, *the* man of God) as an instance of the special use of the article in Hebrew "to denote a single person or thing (primarily one which is as yet unknown, and therefore not capable of being defined) as being present to the mind under given circumstances" (GKC §126.4).

11 *Manoah got up, followed his wife, and came to the man. He said to him, "Are you the man who spoke to this woman?" He said, "I am."*

12 *Manoah said, "Now then, when your words come true, how is the boy's life to be ordered, and what is he to do?"*

13 *The messenger of Yahweh said to Manoah, "You shall take heed of everything that I have said to this woman.*

14 *She is not to eat anything which comes from the vine, and she must not drink wine or strong drink, and she must not eat any unclean thing. You shall take heed of everything that I have commanded her."*

15 *Manoah said to the messenger of Yahweh, "Please let us detain you so we can prepare a kid goat to set before you."*[10]

16 *The messenger of Yahweh said to Manoah, "If you detain me, I will not eat your food; but if you would like to make a burnt offering to Yahweh, do so," for Manoah did not know that he was the messenger of Yahweh.*

17 *Manoah said to the messenger of Yahweh, "What is your name? For your word will come to pass, and then we will honor you."*

18 *But the messenger of Yahweh said to him, "Why do you ask for my name, which is wonderful?"*

19 *So Manoah took the kid goat and the grain offering, and offered them on the rock to Yahweh who works wonders,*[11] *while Manoah and his wife were watching.*

20 *When the flame went up from the altar to the sky, the messenger of Yahweh went up in the flame of the altar while Manoah and his wife were watching. Then they fell on their faces to the ground.*

21 *The messenger of Yahweh did not appear again to Manoah and his wife. Then Manoah realized that he was the messenger of Yahweh.*

22 *Manoah said to his wife, "We are sure to die, for we have seen God."*

23 *His wife said to him, "If Yahweh had meant to kill us, he would not have accepted a burnt offering and grain offering from our hand, or shown us all these things, or informed us now like this."*

24 *The woman gave birth to a son, and called his name Samson. The boy grew, and Yahweh blessed him.*

25 *And the Spirit of Yahweh began to disturb him at Mahaneh-dan, between Zorah and Eshtaol.*

1 The formula that has introduced all the major episodes in the central part of the book now appears for the last time: *Again the Israelites did what was*

---

10. Taking *wᵉnaʿᵃśeh lᵉpānêkā* as a contraction of *wᵉnaʿᵃśeh wᵉnittēn lᵉpānêkā* (see Gen. 18:7-8).

11. Reading *wᵉhûʾ-ʾûmapliʾ*, assuming (with the MT apparatus) that the subject has been omitted by haplography.

evil in the eyes of Yahweh (13:1). As in 6:1, the *evil* is not specified. But as we have seen, 10:6-7 does double duty as an introduction to both the Jephthah and the Samson episodes, and there the evil is spelled out, yet again, as turning from Yahweh to other gods. In particular, the reference in 10:7 to "the gods of the Philistines" foreshadows the appearance of the Philistine god Dagon at the climax of the present narrative (16:23-24).[12] As we shall see, the *forty years* of Philistine oppression of Israel lasted well beyond the death of Samson. For the first time in the book of Judges, the liberation of Israel does not happen in the lifetime of the judge.

2 According to the recurring pattern of the major episodes of this central section of the book, what is expected at this point is a cry to Yahweh for help. But this time no such cry is heard. By the time Samson is born the Philistine dominance over Israel is so complete, and the morale of Israel so low, that even the hope that Yahweh might save them has been extinguished. There is no strength even to cry out.

Instead we find a story beginning whose relevance is not immediately apparent: *There was a man from Zorah* — a town 18 miles (24 km.) due west of Jerusalem, in the low hill country adjacent to the coastal plain. In Joshua it is listed as a town of Judah in 15:33, and of Dan in 19:41. Historically it almost certainly belonged to the Danites first, and became a town of Judah sometime after the Danites left the area and migrated north (ch. 18). In Samson's day the Danites still occupied the area, but their position there was increasingly precarious. The man (who will turn out to be Samson's father) was *from the clan (mišpaḥat) of the Danites.* The use of *mišpaḥat* (clan, family) rather than *sēḇeṭ* (tribe, e.g., 18:30) underscores the weakness of the Danite presence. The man's name, *Manoah,* meaning "rest," is ironical in the circumstances, for rest is exactly what the Danites did not have.[13] At best it expresses a longing, the kind of ache that is still there when hope has died. And to make matters worse, his wife (who remains nameless) was *barren and had not borne children.* Her plight mirrors that of Israel as a whole: disgraced and powerless, with nothing to look forward to but extinction. It is a scene of utter bleakness.

3 The "appearing" *(wayyērā')* of the mysterious *messenger of Yahweh* is the first indication that things are about to change.[14] In 2:1 he went up to Bochim to confront and rebuke Israel, and in 6:11-12 he came and "appeared" *(wayyērā')* to commission Gideon. The present passage has obvious points of connection with the Gideon passage: both have positive consequences for Israel, both involve the commissioning (directly or indirectly) of a deliverer, and in both cases the gradual disclosure of the identity of the

---

12. For the Philistines, see Excursus 4 after 3:1-6.
13. "Manoah" is a longer form of the name "Noah" (Gen. 5:29).
14. See the general comments on the messenger of Yahweh at 2:1a.

messenger climaxes in a fire theophany which at first terrifies those who witness it, but leaves them convinced that they have had an encounter with God which portends good, not harm. It is the powerful injection of hope into their own despair, and that of Israel as well. It sets in motion the whole sequence of events to unfold in the narrative that follows.

The announcement the messenger has come to make is first of all good news for the barren woman. She will be barren no longer; she *will conceive and bear a son.* There is no implication that the conception will be miraculous (without sexual intercourse). Nevertheless, the sudden reversal of her condition, from barrenness to fertility — as announced by the messenger — clearly marks the pregnancy and the son that will come from it as a special gift of God. The word the messenger has brought from God is a creative, transforming word. Furthermore, as the next two verses explain, it is also good news for Israel as a whole.

4-5 The son to be born will be *a Nazirite of God from birth,* and therefore the mother who will carry him in her womb and bring him to birth must abstain from certain kinds of food and drink, and must not cut the child's hair after he is born. The origin and nature of Naziriteship as practiced by the Israelites in the preexilic period is not altogether clear. However, the obvious similarities between the instructions given here and the regulations concerning Nazirites in Numbers 6 make that passage our best guide to reading the present passage in its biblical context.

The term "Nazirite" is related to the verb *nāzar,* "to separate" or "abstain" (Num. 6:1-3). Normally Naziriteship was voluntary and for a limited period, and involved the taking of a vow of separation to Yahweh for some special purpose (see below). During the period of the vow the Nazirite had to observe certain dietary and other rules as outward signs of his separation to God. Numbers 6 specifies abstinence from wine and other fermented drink, as well as grapes and raisins (v. 3), letting the hair of the head grow long (no cutting or shaving, v. 5), and complete avoidance of dead bodies, even of close family members (v. 6-7). In short, he was to keep himself ceremonially clean, in much the same ways as priests did (Lev. 10:8-9; 21:1-24; Ezek. 44:21). At the end of the period of separation the Nazirite had to present certain offerings to Yahweh, and shave off his hair and place it on the altar to be burned (Num. 6:14-18). Then after the priest had performed certain other rituals, the Nazirite was formally released from his vow and free to resume his normal way of life (vv. 19-20).

From the account of the birth of Samuel it seems that in special circumstances parents could take a vow on behalf of their child and thereby effectively consecrate him as a Nazirite for life (1 Sam. 1:11, 24-28).[15] The Old

---

15. The term "Nazirite" is not used in the MT, but the connections with Num. 6

Testament gives almost no information about the kinds of things Nazirites did during the term of their vow. Samuel began as an assistant to Eli the priest, and was subsequently called to be a prophet (1 Sam. 3), but his case was clearly exceptional. If my translation of Judges 5:2 is correct, there may be a hint there that preparation to participate as a volunteer in holy war involved the taking of a Nazirite vow or something similar. Perhaps the young men who comprised the schools of the prophets in the days of Elijah and Elisha (9th cent. B.C.) were Nazirites (2 Kgs. 4:38; 6:1, etc.), but this is speculation. It seems from Amos 2:11-12 that there were numerous Nazirites in the northern kingdom in the days of Amos, but there is no indication of what they did.

Like Samuel, Samson was a special case. No vow is taken; Samson's Naziriteship is divinely determined rather than voluntarily assumed, and for his whole life rather than a limited period. The instructions given to his mother are not exactly the same as those of Numbers 6,[16] but may reasonably be taken as a summary of them. The instruction not to eat *anything unclean* (v. 4) is more general than those in Numbers 6, and would presumably apply to any Israelite (Lev. 11; Deut. 14:1-21). The implication is that Samson's mother should be *particularly* careful to observe the laws about unclean foods because of the holiness of the child she will carry within her. Although it is Samson's mother, in the first instance, that is to obey these instructions, the reason (because her child will be a Nazirite) implies that Samson himself will have to obey them, too. However, the mother is not required to refrain from cutting her hair; this ban (and only this) is for Samson alone, and cannot begin to be observed until he is born. The effect is to give this particular sign of Samson's Naziriteship special prominence, anticipating the significant part it will play in the subsequent narrative.

Finally, and most importantly, the purpose of Samson's separation to God is very clearly stated: *"he will begin to save Israel from the hand of the Philistines"* (v. 5). He is to be a savior; that is the word spoken over him by Yahweh's messenger even before he is conceived. It is his destiny, and it will shape the whole course of his life. But the word *begin (yāḥēl)* is ominous. The Philistines are foes of a different order from former ones, and the struggle to free Israel from them will be hard and long. It will not be completed in Samson's lifetime, but it will be begun; Samson will strike the blow that sets the process of deliverance in motion, and he will not be released from his Naziriteship until he has done this.

---

are clear (v. 11), and 4QSam[a] v. 22 ends with the words, "a Nazirite forever all the days of his life."

16. For example, there is no mention of not eating grapes and raisins, or touching a dead body.

6-7   The woman goes and tells her husband about what she has experienced. Her description of the person she has met raises the question of his identity. To a certain extent this issue, once it is introduced, takes over the whole of chapter 13 and turns it into a "recognition story."[17] In these two verses we see the visitor from the woman's perspective, and share her growing awareness of who he is. She describes him first as *a man of God (ʾîš hāʾelōhîm)* who *came (bāʾ)* to her. Neither expression need denote anyone greater than a prophet.[18] The expression *ʾîš hāʾelōhîm*, with or without the article, is used, for example, of Moses (Deut. 33:1; Josh. 14:6), the anonymous prophet of 1 Samuel 2:27, Samuel (1 Sam. 9:6, 7, 9, 10), and Shemaiah (1 Kgs. 12:22); and the person referred to in the present passage "came" to the woman, just as she has now "come" to her husband. But as the woman's description continues, her awareness that the visitor was no ordinary prophet becomes apparent. Her words associate him with other appearances of such a figure in the past, which the woman has probably heard about: he looked like *the messenger of God* (cf. 2:1; 6:11), so *awesome* that she dare not ask his *name* or *where he was from* for fear of presuming an intimacy with him not proper for a mere mortal.[19] Her reference to him as the messenger of "God" *(ʾelōhîm)* rather than "Yahweh" *(Yahweh)* suggests the same reserve.

In general her report of what the messenger told her simply repeats the details of verses 4 and 5. The lack of any reference to the ban on cutting the boy's hair is strange, but could be taken as implied by the clear statement that he is to be a Nazirite. More striking, and not nearly so easily explained, is the different way she describes his destiny. She makes no mention of the fact that he will "begin to save Israel from the hand of the Philistines," and instead adds words about his death: *he will be a Nazirite of God from birth until the day of his death* (my emphasis). Is it a premonition, perhaps? A gnawing dread of what must be? Whether she knows it or not, her words are prophetic, and will be shown to be so by the way his story ends. Samson's destiny as a Nazirite of God from his mother's womb will be consummated in his death.

8   Manoah's prayer that Yahweh might send the messenger again expresses his entirely natural desire to know more. After all, he is the woman's husband, and the father of the child to be born. But so far the messenger has appeared only to his wife, and spoken only of what she is to do, not what Manoah has to do, or what they are to do as a couple. Furthermore, in her report of what the messenger said his wife has left out the very thing that Manoah wants to know: *what [they] are to do for the child who is to be born.*

---

17. Boling, *Judges,* p. 220.
18. The expression *ʾîš hāʾelōhîm*, with or without the article, is used, e.g., of Moses (Deut. 33:1, Josh. 14:6), Samuel (1 Sam. 9:6, 7, 9, 10), and Shemaiah (1 Kgs. 12:22).
19. Cf. Exod. 3:13-14.

As head of the family, Manoah asks for a second visitation — this time to both of them — so that he will have the knowledge he needs to discharge his proper responsibilities as head of the family.

9-11a God's response to Manoah's prayer is puzzling, and may well have left Manoah feeling aggrieved. Yahweh *listens* to what Manoah has said, and the messenger comes again. But again he comes to Manoah's wife when he is not with her; when she is *sitting in the field* alone (v. 9). If, as seems likely, Manoah's desire is not merely to be given more information but to be acknowledged as head of the family, this is not acceded to. He remains sidelined. His wife has to run and fetch him, and he has to *follow* her back in order to have any part in the proceedings (vv. 10-11a). No explanation is given for why he is treated in this way. To his credit, though, he doesn't seem to take offense, but simply takes the opportunity he has been given to meet the messenger for himself and question him directly.

11b-14 Manoah asks two questions. The first, at the end of verse 11, seeks confirmation of what his wife has just told him: *"Are you the man who spoke to this woman?"* The content of the question is clear, but it is hard to know what to make of its tone, and why Manoah found it necessary to ask it. The reference to his wife as *this woman* (she is still not dignified with a name) and the implication that she might have been mistaken (a woman's testimony is not to be trusted) are both rather disparaging, and may indicate that Manoah feels the need to take control, to assert his authority as her husband. But he could surely have done this more pointedly by referring to her as his "wife," as the narrator has just done (v. 11a). Most likely, though, no slight is intended; Manoah is simply a man of his times. What drives him, though, is clear. He wants to be doubly sure that no mistake has been made because he senses that a great deal is at stake. But the way he addresses the messenger shows that he has not grasped the full significance of what his wife has said. She said that the messenger had "appeared" to her (v. 10); Manoah asks only whether he is the man who "spoke" to her (v. 11). In other words, he is less aware than she is about the true identity of the messenger. Although his access to the messenger is now direct, and no longer mediated by his wife, there is still a gap between what *he* knows and *she* knows. And this gap is never closed. In this chapter Manoah is always trying to catch up with his wife, and never quite able to do so. The answer Manoah is given to his first question is simply *"I am"* — a single word *('ānî)* in Hebrew.[20] It is not evasive, but neither does it provide any unsolicited information. The messenger is not nearly as forthcoming to Manoah as he was to his wife. If Manoah wants to know more (as he clearly does, v. 8), he will have to ask for it.

---

20. Given the lack of any formal correspondence to the famous *'ehyeh* ("I AM") of Exod. 3:14, it is unlikely that there is any allusion to it.

The opening words of verse 12 show that Manoah has no doubt that the promised child will be born. At the very least he accepts that the messenger is a prophet, whose words will *come true* (cf. Deut. 18:21-22). But the question itself shows what his real concerns are. How is the boy's life to be *ordered,* and what is he (the boy) to *do?* As the father, Manoah naturally expects to have a hand in shaping the boy's life. But if he is to be a Nazirite from birth, what about the customary vow, for example? And if he is to begin to deliver Israel, how will he do this, and how can he be prepared for such a task? These are all natural and proper concerns for a man in Manoah's position to have. But again he finds himself pushed firmly into the background: he is simply to take note of the instructions the messenger has already given to his wife, and make sure (as far as he is able) that she carries them out (vv. 13-14). The implication seems to be that Manoah will never "own" the boy as a normal father might; he will be a Nazirite *of God* (v. 7), and it is God, not Manoah, who will shape his life. This will be hard for Manoah, but it is a reality he will have to accept.

15   An invitation to stay for a meal seems strangely mundane after the weighty questions Manoah has been asking. Is there perhaps more going on here than meets the eye? Given the unsatisfactory nature of the answers he has been given, does Manoah perhaps seek to *detain* the visitor in the hope of being able to question him further? This is possible, but unlikely for a couple of reasons. First, Manoah's behavior in the chapter as a whole suggests that he is a rather simple, straightforward character who would be unlikely to use such a ploy. Second, pressing a visitor to stay for a meal is so typical of Near Eastern hospitality in general that we should probably not attribute any ulterior motive to it.[21] It is more likely that Manoah has accepted that he will not be told any more, and is simply making amends for an oversight: he should have offered the visitor hospitality earlier, but has been too intent on questioning him to do so. The least he can do now is offer him a meal before he leaves. But things are about to take an unexpected turn.

16-17   The messenger rejects Manoah's offer of a meal, and instead tells him to prepare *a burnt offering* and offer it *to Yahweh* (v. 16). The parenthetical statement that follows *(for Manoah did not know . . .)* implies that the offer of a meal was based on a false premise. Manoah was treating his visitor as an "ordinary" human being (a prophet) because he did not yet realize that he was more than this. If he had done so, he would not have offered a meal but a *burnt offering,* as he is now told to do. The messenger has begun to nudge Manoah toward a recognition of who he is. His wife had done the same thing back in verse 6 when she told Manoah of the awesome appearance of the man of God who had appeared to her, and her reluctance to ask

21. For example, Gen. 18:1-8; Judg. 19:1-7, 16-21.

who he was for fear of being too presumptuous. But it will take more than nudges and clues to break through Manoah's dullness. Confused, perhaps, by the messenger's strange response, and lacking his wife's sensitivity, he does exactly what she had hesitated to do: he asks the visitor for his name — but not because he suspects he is God; on the contrary, he asks for it because he still thinks the messenger is a prophet, and he at least wants to be able to *honor* him appropriately when his words come true (v. 17). As in his earlier questions, Manoah simply wants the kind of information he needs (as he sees it) to discharge his proper responsibilities when the promised son is born.

18 The messenger's answer this time is evasive in the sense that it does not give Manoah what he has asked for. He asked for the messenger's name, and instead is given a descriptive phrase: it [the name] *is wonderful (peli'y)*. The best clue to the meaning of this is the use of another form of the same word in Ps. 139:6, in a statement about God's total knowledge: "Such knowledge is too wonderful *(pᵉl'iâ)* for me, too lofty for me to attain" (NIV). In such contexts, to say that something is *wonderful* is to say that it is beyond human comprehension. In the present passage, it is the name of the messenger that has this quality; even if the messenger were to tell Manoah what it is, he would not be able to understand it. At the very least it is not the kind of name that Manoah expects it to be, because the messenger is not the kind of person that Manoah thinks he is. But at the same time the messenger's reply is revealing — or very nearly so — because it suggests that there is mystery associated with the name of the messenger, and Manoah's question has brought him very close to the revelation of that mystery. The issue is not what the name of God is; that was revealed to Israel in the time of Moses (Exod. 3:13-15). The issue is what the name (real identity) of the *messenger* is, and the use of the term *wonderful (peli'y)* implies that there is a very close connection between the messenger and God — closer than Manoah has so far realized. The cognate noun, *pele'* (wonder), is used thirteen times in the Old Testament as a whole (in the singular or plural), always in connection with God, especially his acts of salvation and judgment in history, his laws, his final acts of apocalyptic judgment, and (in one case) his Messiah.[22] By locating his name in this class of divine wonders, the messenger definitely claims to be more than a prophet. He does not directly claim to be God, but comes very close to doing so. And his question, *"Why do you ask for my name?"* is a mild rebuke. Manoah has inadvertently trodden on holy ground. If he knew whom he was speaking to, he would have been more circumspect.[23]

---

22. Exod. 15:11; Pss. 77:11 (12), 14 (15); 78:12; 88:10 (11), 12 (13); 89:5 (6); 119:129; Isa. 25:1; 29:14; Lam. 1:9; Dan. 12:6. The messianic reference is in Isa. 9:6 (5).

23. Contrast Moses' more deferential tone and posture in his encounter with God at the burning bush (Exod. 3:5).

19-21   The progressive revelation of the identity of the messenger reaches its climax in these verses. Manoah does what the messenger has told him to do. He takes the *kid goat* he had intended to prepare as a meal (v. 15), adds to it *the grain offering (hamminḥâ)* and offers them up (as a burnt offering) on *the rock* (v. 19).[24] The fact that "grain offering" and "rock" are both definite (*the* grain offering, and *the* rock) is puzzling, since neither of them has been mentioned before in this chapter. The latter is referred to in the next verse as *the altar (hammizbēaḥ,* v. 20). The language suggests that the grain offering and the rock altar were normal, established aspects of the worship Manoah and his wife offered in this place. The differences on this occasion are the addition of a kid goat and the connection with the visit of the messenger. But then, suddenly, something happens that shatters all normalcy: the messenger steps into the rising altar flame and ascends into the sky with it, in full view of Manoah and his wife (v. 20)! There is only one word for such an event, and the previous verses have already given it to us. The expression *Yahweh who works wonders (yhwh ûmapli' laʿᵃśôt)*[25] echoes the "wonderful" *(peli'y)* of verse 18, and the double occurrence of the circumstantial clause, *while Manoah and his wife were "watching"* (literally, "seeing," vv. 19 and 20), highlights the fact that at last Manoah and his wife "see" the same thing. Manoah understands, at long last, who the messenger is (v. 21b). What he and his wife have seen is nothing less than a *wonder (pele'),* a powerful sign of the presence of God. Realizing this, they do the only thing that mere mortals can do in response to such a revelation: they fall face down on the ground (v. 20).

The ascension of the messenger brings the epiphany to an end. And there will be no recurrence: *The messenger of Yahweh did not appear again to Manoah and his wife* (v. 21). From now on Manoah and his wife will recede into the background. The Spirit will replace the messenger, and Samson will replace his parents as the locus of divine revelation.

22-23   In view of the startling intensity of what has just happened we may be forgiven for momentarily losing sight of the fact that the chapter as a whole is not about the identity of the messenger, but the birth of a child! The real climax will not be reached until he is born, in verse 24. But before that, as if to allow us to catch our breath, we are treated to a brief comic interlude. Poor Manoah has spent most of the chapter trying to catch up with his wife, not just physically (to get into the center rather than the margins of the action), but also intellectually (to see things as clearly as she does). No sooner, however, does he finally achieve this than he falls behind her again.

24. Cf. the rock that features in a similar action by Gideon in 6:17-20, also in connection with a visit from Yahweh's messenger.
25. See the footnote to the translation.

Paradoxically, it is only when the messenger has gone that Manoah finally understands who he is (v. 21b). And knowing this, he also knows something else: *"We are sure to die, for we have seen God!"* (v. 22). He is wrong, of course, as his wife at once realizes. But to her credit she does not mock him. Instead she patiently assumes the role of teacher and instructs him about the logic of the situation: *"If Yahweh had meant to kill us, he would not have accepted a burnt offering and grain offering from our hand, nor shown us all these things."* It is true that they have *seen God,* albeit in human form. The one who has appeared to them is *Yahweh* (v. 23). Manoah is not wrong about what *has* happened, but about what is *about to* happen: not their death, but parenthood — the birth of a son. Reminded of that, Manoah's sanity is restored and the episode is set to move to its true climax.

24a The birth announced so simply here is in fact momentous, and what the whole chapter has been leading up to. It is much less dramatic than the messenger's fiery ascent in verse 20, but like it, it does not belong to the category of ordinary things. This too, is a "wonder," for it is a complete reversal of the seemingly irreversible situation with which the chapter opened. The barren woman gives birth, as Yahweh's messenger said she would. God has brought life out of the deadness of her womb. It demonstrates that the issues of life and death are in his hands, and that therefore no situation is hopeless, including Israel's. And in the birth of this baby, to this woman, the change that Israel so desperately needs has already started to happen.

In keeping with the sustained focus on the woman through the whole chapter, it is she rather than Manoah who names the child, and the name she gives him, *Samson (šimšôn),* expresses her confidence that what the messenger has said about him will be fulfilled. It is related to the word *šemeš* (sun),[26] and recalls the closing lines of the Song of Deborah and Barak in 5:31:

> "Thus may all your enemies perish, Yahweh.
> But may those who love you be like the sun
>   going forth in its strength."

She knows the child's destiny, and expects it to be fulfilled. Like the sun he will be strong, and go forth in that strength to defeat Yahweh's (and Israel's) enemies.

24b-25 After the birth and naming of Samson, the narrative picks up speed and moves rapidly to the beginning of his adult life. His childhood is depicted as peaceful: *The boy grew, and Yahweh blessed him* (v. 24b). In the absence of further information, the "blessing" he enjoyed is probably best

---

26. It is a diminutive of *šemeš,* and means "Sunny" or the like (Mobley, *Empty Men,* p. 176), but in its context here it has weightier significance than such a name would normally have.

understood in terms of the natural advantages of good health, normal development, and the care of loving parents who provided a safe, protected environment for him amid the national distress that was all around him. An observer would have seen nothing to indicate that Samson was different from any other boy with good, pious parents. Through those growing years his parents carried the burden of his destiny for him. Samson certainly knew of it as an adult (see 16:17), but if his parents told him of it as a child, we have no knowledge of how, if at all, it affected him.

But eventually the day came when Yahweh claimed him for his mission and his childhood came to an abrupt end: *And the Spirit of Yahweh began to disturb him (lᵉpaʿᵃmô) at Mahenah-dan, between Zorah and Eshtaol* (v. 25). The verb used here to describe the beginning of the Spirit's work in Samson's life is striking, and is used of him alone. Robert Alter comments as follows:

> The usual verb for the descent of the spirit on a judge — a verb which will be applied to Samson at 14:19 — is *ṣālaḥ*. Only here do we have the verb *pāʿēm*, and, indeed, only here in the entire Bible is that verb used in a transitive *(pīʿel)* form. The basic meaning of the root, from a term meaning "foot," is to stamp or pound (thus the sundry modern translations that render it here as "to move" are rather weak). . . . [T]he only other times that the root *pāʿam* occurs in the Bible as a verb are to indicate the inner turmoil of a dreamer awaking from a disturbing dream (Gen. 41:8) and . . . Dan. 2:1 and 3.[27]

However it is best translated, its occurrence here foreshadows the turbulent character of Samson's life that is about to unfold.[28] He becomes restless, passionate, and erratic. But this verse discloses from the outset that, whatever natural desires and peculiarities of temperament may be contributing factors, the underlying cause is the presence and activity of Yahweh's Spirit, propelling Samson into conflict with the Philistines and the eventual fulfillment of his destiny. This verse provides the transition from the account of his birth in chapter 13 to the narrative of his adult life in chapters 14–16.

Zorah and *Eshtaol* lay close to one another 7.5 miles (12 km.) west of Jerusalem, in the low hills adjacent to the coastal plain, on the northern flank of the Valley of Sorek.[29] They were in the original allotment of the tribe of

---

27. "Samson without Folklore," in *Text and Tradition: The Hebrew Bible and Folklore,* ed. Susan Niditch (Atlanta: Scholars Press, 1990), p. 49. Alter himself translates it here as "drive": "The spirit of Yahweh began to drive him."

28. Cognates of the same verb appear repeatedly in ch. 16, at the climax of the narrative (vv. 15, 18, 20, 28). See the comments there.

29. See *OBA,* p. 85. Zorah, identified with Safra (Tel Zorʿa), is mentioned in the Amarna Letters, which date from the time before the Israelite settlement in Canaan.

Dan (Josh. 19:41; Judg. 18:2, 8, 11). Given the uneasy relationship with the Philistines at the time, the *Mahaneh-dan* (camp of Dan), located here between Zorah and Eshtaol, may have been a militia site set up to defend the approaches to the villages.[30] Samson was born into a tense, frontier situation, and was eventually brought back there for burial, with Israel's troubled relationship with the Philistines still unresolved (16:31).

2. Samson's Career, Part 1: From Timnah to Ramath-lehi (14:1–15:20)

This is the first of the two major movements, 14:1–15:20 and 16:1-31, that make up the account of Samson's career. They exhibit a similar symmetry to those of the Gideon narrative, but a much more extensive one. In both movements Samson sees a woman (the Timnite, the harlot of Gaza), becomes involved with a woman who betrays him by revealing a secret (the Timnite, Delilah), is bound and given into the hands of the Philistines (by the men of Judah, by Delilah), and is then empowered by Yahweh to slaughter the Philistines in great numbers (at Ramath-lehi, in the temple at Gaza).[31] The Samson story begins and ends at Zorah and Eshtaol, as the Gideon narrative began and ended at Ophrah. Samson's personal life may be disordered, but the account of it in the following chapters is anything but so.

Samson's marriage, however, as described in chapter 14 and the beginning of chapter 15, is a turbulent affair, and poses some difficulties, not just for Samson himself and his hapless bride, but for contemporary readers. It is fraught with problems from the start: it is cross-cultural, and between peoples (Israel and the Philistines) that are in conflict with one another. As with all marriages, it involves not just the couple themselves but family members, especially parents, who have their own expectations about what should happen. And this particular marriage is complicated by the personality and behavior of Samson himself. In view of all this, it is difficult to know what aspects of the marriage are to be regarded as normal (conforming to convention), and what aspects are irregular and therefore particularly significant in terms of the tensions that develop among the characters and the ways they respond to these tensions. For example, is the fact that Samson's wife re-

---

R. Greenberg, "Zorah," *ABD* 6:1168. Eshtaol "has been identified with Khirbet Deir Shubeib . . . near the village of Ishwah, . . . which retains elements of the ancient name." R. Greenberg, "Eshtaol," *ABD* 2:617.

30. The Danites later gave the same name to another site further north, in the vicinity of Kiriath-jearim (Judg. 18:12).

31. A much more extensive treatment of the symmetry of these two movements is given by Cheryl Exum, "Aspects of Symmetry and Balance." She also sees structural parallels between chs. 14 and 15, *within* the first movement.

mains with her birth family after the wedding, with Samson visiting her there, normal or abnormal? Is the provision of "thirty companions" to accompany Samson during the wedding celebrations simply a matter of convention, or does it have other, more sinister overtones? Is the assumption of the bride's father that Samson has abandoned her reasonable or unreasonable? And is his act of finding another husband for her normal in the circumstances, or a deliberate provocation? Similar issues surround Samson's riddle. Is it a normal piece of marriage entertainment, or is it unreasonably difficult and therefore an affront to Samson's Philistine guests?

In the absence of objective answers, the dynamics of the story itself are the best guide to which answers are more likely to be correct. However, it is potentially helpful to note that, even in a purely Israelite context, the Old Testament recognizes a variety of "partner" relationships between men and women, with different patterns of cohabitation and domestic arrangements for each. For example, "wife" (*'iššâ*) is distinguished from "concubine" (*pîlegeš*); and "maidservant" (*šiphâ/'āmâ*), where it is used formally for a woman's place in a household, is distinguished from both. In Judges, for example, Gideon has many wives, who presumably live with him, plus a concubine in Shechem (8:30-31).[32] The Old Testament also knows of levirate marriage (marriage to a deceased brother's wife in order to provide children to succeed him)[33] as well as normal marriage. Some form of levirate is reflected in the book of Ruth, which is also set in the period of the Judges. As the following treatment of chapters 14 and 15 will show, Samson's marriage is normal in the sense that he takes the Timnite woman as his wife, but her continued residence in her father's house is not normal.[34]

There is a lot of traveling to and fro in chapter 14 between Zorah, where Samson's parental home is, and Timnah, where his marriage takes

32. In Judges *'āmâ* is twice used as a substitute for "concubine," pejoratively in 9:18, and politely (euphemistically?) in 19:19. *šiphâ* is not used at all.

33. Deut. 25:5-10.

34. Contrast Moore (*Judges,* p. 329), who takes 15:1 in particular as evidence that Samson contracted a *ṣadîqâ* marriage, an arrangement in which a woman could marry outside her clan provided she remained with her father and bore children to her own clan. However, Moore's argument for a *ṣadîqâ* marriage entails deleting the reference to Samson's parents in vv. 5, 6, and 10 as later additions which "partly obscure" the real situation. In the text as we have it, it is much more likely that Samson intended to take his wife home with him but left her behind because she had betrayed him, and that his subsequent return to speak with her was an attempt at reconciliation. Compare the Levite's attempt to be reconciled with his concubine in 19:1-3. Lawson Younger notes that, while "visit-type" marriage is attested in Middle Assyrian law, it does not appear to be reflected in Judg. 14–15 since "the context of Samson's departure in rage (14:19) and the actions and comments of the woman's father (14:20; 15:2) suggest that Samson's return was not expected." K. Lawson Younger Jr., *Judges, Ruth,* NIVAC (Grand Rapids: Zondervan, 2002), p. 306, n. 52.

place, and at times this becomes confusing. The direction of the movement is not always clear, nor where certain characters are — especially Samson's parents. For example, in verse 5 his parents go down to Timnah with him, but he seems to be alone when he is attacked by a lion (since they don't know about it). Then, in verse 10 his father goes down to Timnah again, without any intervening statement that he had returned to Zorah. And when Samson goes on his way after finding honey in the carcass of the lion (v. 9), which direction is he going — on to Timnah or back to Zorah? It depends on where his parents are, because when he arrives he gives them some of the honey. These are real difficulties in the narrative which have to be dealt with somehow. They can be "fixed" by performing surgery on the text, and a reasonable case can be made for doing so.[35] However, my reading of the text shows that at least some of the puzzling features that would be eliminated by such a procedure (e.g., the "aloneness" of Samson when he is attacked by the lion) contribute significantly to the presentation of his character and his strained relationship with his parents. So I have assumed that the problems arise partly, at least, from the extreme compression of the narrative (a common feature of biblical storytelling), and tried to show how they function as part of the story's texture. The reader will have to judge how successful I have been. Similar problems exist in relation to the timing of events in the seven-day banquet Samson arranges to celebrate his marriage, and I have treated them in the same way.[36]

a. Samson's Marriage (14:1-20)

1 *Samson went down to Timnah, and saw a woman in Timnah — one of the daughters of the Philistines.*

2 *He went up, and told his father and mother, "I have seen a woman of Philistine descent at Timnah. Get her for me now as a wife!"*

3 *His father and his mother said, "Isn't there a woman among the daughters of your brothers, or among all my people,[37] that you would go and take a wife from the uncircumcised Philistines?" But Samson said to his father, "Get her for me, for she is right in my eyes."*

35. See, e.g., Moore, *Judges,* pp. 329-30.

36. If his wife's tearful entreaties began after the Philistines threatened her on the *seventh* day of the feast (v. 15), how can she be said to have wept before him for all *seven days* of it (v. 17)? The LXX's *"fourth* day" in v. 15 is almost certainly a harmonizing emendation. See the notes to the translation.

37. The singular *'ammî,* "my people," is puzzling after the preceding references to both of Samson's parents. The MT apparatus recommends shortening *'āḇîw wᵉ'immô* to *'āḇîw,* but this is questionable since the full phrase occurs again in v. 4. It is more likely, as Boling suggests (*Judges,* p. 229), that the father speaks for both parents as implied by the final clause of the verse.

4 *His father and his mother did not know that this was from Yahweh, that he was seeking an opportunity against the Philistines. At that time the Philistines were ruling over Israel.*

5 *Samson went down with his father and his mother to Timnah, and they came to the vineyards of Timnah, and suddenly a young lion came roaring to meet him.*

6 *The Spirit of Yahweh rushed upon him, and he tore it in two — like tearing in two a young goat — with his bare hands. But he didn't tell his father or his mother what he had done.*

7 *He went down and spoke to the woman, and she was right in Samson's eyes.*

8 *After some time he returned to take her. He turned aside to see the remains of the lion, and look! there was a swarm of bees in the lion's carcass, and honey!*

9 *He scraped it out into his hands and went off, eating on the way. He went to his father and his mother, and gave some to them, which they ate, but he did not tell them that he had scraped out the honey from the carcass of the lion.*

10 *His father went down to the woman, and there Samson made a feast,[38] for this was the custom of the young men.*

11 *When they saw him,[39] they took thirty companions, and they accompanied him.*

12 *Samson said to them, "Let me give you a riddle. If you fully explain it to me within the seven days of the feast — if you work it out — then I will give you thirty linen garments and thirty changes of clothes.*

13 *But if you are unable to explain it to me, then you will give me thirty linen garments and thirty changes of clothes." They said to him, "Give us your riddle; let's hear it."*

14 *He said to them, "Out of the eater came something to eat, and out of the strong came something sweet." And they were unable to explain the riddle after three days.*

15 *On the seventh day[40] they said to Samson's wife, "Cajole your husband into explaining the riddle for us, or we will burn you and your father's house with fire. Have you invited us here[41] to rob us of our belongings?"*

38. LXX and Syriac add "for seven days."

39. LXX[A], Syriac[h], and OL[L] read "because they were afraid," reflecting the preposition b^e or k^e with *yir'ātām* instead of the MT's *kir'ôtām*. See the exegetical comments on this verse.

40. The LXX has "fourth" — almost certainly a change to harmonize with the *three days* of the preceding verse. See the exegetical comments on vv. 15 and 17.

41. Reading $h^a lōm$ instead of MT's anomalous $h^a lō'$, a variant supported by several Hebrew MSS and recommended by *BHS*.

16 *Samson's wife wept before him and said, "You really*[42] *hate me; you don't love me. You have given a riddle to my people,*[43] *but you haven't explained it to me." He said to her, "But I haven't even explained it to my father or my mother. Why would I explain it to you?"*

17 *She wept before him for the seven days that they held the feast. So on the seventh day he told her, because she had worn him down, and she told the riddle to her people.*

18 *On the seventh day the men of the town said to him, before the sun went down, "What is sweeter than honey? And what is stronger than a lion?" He said to them, "If you had not plowed with my heifer, you would not have worked out my riddle."*

19 *Then the Spirit of Yahweh rushed upon him, and he went down to Ashkelon and struck down thirty of their men. He stripped them*[44] *and gave the changes of clothes to the men who had explained the riddle. With his anger burning he went up to his father's house.*[45]

20 *And Samson's wife became the wife of his companion, who had been his best man.*[46]

1-2 *Timnah* (Tel el-Baṭashi) lay approximately 4 miles (7 km.) west of Zorah and Eshtaol, on the opposite (southern) side of the Valley of Sorek.[47] According to 1:34 the Danites had been unsuccessful in occupying the coastal plain, and been confined to the hills. It is from this higher ground that Samson literally "goes down" to Timnah, which by this time had become a Philistine town. The fact that Samson could go down to it, apparently without difficulty, suggests that the border between Israelite and Philistine territory was open. As subsequent events show, however, this was not because there was peace or equality between the two parties, but because Philistine rule over Israel was an accepted fact (v. 4; cf. 15:11).

The narrative syntax linking 14:1 with the last clause of chapter 13 suggests that Samson's trip to Timnah was the first consequence of the Spirit's activity in his life: "Then the Spirit began to disturb him, . . . and he

---

42. The asseverative use of *raq*, as in Gen. 20:11; Deut. 4:9 (BDB, p. 956).

43. Taking the *bēn* in *libnê 'ammî* as gender neutral, signifying simply "members of the class 'my people.'"

44. Literally, "took their spoil/plunder."

45. Given the way *bêt 'ābîhû* functions here as the polar opposite to Timnah, I have treated it as the name of a place rather than family (household). Contrast the usage in v. 15, and see the comments there.

46. Literally, "[one who] from his companion[s] who was his [chief] companion." The marriage context justifies *best man*, even if there is not an exact correspondence to the contemporary use of the expression. Cf. 15:2.

47. *OBA*, p. 85.

went down." It was to be the first of a series of downward movements as he moved further and further away from the lifestyle expected of him as a Nazirite (14:5, 7, 19; 15:8, 11). The unfolding pattern of his career, like Jonah's, was to be a downward one, both literally and metaphorically.[48] He is presented here as a headstrong youth whose passions are so inflamed by what his eyes see that they blind him to all reason and duty. The result is confusion. In going down to Timnah he crosses the invisible line between Israel and Philistia, friend and enemy. In "seeing" a woman and demanding to have her he blurs the distinction between love and lust. In wanting to marry a *Philistine* woman he breaks the ethnic and religious taboos that support the current social order, and in demanding that his *father and mother* get her for him he overturns normal family relationships (v. 2).[49] If this beginning is any indication of what is to come, Samson looks like being more a chaos monster than a deliverer.

3 Understandably his parents are alarmed and confused. Is this the son that was promised them — a Nazirite of God and deliver-designate of Israel? They try to reason with him. Their reference to the *uncircumcised* Philistines suggests that their deepest concern is that Samson will betray his identity as an Israelite. Marriage involves the deepest union possible between two people; husband and wife become "one flesh" (Gen. 2:24). Circumcision, on the other hand, is the marker, par excellence, of Israel's separation to God as his elect, covenant people (Gen. 17:10). So how can Samson *take a wife from the uncircumcised Philistines* without betraying his separation to God as an Israelite?[50] And if his separateness as an Israelite is compromised, how can his deeper separation to God as a Nazirite be maintained? His parents do not mention this, but it can hardly be far from their minds. Samson's first act after the Spirit begins to disturb him seems to be a denial of every-

48. Jonah went down to Joppa, down into a ship, down into the hold of the ship, and down into the watery depths (Jonah 1:3, 5; 2:6).

49. Not only would a son not command his parents in this way, but a father would normally decide whom his sons would marry (e.g., Gen. 24:4; 38:6).

50. For "uncircumcised" as an expression of contempt for the Philistines in particular see 15:18; 1 Sam. 14:6; 17:26, 36; 31:4; 1 Chron. 10:4. This may reflect the fact that in this respect the Philistines were different, not only from the Israelites, but from most other peoples in the ancient Near East at the time (see R. G. Hall, "Circumcision," *ABD* 1:1025-32). However, in view of Jer. 9:25-26 (where a wide range of nations are said to be uncircumcised), it is probable that, because of important differences in its significance and the ways it was practiced, Israelites considered their own circumcision to be the only valid one. "For instance, circumcision outside Israel was often attached to [pagan] rites of puberty or pre-marriage, and in Egypt it appears to have been restricted to the priests and possibly the ruling class" (Cundall, *Judges,* p. 162). It is also clear from the expression "uncircumcised in heart" in Jer. 9:26 that the word "uncircumcised" was sometimes used metaphorically.

thing that his parents were led to believe he would be and do. No wonder they tried to talk him out of it. But to no avail. Samson's response is chilling: *"Get her for me, for she is right (yāš^erâ) in my eyes."* It subverts the normal, positive sense of *yāšar* (right, upright) by emptying it of all moral content. On Samson's lips it means only "desirable, attractive." Furthermore, the phrase *right in my eyes* anticipates the refrain of the dreadful last five chapters of the book, where everyone does "what is right in his own eyes" *(hayyāšar b^eênāyw).*[51] Samson's going down to Timnah is the beginning of a movement toward moral chaos, not just for himself but for Israel. But Samson is determined; he will have his way, come what will.

4 Samson's parents knew his calling and destiny. What they *did not know* (v. 4) was that his present, erratic behavior was *from* [caused by] Yahweh (v. 4);[52] nor, most likely, did Samson himself. It is we, the readers, who have been told that the Spirit of Yahweh has begun to disturb him (13:25) and have therefore been able to make the connection between this and his present behavior. There is nothing in the narrative to suggest that either Samson or his parents were privy to this knowledge. Samson knows only that he has seen a Philistine woman and wants her, and his parents know only that their son is impervious to all attempts to reason with him. This gap between what we know and what the characters in the story know creates the perfect conditions for irony to flourish, and we will see in due course how it does so.

Our own privileged knowledge is extended by the statement that Yahweh *was seeking an opportunity against the Philistines.* The status quo, which the Israelites had come to accept (15:11), was one of servitude: *the Philistines were ruling over Israel.*[53] Clearly, this situation had to be disturbed if Israel was to be liberated, and the divine intention behind Samson's demand to have a Philistine wife was to bring this about. It is conceivable that such a marriage might have succeeded, and even had a positive effect on Israelite-Philistine relationships.[54] But it was doomed from the start not to do so. Yahweh was intent on provoking conflict with the Philistines, and, given Samson's temperament, he was an ideal tool in his hands to do so. He had become Yahweh's unwitting agent provocateur.

5-7 Samson goes down to Timnah again, this time accompanied by *his father and mother* — presumably to begin the preparations for his mar-

---

51. Judg. 17:6; 21:25.

52. Cf. Gen. 24:50.

53. Note that the expression *at that time* "suggests a date [for the composition or final editing of the text] no earlier than the middle of the reign of David" (Cundall, *Judges, Ruth,* p. 162).

54. Note the use of marriage to promote good relationships between Israel and its neighbors in the period of the monarchy, especially by Solomon (1 Kgs. 9:16; 11:1-3).

riage. His parents seem to have accepted that they cannot prevent it, and decided that it is better to participate in it than to boycott it and thereby lose their son completely. If they remain in contact with him, they may expect to exert at least some influence on him, however minimal.

The *vineyards* of Timnah are an indication of the fertility of the surrounding area, and hence provide a clue to why the Philistines had established a presence there. Compare the way vineyards, along with milk and honey, feature in idealized descriptions of Canaan as the promised land in Numbers 16:14 and elsewhere.[55] In view of this it is ironical that Timnah, a place of vineyards, has become Philistine territory. But vineyards also have other symbolic resonances. They occur again in 9:27 in connection with a Baal harvest festival, and in 20:20-21 in connection with an annual "festival of Yahweh." As part of the associated festivities, young women dance in the vineyards, and are seized and taken by the Benjaminites to be their wives. So, in view of the context here in chapter 14, reference to the vineyards anticipates the wedding and feasting that are about to take place.

But this happy prospect is rudely interrupted by the roar of a *lion* (v. 5b). The lion appears *suddenly,* out of nowhere. Since it is a wild animal, its presence in the vineyards is incongruous and unexpected. As a beast of prey it threatens not only Samson's wedding plans but his very existence, and therefore his destiny. In some ways it is like Samson himself, a beast that breaks boundaries, untameable and unstoppable, driven by animal instincts, and intent on having what its eyes see. Of course, at the surface level of the narrative it is external to Samson. It is a beast; he is a man. It is a lion; he is its prey. But if the vineyards have more than surface significance, so, too, may this lion. It represents the wild, out-of-control aspect of Samson's nature that threatens to destroy him if it is not mastered.[56] A great deal is at stake here; much more than Samson himself is aware of.

Whether or not Samson could have overcome the lion unaided is unclear. David later speaks to Goliath of having killed lions that tried to carry off his sheep (1 Sam. 17:34-36), something that may have been a normal part of life for a shepherd in David's day. But David attributes such victories to Yahweh, who had "delivered" him at such times and could be trusted to deliver him again as he advanced against Goliath — a foe that he *certainly* could not master without Yahweh's help (v. 37). In 2 Samuel 23:20 the killing of a lion in single combat is cited as an exploit that only a great warrior could perform. The fate suffered by a nameless prophet in 1 Kings 13 was presumably more typical: "a lion met him on the road and killed him" (v. 24). A single, unarmed man taken by surprise was normally no match for a lion.

55. For example, Deut. 6:11; Josh. 24:13.
56. Cf. the sin of Cain in Gen. 4:7.

In Samson's case, however, normality is set aside. Everything about his fight with the lion points to supernatural enabling. The *Spirit* that had begun to disturb him in 13:25 now "rushes" upon him, throwing him into a frenzy of destructive strength (v. 6a). He doesn't just kill the lion, but "tears it in two" — *with his bare hands.* There is a significant heightening here of things we have seen in the preceding judge narratives. The Spirit "came" *(hyh)* on Othniel and Jephthah (3:10; 11:29), and "clothed itself" *(lbš)* with Gideon (6:34), but it "rushes" *(ṣlḥ)* on Samson here in verse 6, again in verse 19, and yet again in 15:14. Eglon, Shamgar, and Jael killed their victims with improvised weapons (3:16, 31; 4:21); Samson kills with his bare hands. They stabbed, struck, or hammered; he tears his prey to pieces, as a lion itself would do. In 15:3-5 he will use foxes as weapons. As a man seized by the Spirit, Samson inhabits the borderlands between the civilized and the wild, between man and beast.[57]

In view of the fact that Samson was traveling with his parents (v. 5), it is surprising to read at the end of verse 6 that *he did not tell [them] what he had done.* Would they not have witnessed the event themselves, making such concealment impossible? Evidently not. If we choose to read the text rather than resort to conjectural emendation,[58] there are at least two implications of this statement. First, while Samson's parents accompany him on the journey, he is not under their control. He goes off on his own[59] and has adventures they know nothing about. The parents, who were central in chapter 13, are progressively being marginalized. Second, the parents (especially his mother) were the ones through whom Samson inherited his destiny as a Nazirite. By moving them to the margins of his life, Samson effectively distances himself from the obligations entailed in his calling. At one level he is simply demanding his independence and going his own way. But at a deeper level God, by his Spirit, is claiming him for his destiny. In ways that Samson is not yet aware of, the lion he has killed will play an important part in bringing him into conflict with the Philistines, and hence serve God's purpose of using him to "seek an opportunity" against them (v. 4).

The marginalization of Samson's parents continues in verse 7. They are simply ignored. *Samson* completes the journey to Timnah, and speaks with the woman; and she is right in *Samson's* eyes. What his parents think is irrelevant. The absence of any reference to the woman's parents suggests

57. Cf. Nebuchadnezzar in Dan. 4:28-33.
58. See the discussion at the beginning of this section.
59. Note how, on his return journey, he has to *turn aside* from the main path to see the remains of the lion (v. 8). The LXX makes this explicit in v. 5 as well. Instead of the MT's *wayyābō'û,* "they came [to]," LXX[A] has *exeklinen,* "he turned aside," and LXX[B] has *ēlthen,* "he came." But this is unnecessary. The MT conveys the same information more subtly, and is to be preferred as the harder reading.

that, as far as Samson was concerned, they, too, were irrelevant. He saw the marriage as a matter between him and the woman alone. It is hard to know exactly what to make of the statement that he *spoke* to her. It is more bland than the "persuade" (speak to the heart) of 19:3.[60] At the very least it implies that something more than her physical appearance mattered to Samson, and that he chose to disclose his intentions to her. And the fact that the "speaking" is followed by a reaffirmation that she was *right in his eyes* suggests that his choice of her was confirmed by the conversation. But she remains nameless, and there is no explicit love language.[61] She is essentially passive, and it is doubtful that she was given any real power to choose.

8-9 The opening words of verse 8, *After some time,* pass over the period of betrothal in silence and bring us at once to the time when the wedding is to take place. Samson goes down to Timnah again, this time to *take* the woman as his bride (v. 8). The language confirms the impression of the woman as essentially passive. She is simply an object of desire.

There is also something else that attracts Samson's attention, however. His trip back to Timnah brings him again into the vicinity of the vineyards (v. 5). He turns aside to see *the remains of the lion* that he had killed (v. 6) and discovers, not just a *corpse,* but a *swarm of bees* living inside it — *and honey!*[62] The use of the particle *hinnê (look!)* suggests surprise, and the way the phrase *and honey* is syntactically isolated at the end of the sentence implies that this in particular was not something Samson was looking for. He turned aside simply out of curiosity, and perhaps to re-live his adventure by viewing the surviving evidence of it. But what happens next is reminiscent of something that happened in another place and time: he saw, he took, he ate (v. 8). On the surface it is a purely innocent act; but the reference, not just to the remains of the lion, but its *carcass (gᵉwîyaṯ)* suggests that the resonance with Genesis 3 (eating something forbidden) is not coincidental. This is confirmed by the fact that after the "seeing," "taking," and "eating" comes the "giving" of the honey to someone else (Samson's parents), who also "eat" (v. 9; cf. Gen. 3:6). Finally, the negative significance of the whole sequence of acts is confirmed by the pregnant statement at the end of verse 9: *he did not tell [his parents] that he had scraped out the honey from the carcass (gᵉwîyaṯ) of the lion.* Samson has implicated his parents in something he knows they would not approve of. The term *gᵉwîyaṯ* simply means "body," not necessarily "corpse."[63] But combined here with *re-*

---

60. Cf. Isa. 40:2.

61. Contrast 16:4, 15.

62. Boling (*Judges,* p. 230) notes that "In Israel it was widely understood that honey held enlightening and courage-producing potential, as in the story of Jonathan (1 Sam. 14:24-30)."

63. See Gen. 47:18; Neh. 9:37; Ezek. 1:11, 23; Dan. 10:6.

mains and *after some time,* it can be nothing else: by the time Samson revisits the lion, its body is a decaying corpse (as in 1 Sam. 31:10, 12; Ps. 110:6; Nah. 3:3). David Grossman has nicely captured the pathos in the picture of Samson going on his way eating the honey which he has scraped *into his hands:* "Take a look at him: a he-man with a little licking boy inside!"[64] But the darker significance of it lies in the instruction that was given to his mother in 13:4-5: "Now take care that you don't drink wine or strong drink, *nor eat anything unclean,* for . . . the boy will be a Nazirite of God." It will become clear in 16:17 that Samson has known all along that he is a Nazirite, and his concealment of the source of the honey from his parents can hardly mean anything else than that he knows that food from such a source was "unclean," and therefore forbidden. After distancing himself from his parents by disregarding their wishes and acting independently of them, Samson draws them into complicity with him by giving them some of the honey to eat, too (v. 9). In so doing he dishonors his parents in a particularly cynical way. Even in eating honey, he is not the "little licking boy" he seems to be.

10-11   The opening clause of this verse, *His father went down,* implies that Samson's father (and therefore his mother, too) had returned home at some point, and that Samson had doubled back to give them the honey before continuing on his way to Timnah. (See the discussion at the beginning of this section.) Samson's father now comes down to Timnah again *to see the woman,* that is, to meet (at last) the woman that Samson has chosen to marry. But again he is marginalized. If he hoped to play a significant role, such as formally giving his approval or negotiating the dowry, he is mistaken. He simply disappears from the narrative! It is *Samson* who makes arrangements for the reception (he "makes a feast"). The explanation, *for this was the custom of the young men (kēn ya'ăśû habbaḥûrîm)* probably refers to what was normal among the Philistines. Whatever may have been their practice in the past, it was now normal for the young men themselves, not their parents, to organize the wedding celebrations. Samson is behaving like a Philistine. His father has lost his son to them, and has no say in the matter. If this is a correct reading of verse 10, what the Philistines do in verse 11 should probably also be seen in the same light. When they see Samson, they choose thirty young men to "accompany" him, that is, to assist him in an official capacity in the wedding celebrations. This, too, was probably customary, though special arrangements may have been necessary for Samson. Since he was getting married in a setting where he could not provide the members of his own wedding party, the Philistines had to do it for him (v. 11). But the expression *when they saw him* suggests that there was some-

---

64. David Grossman, *Lion's Honey: The Myth of Samson* (Melbourne: Text Publishing, 2006), p. 54.

thing about him (his foreignness and/or his impressive physique) that convinced them that a large number of attendants should be provided, though whether this was simply a mark of respect is not clear. They may also have seen him as dangerous, and provided *thirty* men to accompany him as a precaution. If so, their instincts were correct.

12-14 *Seven days* was the customary period for the observance of a religious festival *(ḥag)* in Israel,[65] and may also have been the customary length of a marriage feast *(mišteh),* although we have no direct evidence of this.[66] However, given the allusions to Philistine custom that we have already observed in the previous verses, it is likely the seven days of Samson's "Philistine" marriage followed the established practice in Timnah. Given the impossibility of continuous eating and drinking for such a period, entertainment was an essential part of such a feast, and Samson (probably again in keeping with the traditional role of the host/bridegroom) was happy to oblige. He proposes a riddle with a wager attached.

The wager involves *linen* garments (plain undergarments) and *changes of clothes* (sets of outer garments). If his thirty companions can *fully explain (haggēd taggîdû)* the riddle to him, he will give each of them a set of the garments (v. 12); if they cannot, each of them will give him the same (v. 13). Either way, a considerable amount of property will change hands, with Samson standing to benefit thirty times as much as any of his companions. The riddle itself is based on his discovery of bees and honey in the carcass of the lion:

> *"Out of the eater came something to eat,*
> *and out of the strong came something sweet"* (v. 14a).

Not surprisingly, after *three days* of trying they were still not able to explain it (v. 14b). The riddle was impossibly difficult since no one knew about his adventure with the lion. He had given his parents some of the honey, but had not told even them where it had come from (v. 6). Only if "carcass beehives" were commonplace would Samson's companions have a chance of guessing what the riddle referred to. But verse 8 strongly suggests that this was not the case; Samson was not looking for honey when he turned aside to see the remains of the lion, and was taken by surprise when he found it. It was not a common sight.

Given all this, Samson's riddle turns out not to be the light-hearted piece of entertainment that it promised to be. On the contrary, in view of its

---

65. For example, Exod. 12:15 (the Passover); Lev. 8:33 (the ordination of priests); 23:34 (the Feast of Tabernacles); 1 Kgs. 8:65 (the dedication of the temple); and Ezek. 43:25 (the dedication of the altar of burnt offerings).

66. But note the seven-day feast *(mišteh)* given by Ahasuerus in Esth. 1:5.

difficulty and the high stakes attached to it, it can hardly be seen as anything less than a deliberate provocation. Why Samson proposed it we can only surmise, but at least we do have some clues in the preceding narrative to work with. First, the riddle is entirely in keeping with Samson's character as we have come to know it, especially his immaturity in demanding to have what his eyes see, and the way he has treated his parents — totally disregarding their wishes, marginalizing them, and cynically "playing" with them by manipulating them into eating honey from a source that would horrify them. Samson is the sort of brash young man who must be the center of attention, and enjoys manipulating those around him. Second, however, and more seriously, it sends a strong message to the Philistines that, though Samson may come among them, marry one of their women, and fit in with their cultural norms to some extent, they will never "own" him. He will always be his own man and relate to them on his own terms. They will never be able to control him, any more than his own parents could. It is Samson who will call the tune, not the Philistines. Finally, since the whole chain of events which led to the riddle was set in motion by the Spirit of Yahweh rushing upon Samson back in verse 6, all this is part of God's deeper purpose of "seeking an opportunity" against the Philistines (v. 4). Behind the provocation of Samson lies the provocation of God. Samson himself is not as much in control as he thinks he is; nor are the Philistines. They are all in the hands of God, who is shaping things toward an end that he, not they, will finally bring about (13:5).

15 The *three days* of verse 14 have now become *seven*. The time for solving the riddle is about to expire (v. 12), and Samson's companions can bear their humiliation no longer. They sense (rightly as it turns out) that Samson's one point of vulnerability is his newly acquired bride, and determine to get the answer they need through her. They approach her with a demand and a threat. They tell her to *cajole (pattî)* Samson, that is, use her womanly wiles to persuade him to divulge the answer to his riddle to her, and therefore (indirectly) to them. The threat they use to pressure her is an extreme one: do as we say, or *we will burn you and your father's house with fire*. The conjunction of *you* (her person, body) with her *father's house (bêt 'ābîk)* suggests that the latter, too, refers to persons rather than just a building. They threaten to immolate with her all her family, including servants (her father's "household"). She is already caught in the power play between the dominant males (Samson and his male companions), but it is not just them she has to choose between. Now she has to choose between compliance and death; between Samson and her entire family. But she has hardly had time to bond with Samson in a way that would justify sacrificing everything for him, especially since she may never even have wanted the marriage as he did.[67] The

---

67. See the comments on v. 8.

Philistines have rightly sensed her vulnerability, and hence Samson's. Their closing question in this verse alludes to the wager attached to the riddle: *"Have you invited us here <u>to rob us of our belongings</u>?"*[68] The wedding invitation has turned out to be a trap, and the expense and loss of face they would suffer by giving Samson thirty sets of clothes after what he has done to them is something they simply cannot countenance.

16-17   Samson's wife has made her choice, and sets about "cajoling" Samson with tears, and an accusation: *"You really hate me; you don't love me. You have given a riddle to my people, but you haven't explained it to me."* The expression *my people* is telling, and indicates where her allegiance lies, and the accusation entails an implicit justification for the course of action she has embarked on. She herself has already been betrayed by Samson. He who professed to *love* her by choosing her as his bride has *hated* her (betrayed that love) by shutting her out of his inner world where the answer to the riddle lies. Since this secret is his means of manipulating people he wants to humiliate, concealing it from her is incompatible with loving her. If he continues to conceal it, she is justified in betraying him because he has already betrayed her. The trap she has set for him, however, is that by accepting the challenge to truly *love* her, he will betray himself, for she, too, has a secret: she is his enemy. She may be vulnerable, but she is not as vulnerable as he is at this moment. She is the predator; and he is the prey. Samson senses danger, but his wife's cajoling has seriously weakened his resolve. All he can offer now is token resistance: *"I haven't even explained it to my father or my mother. Why would I explain it to you?"* In view of how Samson has treated his parents in the preceding narrative this is a feeble excuse, entirely lacking in conviction. He has already nullified "duty to parents" as a reason for refusing her. His resolve is gone; all he is doing now is stalling.

The statement that Samson's wife wept before him for all *seven days* of the feast (v. 17) is puzzling after verses 15-16, which seem to say that she began her tearful entreaties only on day seven. What it effectively does, however, is to set the events of the seventh day in a larger context. Apparently Samson's wife had been upset from the very beginning that Samson had not shared the answer to his riddle with her, and if this was known, it may well have suggested to the Philistines that she would be susceptible to blackmail: a weeping, disaffected wife would be much more likely to betray her husband than a happy one. At any rate, the events of the seventh day simply brought matters to a head. She had *worn him down* with her weeping, so he *told her* the answer to the riddle, and she told her people. The deed was done.

18-19a   All the foregoing had taken precious time, but it paid off. According to the traditional Israelite way of defining days, the *seventh day* would

68. Literally, "to dispossess us *(halyār^ešēnû)."*

end at sundown,[69] and it was then — at the very last minute — that the Philistines gave Samson the answer to his riddle. Samson is furious, of course. Instead of accepting defeat graciously he hurls another riddle at them:

> *"If you had not plowed with my heifer,*
> *you would not have worked out my riddle."*

Everything about this riddle is insulting and expresses Samson's suppressed rage at those who have colluded against him. His wife is a *heifer,* a young cow, who has bowed to the yoke and served her enemies. "Plowing" does double service as both an agricultural and a sexual metaphor. The common element is penetration, and illicit use of Samson's "property." His opponents in this contest have been progressively redefined, from "thirty companions" (v. 11), to "his wife's people" (vv. 16, 17), to *the men of the town* (here in v. 18). The entire male population of Timnah now stands over against Samson as gloating enemies, aligning themselves with the original thirty. They are men of Timnah; Samson is not, and now never can be. He has alienated them all. They have more than answered his provocation, and it is hard to see how the breach between them and Samson can ever be healed.

In these circumstances, the sudden "rush" of the *Spirit* upon Samson for a second time in verse 19 is a reminder of God's involvement in Samson's life, and the purpose of it. The first onrush of the Spirit in verse 6 set in train the series of events which led to the breach between Samson and the Philistines which has now occurred. The second onrush starts a second, shorter sequence that widens that breach and makes it utterly irreversible. Instead of waiting for his anger to subside, and then coming to some arrangement with his opponents about fulfilling the obligation he has incurred, he acts in a way that can only make him more enemies. *Ashkelon* was a major city in the Philistine heartland, 25 miles (40 km.) west-southwest of Timnah on the Mediterranean seaboard.[70] Samson goes down there, kills thirty men, strips them, and gives their clothes to his opponents back in Timnah in fulfillment of his wager. Nothing could have infuriated the Philistines in both places more, or better served Yahweh's purpose of "seeking an opportunity" against them (v. 3). Like the bare-handed slaughter of the lion, it happens immediately after the Spirit rushes upon Samson, and requires double causation to fully explain it. Samson is an immature, incensed, out-of-control youth; but at the same he is a weapon in God's hand, being propelled relentlessly and unerringly toward his destiny as Israel's savior.

19b-20 Verses 19b and 20 bring partial closure to the narrative at

---

69. Cf. Gen. 1:5b; Josh. 10:12-14.
70. *OBA,* p. 85.

this point. Samson's return to *his father's house* completes, for the time being, the series of movements between there and Timnah that have spanned chapter 14. Furthermore, with the riddle solved and the wager settled, that complex of events, too, appears to have run its course. But Samson doesn't return home as a repentant prodigal. Far from it; his anger still "burns," and we can take it as given that the Philistines of Ashkelon, too, will not meekly let matters rest. There will certainly be a sequel.

Of course, in view of the betrayal that has taken place, Samson's marriage is in ruins, and the chances of recovering it look slim, to say the least. The chapter that began with his demanding to have a Timnite woman ends with his going home without her, leaving her like a piece of abandoned property to be given to another (v. 20).[71] With her return to her people, and Samson's return to his, a space has been opened between the parties in conflict. The first round of Samson's engagement with the Philistines has been completed.

b. Growing Conflict with the Philistines (15:1-8)

1 *After some time, in the days of the wheat harvest, Samson visited his wife with a kid goat. He said, "Let me go in to my wife, to her room." But her father would not permit him to go in.*

2 *Her father said, "I was certain that you thoroughly hated her.[72] So I gave her to one of your companions. Isn't her younger sister better than she? Please take her instead."*

3 *Samson said to them,[73] "This time I am blameless with regard to the Philistines when I bring trouble on them."[74]*

4 *Then Samson went and caught three hundred foxes. He took torches, turned them tail to tail, put a torch between each pair of tails,*

5 *set fire to the torches, and sent them into the Philistines' standing grain. He set fire to the stacked grain and standing grain, the vineyards and olive groves.*

6 *The Philistines said, "Who has done this?" They said, "Samson, the son-in-law of the Timnite, for he took his wife and gave her to his companion." So the Philistines went up and burned her and her father's house[75] with fire.*

---

71. See the footnote to *best man* in the translation of this verse.

72. He had effectively divorced her (Deut. 24:3-4). Cf. Boling, *Judges*, pp. 234-35.

73. LXX^A has *autō*, "Samson said *to himself*." LXX^B agrees with the MT.

74. The LXX, the Vulgate, and one Hebrew MS read "on *you*" (*'immākem*).

75. Reading *bêt 'ābîk* with LXX, Syriac, and many Hebrew MSS instead of the MT's *'ābîhā;* cf. 14:15. The *bêt* has been lost from the MT by haplography after the object marker, *'et*.

7 *Samson said to them, "Since this is how you behave, I will surely avenge myself upon you. Then I will stop."*

8 *So he struck them down, leg on thigh — a great slaughter. Then he went down*[76] *and stayed in the cleft of the Rock of Etam.*[77]

1-2 *After some time* has passed and his temper has cooled, Samson sets out for Timnah again to visit his wife, and with that the narrative starts to move forward again. Positive resonances are set up by the references to *the days of the wheat harvest* (spring time),[78] and the *young goat* that Samson brings with him is presumably a gift for his wife and/or her family.[79] The expression *his wife* implies that Samson thinks the marriage is still intact, despite the period of separation. He seems intent on normalizing the relationship,[80] though whether this would involve taking her back with him to his own father's house is not clear.[81] When he arrives, he uses the same expression as the narrator to assert his right to see her privately: *"Let me go in to my wife, into her room."* The irony, of course, is that we the readers know that she is no such thing (14:20). Samson is about to be disabused of his naïve confidence that he can simply erase the past and start again.

The woman's father refuses point blank to give Samson access, and tells him by way of explanation what we already know: she has been given to one of the young men who were Samson's "companions" at the wedding (v. 2). He had thought, in view of what had happened in connection with the riddle and Samson's subsequent behavior, that Samson *thoroughly hated* her, and made the best of a bad situation by finding her another husband. Samson could hardly blame him. Furthermore, while firmly shutting the door against any undoing of what has been done, the father offers Samson an alternative: the woman's *younger sister,* who is *better than she.*[82] But Samson will not be

76. Some Hebrew MSS and the Syriac read, "he went" *(wayyēlek).* For the significance of the MT's *wayyēred* see the exegetical comments on this verse.

77. The LXX has *para tō cheimarrō en tō spēlaiō Ētam* ("by the brook in/by the Etam cave").

78. The book of Ruth, which opens a window on the peaceful interludes of the judges period, tells a story of courtship and marriage set against the backdrop of the barley harvest. The Pentateuch locates the beginning of the harvesting of grain crops in the springtime (May-June), when the Feast of Weeks was to be celebrated, fifty days after Passover.

79. Cf. 6:19, where Gideon prepares a *young goat* (same expression) to serve to Yahweh's messenger.

80. Cf. the Levite's attempt to seek reconciliation with his estranged concubine in 19:1-3.

81. See the discussion at the beginning of 14:1-20 on the nature of Samson's marriage.

82. Cf. Laban's offer to Jacob in Gen. 29:21-26.

376

placated. He who demanded to have the woman in the first place will not lightly accept her being taken from him. Samson is at odds with the Philistines again, and a second cycle of violence is about to unfold.

3-5   There are some textual uncertainties in verse 3 that make it difficult to know for sure whether Samson is talking to himself or addressing the Philistines.[83] But the substance is clear. He believes he has been badly wronged. Whatever may have been the rights or wrongs of his previous treatment of the Philistines (e.g., his slaughter of thirty of them in Ashkelon, 14:19), *this time (happa'am)* Samson believes he is fully justified in taking vengeance on them. The way he does so is highly original, to say the least!

For a second time we see Samson associating with animals and demonstrating mastery of them. In 14:6 it was a lion; here it is *foxes,* or perhaps jackals,[84] and in verses 15-17 it will be the jawbone of a donkey. It is part of the sustained depiction of Samson as a warrior and wild man (see the comments on 14:5-7), but also as an "Adam-gone-wrong" whose mastery of the animals is violent and exploitative rather than responsible, and in the service of war rather than peace.

Like the bare-handed tearing apart of the lion, the catching, harnessing, and deploying of *three hundred* foxes as incendiary weapons is a feat of such an extraordinary nature that it must either be dismissed as fiction or attributed to a power greater than Samson himself. The issue is more complicated than it was with the lion because here there is no reference to the Spirit of Yahweh rushing on Samson, so divine involvement cannot simply be read off the surface of the narrative. Furthermore, if Samson is driven by anything here, it would seem to be white hot anger and a desire for revenge more than anything else. Nor is Samson fighting for his life here as he was with the lion, so there is no necessity for divine intervention to secure his continued existence and the fulfillment of his destiny. Nevertheless, this feat with the foxes does dramatically escalate the growing conflict with the Philistines, and therefore serves the divine purpose of "seeking an opportunity" against them (14:4). The damage Samson inflicts on the Philistines on this occasion is extensive. He destroys all their *grain* (both *stacked,* awaiting removal to storage, and *standing*), as well as their *vineyards* and *olive groves* (v. 5). Their entire agricultural production in the Timnah area is

83. See the notes to the translation.
84. The English versions sometimes render *šûʿālîm* as "foxes" and sometimes as "jackals," with a preference for the latter in contexts of ruins and dead bodies (Ps. 63:10 [Heb. 11]; Lam. 5:18). Jackals are similar in appearance to foxes, but hunt in packs while foxes typically hunt alone. The association here with destruction, and the large number caught in a (presumably) short time marginally favors "jackals." But the unnaturalness of the whole episode makes such considerations irrelevant, so nothing is to be gained by departing from the traditional translation.

wiped out. Unconventional it may be, but this operation is similar in its effects to the depredations caused by the marauding Midianites back in 6:4.[85] It is in effect a declaration of war.[86] There can be no turning back now; Samson will have to fight the Philistines to death. Given the perfect alignment with God's declared purpose for Samson, and its more-than-human character, we are clearly meant to attribute Samson's remarkable, single-handed devastation of the Philistines to God, whose agent he is. Indeed, the logic of the story from beginning to end requires us to do this, even when (as here) there is no explicit reference to divine agency. As Samson himself will finally affirm in 16:17, the secret of his supernatural strength at every point has been his separation to God.

6-8 News travels quickly in a small town, so by the time the question, *"Who has done this?"* is asked, some already know who *(Samson),* and why (because of what has been done with his wife) (v. 6; cf. v. 2). The situation is similar to that in 6:29 when the men of Ophrah discover the demolished Baal altar: the community as a whole is outraged and want to find the culprit at once and punish him. The unidentified informants (*"They* said") are probably relatives and neighbors who were close enough to witness what had provoked Samson. But there are hints that this has already become more than a family or small-town affair. Those who demand answers are referred to generally as *the Philistines* (contrast "men of Ophrah" in 6:29), and Samson's father-in-law (who remains nameless) is referred to by the informers as *the Timnite,* a descriptive term that would seem to be appropriate only if those asking the question were, or included, people who were from further afield. What has happened is local, but it has stirred the passions of the Philistines more generally. The arena of the conflict, not just its intensity, is rapidly expanding.

The family of *the Timnite* has become a source of trouble for the Philistines. Its domestic affairs have already had disastrous repercussions in Ashkelon, as described in 14:19. Now they have caused trouble again. Better, it seems, to get rid of them root and branch than risk further and possibly worse problems. Determined to act, the Philistines "go up" *(wayyaʿalû),* presumably from one or more of the Philistine cities to the southwest on the coastal plain, and Samson's hapless wife suffers the fate she had desperately tried to avoid in 14:15. They destroy her and her whole family *(father's house)* with *fire,* as Samson had destroyed the Philistine crops. So fire is answered by fire, but it is only a first step. Now Samson himself will have to be dealt with, and that will prove considerably more difficult, for the destruction

---

85. But more localized.

86. Samson and his "three hundred" (v. 4) are reminiscent of Gideon and his unconventional army of the same number.

of his wife and her family has confirmed his belief that the Philistines are wholly evil and roused him to even greater heights of fury against them. There is no question in his mind that he is in the right, and totally justified in continuing his conflict with them. Nor does he hesitate. After a brief declaration of intent (v. 7) he launches an all-out attack (v. 8a).

Pre-battle parley is a common feature of warfare in heroic literature,[87] and is attested elsewhere in Judges (e.g., 20:12-13). The preface to it here in verse 7 *(Samson said to them)* is extremely brief, perhaps reflecting his anger and eagerness for action. In this respect it contrasts strongly with the much longer and more formal exchange with the king of Ammon in 11:12-28, conducted at a distance through messengers. There is no such explanation here of how Samson *said* what he did to the Philistines before attacking them, and, unlike Jephthah, he does not speak for Israel, but purely for himself. Nevertheless, and somewhat surprisingly in view of what we have previously seen of him, there is some evidence of rationality here. What he says has the following elements:

Accusation	*"Since ('im) this is how you behave* [protasis],	Actions have been committed against Samson which require a retributive response.
Oath	*I will surely (kî'im) avenge myself (niqqamtî) upon you* [apodosis: an oath of vengeance].	Samson swears to take the action he is entitled/obliged to take.
Limitation	*Then I will stop."*	Samson's action will not be unrestrained. He will stop when its objective has been achieved.

Vengeance taking *(niqqamtî)* of the kind spoken of here is a principle of justice recognized in Genesis 9:5-6, and given formal expression in the law of Moses. For example, Exodus 21:20: "When a man strikes his slave, male or female, with a rod and the slave dies under his hand, he shall be avenged *(nāqōm yinnāqēm)*" (ESV). Furthermore, if Samson's vow, *"I will surely avenge myself,"* can be taken as shorthand for "take vengeance for the murder of my wife and her family by killing those who did it," then what is in view is the same in substance as what the Mosaic law provides for in material dealing with the rights and obligations of the "avenger of blood" *(gō'ēl haddām)* (Num. 35:19-27; Deut. 19:6-12). To what extent Samson may have known of such provisions, still less been consciously acting in accordance with them,

---

87. As, e.g., in Homer's account of the way the Greek heroes behaved in the Trojan War.

is difficult if not impossible to know.[88] What is clear, though, is that at this point at least Samson shows some capacity to act in a considered and measured way. This is surprising, to say the least, in view of his previous behavior and the extreme provocation he has suffered. It shows that he is beginning to show some of the qualities required in a leader, and prepares the way for the statement in 15:20 and 16:31 that he "judged Israel for twenty years." Samson has begun to grow up.

The clash itself is described just as succinctly as the parley that preceded it (v. 8). The expression *leg on thigh (šôq 'al-yārēḵ)* is clearly idiomatic. It occurs only here, so there is no way of pinning its significance down precisely, though the words themselves and the battle context provide helpful clues. Daniel Block is probably close to the mark with his suggestion that it is "presumably a wrestling idiom for total victory."[89] However, the total victory in this case entailed something far more bloody and permanent than the winning clinch of a wrestling match, namely, *a great slaughter (makkâ gᵉḏôlâ).*[90] No details are given about, for example, the number of the slain (though the word *great* suggests many) or the means Samson used. Again, there is no reference to the Spirit rushing on him. But as in all his battles, he probably fought single-handedly, and since the remarkable outcome served God's purpose a presumption of divine involvement is again reasonable.[91]

The precise location of *Etam* is not known. In 1 Chronicles 4:32 it is referred as a village *(ḥāṣēr)* in the territory of Simeon, which was within Judah according to Joshua 19:1-9. It was later fortified by Jeroboam, and is listed between Bethlehem and Tekoa in 2 Chronicles 11:6, implying a location somewhere in the hill country south of Jerusalem. The most likely site is "in the vicinity of Khirbet el-Khokh . . . about 2 miles [3.5 km.] SW of Bethlehem near the modern village of Artas."[92] The *rock of Etam* was presumably a place well known to the Israelites of the area in Samson's day, and the *cleft (sᵉᶜîp)* in it a cave or fissure in which someone on the run could hide, especially from pursuers (such as the Philistines) who did not know the area as the "natives" did. The fact that Samson *went down (wayyēreḏ)* to it suggests that it was located in a (possibly narrow) valley or dry creek bed, and was therefore not visible from a distance. According to verse 8, Samson withdrew

---

88. He does, however, seem to be aware in 16:17 of some form of the Nazirite traditions enshrined in Num. 6.

89. Block, *Judges, Ruth,* p. 442.

90. Cf. Boling's more colorful description: "a tangle of legs and thighs" (*Judges,* p. 235).

91. See the comments above on vv. 3-5.

92. Wade R. Kotter, "Etam," *ABD* 2:643. Cf. *OBA,* p. 85. Kotter thinks that the biblical data implies there were two Etams, with Khirbet el-Khokh the probable site of only one of them, and that neither should be confused with the Rock of Etam of Judg. 15.

there after the fight and *stayed (wayyēšeḇ)* there for a time. It may have been because of exhaustion and the need for rest, or it may have been a quite deliberate cessation of hostilities on his part in line with his declaration in the previous verse, "Then I will stop." He may have believed he had avenged himself fully on the Philistines for the wrongs they had done him, and now desired only that they would leave him alone.[93] If so, it was a vain hope. The Philistines saw it quite differently, and would not let matters rest.

c. Climax 1: Confrontation and Victory at Lehi (15:9-19)

This important narrative unit is framed by the references to Lehi in verses 9 and 19. It begins with the Philistines arriving and taking up their positions there, and ends with Samson arriving there and killing them in large numbers.

9 *The Philistines went up and camped in Judah. They deployed themselves against Lehi.*

10 *The men of Judah said, "Why have you come up against us?" They said, "We have come up to tie up Samson — to do to him as he has done to us."*

11 *Three thousand men from Judah went down to the cleft of the rock of Etam. They said to Samson, "Don't you know that the Philistines rule over us? Why have you done this to us?" He said to them, "As they have done to me, so I have done to them."*

12 *They said to him, "We have come down to tie you up and hand you over to the Philistines." Samson said to them, "Swear to me that you won't attack me yourselves."*

13 *They said to him, "No, we will just tie you up securely and hand you over to them. We certainly won't kill you." Then they tied him up with two new ropes, and took him up from the rock.*

14 *But when he came to Lehi and the Philistines came shouting to meet him, the Spirit of Yahweh rushed upon him, and the ropes which were on his arms became like flax which has caught fire, and his bonds melted away from his hands.*

15 *He found a fresh jawbone of a donkey, reached out his hand and took it, and struck down a thousand men with it.*

16 *Samson said,*
"With the jawbone of the donkey, [I've made] heap on heap,
with the jawbone of the donkey, I've struck down a thousand men."

93. The paragraph division in the MT at this point (marked by a *samek* in *BHS*) implies the end of a segment of the narrative.

381

17 *When Samson had finished speaking, he threw away the jawbone and called that place Ramath-lehi [Jawbone Hill].*

18 *Then he became very thirsty, and cried out to Yahweh, and said, "You have given this great deliverance by the hand of your servant. Shall I now die of thirst and fall into the hand of the uncircumcised?"*

19 *Then God split open the depression [in the ground] which is at Lehi, and water came out of it. So he drank, his spirit revived, and he lived. So he called it En-hakkore [Caller's Spring], and it is at Lehi to this day.*

9-10 Having apparently concluded that only a concerted effort can solve the Samson problem, the Philistines launch an all-out military assault. They "go up" from their own territory on the coastal plain into the higher country to the east and set up camp in *Judah,* the homeland of Israel's leading tribe (see 1:1-2). It is crisis time; Samson's activities have provoked a confrontation of the first order between Israel and its Philistine enemy. The Philistines "deploy themselves" (take up their positions) in readiness to attack *Lehi,* hoping to find Samson there, or perhaps just to seize and occupy it as a forward base for the next stage of their operations. *Lehi* is short for Ramath-lehi (Jawbone Hill), but the name is anachronistic here, since according to verse 17 the place was called this only after (and because of) the events about to be described.[94] Its exact location is uncertain, but it must have been somewhere between the central highlands and the coastal plain, close to where the territories claimed by the Philistines and Judah intersected. If so, it was roughly along the route of Samson's withdrawal, but about 8 miles (13 km.) short of Etam, where he was hiding (v. 8).[95]

Given the general location where contact is made, the *men of Judah* (*ʾîš yᵉhûḏâ*) who appear in verse 10 are probably militiamen who have been deployed to intercept and repel the invaders. Again we have a standoff, with the opposing sides drawn up and the traditional exchange of words before the battle is joined (cf. v. 7). The Judahites are apparently unaware of Samson's activities, and demand to know why the Philistines have moved against them (v. 10a). The reply is that they have come to *tie up (leʾᵉsôr)* Samson, *to do to*

94. But note the suggestion of F. F. Bruce, "Judges," p. 271: "The place [Lehi] (meaning 'cheek', 'jawbone') may have been so called from the appearance of its crags, and can be identified with modern Khirbet es-Siyyaj ('the ruin of Siyyaj'), where Siyyaj seems to be a loanword from Greek *siagōn* ('jawbone'), which is the rendering of Lehi found in Josephus and some Greek versions of the OT." As with other identifications based on etymology (especially of sacred sites), it is hard to know how much factual basis this one has.

95. It is identified conjecturally as Beit ʿAtab in *OBA,* p. 213 (see the map on p. 85).

him as he has done to us. As far as the Philistines are concerned, Samson has done much more harm to them than they have to him. He cannot be allowed simply to go away without paying for what he has done, and they intend to make sure he doesn't. The "binding" they have in mind (as we are about to see) is quite literal and, because of Samson's great strength, a necessary preliminary to punishing him. "Binding" Samson becomes an obsession which the Philistines pursue through the rest of this chapter and well into the next. They do not finally achieve it until 16:21, where they bind him with bronze shackles, and even then he manages to turn the tables on them. Samson was a very hard man to restrain!

In contrast to "binding," the stated purpose *(to do to him as he has done to us)* is nonspecific. The Philistines can hardly mean that they will literally do to Samson everything he has done to them, and subsequent events bear this out. Rather, it is a general statement of principle: Samson has inflicted suffering and loss on them, so they are justified in doing the same to him. As in conflicts in general, both parties have legitimate grievances and believe their reactions are justified. But the Philistines are doing more here than explaining themselves; they are also issuing a warning. Samson's statement of intent back in verse 7 had an explicit clause of limitation ("Then I will stop"). In the case of the Philistines the limitation is implicit. They have no quarrel with the people of Judah or the Israelites in general. They have crossed into Judah's territory solely to capture and bind Samson so they can take him back with them and punish him appropriately. The men of Judah should let matters take their course rather than inflame the situation and escalate it into an all-out war with the Philistines. They should carefully weigh the cost of defending Samson before going any further. And they don't take long to make up their minds.

11-12a Any deliberations the men of Judah may have had over the issue are passed over in silence, together with any inquiries they may have had to make to determine his whereabouts. In narrated time the action they take in verse 11 follows immediately upon their hearing the ultimatum the Philistines have given them. *Three thousand* of them go down to Samson's hiding place to arrest him and hand him over (v. 12). Whether the "three thousand" is taken at face value, or as an instance of the exaggeration typical of heroic literature, or read as three contingents (about seventy-five men),[96] the implications are the same. The men of Judah are now fully aware of the danger Samson poses, and in view of his great strength they are taking no chances. Just as the Philistines mounted a full-scale military operation to find and bind Samson, so now do the men of Judah who have become their lackeys.

96. See the discussion of the large numbers of Judges in Section IX.C of the Introduction.

But there is one more exchange of words before the fateful action is taken. This time, tragically, it is between representatives of two Israelite tribes (the men of Judah and Samson the Danite) who have effectively become enemies under the pressure that the Philistines have brought to bear on them. Both feel the need to justify their actions, and try to do so. The men of Judah accuse Samson of acting irresponsibly: *"Don't you know that the Philistines rule over us?"* (v. 11a). As they see it, Samson has endangered them all by provoking the Philistines needlessly, without regard for the realities of the situation and the likely consequences of his actions. But Samson is unrepentant: *"As they have done to me, so I have done to them"* (v. 11b). He has only defended his rights and honor. What self-respecting man, Israelite or otherwise, would not do the same?[97] Whether intended or not, this is a cutting indictment of the men of Judah who, at this moment, are acting cravenly by giving in to Philistine pressure and doing what is expedient rather than what is just. Of course the situation is more complex than this. Neither the men of Judah nor Samson is wholly in the right or in the wrong. Nor are any of them aware of the hidden hand of God in the course of events that they are all caught up in. But if honor is an issue, none of them come off very well. This is a day of shame, not just for Samson and those who have come to arrest him, but for Israel as a whole.

We have come to a point in Judges where to fully grasp the significance of what is happening we need to reflect on how the book opened. There a united Israel inquired of Yahweh about how they should proceed in carrying out the mandate Joshua had given them to complete the conquest of Canaan. The answer was that the tribe of Judah should lead them, and that if it did so, victory was assured (1:1-2). Now here in chapter 15 there is no seeking direction from God and no victory. Israel's subjection to the Philistines is accepted as an established fact. There is no cry for deliverance. The only person who fights the Philistines is Samson, and he does so only when his attempt to intermarry with them is thwarted. And although he is destined eventually to begin to save Israel, the men of Judah (yes, Judah!) see him only as a threat to the status quo, and arrest him in order to hand him over to their Philistine masters. What a fall there has been from the expectations with which the book began! The whole downward spiral of the central part of the book reaches rock bottom here. Surely only a remarkable act of God can save Israel now.

12b-13 Samson's submission to his betrayers is full of pathos. He has no desire to fight his fellow Israelites, but neither does he trust them, and fears what may happen if he is forced to defend himself against them. (He is beginning to fear his own strength.) So he negotiates terms of surrender. He makes them swear not to attack him themselves (v. 12b). Then, like a man

97. Certainly not the Philistines! See v. 10.

reconciled to what must be, he allows them to bind him *securely* with *two new ropes* (they don't trust *him* either) and take him out of hiding to meet his fate. *New ropes (ʿăbōṯîm ḥăḏāšîm)* will appear again in 16:11, in another episode of betrayal, and in retrospect we will see that it is not the ropes that bind Samson here, but something deeper: a sense of hopelessness, perhaps, or the awareness of a destiny he is powerless to resist.

14-19   Now things take an unexpected turn, and the pace suddenly picks up again. There is no prisoner transfer of the kind we were expecting, and the men of Judah simply disappear, as of no further interest to the narrator. Instead, God himself suddenly takes charge of the prisoner, and all attention is focused on him. It is *he*[98] (Samson) who arrives back at Lehi where Philistines are waiting. His captors are invisible, like the "nobodies" they have become.

In its basic elements what follows is like a replay of Samson's fight with the lion in the vineyards of Timnah:

14:5-6	*15:14-19*
A lion comes "roaring" *to meet him.*	The Philistines come "shouting" *to meet him.*
The Spirit of Yahweh rushes upon him.	*The Spirit of Yahweh rushes upon him.*
He "tears" the lion in two.	He "strikes down" the Philistines.

The central reality in both cases is the Spirit's sudden seizure of Samson. So there is no point in asking whether what Samson now does at Lehi is humanly possible, any more than what he did at Timnah was. It is simply not that kind of thing. This is another moment when God breaks in like a rushing wind and makes the impossible happen.

The events at Timnah and Lehi, then, have the same basic character. But there is a vast difference in the way they are treated. The first is dealt with in summary form, with a minimum of artistry. The second is narrated in much more detail, with wordplays, embedded discourse (a monologue), a couple of lines of verse (a victory song), and two acts of naming to mark the event's enduring significance. What we have here in 15:14-19 is not just another incident in Samson's hectic career, but the crashing climax of the whole train of events that was set in motion by his trip to Timnah and demand to have a Philistine wife at the beginning of chapter 14.

---

98. The pronoun *he (hû')* is in the emphatic first position in the clause. It is "Samson" who arrives, not the men of Judah and their prisoner.

14   The *shouting* of the Philistines, like the "roaring" of the lion back in 14:5, expresses not just excitement (Samson is a great prize; they can hardly wait to get their hands on him), but predation. Samson's enemies are aroused, and he must fight them or be devoured by them. Moreover, the odds are overwhelmingly stacked against him. He is a solitary man facing an army, and he is unarmed. Not only does he hold nothing in his hands, but his *hands* and *arms* are bound so that he cannot use them. In keeping with the dramatic nature of the presentation, we are given more detail here than in verse 13. The *ropes* (*ʿᵃḇōṯîm*) are around his arms, and for added security *bonds* (*ʾᵉsûrîm*) have been placed on his hands, perhaps tying them together behind his back. If he is to fight at all, he must first be freed — which is the first effect of the sudden "onrush" *(tiṣlaḥ)* of the *Spirit (rûaḥ) of Yahweh*. The basic image is of wind, as suggested by both the "rushing" and the word *rûaḥ* (wind, breath, spirit). But there is also fire.[99] When the Spirit rushes upon him, his bonds *burn* like flax in a fire *(bāʾēš),* and the bonds *melt* off his hands. The men of Judah had intended to hand Samson over to his enemies, but Yahweh has freed him to fight them.

15-17   This important unit is framed by Samson's finding a *jawbone of a donkey* in verse 15, and his naming a place after it — *Ramath-lehi* [*Jawbone Hill*] — in verse 17. The intervening material tells what he did with it. His conflict with the Philistines, which has been developing in stages through the whole of chapters 14 and 15, reaches a climax here, and a resolution of sorts. Samson's victory is so comprehensive that his dominance over the Philistines is established and he effectively replaces the men of Judah as Israel's divinely authorized leader. He is another, but greater, "Shamgar" (3:31).

In view of the explicit intervention of God in verse 14, Samson's "finding" *(wayyimṣāʾ)* of the jawbone must be seen, not as fortuitous, but as providential. As with Abraham's "looking up and seeing" a ram caught in a thicket, what Samson "finds" is God's timely provision for his need. As if in recognition of this (though perhaps just with surprise and relief at this moment) he "reaches out" *(wayyišlaḥ)* one of his freed hands and takes hold of it. For the third time in chapters 14 and 15 Samson reaches into the animal world and conscripts them into his service. First he killed a lion and drew honey from its carcass (14:5-9). Then he caught foxes and used them as fire-

---

99. In fact, "the Samson story abounds in fire images — the flame in which the announcing angel ascends to heaven, the fire that consumes Samson's wife, the torches bound to the fox-tails that carry conflagration through the Philistine fields, the cords binding Samson that snap like flax in flame — so that fire is at once associated with the powerful destructive energy he exerts and with the destruction he courts." Alter, *Samson without Folklore,* pp. 50-51. Cf. the conjunction of wind/Spirit and fire on the day of Pentecost (Acts 2:2-3).

wielding agents of his vengeance (15:4-5). Now he takes the jawbone of a donkey and uses it to kill his enemies. Under the influence of the Spirit he exercises dominion over the animals: even in death they serve him! Again there are traces here of the dominion originally given to Adam (see the comments on previous two passages), and this time there is no question of his misusing that dominion. The donkey (represented by the jawbone) is reclaimed from death to serve God's purposes through Samson. In his hand it becomes a mighty weapon.

The word *fresh* (*ṭᵉrîyâ*) suggests that the jawbone was not yet dried out and brittle, and was therefore less likely to break in Samson's hand.[100] It would also, of course, probably be damp and bloody, and therefore a gruesome object, and — like the lion's carcass of 14:8-9 — unsuitable in normal circumstances for a Nazirite to use, or even touch (Num. 6:6; cf. Judg. 13:7). But these were not normal circumstances, and, as we have noted, the provision of this particular jawbone was providential. It would therefore be reading against the whole tenor of the text to suggest that Samson was at fault in taking up this jawbone, any more than the priest Ahimelech later was in taking the consecrated loaves and giving them to David and his men to eat (1 Sam. 21:1-6; Mark 2:26). Some things are simply more important than others!

The casualty count, *a thousand men* (*'elep 'îš*), at the end of verse 15 is the bridge into Samson's exultant victory song in the following verse. The roundness of the number and the ambiguity of the term *'elep*, would permit the reduction of the traditional "thousand" men to "a [whole] contingent," about twenty-five men.[101] But the descriptive expression, "heap on heap," in verse 16 favors the traditional rendering of *'elep* as "a thousand," even if (as seems likely) it is an approximation. This is entirely in keeping with the convention, in heroic literature, of depicting champions and their exploits as larger than life. The difference here is that the superhuman quality of this hero's achievements is attributed to the onrush of the Spirit of Yahweh (v. 14). In other words, the real hero is not Samson but Yahweh, who really *is* "larger than life" (at least life as we normally experience it) and not limited by the weakness of those he chooses to use.

16 The singing of a joyful song in response to a great victory achieved with God's help is a tradition reflected classically in the Old Testament by the Song at the Sea (Exod. 15) and within the book of Judges itself by the Song of Deborah and Barak (Judg. 5). Samson's song is much briefer — just a single verse of two lines:

100. Boling, *Judges,* p. 239.
101. Boling, *Judges,* p. 237. See the discussion of the large numbers of Judges in Section IX.C of the Introduction.

bilḥî haḥ^amôr/	*"With the jawbone of the donkey/*
ḥ^amôr ḥ^amōrāṯāyim	*[I've made] heap on heap,*
bilḥî haḥ^amôr/	*with the jawbone of the donkey/*
hikkêṯî 'elep 'îš	*I've struck down a thousand men."*

The two lines have two cola each, with a strong, rising 2-2//2-3 rhythm, and exhibit the parallelism typical of classical Hebrew verse. The first parts of the two lines are identical. The cryptic second half of the first line, *"[I've made] heap on heap,"*[102] is interpreted by the corresponding part of the second line, *"I've struck down a thousand men."* The effectiveness of the whole is enhanced by assonance (e.g., *î, im, î, 'îš*), and a play on the two meanings of *ḥ^amôr* ("donkey" and "heap"). In contrast to Exodus 15 and Judges 5, this song makes no reference to God. That comes later, in verse 18, when Samson's excitement has passed and a more sober grasp of reality has taken hold. But given the fact that acknowledgment of God is close at hand, it is probably best to read the song of verse 16, not fundamentally as a piece of boasting, but as an expression of sheer astonishment at what has happened.[103] Samson finds it just as hard to believe as we do!

17 In view of the rhythmic, poetic quality of the previous verse, *speaking (dabbēr)* seems to be a very understated way of referring to what Samson has been doing! It does, however, nicely reflect the change of tempo and mood as we move from the song itself to what follows.[104] Exhausted at last, Samson throws the jawbone away (it has served its purpose), but then, almost as an afterthought, reclaims it from oblivion by incorporating it into a name for the place where all this happened: *Ramath-lehi* (Jawbone Hill).[105] *Lehi,* the shorter form of the same name, has occurred anachronistically in verses 9 and 14, but now the full form of the name identifies this as the actual moment when it was coined.[106] The story of "Jawbone Hill" is almost fin-

---

102. An almost identical form of the same expression occurs in Exod. 8:10 (Eng. 14): "heaps and heaps *(ḥ^omārim ḥ^omārim)* of frogs."

103. Contrast the song of Lamech in Gen. 4:23-24, which is pure boasting with no accompanying acknowledgment of God.

104. The *wayyō'mer (said)* at the beginning of verse 16 has a similar bland quality, but by the time we get to the end of the verse it has been colored and filled out by the content of the song itself. What follows the *ledabbēr* of v. 17, however, is of an entirely different kind, and does not condition the introductory verb in the same way.

105. Block (*Judges, Ruth,* p. 446) takes *Ramath-lehi* to refer, not to the place in general, but to a mound Samson made with the corpses of the Philistines. But this is unlikely in view of the use of the term *māqôm,* "place," to designate what is named.

106. The name does not occur before Judg. 15, and occurs again only in 2 Sam. 23:11 with reference to the exploits of one of David's mighty men. The bestowal of the name occurs only in Judg. 15:17.

ished, but not quite. There is to be one more development, and like a rabbit produced suddenly from a hat, it will turn out to be the most significant thing of all, and the true climax of the passage.

18-19 With his strength spent, Samson becomes acutely aware of the fact that, in spite of what has just happened, he is not a superman but a real man with real needs. He is *thirsty,* so much so that he fears he will *die of thirst* (v. 18). But there is something he fears more than dying. To *fall into the hand of the uncircumcised*[107] would effectively mean to surrender himself in death to the Philistines, and allow them to misrepresent everything that has happened by taking his body home and displaying it as proof that they had vanquished Samson instead of he them (cf. 1 Sam. 31:8-10). For Samson to die of thirst here, now, would be to lose more than his life; it would be to lose everything. So in his extremity, Samson "cries out" *(wayyiqrā')* to Yahweh, and with that we have reached a moment of great significance.

"Crying out to Yahweh" has been part of the repeating pattern of the book from the account of the first judge onward (3:9, 15; 4:3; 6:6, 7; 10:12). Only here, in the Samson story, has it not occurred — until now.[108] In Samson's day Israel had lost its voice because it had lost all hope of deliverance. Samson, and only he, cries out, first here in 15:18, and again in 16:28. He cries out for himself, of course, lest he fall into Philistine hands. But there is an added dimension that closer attention reveals. The expression *this great deliverance (hatteṣû'â)* echoes the words spoken to his mother before he was born: "he will begin to save [i.e., deliver, *leĥôṣîa'*] Israel" (13:5). Furthermore, Samson acknowledges that he has been Yahweh's *servant*[109] and that the deliverance he speaks about has been brought about *by* his (Samson's) *hand (beyad-'abdeĥā).* In other words, Samson recognizes himself as the agent, not just the object, of the "great deliverance" God has brought about. It is the first hint that he has begun to recognize the larger significance of his conflict with the Philistines. It is not just Samson's life and honor that are at stake here, but Israel's bondage to the Philistines, and God has begun to do something about that through Samson, his *servant.* Of course it is impossible to know how much of this was present to Samson's mind at the time. Perhaps he spoke better than he knew,[110] but this is certainly the implication of the words he uttered. Aware of it or not, this is one of Samson's finest moments.

107. See the comments on 14:3, including footnotes.

108. In the case of Samson *qr'* is used rather than the *z'q* of 3:9 etc., but there is no semantic difference; both refer to a cry for help.

109. Cf. Josh. 1:1, where the same term is used of Moses.

110. Block (*Judges, Ruth,* p. 447) thinks that his motives were purely self-serving and hypocritical, especially his reference here to the Philistines as *the uncircumcised:* "Where was this sensitivity to contamination when his parents had protested his desire to marry one of these uncircumcised?" But *the uncircumcised* may be used here simply as a

Verse 19 describes God's response. Samson's cry is heard and answered at once. The term *hammaktēš*, which I have translated as *the depression [in the ground]*, is a rare word, and of uncertain meaning in this context. There are only two other occurrences in the Old Testament: Zephaniah 1:11, where it is a place-name, and Proverbs 27:22, where it is a bowl for crushing grain. Whatever its precise meaning here in Judges 15:19, it is the source from which a spring suddenly emerges. If there had ever been a spring there before, nothing remained of it but a dried-out hollow in the ground. But in answer to Samson's cry it broke open again, and Samson's life was saved: *he drank, his spirit revived, and he lived.* Like Israel in the wilderness, Samson has been saved by the provision of miraculous water. The naming of the spring *En-hakkore [Caller's Spring]* underscores the significance of the moment and memorializes it for future generations. The fact it was *still there at Lehi* in that writer's day suggests that it was a spring that never ran dry, and became the symbol of a profound truth. However bleak things may be, there is always hope for those who "call" on Yahweh — including Israel, and us![111]

d. Epilogue (15:20)

20 *He judged Israel in the days of the Philistines for twenty years.*

This formal notice stands outside the frame of the Lehi episode of verses 9-19 and marks the end of the whole first phase of Samson's career that spans chapters 14 and 15. It does more than this, however. It tells us that as a consequence of what has gone before (especially the "great deliverance" that happened at Lehi) Samson effectively replaced the men of Judah as Israel's leader, and was recognized as such by his compatriots. He became Israel's judge (in the sense that term has in Judges), and exercised leadership in that capacity for twenty years. By being where it is, this notice confirms that the Lehi episode of verses 9-19 was a kind of rite of passage for Samson, a moment of self-understanding and of his identity as Yahweh's servant which was indispensable for his transition to judgeship. However, the phrase *in the days of the Philistines* is a reminder of his limitations, even in this high office. He will not deliver Israel in the full sense that the other judges have done. His judgeship will both begin and end *in the days of the Philistines.* He will not bring their oppression of Israel to an end, but he will "begin" to end it (13:5). Others will have to complete what Samson begins.

---

derogatory term reflecting Samson's very changed view of the Philistines in light of all he has now experienced of them. Block's negative interpretation is hard to square with the reference to Samson as a hero of faith in Heb. 11:32.

111. Joel 2:32; Rom. 10:13.

This notice occurs again, in a slightly different form, at 16:31, and we will reserve further comment on it until then.

3. Samson's Career, Part 2: From Gaza to Gaza (16:1-31)

The second phase of Samson's career begins with his going to Gaza (16:1), and ends (apart from a brief epilogue) with his dying there in the temple of Dagon (16:23-30). In between he escapes from Gaza (v. 3), but he is eventually caught and taken there again (v. 21). Gaza lay close to the coast approximately 13 miles (21 km.) south of Ashkelon, deep in Philistine territory.[112] The way it features in verses 23-30 reflects its importance as the chief city of the Philistine pentapolis,[113] and therefore the logical place for Samson's final confrontation with the Philistines to take place. In chapter 16 as a whole it functions as a kind of magnetic pole to which Samson is irresistibly drawn. It is the place of his destiny.

a. Samson and the Prostitute (16:1-3)

Gateless in Gaza

This is a brief unit, but its significance should not be underestimated. Robert Alter has noted that in chapters 14–16 "Samson passes through a series of three women who mark the spectrum of female sexual partners — wife, whore, and mistress (see Vickery)," and that this consists of three episodes with an ABA pattern: "two protracted involvements sandwiching a one-night stand."[114] In view of this, 16:1-3 can be seen as the pivot on which the entire account of Samson's adult life turns. We have already noted how it triggers the second phase of Samson's career. It also serves as a backdrop to his affair with Delilah, and contributes to the motifs of Samson's great strength, and his sightedness and blindness, both of which are key elements of the thematic texture of chapter 16 as a whole.

1 *Samson went to Gaza, where he saw a woman who was a prostitute and went in to her.*

112. See *OBA*, p. 15.
113. In pre-Israelite times it had been the capital of the Egyptian province of Canaan. See H. J. Katzenstein, "Gaza," *ABD* 2:912-15. It has given its name to the whole Palestinian territory known today as the Gaza Strip.
114. "Samson without Folklore," p. 48. The article by Vickery to which he refers is J. B. Vickery, "In Strange Ways: The Story of Samson," in *Images of Man and God: Old Testament Short Stories in Literary Focus,* ed. B. O. Long (Sheffield: Almond, 1981), pp. 58-73.

2 *The people of Gaza [were told],*[115] *"Samson has come here." So they surrounded [the place],*[116] *and lay in wait for him all night*[117] *at the city gate. They kept quiet all night, thinking, "[We'll wait] until dawn breaks, and then kill him."*

3 *Samson lay down until the middle of the night, and then got up in the middle of the night. He grasped the doors of the city gate and the two doorposts. He pulled them up, along with the bar, put [them] on his shoulders, and took them up to the top of the hill that is opposite Hebron.*

1 The continuation of the narrative after the victory at Lehi, and especially after the formal closure made in 15:20, is unexpected, and is part of the reason why chapter 16 has often been viewed as secondary.[118] Secondary or not, however, chapter 16 is part of the narrative as we have it, so our task here is to consider how it functions, especially in relation to what precedes it.

While the wording is not identical, this chapter begins very similarly to chapter 15: Samson "goes" (in ch. 14 he "goes down"), and "sees . . . a woman." We are apparently at the beginning of another phase of Samson's career that will be similar in some respects to the previous one. This is a reasonable expectation, and what follows confirms that it is a right one. To grasp the full significance of chapter 16, we must read it with chapters 14–15 constantly in mind, but the differences will turn out to be just as significant as the similarities. We have already seen a striking example of this in the two major phases of Gideon's career (chs. 6–7, and ch. 8 respectively). In fact, repetition with variation is intrinsic to the structure of Judges as a whole.

One way the relationship between the present chapter of Judges and the preceding two has been understood is represented by the LXX, which has *ekeithen* in verse 1: "And Samson went *from there* [Lehi] to Gaza." That is, he went to Gaza directly after his defeat of the Philistines at Lehi. In terms of the syntax of the passage, this is perfectly reasonable. In the underlying Hebrew, the clauses of 15:19–16:1 are linked in the normal way for a continu-

---

115. The verb is missing in the MT, which begins this verse abruptly with *laʿazzātîm*, "to the Gazites." The translation follows the LXX, which opens the verse with *kai apēngelē* (= Heb. *wayyuggaḏ*), "it was told/reported." Cf. NIV and most other English versions.

116. Implied. Literally just, *they surrounded (wayyāsōbbû).*

117. *BHS* recommends reading *kol-hayyôm* (all day) here, to complement the *kol-hallaylâ* (all night) of the second half of the verse. But the verse makes sense as it stands, and the proposed emendation lacks any hard evidence to support it.

118. So, e.g., Boling, *Judges,* pp. 29-38, who sees 16:1–18:31 and 19:1-21 as part of a two-stage expansion of an earlier form of Judges that consisted of only 2:6–15:20. See the comments on the history of the formation of Judges in Section III of the Introduction.

ous narrative.[119] There are two problems with this reading, however. First, it is unlikely that Samson, directly after praying that he would not fall into the hands of the Philistines (15:18), would go to Gaza, one of their major cities. Second, and more telling, is the fact that 16:1 does not follow directly after the Lehi episode of 15:9-19, but after the notice about Samson judging Israel for twenty years in 15:20. In contrast to the LXX, the standard Hebrew text (the MT) recognizes the importance of this by leaving a paragraph break between 15:20 and 16:1.[120] The implication is that Samson's going to Gaza did not occur directly after the Lehi episode, but toward the end of his twenty-year judgeship. By this time the relationship between Israel and the Philistines may have cooled sufficiently for him to go to Gaza, with appropriate caution, and if he had reason to do so, just as he had been able to go to Timnah at the beginning of chapter 14. This makes much better sense, and is the way the relationship between the present chapter and the preceding two will be understood in what follows. Samson's going to Gaza happened late in his twenty-year judgeship, and sparked a second cycle of conflict with the Philistines that brought his rule as judge (and his life) to an end.

We are not told why Samson went to Gaza, whether officially (as Israel's judge) or for purely personal reasons. Nor are we told whether he went openly, or covertly, like Gideon going down into the Midianite camp in 7:8b-14. The way the Philistines react when they are informed of his presence (v. 2) certainly suggests that his visit was unexpected. What the text clearly implies, however, is that he did not go to Gaza with the express intention of visiting a prostitute. The sequence of events is the same as in 14:1: he *went,* and (while he was there) he *saw* a woman. The "seeing" in both cases is literal (with his eyes), not metaphorical (visited, had intimate relations with). His "seeing" in the latter sense is conveyed by a second verb: he *went in* to her. It may have begun by simply entering her house, perhaps to hide,[121] but (knowing Samson as we do) probably went further. This kind of "seeing" corresponds to his demanding to have the woman he had "seen" in Timnah as his wife in 14:2; it follows on, as a sequel, to "seeing" her in the normal sense. There are echoes in both places of the seeing, taking, and eating of Genesis 3:6. Samson was taking a risk in going to Gaza at all. But he increased the risk exponentially by following his eyes and "going in" to the prostitute. It was a relapse (a "fall," we might say) into the kind of immature and irresponsible behavior that had brought him into conflict with the Philistines in the first place.

---

119. A sequence of *wayyiqtol* verb forms. The only aside is for the conferral of the name Ramath-lehi in v. 19b.
120. Represented by a strong paragraph marker *(pēh)* in *BHS*.
121. Like the Israelite spies of Josh. 2:1.

2-3 Samson has already been betrayed by his wife (14:17), and by the men of Judah (15:12). Now he is betrayed by informers who have seen him go into the harlot's house (v. 2). Those they alert to his presence are described as *the people of Gaza ('azzātîm)*. The expression is general, but can hardly refer to the inhabitants of Gaza as a whole, since when *they* respond by setting an ambush and lying in wait for Samson, it is clearly a particular group who are in view, presumably the leading men of the city or their representatives. The fact that they are called "Gazites," however, suggests that those who betrayed Samson to them on this occasion were not Gazites themselves, but resident aliens, as David and his men were (in Gath, another Philistine city) at a later time (1 Sam. 27). Whoever they were, they must have felt that it was in their interests to side with the Gazites against Samson, and effectively handed him over to his enemies as the men of Judah had done. The men of Judah did it openly, by binding Samson. These do it secretly, by telling the Gazites of his whereabouts.

The debacle at Lehi has taught the Philistines the need for caution. There is no shouting this time, or headlong rush as there was in 15:14, but careful planning. A double trap is set for Samson, around *the place* (house) he has gone into,[122] and at *the city gate,* which was presumably the only way out of Gaza. Then they lie in wait for him *all night* in readiness to take him at first light, when he will be deprived of the cover of darkness but still drowsy and sated, they hope, from his night's activities. But Samson takes them by surprise. He shares the prostitute's bed only until midnight, then rises. Has he heard something that has made him uneasy, or had it always been his plan to slip out in the dead of night as a precaution? We are not told. But at some point (after coming out of the house if not before) he must have realized that he was being watched, and decided to leave Gaza at once. And since there is only one way out, and secrecy is no longer possible, Samson goes to the opposite extreme. He doesn't just break through Gaza's gates, but takes them with him! The Philistines, who had thrown a double cordon around him, are not even mentioned. The narrator, like Samson, treats them with utter contempt. When Samson is aroused, it is as if they and all their carefully made plans are reduced to nothing. Samson leaves the Gazites, like their city — breached, broken, and utterly humiliated.

The detail with which the gate is described — its *doors,* its *two doorposts,* and its *bar* — imply that it was substantial. If it conformed to the normal pattern of Canaanite city gates of the period, it would also have had six guard posts, three on each side of a passage leading to the doors themselves.[123]

---

122. See the note on the translation at this point.

123. See the diagram of a typical Canaanite/Israelite city gate in Block, *Judges, Ruth,* p. 450.

It would have been a formidable barrier, especially when fully manned. But Samson has spent all his life breaching barriers: between the permissible and the forbidden, holy and profane, man and animal, Israelite and Philistine, Naziriteship and normality. Barriers have never been able to contain him. They appear to him only as challenges which rouse him to a renewed frenzy of breaking through. So it is here again. His "grasping," "pulling," "putting," and "taking" (v. 3) transgress the boundary between the possible and impossible, the human and superhuman. No normal person could do what he did. But Samson is not normal; that is his glory and his torment. The Philistines will never be able to contain him until they discover the secret of his great strength and find a way to neutralize it. That is the message for the Philistines here, and we will see in what follows how they respond to it.

However, there is also a message here for the people of Judah, especially their leaders, and it is conveyed by what Samson did with Gaza's gates after he uprooted them: *he put [them] on his shoulders and took them up to the top of the hill that is opposite Hebron* (v. 3). Hebron (formerly known as Kiriath-arba) was situated in the central hill country 39 miles (62.5 km.) east of Gaza and 927 meters above sea level.[124] It was the highest town in Palestine. It had been conquered by Caleb and given to him as a family possession (Judg. 1:20). David was later anointed there as king of Judah, and two years later as king of Israel (2 Sam. 2:4; 5:3). It remained the capital city for seven and a half years (2 Sam. 5:5). In Samson's day it was already the leading city of Judah.[125] The route from Gaza to Hebron was uphill all the way. The unnamed hill *opposite Hebron* must have been to the west, on the last ridge before Hebron itself.

As a feat of strength, Samson's shouldering the gates of Gaza and carrying them all the way up to Hebron surpasses, if anything, his uprooting them in the first place. It is a labor of truly Herculean proportions. And it is performed with such deliberateness that it cannot fail to be significant — for Samson himself, and for the development of this final phase of his career. For some reason Samson wanted to show himself to the people of *Hebron* in this way, exhausted but triumphant, with Gaza's gates on his shoulders. They are a war trophy, the proof of a victory. They announce that Samson has opened a new round of conflict with the Philistines, and say to the people of Hebron, the leading city of Judah, that this time there will be no craven capitulation; no binding of Samson to hand him over. It is not a rallying call, like Ehud's trumpet blast in 3:27, for Samson has never been a leader of men. He will fight the Philistines alone, in his own way, and beat them. The people of Hebron stare at him across the valley with a mixture of awe and dread. There will never be peace with the Philistines while this man lives.

124. See *OBA*, p. 85.
125. F. F. Bruce, "Hebron," *NBD*, pp. 471-72.

b. Samson and Delilah (16:4-22)

This deservedly famous passage brings us to the last of Samson's affairs with women. It is in the nature of a fatal character flaw that it exposes the person who has it to danger again and again, until it finally destroys him. After what happened at Gaza Samson has every reason to avoid the Philistines, or approach them only with extreme caution and thorough preparation. But that is not how Samson operates. Nor is it the way God uses him. He is moved much more by powerful urges than by rational thought and careful planning, and his conflict with the Philistines always arises as a by-product of something else. He sees the Philistine women and finds them irresistible, and goes to them again and again, reckless of danger and sober responsibility. And now he does so for what will be his last time. This passage has an aura of déjà vu about it. But there are important differences this time that seal Samson's fate and bring the repeating cycle of his life to an end.

4 *Afterward he loved a woman in the valley of Sorek whose name was Delilah.*

5 *The lords of the Philistines came up to her and said to her, "Cajole him and find out how he has such great strength, and how we can overcome him and tie him up so that we can torment him,*[126] *and we will each give you eleven hundred [pieces] of silver."*

6 *So Delilah said to Samson, "Please tell me how you have such great strength, and how you can be tied up so that someone could torment you."*

7 *Samson said to her, "If they were to tie me up with seven fresh cords which have not been dried, then I would become weak, and would be like any [other] man."*

8 *So the lords of the Philistines brought up to her seven fresh cords which had not been dried, and she tied him up with them.*

9 *While they lay in wait for her in the inner room, she said to him, "The Philistines are upon you, Samson!" But he snapped the strings as a strand of fiber is snapped when it comes near fire. So [the secret of] his strength remained unknown.*

10 *Delilah said to Samson, "See how you have mocked me and told me lies! Now please tell me how you may be tied up."*

11 *He said to her, "If they were to tie me up fast with new ropes with which no work had been done, then I would become weak and would be like any [other] man."*

126. That is, "to afflict him" *(leʿannōtô),* but the stronger translation is fully justified by the context. Cf. Alter, "Samson," p. 53, who translates it as "to torture him." The expression is repeated by Delilah in v. 6.

12   *So Delilah took new ropes and tied him up with them. She said to him,*
"The Philistines are upon you, Samson!" Now they were lying in wait
in the inner room, but he snapped the ropes off his arms like a thread.

13   *Delilah said to Samson, "Until now you have mocked me and told me*
lies. Tell me how you may be tied up." He said to her, "If you were to
weave the seven locks of my head into the web [and fasten it with the
pin, then I would become weak and be like any (other) man." So
Delilah put him to sleep and wove the seven locks of his head into the
web,][127]

14   *and fastened it with the pin, and said to him, "The Philistines are*
upon you, Samson!" He woke from his sleep and pulled up the pin, the
loom, and the web.

15   *She said to him, "How can you say, 'I love you,' when your heart is*
not with me? This is now three times you have mocked me, and not
told me how you have such great strength."

16   *When she had worn him down with her words day after day, and pres-*
sured him, he became exasperated to the point of death

17   *and told her all his heart. He said to her, "No razor has ever come*
upon my head, for I have been a Nazirite of God from my mother's
womb. If I were to be shaved, then my strength would depart from me,
and I would become weak and be like every other man."

18   *When Delilah saw that he had told her everything that was in his*
heart, she sent and summoned the lords of the Philistines, saying,
"Come up at once, for he has told me everything that was in his
heart." So the lords of the Philistines went up to her and brought their
money with them.

19   *She put him to sleep on*[128] *her knees, and called a man*[129] *who shaved*
off the seven locks of his head. Then she began to torment him,[130] *and*
his strength departed from him.

127. The words in this set of brackets are restored from the LXX, which almost
certainly preserves the original text. The scribe's eye appears to have moved inadvertently
from the first occurrence of *hammassāket* (the web) to the second, resulting in the loss of
all the intervening words. This follows the recommendation of the MT apparatus, except
that I have ignored LXX's *eis ton toichon* (to the wall), because if this were an original
part of the MT, we would expect some reference to it in what follows in v. 14. Cf. the English versions in general.

128. The *BHS* apparatus recommends reading *bên* (between), in line with the *ana
meson* of LXX[A]. However, LXX[B], which has *epi* (on), supports the MT.

129. I assume that the lengthening of the vowel of the preposition in *lā'îš* is because *'îš* is a one-syllable word, rather than because it is definite.

130. The LXX has *ērxato tapeinousthai*, "and he began to be humbled/brought
low" *(= wattāḥel lē'ānôt).*

20 *She said, "The Philistines are upon you, Samson!" He woke up from his sleep, and said [to himself], "I will go forth as before and shake myself free." But he didn't realize that Yahweh had departed from him.*

21 *The Philistines seized him and gouged out his eyes. They took him down to Gaza and bound him with bronze fetters, and he ground [grain] in the prison.*[131]

22 *But the hair of his head began to grow again after it had been shaved.*

4 The *valley of Sorek* forms a natural access corridor between the coastal plain and the high country around Jerusalem. Today a railway line ascends through it. In Samson's day it was the crossover point between Israelite and Philistine territory, with the Danite villages of Zorah and Eshtaol just north of it, and Timnah (where a Philistine woman first caught Samson's attention) and Ekron, the northernmost city of the Philistine pentapolis, just south of it.[132] So with Samson in the valley of Sorek here in verse 4, the story of his life has come full circle; he is back in the vicinity of Timnah where his troubles with the Philistines began. The opening expression, *Afterward (ʾaḥᵃrê kēn),* both links what he does here with what has gone before, and separates it from it. Enough time has passed for Samson's rage against the Philistines to settle and his attraction to their women to reassert itself, so he begins to flirt with danger yet again. If his experience in Gaza contributes anything to what he does now, it may be by enabling him to think (foolishly) that he is invincible.

The first major difference from Samson's previous affairs with women is that this time the woman is named. The meaning of the name *Delilah (dᵉlîlâ)* — if it has one — is uncertain. Boling relates it to the Arabic *dallatum,* "flirt," and hence "flirtatious."[133] Younger thinks it more likely to be related to a class of names derived from Akkadian *dalālum,* "to praise, glorify," which is widely attested in ancient Near Eastern sources contemporary with the Old Testament (Ludlul-Sin, Adalal-Sin, Dilīl-Adad, etc.).[134] Both are possible, but neither is certain, and other, older suggestions (e.g., "languishing," "delicate") have not proved convincing either.[135] More significant for our purposes is the sound of the name and the echoes it produces in its present context. "Delilah" *(dᵉlîlâ)* sounds very similar to *hallaylâ,* the Hebrew word for "night," which has occurred four times in verses 2 and 3 in connection with Samson's visit to the prostitute in Gaza. With Delilah darkness starts to close around Samson again, and another trap that the Philistines will set for him. And this time he

---

131. Reading the Qere, *hāᵃsûrîm.*
132. See *OBA,* p. 85.
133. Boling, *Judges,* p. 248.
134. Younger, *Judges, Ruth,* p. 315.
135. Moore, *Judges,* p. 351.

will not escape. In view of her Hebrew-sounding name, it is possible that Delilah was an Israelite; but where she lived and how she behaved make it far more likely that she was a Philistine.[136]

The second major difference is the simple statement that Samson *loved (wayye'ĕhaḇ)* her. This is not said of his half-night with the prostitute. There was no love in that. He just "saw," "went in," and "lay" with her (16:1-3). In his brief marriage in chapter 14, "love" occurs only as a reproach on the lips of his wife: "you don't *love* me *(lō' 'ăhaḇtānî),*" and judging from the data the text gives us, she is right. Samson "sees," evaluates (she was "right" in his eyes), and orders his parents to "get her" for him (14:1-3). When he is pressed to open his heart to her, however, he rates her as even less entitled to that than his parents (14:16). She is a valued acquisition, but never his soul mate. He never "loved" her. But here it is different. Delilah is not just a prize acquisition, or sex provider. She has a name, and "love" stands at the beginning as the narrator's own term for how Samson perceived her and desired her: *he loved a woman . . . whose name was Delilah.* This love blinded him to the dangers involved, and eventually led to his being literally blinded, in the most brutal way imaginable (v. 21).

5 The Philistines were quick to realize Samson's vulnerability and exploit it. In the Old Testament the word translated *lords (sarnê)* in this verse is used exclusively of the Philistines, and alludes to their distinctive political system.[137] It is not clear here in verse 5 whether the *sarnê* in view are the rulers of the five Philistine cities, or advisors to them, or generals who led their armed forces, or whether they functioned in some combination of these roles. Later, in the climactic episode of the narrative, it seems to refer to all Philistine leaders, of whatever kind. In 1 Samuel 27 and 29, however, which refer to events not long after the judges period, Achish, the Philistine ruler of Gath who gave David sanctuary from Saul, is called a "king" *(meleḵ),* and there is a difference of opinion between him and the "lords" *(sarnê)* over the degree to which David should be trusted (1 Sam. 27:2; 29:6-7). Whatever the particulars of their office may have been, the *lords of the Philistines* in the present passage were high-level representatives of the entire Philistine confederacy. Their "going up" to Delilah *(wayya'ălû 'ēlêhā)* may be geographical, that is, "northward" from the Philistine cities south of the Sorek Valley,[138] or simply metaphorical, meaning they "approached" her.[139]

---

136. "Recent Philistine inscriptions demonstrate a strong tendency among them to adopt Semitic names." Younger, *Judges, Ruth,* p. 316, n. 73.

137. For example, Josh. 13:3; 1 Sam. 5:8, 11; 6:4, 12, 16, 18; 7:7; 1 Chron. 12:19. Contrast Jeremiah, who, in the late 7th/early 6th century, refers to "all the kings *(malḵê)* of the Philistines" (Jer. 25:20).

138. Cf. Gen. 44:17, 24, 34, of Joseph's brothers "going up" from Egypt to Canaan.

139. Cf. Deut. 25:7, of "going up" to the elders at the town gate.

What we are seeing here is a rerun of the events of chapter 14, but with the stakes now much higher. Again the Philistines are seeking the answer to a riddle, not this time a riddle Samson has framed in words, but one he has presented by his actions, especially in stripping Gaza of its gates, namely, what is the secret of his *great strength?* And those who are trying to solve the riddle this time are not merely intent on winning a wager, but on "overpowering" Samson, so that they can *tie him up [to] torment him.* Furthermore, sensing that Delilah is a very different kind of woman from the young bride of chapter 14, they do not threaten her, but offer her money — a great deal of it — in return for her cooperation. Given all the variables involved, it is difficult to translate the amount of the bribe into a modern equivalent.[140] However, assuming there were five *lords* (one for each city of the Philistine pentapolis) and that the monetary unit in view is the shekel, the total would be 5,500 shekels, which we might compare with the "four hundred shekels Abraham paid for a family burial place (Gen. 23:15, 19), the fifty David paid for the oxen and threshing floor of Araunah (2 Sam. 24:24), the seventeen Jeremiah paid for a piece of property (Jer. 32:9), and the thirty shekels the covenant code sets as the value of a slave (Exod. 21:32)."[141] It was a huge sum,[142] and given that it is effectively the price of a man's life, Victor Matthews has nicely captured the cool manner in which (by implication) it is accepted: "There is no sense of coercion or, for that matter, of reluctance on Delilah's part to betray her lover. Nor is there any real malice on her part either. It is simply a matter of business for this very business-like woman."[143] She is every bit as mercenary as the prostitute of Gaza, but far more up-market — and lethal. She is now entirely an agent of Samson's enemies; all that remains is for the betrayal to be enacted.

6-9 The betrayal unfolds in a repeating pattern through three episodes in which Samson keeps his secret (vv. 6-9, 10-12, and 13-14), to a fourth in which he reveals it and suffers the consequences (vv. 15-21). It is a kind of ritualized dance of death. Astonishingly, Delilah begins working on Samson by telling him at once what he may expect from the Philistines if she should betray him to them. She even uses the very words ("tie up," "torment") that they have used in recruiting her (v. 6)! It is a very odd way, we might think, of "cajoling" him into confiding in her! Wouldn't it have exactly the opposite effect? The answer is no, for two reasons. First, since the secret of Samson's great strength is what every Philistine wants to know but cannot,

---

140. Younger estimates it as "in the $15 million category" (*Judges, Ruth,* p. 316, n. 75).

141. Boling, *Judges,* p. 249.

142. Cf. the ten pieces of silver a year offered to a Levite as his wage in 17:10.

143. Matthews, *Judges and Ruth,* p. 160.

to ask him to reveal it to her alone is to tell him she wants to be his soul mate, to know him as no one else does, to be as close to him as only a lover can be. In a paradoxical way, it is a declaration of her professed love for him. And since Samson, for his part, already loves her, it is a challenge he will find hard to resist. Second, it shows us just how well Delilah knows her man. She knows that Samson is the kind of person who is aroused by danger rather than repelled by it. She challenges him to live dangerously with her, and revel in the excitement of it. Again, it is something that this particular man, who has never fully grown up, will find hard to resist. Delilah has read him well.[144]

Samson's love for Delilah and his daredevil temperament have made him doubly vulnerable. The danger is too real, however, and too great for even him to be totally indifferent to it. So instead of rebuffing her and risk losing her, he embarks on a hazardous game of brinkmanship by teasing her with false answers. "If *they* were to tie me up *(ya'asrunî)*," he says. Why the indefinite form of the verb? Who could *they* be but the Philistines? Does Samson hint that he already suspects that Delilah is in collusion with them? Or is it simply a case of the not-uncommon use of the indefinite active as a virtual passive, "If I should be tied up"? Either is possible, and the latter is only slightly less loaded than the former. It is all part of the game they are playing: tease and countertease, hint and suggestion. Who will come clean and be the first to lower their defenses and speak plainly? The *fresh cords* *(yᵉṭārîm laḥîm)* of verse 7 may have been raw sinews, or pieces of animal gut, or something such as bowstrings or tent ropes made from gut but not yet *dried* out (i.e., *lō'-ḥōrāḇû*).[145] If so, they are reminiscent of the "fresh jaw-bone" of 15:15 which Samson used to kill the Philistines.[146] Perhaps he is suggesting that his enemies should try to turn the tables on him by using something *fresh* themselves! But of course he mocks them. It is a much too easy answer to Delilah's question, as events are about to show. In an Israelite context, the number *seven* has connotations of completeness,[147] and may have had other (perhaps magical) associations for the Philistines. The expression *become weak like any [other] man* simply means, on the face of it, what it says: Samson's great strength will desert him. But both this and the number seven will recur and take on deeper significance as the passage unfolds.

144. Cf. Alter, "Samson without Folklore," p. 53: "The glint of the dagger in the velvet hand of love is what has excited him from Timnah onward."

145. See the use of *yeṭer* in Ps. 11:2 ("bowstring") and Job 4:21 (perhaps "tent rope"). Cf. Boling, *Judges,* p. 249.

146. A different word is used in 15:15, but the sense (raw, not dried out) is the same.

147. Note the seven days of Samson's wedding feast in 14:12, and cf. Gen 2:2; 7:4; 41:29-30, etc.

401

With Delilah in possession of Samson's answer to her question, things follow as a matter of course with only the barest essentials being told. The Philistines bring her the required cords, and secretly wait to see the result. Delilah ties up Samson with them, and then tells him the Philistines are *upon* him (have come to seize him), whereupon Samson (of course) snaps the cords as though they are bits of fiber in a flame, *so [the secret of] his strength remained unknown* (vv. 8-9). The first episode of the drama is finished. It has already become a farce, but the laugh isn't only on Delilah because Samson has been tricked, too. Samson has kept the secret of his great strength; Delilah has hidden her accomplices in an *inner room* (v. 9). So Samson is kept guessing about what she is up to. Is this just a game, or something more sinister? Is Delilah a tease or a traitor? It is a dangerous thing to be uncertain about.

10-12   The second episode begins with Delilah reproaching Samson for mocking her by telling her lies (v. 10). From there on this episode is a virtual repeat of the first, with only minor changes. Interestingly, she drops the reference to "torment," probably to make her "game" sound more innocent than it is. Now she merely asks how he can be *tied up,* and Samson replies, *with new ropes (ba'ăḇōṯîm ḥăḏāšîm)* — ropes that have suffered no wear and tear from being used. But of course that has already been done (15:13),[148] and proves no more effective this time than before. When Delilah sounds the alarm, he "snaps" the ropes off his arms like *a thread* (v. 12) — a flimsy piece of cotton or measuring tape.[149]

13-14   Much more significant changes occur in this third episode. The introductory exchange between Delilah and Samson is condensed to the barest minimum. Even the imperative, *Tell me,* is condensed from *haggîḏā-nā'* to *haggîḏā,* perhaps reflecting a growing impatience on Delilah's part.[150] What follows, however, is described in much more detail than previously. Now, for the first time, Samson mentions his hair, which he specifies as *the seven locks of my head* (v. 13). He no longer speaks vaguely about "them" but *you,* and introduces an entirely new way of tying him up. His reference to his *seven locks* suggests that his hair is special to him in some way, and that he has taken care to maintain it in this form. He is coming perilously close at this point to divulging the deepest secret of his life. But not yet; he will tease Delilah again, perhaps just because he enjoys doing so, and/or because he realizes how close he has come to giving her the secret she is seeking and is

---

148. Delilah may be ignorant of this because there had been no survivors. Younger, *Judges, Ruth,* p. 317, n. 77.

149. See, e.g., Gen. 14:23; Song 4:3; 1 Kgs. 7:15.

150. On whether the presence or absence of the particle *nā'* has any semantic value see Arnold and Choi, *Biblical Hebrew Syntax,* p. 65.

still in two minds about doing so. For whatever reason, he decides to play with her (and his secret) one more time.

The reference to thirty "linen garments" *(sᵉdînîm)* back in 14:12 implies that clothes made from woven cloth were common among the Philistines. So it is not surprising that there was a *loom ('ereg)* in the room where Samson and Delilah were closeted, most likely in Delilah's home (v. 14). On the loom was some *web (massāket)* — unfinished woven cloth — and a *pin,* probably made of wood, used to *fasten* each new row of thread by tapping it tightly into place against the previous rows.[151] Samson tells Delilah to weave the seven locks of his hair into the web and fasten it with the pin.[152] *Until now* he may have mocked her and told her lies (v. 10), but this time (he implies) his strength really will leave him (v. 13). Delilah, too, treats this time as special. She puts Samson to *sleep* (he is like Sisera in Jael's tent, or a child on its mother's lap), and while he sleeps, she does as he has told her to do. But when she sounds the alarm, his strength is still there. He wakes and gets up, pulling everything up with him — *peg, loom,* and *web,* and, of course, hair — making Delilah look stupid yet again, and very, very angry!

Samson's hair was the only part of him that had not been bound in the previous two episodes; the cords and ropes had presumably been tied around his limbs and torso, immobilizing everything but his head. In this third episode the situation is reversed; only the locks of his head are bound, leaving his body and limbs free. Furthermore, given the domestic setting, the loom would not have been very large. It would have been fastened to the floor in some way, but a strong man like Samson, with his limbs free, would not have had much trouble dislodging it and freeing himself from it. So how could it have seemed possible to Delilah that Samson had told her the truth on this third occasion? The most likely answer is that Samson's reference to his hair as *seven locks* had suggested to Delilah that his hair had some kind of magical potency, and that this potency could somehow be neutralized by doing as he had told her; in short, that the "binding," in this case, was magical rather than (merely) physical. It didn't work, of course, because the secret of Samson's strength had nothing to do with magic. But the way this episode draws attention to Samson's hair prepares the way for the fourth and final episode, which now follows.

15-22 Delilah's final attempt to elicit the secret of Samson's great strength is described much more fully than the preceding three. The word

---

151. See the description of a loom of the kind envisaged here in J. H. Walton, V. Matthews, and M. W. Chavalas, eds., *The IVP Bible Background Commentary: Old Testament* (Leicester: Inter-Varsity Press, 2000), p. 269.

152. "Delilah's tightening *(tāqaʿ)* of Samson's hair with a pin *(yātēd)* (16:14) recalls Jael's striking *(tāqaʿ)* the tent peg *(yātēd)* into Sisera's temple (14:21)." Younger, *Judges, Ruth,* p. 319.

"love" *(wayye'ᵉhaḇ)* that opened the whole account of Samson's dealings with Delilah (v. 4) returns now to introduce the last, climactic episode of the passage: *"How can you say, 'I love you ('ᵃhaḇtîk),' when your heart is not with me?"* (v. 15). The narrator has used the word "love"; now Delilah uses it, and apparently Samson has used it, too: he has "said" it to Delilah, that is, declared his love for her. So "love" here is something much more than sex or possession. There is romance in it, at least on Samson's side. And used in close proximity to the word "heart" *(lēḇ)* here, it acquires added force. Love, as both Samson and Delilah speak of it, is something that engages the heart, the very core of a person's being. In short, it gives access to his secrets, and is therefore Delilah's most potent weapon. In effect, she tells him he must open his heart to her or lose her. The same tactic was used successfully in Timnah, when much less was at stake and there was much less reason to think that real love was present (14:16). Now it is deployed again, by a much more powerful woman, when everything is at stake and when love has all but broken through Samson's defenses. Delilah has already taken his hair in her hands; now she asks for his heart. Her words are accusatory *("three times you have mocked me"),* but her "love" and "heart" language soften her speech and give it a cajoling rather than bitter tone. The truth is that the "mocking" she accuses him of has really been a case of teasing, a form of love play, that has brought her to the point of pleading, and him to the brink of yielding completely. Delilah probably senses this. In any case, having already deployed her most powerful weapon, all she can do now is thrust at Samson with it again and again, hoping that by sheer perseverance she may at last break through. And finally she does: *When she had worn him down with her words day after day, and pressured him, he became exasperated (wattiqṣar napšô) to the point of death and told her all his heart* (vv. 16-17a). At last she has him.

This is the second time in Judges that we have encountered the expression *wattiqṣar napšô,* he [literally, *his heart*] *became exasperated.* Back in 10:16, it was used with reference to Yahweh, who "became exasperated with Israel's misery" and finally gave them what they had asked him for (deliverance from the Ammonites). In the present passage Samson becomes exasperated with Delilah's persistent pleading and finally gives her what she has been asking for (the secret of his great strength). The difference is that Yahweh was fully aware that Israel would betray him (by turning back to its old ways), whereas Samson did not know whether Delilah would betray him or not. In Yahweh's case, yielding was an act of grace, not weakness. In Samson's case, it was pure capitulation. His defenses had been broken down, and he could not resist Delilah any longer. What would be would be; his love for her had blinded him. At last *he told her all his heart,* and placed himself completely in her power. The reference to *death* at the end of verse 16 is a dark premonition of where all this is leading.

When Samson opens his heart, we find something there which we had always expected but had never been sure of. Samson's actions have been so at variance with what was said to his mother in chapter 13, and the law of concerning Nazirites in Numbers 6, that there has always been a question mark about whether he really knew who he was. But now that doubt is removed: *"I have been a Nazirite of God from my mother's womb. If I were to be shaved, then my strength would leave me, and I would become weak and be like every other man"* (v. 17; cf. 13:5). The ban on shaving his head was the only prohibition that was specifically said to apply to Samson himself rather than his mother. Given the special nature of his Naziriteship, it had always been a moot point whether or not he had to observe all the bans applicable to Nazirites in general. About his hair, though, there had never been any doubt. His unshaven head was to be the mark, par excellence, that this particular man had been claimed by God from his mother's womb to be a lifelong Nazirite. And Samson knew it. The secret of his great strength lay in his hair because it lay in his Naziriteship — his separation to God. To shave it off would be to symbolically cancel his Naziriteship, and make him "weak, *like every other man (keķol-hā'āḏām)."* There is a subtle change of wording here that has been described by David Grossman as follows:

> 'As *every* other man', he literally said. But earlier, when Delilah had bound him, he said to her — twice — that he would weaken *ke'achad ha'adam,* like *any* other man, the word *achad* meaning 'one', as if still wanting, unconsciously, to retain his individuality. Now he forfeits this too, and reveals to her how he can become like every man, tasting these words for the first time.
>
> But maybe it is not a weakness, an illness, to be like everyone else. Maybe this is what Samson, in his heart of hearts, has wanted his whole life.[153]

The fact is that Samson has always been in rebellion against his separation to God. He has never wanted to fight the Philistines as he was destined to do. He has wanted to mix with them, intermarry with them, and party with them. He has especially wanted to have this woman, Delilah, because he loved her. But his separateness has always caught up with him, and turned his relationships with the Philistines sour. It is the Spirit that has propelled him into conflict with them. When he wanted to stop (15:7), he was not allowed to; the men of Judah took him out of hiding, and the Spirit had seized him and thrust him into battle with the Philistines again (15:14). And after that there had been no turning back. He couldn't even find relief by visiting a prostitute without be-

---

153. *Lion's Honey: The Myth of Samson* (Melbourne: Text Publishing, 2006), pp. 133-34.

ing ambushed (16:1-3). He had to fight them, but it was never what he wanted. All he had wanted was what *every* man wanted if he dare admit it: sex, love, and freedom from the too narrow confines of his upbringing. But Samson's Naziriteship had dogged him at every turn, and become an unbearable burden. That is what he told Delilah when he opened his heart to her. I don't want to be special any more. Bring the nightmare to an end. Shave my head and make me normal.[154]

Meanwhile, the Philistines have apparently left, thinking Delilah would never succeed. But now that she knows that she has, she calls them back, and they return, bringing the money they have promised her (v. 18). Presumably the ambush is again set, as in verse 9. With everything in readiness, Delilah again puts Samson to sleep, this time *on* [or *between*][155] *her knees* (v. 19), like a newborn baby. She calls *a man,* to bring a razor perhaps, or to assist her in some other way. But it is she herself (the verb is feminine) who quietly shaves off his seven locks as he sleeps. It is an episode full of pathos, intensely intimate and at the same time completely public, with the hidden Philistines watching like voyeurs, relishing every moment.[156] It is as though, for a little while, time stands still. Everything is in slow motion. But then it is over, and things move quickly to their dreadful end.

Having gotten what she wants, Delilah gives up all pretense to being Samson's lover. She herself begins to *torment*[157] him (presumably to begin waking him up) even before she sounds the alarm, and immediately his strength leaves him (v. 19). When he does wake, Samson momentarily forgets what he has done. He says [*to himself*], *"I will go forth as before and shake myself [free]"* (v. 20). But this time he is not bound by anything but normality — no cords, ropes, or loom, and no Naziriteship. He has nothing to "shake off" anymore! But his freedom is illusionary, for he still has enemies, and now he has no more power to resist them than a "normal" man would. In those first,

---

154. Cf. Samson's lament in John Milton's *Samson Agonistes,* lines 63-64:

God, when he gave me strength, to show withal
How slight the gift was, hung it in my hair.
But peace! I must not quarrel with the will
Of highest dispensation, which herein
haply had ends above my reach to know:
Suffices that to me strength is my bane
And proves the source of all my miseries. . . .

155. See the note on the translation.

156. See the artistic portrayals of the episode from the 17th to 20th centuries in Gunn, *Judges,* pp. 216, 218.

157. It is the same word that the Philistines used back in v. 5. See the comments on the translation of v. 15.

confused, waking moments he *didn't realize that Yahweh had left him* (v. 20). Soon he did realize it, however, because the *Philistines seized him and gouged out his eyes* (v. 21a). There is heavy irony here. Samson's wild career began when he "saw" a woman, and demanded to have her because she was "right in his eyes." Now he has lost those eyes and sees nothing. What Samson did to Gaza has now been done to him: eyeless Samson, like gateless Gaza, has become violated and defenseless. Gaza has risen again and taken vengeance on him. The Philistines *took him down* there, *and bound him with bronze fetters,* and set him to work, "grinding grain" like an animal (v. 21b).[158] The man who despised his Naziriteship (as Esau despised his birthright) has lost his humanity as well. He is completely undone. And there his story might have ended, *but the hair of his head began to grow again* (v. 22). It is one of those wonderfully pregnant lines that contains so much more than it says.[159] The man who wanted to be "like every man" will not be allowed to be, for Yahweh has begun to claim him back to do at last what he was always destined to do.[160] Verse 22 is the bridge into the final, crowning episode of Samson's tragic life.

c. Samson Fulfills His Destiny (16:23-30)

Nothing in his life became him like the leaving of it.[161]

Samson's destiny has cast a long shadow before it. Before his birth his mother was told he was to be a Nazirite who would begin to deliver Israel

---

158. This "taking" down of Samson here is the climax of all his "goings" down in the course of the narrative (14:1, 5, 7, 19; 15:8). Cf. Exum, "Aspects of Symmetry," p. 13, who comments with particular reference to ch. 14: ". . . while going down impels the narrative forward, coming up in conjunction with going down forms an inclusion around it, vv. 1-2 and 19-20." The same may be said of chs. 14–16 as a whole (note the inclusion formed by 14:1-2 and 16:31).

159. Cf. James L. Crenshaw, who has aptly described it as "one of those pregnant sentences that is the mark of genius." "The Samson Saga: Filial Devotion or Erotic Attachment?" *ZAW* 86 (1974): 501.

160. Cf. the words of Manoah in Milton's *Samson Agonistes,* lines 1495-1501:

And I persuade me God had not permitted
His strength again to grow up with his hair
Garrisoned around him like a camp
Of faithful soldiery, were not his purpose
To use him further yet in some great service,
Not to sit idle with so great a gift
Useless, and thence ridiculous, about him.

161. Malcolm, in Shakespeare's *Macbeth,* Act 1, Scene 4.

from the Philistines (13:5). His mother herself, as though voicing a grim premonition, spoke of him being a Nazirite "until the day of his death" (13:7). In this final momentous episode both of these weighty predictions are fulfilled. Samson's Naziriteship is consummated in his death, and in dying as he does he begins the deliverance of Israel.

23 *Now the lords of the Philistines gathered to offer a great sacrifice to Dagon their god, and to rejoice.*[162] *They said, "Our god has given into our hand Samson, our enemy."*

24[163] *The people saw him and praised their god, for they said,*[164] *"Our god has given into our hand our enemy, who laid waste our land and multiplied our slain."*

25 *Now when their spirits were high, they said, "Call Samson, so that he can entertain us." So they called Samson from the prison, and he entertained in their presence. They made him stand between the pillars.*

26 *Samson said to the boy*[165] *who held him by the hand, "Put me where I can feel*[166] *the pillars on which the temple*[167] *is founded, so that I can lean on them."*

27 *Now the temple was full of men and women. All the lords of the Philistines were there, and on the roof were about three thousand men and women who were watching while Samson entertained.*

28 *Samson called out to Yahweh, "O my lord Yahweh, please remember me. Please strengthen me just this once, O God, so that I can avenge myself on the Philistines with the revenge [they deserve] for [at least] one of my two eyes."*[168]

---

162. The noun *śimḥâ*, "joy," is used with the preposition *l^e* as an infinitive.

163. *BHS* recommends relocating v. 24 to after v. 25. See the exegetical comments on v. 24.

164. MT suggests deleting *'ām^erû* (they said) on the grounds that it is absent from LXX[B]. It may have been added under the influence of v. 23. But given its presence there, it would have to be understood, in any case, in v. 24. There is nothing at stake semantically in its inclusion or omission.

165. The Hebrew word *na'ar* has a range of meanings, including "youth" (young man), "servant," and "boy" (as, e.g., in Exod. 2:6, where it is synonymous with *yeled*). See the exegetical comments on this verse.

166. Reading the Qere, *wah^amiššēnî*, from *mšš* (Hiphil), "to touch, feel," with *BHS* and the English versions in general.

167. Literally, "house" *(habbayit)*, as in v. 27.

168. Cf. Moore, *Judges*, p. 363, and Keil and Delitzsch, "Judges," p. 425. Contrast LXX and the English versions in general, which take *'aḥat* with *n^eqam*, "one [act of] vengeance for my two eyes." But when the numeral "one" qualifies a preceding noun, the noun is normally absolute (e.g., Gen 1:9; 2:24), not construct as *n^eqam* is here. Also, the feminine form of the numeral *('aḥat* rather than *'eḥād)* suggests that it qualifies *'ênay*

29 *Then Samson grasped the two middle pillars on which the temple was founded, and braced himself against them, one with his right hand and the other with his left.*

30 *Samson said, "Let me die with the Philistines!" Then he pushed hard, and the temple fell upon the lords and upon all the people who were in it. The dead whom he killed in his death were more than those he killed in his life.*

23-24   At last the Philistines have something to celebrate. The expression *the lords of the Philistines* is here used more inclusively than in verses 5, 8, and 18 — not just the heads of the five Philistine cities or their delegates, but all Philistine leaders of whatever rank, and probably their staff and other leading citizens as well. According to verse 27, *all* the rulers were there, plus about three thousand others. It was a great gathering. The place is apparently Gaza, since Samson had been imprisoned there (v. 21) and must have been close at hand since he is easily "called for" and brought out before the crowd in verse 25. The specific location, as we are about to see, is the temple of the god Dagon, and the purpose is to celebrate the capture of Samson, who by this time had eluded the Philistines for twenty years (15:20; 16:31).[169]

The significance of the name *Dagon (dāgôn)* is uncertain. Earlier Jewish and Christian commentators related it to the Hebrew word *dāg,*[170] "fish," and hence "fish god," or the like. But this is generally discounted these days, and most scholars now think that it is related to *dāgān,* the common Hebrew word for grain, and hence "grain god." The Hebrew term *dāgān* may be derived from the name Dagon, or the name Dagon may be derived from an earlier, pre-Israelite cognate of *dāgān.* The discovery of a temple of Dagon at the pre-Israelite (14th cent.) site of Ugarit in northern Palestine has made the second of these two possibilities more likely to be the correct one.[171] It also shows that although the Philistines refer to Dagon as *our god,* they had actually inherited him — or at least his name — from the Canaanites. In Samuel's time there was a temple to Dagon in Ashdod (1 Sam. 5:2-7), and in the days of Saul and David there was one in Beth-shan, near the eastern end of the valley of Jezreel (1 Sam 31:10; 1 Chron. 10:10).[172] So

---

(feminine) rather than *nᵉqam* (masculine). The LXX reading makes easier sense, but this is hardly a good enough reason to follow it. See the exegetical comments on this verse. "One" and "two" appear again in the next verse, where Samson takes hold of the two pillars, one with his right hand and one with his left.

169. See the comments on these verses.

170. As the name *šimšôn,* "Samson," is (probably) related to *šemeš,* "sun." See the comments on 5:31 and 13:24.

171. K. A. Kitchen, "Dagon," *NBD,* p. 258.

172. See *OBA,* p. 84.

the worship of Dagon extended over centuries and across ethnic boundaries, and the Philistines themselves worshiped him in more than one place. But it can hardly be coincidental that Samson finally encounters him in Gaza. There is a kind of grim poetic justice in it. Samson, who tore off Gaza's gates, has been imprisoned in Gaza, and the destroyer of Philistine grain (15:5) is about to be arraigned before the Philistine grain god.

The Philistines are jubilant, and attribute the remarkable reversal in their fortunes to Dagon: *"Our god has given into our hand Samson, our enemy."* They first "say" it, perhaps when they first hear the news (v. 23), and then repeat it in a longer form when they "see" Samson (v. 24). The text as we have it does not follow a strictly chronological order, since the people's "seeing" of Samson in verse 24 presumably happened after, rather than before, his being summoned and brought out to them in verse 25. In view of this, the *BHS* apparatus recommends reversing the order of these two verses.[173] However, there is no hard manuscript evidence to support such a change. It seems, rather, that some liberty has been taken with the chronology in order to bring material of a similar kind together to create the following structure:

vv. 23-24	Worship (of Dagon)
v. 25a	*Transition:* Samson brought out
vv. 25b-30	Entertainment (by Samson)

As we will see, worship and entertainment are both presented ironically: in both cases the reality is different from what the Philistines intend.

The Philistine worship consists of the offering of a *great sacrifice* (unspecified), "rejoicing," and "praising" Dagon in the hymn[174] summarized in the poetic lines of verses 23b and 24b:

"Our god has given into our hand Samson, our enemy . . .
Our god has given into our hand our enemy,
who laid waste our country and multiplied our slain."

The poetic form of the lines suggests that they were sung. However, the introductory words in verse 24, *[They] praised their god, for they said,* implies that what follows is the reason for the praise rather than the praise itself: they *praised their god* [in some unspecified way], *for they said* [to themselves and/or one another], *"Our god has given into our hand our enemy. . . ."* Either way, the lines in question express the Philistine perception of what had happened. The parallel expressions, *our god* (Dagon) and *our enemy* (Sam-

173. See footnotes on the translation of v. 24.
174. See the comments on 15:16 (Samson's victory song) and ch. 5 (the song of Deborah and Barak).

son), indicate that while, at one level, the conflict had been between them and Samson (he had ravaged their land and killed many of their people), the deeper reality, as they see it, was that it had been between Samson and Dagon, and that Dagon had triumphed. The victory they have come to celebrate was not their own achievement, but Dagon's, and hence the *great sacrifice to [him]*. He, Dagon, had *given* Samson into their hand. They are wrong, of course. Samson was not given into their hand because Dagon had defeated him, but because Yahweh had left him (v. 20) — and did so just long enough for the Philistines to be able to blind him, bind him, and bring him down to Gaza, and (after his hair had begun to grow again) into the very temple of their god Dagon, where they are about to learn, to their cost, just how mistaken they are.

25a   At some point, when *their spirits were high,* the Philistines decide to treat themselves to some fun at Samson's expense; to revel in the mastery of Samson that (as they think) Dagon has given them.[175] The cry, *"Call Samson, so that he can entertain us,"* may have been an order issued by the "lords" of verse 23, or just a spontaneous cry of the high-spirited crowd (v. 24). In either case it was promptly acted upon, and the public humiliation of Samson began. He was called from the *prison* where he was shackled (v. 21), which was presumably close by, and *entertained* them as they had demanded he should. The text is mercifully reticent about the details, but the biting sarcasm of the single word, *entertained (śāḥaq),* says it all. What did he do? And under what cruel goadings? While *śāḥaq* commonly has positive connotations (joy, laughter, dance, music),[176] here the implied joy is vindictive and the laughter derisive.[177] Samson "entertains" his audience (whom he cannot see) by appearing before them as a pathetic, laughable caricature of his former self. The Philistines' desire to "bind" Samson had always been so that they could "torment" him (16:5, 6, 19), and now that desire is given full rein. It is the nadir of Samson's career, and his darkest moment.

25b-26   At some point Samson's tormentors *made him stand between the pillars* (v. 25b). According to the next verse, they were *the pillars on which the temple [was] founded,* that is, its two central pillars. Why they did so is not stated, but the coercion involved suggests that it was part of the "entertainment" they were forcing him to provide. If in Philistia, as in Israel, temples doubled up as places of sanctuary for wrongdoers until their fate was deter-

---

175. There is no reference to drunkenness, although that may have played a part.

176. For example, 2 Sam. 6:5; Jer. 30:19; 31:4; Job 40:20; Prov. 31:25; Eccl. 3:4. The fuller expression, *entertained in their presence (wayᵉśaḥēq lipnêhem),* has the same verb, followed by the same preposition, as in David's "dancing before Yahweh" in 2 Sam. 6:21.

177. Cf. the use of *śāḥaq* in Pss. 2:4; 37:13; 52:6-7; Prov. 1:26; Job 5:22; Lam. 1:7.

mined,[178] it could be that Samson was made to stand between the pillars in order to mock him as Israel's judge. Let him perform that role now by passing judgment on his tormentors! Whatever the reason, it was a fatal mistake.

The picture, in verse 26, of Samson being *held* (literally, "strengthened," *maḥᵃzîq*) by a *boy (naʿar)*[179] is full of pathos, which is compounded when he asks the boy to help him by "putting" him where he can feel the pillars and *lean* on them. How the strong man has been humbled! This is a new Samson, who has been taught by suffering to know his weakness as never before.[180] However, there is more going on than we are presently aware of. The pathos will become far more complex when we find out — as we soon will — what is taking shape in Samson's mind. He is about to die, taking this boy and thousands of his fellows with him. The boy appears to be leading the man, but actually it is vice versa. The man is leading the boy — to his death. And in the context of the story as a whole, God is "leading" them both, for what they are both caught up in is something God has determined should happen from the beginning (13:5; 14:4).

27 The word *lean (wᵉʾeššāʿēn)* at the end of verse 26 sounds innocent enough. After what he has been subjected to, Samson can barely stand, and he asks the boy to help him get some respite for a moment or two by leaning against the pillars. It is not clear whether he always intended to do more than this, or whether the idea came to him suddenly and unbidden (like the onrush of the Spirit in 15:14) as he leaned there. Samson was blind, of course, but verse 27 shows us the episode as it would have appeared to someone standing where he was. The syntax marks it as an aside[181] in which we are invited to take in the situation before the forward movement of the narrative is resumed in verse 28.

From the description given in verse 27, the *temple* (literally, "house") in which all this was taking place appears to have been a substantial building, with a large central courtyard surrounded by a *balcony (gāg)*[182] from which

---

178. 1 Kgs. 2:28-35; cf. Num. 35:6-28.

179. See the note on *boy* in the translation. Given that the purpose was to ridicule the "mighty" Samson, it is likely that he was deliberately shown to the crowd being led about by a mere boy in order to provide an appropriate spectacle for them to enjoy. Cf. the positive counterpart in Isa. 11:6, "a little child *(naʿar qāṭōn)* will lead them" (NIV).

180. In 15:18, after a great victory, he asked God to help him. Here, after being tormented, he asks a boy.

181. The *wayyiqtol* sequence of the main narrative thread is interrupted by a series of disjunctive clauses, with subjects in the first position followed by non-finite verb forms (participles, infinitives, or their equivalents).

182. The word *gāg* is the normal Hebrew word for "roof," but must refer here either to an open roof of some kind, or balcony, since those standing on it can look down into the interior temple.

people could watch what was happening below. The number *(three thousand)* for those on the balcony alone is huge, but is a round number, more significant for the impression it creates than for its literal accuracy. It shows us a building that is dangerously overcrowded, filled to overflowing with both *men and women* on both levels. Most significantly, <u>all</u> *the lords of the Philistines (kōl sarnê pᵉlištîm)* are there in the temple, with the balcony and its huge press of people above them, totally absorbed in the spectacle Samson presents to them, and unaware of how vulnerable they are. If the building were to collapse now, it would wipe out a large, representative slab of the Philistine population, including the entire top echelon of its leadership.[183] This sets the scene for the last, crowning deed of Samson's tragic career to be enacted.

28 For the second time, Samson "cries out" to Yahweh (see the comments on 15:18). He has not seen the situation as we have just been shown it (v. 27), but he may well have sensed it. Does he perhaps see more in his blindness than he did when sighted? Certainly he realizes that an opportunity exists at this moment for one final act of vengeance on his enemies. The bitterness he feels is powerfully expressed in his terse reference to revenge *for [at least] one of my two eyes.*"[184] Nothing can compensate Samson for what the Philistines have done to him, and to fully punish them as they deserve is beyond him. But at least partial satisfaction is within his grasp now, at this moment, if only God will listen to his cry and *strengthen* him *just this once.*

There is desperation in the way Samson appeals to God here. But there is also something very poignant. The words, *just this once,* acknowledges how little right he has to expect anything from God. But at the same time it appeals to precedent. God has strengthened him at moments of great need in the past. If he will do so just once more, Samson will never trouble him again. It is the language of a beggar. But the plea that God would *remember* him is much more than this. Remembrance is a very significant motif in the Old Testament, beginning with the promise made by God after the flood: "I will remember my covenant between me and you and every living creature with you, a covenant for all generations to come" (Gen. 9:15 NIV). According to Exodus 2:24, the exodus happened because God "remembered his covenant with Abraham" (NIV). In such passages remembrance entails being faithful to a relationship by fulfilling the obligations entailed in it. In the Psalms it is frequently the basis of appeal to God to act because of his special relationship with Israel, or with the psalmist personally.[185] Samson's cry in

---

183. See the comments on *sarnê pᵉlištîm* in 3:3 and 16:5.
184. See the note to the translation.
185. For example, Pss. 25:6; 74:2; 89:50; 106:4; 119:49; 132:1.

the present passage stands within this tradition. It is an appeal to God to act on the basis of the special relationship he had established with Samson even before he was born: "[He] will be a Nazirite of God" (13:5). There is grim irony in the fact that Samson should invoke this relationship now, given that he himself has shown so little regard for it in the preceding narrative. In fact, it was his effective repudiation of it by allowing Delilah to cut his hair that has led to his present distress. Nevertheless, the enigmatic statement about his hair beginning to grow again back in verse 22 implied that God intended to use him against the Philistines again. So far, though, Samson has known only weakness. Strength has lain entirely with his captors and tormentors. But now in his extremity he dares to hope that Yahweh may not, after all, have utterly abandoned him. It is not a cry of repentance, and there is nothing noble about it. All Samson wants is vengeance for the personal wrongs he has suffered. God wants something more, but at least there is a confluence of their two desires: what Samson wants for his own reasons, God wants for other, greater reasons. So Samson's prayer is answered.

29-30 Our attention has already been drawn repeatedly to the two *pillars* which feature here. First they were just "the pillars" (v. 25b), then in Samson's own words, "the pillars on which the temple is founded" (v. 26b), and now in the voice of the narrator, and most fully, *the two middle pillars on which the temple was founded* (v. 29). Everything depends quite literally on these two pillars and their capacity to withstand the pressure being applied to them. They are already under enormous strain because of the overcrowding of the structure they support. Now Samson grasps them and braces himself against them, *one with his right hand and the other with his left* (v. 29), and in this cruciform position utters his final prayer: *"Let me die with the Philistines!"* (v. 30a). His life has been inextricably bound up with the Philistines from the beginning. Their name was spoken over him before he was born (13:5). He has loved them, clashed with them, killed them, and been blinded and tormented by them. Paradoxically, the only way he will ever be free of them is by dying with them. That is what he has asked God to strengthen him for. Now, relying on God to grant his wish, he "pushes hard" against them, and what he has asked for is granted: *the temple fell upon the lords and upon all the people who were in it* (v. 30b), including Samson himself.

It was not Samson's finest hour in a moral or spiritual sense; it was too clouded with bitter self-interest for that. But it was certainly his greatest achievement. That is the implication of the narrator's grim summary at the end of verse 30: those Samson killed in his death were *more than those he killed in his life* — "more" indeed, not just because they were more numerous, but because they included "all the lords of the Philistines" (v. 27), and even "their god" (v. 23)! The conflict with the Philistines was far from finished, of course. It was to continue for another two hundred years. But the struggle against them would never be quite the same after Samson's death, for he had demonstrated the vulnerability of their leadership and Yahweh's supremacy over their god. When the Philistines temporarily captured the ark, Dagon fell again, as he had done when they captured Samson (1 Sam. 5:1-5), and David ended their power forever (2 Sam. 5:17-25). But there is an important sense in which David merely completed what Samson had begun. In terms of both its size and significance, his victory in Dagon's temple can rightly be seen as the consummation of his Naziriteship, and the full realization of his destiny. Samson did not deliver Israel from the Philistines, but he did "begin" to do so, just as Yahweh's messenger said he would (13:5).

d. Epilogue (16:31)

31 *Then his brothers and all his father's house came down and took him and brought him up and buried him between Zorah and Eshtaol, in the tomb of his father Manoah. He had judged Israel for twenty years.*

31 This quiet epilogue brings closure by telling how Samson was brought back at last to the place, *between Zorah and Eshtaol,* where the Spirit had first begun to move him (13:25). It also shows us how, in the respect shown to him by *his brothers and all his father's house,* he was at last reconciled to them, and they to him. His being laid in *the tomb of his father Manoah*[186] completes the theme of reconciliation and brings the whole frenzied movement of his life to its eventual point of rest.

The final note, about his judging Israel for *twenty years,* corresponds to the similar note in 15:20, but with a significant difference. The note in 15:20 is linked sequentially with what has gone before: Samson defeated the Philistines at Lehi "and judged" Israel.[187] Here in 16:31 the syntax is disjunctive,[188] requiring the translation, "he *had* judged Israel." Taken together, the two notices indicate that Samson's judgeship effectively began with his victory at Lehi and ended with his victory and death in Gaza: twenty years in all. As far as we know, Samson never led Israel in battle, or "sat" dispensing justice in an ongoing way like Deborah (4:4-5). But whatever else he may or may not have done, the narrator is insistent in these two notices that he did *judge Israel,* just as surely as any of the other judges did. And the way he did it is what the battles at Lehi and Gaza show us: he inflicted defeat after defeat on the Philistines, and by so doing began to deliver Israel from them. The

---

186. Cf. Gideon, who "was buried in the tomb of his father Joash" (8:32).

187. The verb is in the normal first position and is a *wayyiqtol (wayyišpōt).*

188. The clause begins with the subject, $w^e h \hat{u}$, and the verb, which is displaced to the second position, is a *qatal (šāpaṭ).*

narrator is just as determined to honor Samson in his own way, as his family did in theirs.

Summary Reflections on 13:1–16:31

Now for some reflections on the Samson story as a whole. Given the heavy blend of passion, heroism, and tragedy that it contains, it is not surprising that the story has attracted the attention of great creative artists. No one can view "Samson and Delilah" (Rubens, 1577-1640) or "Samson Killing the Lion" (Léon Bonnet, 1833-1922), or hear Handel's "Samson" oratorio (1740), or read John Milton's *Samson Agonistes* without being aware of both the creative power of the artists and the greatness of the work that inspired them. Handel's oratorio was composed in the same year as his "Messiah"; Milton's poem followed hard on *Paradise Lost,* and the treatment in both cases shows that they did not regard the Samson story as an item of comic relief after the treatment of nobler themes. They took Samson seriously, and the author of Judges clearly wants us to do the same. That is not to say that the story has no humor in it. The sight of Samson bursting out of Gaza at midnight, for example, like a crazed orangutan escaping from a zoo, taking the gates with him, is a moment to be relished — especially since the joke is on the Philistines, Israel's enemies. But beneath all the surface chaos, and the mad careering here and there of the wild-man hero, there is a steady building toward a predetermined climax of profound theological significance. For Samson is not just Samson; he is also Israel. He is separated from other men, but he longs to be like them, just as Israel is separated from other nations, but is continually drawn to them. He goes after foreign women, as Israel goes after foreign gods. He suffers for his willfulness, as Israel does for its. And in his extremity he cries out to Yahweh, as Israel has repeatedly done. But now it is Samson *alone* who does so; he is remnant Israel; Israel reduced to a single man.[189] It is this implicit identification of Samson with Israel that gives the climax of the story its twin qualities of hope and grim foreboding. To

---

189. Edward L. Greenstein, "The Riddle of Samson," *Prooftexts* 1, no. 3 (1981): 24, argues that the riddle formula (what appears to be x can later be recognized as y) pervades the entire narrative of Samson and provides the key to its interpretation. The "solution" he proposes to the narrative as a whole considered as a riddle is, "What appears to be Samson is the people of Israel; what appears as the Naziriteship of Samson is the Israelite covenant." Cf. Vickery, "In Strange Ways," p. 62. Although Vickery does not press the analogy as far as Greenstein, he, too, notes "the parallelism of individual behaviour and national fate" in the Samson story, so that Samson is not only Samson, but also "the figure of Israel." A similar point is made by the chorus in Milton's re-creation of the story in his epic poem, who cry, when they see the blinded Samson, "O mirror of our fickle state" (Milton, *Samson Agonistes,* line 164).

what terrible straits will Yahweh have to reduce Israel before it, too, is reconciled to its separateness? In the broader sweep of Old Testament history the blinding of Samson, Israel's last judge, and his being taken down to Gaza, foreshadow the blinding of Zedekiah, Israel's last king, and his deportation to Babylon (2 Kgs. 25:7).[190]

Other perspectives on Samson are suggested by the few (and in two cases, doubtful) references to him elsewhere in the canon. In the review of God's past acts for Israel in 1 Samuel 12:11, it is more than likely that in the list, "Jerubbaal, Bedan (= Barak?), Jephthah, and Samuel," the last should be "Samson" rather than "Samuel," as in some manuscripts of the LXX and the Syriac.[191] If so, Samson is recognized by Samuel himself and the biblical author, without any apparent embarrassment, as someone by whom Yahweh had delivered Israel before they had a king — an indication of the positive potential of the Samson tradition. Of particular interest for Christian readers, of course, is the way this is picked up and developed in the New Testament. Care is needed, however, lest we see allusions to Samson where they are probably not intended. The view that Matthew 2:23, "He [Jesus] will be called a Nazarene *(Nazōraios)*" (NIV), alludes to Judges 13:5, "the boy [Samson] will be a Nazirite *(nāzîr)*," has a long history, and has been advocated by many weighty commentators, including John Calvin. It is generally discounted these days, however, because it has no apparent connection with what Matthew is saying in the immediate context: that Jesus grew up in Nazareth, a relatively obscure and despised place (John 1:46; Acts 24:5). If so, his claim, in the same verse, that this happened so that "what had been spoken by the prophets might be fulfilled" (NIV) is not an allusion to Judges 13:5, but to the fact that the Old Testament prophets in general had foretold that the Messiah would be despised.[192]

We are back on solid ground, though, when we come to Hebrews 11:32. Here Samson is explicitly named in another review of Israel's history, this time with a focus on faith, which the writer defines at the outset as "the assurance of things hoped for, the conviction of things not seen" (v. 1 ESV). Many examples are given, ranging from Abel (v. 4) right through the Old Testament canon and beyond, to "Jesus, the founder and perfector of *our* faith" (12:2 ESV, my emphasis). Samson is unabashedly cited, along with Gideon, Barak, Jephthah, David, and the prophets, as someone who exhib-

190. I owe this observation to David Pennant, formerly of Trinity College in Bristol, UK. For the reason why I understand Samson, not Samuel, to be Israel's last judge, see Section III of the Introduction.

191. See the MT apparatus, and the NRSV.

192. So D. A. Carson, "Matthew," in *The Expositor's Bible Commentary, Volume 8,* ed. F. E. Gaebelein and J. D. Douglas (Grand Rapids: Zondervan/Regency, 1984), p. 97. I am indebted to Carson for the substance of the preceding paragraph.

ited such faith (v. 32). This is rather surprising, of course, in view of his general character and conduct as we have seen it in Judges. However, at the very least it should provoke us to go back and look at the Samson of Judges 13–16 again, not to read faith back into it, but to see whether it may be there in ways we haven't adequately appreciated.

The list of worthies in Hebrews 11:32 is followed immediately, in verse 33, by the qualifying clause, "who through faith conquered kingdoms" (NIV). In view of this the most obvious parts of the Samson story to reconsider are his victories over the Philistines at Lehi and Gaza, at the end of chapters 15 and 16 respectively. On any reckoning these are the two crowning moments of his career, and the only two places where he cries out to God. In the first, he cries out for life, and is given it; in the second, he asks for death, and is given that. In the first he confesses himself to be Yahweh's servant (15:18). In both he acknowledges his total dependence upon God for what he does not yet have (rescue from death, vengeance on the Philistines). In the second he effectively claims what he has asked for by pushing hard against the two pillars, and, as he does so, receives it. In both cases his victory over the Philistines is God-given (15:18; 16:28-30). Is it any wonder, then, that the author of Hebrews 11 saw Samson *at his best* as someone who exhibited the kind of faith he was speaking about?

Finally, we need to consider the significance of the fact that the review of Old Testament people of faith in Hebrews 11 reaches its climax in the achievement of Christ, "the author and perfecter of our faith" (12:1-2 NIV). At the very least this must mean that the figures of Hebrews 11 were forerunners, in some sense, of Jesus, the perfectly faithful one. The fact that they were similar to Jesus in terms of their faith does not, of itself, justify extrapolation to other qualities. For example, in terms of his character and motivations Samson was utterly unlike Jesus, and the same is true, to varying degrees, of all the other persons listed. In fact, the term *perfecter (teleiōtēn)* implies that, even in the matter of faith, those who came before were different from Jesus as well as similar to him. Nevertheless, other points of correspondence do exist. For example, "the prophets" of verse 32 were definitely forerunners of Christ, through whom God has spoken in "these last days" (1:1-2 NIV). And the persecution and mistreatment suffered by the martyrs of verse 37 anticipate the opposition and shame suffered by Christ (12:2-3). In the same way, Christian readers can hardly fail to notice a number of points of correspondence between the broad structure of Samson's career and that of Christ: his annunciation by a divine messenger, his marvelous conception, his holiness as a Nazirite, his endowment with the Spirit, his rejection by his own people, his being handed over by their leaders, the mocking and scorn he suffered at their hands, and the way his calling was consummated in his death, by which he defeated the god Dagon and laid the foundation for a deliverance to be fully realized in a day to come. The correspondences are too numerous, and too germane to who Samson was, for what he achieved to be simply brushed aside as fanciful. The fact is that when the story is read in the context of the Bible as a whole, we discover even here, in the most unlikely of places, intimations of things to come.[193]

III. EPILOGUE (17:1–21:25)

A collection of unhappy stories[1]

As noted in Section IV of the Introduction, chapters 17–21 contain two major narrative complexes, in chapters 17–18 and 19–21 respectively, which are clearly different in kind from those that have gone before. They are formally distinct in that they stand outside the editorial framework, with its repeating pattern, that unifies 3:7–16:31. They are also distinct in content, in that neither of them features the career of a judge. They are set in the same general period as the judge narratives from Othniel to Samson, but do not follow them chronologically. The entire epilogue is spanned by a refrain that appears in an expanded form in 17:6 and 21:25, and an abbreviated form in 18:1 and 19:1, giving the following inverted pattern:

A   (17:6)   *In those days there was no king in Israel;*
               everyone did what was right in their own eyes.

B   (18:1)   *In those days there was no king in Israel.*

B′   (19:1)   *In those days there was no king in Israel.*

A′   (21:25)   *In those days there was no king in Israel;*
               everyone did what was right in their own eyes.

The two narratives linked by this structure have so much in common that the conjunction is a very natural one. They both feature a Levite who, in each case, has connections with "Bethlehem in Judah" on the one hand, and "the hill country of Ephraim" on the other (17:7-8; 19:1). The Levite of the first story resides in Bethlehem but travels to the hill country of Ephraim; the Levite in the second resides in the hill country of Ephraim but travels to Bethle-

---

193. For a historical review of Samson in Christian typology, see Gunn, *Judges,* pp. 180-82. Luther and Calvin both viewed Samson as a type of Christ.
1. Mobley, *Empty Men,* p. 225.

hem.[2] In both cases the personal fortunes of the Levite become the occasion for larger action. In the first story it is the presence of the Levite in Micah's house that attracts the attention of the Danites (18:3), who transfer both the Levite and Micah's image to Dan. In the second story it is the presence of the Levite and his concubine in Gibeah that triggers the outrage committed there and the war that follows (19:22). The first narrative concludes with a reference to the sanctuary at Shiloh (18:31); the second concludes with the abduction of "the daughters of Shiloh" (21:19-23). The central section of the book dealt with a series of external threats to Israel's existence in the form of foreign invasion and oppression. The epilogue focuses on the internal threat to its existence posed by its near collapse into moral and spiritual chaos.

It is possible, indeed likely, that these narratives were once separate from each other, and were brought together and put where they now are as part of the final stages of the formation of the book. The presence in both of them of wandering, unemployed Levites suggests a time after the separation of Israel (the northern kingdom) from Judah, when Jeroboam I appointed non-Levites as priests (1 Kgs. 12:31), or after the reforms of Hezekiah in the eighth century B.C., or Josiah in the seventh century, which involved the closure of many shrines in both the south and the north (2 Kgs 18:1-4; 23:1-20). The reference to "the captivity of the land" in 18:30 implies that at least the second of the two narratives was either written, or received its final editing, after the deportation of the population of Dan to Assyria by Tiglath-pileser III in 734 B.C.[3] In these settings the stories may have served to support the Davidic monarchy as an institution, and the reforms of Hezekiah and/or Josiah in particular. Negatively they may have served to attack idolatry and its associated evils (as in the reign of Manasseh), or the corrupt worship at the northern shrines, especially at Dan. The extremely negative portrayal of the Benjaminites in chapters 19–21 may reflect the conflict between David and Saul (a Benjaminite) in the early period of the monarchy. The refrain, which anticipates the rise of kingship, and the references to Shiloh in 18:31 and 21:12-21 suggest a strong, perhaps original link with the opening chapters of 1 Samuel.

All these possibilities exist, and there is no way, finally, of adjudicating between them. What is clear, however, is that whatever their original provenance and purpose may have been, these two narratives now form a most appropriate epilogue to Judges. Among other things they provide, in chapters 17 and 18, an account of the forced migration of the Danites that was foreshadowed in 1:34. And the way the question that is asked in 20:23

2. Cf. Boling, *Judges,* p. 42. This inversion of corresponding narrative elements mirrors the inverted pattern of the editorial refrain noted above.

3. So Block, *Judges, Ruth,* p. 513.

echoes the one that was put in 1:1-2 prompts us to read the end of the book in the light of its beginning, bringing closure to the whole.[4]

A. RELIGIOUS CHAOS: MICAH AND THE DANITES (17:1–18:31)

They did it their way.[5]

In this first major narrative, the editorial comments at 17:6 and 18:1 occur at nodal points in the development of the plot: points of discontinuity, at which one episode reaches a point of rest and a further development is initiated from a different direction.[6] The resulting three-part structure is as follows:

> 17:1-5 Micah acquires an idol and installs it, along with an ephod and teraphim, in his private shrine in the hill country of Ephraim.
>
> [Break]
>
> 17:7-13 A Levite from Bethlehem in Judah travels to the hill country of Ephraim, meets Micah, and is installed by him as a priest in his shrine.
>
> [Break]
>
> 18:1b-31 The Danites, in the course of migrating northward, come to Micah's shrine. They take both his idol and his priest and install them in their own newly established shrine at Dan.[7]

1. The Establishment of Micah's Shrine (17:1-5)

1 *There was a man from Mount Ephraim whose name was Micah.*
2 *He said to his mother, "The eleven hundred [pieces] of silver which*

---

4. See Section IV of the Introduction.

5. The heading is an allusion to the song "I Did It My Way," popularized by Frank Sinatra.

6. The same phenomenon appears in the plot structure of the Deborah-Barak narrative. I owe this definition of nodal point to D. F. Murray, "Narrative Structure and Technique in the Deborah-Barak Story, Judges iv 4-22," in *Studies in the Historical Books of the Old Testament,* ed. J. A. Emerton (Leiden: Brill, 1979), p. 159.

7. Cf. Amit, "Hidden Polemic," p. 5. Amit herself holds that the final part of the narrative ends with v. 30, and that v. 31 is attached to provide a connection [via Shiloh?] with what follows.

were taken from you, about which you yourself uttered a curse,[8] *and even said it in my hearing — well, that silver is with me — I am the one who took it, but now I will return it to you."*[9] *And his mother said, "Blessed be my son by*[10] *Yahweh."*

3 *He returned the eleven hundred [pieces] of silver to his mother, and his mother said, "I had wholly consecrated*[11] *the money to Yahweh from my own hand for my son, to make an idol of cast metal."*[12]

4 [13]*Then his mother took two hundred [pieces] of silver and gave it to the silversmith, and he made it into an idol of cast metal, and it ended up in the house of Micah.*

5 *Now this fellow Micah had a house of God, and made an ephod and teraphim, and consecrated one of his sons, who became his priest.*

This opening episode of the narrative is framed by the references to *Micah* in verse 1 and verses 4b, 5. Verse 1 provides background information, the action

8. Literally just "you swore *('ālît)* [an oath]." I have rendered it "uttered a curse" because of the consistently negative connotations of *'lh* in the Old Testament (*HALOT*, p. 51; see, e.g., Deut. 29:20 [Heb.]; 1 Sam. 14:24 [where it is specified by *'ārûr*, "cursed"]; Hos. 4:2; 10:4; 1 Kgs. 8:31; Zech. 5:3, etc.). Even when it is used to confirm the truth of someone's words, such an oath is in effect self-cursing (e.g., Num. 5:21). Hence the oath taking here in v. 2 cannot be the vow of consecration referred to retrospectively in v. 3, which, in any case, must have preceded it.

9. The text as it stands is not entirely coherent, since Micah returns the silver to his mother twice, at the beginning of v. 3 and again at the beginning of v. 4. With *BHS* apparatus and most commentators, I have restored *"but now I will return it to you"* from the end of v. 3 to follow *"I took it"* here in v. 2, where it logically belongs. Cf. HCSB. I have also dropped the second statement that Micah returned the silver to his mother from the beginning of verse 4, since its occurrence there was probably caused by the misplacement of the clause that I have restored to its correct position in v. 2.

10. The preposition on *la-Yahweh* expresses agency, as in Gen. 14:19, "Blessed be Abraham *by* God Most High *(l⁰ʾēl ʾelyôn)*." Arnold and Choi, *Biblical Hebrew Syntax*, p. 114.

11. Or "I hereby consecrate" (the performative perfect); cf. ESV, NIV, HCSB, etc. Either translation of *haqdēš hiqdaštî* is possible, but the retrospective rendering makes better sense of both the woman's extreme reaction to the theft of the money, and what she does with it when she gets it back. Cf. LXX, KJV, and Boling, *Judges,* p. 254.

12. See the textual note on *"but now I will restore it to you"* at the end of v. 2. The Hebrew *pesel ûmassēkâ*, "a graven image and a molten image," is a hendiadys. Also in v. 4, where the singular verb, *wayᵉhî* (and it was . . .), confirms that a single object is in view. The splitting open of this hendiadys in 18:17 may simply be a stylistic device. The resulting envelope construction encloses "ephod and teraphim," the pair first introduced in 17:5. Cf. Boling, *Judges,* pp. 256, 264.

13. At this point the MT has the words *wayyāšeb ʾet-hakkesep lᵉʾimmô*, "and he returned the silver to his mother." For an explanation of why I have deleted them see the textual note on *"but now I will return it to you"* in v. 2.

happens in verses 2-4 (money changes hands and an idol is created), and verse 5 fills out the episode by providing more detailed information about the situation in which the action has taken place.

1 With the economy typical of Hebrew narrative we are introduced at once to the central character, and told his name, *Micah (mîḵāyᵉhû)*. It means, "Who is like Yahweh?"[14] It has a significance in the narrative that is not yet apparent. We are also told his place of origin. He was *from*[15] *Mount Ephraim,* the central high country immediately north of Jerusalem, in the territory of the most prominent and powerful of the tribes.[16] Geographically, it lay at the center of Israelite territory, which is probably why Ehud blew the trumpet there to rally the Israelite tribes to his cause (3:27), and why Deborah later sat there judging Israel (4:4-5). Anything that happened there was likely to have much more than purely local significance. *Mount Ephraim* was no backwater!

2-4 The narrative proper gets under way with a conversation between Micah and his mother. The *eleven hundred [pieces] of silver* (v. 2) he speaks of is the same as the amount each Philistine lord had offered to Delilah for betraying Samson — a sizeable amount of money.[17] There are some obscurities in these three verses due, in part at least, to damage the text has suffered in transmission. My translation reflects a couple of emendations which are explained in the footnotes to verse 2. The basic sequence of events is as follows:

Verse 2
a. Eleven hundred pieces of silver are stolen[18] from Micah's mother.
b. She utters a curse *('lh)* on the person who did it, not knowing it was Micah.
c. Micah hears her utter the curse.
d. He tells his mother that he is the one who took the money, and says he will return it to her.
e. On hearing this, his mother blesses *(brk)* Micah in the name of the Yahweh.

---

14. The same form of the name, with slightly different vocalization, occurs in 1 Kgs. 22:9 (Micaiah ben Imlah). Another form *(mîḵāyâ)* occurs in Jer. 26:18 (Micah the Morashite). Cf. *mîḵā'ēl* (Who is like El?) in Num. 13:13; Dan. 10:13; 1 Chron. 5:13, etc.

15. The use of *min* to indicate source, as in 12:8. Contrast *bᵉhar 'eprāyim (in Mount Ephraim)* in 2:9; 3:27; 4:5. The *from* of 17:1 reflects the standpoint of the author, who writes after Micah's relocation to Dan in ch. 18.

16. See 8:1 and 12:1.

17. See the comments on 16:5.

18. Literally, "taken" *(luqqaḥ).* Cf. the use of the same verb in 18:17.

Verse 3

f. Micah returns the money as he said he would do.

g. On receiving it, Micah's mother tells him that before it was stolen she had consecrated *(qdš)* the money to Yahweh to be made into an idol for her son (i.e., for Micah).

Verse 4

h. She then takes two hundred of the eleven hundred pieces of silver and gives them to the silversmith, who uses them to make an idol.

i. The idol ends up in Micah's house, as his mother had intended.

At one level, then, this is a story with a happy ending: curse turned to blessing, and the consecration of something to Yahweh. Evil is overcome by confession, and a mother's intentions for her son are realized. Broken relationships are healed, and Yahweh is worshiped. But of course, this leaves us with a number of unanswered questions. Why would Micah's mother consecrate silver to *Yahweh,* to be made into an *idol?*[19] And having consecrated all *eleven* hundred pieces of silver for this purpose, why did she give only *two* hundred of them to the silversmith? What happened to the other nine hundred? This strange conjunction of devotion to Yahweh and idolatry, and disconnection between word and act, gives the episode a satirical quality which, as we are about to see, turns out to be characteristic of the whole narrative.

The reference to Micah's *house (bayit)* at the end of verse 4 may simply mean his "home." It would not be the first or last time household gods have featured in Israel's history.[20] But the term normally used for them is *tᵉrāpîm (teraphim).* The terms used of Micah's idol *(pesel* and *massēkâ,* v. 3) normally refer to the kinds of objects found at public shrines of various kinds.[21] More light is thrown on the issue of Micah's *bayit* in verse 5, which completes this opening episode of the narrative.

5 Micah's *house* is clearly something far more than a simple domestic dwelling. It has all the paraphernalia of a shrine, including an *ephod, teraphim* (household gods), and a *priest,* as well as his newly acquired *idol* (v. 4). It may have been a separate structure, or a part of his own house (in the domestic sense) that was set apart and furnished as a shrine.[22] The fact that he

---

19. Contrast Deut. 5:8 (cf. Exod. 20:4; 34:17)! The incongruity of her vow is typical of the way the whole scene is handled.

20. For example, Gen. 31:19, 34, 35; 2 Kgs. 23:24; Hos. 3:4; Zech. 10:2.

21. For example, Exod. 32:4; 2 Kgs. 21:7; 2 Chron. 33:7; Nah. 1:14.

22. "Archaeological excavations at sites throughout Syria-Palestine have uncovered house-shrines. These private sanctuaries would have served the needs of households and perhaps extended families within a village culture (the plaster fragments from Tell

was able to set up and maintain such a place suggests that he was a wealthy man. That his mother was able to set aside eleven hundred pieces of silver for an idol is suggestive of the same thing; he certainly belonged to a family of no small means. The *ephod* was a priestly garment, but given the environment in which we find it here, and the fact that Micah *made* it, it is unlikely that it bore much resemblance to the splendid high-priestly garment of that name described in Exodus 28:6-13; 39:2-7.[23] The *teraphim,* also purpose-made by Micah himself, were small household gods, thought, among other things, to bring luck and prosperity to the family.[24] Many examples have been found in Mesopotamia and Syria-Palestine, mainly in private homes rather than at public shrines. They stand in contrast here to the much grander idol made from his mother's silver. Finally, to complete the setting up of his shrine, Micah *consecrated one of his sons, who became his priest.* Literally, he "filled the hand" *(way^emallē' 'et-yad)* of one of his sons. This is the normal idiomatic expression for consecrating a priest.[25] What is not normal, of course, is whom he appoints. There has been nothing in the preceding verse to suggest that Micah himself was a Levite (he was just "a man from Mount Ephraim"), so we have no reason to think his son was either, and subsequent events will confirm that he wasn't. So the priest that Micah appointed was just as makeshift and irregular as everything else in his shrine.

The expression used to describe the entire installation with its silver idol, teraphim, ephod, and priest, is *bêt 'elōhîm,* which I have translated *house of God.* But the last term, *'elōhîm,* is ambiguous, especially in this context. It is plural in form, but may mean either "God" (as when *bêt 'elōhîm* is used of the Jerusalem temple),[26] or "gods" (as in the expression *'ah^arê 'elōhîm,* "other [pagan] gods").[27] In the present context, the fact that Micah's mother has blessed him in the name of Yahweh (v. 2) and consecrated the silver she gave him to Yahweh (v. 3) suggests that his *bêt 'elōhîm* should be thought of as a "house of *God.*" But the fact that it houses an *idol* (v. 4) and

---

Deir ʿAlla may be associated with such a shrine, as may the Kuntillet ʿAjrud inscriptions). In larger population centres, more formal temples and shrines also existed." *BBC,* p. 271.

23. Compare Gideon's homemade ephod in 8:27.

24. Something of their importance can be seen in Laban's frantic desire to recover the *teraphim* that Rachel had stolen from his home (Gen. 31:19-35). See the comments on v. 4, and cf. *BBC,* p. 63.

25. As in, e.g., Exod. 28:41; 29:9, 29, 33, 35; Lev. 8:33; 16:32; 21:10. Its significance is unknown. It may have consisted of placing something, such as a sacrificial animal (Exod. 29:24) or some other symbol of office, in the priest's hand.

26. For example, Pss. 42:4; 52:8 (Heb. 10); 55:14 (Heb. 15); 84:10; Ezra 8:33; 1 Chron. 10:10; 2 Chron. 34:9, etc.

27. As frequently in Deuteronomy, and in Josh. 23:16; 24:2, 16; Judg. 2:12, 17, 19; 10:10, etc.

teraphim (v. 5) implies that it is in fact a "house of *gods.*" In translation we are forced to choose between the two or use a neutral term such as "shrine." But the ambiguity of *bêt ʾelōhîm* is not a problem to be solved, for it captures and completes the satirical irony of the entire passage: Micah's "house of God" is in fact a "house of gods," but neither Micah nor his mother seems to be able to tell the difference. The body of the book has shown us the nation of Israel vacillating between faithfulness to Yahweh and going after other gods, but at least able to know they were doing so (as, e.g., in 10:15-16). The present passage shows us that, at the domestic and village level, even this ability has been lost. The man whose name means "Who is like Yahweh?" can become the owner and patron of a house of idols! It is an episode of complete religious chaos.

2. Break: The First Occurrence of the Refrain (17:6)

> 6 *In those days there was no king in Israel. Everyone*[28] *did what was right in their [own] eyes.*

6 This is the first occurrence of the refrain that runs through chapters 17–21, and it serves at least three functions. First, it helps to link the body of the book to the epilogue, which begins here in chapter 17. The body of the book ended with the story of Samson, who "saw" a woman in Timnah and demanded to have her because, as he put it, she is "right in my eyes" (*yāšerâ beʿênāy,* 14:3). So the last judge was a man who did what was right in his own eyes, and from there we move on to the epilogue, in which *everyone [does] what* [is] *right in their [own] eyes (hayyāšār beʿênāy).* The repetition of this key expression helps bind these two parts of the book together. Second, as we have already noted, it marks a point of discontinuity (a nodal point) in the Micah narrative itself. Third, it generalizes from the particular situation depicted in verses 1-5. In the days of the judges, "everyone" did what was right in their own eyes. In other words, Micah and his mother were typical rather than exceptional. Fourth, it hints at the next major development to take place in Israel's development as a nation — the emergence of kingship — and in effect offers an apology for it. The institution of the monarchy was needed to bring some kind of order out of the religious chaos of the judges period.[29] It

---

28. Literally, "*a man (ʾîš)*." Mobley, *Empty Men,* p. 148, suggests that *ʾîš* might mean that "in those days, when there was no king, it was every 'patriarch,' every 'warlord,' every 'patron' . . . who did what was right in his own eyes," and hence that "man" should be retained in translation. But this is unlikely, in my judgment, because of the prominent role Micah's *mother* plays in the story.

29. Cf. Cundall, "Judges — An Apology for the Monarchy?" pp. 180-81.

also, incidentally, provides some data relevant to the question of the time of the final editing of the book.[30]

3. The Appointment of a Levite as Micah's Priest (17:7-13)

7 Now it happened that there was a young man from Bethlehem in Judah, from the clan of Judah, who was a Levite and was sojourning there.

8 The man left the town of Bethlehem in Judah to sojourn in whatever place he could find, and he came to Mount Ephraim, to the house of Micah, as he made his journey.

9 Micah said to him, "Where do you come from?" And he said to him, "I am a Levite from Bethlehem in Judah, and am on my way to sojourn in whatever place I can find."

10 Micah said to him, "Stay with me and become my father and priest, and I will give you ten [pieces] of silver a year, and a set of clothes, and your upkeep." So the Levite went [with him].

11 The Levite was happy to stay with the man; so the young man became to him like one of his sons.

12 Micah consecrated the Levite, and the young man became his priest, and took up residence in Micah's house.

13 Micah said, "Now I know that Yahweh will treat me well, because the Levite has become my priest."

This second episode is entirely taken up with how a wandering Levite came into contact with Micah and was installed as priest in his shrine. It has two parts. The first is framed by the *way*ᵉ*hî* of verse 7 which opens it *(Now it happened that there was a young man from Bethlehem in Judah)*, and the double *way*ᵉ*hî* of verse 12 that closes it *(and the young man became his priest, and took up residence in Micah's house)*.[31] The second part, verse 13, ends the entire episode on a highly ironic note which sets Micah up for the catastrophic fall he will experience in chapter 18.

7-8   The *young man* we meet here was a member of the priestly tribe of Levi (Deut. 33:8-11). Only descendants of Aaron were supposed to be actual priests; the rest were to be assistants (Num. 8:5-26). With no tribal territory of their own, they lived among the other tribes. Although allotted specific towns,[32] they were not confined to these, especially in the chaotic conditions of the judges period.[33] This particular Levite was from *Bethlehem*

---

30. See Section III of the Introduction, on the history of the book's formation.

31. Cf. Boling, *Judges,* pp. 256-57.

32. See Num. 35:1-5; Josh. 21:1-42.

33. So *NBC,* p. 282. See the comments above in the introduction to chapters 17–21 as a whole on the possible background(s) of this narrative and the following one.

in Judah,[34] where he had been *sojourning* (living as a landless foreigner). In view of this, the statement that he was *from the clan of Judah* is puzzling, and has been deleted by some as a gloss.[35] There is very little manuscript evidence for this, however. The only significant ancient text or version that lacks it is the Syriac, where its omission is as likely to be an emendment to remove a perceived difficulty as a witness to a different original. The LXX supports the MT. As part of the text as we have it, it seems to indicate two things. The word *clan (mišpaḥaṯ)* may allude to the weakness of even the tribe of Judah at this time.[36] And the whole phrase, *from the clan of Judah,* probably indicates the place and circumstances of this Levite's birth: that is, that he was born to parents who were already living among the people of Judah.[37] At any rate, the young man apparently concluded that he had no long-term prospects there, and went away in search of a better life for himself elsewhere (v. 8a). And so he came to the house of Micah, not, evidently, as his consciously chosen destination, but *as he made his journey (laʿᵃśôṯ darkô,* v. 8b).

9-12 It is evident from what takes place here that, in their chance meeting, both Micah and the Levite see an opportunity to better themselves. In spite of the impression of total confusion conveyed by Micah's previous conduct, he shows here that he is at least aware of a traditional connection between Levites and priesthood.[38] So he offers the Levite *ten [pieces] of silver a year, a set of clothes, and [his] upkeep* if he will stay and become his priest. It is a further indication of Micah's wealth (cf. v. 5 and comments), and apparently an offer the Levite finds more than attractive! He accepts at once, and *goes* with Micah; that is, after being *consecrated* (v. 12) he moves in with him and becomes a key member of his household, like *one of his sons* (v. 11). We cannot help but recall, at this point, that Micah has already consecrated one of his own sons as priest back in verse 5! What happened to this son? Was he replaced, or demoted, or has he simply gone missing, like the nine hundred pieces of silver that went missing in verses 1-4? No one seems to know or care; least of all Micah and his new employee, who settle at once into a cozy "father/son" relationship. In religious matters it is the Levite who is *father* to Micah (v. 10), while in domestic affairs (by implication) it is Micah who is father to the Levite (v. 11).

34. Cf. the other, northern Bethlehem of 12:8.

35. See the note in the apparatus of *BHS.*

36. See the comments on 15:11-12, and note how the Danites are referred to as a clan *(mišpaḥaṯ)* in 13:2, but a tribe *(šēḇeṭ)* in 18:30 after they have established themselves in the north.

37. Cf. Samuel, who was an Ephraimite by birth (1 Sam. 1:1) but was identified as a Levite in 1 Chron. 6:26. See the other possibilities suggested by Daniel Block in *Judges, Ruth,* pp. 485-86.

38. See the comments, above, on v. 7.

13 The episode ends with Micah confident that his future is now well secured:

> *"Now I know that Yahweh will treat me well,[39]*
> *because the Levite has become my priest."*

He is wrong, of course. In fact, he is standing on the edge of a chasm, for we have come to a major turning point in the development of the plot. Micah's personal fortunes, which have risen steadily throughout the first two episodes, are about to undergo a sudden reversal. From now on nothing will go right for him. It is a moment of the most exquisite irony.

4. Break: The Second Occurrence of the Refrain (18:1a)

1a *In those days there was no king in Israel.*

See the comments on the longer form of the same refrain at 17:6. The longer form has two parts, which together constitute a diagnosis of the chaotic state of Israel as depicted in chapters 17–21. The second part of the refrain (not repeated here) refers to what was wrong at the micro-level, namely, extreme individualism: everyone doing what was right in their own eyes. The first part (which *is* repeated here) refers to what was amiss at the macro-level, namely, the absence of any strong central authority capable of rectifying the situation: *there was no king in Israel.* Here, as in 17:6, the refrain marks a point of discontinuity in the development of the plot. What follows is a new narrative episode that at first seems to be quite independent of what has gone before, and does not intersect with it until some spies sent out by the Danites come into the vicinity of Micah's house on their way north and happen to hear a voice they recognize (vv. 2b-3).

The fact that only the shorter form of the refrain occurs here and in 19:1 has two effects. First, by implication, it emphasizes the absence of a strong central authority as the primary problem. This anticipates, in a positive way, the emergence of kingship in 1 and 2 Samuel, and the role the Davidic kings in particular will play in establishing Jerusalem and the temple as the regulating center of Israel's administration and worship. It also foreshadows the key role that kings like Hezekiah and Josiah will play in abolishing shrines such as those of Micah and the Danites, and centralizing all worship in Jerusalem. Second, as we noted earlier, the shorter form of the refrain here and at 19:1 gives the fourfold repetition of the refrain a heightened structural significance by forming it into a chiasm. This suggests that the two

---

39. Literally, "do me good" *(yêṭîb).*

major narratives of chapters 17–21 are not merely two miscellaneous items in an appendix, but parts of a very intentional literary composition spanning all five chapters.

5. The Migration of the Danites and the Transference of Micah's Idol to the Shrine at Dan (18:1b-31)

This final episode of the narrative is much longer and more complex than the first two. After the introduction in verse 1b, it consists of two major parts, each involving a series of scenes linked by bridging narrative.[40] The first spans verses 1b-10, and deals with a reconnaissance mission carried out by spies sent by the Danites to find a suitable place for them to migrate to, and concludes with their returning and reporting their discovery of Laish, in the far north. The second, in verses 11-31, describes the subsequent migration of the Danites and their conquest and occupation of Laish. It ends with their re-naming it after their ancestor, Dan, and setting up a shrine of their own there. Micah, his idol, and the Levite he had appointed as his priest feature in both parts of the narrative. In the process Micah loses everything he had acquired in chapter 17, and his idol and priest end up in the new shrine at Dan.

a. The Selection and Commissioning of the Spies (18:1b-2)

1b *In those days the tribe of the Danites was seeking for itself an allot-ment [of land] to live in, for to that day no allotment[41] had fallen to it among the tribes of Israel.*

2 *The people of Dan sent five men from all parts of their clan[42] — val-iant men — from Zorah and Eshtaol, to spy out the land and explore it. They said to them, "Go, explore the land." So they came to Mount Ephraim, to the house of Micah, and lodged there.*

1b The situation summarized here reflects the description of the plight of the Danites in 1:34 and Joshua 19:40-47a. In the time of Joshua they had been given an *allotment [of land]* in the vicinity of Zorah and Eshtaol in the south, but had not been able to get a secure foothold there because of pres-

---

40. Cf. Alter, *The Art of Biblical Narrative,* p. 63: "A proper narrative event oc-curs when the narrative tempo slows down enough for us to discriminate a particular scene." Biblical scenes in this sense characteristically feature dialogue.

41. The preposition on *bᵉnaḥᵃlâ* is best understood as an instance of the *beth essentiae* (GKC #119 i). The retention of the subject to the end of the sentence makes it emphatic, something difficult to capture in translation without undue woodenness.

42. Reading the singular, with the MT. The LXX and Targum read the plural, "clans."

sure from the local Canaanite population and later the Philistines (see the comments on 1:34). So although land had been allotted to them, it had not *fallen* to them in the sense of fully becoming theirs, and their hold on the part of it they had managed to occupy became increasingly tenuous over time. The events of the Samson story may belong to the latter part of this period, or to the period following the migration of the Danites, when a remnant that remained in the south had effectively been absorbed into the tribe of Judah.[43]

2 The previous verse spoke of the "tribe" *(šēbeṭ)* of the Danites. Here they are referred to as a *clan (mišpaḥâ),* alluding, perhaps, to their enfeebled state at the time.[44] Nevertheless, it was a clan of some complexity, with various *parts (qᵉṣôṭ),* from which *five . . . valiant men* were chosen to go on a reconnaissance mission to find an alternative place for the Danites to live. This is the first indication that what follows is going to unfold in a way that echoes, at many points, the traditional accounts of Israel's exploration, conquest, and settlement in the land of Canaan (as in Num. 13–14; Deut. 1). That operation, too, began with the sending out of spies (Num. 13:2). We will need to keep this comparison in mind as we read on because, as we will see, it is of particular importance for the way the Danite migration is viewed in this chapter.

The reference to *Zorah and Eshtaol* is another obvious point of connection with the Samson story of chapters 13–16. It was here, between Zorah and Eshtaol, that the Spirit first began to disturb Samson (13:25). Now something else is set in motion from the same locality, but this time there is no reference to divine initiative, even beneath the surface of things. The spies are simply *sent* by their fellow clansmen. There is nothing remarkable about this in itself, but the comparison with 13:25, and the sustained absence of God in all that follows, will turn out to be a distinctive and significant aspect of how this particular narrative is constructed. The "between-ness" of 13:25 (*"between* Zorah and Eshtaol") and the "and-ness" of the way the same locality is described here ("from Zorah *and* Eshtaol") suggest that, while this may have been the clan's heartland, it had no real center, and certainly no town or city of any size or strength. It is another indication of Dan's weakness. It was decentered; or, to put the same thing in a more forward-looking way, it needed a center. Hence the sending out of spies. The narrative will end with this need being met, albeit in a highly dubious fashion (vv. 27-29).

According to 1:34, the Danites had already been denied access to the coastal plain. With the Philistines to the south, and the areas to the east already settled by the tribes of Judah and Benjamin, the only logical direction for the spies to go was north, through the central highlands. So their arrival on *Mount Ephraim,* in the vicinity of Micah's house, toward nightfall, is un-

---

43. Which would explain the leading role played by the men of Judah in 15:9-13.
44. Cf. 13:1, 1:34, and the reference to the "clan of Judah" in 17:7.

derstandable (cf. 19:11). It is also one of those convenient coincidences that enable a story to take the particular shape that it does. In this particular case, of course, it enables the developing narrative of this chapter to intersect with that of chapter 17. We have already noted the indications of Micah's wealth. So finding the space and welcome they needed, the Danite spies *lodged there* for the night — which provides the setting for the next scene of the narrative.

b. The Spies Inquire of Micah's Levite (18:3-6)

> 3 *While they were at the house of Micah, they recognized the voice of the young Levite, so they turned in there. They said to him, "Who brought you here? What are you doing in this [place]? What is your business here?"*
> 4 *He told them, "This is what Micah did for me — he hired me, and I became his priest."*
> 5 *They said to him, "Please inquire of God so that we may know whether our journey which we are undertaking will be successful."*
> 6 *The priest said to them, "Go in peace. Your journey which you are undertaking is under Yahweh's favor."*

3-4 These verses backtrack briefly to explain how it was that the spies were drawn to Micah's house. It wasn't just their proximity to it, the time of day, or their need of lodging, but something they heard and *recognized,* namely, *the voice of the young Levite.* The recognition may have had something to do with the way the Levite spoke — not like a native of the area, but like someone from their own general locality. We have already seen in the Samson story the close connection between the Danites and the people of Judah, among whom the Levite had been living (see the comments on 15:9-11a; 16:3). Like the Danites themselves, he had traveled north seeking a better life for himself. It is not unlikely, therefore, that his accent identified him as someone from further south. In view of what follows, however, it is more than likely that the Danites actually knew the Levite from a previous encounter. This would better explain how they were attracted to Micah's house by the sound of the young man's voice, and the familiar terms in which they begin their conversation with him (v. 3b).

The Danites ask the Levite how he came to be in Micah's house, and what he is doing there. His reply is straightforward, and effectively a summary of what has already been narrated in 17:7-13. There is one significant difference, however. The Levite says:

> *"This is what Micah did for me — he hired (śkr) me,*
> *and I became his priest"* (v. 4).

432

Back in 17:12 the narrator had put it rather differently: literally, "Micah *filled the hand of* the Levite, and the young man became his priest." As we noted there, the expression "to fill the hand" is idiomatic for "consecrate" (see, e.g., Exod. 28:41; 29:9, 29, 33, 35; Lev. 8:33), and probably refers to the ceremonial filling of the appointee's hand with some token of his office. But the use of the term *hired (śkr)* here in 18:4 suggests that it is the filling of the hand in quite another sense that occupies the Levite's mind! The hint is not lost on the Danites, as we are about to see.

5-6 On finding that the Levite is a priest, the Danites ask him for an oracle regarding their journey — whether it will prosper *(taṣlîaḥ)*, that is, be *successful*. Their inquiry may have been prompted, not just by the Levite's official position, but by the presence of an ephod and teraphim in the shrine at which he served (17:5). The ephod as a sacred object is associated elsewhere in the Old Testament with oracular inquiry, especially before some dangerous activity is undertaken (e.g., 1 Sam. 23:1-12; 30:7-8; Ezek. 21:21),[45] and teraphim in particular seem to have been valued as a means of securing the wealth and prosperity of families or clans (Gen. 31:14-34). The request for Micah to "inquire of *ʾelōhîm*" (*God*, v. 5) recalls the reference to Micah's shrine as a "house of *ʾelōhîm* (God/gods)" back in 17:5. True to his character as a priest-for-hire, the Levite tells the Danites what they want to hear: *"Go in peace. Your journey which you are undertaking is under Yahweh's favor"* (v. 6). Literally, he tells them that their journey is "before *(nōkaḥ)* Yahweh," but preceded here by *peace (šālôm)* it can only mean that he looks upon it with favor. This completes the scene that began with the spies' arrival at Micah's house.

c. The Spies Discover and Appraise Laish (18:7)

7 *So the five men went off and came to Laish, and saw that it was inhabited and secure. The people who were in it were living according to the custom of the Sidonians, quietly and securely, with no [enemies] humiliating them because of anything in [their] land, for they were a long way [even] from the Sidonians, and had no formal ties with anyone.*[46]

45. Gideon's ephod was also probably intended to serve such a purpose. See the comments on 8:22-27.

46. Or, with *Aram* (Syria), if *ʾādām* is a corruption of *ʾᵃrām* (Boling, *Judges*, p. 260). The text of this verse is very repetitious and syntactically confused, possibly because of the merging of two sources, one referring to the city (feminine), and the other to its people (masculine) (Moore, *Judges*, p. 390). With *BHS* I have taken the clause *yôšebet* (feminine)-*lābeṭaḥ kᵉmišpāṭ ṣidōnîm* as referring to the city, and *šōqēṭ ûbōṭēaḥ* (masculine), and the words which follow them, as referring to the people, and rearranged the order of the text accordingly. I have taken *yôšebet* to mean "inhabited" in line with the nor-

7 See the footnotes to the translation for the various textual and translation difficulties relating to this verse. *Laish* (or Leshem, Josh. 19:47) lay at the sources of the Jordan, 29 miles (39 km.) north of the Sea of Galilee, just outside Israelite territory. The statement that its people were living "according to the *mišpāṭ* of the Sidonians" cannot mean that they had a formal treaty with Sidon, since (if our translation of the last clause of the verse is correct), Laish *had no formal ties with anyone.*[47] In this context *mišpāṭ* must refer rather to their general way of life (their culture, or *custom*), which was akin in some respects to that of the Sidonians, a seafaring people known for their commerce rather than military activity.[48] This cultural influence most likely came about through trade, and was not unique to Laish. Like the other inland towns, Laish would have had to depend on the Phoenician coastal cities, especially Tyre and Sidon, for their access to the Mediterranean world and the commerce associated with it. But although their closest cultural ties were with Sidon, they were *a long way* from it. It was 30 miles (48 km.) to the northwest. According to verse 28, Laish was in "a valley belonging to Beth-rehob," which was about 5 miles (8 km.) to the east. It later became a city-state hostile to Israel (2 Sam. 10:6). For now, however, it posed no threat. But it could not be counted on as an ally either, for Laish had *no formal ties* with anyone, including Israel. It was *secure (beṭaḥ),*[49] not in the sense that it had strong fortifications or powerful allies, but because, as far as its citizens knew, it had no need of them. In short, it was just the sort of prize the Danites had been looking for. It was an *inhabited,* functioning city rather than a ruin. It was defenseless. They could take it without coming into conflict with their fellow Israelites, or anyone else for that matter. And it would give them the kind of access to trade that had been denied them in the south (1:34). As they gazed at it, it must have seemed to the spies that the oracle of Micah's Levite was true; that Yahweh had favored their journey (v. 6).

---

mal sense of the verb *yšb* when it is used of cities (e.g., Jer. 17:25; 50:39; Ezek. 26:20; 29:11; 36:35; Isa. 13:20; Zech. 2:4 [Heb. 8]; 9:5; 14:11). With Boling (*Judges*, p. 263), I take *dābār* as referring to a contractual arrangement, as in 11:10, 11, 28. For a review of the various proposals that have been made in relation to the textual and translation problems of this verse, see Block, *Judges, Ruth*, pp. 498-501.

47. See the notes to the translation.

48. Though, for an exception, see 10:12. The expression "ships of Tarshish," which originally referred to Phoenecian ships plying the Mediterranean sea lanes as far as Tarshish in Spain, became proverbial for trading ships in general (e.g., 1 Kgs. 10:22; 22:48; 2 Chron. 9:21; Ps. 48:7; Isa. 2:16; Ezek. 37:25, etc.).

49. The same expression, *yôšebet-lābeṭaḥ*, "inhabited and secure," is used of Babylon in Isa. 47:8 and Nineveh in Zeph. 2:15, where (in both places) it carries overtones of complacency and pride.

d. The Spies Report Back (18:8-10)

8 *They went to their brothers at Zorah and Eshtaol, and their brothers said to them, "How have you fared?"*

9 *They replied, "Come on, let's go up against them, for we have seen the land, and look, it is very good, but you are doing nothing. Don't be slow to go and take possession of the land.*

10 *When you go, you will come to a [mistakenly] secure people. The land is broad in both directions — surely God has given it into your hand — a place where there is no lack of anything on earth."*

8-10   The spies' return to *Zorah and Esthtaol* sets the stage for the next scene, in which they report back to those who sent them — their *brothers* or clansmen (see v. 2). Again there are superficial similarities to the story of the Israelite spies in Numbers 13. Both lots of spies tell of seeing a good, desirable land. But in other respects the two narratives diverge sharply. The spies of Numbers 13 speak of large, powerful people and fortified cities, and are divided over whether or not their fellows should attempt to take the land (Num. 13:26-33). The Danite spies speak only of *[mistakenly] secure people* (*'ām bōṭēaḥ*),[50] living in a *very good . . . broad* land, with *no lack of anything,* and are unanimous that their fellows should go up at once and take it (vv. 9-10). It is interesting to compare the description here with that in verse 7. The participle *bōṭēaḥ* here in verse 10 echoes the two expressions from the same root in verse 7 *(lāḇeṭaḥ and ûḇōṭēaḥ),* as I have tried to let show in my slightly awkward translation. The unsuspecting, false security of the people is a key feature of the situation. But other aspects of the former description (the absence of enemies or allies) are omitted, while some new elements (the goodness, breadth, and abundance of the land) are added. In general, the emphasis in verses 9-10 falls on the *land,* especially its goodness *(ṭôḇâ),* in ways that echo the descriptions of the land of Canaan in the spies' reports of Numbers 13:27 and Deuteronomy 1:25. The description of it as *broad in both directions (raḥᵃḇat yāḏayim)* is slightly suspect in view of the later reference to Laish being in a valley (v. 28). But spies are in the business of persuasion, and their excitement is palpable. The picture of a broad land, with plenty of room for expansion, would have been particularly attractive to the Danites, given the confined nature of their situation in the south (1:34).

Above all, the spies are so convinced that what they and their fellow Danites have been presented with is a God-given opportunity that it would be reprehensible not to take it up: *"Don't be slow. . . . God has given it into your*

---

50. Cf. *yôšeḇet-lāḇeṭaḥ* in v. 7.

hand" (vv. 9, 10). They sound just as positive, and even more convinced of God's involvement, as Caleb in Numbers 13:30 (cf. Deut. 1:25). But the role that Micah's Levite has played in shaping their perceptions still hovers in the background as a complicating factor.

e. The Danites Begin Their Migration (18:11-12)

11 *Six hundred men from the clan of the Danites, equipped with weapons of war, set out from there, from Zorah and Eshtaol.*

12 *They went up and camped at Kiriath-jearim in Judah. Hence that place is called Maheneh-dan [Camp of Dan] to this day. It is there, just west of Kiriath-jearim itself.*

11 A new journey begins here which basically follows the same route as that of the five spies in the first half of the chapter. But now a much larger company is on the move, including armed men (v. 11), children (and therefore, by implication, whole families), their cattle, and their belongings (see v. 21). And this time there will be no coming back. The migration of a whole clan, or at least a large part of it, is under way. The starting point, as before, is *Zorah and Eshtaol* (see the comments on 13:2 and 13:25). The *six hundred* armed men is a small force compared with Barak's ten thousand (4:6), Gideon's (initial) twenty-two thousand (7:3), or the hundreds of thousands fielded in the civil war of chapter 20 (twenty-six thousand Benjaminites and a combined total of four hundred thousand for the other tribes, 20:15, 17).[51] But it shows that the Danites, even in their reduced state,[52] were still a force to be reckoned with,[53] and expected to have to fight to achieve their objective.

12 The first stopping place was *at Kiriath-jearim* (Town of Forests) *in Judah,*[54] not in the town itself itself, but just west of it. The sight of so many fellow Israelites on the move must have been remarkable. It certainly made a lasting impression on the local population, since the writer tells us that the place where they camped was still known as *Mahaneh-dan [Camp of Dan]* in his own day. The location of ancient Kiriath-jearim is not definitely

51. See the note on the large numbers in Section IX.C of the Introduction.

52. They are again referred to as a *clan (mišpāḥâ)* rather than a *tribe (šēḇeṭ).* Cf. 18:2.

53. Cf. Saul's six hundred men in 1 Sam 13:15; 14:2, and David's six hundred in 1 Sam. 23:13; 27:2. But see 2 Sam. 15:18, where the six hundred Gittites are one contingent in a much larger army.

54. Kiriath-jearim is listed as a town of Judah in Josh. 15:60, where it is also called Kiriath-baal, suggesting that in pre-Israelite times it had been a Canaanite high place (a place of Baal worship).

known, although most scholars put it about 8 miles (14 km.) northwest of Jerusalem.[55] If so, the Mahaneh-dan referred to here cannot be the same as that of 13:25, which lay between Zorah and Eshtaol, where the present journey began. The distance between the two, about 7 miles (12 km.), was the distance traveled on the first day.

f. They Acquire Micah's Priest and Idols (18:13-21)

13 *From there they passed through Mount Ephraim, and came to the house of Micah.*

14 *The five men who had gone to spy out the land at Laish[56] said[57] to their brothers, "Do you know that in [one of] these houses there are an ephod and teraphim, and an idol of cast metal?[58] So now consider what you will do."*

15 *They turned aside [to go] there, and came to the house of the young Levite (the house of Micah)[59] and asked him how he was.*

16 *The six hundred Danites,[60] girded with their weapons of war, were standing at the entrance of the gate.*

17 *The five men who had gone to spy out the land went up [to the gate],[61] entered, and took the idol of cast metal,[62] the ephod, and the teraphim,*

---

55. At Tell el-Azhar or Kiryat-el-enab. See F. Weddle, "Mahaneh-Dan," *ISBE* 3:223.

56. The expression *hā'āreṣ layiš* is not in the normal form of a construct chain. MT recommends omitting *layiš* as a gloss. It is absent from LXX[A], but present (as *Laisa*) in LXX[B], which is generally regarded as representing an earlier form of the text of Judges. (See the section on the text of Judges in the Introduction.) Whether a gloss or not, it functions as an explanatory comment on *hā'āreṣ* (the land).

57. Literally, "answered" *(wayya'ănû)*. See the exegetical comments.

58. Taking *pesel ûmassēkâ* as a hendiadys, as in vv. 4-5.

59. The *BHS* apparatus suggests that *bêt mîkâ* is a gloss. But it is exegetically significant (see the comments on this verse).

60. The syntax is rough and disjoined, perhaps because the text has suffered some disturbance in translation. My translation incorporates some minor emendations recommended in the *BHS* apparatus, in which nothing of exegetical significance is at stake.

61. This use of *wayya'ălû* here is unusual, since the verb *'lh* nowhere else means "to approach" something. It's possible that it has its normal sense here, and that the five men "go up" to the gate because it is uphill. *BHS* notes the suggestion that it be emended to *wayyô'îlû*, "they wanted, were resolved [to enter]," but this would require a following infinitive, which is lacking here.

62. With Boling (who cites Freedman) I recognize an envelope construction here and in v. 18, in which the hendiadys of 17:4 *(pesel ûmassēkâ)* has been broken open to frame "ephod and teraphim" (Boling, *Judges*, p. 264). My translation does not, in every case, use exactly the same terms as Boling's, but adopts the same principle, namely, that the opening of the hendiadys is for purely stylistic reasons. Cf. Block, *Judges, Ruth,*

while the priest stood at the entrance of the gate with the six hundred men who were girded with weapons of war.

18 *When[63] these [five] men had entered the house of Micah and taken the idol of cast metal,[64] the ephod, and the teraphim, the priest said to them, "What are you doing?"*

19 *They replied, "Be quiet. Put your hand over your mouth, and come with us, and become our father and priest. Is it better for you to be priest to one man's household, or to be priest to a tribe and clan in Israel?"*

20 *The priest was pleased with this, so he took the ephod, the teraphim, and the idol,[65] and went into the midst of the people.[66]*

21 *They turned and went off, and placed the children, livestock, and [other] valuables[67] at the front.*

13 The next stage of the narrative begins with the Danites leaving the territory of Judah, heading north to Mount Ephraim (see the comments on v. 2), and coming eventually to Micah's house — the point where all three strands of the narrative of chapters 17–18 intersect. Micah has established a shrine there, the spies have lodged there, and now the larger company of Danites arrives there. The spies, having arrived in the general area, were drawn to it by their need of accommodation and the sound of the Levite's voice (which they recognized, v. 3). It follows almost as a matter of course that the migrating Danites should arrive at the same point, not only because it lay in their path, but because they were effectively retracing the steps of the spies. Indeed, the

---

p. 506, n. 134, who says that the hendiadys "has been split to frame the entire list and focus attention on the image." The fact that there are still only three items, not four, in v. 20 suggests that this is correct.

63. The opening clause of this verse is considered an addition in the *BHS* apparatus, and therefore, by implication, redundant. But in fact it is a flashback, as indicated by the disjunctive syntax, and necessary after the parenthesis in v. 17b to provide the proper context for the priest's question which follows. Cf. Boling, *Judges,* p. 264.

64. See the note on this expression in the previous verse. The absence of the article on *pesel* here, and of the conjunction and object marker before *hā'ēpod,* is anomalous, but does not affect the sense in any way.

65. Both the A and B texts of LXX Judges have the full expression, *to glypton kai to chōneuton* (= *wᵉ'et-happesel wᵉ'et-hammassēḵâ*) here (cf. 17:3-4). Boling (*Judges,* p. 264) suggests that the MT has lost the second word "due to homoeoarcton."

66. In other words, he went in among them so that the traveling Danites formed a kind of protecting shield around him.

67. The word I have translated *valuables* is *kᵉḇûddâ,* literally "heavy [stuff]," and is so translated by Boling (*Judges,* p. 261), following LXX[B] (*baros*). However, LXX[A] takes *kᵉḇûddâ* in the metaphorical sense and renders it as *endoxon* (glorious [stuff]). My translation reflects the latter option, which makes better sense in the context.

opening part of verse 14 suggests that the spies were actually functioning as guides. So while the convergence that happens here is clearly part of the literary design of the narrative, there is nothing implausible about it from a historical point of view.[68]

14   After giving their report back in verses 8-10, the spies receded into the background. Now they reappear in the role of consultants and guides. The verb rendered *said* in the translation of this verse is literally "answered" *(wayya'anû)*. The Danites have apparently asked the spies a question of some kind (such as the best route to take, or the best place to pitch camp again), and they respond by drawing the attention of their *brothers* (fellow Danites) to certain *houses (bāttîm),* and particularly to *one*[69] of them in which a shrine is located. The plural, *houses,* is puzzling, since it is clearly Micah's shrine they are referring to, and in 17:4-13 we have heard only of Micah's house (singular). However, it was not clear there whether Micah's shrine was located inside his house, or in a separate structure (see the comments on 17:5). The plural *houses* here in 18:14 may be taken as confirming that the shrine was in fact housed separately. Or it may simply refer to a cluster of dwellings that comprised a small settlement,[70] Micah's house being the one of special interest because it contained a shrine. Both readings are possible.

Much more significant is why the spies draw attention to the shrine at all, and here, too, there are ambiguities that resist complete resolution. One possibility emerges fairly straightforwardly from what the spies say, and what they themselves did when they visited this same shrine on their own journey northward. They refer to the contents of the shrine *(an ephod and teraphim, and an idol of cast metal),* and advise their fellow-Danites to *consider what you will do.* As we noted previously, ephod(s) and teraphim, as cultic objects, were associated with oracular inquiry and prosperity (see the comments on 8:27 and 18:5). Furthermore, what the spies themselves had done when they visited this shrine was to seek an oracle concerning the likely success of the journey they had embarked on (18:5). The oracle was favorable, and their subsequent journey was successful, as their fellow Danites now knew. So they may be suggesting that their Danite brothers should do what they themselves had done: go to Micah's shrine and seek a similar oracle concerning the present journey. But if this is what they mean,

68. There is no fundamental incompatibility between "story" and "history" as literary genres. For an excellent treatment of this important issue see Provan, Long, and Longman, *Biblical History,* pp. 75-97.

69. The word *one* does not occur in the text, but is implied by the fact that only a single shrine is in view (namely, Micah's), which we know from 17:4 was in "his [singular] house."

70. See the comments on v. 16.

why do they not say so directly? Why, *"consider what you will do,"* instead of, "Let us go there and inquire of God," or the like? And why not mention that there is a Levite at the shrine, given the need of such a person to seek an oracle on their behalf? The ambiguity of their words suggests that they may be hinting at something more sinister. Perhaps they have mentioned only the ephod, teraphim, and idol because it is these objects themselves they are interested in at this moment, rather than their usefulness in seeking an oracle. In short, they may be intentionally planting the idea of theft. What follows shows that, whether intended or not, it is this second meaning of what the spies have said that registers in the minds of their fellow Danites and spurs them into action.

15 The Danites act on what they have heard the spies say by turning aside and going to the shrine. The way it is first called *the house of the young Levite,* and only secondly, by way of explanation, *the house of Micah,* suggests that by this time the Levite has in effect replaced Micah as head of the house, at least as far as the Danites are concerned. In this entire scene they speak only to the Levite. Even when some of them go into "the house of *Micah*" to rob it (v. 18), it is only the Levite who protests. It is as though Micah is simply not there. It is the beginning of his decline into nothingness. He is of no importance as far as the Danites are concerned. It is only the Levite and the cultic paraphernalia of what has in effect become "his" shrine that interest them.

They greet the Levite as though they already know him, just as the spies did back in verse 3. Literally, they "asked him about shalom" *(wayyišᵃʾlû-lô lᵉšālôm).* Although *shalom* can mean, among other things, health, welfare, prosperity, or peace, the greeting is entirely conventional and straightforward.[71] It is the Levite's "shalom" they inquire after, not their own (they are not asking for an oracle), and there is no hint in their greeting of what they are about to do.

16 We learn here that the settlement where Micah's house was situated had a *gate.* It was probably what we would call today a compound,[72] with an encircling wall of some kind for security. The picture here of six hundred armed Danites standing at *the entrance of the gate* (the only way in or out), jars menacingly with the friendly greeting of the previous verse. What are they doing there (since no enemy is in sight) if not to intimidate? And even if that was not their intention, it would certainly be the effect on anyone who saw them, especially those, like Micah and his Levite, who were inside. This is the point in the narrative where tension starts to build.

71. See, e.g., Gen. 43:27; 1 Sam. 10:4; 30:21.
72. See Block, *Judges, Ruth,* p. 505, who suggests that the expression *bêt mîkâ* in v. 15 may be understood as the name of the site as a whole.

17-18 In these two verses the real intent of what the spies had said back in verse 14 becomes apparent. "Now consider what *you* will do," they said to their clansmen, but now it is they themselves who do what they had been hinting at. They *(the five men who had gone to spy out the land)* go up to the gate, through it, and into Micah's house, and take his *idol, ephod, and teraphim* (v. 17a). The statement that the priest *stood at the entrance of the gate with the six hundred* armed men (v. 17b) is puzzling. Why is he standing there? It appears to implicate him in the crime as much as those he stands with. But what follows shows that, at this stage at least, he is not party to the crime, since his question at the end of verse 18 shows that he didn't know what was happening until the five men came out again with their stolen property. In fact, his question is effectively a protest: *"What are you doing?"* So it appears that he was standing at the gate with the armed men for some other reason — perhaps to ask them the same question! — but before he could do so (or anything else for that matter) the crime was committed, and he became merely a witness to it, a helpless bystander.

19-20 Since the Levite's question in verse 18 ("What are you doing?") was addressed to the five spies, it is most natural to see them in particular as those who address the Levite here in verse 19. In the first part of their response they do not answer his question at all, but order him to *"Be quiet,"* most likely because they do not want his master Micah to know what is happening. The fact that Micah himself neither speaks nor is spoken to in the preceding verses suggests that what has happened so far has been without his knowledge, and the fact that he enters as a participant in the narrative only belatedly (in vv. 22-23) confirms this. As someone who owed his position and livelihood to Micah, the Levite's first duty in these circumstances was to sound the alarm. So with the command to be quiet the Levite is already being asked, by implication, to betray his master. Then he is encouraged to do so by an appeal to his venality. As we saw, the Levite had already shown this aspect of his nature to the spies on their previous visit by his reference to being "hired" *(śkr)* by Micah (18:4). Now, as spokesmen for their fellow Danites, the spies shrewdly exploit this venality by offering the Levite far better terms of employment than he could ever hope to have by remaining with Micah. The position of *father and priest* is what Micah had offered him back in 17:10. The spies now use the same phrase but outbid Micah by offering him far more: not just father and priest to one man's household, but to an entire *tribe and clan* in Israel (v. 19).

The use of the two terms, *tribe* and *clan,* here at the end of verse 19 is puzzling. Why both terms when one of them would have been sufficient? The answer probably lies in the oscillation between the two terms throughout chapter 18 as a whole. We may represent this as follows:

441

tribe *(šēḇeṭ)*	clan *(mišpāḥâ)*
18:1	
	18:2
	18:11
18:19	18:19
18:30	

What this suggests is that in this migration of the Danites, they are in transition between "clan" and "tribe" status. Because of the difficulties they have experienced, they have been reduced to clan status;[73] but they have been a tribe (v. 1), and will be so again (v. 30). Both terms are used here in verse 19 for rhetorical effect. The Danites are hinting that, whatever they may be at present (clan or tribe), they are on their way to something greater. They are in transition, and urge the Levite to join them and be in transition himself, from priest to a single household to priest to a whole evolving people.

It is an offer that a man of this Levite's character cannot refuse. He is *pleased* — so much so, in fact, that he acts without delay. He takes the *ephod, teraphim, and idol* from the five men who have just stolen them, and moves *into the midst of* the people (the Danites). Both acts have symbolic significance. By taking these tokens of priestly office from the five men, he effectively accepts reconsecration at their hands,[74] and by moving into the midst of the migrating Danites he symbolically cuts himself off from Micah and accepts them as his new constituency. It is a complete act of betrayal, but entirely in keeping with the Levite's character as we have observed it. The fourfold repetition of the word *priest* in this context stresses the office (and the prestige associated with it) rather than the eligibility for the office entailed in his being a Levite.

21   The present scene began with the Danites arriving in the vicinity of Micah's house and, on advice from the five spies, "turning aside" *(wayyāsûrû)* to go into it (v. 15). Having achieved their purpose, the Danites now "turn" *(wayyipnû)* to leave it, and go on their way. Given what they have just done, the reason they put their children, livestock, and (other) valuables[75] *at the front* was probably that they expected to be pursued, and therefore any attack would most likely come from behind. This way they could keep their six hundred armed men between the attackers and the persons and property they needed to protect. The priest and his religious artifacts were "in the

---

73. See 1:34 and 13:2, and notice that in Num. 26:42-43 the descendants of Dan are comprised of only one clan, in contrast to the descendants of Reuben, Simeon, and Gad, who are comprised of several clans (vv. 5, 12, 15).

74. He allows them to "fill his hand" with them. See the comments on 17:12.

75. Literally, "heavy (stuff)" *(keḇûddâ)*. See the notes on the translation.

midst" of the people (v. 20), surrounded on all sides, and therefore in the safest position of all.[76]

g. Micah's Fruitless Pursuit (18:22-26)

This short scene begins with Micah initiating his pursuit (v. 22), and ends with him giving it up and returning to his house (v. 26).

22 *They had gone far from Micah's house when Micah[77] and the men who were in the houses near Micah's house assembled[78] and caught up with[79] the Danites.*

23 *They called out to the Danites, who turned to face them and said to Micah, "What is the matter with you, that you have assembled [with your men]?"*

24 *He said, "My gods that I made for myself[80] — you have taken! And the priest! And you have gone away! What do I have left? How can you say to me, 'What is the matter with you?'"*

25 *The Danites said to him, "Don't raise your voice at us lest some angry men[81] attack you, and you forfeit[82] your life and the lives of your household."*

26 *Then the Danites went on their way. Micah saw that they were too strong for him, so he turned and went back to his house.*

22 The Danites have already gone *far from Micah's* house before the pursuit begins. The slowness of Micah's response reinforces the impression

---

76. Compare the location of the tabernacle during Israel's progress through the wilderness.

77. With the LXX, which has *Micha kai hoi andres*. The MT has lost *wᵉmîkâ* after the preceding *mîkâ* by either haplography or homoeoteleuton.

78. Since Micah himself is included in the subject, *nizʿᵃqû* must be understood in the middle sense (assembled) rather than the passive (were called out).

79. Cf. Gen. 31:23, where the Hiphil of *dbq* followed by the object marker clearly has this sense.

80. With LXX^A and the Vulgate. The MT has only *ᵃšer-ʿāśîtî* (which I made). However, it is likely that the versions preserve the original reading here, for three reasons: first, the indirect object is normal after *ʿśh* where it refers to the making of idols "for oneself" (Exod. 20:4; 34:17; Deut. 5:8; Isa. 63:14; cf. Isa. 43:21); second, it is especially appropriate here, where ownership is the point at issue; and finally, it could easily have been lost by haplography, since the following word begins with *lamed* (see *BHS* apparatus).

81. Literally, "men bitter of soul" *(mārê nepeš)*. Cf. 2 Sam. 17:8, where the same idiom clearly means "angry, enraged."

82. Literally, "gather your life" *(wᵉʾāsaptâ napšᵉkā)*, a form of the idiom "to be gathered to one's people (in death/the grave)," e.g., Gen. 25:8. Here the thought is that Micah is in danger of making this happen, to both himself and his household.

verses 13-21 have already given us that he was absent when the pillaging of his shrine took place. The threefold use of his name in verse 22[83] suggests that the present scene will be fundamentally about him, and what follows confirms this. His story began in 17:1-2 with his confession that he had stolen his mother's silver. It ends here with his having to accept that the Danites have stolen his gods (v. 24). There is no reference to Yahweh's involvement, but there is a sense of poetic justice in what happens: the robber is robbed; Micah gets what he deserves. There is also a sense of inevitability about what happens, since Micah is powerless either to prevent it from happening or to reverse it when it does happen. The story as a whole will end with the Danites themselves being robbed (v. 30). There are similarities, in this respect, to the story of Abimelech in chapter 9.[84] There we were left in no doubt about God's involvement (9:23). Here we can only speculate about it, but the precision with which retribution takes place strongly suggests that more than chance is involved.

The way Micah's neighbors come so readily to his assistance suggests that he is a respected member of the community, and most likely the leader of it (like Joash in 6:31-32, who was also the owner/patron of a shrine). The apparent ease with which his company was able to overtake the Danites in spite of their considerable head start is probably because, unlike them, Micah's men were not encumbered with goods, livestock, and dependents.[85] Although his personal fortunes are in decline, Micah does have some dignity and success in this opening verse of the scene; but it is not to last.

23-24 Micah and his men succeed in getting the attention of the Danites by "calling out" to them; but from then on they have no success at all. The Danites have been expecting them, as we have seen, and from the moment they turn to respond, it is clear that Micah can do nothing. The way the dialogue in these verses is both initiated and ended by the Danites mirrors the fact that they, not Micah, are in the position of power. And it is clear from the start that they are not going to make any concessions. Their opening question, *"What is the matter with you?"* is effectively a taunt rather than a genuine query, calculated to enrage Micah rather than draw him into any meaningful engagement with them. They doubtless listened to his response with amused satisfaction, for there is nothing dignified about it. The broken syntax[86] and the content are both expressive of Micah's agitated state. It is

83. See the notes to the translation.

84. Cf., too, the striking similarity between what the Danites say to the Levite in 18:19, and what Abimelech says to the citizens of Shechem in 9:2.

85. Cf. Block, *Judges, Ruth*, p. 507.

86. Particularly the way in which the two objects of the verb *leqaḥtem (you have taken)* are separated from one another, one before the verb, the other after it, gives the impression that the second one is an afterthought.

the speech of a man who is so beside himself with anger that all he can do is blurt out accusations.

Micah's basic accusation is that the Danites have *taken* (stolen) his property (v. 24). They have taken both his *gods* (*ᵉlōhîm*) and his *priest,* but it is the former which seems to be his main concern. They are the first thing he mentions when he opens his mouth,[87] and his right to have them is emphasized by the threefold use of first person expressions (*"my gods which I made for myself"*).[88] This is highly ironical, of course, since "making a god/idol for oneself" is exactly what the Israelites were forbidden to do in the second commandment (Exod. 20:4). So any claim to rightful ownership based on having done such a thing is invalid. Furthermore, the very idea that one can *make* a god at all is absurd, and is a key part of the critique of idolatry in the Old Testament as a whole, from the incident of the golden calf in Exodus 32 onward (see esp. Isa. 43:9-20). In better days Micah had prided himself on having a Levite as his priest, confident that this legitimized his shrine and guaranteed Yahweh's favor (17:13). But now, when trouble has come, it is his *gods* he is most desperate to recover; *the priest* is mentioned almost as an afterthought. The truth, of course, is that both his gods and his priest have failed him, and the confidence he placed in them has been exposed for the folly it always was. His life has revolved around these things, and without them he is nothing. His question, *"What do I have left?"* is an admission of this painful reality. He has been completely undone.

25-26 The Danites have no sympathy for Micah, and have no intention of giving him what he wants. But neither do they want to kill him; after all, he and his followers are fellow Israelites. They just want to get rid of him. So they respond to his question, "What do I have left?" by pointing out that he still, at least, has his life, but warn him that he is in danger of losing even that if he doesn't desist — and the lives of his men as well. Their reference to *some angry men* (v. 25) is a way of threatening him with violence without accepting responsibility for it. Some hotheads among them might lose patience with Micah and take matters into their own hands, so Micah had better leave at once. Finally, the Danites show their contempt for Micah by simply resuming their journey as though he is no longer there. Seeing that he is powerless to stop them, Micah accepts the inevitable, turns around, and returns to his house (v. 26). The singularity of the language, *"he returned to his house,"* adds one final dimension to his loss. It's as though the company that came with him no longer have any significance, because he has lost the status that made him someone to follow. He goes back alone, socially if not physically — an empty man to an empty house. It is a pathetic exit.

---

87. They are in the first position in the sentence, which is emphatic in Hebrew.
88. See the notes to the translation.

h. The Danites Complete Their Migration (18:27-31)

This final scene is framed by the references to Micah's idol in verses 27 and 31 respectively. Micah has gone (he's as good as dead), but his idol lives on.

27 *After they took what Micah had made,*[89] *and the priest who had belonged to him, the Danites came against*[90] *Laish, against people [living] quietly and securely,*[91] *and smote them with the edge of the sword, and burned the city with fire.*

28 *There was no deliverer, because it was far from Sidon and had no formal ties with anyone.*[92] *It was in the valley which belongs to Beth-rehob.*[93] *They rebuilt the city and lived in it.*

29 *They called the name of the city Dan, after the name*[94] *of their ancestor Dan, who was born to Israel; but Laish was the previous name of the city.*

30 *The Danites set up the idol for themselves, and Jonathan, the son of Gershom, the son of Moses*[95] *— he and his sons were priests to the tribe of the Danites until the day of the captivity of the land.*

31 *They set in place for themselves Micah's idol, which he had made, for the whole time that the house of God was at Shiloh.*[96]

27-28a In the previous two scenes the pace of the narrative had slowed down considerably because of the predominance of dialogue. Now it picks up again, and the story begins to move quickly to its conclusion. The time for talk is over; the time for action has come. The rest of the journey is passed

---

89. A couple of Hebrew MSS have *happesel* (the *idol* that Micah had made). *BHS* suggests *hāʾĕlōhîm* (*the gods* that Micah had made), in line with v. 24. But the supporting evidence is weak, and the text makes perfect sense as it stands.

90. LXX[A] has *heōs* (= *ʿad,* "up to, as far as"). But in situations of conflict (as here) the MT's *ʿal* normally has the sense "against" (Judg. 3:12; 4:24; 6:2, 3, 4, 31; 9:18, 31, 34; 15:14). This is supported by LXX[B], which has *epi Laisa* (*against* Laish); cf. the use of *epi* in Matt. 10:21.

91. Heb. *šōqēṭ ûḇōṭēaḥ,* as in v. 7. See the comments there.

92. See the comments on v. 7.

93. See the comments on v. 7.

94. *BHS* recommends, in line with some witnesses, reading *kᵉšēm* for MT's *bᵉšēm.* But the use of *bᵉšēm* in the construction, "call X *after the name of* Y," is attested elsewhere (e.g., Num. 32:42).

95. Or *Manasseh.* See the comments on this verse.

96. *BHS* notes that some have proposed emending *bᵉšilō* (in Shiloh) to either *bᵉlāyᵉšâ* (in Laish) or *bᵉšalwāh* (in [a state of] prosperity; cf. Jer. 22:21; Ezek. 16:49; Ps. 122:7; Prov. 17:1). But there is no hard evidence to support these emendations, and the text makes perfect sense as it stands. We will meet Shiloh again in 21:19.

over in silence, and we find ourselves immediately back at *Laish,* in the far north. With Micah's man-made gods and hired priest now firmly in their possession, the Danites move swiftly against the unsuspecting city, putting its entire population to the sword and turning the whole place into a blazing funeral pyre. The details about the peacefulness and relative isolation of Laish and its people in verse 7 are repeated here, as if to underline their victim status. The one detail that receives elaboration is the total defenselessness of the city. In view of its proximity, *Beth-rehob* was the one place that might have offered support if it had reason or inclination to do so, but it had neither.[97] So Laish, in its hour of need, had *no deliverer,* and its fall was inevitable. This means, among other things, that the conquest of Laish does not reflect well on the Danites. It is an inglorious affair, the final stage in their movement away from their true inheritance and toward idolatry as the constitutive center of their tribal existence (see the Excursus below on the migration of the Danites as an anti-conquest narrative).

28b-29   The Danites complete their conquest of Laish by effectively destroying even the memory of it. They rebuild the city and live in it, but show by renaming it that it is not Laish resurrected, but something entirely new and entirely their own. Laish is no more. It has been obliterated and replaced by *Dan,* a Danite city, so named after Dan, *who was born to Israel* (Gen. 30:1-6). This is surely an allusion to the renaming of Jacob in Genesis 32:28: "Your name will no longer be Jacob, but Israel, because you have struggled with God and with man and have overcome" (NIV). As Jacob was reborn as Israel, Laish has been reborn as Dan, and the Danites have been reborn as a tribe, with (at last) a land and city to call their own. It is a bold claim to have overcome — even God himself! — as Jacob once fought and overcame him at Peniel, and was transformed in the process from a deceiver and thief to a man of honor. But in fact Dan's conquest of Laish has the same kind of ambiguity about it as Jacob's "conquest" of God in Genesis 32. In reality it was not Jacob who prevailed at all, but God (as evidenced by Jacob's dislocated hip; Gen. 32:31-32). And here in Judges 18 it is not really Dan who has conquered Laish, but Laish that has conquered Dan, as the helpless bait on a hook effectively "conquers" the fish that takes it. By conquering Laish, Dan has not contributed to Israel's conquest of Canaan at all, but to Canaan's conquest of Israel. For it will not be Yahweh who is worshiped there, but Micah's idol. In other words, the renaming of Laish after *Dan, who was born to Israel,* is highly ironical.

30-31   The entire story of Micah and the Danites concludes with the establishment of a new shrine in Dan. The first act of the Danites after conquering and occupying and renaming Laish was to *set up the idol for themselves* (v. 30). The idol *(happāsel)* needs no qualification to identify it; the whole story

---

97. See the comments on Beth-rehob at v. 7.

tells us that it was Micah's. Nor is the "setting up" of it sanctioned by any divine command or royal authority; the Danites simply set it up *for themselves* (v. 30). It is a unilateral act; the shrine, like the idol itself, is man-made, and exists only to serve the interests of its makers. Its only claim to legitimacy was the priesthood that subsequently served there, namely, *Jonathan, the son of Gershom, the son of Moses — he* [Jonathan] *and his sons* (v. 30).

Given all that has gone before, the "Jonathan" in the expression *Jonathan, the son of Gershom, the son of Moses* of verse 30 can be none other than Micah's Levite. But what exactly are we to make of the term *son* here? The Hebrew term *bēn* (son) is commonly used in the Old Testament, as in English, in its straightforward, literal sense. However, it is also used metaphorically for "descendant," with the issue of how close or distant the relationship was left open.[98] The issue is particularly complicated in the case of genealogies. It is clear that in some cases genealogies are compressed by leaving out one or more generations without any variation in terminology. For example, the list of Aaron's descendants in Ezra 7:1-7 omits six names that occur in 1 Chronicles 6:3-14, but still uses "son" as the linking term.[99] So, in lists of ancestors, "son" *(bēn)* does not have a single, fixed meaning; its sense in any given situation depends on context, and whatever light may be thrown on the case in point by other relevant data. With this in mind, what can we say about the use(s) of the term in the account of Jonathan's family history in Judges 18:30? From the opening chapters of Exodus it appears that Moses belonged to the tribe of Levi (6:16-20), and that *Gershom* was his literal son by Zipporah (2:22). No such grounds exist, however, for identifying the *Jonathan* of verse 30 as the literal son of Gershom. Furthermore, every other Jonathan in the Old Testament is either a non-Levite, and/or too far removed in time to be the Jonathan of Judges 18.[100] All we can say on the evidence available to us is that Judges 18:30 identifies Micah's Levite as a "descendant" of Gershom, the son of Moses.

The revelation of the name and ancestry of Micah's Levite in verse 30 comes as a complete surprise, and has almost certainly been withheld until now precisely to achieve this effect. The Levite's bad character has been too clearly established by this point for the revelation that he is a descendant of Moses to redeem him. Indeed, it does exactly the opposite. Here is the crowning scandal of the Danites' idolatrous shrine: it brought dishonor even on the revered name of Moses! Indeed, so great was the scandal that the scribes who copied the passage as scripture inserted a small, superscript *nun*

---

98. As, e.g., in the expression "sons/children of Israel" (Gen. 32:32; 36:31; Exod. 1:7, etc.).

99. Except that Ezra 7 uses *bar,* the Aramaic equivalent of *bēn.*

100. The data is summarized in T. H. Jones, "Jonathan," *NBD,* p. 614.

between the *mem* and *shin* of *mšh* (Moses) to indicate that it should be read as *m^nšh* (Manasseh) to avoid publicly sullying Moses' great name.

Verses 30 and 31 also give us two pieces of information about the later history of the Danite shrine:

i. Jonathan and his sons served as priests there *until the day of the captivity of the land* (v. 30), and
ii. Micah's idol remained in place there *for the whole time that the house of God was at Shiloh* (v. 31).

Since Jonathan's *sons* are not named, and there is no other data about them available to us, the statement that Jonathan and his sons served at the shrine for the whole time it existed cannot be used to restrict the time in question to a single generation. *Sons* may be metaphorical here, just as in *son* (descendant) *of Gershom* (see above). So the shrine may have been serviced by Jonathan's descendants for one generation or many. This depends on how we understand the two expressions, *until the day of the captivity of the land* (v. 30) and *the whole time that the house of God was at Shiloh* (v. 31).[101] However, they cannot simply be equated, because the first refers to how long Jonathan's descendants served at the shrine, and the second to how long Micah's idol remained in place there, which may have been for a much shorter period. No more is heard of Shiloh as a functioning shrine after the time of Eli and Samuel (11th cent. B.C.), but Dan continued to figure (infamously) as a major shrine until the deportation of its population to Assyria by Tiglath-pileser III in 734 B.C. (2 Kgs. 15:29).[102] Taken together, what verses 30 and 31 indicate is that the descendants of Jonathan served at the shrine in Dan right down to 734 B.C., but Micah's idol remained in place there only until the fall of Shiloh in the eleventh century B.C. (a much shorter period).[103] It was eventually replaced by a golden calf early in the reign of Jeroboam I (about 930 B.C.). We do not know what idols, if any, were housed there in the interim, but Jeroboam's action was entirely in keeping with Dan's earlier history and confirmed its status as a shrine famous for its idolatry. It was idolatrous from its inception.

In view of this, the statement about the Levite's ancestry in verse 30 has the same status as Micah's confident assertion back in 17:13: "Now I

---

101. See the comments below on the location and theological significance of Shiloh.

102. Cf. Block, *Judges, Ruth,* p. 513.

103. By the time of Saul, about 1050 B.C., the priesthood had moved to Nob (1 Sam. 22:11), and Shiloh was no longer a significant shrine (cf. Jer. 7:12, 14; 26:6, 9). We do not know why Micah's idol remained in use at Dan only until the fall of Shiloh. However, the fall of Shiloh may have triggered a reform movement, as the earlier capture of the ark had done (1 Sam 7:2-9).

know that Yahweh will treat me well, because the Levite has become my priest." Like everything else in this narrative, it is deeply ironical and a prelude to disaster. The Danites have repeated Micah's sin, and will suffer the same consequences he did. Having this Levite and his descendants as their priests will not attract Yahweh's favor to their shrine, but — like the idol they have installed there — make his judgment inevitable. This shrine will endure only until, like its predecessor in Micah's house, it, too, is invaded, plundered, and reduced to nothing. Neither will Jeroboam's elevation of it to one of the two leading shrines of the northern kingdom[104] save it, but only confirm its corrupt nature, prolong Micah's sin, and guarantee its destruction.

It is surely a sign of the remarkable skill of the author that the very last word of the whole story is not Dan, where Micah's idol was set up, but *Shiloh* (v. 31b). For what appears to be merely a piece of chronological data (see above) is in fact the final, masterly stroke that completes all that has gone before. *Shiloh,* like the house of Micah, lay in the central hill country of Ephraim, 19 miles (30 km.) north of Jerusalem.[105] It was here that the tabernacle was first set up after Israel's arrival in Canaan, and here that the land was divided up by lot among the various tribes (Josh. 18:1, 8-10; 19:51). By the time of the judges, even Shiloh was beginning to be affected by the general trend toward corruption,[106] but it was still the symbolic center of Israel's life in Canaan, something still recognized by the annual "festival of Yahweh" that was held there (Judg. 21:19 NIV), and the reference here in 18:31 to the fact that the tabernacle still stood there. But the author has chosen his words carefully. He doesn't call the tabernacle the *'ōhel mô'ēd* (tent of meeting), as in Joshua 18:1, but *bêt-hā'elōhîm (house of God),*[107] the same phrase he had used for Micah's shrine back in 17:5. The only difference is the definite article: Micah's shrine was *bêt 'elōhîm, "a* house of gods"; but the tabernacle in Shiloh is still "*the* house of God." So with one deft stroke he has brought the narrative full circle, not just from the hill country of Ephraim, via Laish/Dan, back to the hill country of Ephraim, but from Micah's "house of gods," via its reincarnation in Dan, back to the *house of God* in Shiloh. And Shiloh, in the end, with its tabernacle housing the ark of the covenant and the ten words of Moses, becomes the final standpoint from which everything that has gone before is assessed. It is all "off-center," deviant, as idolatry always is.

104. 1 Kgs. 12:28-29.

105. Normally identified with the modern *Seilun.* Excavations of the site have shown evidence of Middle Bronze occupation, and reoccupation between 1200 and 1050 B.C., roughly the time of the judges. J. B. Taylor and J. Woodhead, "Shiloh," *NBD,* p. 1194.

106. See the comments on 21:19.

107. This may have been the tabernacle itself, or something more substantial that replaced it, as suggested by the term *hêkal* (temple) in 1 Sam. 1:9; 3:3.

Summary Reflections on 17:1–18:31

There is no doubt that the story as a whole is a telling critique of the shrine at Dan, and could have served, or even been written originally, as an attack on the religious policies of Jeroboam I and his successors. But here, as part of the epilogue to the book of Judges, it serves a purpose that is both more particular and more general than this. First, it probes more deeply the "evil" *(hāra')* that Israel did again and again in the period of the judges. The introduction has described it generally as "forsaking Yahweh" and "serving the Baals" (2:11-12). The body of the book has given some particular instances of this: Gideon's "ephod" (which ended up functioning just like a Baal altar; 8:27), the worship of "Baal-berith," especially by the citizens of Shechem (8:33; 9:4; cf. 9:46), and the worship of the gods of Aram, Sidon, Moab, the Ammonites, and the Philistines (10:6). The worship of Gideon's ephod and Baal-berith (Covenant Baal) may have been corrupt forms of Yahweh worship, while the worship of the gods of foreign nations such as Aram and Moab could hardly be construed as the worship of Yahweh at all. Against the backdrop of the Sinai covenant, which is referred to repeatedly in the speeches of rebuke in the book of Judges (2:1-3; 6:7-10; 10:11-14), all such worship involved unfaithfulness to Yahweh tantamount to spiritual prostitution (8:33). In practice, what is common to all these deviant practices is idolatry in one form or another. What the present narrative does is to lay aside, for a while, all the other matters that the episodes in chapters 3–16 have been about, and focus on this particular one so that we can understand it at greater depth. It shows us the shape that the religious life of everyday Israelites took among members of the post-Joshua generation, when apostasy began to take hold (2:10-12).

It is precisely by being so focused in this way, however, that the story of Micah and the Danites is able to transcend its particular context and speak to worshipers of the God of Israel in whatever age they live, including our own. For from beginning to end it is a story about the folly of idolatry, which is a universal and perennial problem. It shows how it arises from ignorance. The characters in the narrative from beginning to end (Micah's mother, Micah himself, his Levite, and the Danites) are ridiculously unaware of the incongruity of their actions. Micah's mother consecrates money to Yahweh for the making of an idol. Micah, whose name means "Who is like Yahweh?" creates "a house of gods." The Levite is happy to serve at Micah's idolatrous shrine, and Micah thinks that Yahweh is sure to bless him because he has acquired the services of this Levite. And the Danites repeat all the sins of Micah, only on a grander scale! What we are being shown is how people behave who have a background of covenant faith, but have lost touch with the saving acts of God that brought it into being and the word of God that prescribed

451

how it should be lived out (2:1-3). It is a story of "another generation" that has only a vague awareness of where it came from, and is no longer moored securely to its gospel foundations. It shows us how people behave when they are still religious but no longer know what truly pleases God. They do "whatever is right in their own eyes" and expect Yahweh to bless them for doing so (17:13). In such a confused environment religion becomes merely a means of self-advancement, and provides fertile soil for a host of other evils to take root and flourish: lying, theft, the buying and selling of religious services and offices, and unwarranted violence. The grim humor of the story reinforces the message that such religion is both absurd and tragic.

In its fundamental subject matter and message, then, the story of Micah and his idols is one with the accounts of Aaron and the golden calf, the syncretism of Jeroboam I and his successors, and the prophetic denunciations of idolatry that arc right across the Old Testament and continue (via the intertestamental literature) into the New, from Exodus 20 to Romans 1, and on through 1 Corinthians 8 and 10 to the very end of the canon. The last book, Revelation, speaks of idolatry as an evil that rebellious human beings will persist in to the very end (Rev. 9:20). And the church is no less immune to it than Israel was if it loses touch with its gospel foundations. Hence the warning of the aged apostle John, "Dear children, keep yourselves from idols" (1 John 5:21 NIV).[108] It would serve just as well as a closing reflection on the story of Micah and the Danites.

Excursus 7: The Migration of the Danites as an Anti-Conquest Narrative

We have noted in passing some echoes, in Judges 17–18, of the traditional accounts of the Israelite conquest of Canaan. Since this comparison is so significant for the way the whole migration of the Danites is viewed in Judges 18, we pause here to note that comparison again, including some aspects of it that we have not so far mentioned.

An analogy with the traditional account of the *national* migration, conquest, and settlement is suggested by the comparison between Dan and Shiloh drawn in verse 31, as we have seen. In the course of their migration, the Danites acquire a Levite-priest and idols at Micah's house, as the Israelites had acquired the Levitical priesthood and furnishings of the tabernacle at Sinai. The mission of the spies in Judges 18 is strikingly reminiscent of that in Numbers 13–14 and Deuteronomy 1, and the *six hundred men* of Judges 18:11, 16, and 17[109] recall

108. Cf. 1 Cor. 10:14 (NIV): "Therefore, my friends, flee from idolatry."
109. Cf. the "six hundred men" of 20:47 — a further link between the two narratives of this closing part of the book.

the "six hundred thousand men (or contingents)" of Exodus 12:37 and Numbers 11:21.[110] The Danites slaughter all the inhabitants of Laish as the Israelites had slaughtered the inhabitants of Jericho.

The basic pattern is the same,[111] but key elements appear in inverted form in Judges 18, giving the account of the Danite migration a markedly satirical thrust. The Israelites were engaging in holy war; the Danites were not. The cities of Canaan were heavily fortified; Laish was defenseless. The Israelites were authorized by Yahweh; the Danites were not. Yahweh gave Israel victory but is totally absent from the account of the Danite campaign. Israel was advancing into the heart of the land to claim their promised inheritance; the Danites were withdrawing from theirs (18:1; cf. 1:34). And the final, most scandalous point of the implied comparison is that the Danites complete their journey by setting up Micah's idol in Dan (Judg. 18:30) as Israel had once erected the tabernacle in Shiloh (Josh. 18:1).

B. MORAL CHAOS: THE OUTRAGE AT GIBEAH AND ITS CONSEQUENCES (19:1–21:25)

This time the editorial comments about there being no king and everyone doing what was right in their own eyes do not occur in the body of the narrative as in chapters 17 and 18, but at its two extremes (19:1 and 21:25). This difference is in keeping with the fact that the plot of this second narrative does not have points of discontinuity comparable to those at 17:6 and 18:1 in the first narrative but is unilinear, each development emerging directly out of the one that precedes it.[1] There are four episodes, as follows:

Transition	No king in Israel (19:1a)
I	The outrage at Gibeah (19:1b-28)
II	Preparations for war (19:29–20:11)

110. See the discussion of the meaning of 'elep at 1:4.

111. Compare Abraham Malamat, "The Danite Migration and the Pan-Israelite Exodus-Conquest: A Biblical Narrative Pattern," *Biblica* 51, no. 1 (1970): 1-16. Malamat studies the content and structure of the two accounts in detail and concludes that "they are individual models of different scale, following a basic pattern which evolved for biblical narratives of campaigns of inheritance" (p. 16).

1. Compare and contrast M. Noth, "The Background of Judges 17–18," 68-85. In relation to 17:6 and 18:1a, Noth comments that "they have been placed in their present location by someone who comprehended the interior structure of the narrative" (p. 79). But he argues that the placement of 19:1a and 21:25 at the extremes of the second narrative is evidence that they are secondary to the similar comments in chs. 17–18, and were taken over from there when the complexes of 17–18 and 19–21 were joined together. The general point he is making about the editorial history of the text may well be correct, but this particular reason for it fails to appreciate the difference of plot structure to which I have referred.

III   The war itself (20:12-48)
IV   Postwar reconstruction (21:1-24)
Epilogue No king in Israel (25)

The principal action takes place in the third episode. The first two trace developments that lead up to it, and the last shows the consequences that flowed from it.

1. Transition: No King in Israel (19:1a)

1a *In those days when there was no king in Israel. . . .*

Only the shorter form of the refrain occurs here and in 18:1. However, given the connotations of chaos that both forms of the refrain have picked up through their occurrence in chapters 17–18, its reappearance at this point of transition is rather ominous.[2] It predisposes us to expect that the chaos will continue in what follows, though what form it will take remains to be seen. (See also the comments on 17:6, 18:1, and 21:25.)

2. Episode 1: The Outrage at Gibeah (19:1b-28)

This section provides the background to the outrage committed in Gibeah, and establishes the narrator's perspective[3] on the characters involved in it. It unfolds in two main parts, centered in Bethlehem and Gibeah respectively, each consisting of a series of scenes that follow the same basic pattern: journeying, arriving, staying, and leaving. In Part 1 the journeying and arriving are combined in one scene. In Part 2, which is longer, they occur in two separate scenes.

a. Part 1: Five Days (and Four Nights) in Bethlehem (19:1b-10a)

(1) Scene 1: Journeying and Arriving (19:1b-3)

1b *. . . a man who was a Levite was sojourning in the remote parts of Mount Ephraim. He took for himself as a concubine a woman from Bethlehem in Judah.*

2. It should be noted, at this point, that neither part of the refrain, in itself, necessarily implies chaos. Having no human king does not entail chaos unless one is prepared to consign the whole premonarchic period of Israel's existence to chaos. And "everyone doing what is right in their own eyes" doesn't necessarily entail chaos unless Israel was also in a state of chaos under Moses (Deut. 12:8).

3. The second episode will provide a different, contrasting perspective on the same event. See below.

2 *His concubine played the harlot[4] against him, and left him for her father's house at Bethlehem in Judah; and she was there for some time — four months in all.*

3 *Then her husband stirred himself into action and went after her, to speak kindly to her and bring her back.[5] His young man was with him, and a pair of donkeys. She brought him[6] to her father's house, and when the young woman's father saw him, he was delighted to meet him.*

1   A *Levite* and *Mount Ephraim (har-'eprayim)* both feature in this story as in the previous one. But the starting point is different. This Levite is already living in Mount Ephraim, but in its remote parts *(bēyark'tê)*, not as close to the north-south route normally taken by travelers as the place where the first Levite had found employment. But this Levite, too, had traveled, apparently, for he had acquired a *concubine* in the same place that the first Levite had come from, *Bethlehem in Judah,* and brought her home with him. Whether or not he had found employment, as Micah's Levite had done, we don't know; nothing is said of it because it is not relevant to the present narrative. The initial impression is of a couple living a settled life in a relatively remote, rural setting.

But there are already hints that everything may not be quite as blissful as it seems. Since only one man and his partner are mentioned, we might have expected her to be called his wife *('iššâ),* as in the case of Achsah and Othniel (1:13), Deborah and Lappidoth (4:4), Jael and Heber (4:21), Samson's mother and Manoah (13:2), and Samson's own wife in Timnah (14:2). But no, she is the Levite's *concubine (pîlegeš)* which, at the very least, accords her a lower status than "wife."[7] And the way the beginning of their relationship is described *(he took [her] for himself)* suggests that she had no say

4. The MT is suspect, since no exact parallel to the construction *znh 'l* is attested elsewhere. Moreover, the *ōrgisthē,* "became angry [with]," of LXX[A], favored by most commentators, is regularly rendered by *ḥrh 'p* in Judges (2:14, 20; 3:8; 6:39; 9:30; 10:7; 14:19), and it is difficult to see how the MT of 19:2 could be a corruption of this. The *eporeuthē ap' autou,* "she deserted him," of LXX[B] appears to be an interpretation of the MT rather than a translation from an alternative text. See Moore, *Judges,* 409. The MT appears to be original.

5. Reading the Qere, *laḥªšîbâ,* which is clearly required here, rather than the Ketib, *lahašîbō* (to bring *him* back).

6. LXX[A] has merely *eporeuthē,* "[when] *he came* to her father's house," but LXX[B]'s *eisēnenken* supports the MT, which is the harder reading and therefore more likely to be original (cf. Song 8:2).

7. The full expression is *'iššâ pîlegeš,* in which *pîlegeš* qualifies *'iššâ,* making it clear that here *'iššâ* is to be understood as "woman" rather than "wife": a woman who was a concubine.

in the matter,[8] and that he regards her more as his property than his partner. It doesn't necessarily imply this,[9] but in conjunction here with *concubine,* it is at least open to that possibility. The same is true of the title "Levite." There is no reason why it should have negative connotations for us except that it has been colored by the way a Levite has featured in chapters 17–18. One thing is clear, though: the last (and only) time that the word *concubine* occurred in Judges it spelled trouble.[10] And as we are about to see, the same will turn out to be true here also.

2   What we suspected as being under the surface in the previous verse breaks out into full view here. The Levite's concubine *played the harlot (wattizneh)*[11] *against him* [*the Levite*], went to her father's house in Bethlehem, and remained there for four months. Her behavior could hardly be more damned than by calling it harlotry *(znh).* Furthermore, she who "plays the harlot" here ends up becoming the common property of the men of Gibeah in 19:25, suggesting (with grim irony) that, from the narrator's point of view, there was an element of justice in the concubine's fate. We are reminded of Samson, who did what was right in his own eyes and ended up having his eyes put out (14:3; 16:21), or Abimelech, who killed his brothers on a stone and was finally killed himself by having a stone dropped on his head (9:5, 53). However, the censure is muted somewhat by the narrative details. Damning though it is, it seems that *znh* is used metaphorically rather than literally here: the "harlotry"[12] the concubine committed was nothing more, as far as we know, than walking out on her husband; and then, far from giving her favors to other men, she went straight home to her father and stayed there. Her only motive, it seems, was to escape from a situation that she found intolerable. As we will see, the Levite will not escape the narrator's censure either. In fact, all the characters in this narrative will turn out to be culpable in one way or another, and the Levite most of all.

3   After four months the Levite at last sets out for Bethlehem to try to get his estranged concubine back. Samson, we recall, had done the same with respect to his wife (15:1). The Levite's intentions seem honorable. There is no mention of a gift as there was with Samson, who brought his wife

8. Contrast Rebekah in Gen. 24:58.

9. For example, the same language is used in Gen. 24:3 of Abraham's servant getting a wife for Isaac.

10. Abimelech was the son of Gideon's concubine (8:31). Cf. Block, *Judges, Ruth,* 522.

11. See the note to the translation.

12. Cf. Boling, *Judges,* 274: "MT is interpretive. As Israelite law did not allow for divorce by the wife, she became an adulteress by walking out on him." A similar understanding of the MT is reflected in the Jewish commentators. For references see Moore, *Judges,* 409.

a young goat, but the references to his *young man* and *two donkeys* are indications of serious intent; this is no casual affair, but a mission planned and undertaken with care. Furthermore, the fact that he goes to *speak kindly* (literally, "to speak *to her heart*" [*'al-libbâ*]) suggests that she had not left without provocation, and that the Levite intends to win her back by gentle persuasion rather than simply demanding that she return and that her father hand her over to him. The way he is greeted on arrival, too, suggests that both the concubine and her father are eager for reconciliation rather than confrontation. She "brings him in" to her father's house, and her father is *delighted* to meet him.[13] This is already turning out to be a rather complex narrative that oscillates between foreboding and hope, censure and a readiness to recognize good when it is present.

(2) Scene 2: Staying (19:4-8)

4 *The young woman's father prevailed upon[14] his son-in-law [not to leave], so he stayed with him for three days; they ate and drank and spent the night there.*

5 *On the fourth day they rose early in the morning and got ready to go. But the young woman's father said to his son-in-law, "Please, fortify yourself with a bit of food, and then go."*

6 *So the two of them sat down and ate together, and drank. And the young woman's father said to the man, "Please agree to spend the night and enjoy yourself."*

7 *The man rose to go, but [again] his father-in-law pressured him, so he turned back[15] and spent the night there.*

8 *He got up to go early on the morning of the fifth day, but the young woman's father said, "Please fortify yourself [with some more food], and wait till the day wears on." So they both ate.*

4   The young woman's father *prevails upon (wayyeḥᵉzaq)* the Levite not to rush away, but stay and enjoy his hospitality. Is it just customary courtesy, we wonder, or is something more intended? The use of the term *son-in-law (ḥōṯēn)* indicates full acceptance of his daughter's relationship with the Levite as formal and approved. At the very least he seems to want to give the relationship between his daughter and the Levite a better chance of success in the long term by building a stronger personal relationship with his guest.

---

13. That is, to meet him *again,* presumably.

14. Reading, with many MSS and edd., the Hiphil of *ḥzq,* rather than the Qal of the MT.

15. One Hebrew MS and several MSS of the LXX have *wayyēšeḇ,* "he stayed."

457

And it seems that the feeling is mutual: *he stayed with him for three days; they ate and drank and spent the night there.* But who is the subject of the last three verbs? The last, *"they* spent the night *(wayyālînû)* there," would most naturally include the concubine, since the verb *lyn* normally means to lodge somewhere as guests, and only the Levite and his concubine are guests. But the way the string of verbs begins, *he* [the Levite] *stayed with him* [the father], suggests that the primary referent of at least the next two verbs, *they ate and drank,* is the two men. In short, the daughter may be present, but she is at best marginal to the action. When, we wonder, will the Levite *"speak kindly* to her" (literally, "speak *to her heart"*), as he intended to when he set out (v. 3)?[16]

5 On the fourth day *they* rise early in the morning and prepare to leave. Here there is no ambiguity about the subject of the verb: the early risers are the Levite and his concubine. Since they rise together and prepare to leave together, we may be meant to understand that the intended reconciliation has taken place. But the father is not ready to release them yet. He urges them to stay and "fortify themselves" with some more food before leaving. Literally he says, "support/sustain *your heart (libb'kā)* with a piece of bread/food." He may simply be using the normal idiom for such an invitation,[17] and there may be nothing unusual in a host wanting to retain guests for a further meal before they go. Nevertheless, with "speaking to the heart" of the concubine announced as the purpose of the Levite's mission only two verses previously, the use of the term "heart" again here is potentially significant. Is it a clue, for those attuned to hear it, that more is going on here than a simple offer of further hospitality? Is the father hinting that the Levite's mission is not yet fulfilled, and that he should not leave until it is?[18] It can only be a question at this stage, but there are sufficient grounds for staying alert for any further uses of "heart" language.

6-7 In terms of the way the story is told, two significant things happen in verse 6. First, the marginalization of the concubine becomes explicit. Given that, in verse 5, it is specifically her husband that her father has invited to stay for a meal *("Please fortify <u>yourself</u>* [masculine singular] *with a bit of food"), the two of them* who sit down to eat and drink here in verse 6 must be the two men (the father and the husband). The young woman herself is either absent or ignored. Second, when, at the conclusion of the meal, the young

---

16. For this suggestion and the further treatment of the "heart" motif in what follows I am indebted to Jacqueline Lapsley's insightful treatment of this passage in *Whispering the Word: Hearing Women's Stories in the Old Testament* (Louisville: Westminster John Knox, 2005), 35-67.

17. As the narrator uses similar language in 19:22: "they were all *enjoying themselves" (mêṭîbîm 'eṭ-libbām).*

18. Lapsley, *Whispering the Word,* 39.

woman's father urges his guest to stay for another night, he again uses the word "heart"; *enjoy yourself* is literally "let *your heart (libbekā) be good.*" This is the third time the word has been used in this scene, and each occurrence increases the probability of its significance as a clue to the real reason behind the father's reluctance to let the Levite go.

There is a puzzling contradiction in his behavior, however. If he detains the Levite in the hope of a full reconciliation with his daughter, why does he pay so little attention to her? The impression we get is that he is intent on cultivating the connection with the Levite for his own sake rather than hers; the Levite's relationship with his daughter is merely what has given him the opportunity to do so. We are reminded of how Micah and the Danites saw a Levite as a desirable acquisition in chapters 17–18. There is no reference to a shrine in the present narrative, but given the confused environment of the time, a family connection with a Levite may well have had some superstitious value and been regarded as socially advantageous. The young woman's father certainly seems to think so, and this is in all probability the main reason why he was "delighted to meet him" back in verse 3.

The focus remains firmly on the two men in verse 7: *The man rose to go, but* [again] *his father-in-law pressured him, so he turned back and spent the night there.* The young woman has neither presence nor voice. She is at best a pawn in the game being played by her husband and father.

8 The young woman is almost invisible in this verse, too. There are only two merest hints of her presence. The first is the plural form of the imperative, *wait (hitmahm ͤhû).* But this is curious, to say the least, given the fact that the verse begins by referring only to the Levite *("He got up early"),* and that the immediately preceding imperative, *"Please fortify yourself (s ͤ'ād-nā' l ͤbāb ͤkā)"* is masculine singular. In view of this the final clause, *So the two of them ate,* is best taken as referring to the two men, as in verse 7. Verse 8 begins with the Levite rising early, and ends with him and his host feasting together for another day. In between, the young woman, at the very best, hovers on the margins of the scene, barely visible. The anomalous plural imperative, *wait,* hints at her presence, nothing more.

There is another hint of her presence, however, that is equally hard to spot, but potentially more significant. In verse 8 the word "heart" occurs for the fourth time in the scene, again on the lips of the young woman's father. As in verse 7 he says, literally, "fortify *your heart*" (l ͤbāb ͤkā). The hospitality he is showing the Levite has become farcical by this stage. But the way the word "heart" keeps occurring again and again reminds us why the Levite came in the first place (v. 3), and serves as a plausible explanation for the host's strange behavior. There is a "matter of the heart" that has fallen into the background and almost been forgotten, like the young woman herself. She has been so marginalized that she is barely discernible; but she is still present, if only subconsciously, in the minds of the two men. She is the reason they are there, and the invisible link between them.

(3) Scene 3: Leaving (19:9-10a)

9 *The man rose to go — he and his concubine and his young man. But his father-in-law (the young woman's father) said to him, "Please, look, the day is declining toward the evening. Please spend the night. Look, the day is coming to an end.*[19] *Spend the night here so you can enjoy yourself. Then you can rise early [tomorrow] for your journey, and go home."*[20]

10a *But the man was not willing to spend the night, so he got up and left. . . .*

9-10a   The mix of singular and plural forms in the Hebrew text of these verses reflects the fact that it is the Levite, his concubine, and his servant who are about to leave, but that the decision to leave or stay is the Levite's alone.[21] Similarly, the rather cumbersome, repetitive style, especially of verse 9, is best seen as an indication, not of textual corruption,[22] but of the agitated state of the concubine's father. He is desperate to keep the Levite from leaving, but has run out of things to say: all he can do is plead, and repeat himself. But the Levite has become exasperated at his host's continued importunity. He finally draws the line and takes his leave about mid-afternoon of the fifth day (v. 10).

Two things are noteworthy in verse 9. First, the word "heart," whose key significance was flagged at the outset of the scene (v. 3), is here used for the fifth and last time as it draws to a close: "*Spend the night here so you can enjoy yourself (l^{e}bāb^{e}kā)*." Whether or not the father is consciously hinting at the purpose of the Levite's visit remains unclear. But the way "heart" keeps occurring keeps us readers wondering: Has the Levite done what he came to do? Has reconciliation happened or not? Does the concubine go with him willingly or unwillingly? And is there a related significance in her father's exaggerated, and finally desperate, hospitality? We do not know, but the fact that only the Levite is mentioned in verse 10 suggests that, although they both leave with him, the concubine is no more valued by the Levite than his

---

19. The words, *"Please spend the night. Look, the day is coming to an end,"* are absent from the both LXX^A and LXX^B. But see the exegetical comments.

20. Literally, "go to *your tent" (l^e'ōhāle\underline{k}ā)*. Many medieval Hebrew MSS have the plural, "your tents." See the exegetical comments.

21. Keil and Delitzsch, "Judges," 443.

22. See the notes to the translation.

servant. All the text says is that *he [the Levite] got up and left.* There are no textual grounds for thinking that genuine reconciliation has taken place.

The second noteworthy thing is the way the concubine's father refers to the Levite's destination at the end of verse 9: *"go home"* is literally, *"go to your tent (leʾōhālekā)."* Whether or not the Levite literally lived in a tent (as Boling asserts),[23] the rhetorical significance of the term in this context lies not so much in what it denotes as in how it functions. The Levite's "tent" stands in contrast to the host's "house" *(bayit)* back in verses 2 and 3. The word "tent" can hardly be disparaging, since the last thing the concubine's father wants to do is offend the Levite. Rather, by this use of the term he makes one last attempt to persuade the Levite to stay. He won't have the same level of accommodation and cuisine he had enjoyed for the last five days when he gets back to his "tent" in the remote parts of Mount Ephraim (v. 1), so why leave before he must? The contrast may also hint at one of the reasons why the Levite's concubine left him: she missed the comforts of "her father's *house"* (v. 2).

b. Part 2: One Night in Gibeah (19:10b-28)

This passage, too, begins with arrival and ends with departure, and involves the Levite being shown hospitality. But this time the place is Gibeah, the arrival and departure are both more fraught than in the previous passage, and the hospitality far more dark and twisted. It unfolds through four scenes. The first, transitional scene explains why the Levite and his companions decided to seek lodgings in Gibeah (vv. 10b-14). The second deals with how they came to spend the night in the home of a particular old man there (vv. 15-21). The third scene deals with the horrors that led to the Levite leaving with his concubine apparently dead in the fourth (vv. 22-28).

(1) Scene 1: Journeying (19:10b-14)

10b   *. . . and arrived opposite Jebus (that is, Jerusalem). With him were [his] pair of saddled donkeys; and his concubine [also] was with him.*[24]

11   *When they were near Jebus and the day was far spent,*[25] *the young*

---

23. Boling, *Judges,* 275.

24. Instead of *ʾimmô* here, LXX[L] has *weναʿărô* ("and his young man") — a reading recommended by *BHS.* But *ʾimmô* is more likely to be original for three reasons: it is supported by both LXX[A] and LXX[B], it is the harder reading, and it is difficult to see how it could have arisen as a corruption of *weναʿărô.*

25. With *BHS* taking *rad* as an abbreviated form of the Qal perfect, *yārad.*

man said to his master, "Come on, let's turn aside to this city of the Jebusites, and spend the night in it."

12 *But his master said to him, "We won't turn aside to a city of foreigners,*[26] *who do not belong to people of Israel;*[27] *we'll go on to Gibeah."*

13 *He said to his young man, "Come on, let's approach one of [these] places, and spend the night at Gibeah or Ramah."*

14 *So they kept on going, and the sun went down on them near Gibeah, which belongs to [the tribe of] Benjamin.*

10b-14   The first part of the Levite's journey is passed over quickly: "he got up, and left, *and arrived.*" The series of three verbs in quick succession nicely captures the Levite's loss of patience with his host, and his desire, now, to get home as quickly as possible. But he has left too late, and so, as evening closes in, he finds himself well short of his goal: not home, but *opposite Jebus,* just 12 miles (8 km.) from his starting point.

The Levite's traveling party is made up, beside himself, of two *saddled donkeys, his concubine* (v. 10b), and his *young man,* who makes his presence felt by addressing his master in verse 11. We have heard of them all before, of course, but are reminded of them here because of the way their presence complicates the Levite's dilemma: a lone traveler may perhaps find overnight lodgings easily enough; it may be more difficult, though, for a company of this size. More serious, however, is the nature of the place they have arrived at. Jebus has already been a place of conflict between Israel and its native population (see 1:8, 21 and comments), and for the time being at least is firmly in the latter's hands: *Jebus,* as its name implies, is a *city of the Jebusites* (v. 11; see further below). But the need is urgent, and the Levite's *young man,* apparently less aware of the complexity of the situation than his master, sees turning in there as the only practical option, and says so. The Levite, though, is not convinced that they will receive a friendly welcome there, and insists that they press on to *Gibeah,* a further 2.5 miles (4 km.) north. Though it is not apparent at this stage, this will prove to be a bad mistake, and the effective trigger for all the horrendous events that follow.

In verses 13-14 the narrative fast-forwards again to the point where the Levite and his company are close to *Gibeah.* This time it is the Levite himself who proposes that they turn in and seek lodgings for the night. The fact that he also mentions *Ramah,* a further 3 miles (5 km.) beyond Gibeah, is

26. Following MT and LXX^A *(allotriou),* which take *nokrî* (masculine singular) as a gentilic, functionally equivalent to *mibbᵉnê yiśrāʾēl* in the next clause. LXX^B has *allotrian (= nokrîyyā),* "foreign city."

27. The feminine plural form *hēnnâ* is an obvious scribal error for *hēmmâ,* since the only possible referent is *bᵉnê yiśrāēl,* which is masculine plural. See the *BHS* apparatus.

again indicative of his desire to get home: he wants to make the most possible distance on this first day. So they travel on, but the issue of how far they will get is finally decided by the sun. It sets when they come *near Gibeah,* so they give up hope of going further and turn in there. If the Levite had listened to his servant, they would have stayed in Jebus; and if his host in Bethlehem had not been so hard to get away from, they might have gotten all the way home, or at least as far as Ramah. But a whole series of apparently unrelated circumstances, including the time of sunset on the day in question, have conspired to bring them (by fate, or is it providence?) to Gibeah, where their simple homeward journey is about to turn into a nightmare.

The statement that the Gibeah in question belonged to [*the tribe of*] *Benjamin* (v. 14) accords with Joshua 18:28, where Gibeah and "the Jebusite city (that is, Jerusalem)" (NIV) are both identified as lying within the territory of Benjamin. But Judges 1:21 speaks only of Jebus as a place from which the Benjaminites had failed to expel the Jebusites. This confirms that, in a general sense at least, the Levite has received what he wanted: he has avoided a town that is not yet Israelite, and arrived at one that is. But what follows is not what he expects.

(2) Scene 2: Arriving (19:15-21)

15 *So they turned aside there to go and spend the night at Gibeah. They entered [it] and sat down[28] in the open square of the city. But no one would take them home to spend the night.*

16 *But then an old man turned up, coming in at evening from his work in the field. He was from Mount Ephraim and was residing in Gibeah. But the local men were Benjaminites.*

17 *He looked up and saw the traveler in the open square of the city. The old man said, "Where are you going, and where do you come from?"*

18 *He replied to him, "We are passing through from Bethlehem of Judah to the remote parts of Mount Ephraim, where I come from. I went to Bethlehem of Judah, and I am going [back] to my home,[29] but no one is taking me into his house.*

---

28. The MT has the singular of both verbs: "he [the Levite] entered [it] and sat," but the context requires plural, as in the LXX. The final *waw* was probably lost from *wayyābō'* by haplography (the next word begins with the same letter). The loss of the same letter from the second verb *(wayyēšeb)* is harder to explain, but was probably a secondary development, influenced by the first.

29. The MT's *we'et-bêt Yahweh,* "and [object marker] the house of Yahweh," is almost certainly corrupt. At the very least we would expect "to" (either *'el* or *lᵉ*) here with "I am going" *(ᵃnî hōlēk),* rather than the object marker. And "the house of Yahweh" *(bêt Yahweh)* makes little sense in this context. Even if (as seems unlikely) the Levite is allud-

19 *We have both straw and fodder for our donkeys, and there is also bread and wine for me, your maid-servant, and the young man who is with your servants; we have no need of anything."*

20 *The old man said, "Welcome. Please, let me supply all your needs; don't spend the night in the open square."*

21 *So he brought him into his house and fed[30] the donkeys, and they washed their feet and ate and drank.*

15 Instead of being welcomed as fellow Israelites, the Levite and his party are left sitting in the open square of the city: *no one would take them home to spend the night* (v. 15). It is a complete contrast to the way the Levite had been treated in Bethlehem (v. 3), and to what he had expected here in Gibeah. It suggests that all is not well in Gibeah, and in the relationship between Benjamin and the rest of Israel.

16-21 Things begin to look up when an old man appears, *coming in at evening from his work in the field.* Significantly, he is not a Benjaminite, but from *Mount Ephraim,* the same general locality as the Levite himself (v. 1). He was not born in Gibeah, but merely "resides" *(gār)* there as a stranger, without full citizenship rights.[31] There may be a further hint of his "stranger" status in the fact that the labor he does is called "*his* work," but the place where he does it is simply "*the* field"; he works on land that is not his.[32] But these indications of difference are purely formal and material. The significant difference between this old man and *the local men,* who were *Benjaminites,* lies in how he behaves. Instead of ignoring the *traveler (hā'îš hā'mōrēaḥ)* in the town square as the locals do, he "looks up," "sees" him, and inquires about where he is from, where he is going, and (by implication) why he is still outside with night closing in; by now he should have found lodgings. The way the dialogue is presented as an exchange between two in-

---

ing to an intended visit to the shrine at Shiloh on the way home, we would have expected *bêt-hā'elōhîm* rather than *bêt Yahweh,* since that is how it has been referred to in 18:31 (cf. Block, *Judges, Ruth,* p. 531, n. 227). The translation above follows the LXX, which has *eis ton oikon mou.* It is possible, as Block and others have suggested, that *bêtî* was mistakenly taken, at some point, as an abbreviation of *bêt Yahweh.* See the references in Block's footnote to the fuller discussions by O'Connell and Tov.

30. The K and Q are both variants of the *wayyiqtol* of *bll,* "to feed [animals], give provender," a denominative from *belîl,* "fodder" (Isa. 30:24; Job 6:5; 24:6). Moore, *Judges,* p. 417.

31. Cf. the use of the same term in Judg. 17:7; Exod. 12:49, Lev. 16:29, etc., and the cognate noun *gēr* (sojourner, stranger, foreigner) in such places as Gen. 15:13; 23:4.

32. This is not a necessary implication of *haśśādeh* (see, e.g., Gen. 4:8; and within Judges, 1:14; 9:27, 42). What is suggestive in the present context is the contrast between "*his* work" and "*the* field" in proximity to *gār.*

464

dividuals (the old man and the Levite) draws attention to the affinity between them: they are both from the hill country of Ephraim, and are both strangers in Gibeah. But, of course, they are not alone (as the old man can hardly have failed to notice), and the Levite responds as spokesman for his whole party ("*We are passing through*," v. 18), presumably as he was expected to do.

This introduces a potential obstacle, however. The old man may be well disposed toward them, but does he have a large enough house and sufficient provisions to cater to such a company? The Levite anticipates this problem by assuring the old man at once of their self-sufficiency in terms of food and provisions for both themselves and their animals: "*we have no need of anything*" (v. 19) — anything, that is, except lodgings. And his tone is appropriately deferential for someone in such circumstances, referring to himself and those with him as *your servants.* They are at the old man's mercy, and the Levite knows it. He does not need to beg, however, for the old man is more than willing to help. Without hesitation he welcomes the Levite,[33] offers to *supply all [his] needs,* brings him into his house, and (personally, it seems)[34] feeds the donkeys (v. 21a). He is a veritable "good Samaritan."[35] His only concern is that the Levite should not spend the night outside (v. 20b). The scene ends with all of them inside, eating and drinking together.

(3) Scene 3: Staying (19:22-25)

22 *They were enjoying themselves when suddenly the men of the city, worthless fellows,[36] surrounded the house, and began to pound[37] on the door. They said to the old man, the owner of the house, "Bring out the man who has come to your house, so we can have sex with him."*

23 *The man who owned the house went out to them and said to them, "No, brothers! Please don't act wickedly, for this man has come to[38] my house. Don't commit this folly!*

24 *Look, my virgin daughter and his concubine[39] — please let me bring*

---

33. Literally, "Peace (*šālôm*) to you [singular]."

34. The sequence of two *wayyiqtols* (he *brought them in* and *fed* their donkeys) implies that the same person did both.

35. Luke 10:25-37.

36. Literally, "men of the sons of Belial" ('*anšê b*ᵉ*nê-b*ᵉ*lîya'al*), but '*anšê* is redundant here, and may have arisen under the influence of the preceding phrase, "men of the city" ('*anšê hā'îr*). It is absent from the LXX and the Vulgate.

37. Taking the participle in the ingressive sense after *nāsabbû* (they surrounded).

38. The anomalous form '*al* is a mistaken pointing of '*el* in the Leningrad Codex.

39. *BHS* recommends deleting *and his concubine* (*ûpîlagšēhû*) and emending the object '*ôṭām* (let me bring *them* out) to '*ôṭâ* (let me bring *her* out), and likewise with the other plural suffixes in this verse, to harmonize with v. 25, where only one woman is

them out. Rape them. Do with them as you please. But to this man do not do this foolish thing!"

25 *But the men would not listen to him. So the man took hold of his concubine and sent [her] outside to them. They had sex with her and abused her all night long until the morning, and discarded her as dawn was breaking.*

22 The atmosphere quickly lightens as host and guests settle down to a convivial evening together (v. 22). But then suddenly *(wᵉhinnê)* the worst elements of the local population gather outside and begin to beat on the door, demanding that the host send his principal guest out to them so they can rape him! The expression, *men of the city,* identifies the rabble at the door as "native" Gibeonites, in contrast to both the old man, who is from Mount Ephraim (v. 16), and his guests, who are travelers passing through. The further description of them as *worthless fellows* (literally, "men of belial" [*bᵉnê-bᵉlîyaʿal*]) is a damning indictment of Gibeonite society, even before we hear what they want. The etymology of *bᵉlîyaʿal* is uncertain, but it is most likely a combination of the negative particle *bᵉlî* (not, without) and the noun *yaʿal* (worth), from a root meaning "to be worthy."[40] It occurs twenty-seven times in the Old Testament, regularly with reference to people of bad character,[41] and once of a disease from which the sufferer is not expected to recover (Ps. 41:8 [Heb. 9]). In the poetry of Ps. 18:4-5 (Heb. 5-6) *bᵉlîyaʿal* is parallel to *māwet* and *šᵉʾôl* ("death" and "Sheol"). It is probably this poetic use of the term which paved the way for its use as the name of a supernatural evil being ("Belial" or "Beliar") in intertestamental and rabbinic literature. In the New Testament the Greek form of the word occurs once as a name of Satan (2 Cor. 6:15). Here in Judges 19:22 it is used idiomatically with *bᵉnê* (sons of) as a descriptive term for a class of people who are symptomatic of the sick state of society in Gibeah. They use the normal euphemism for sexual intercourse: *"Bring out the man . . . so that* [literally] *we can know him"* (wᵉnēdāʿennû).[42] But there is nothing subtle about their behavior (pounding on the door), nor

---

thrust out. On this reading the old man offers only his own virgin daughter to the mob. But since it is not she, but the Levite's concubine that is thrust out in v. 25, one would then have to suppose that the Levite gratuitously substitutes his own concubine for the woman who was offered. This is possible, but unlikely. Why would he do so? The basic problem with the suggestion, though, is that it involves emendation with no hard (textual) evidence to support it.

40. Block, *Judges, Ruth,* p. 535; T. J. Lewis, "Belial," *ABD* 1:654-56; cf. *HALOT,* 1:133, 420.

41. Deut. 13:13; 15:9; 1 Sam. 1:16; 2:12; 10:27; 25:17; 30:22; 2 Sam. 16:7; 20:1; 23:6; Nah. 1:11, 15; Ps. 101:3; Job 34:18; Prov. 6:12; 16:27; 19:28; 2 Chron. 13:7.

42. Cf. Gen. 4:1; 24:16; 38:26; 1 Kgs. 1:4, etc.

any doubt about what they intend. What they want is neither consensual nor natural; it is homosexual pack rape (men having forced sex with a man).

Now at last the full irony of the Levite's decision to travel on to Gibeah becomes apparent. Having eschewed the hospitality of "foreigners" and entrusted himself to Israelites, he finds himself in a virtual Sodom,[43] and he himself (a "foreigner" in Gibeah) is the main object of attack! The extensive verbal parallels between the present scene and that in Genesis 19:4-9 are obvious, and serve to emphasize this moment as one of particularly gross depravity. The fact that it takes place in an Israelite rather than a foreign city makes it especially scandalous.

23-24 Everything we have seen about the owner of the house so far has been positive. He is socially aware, hospitable, and generous to a fault, and all in all a complete contrast to the native Gibeonites among whom he lives. Now he is faced with a crisis to which he first responds with considerable courage, putting himself at risk by going outside to face the crowd and try to reason with them:

> *The man who owned the house went out to them and said to them, "No, brothers! Please don't act wickedly, for this man has come to my house. Don't commit this folly!"*

He appeals to them, for persuasive purposes, as *brothers* (fellow Israelites), urging them to desist from behavior that should be as abhorrent to them as it is to him. But it's of no use; they will not be deterred. So he offers them an alternative:

> *"Look, my virgin daughter and his concubine — please let me bring them out. Rape them. Do with them as you please. But to this man do not do this foolish thing!"*

It is not clear whether he already had this in his mind as a fall-back option, or whether it just occurred to him in the pressure of the moment. It depends on whether the introductory *hinnê (Look)* is a rhetorical device, or an indication of sudden inspiration. What is clear is that he would not have offered this alternative if he did not feel he had to. But offer it he does, and by so doing he unwittingly sets in train a series of events that will bring Israel to the brink of

---

43. The extensive verbal parallels are listed by, among others, Burney (*Judges*, p. 274) and Block (*Judges, Ruth*, pp. 533-34). While literary dependence is generally acknowledged, which is dependent on which is disputed. Block thinks Judges 19 echoes Genesis 19. Niditch thinks the Judges narrative is primary. S. Niditch, "The 'Sodomite' Theme in Judges 19–20: Family, Community, and Social Disintegration," *CBQ* 44, no. 3 (1982): 365-78.

total self-destruction. Again this dark narrative is deeply ironical. The model host turns out to be the one who conceives the idea of throwing the two women to the dogs. That he should volunteer the Levite's concubine as well as his own daughter is surprising, to be sure.[44] Perhaps the rules of correct behavior in such circumstances, as he understands them, apply to male guests only, or, more likely, he is just doing the best he can: two women instead of one man; at least he will have saved his principal guest. The fact that his own daughter is a *virgin* adds a special poignancy to the horror of what happens here. For a second time in Judges a virgin daughter is sacrificed to a father's perverted sense of moral obligation (cf. 11:39). And more young women will fall victim to similar abuse before this story has run its course (21:19-22).

The ethical confusion in the mind of the host is nicely mirrored by the moral terms he uses: *"do not act wickedly" (tārēʿû)* (v. 23); *"do not do this foolish thing" (hannᵉbālâ)* (v. 24); *"Do with them* [the two women] *as you please"* (literally, "what is *good* in your own eyes"; *haṭṭôb bᵉʿênêkem*) (v. 24). In other words, what is acceptable to him as an alternative to "wickedness" and "folly" is "doing what is good in one's own eyes." But 17:6 and 21:25 tell us that this is in fact the fundamental problem — the one evil that underpins all the others, and the host has, albeit reluctantly, committed this same evil himself. He is just as responsible, in his own way, for what happens to the two young women as the mob outside his door are. The model host and the rabble outside are not as different from each other as they first seem to be. They are both enmeshed in the same evil, and symptomatic of the same basic, moral sickness.

25 The focus narrows now to the Levite and the concubine. In view of the offer made in verse 24, the words *the man took hold of his concubine* could be taken to mean, "the host took hold of the Levite's concubine." However, the opening words of verse 25 *(But the men would not listen to him)* make this unlikely. The host has been rebuffed by the mob at his door; they show no indication of being willing to accept the alternative he has offered them. What follows is not the host doing what he promised (bringing out his virgin daughter and the concubine), but the Levite, whose fate now seems to be sealed, taking matters into his own hands and making a last-ditch attempt to save himself. He grabs his concubine and thrusts her out.[45] Whereupon the mob, with the concubine actually in their hands now, act as creatures of appe-

---

44. See the notes on the translation. This puzzling feature of the text does serve, however, to underscore the allusion to the corresponding episode in Sodom (Gen. 19:8).

45. Cf. Boling, *Judges,* p. 276, who comments that *the man* of v. 25 "is probably the Levite, whose story is being told. Other protagonists in chs. 19–21 — the father-in-law, the master of the house — are regularly identified by some such title." Cf. Moore, *Judges,* p. 418: "The Levite gives up the woman to save himself."

tite rather than reason and settle for immediate gratification. We are spared the harrowing details of what she suffered at their hands. Three graphic verbs in quick succession tell it all: they *had sex with her* (literally, "*knew* her"),[46] *abused* her, and then *discarded* her. They are true (literally) "sons of Belial" (v. 22); their appetites and motives are uncomplicated and brutal. They are the chief culprits, but they are not the principal characters in this closing part of the scene. What they do takes place offstage, and is left largely to our imagination. The two characters whose actions have been subject to the most scrutiny are those still inside the house, the host and the Levite, and neither of them has fared well — especially the Levite.

(4) Scene 4: Leaving (19:26-28)

26 *Early in the morning the woman came and fell at the door of the man's house where her lord was, [and remained there] until it was light.*

27 *Her lord got up in the morning, opened the doors of the house, and went out to go on his way. But there was the woman, his concubine, fallen at the door of the house, with her hands on the threshold!*

28 *He said to her, "Get up, and let's go." But there was no reply. So he took her [and put her] on the donkey. Then the man set out and went to his own place.*

26-28 *Early in the morning,* while it is still partly dark, the discarded concubine falls at the door of the house, too weak to knock or cry out, perhaps already dead (v. 26). Inside, at daybreak, the Levite "gets up" (*wayyāqām,* v. 27). The expression is chilling in what it implies by its sheer ordinariness. After thrusting out the concubine, and seeing that he himself is no longer personally threatened, the Levite has retired to bed. In the morning he rises without any apparent remorse for what he has done or concern for his concubine. In fact, he appears to give no thought to her at all until he is preparing to leave and finds her (*wᵉhinnê, There* she was!) on the doorstep, and tells her with almost unbelievable callousness to *"Get up"* because he is ready to go. But there is no answer. So he picks her up, puts her on his donkey, and completes his journey home (v. 28).

Twice in this final scene the Levite is referred to as *her lord* (*'ᵃdōneyhā,* vv. 26, 27). At the outset of this story he had been her "husband" (*'îšāh*), who had set out to speak *kindly* to her (*'al-libbâ,* v. 3). The term *'îš* occurs again in the final clause, but now it is colored by the double use of *'ᵃdōneyhā* that precedes it, and by its absence of a possessive suffix: not "*her*

46. Cf. v. 22.

husband," but simply *"the* man *(hā'îš)."* He may be the same "man" in one sense, but now we know that he is no true "husband" to the concubine; he is not "hers" by any ties of affection or accepted obligation. His relationship with her is now defined purely in terms of rule and power. He takes her home because she is his property, nothing more, and because, dead or alive, he still has some use for her, or at least what's left of her, and we are about to see what "use" it is.

3. Episode 2: Preparations for War (19:29–20:11)

In the first episode hospitality went wrong because of the moral blindness of a host. In this second episode another Israelite institution goes wrong, but for more sinister reasons: a man of bad character deliberately manipulates it for his own ends.

The passage begins with the Levite calling on Israel to gather in order to confer and decide on a course of action (19:29-30), and ends with a large force of fighting men deployed against Gibeah (20:11). All the intervening material is taken up with the proceedings of the assembly (the *'ēḏâ* or *qāhāl*) that lead to this outcome.[47]

Assemblies like this occur repeatedly in Judges, from the initial one in 1:1-2 to the final one in 21:2-14. An assembly is convened in 10:17-18, and similar assemblies are probably to be taken as the setting for every occasion on which Israel cries out to Yahweh for help and/or is addressed by him or by someone who speaks for him (2:1-5; 3:9, 15; 4:3; 6:6-10). They typically occur in times of crisis, and much depends on what happens at them. They were a vital part of Israel's life as a tribal confederacy in the judges period.[48] But this particular assembly will turn out to be a farce because of the bad character of the one who convenes it. The satirical tone of the previous episode is maintained in this one.

29 *When he came to his home, he took his knife,[49] took hold of his concubine, cut her up into twelve pieces, and sent her throughout all the territory of Israel.*

30 *Everyone who saw it said, "Such a thing as this has never happened or been seen from the day the Israelites came up from the land of*

47. See 20:1; 21:10, 13, 16 (*'ēḏâ*) and 20:2; 21:5, 8 *(qāhāl).* The synonymity of the two expressions is implied by the statement *wattiqqāhēl hā'ēḏâ* (the assembly gathered) in 20:1.

48. See the Section II.C of the Introduction.

49. Literally, *"the* knife" *(hamma"kelet),* an example of the use of the article to indicate focused attention on something under particular circumstances (GKC #126r). It suggests the deliberation with which the Levite performs the action.

Egypt until this day.[50] *Put your mind*[51] *to it! Confer [about it], and speak."*

1 *Then all the Israelites came out, and the assembly gathered as one man to Yahweh at Mizpah, from Dan to Beersheba, including the land of Gilead!*

2 *The leaders of all the people — all the tribes of Israel — took their places in the assembly of the people of God — four hundred thousand*[52] *foot-soldiers, armed with swords.*

3 *The Benjaminites heard that the Israelites had gone up to Mizpah. The Israelites said, "Speak up! How did this evil thing happen?"*

4 *The Levite fellow, the husband of the murdered woman, answered, "It was to Gibeah, which is in Benjamin, that I came — I and my concubine — to spend the night.*

5 *The rulers*[53] *of Gibeah rose up against me; they surrounded the house because of me at night — it was me they intended to kill, but it was my concubine they raped, and she died.*

6 *So I took hold of my concubine, and I cut her up and sent her into all the territory of Israel's inheritance, for they had done a wicked, foolish thing in Israel.*

7 *So now, all you Israelites, give your considered verdict*[54] *here [in the assembly]."*

8 *All the people rose as one man, and said, "Not one of us will go to his tent, or return to his home.*

9 *But now this is the plan we will carry out against Gibeah: we will go up against it*[55] *by lot.*

---

50. The LXX has a longer form of this verse. After *until this day* it has *and he [the Levite] commanded the men he sent, "Say this to all the men of Israel, 'Has anything like this happened from the day the Israelites came up out of Egypt until this day?'"* Since this ends with exactly the same words *(until this day)* as what immediately precedes it, it is easy to see how it could have been accidentally omitted by haplography. However, restoring the whole of it to the MT results in a text that is repetitive and doesn't make complete sense. Most likely the LXX represents the conflation of two variants that can't be satisfactorily harmonized by simply adding the wording of one to the wording of the other. The translation follows the MT, which is the harder reading, and therefore most likely to be original.

51. Taking *lākem* as a contraction of *lᵉbabkem* (to your heart/mind). Cf. *BHS* apparatus.

52. Or *four hundred contingents.* See Section IX.C of the Introduction.

53. The expression is *baʿᵃlê haggibʿâ*, which could mean either "lords, rulers" (cf. Isa. 16:8) or just "citizens, inhabitants" (cf. Josh. 24:11). Cf. the *baʿᵃlê šᵉkem* of Judg. 9:2, 3, 6, etc.

54. Taking *dābār wᵉʿēṣâ* (word and counsel) as a hendiadys.

55. Assuming that the verb *naʿaleh* has dropped out before *ʿālêhā* by homoeo-

10 *We will take ten men from a hundred from all the tribes of Israel, and a hundred from a thousand, and a thousand from ten thousand, to take provisions for the people so that they can go in and take action against[56] Gibeah[57] of Benjamin for[58] all the folly it has committed in Israel."*

11 *So all the men of Israel were gathered against the city, united[59] as one man.*

19:29–20:1   When the Levite gets home, he calmly takes his knife, lays hold of his concubine, cuts her up into *twelve pieces* — one for each tribe — and sends them to all parts of Israel. As indicated in the translation, it is literally *her* he sends in this gruesome form. This is the final, ultimate violation of her personhood. She is denied even the dignity of burial. Furthermore, a special horror is added by lingering doubt about whether she was already dead or merely unconscious when the dismemberment took place. Note, for example, the contrast between 5:27, where we are told that Sisera "fell — *dead,*" and 19:26, where we are told only that the concubine "fell" at the door of the house. Was she dead or merely senseless? Was it the Levite himself rather than the rapists of Gibeah who killed her? We cannot know, but the question is a natural one, and our inability to answer it cannot help but color our perception of the Levite's character. He, in any case, would not care what the answer was; he had no further use for her as a person — only as an object to inspire horror and bend others to his will.

The Levite's treatment of his concubine picks up further resonances from its literary context. Within Judges it recalls Jephthah's sacrifice of his daughter (11:34-39).[60] The concubine is the second woman to be "sacrificed" by a man who should have been her protector. And it anticipates the forcible

---

teleuton (they have the same endings in the consonantal form of the text). Cf. the LXX, which has *anabēsometha ep' autēn.*

56. The MT's *la'a'ṣôt lebô'ām* has probably arisen through a conflation of variants (Boling, *Judges,* p. 284), or (as my translation suggests) by the accidental transposition of the two infinitives (Block, *Judges, Ruth,* p. 556, n. 314). The LXX has *tois eisporeuomenois epitelesai.*

57. Reading *gib'ā* instead of the MT's *geba',* with the LXX and the English versions in general. Although Gibeah and Geba are distinguished in Josh. 18:24, 28 and Isa. 10:29, there can hardly be any doubt that the same town is in view here in v. 10 as in v. 9.

58. Taking *ke* of *kekol-hannebālâ* in the sense of "in accordance with," "as warranted by," as in Gen. 6:22; Exod. 21:30; Num. 30:2; 1 Sam. 25:30, etc. Cf. *BDB,* p. 454.

59. Taking *ḥaberîm* (companions, associates) in the adverbial sense, "*as* companions" (i.e., *united*).

60. Did he, too, perhaps cut the victim into pieces, as stipulated for a burnt offering in Lev. 1:6, 8, and 12?

abduction of the young women of Shiloh in 21:15-23. "Everyone doing what is right in their own eyes" produces a society in which both sexes lose their humanity, but it is women who suffer most.

The Levite's action is effective, however. All who receive the gruesome remains agree that such a thing has never before happened in Israel's history, and demands a response (v. 30). Given, though, that the assembly does not convene until 20:1, the imperatives at the end of v. 30 must be taken as something that happens prior to this.[61] Local people demand action from their leaders. The result is a great, all-Israel assembly: *all the Israelites* (i.e., their leaders, v. 1), from *Dan* in the remote north to *Beersheba* in the far south,[62] *including the land of Gilead* (i.e., from east of the Jordan as well as west of it), gather *as one man* to Yahweh at Mizpah (20:1).[63] Ironically, this is a greater response than any of the judges had achieved, as far as we know. Only the phrase *to Yahweh* (20:1) hints at a limitation to the Levite's influence. Yahweh remains the supreme ruler of Israel, as the leaders will later acknowledge by inquiring of him (v. 18). But by then the Levite will have disappeared from the narrative without any hint that he was raised up by Yahweh as the judges had been. The Levite is at best a caricature judge who almost destroys Israel rather than saving it. But he is certainly influential: it is his summons that brings Israel's leaders out as one man.

The manner in which he galvanizes Israel into action is without precedent in the Old Testament. However, it does have striking resemblances to the way Saul later summons Israel to war in 1 Samuel 11:1-8. When Saul hears that Nahash the Ammonite has threatened to gouge out the eyes of his fellow Israelites in Jabesh-gilead, the Spirit of God rushes on him. He immediately becomes incensed, and in hot anger grabs two oxen, cuts them to pieces, and sends them throughout Israel, threatening to do the same to the oxen of anyone who doesn't answer his call. A holy dread (the terror of Yahweh) falls on all who receive the gruesome pieces, and they come out "as one man" to follow Saul in battle. The similarities to the present passage are obvious. But the differences are equally striking, and arguably more significant in the backward light they throw on it. In the case of the Levite there is no onrush of the Spirit, or any divinely inspired dread. In fact, there is no involvement by Yahweh at all. Nor is there any hot anger. In contrast to Saul, the Levite does his grizzly work without any apparent emotion at all. But the most chilling dif-

61. See the notes to the translation of v. 30.

62. Biblical Beersheba lay approximately 47 mi. (77 km.) south-southwest of Jerusalem, midway between the southern Dead Sea and the coastal plain.

63. The *Mizpah* in view here is almost certainly not the place of the same name in 11:11. That was in Gilead in Transjordan; this one is in central Canaan. It is generally identified with the modern site of Tell en-Nasbeh, 6.5 mi. (10.5 km.) north of Jerusalem and about 6 mi. (9.5 km.) north-northwest of Gibeah (Boling, *Judges,* p. 550).

ference of all is the victim: not two oxen, but a human being. It is this that gives the Levite's action its distinctively un-Israelite quality, and justifies seeking whatever antecedents it might have *outside* Israel rather than in it. A striking instance is the following text from the royal archives of Mari, in present-day Syria, from the first half of the second millennium B.C. It is from a letter to King Zimri-Lim, who reigned from 1782 to 1759. The writer, Bahhdi-Lim, is frustrated that the inhabitants of a particular area have so far ignored his repeated calls to come and support him in an urgent military campaign:

> Now if I had my way, a prisoner in jail should be killed, his body dis-membered, and transported to the area between the villages as far as Hudnim and Appan in order that the people would fear and gather quickly, and I could make an attempt, in accordance with the command which my lord has given, to carry out the campaign quickly.[64]

Without further evidence it is impossible to know how widespread the practice was, but the response to the Levite's use of it in Judges suggests that it was not unknown in Israel's world in the judges period either. If so, it is another example of the deep inroads that pagan practices made into Israel's life at the time.[65]

2-3a The nature and purpose of the assembly are indicated here by a double set of contrasts. On the one hand, it is a religious gathering: *the assembly of the people of God,* gathered, as we saw in verse 1, "to Yahweh." But it is also a military muster, as shown by the *four hundred thousand*[66] *foot-soldiers, armed with swords.*[67] The implication is that what is in view in this assembly is holy war. A further indication of this will follow. The second contrast is between the "all Israel" nature of the assembly on the one hand

---

64. *ARM* 2.48. English translation as cited by Block in *Judges, Ruth,* p. 546. G. Wallis drew attention to this letter in "Eine Parallele zu Richter 19 29ff. und 1 Sam. 11 5ff. aus dem Briefarchiv von Mari," *ZAW* 64 (1952): 57-61.

65. Cf. especially the sacrifice of Jephthah's daughter.

66. See the note on this number in the translation. Ironically, if it is taken at face value and compared with figures in the census lists of Num. 1 and 26, it is a surprisingly *low* number! It suggests that the population of Israel as a whole was only about two million, a third less than the number that left Egypt. But perhaps this is not so surprising, given the rigors and disasters of the journey through the wilderness, in which an entire generation died, and the warning of Deut. 28:18 that if Israel rebelled against Yahweh, it would be cursed with infertility. Cf. Block, *Judges, Ruth,* p. 550.

67. It is possible that the term (*pinnôṭ,* literally, "corners"), translated as *leaders* in v. 2, may be a technical term for military officers (cf. 1 Sam. 14:38). But the following explanatory phrase, *all the tribes of Israel,* suggests that they were tribal leaders, perhaps a mixture of military leaders and tribal elders, as in 10:17-18, 11:6. But all were *armed* (v. 11).

("leaders of *all* the people — *all* the tribes of Israel"), and the fact that one tribe, Benjamin, is absent. The *Benjaminites* [only] *heard* that *the Israelites* had gone up to Mizpah. The implication is that Benjamin is no longer part of Israel. Either it was not invited, or it chose not to come. The breach between Benjamin and the other tribes that is already hinted at here will soon take the form of all-out war between them.

3b-7 When he is asked to explain his summons, the Levite gives a carefully tailored version of events. The facts are not grossly distorted, but he gives quite a different impression of what happened than the narrator did in the previous episode. In the narrator's account the rapists were "men of the city, worthless fellows" (19:22); the Levite speaks of the *rulers (ba*ᵃ*lê)* of Gibeah rising against him (v. 5; cf. 9:2). To the members of the assembly, who do not know the facts as we do, this would presumably be taken at face value as an assertion that the crime was not the work of an unruly rabble, but something in which Gibeah's leading citizens were implicated. In the narrator's account the offenders demand that the host bring the Levite out so that they can "have sex with him" (19:22). The Levite says that they *intended to kill* him (v. 5). Considering what happened to the concubine, it is perhaps a reasonable inference that they intended more than a mere sex orgy. But the Levite's choice of words lays particular stress on the threat to himself, thereby diminishing his responsibility by implication. In the absence of further information, what he says could conjure up a totally different scenario from the actual one; for example: his life was threatened; he escaped, but his concubine was caught and raped; he later recovered her body, and so on. Finally, as we have seen, the narrator's account was suggestively vague about whether the concubine dies solely as a result of the rape, or as a result of the combined effect of the rape and the Levite's subsequent treatment of her. Was she unconscious or dead on the doorstep? Did she die while the Levite was taking his rest, during his preparations to leave, or on the journey home? As we have seen, the narrator's account even allows us to entertain the suspicion that, having turned her out to the mob, the Levite considered her as good as dead,[68] but then, having conceived the possibility of using her corpse to avenge himself on the men of Gibeah, deliberately contributed to her death or even caused it directly with his knife when they got home.[69] This would explain the extraordinary callousness he displays. In contrast, the Levite's own account is deceptively simple: *"my concubine they raped, and she died"* (v. 5). He implies that she died solely as a result of what the mob did to her, without any mention of the fact that he thrust her out to them to save himself. His speech arouses none of the suspicions the narrator's account did, and actually withholds details that

---

68. Or at least as polluted and of no further use to him as a concubine.
69. Cf. Polzin, *Moses and the Deuteronomist,* pp. 200-202.

might reflect badly on the Levite himself. This is the second time we have seen the Levite doing this. His speech to the old man on his arrival in Gibeah in 19:18-19 does not have the same sinister overtones as the present one, but it displays the same kind of strategic omissions in order to elicit a desired response.[70] He also knows what to include. He climaxes his appeal to the assembly here in chapter 20 by referring to the land as *Israel's inheritance* (*nah̬ᵃla̲t yiśrā'ēl*, v. 6), implying that everything involved in Yahweh's original gift of it to Israel's twelve tribes is now at stake,[71] and therefore urgent united action is essential. The Levite is not a truth-teller, however, but a truth-manipulator, and here it is Israel as a whole that is being manipulated. Hence its *considered verdict* (v. 7) is compromised even before it is given, and will inevitably lead to flawed action: not true holy war, but a parody of it.

8-11 The members of the assembly are as impressed by the Levite's speech as they were by his grisly summons. But the Levite himself begins to fade into the background at this point; from now on attention is focused on the assembly itself and the actions it takes. Presumably leadership was exercised by one or more persons, but no names are given so that the emphasis can fall on the total unity with which the members of the assembly act. They rise *as one man* and declare that no one will return to either his *tent* (at the assembly site) or his *home* until the matter is dealt with. However, there is no sense here of precipitous action, like that of a mob whipped into a frenzy by the Levite's rhetoric. On the contrary, the members of the assembly give every evidence of trying to act in a careful, responsible manner. They announce a *plan* (literally, "thing") they have agreed on: *"we will go up against [Gibeah] by lot"* (v. 9).

The verb *'lh,* "to go up," which was a key term in the operations against the Canaanites in 1:1–2:5, reappears here. Here, though, it probably means simply to advance, since the movement involved is not from lowlands to highlands but from one location in the highlands to another. And although there is no explicit reference to seeking Yahweh here, as Israel did in 1:1, their decision to go up *by lot (bᵉgôrāl)* invests their action with particular solemnity, and indicates their intention to act in accordance with established practice. To this point in the biblical account of Israel's history, the expression *bᵉgôrāl* has been used almost exclusively of the method by which the various tribes were assigned their respective territories in the land Yahweh

---

70. He tells of his visit to Bethlehem because he wishes to present himself as travel-weary, but does not mention the reason for the visit because this might raise questions about the good character of him and/or his concubine. The deferential "for me and your maid-servant" (v. 19) is calculated to win the host's favor while conveying minimal information.

71. Cf. the reference to the land as Israel's *nah̬ᵃlâ* in Exod. 15:17; Deut. 4:38; 15:4, etc.

had given them.[72] In Joshua 18–19, in particular, Joshua, Eleazar the priest, and the other tribal leaders are said to have given each tribe its "inheritance" *(naḥªlâ)* "by lot" *(beḡôrāl)* "before Yahweh" *(lipnê Yahweh)* at Shiloh[73] — a very significant event. The context suggests that the process involved the use of the priestly Urim and Thummim.[74] In the present passage the Israelites are at Mizpah rather than Shiloh, and there is no mention of a priest. However, the references to assembling "to Yahweh" *('el-Yahweh,* v. 1), to the land as Israel's inheritance *(naḥªlâ,* v. 6), and to the use of the lot *(gôrāl,* v. 9) all draw attention to the weightiness of the occasion, and suggest that those involved are attempting to act in accordance with Israel's sacred traditions. By using the lot after assembling to Yahweh, they implicitly defer to him and appeal to him to guide their decision making.

For all this, though, it is not entirely clear what they intend to determine by means of the lot. Is it the order in which the advance will be made: which tribe will go first, which second, and so on? The question about who will go first was certainly asked at the beginning of the book and will soon be asked again (v. 23). But a different matter seems to be in view here, as indicated by verse 10. The Israelites have agreed that 10 percent of the manpower available to them should be set aside for vital noncombat duties, and that the lot should be used to select them — presumably so that the process can be seen to be impartial. This 10 percent is to be assigned provisioning duties, so that when the operation reaches its final stage, it will not falter because of inadequate supplies for those on the front line. Despite the numerical imbalance between the two sides, the leaders clearly respect the fighting ability of the Benjaminites,[75] and take measures to make sure, as far as possible, that their mission will not fail for lack of careful planning. They want to be sure their men can complete what they are about to begin. This will involve their "going in" to Gibeah (v. 10), as their forebears had gone in to Jericho[76] with similar consequences. But this time it will be Israelites who will die.

The description of what the Gibeonites have done at the end of verse 10 *(kol-hann^ebālâ, all the folly)* echoes the words of both the host back in 19:23-24 and the Levite in 20:6. But the word *all (kol)* is new, and indicates the justification and intent of the massive military operation the Israelites are about to embark on. They intend to inflict a punishment on Gibeah fully

---

72. Num. 26:55; 33:54; 34:13; 36:2; Josh. 14:2; 19:51; Judg. 1:3. In Josh. 21:4-8 and 1 Chron. 6:46-50 (Eng. 61-65) it is used with reference to assigning cities to the Levites. The only other occurrence is in Mic. 2:5: "Therefore you will have no one in the assembly of the Lord to divide the land *by lot*" (NIV).

73. See esp. Josh. 18:1-2 and 19:51.

74. See the comments on 1:1-2.

75. See v. 16, and cf. 1 Chron. 12:1-2.

76. Josh. 6:21-22.

commensurate with the wrong it has done — to fully satisfy the demands of justice. But they do not know all the facts as we do, and so the Levite, who is at least as guilty as the Gibeonites, will go unpunished. Hence the impressive unity of verse 11 *(all the men of Israel were gathered against the city, united as one man)* is unity in a cause that is flawed from the beginning. One wonders what will become of an Israel whose leaders are so swayed by a man of this Levite's character. That is the serious issue posed by the satirical portrayal of the assembly in this episode.

4. Episode 3: The War Itself (20:12-48)

The outcome of the assembly's decision is a holy war,[77] an institution especially associated with Israel's heroic age in the biblical traditions. The present narrative includes nearly all its formal features, distributed over Episodes 2-4 as follows: the summons, the assembly of the people of God, the vow of concerted action (Episode 2); the inquiry for divine guidance, offerings in the face of reverses, divine assurance of victory, panic among the enemy, the execution of the ban (Episode 3); dispersal of the assembly (Episode 4).[78] The peculiar horror of the present account is that it is one of the tribes of Israel that is the enemy, and that the war is prosecuted with a determination and thoroughness surpassing anything seen in Israel's wars against the Canaanites elsewhere in Judges. The action in Episode 3 alternates between engagement with the enemy and inquiry of Yahweh, giving the following compositional pattern:

> Attempt at negotiation
> > Inquiry of Yahweh
> Defeat
> > Inquiry of Yahweh
> Defeat
> > Inquiry of Yahweh
> Victory

This alternating pattern reflects the protracted nature of the struggle, the complicated relational dynamics involved (Israel struggles with Yahweh as

77. Or "Yahweh war." Janet Tollington, "The Ethics of Warfare and the Holy War Tradition in the Book of Judges," in *Ethical and Unethical in the Old Testament: God and Humans in Dialogue,* ed. Katharine Dell (New York and London: T&T Clark, 2010), pp. 71-87.

78. Cf. the characteristics of holy war narrative listed by Gerhard von Rad in *Heilige Krieg im altern Israel,* 4th edn. (Göttingen: Vandenhoeck & Ruprecht, 1965), pp. 6-14.

well as with Benjamin), and the painfulness of the path to victory (it comes only after Israel is twice defeated). On the large numbers of men involved, see Section IX.C of the Introduction.

a. Attempt at Negotiation (20:12-17)

The verbal exchange before battle that we see here is reminiscent of Jephthah's exchanges with the king of Ammon in 11:14-28, and with the Ephraimites in 12:1-3. In neither case was there much hope of a positive outcome, and probably none was expected (especially on Jephthah's part). Their main function was to justify the action about to be taken, and perhaps buy time for necessary preparations. The same is true here. The failure of negotiation has been made all but inevitable by developments that have occurred in the previous two episodes.

12 *The tribes of Israel sent men throughout the whole tribe[79] of Benjamin, saying, "What about this evil that has been committed among you?*

13 *Now hand over the men — worthless fellows — who are in Gibeah, so we can put them to death and purge the evil[80] from Israel." But the Benjaminites[81] were not willing to listen to what their Israelite brothers said.*

14 *So the Benjaminites came together from the towns to Gibeah, to go out to war against[82] the Israelites.*

15 *On that day the Benjaminites mustered from the towns twenty-six thousand men armed with swords, apart from the inhabitants of Gibeah, [who] mustered seven hundred chosen men.*

16 *Out of all these people there were seven hundred chosen, left-handed men, each of whom could sling a stone at a hair and not miss.*

17 *The Israelites who were mustered, apart from Benjamin, were four hundred thousand men armed with swords, each of them a warrior.*

12-14 The sending of men *throughout the whole tribe of Benjamin* is an attempt to isolate Gibeah by appealing to the residents of the other towns to break solidarity with it. The *evil* in question (v. 12) has not been committed

---

79. Reading the construct singular, with the LXX and Vulgate. The MT's *šiḇṭê*, pointed as a construct plural, may in fact be a singular with an archaic genitive case ending (Boling, *Judges,* p. 284).

80. Reading *hārāʿâ* (with the article) instead of the MT's *rāʿâ*. The article was probably omitted by haplography after the final *h* of the previous word.

81. Reading *bᵉnê-ḇinyāmin*. The *bᵉnê* has been omitted by homoeoarcton.

82. For this sense of *ʿim* in military contexts see BDB, p. 767.

479

by all the Benjaminites, or in all its towns. It has been done by certain men —
worthless fellows[83] — *who are in Gibeah* (v. 13). If the Benjaminites in general can be persuaded to hand these men over (or perhaps force the leaders of
Gibeah to do so), the evil can be purged *from Israel* (v. 13), and war averted.
Significantly, the Israelites who deliver this ultimatum on behalf of the assembly do not use the same terminology that the Levite himself did in addressing the assembly back in verse 5. He said that the crime was committed
by "the *rulers (ba'ălê)* of Gibeah." The Israelites speak only of *worthless men*
[*bᵉnê-bᵉlîya'al*] who are *in Gibeah,* echoing the narrator's own account of the
affair in 19:22. The difference may simply be for diplomatic reasons: the Israelites want to enlist the many against the few. But it also hints subtly at the
declining influence of the Levite. The focus is no longer on the Levite's involvement in what happened in Gibeah, but on the seriousness of it in its own
right. The Levite triggered the action now taking place, but his influence on
the way it is executed has diminished. He is fading into the background.
Other men, of better motives, are now in charge. But the Benjaminites refuse
to cooperate, and reject the olive branch that has been offered: they are not
willing to listen to *their Israelite brothers,* and instead make their own preparations for war (vv. 13b-14).

This response is hardly surprising. In Episode 1 the citizens of Gibeah
abuse the Levite and his companions (fellow Israelites) passively by refusing
them hospitality, before the rapists abuse them actively (19:15, 22). In Episode
2 the Benjaminites in general hear of the assembly but do not attend it. Now
they openly declare their solidarity with the rapists by refusing to extradite
them. The evil committed in Gibeah has now led to an open breach between
one whole tribe and the rest of the federation. Israel has begun to disintegrate.

15-17 These verses present a number of difficulties. The numbers
are very large, but consistent with those in the census lists of the book of
Numbers and elsewhere.[84] In addition to this general issue, however, there
are problems related to the meaning of verse 15, and to the two references to
"seven hundred men" in verses 15 and 16 respectively. The most straightforward translation of verse 15 would be as follows: "On that day the
Benjaminites mustered from the towns 26,000 men; apart from the citizens
of Gibeah they mustered 700 chosen men." That is, 25,300 were mustered
from Gibeah, and only 700 from all the other towns of Benjamin combined.
Assuming that the ratio of fighting men to total population is roughly the
same, this would make Gibeah 36 times larger than all the other towns of
Benjamin combined! My translation, with the LXX and most English ver-

---

83. The expression is literally "sons of Belial" (*bᵉnê-bᵉlîya'al*), as in 19:22. See
the comments there.

84. See Section IX.C of the Introduction on "The Problem of the Large Numbers."

sions, takes *hitpāq^edû š^eba' mē'ôṯ 'îš bāḥûr* as a relative clause: *apart from the inhabitants of Gibeah, [who] mustered seven hundred chosen men.* This reverses the proportions (700 from Gibeah to 26,000 from elsewhere), and agrees much better with Joshua 18:21-28, which lists Gibeah as one of twenty-six Benjaminite towns. The occurrence of the number 700 again in verse 16 is puzzling. But the text as we have it makes clear that they are not the same 700 as in verse 15. Those in verse 15 were from Gibeah alone; these are from "*all* these people," that is, from the entire Benjaminite fighting force. What distinguished them was not their "chosenness" as elite warriors — the 700 from Gibeah were the same — but that they were left-handed, amazingly accurate marksmen. In contrast to swordsmen, they were able to strike the enemy with deadly accuracy before hand-to-hand combat began. The relevance of their left-handedness is less clear, unless, like Ehud's,[85] it gave them the advantage of surprise: they appeared less adept, but were actually more so. Although Benjamin is outnumbered fifteen to one (400,000 to 26,700), they will not be easy to overcome.

In general, the head count of fighting men mustered by the opposing sides in verses 15-17 indicates the complete breakdown of negotiation, the determination of the parties to decide the issue by force of arms, and the massiveness of the conflict about to unfold. They also show something else which becomes apparent only when these totals are compared with the corresponding ones in Numbers. The stress in Judges 20 on the totality and unity of the response (*all . . . as one man,* 20:1, 8, 11) suggests that all men qualified for military duty were called up. If this is so, the relevant data is as follows:

Men able to go to war	Numbers 26	Judges 20
Benjamin	45,600	26,700
The other 11 tribes combined	556,130	400,000
All Israel	601,730	426,700

Assuming that the ratio between the number of men eligible for call-up and the total population remains relatively constant, these figures indicate a decline of almost 30 percent in Israel's population in the Joshua-Judges period. Despite the victories under Joshua, Israel has not prospered since its arrival in Canaan.[86] The further, substantial losses to be sustained in the civil war about to take place will be the final stage in this decline, and bring Israel to the brink of extinction.

---

85. The same idiomatic phrase, *'iṭṭēr yaḏ-y^emînô* (bound/restricted in the right hand) is used of both (3:15; 20:16).

86. As foretold in Deut. 28:29.

b. Inquiry of Yahweh (20:18)

> 18 *They set out and went up to Bethel; and the Israelites asked God, "Who will go up for us first to the battle with the Benjaminites?" Yahweh replied, "Judah[87] first."*

18 On *Bethel* (= Bochim) see the comments at 1:22 and 2:1. It is 3 miles (5 km.) northwest of Mizpah, where the assembly was convened at the beginning of this chapter. The reason for recourse to Bethel rather than Mizpah on this occasion appears to be that the express purpose now is to inquire of Yahweh, and the logical place to do that was Bethel because (as we are told later) the ark of the covenant was there, attended by Phinehas the priest, the grandson of Aaron (v. 27). Bethel will continue to be the main assembly point for the Israelites for the rest of the war (20:26; 21:2). And as the war unfolds, and setbacks take a heavy toll, it will again become a place of weeping as it was in 2:4. Given the large numbers of men involved, the movements to and from Bethel can hardly have involved all of them, but leaders who represented the whole. The extreme compression of the narrative makes assumptions like this natural and required at certain points. Verse 26, where we are told that they "all" went up, is the exception.

The Israelites, then, do not begin the battle at once, but first go to Bethel to inquire of Yahweh, in effect recognizing him as their commander-in-chief. And their inquiry at this point reflects their confidence about the rightness and eventual outcome of their cause. They are committed to the war, and Yahweh's approval is assumed. So they raise a purely procedural matter; how is the campaign to be conducted? In particular, who is to lead it? The Levite who convened the assembly is completely out of the picture. No one seems to have any expectation that he will lead the Israelites in the field. If he is like a judge at all, he is more like a Deborah or a Samuel who sets things in motion but leaves the fighting to others. The situation is not unlike that in 1:1-2 and 10:18. Action is imminent, so the question of leadership has become critical: *"Who will go up for us first to the battle with the Benjaminites?"* Now, for the first time in this narrative, Yahweh himself becomes directly involved in the action. He nominates Judah to lead, appropriately so since the ravished concubine was a Judahite.[88] But in contrast to 1:2 there is

---

87. The LXX has *anabēsetai (= ya'aleh)*. The verb may have been omitted accidentally because of its similar ending to *yehûdâ* in the consonantal text. But see the exegetical comments.

88. An analogy on the personal level is to be found in the legislation regarding the avenging of blood in Num. 35:19ff. While it was ultimately the responsibility of the community as a whole to punish the slayer, the chief responsibility fell on the *gō'ēl* (avenger/

no promise of victory, and Yahweh's response is terse, to say the least; just two words: Judah first.[89]

We noted in the introduction the significance of the comparison and contrast between this inquiry and response and those in 1:1-2 for both the whole shape of the book and the picture of Israel's decline that it represents. Judges begins and ends with war, but at the beginning Israelites fight Canaanites; here they fight *Benjaminites.* Israel has failed in the war of conquest, and turned on itself, and Yahweh is not pleased.

c. Defeat (20:19-22)

19 *The Israelites set out in the morning and encamped against Gibeah.*

20 *The men of Israel went out to battle against Benjamin. The men of Israel[90] drew up their lines for battle against them at Gibeah.*

21 *The Benjaminites came out from Gibeah and destroyed in Israel that day twenty-two thousand men, [striking them] to the ground.[91]*

22 *But the people, the men of Israel, rallied,[92] and again drew up their lines for battle at the place where they had drawn them up on the first day.*

19-22 At first light the next day the Israelites return to their camp near Gibeah and immediately prepare to fight. They go out and take up forward positions, "drawing up their lines" against Gibeah, presumably with Judah in front. But the Gibeonites are too smart for them. They have been waiting for them and seize the initiative by acting first, probably before the Israelites are fully set. The result is carnage, all of it, as far as we know, on the Israelite side: *twenty-two thousand men* either killed or so severely wounded that they can play no further part in the war.[93] The number, like all the others in this narrative, is large, but is only 5.5 percent of Israel's total fighting force as given in verse 17.[94] So despite heavy losses the Israel-

---

redeemer), who was a kinsman of the victim. The Judahite Levite has in effect called on the Israelites to assist him in avenging the death of his concubine.

89. But see the note on the translation.

90. This second occurrence of *'îš-yiśrā'ēl* is awkward, and appears to be redundant. It is omitted in LXX[B].

91. See the exegetical comment (with footnote) on this unusual idiom.

92. Literally, "strengthened themselves" *(wayyiṯḥazzēq).* This clause is clearly contrastive, even though there is no disjunction in the syntax. *BHS* suggests that it should be moved to follow v. 23, where it would follow from what precedes it more naturally.

93. The idiom *destroyed . . . to the ground (wayyašḥîṯû . . . 'ar'ṣâ)* is ambiguous. Contrast v. 31, which is more explicit.

94. Of course, it may have been a bigger proportion of those actually deployed in this first engagement.

ites were able to "rally" and close ranks and (by the following day) take up the same positions they had taken up on the *first day* (v. 22).[95] It was not a rout, but a setback severe enough to badly affect their morale, as the following verse shows.

d. Inquiry of Yahweh (20:23)

> 23 *The Israelites went up[96] and wept before Yahweh until evening. They inquired of Yahweh, "Shall we again draw near for battle with the Benjaminites, our brothers?" Yahweh replied, "Go up against them."*

23 The chastened Israelites (or their representatives)[97] "go up" for a second consultation with Yahweh. The place is not mentioned, but by implication it is again Bethel, as in verse 18.[98] Their second inquiry shows the drastic loss of confidence the Israelites have suffered as a result of their disastrous defeat. They are now doubtful about the wisdom, and perhaps also the rightness, of continuing the war. They "weep" before Yahweh, as they had in 2:4. A conciliatory note is struck by the reference to the Benjaminites as *our brothers*. There may also be significance in the change here from the generic *ᵉlōhîm* (God) of verse 18 to the personal name *Yahweh*. The Israelites are less casual in their inquiry this time, alluding to the covenant ties and obligations involved in Yahweh's special relationship with both themselves and the Benjaminites. But Yahweh's response is again terse. He sends them into battle again, to (as we are about to see) another severe mauling at the hands of the Benjaminites.

e. Defeat (20:24-25)

> 24 *The Israelites advanced toward the Benjaminites on the second day.*
> 25 *Benjamin went out from Gibeah to meet them on the second day, and destroyed eighteen thousand more men among the Israelites, [striking them] to the ground — all of these armed with swords.*

24-25 The inquiry and weeping of verse 23 have completed the first day ("until evening"). Here in verses 24-25 we reach the *second* day of verse 22.

---

95. In terms of chronology v. 22 skips forward to the *next* (second) day of v. 24. See the comments there.

96. *BHS* recommends inserting *bêt-'ēl*, "[to] Bethel" here, but in the light of v. 18, this is already implied. The proposed amendment is unnecessary and lacks textual support.

97. See the comments on 20:18.

98. See the notes on the translation.

Again, only the briefest account is given of this second engagement between the two sides. The Israelites, it seems, have learned nothing from their defeat. The Benjaminites again seize the initiative and inflict almost as many casualties as in the first encounter — *eighteen thousand,* or 4.8 percent, of the remaining 378,000-strong Israelite fighting force (v. 25). The added detail this time, that all the fallen were *armed with swords,* underlines the heavy nature of the loss, and also hints at one of the contributing reasons for it. The Israelites have only swordsmen, while the Gibeonites have a 700-strong contingent of skilled marksmen (v. 16), which has so far made it impossible for the Israelites to get close enough to engage them and inflict casualties of their own. Clearly, their superior numbers alone are not sufficient. They need better tactics if they are to succeed — tactics that use their superior numbers to better advantage.

f. Inquiry of Yahweh (20:26-28)

26 *All the Israelites, the whole fighting force,[99] went up and came to Bethel.[100] They wept and sat there before Yahweh, and fasted that day until evening, and offered burnt offerings and peace offerings before Yahweh.*

27 *The Israelites inquired of Yahweh (the ark of the covenant of God was there in those days,*

28 *with Phinehas, the son of Eleazar, the son of Aaron, ministering before it),[101] "Shall I again go out to battle against the Benjaminites, my brother, or shall I stop?" But Yahweh replied, "Go up, for tomorrow I will give him into your hand."*

26-28   This third inquiry is described in much more detail than the previous two, and everything about it reflects the agony of indecision and reluctance that the Israelites now find themselves in. Everything is intensified.[102] Now it

---

99. Literally, "all the people" *(ḳol-hā'ām).* But in this military context *'ām* clearly refers to members of the armed militia, not the people in general, as recognized in most English versions.

100. The KJV's translation of *wayyābō'û bêt-'ēl* as "came into the house of God" is unlikely to be correct in view of the use of *bêt-'ēl* as a town name in v. 18, and the apparent reference to it as a town rather than a building in v. 27. The reference to a Yahweh festival in Shiloh in 21:19 suggests that this, not Bethel, was the location of the tabernacle, as in Josh. 18:1 (cf. 1 Sam. 1:3-9).

101. LXX[B] keeps this entire parenthesis together by beginning v. 28 immediately after *The Israelites inquired of Yahweh* in v. 27. See *BHS* apparatus.

102. For the substance of what follows I am indebted to Block, *Judges, Ruth,* p. 560.

is not just the "Israelites" who go up, but *All the Israelites, the whole fighting force*. They don't just "go up," but "go up *and come*" to Bethel. They don't just "weep" before Yahweh; they "sit and weep and fast all day until evening, and offer burnt offerings and peace offerings before Yahweh" — all before making their inquiry (v. 26)! And they don't just refer to the "Benjaminites" (as in the first inquiry), or even "the Benjaminites our brothers" (as in the second), but "the Benjaminites, *my* brother (*'āḥî*)," intensifying the relational aspect of what is at stake by using the first person pronoun. We have clearly reached a crisis point. The Israelites have no more stomach for the fight, and will go on only if they are forced to do so. They even name the alternative as a possibility they hope for: *"Shall I go out again . . . or stop?"* (v. 28a). Yahweh, too, uses more words this time. His response is less terse than previously, and both more sensitive to their pain and more encouraging. He echoes the Israelites' own use of the personal pronoun (showing he has noticed it), and adds a promise, this time, to his command to go on: *"Go up, for tomorrow I will give him into your hand"* (v. 28b).

As we noted earlier, the parenthesis concerning *the ark of God* and *Phinehas* the priest in verses 27b and 28a explains why the Israelites have gone to Bethel on all three occasions to make their inquiries. We have already seen in 18:3-6 an instance of recourse to a priest in order to inquire (through him) of Yahweh. Here, though, the priest in question is no mere Levite of dubious credentials, but a grandson of Aaron himself![103] The ark may have been at Bethel *in those days* (v. 27), rather than at Shiloh, precisely because of the crisis situation, and the need for those involved to consult with Yahweh. According to Genesis 28, it was at Bethel that the patriarch Jacob had an encounter with Yahweh, also in a time of crisis, which understandably gave the place a special sanctity in the minds of his descendants. The fact that the bringing of the ark to the scene of a battle later became tinged with superstition, for which Israel paid a heavy price (1 Sam. 7), and that Bethel later still became the site of an idolatrous shrine (1 Kgs. 12:29), does not necessarily mean that the Israelites did wrong to seek Yahweh there in the present narrative. There is none of the heavy irony here that there was in connection with the shrine at Dan in chapters 17 and 18. In terms of its function, the parenthesis in verses 27b-28a appears to be purely explanatory rather than derogatory, though we may well be intended to compare and contrast the presence of the ark in Bethel, served by a grandson of Aaron, with the presence of Micah's idol in Dan, served by a grandson of Moses (18:30). The third inquiry of Yahweh at Bethel has a positive outcome. It meets with a promise, and issues, at last, in victory.

103. We are probably meant to contrast this endorsement of Phinehas with the ironic identification of the Levite of chapters 17 and 18 as a grandson of Moses (18:30).

g. Victory (20:29-48)

29 Then Israel set men in ambush around Gibeah.

30 The Israelites went up against the Benjaminites on the third day and drew up their lines against Gibeah as before.

31 The Benjaminites went out to meet them[104] (they were drawn away[105] from the city) and began to strike down some of them, slain as before on the roads (one of which goes up to Bethel and one to Gibeah) [and] in the open country — about thirty men of Israel.

32 The Benjaminites said, "They are smitten before us as before." But the Israelites had said, "Let's flee and draw them away from the city onto the roads."

33 Then all the men of Israel rose up from their place and drew up their lines at Baal-tamar, and the Israelite ambush came rushing out from its place west of Gibeah:[106]

34 ten thousand chosen men from all Israel came out opposite Gibeah. But the battle was fierce, and they hadn't realized that the counterattack against them would be so severe.

35 Then Yahweh struck down Benjamin before Israel, and the Israelites destroyed in Benjamin that day twenty-five thousand one hundred men, all of whom were armed with swords.

36 The Benjaminites saw that they had been struck down. The men of Israel gave ground to Benjamin because they trusted in the ambush they had set against Gibeah.

37 The ambushers had suddenly made a raid on Gibeah, and proceeded to put the whole city to the sword.

38 Now the signal[107] the men of Israel had agreed with the ambushers was for them to send up a great cloud of smoke from the city.

39 So the men of Israel turned back in the battle. Benjamin had begun to strike down slain about thirty among the men of Israel. Indeed, they

---

104. Literally, "the people" (hā'ām), which, in this military sense, means "militia, army."

105. The absence of a conjunction on hān⁽ᵉ⁾t⁽ᵉ⁾qû is puzzling. Contrast Josh. 8:16, which, in a similar context, has the expected form wayyinnāt⁽ᵉ⁾qû. However, it is difficult to see how hān⁽ᵉ⁾t⁽ᵉ⁾qû could have arisen from this as a corruption, and should therefore be retained. The syntax, which is admittedly rough, clearly marks hān⁽ᵉ⁾t⁽ᵉ⁾qû min-hā'îr as a parenthesis.

106. Following the LXX, which has apo dysmōn tēs Gabaa (= ma'rābâ laggib'â). The MT's mimma'ᵃrê-gāba' (from the plain of Geba) makes little sense, and is almost certainly a corruption of this, as recognized by the English versions in general. Cf. v. 10, and Boling, Judges, p. 287.

107. Literally, "the set time" (hammô'ēd).

said [to themselves], "Surely they are being completely struck down before us, as in the first battle."

40 *But when the cloud began to go up from the city — a column of smoke — Benjamin turned to look back, and saw the whole of the city gone skyward.*

41 *When the men of Israel turned back, the men of Benjamin were terrified, for they saw that disaster had struck them.*

42 *They turned before the men of Israel [and fled][108] toward the desert, but the battle followed hard after them, with those from the city[109] wreaking havoc among them.*

43 *They [the Israelites] surrounded Benjamin; they pursued him from Nohah;[110] they trampled him down as far as a point opposite Geba[111] to the east.*

44 *Eighteen thousand men of Benjamin fell — all of them substantial men.*

45 *They turned and fled to the desert, to the Rimmon Rock. They ruthlessly cut down five thousand men on the roads, and went after them in hot pursuit as far as Gidom, and struck down two thousand of them.*

46 *The number of men from Benjamin who fell that day was twenty-five thousand men armed with swords — all of them substantial men.*

47 *But six hundred men turned about and fled to the desert, to the Rimmon Rock. They stayed at the Rimmon Rock for four months.*

48 *But the men of Israel went back to the [other] Benjaminites and struck them down with the sword — from town to town,[112] man[113] and beast — everything they found; and all the cities they found they set on fire.*

29-32 With the promise of victory, the Israelites resume the battle with renewed enthusiasm and greater wisdom. They use a classic military tactic that makes the most of their superior numbers and takes the now overconfident

---

108. The verb *wayyānusû* (and fled), which is implied here, occurs in vv. 45 and 47.

109. The MT's *min-he'arîm* (from the cities) makes little sense. It is much more likely that only one city is on view — the one (Gibeah) mentioned in the previous verse. The plural form has probably arisen by duplication of the *mem* that begins the following word, and the subsequent reversal of the *ayin* and *resh*. See the *BHS* apparatus.

110. With LXX[B]. MT's *menûḥâ* (rest, security) makes no sense, and is syntactically isolated. Cf. NRSV, and Boling, *Judges*, p. 287.

111. Reading *geba'*, a proposal noted in the *BHS* apparatus. See the exegetical comments.

112. Assuming, with *BHS*, that *wā'îr* has been omitted after *mē'îr* by haplography.

113. Reading *metim* (defective *metîm*, "men") instead of the MT's *metōm* (soundness), which hardly makes sense in this context.

Gibeonites by surprise. They secretly *set men in ambush* around Gibeah before drawing up the bulk of their force for a frontal assault on the city as before. This time there are far fewer casualties (only *about thirty* Israelite men) because, instead of trying to stand their ground as previously, they deliberately draw back, pretending to flee, and draw the unsuspecting Gibeonites after them in hot pursuit, leaving the city exposed to the ambush. Abimelech used similar tactics against Shechem (9:30-45). But the narrative that bears the closest resemblance to the present one is the Israelites' second, successful campaign against Ai, when they, too, had inquired of Yahweh after experiencing defeat.[114] There the ambush strategy was explicitly given to Israel by Yahweh (Josh. 8:2). We are not told that here in Judges; simply that the Israelites used it. But the general pattern of the two narratives is the same, and in both cases it is not the strategy alone that produces the outcome, but Yahweh's intervention at the critical moment to "give" the Israelites the victory he has promised them.[115] Here in Judges, however, the situation is essentially tragic rather than glorious since it is not a campaign of conquest, or a struggle against oppression, but a painful internal conflict where brother fights brother. Nevertheless, the fact that Yahweh is now directly involved, giving victory as promised, provides grounds for hope that something may yet be salvaged from the mess that the Israelites have gotten themselves into.

33-34   The narrative, which has been rather tightly written to this point, now opens out into a much more expansive one, in which fighting ebbs and flows, stands and reverses, and confusion reigns among the Gibeonites as the ambush that has been set against them is sprung with deadly effect. The untidy, repetitious nature of the narrative reflects the general messiness of the struggle.[116] But the outcome is never in doubt, and the promised victory is eventually achieved.

The general picture of what happens in verses 33 and 34 is clear, even if some of the detail is less so. The expression <u>all</u> *the men of Israel* at the beginning of verse 33 cannot literally be *all,* since those who were set in ambush are referred to as a distinct group in the second half of the verse. It must mean all those involved in the mock retreat, which took place along the roads to the east-northeast of Gibeah, the direction the Israelites had come from. The location of *Baal-tamar* is unknown, but it must have been somewhere along one of these roads. At a certain point, these Israelites gave up the pre-

---

114. Josh. 7:6-9; 8:1-2.
115. Josh. 8:18-19; Judg. 20:35.
116. Many scholars attribute the untidiness of the narrative to the blending of two original, separate accounts of the battle. In what follows we will attempt to make sense of the admittedly complex narrative as it unfolds step by step. Cf. Philip E. Satterthwaite, "Narrative Artistry in the Composition of Judges XX 29ff," *VT* 42, no. 1 (1992): 80-89.

tense of flight, *rose up* against their pursuers, and *drew up their lines* for battle. The expression *their place* refers to the spot where they did this, in accordance with the plan they had made before the battle began. This sudden reversal took the Gibeonites by surprise. Suddenly, when they least expected it, they had a real fight on their hands.

At the same prearranged moment, the Israelite *ambush* force *came rushing out of its place west of Gibeah* (v. 33b). And now, for the first time, we are given details about them — *ten thousand chosen men from all Israel* (v. 34). They are the elite fighters, carefully selected for this critical maneuver. They come out *opposite Gibeah (minneged laggib'â),* between the city and the Gibeonites who have been drawn away from it, cutting off their line of retreat and forcing them to fight on two fronts simultaneously, on the east and on the west, in front of them and behind them. Everything has gone to plan for the Israelites, and with their superior numbers and tactical advantage they may have expected victory to follow as a matter of course. But they, too, are taken by surprise. The battle is *heavy,* and *they* (the Israelites who have rushed into position opposite Gibeah) have underestimated the determination and capacity of the Benjaminites to fight back, even with the odds stacked so much against them: *they hadn't realized that the counterattack against them would be so severe* (v. 34b).[117] So as we reach the end of verse 34, the outcome is still uncertain. The vastly superior tactics of the Israelites in this third engagement have still not secured certain victory for them.

35 This verse stands alone as the pivot on which the whole narrative turns. When the battle is most fierce, and everything hangs in the balance, Yahweh intervenes and gives victory, at last, to the Israelites. Suddenly the situation is reversed, and the huge casualty count is now among the Benjaminites rather than Israel: *twenty-five thousand one hundred men.*[118] The significance, though, lies not in the raw number, but in the fact that it represents no less than 94 percent of Benjamin's total fighting force of only twenty-six thousand seven hundred (v. 15)! And the fact that all of them are identified as *men armed with swords* suggests that Benjamin's seven hundred skilled marksmen, who had given it a huge tactical advantage previously, are now no more (v. 16). It is an overwhelming defeat from which Benjamin will never recover. And what has

---

117. The English versions assume a change of subject here, and understand *wᵉhēm lō' yāḏᵉʿû (but they did not realize)* to refer to the Benjaminites. But the subjects of all the verbs in vv. 33 and 34 to this point have been the Israelites, and there is nothing to indicate a change of subject here in either the MT or the LXX. The contrast implied by the disjunctive syntax is between the success with which the Israelites have employed their new tactics, and their underestimation of the severity of the battle that would still have to be fought before victory would be achieved.

118. A more precise breakdown of the casualties and survivors is given later, in vv. 44-46. See the comments there.

brought them down, in the end, is not Israel's superior numbers or clever tactics, but the fact that Yahweh has stepped in and taken sides against them. He has "struck them down" *(wayyiggōp̄)* and put them completely at the mercy of the other eleven tribes who had united against them.

36   This verse repeats in summary form the content of the previous seven verses (29-35). The key to this apparently tedious repetition is given in the clause that introduces it: *The Benjaminites saw (wayyir'û) that they had been struck down.* In other words, there is a change of perspective at this point; we are taken inside the heads of the defeated Benjaminites to "see" what they now see, and see it through their eyes. They *saw* that they had suffered a devastating defeat because the Israelites had deliberately "given ground" because *they trusted in the ambush they had set against Gibeah.* That is, the Benjaminites see that they have been outsmarted by their enemies, who formulated a well-thought-out plan and worked cooperatively to implement it (v. 36). This change of perspective does two things. By lingering for a while on what has just happened, the narrator underlines the magnitude and significance of it. And by showing it to us through the eyes of the defeated Benjaminites, he enables us to feel it as they do and produces a degree of empathy with them. In the last episode of the narrative, this empathy will surface again as something that Israel as a whole feels, and will become the trigger for the events that bring the story to a close, and to a resolution of sorts (21:2, 24). In terms of its function, then, this verse anticipates what is to come and helps to give the plot coherence. When their blood cools, the victors will feel what we feel, and act upon it. For the present, they are intent only on finishing what they have begun, and what follows shows us just how ruthlessly they did it.

37-41   After the brief reprise of verse 36 the narrative appears set to move forward again. Instead, however, it doubles back on itself to the point (in v. 33) where the men in ambush first make their appearance. Such repetition is characteristic of this narrative, as we have begun to see. But it is never repetition without purpose. Every time it occurs there is a change of perspective (as in v. 36), or the addition of details which acquire a particular significance by being withheld until this moment. This was the case in verse 36, and it is so again here, as we are about to discover.

Verses 37 and 38 expand on the statement, in verse 36, that *the men of Israel . . . trusted in the ambush they had set against Gibeah* by taking us back to the moment (in v. 34) when the ambushers first sprang into action. Before engaging the Benjaminites from behind, they rush into Gibeah, put the whole city to the sword, and set it ablaze. The resulting *great cloud of smoke*[119] was the prearranged *signal* for the Israelites to turn around and start

---

119. Cf. v. 40, which describes the same phenomenon as a "*column ('ammûd)* of smoke."

fighting their pursuers. This puts the *great cloud of smoke* at the center of narrative attention, the reference point for seeing the true significance of everything else. For the Israelites it is a sign of victory — proof that their ambush strategy has worked, and that they have at last gotten the upper hand over Gibeah and its supporters. There is more fighting to be done, but the outcome is no longer in doubt. For the Benjaminites it is a symbol of doom that presages their complete undoing. When they see it, they know that *disaster* has come upon them, and they are *terrified* (vv. 40-41).

Its deeper significance, though, lies in the way it completes the pattern of allusion to Israel's campaigns of conquest in the book of Joshua. The Israelites have done to Gibeah as Joshua and his men did to Ai.[120] In other words, they have treated it as one of the Canaanite cities that Israel was commanded to utterly destroy.[121] It is a further, wry comment on the fact that all the present troubles began when the Levite refused to stop in Jebus, "a city of foreigners, who do not belong to the people of Israel," and went on instead to Gibeah (19:12-14), which turned out to be a virtual Sodom. The smoke rising up from Gibeah marks it as a symbol of everything Yahweh hates and has consigned to destruction. For all that, however, Gibeah is (or was) part of Israel — part of its God-given inheritance in the promised land.[122] Hence the *great cloud of smoke* going up from it now also has a very tragic significance. It represents the terrible cost at which this victory has been achieved. In order to deal with the outrage in Gibeah, Israel has had to utterly destroy part of itself, and therefore it poses in a particularly graphic way the issue the whole of chapter 21 will wrestle with: Can the wound that Israel has inflicted on itself be healed? Can Israel as it used to be ever be recovered, or is it gone forever?

42-47 These verses describe the rout that began when the Benjaminites saw the column of smoke rising from Gibeah and realized that their cause was lost. Flight now became their only option. They *turned* and fled *toward the desert (ʾel-derek hammidbār).*[123] In view of the further details given in verses 43-47, this is best taken as a general reference to what is now the Syrian Desert east of Amman. It doesn't indicate their goal so much as the general direction of their flight: to the east. But they didn't get far, because *the battle followed hard after them* (v. 42). The rather enigmatic final clause of verse 42 probably refers to the men who had raided and destroyed

120. Josh. 8:19, 24.
121. Deut. 7:1-2; 20:16-17. Cf. also Deut. 13:12-18, where an Israelite city whose people have been persuaded to turn away from Yahweh and worship other gods is to be treated in the same way. Gibeah has become a Canaanite city, and is to be treated as such.
122. Josh. 15:57; 18:28.
123. Verse 45 uses the shorter equivalent, *hammidbārâ.*

Gibeah.[124] They showed similar zeal in pressing home Israel's advantage. Seeing that the Benjaminites had begun to flee, they joined in chase and "wrought havoc" *(mašḥîṯîm)* among them. Of all the Israelite warriors, these men were the destroyers par excellence.

Verse 43, too, has a number of obscurities, probably caused in part by minor corruptions of the text.[125] As indicated in the translation, the referent of the opening verb, *kittᵉrû (they* surrounded), is best taken as referring to the Israelites in general rather than the ambush contingent on the previous verse,[126] and to the fact that the strategy the Israelites used had succeeded in trapping the Benjaminites in a pincer movement. The location of *Nohah* is unknown. This is the only occurrence of *Nohah* as a place-name in the Old Testament, but it does occur in 1 Chronicles 8:2 as the name of one of Benjamin's sons, making it entirely plausible that it doubled up as the name of a Benjaminite town. It is mentioned here as the place at which the Benjaminites turned and started to flee, and must therefore have been to the east of Gibeah, and not far from it. According to the MT, they were pursued until they were opposite "Gibeah" *(haggiḇ'â).* But this cannot be correct, since the place in view is the terminus of Benjamin's flight eastward, away from Gibeah.[127] The alternative, *Geba,* adopted in the translation, requires only minor emendation of the text, and is a site generally located about 3 miles (5 km.) northeast of Gibeah.[128] The pursuit was relentless and brutal. The battle *followed hard after* the Benjaminites (v. 42), and their pursuers *trampled [them] down (hiḏrîḵuhû)* as they fled (v. 43).[129]

The grim count of Benjaminite casualties begins in verse 44 and continues through the next three verses. The number for each phase of the conflict is given in turn: eighteen thousand in the initial clash, when the Israelites turned back and attacked their pursuers (v. 44); *five thousand* as the rest fled toward the desert (v. 45a); and a further *two thousand* at the end of the pursuit, when most of the remaining Benjaminites were too exhausted to flee any longer (v. 45b) — *twenty-five thousand* in all (v. 46). Only six hundred escaped (v. 47). This does not tally exactly with the total of *twenty-five thousand one hundred* of verse 35, but it may include casualties inflicted in the

---

124. See the textual comments on the translation.

125. See the notes to the translation.

126. The fact that v. 43 begins with a *qatal* verb form rather than a *yiqtol* tends to confirm this. Verse 43 does not continue the narrative of the previous verse, but deals with another, complementary aspect of the conflict.

127. Presumably to the northeast, toward *Geba* (v. 43), rather than directly east into the Israelites who were blocking their path.

128. See, e.g., *OBA,* p. 92, and *NBD,* p. 398.

129. The unusual use of the Hiphil of *rdp* (to pursue) also suggests intensity. Boling translates it as "pursued vigorously" *(Judges,* p. 283).

assault on Gibeah itself (v. 34). In any case, given the realities of war and the imprecision of such terms as "fell," "struck down," and so on, discrepancies are only to be expected and, if anything, enhance the authenticity of the account. The statement that the fallen were all *substantial men* (v. 46) emphasizes the magnitude of Israel's victory, but at the same time shows respect for the vanquished. The Benjaminites were overcome on this occasion by the Israelites' superior strategy and overwhelmingly greater numbers; but they were no weaklings, as their previous two victories have shown.

Gidom (v. 45) must have been at the *point opposite Geba* referred to in verse 43, but is otherwise unknown. The *Rimmon Rock* (*sela' hārimmôn,* vv. 45, 47), where the last six hundred took refuge, is generally associated with the modern village of *Rammun,* 6 miles (9 km.) north-northeast of Gibeah.[130] Subsequent events will show that the Israelites knew the remaining Benjaminites had taken refuge there,[131] but chose to ignore them for the time being.

48 Formally the count of the casualties in verses 44-47 corresponds to the tally of the recruits in verses 14-17, and these two passages frame the intervening account of the war itself. What follows, in verse 48, is technically the mopping up operation that followed the war, though that expression hardly does justice to the extent and severity of the action involved. The background to it is the reference in verses 14 and 15 to Benjaminite "towns" (*'ārîm*) that had supported Gibeah by sending men to participate in the war. In contrast to the Benjaminites who "stayed" (*wayyēš^ebû*) at Rimmon Rock (v. 47), the Israelites now "go back" (*šābû*) to punish these towns. The punishment is so terrible in its thoroughness that it brings the tribe of Benjamin to the brink of extinction. The victorious Israelites go from *town to town,* putting all their human and animal inhabitants to the sword, and setting the towns themselves on fire. In short, they totally destroyed them, as Gibeah itself was destroyed (vv. 37-38). And the repeated expression, *all they found (kol-hannimṣā'),* suggests that the destruction knew no limits. Perhaps all the Benjaminite towns had sent fighters, but in the end it mattered not. Simply being Benjaminite was enough. The Israelites destroyed everything they found.

There are obvious similarities to the holy war material of Deuteronomy and Joshua.[132] But these serve only to highlight the differences. Israel

---

130. It is literally "Pomegranate Rock." P. M. Arnold ("Rimmon," *ABD* 5:773-74) locates it closer to Gibeah and identifies it as the el-Jaia cave in the Wadi es-Swenit, "some 30m high, pitted on the inside with hundreds of small caves and holes, and thus resembling a split pomegranate."

131. See 21:13.

132. Especially the occurrence of the unusual expression *metîm* (men) in v. 48 and Deut. 2:34, as noted by Boling (*Judges,* p. 288). The reality represented by the typical holy war term, "totally destroy" (*ḥrm),* is clearly implied.

destroyed part of itself when it destroyed Gibeah. Now it is going much further — virtually destroying a whole tribe. And it is doubtful, to say the least, that it has divine warrant for doing so. The promise of victory given in verse 28 was fulfilled in verse 35. This is something more, and it is Israel's own doing. There is no suggestion of Yahweh's involvement.

5. Episode 4: Postwar Reconstruction (21:1-25)

Just as the narrative seems set to move swiftly and smoothly to its conclusion, a fresh complication appears with the revelation that the Israelites had sworn an oath at Mizpah not to give their daughters in marriage to the Benjaminites (21:1; cf. 20:1). To this ill-considered oath they have now added excessive slaughter. In the heat of battle the passion for revenge seems to have gotten the upper hand (the Benjaminites had inflicted heavy losses on the other tribes in the first two engagements). Only now, with passion spent and a more sober perspective restored, do the claims of brotherhood begin to influence behavior again (21:6; cf. 20:23, 28). But the damage has already been done; all the Benjaminite women have been slaughtered (20:47-48; 21:16), and because of the oath the six hundred male survivors must die childless and the tribe become extinct. That is the problem this final chapter wrestles with. The solution emerges gradually, and the whole is rounded off by the final occurrence of the refrain that links the two parts of the coda (chs. 17–18 and 19–21) together. The resulting structure is as follows:

The problem	vv. 1-4
An apparent solution	vv. 5-12
A further problem	vv. 13-18
The final outcome	vv. 19-24
Closing refrain	v. 25

This final episode shows a morally bankrupt Israel resorting to casuistry of the most dubious kind to rescue itself from dilemmas of its own making. The treatment is highly ironical, bordering at times on farce. But the underlying message is serious. This final episode completes the picture of moral chaos presented in the previous three.

a. The Problem (21:1-4)

1 *Now the men of Israel had sworn an oath at Mizpah, "No one among us will give his daughter as wife to a Benjaminite."*
2 *The people came to Bethel and sat there until evening before God. They lifted up their voices and wept a great deal.*

3 *They said, "Why, Yahweh, God of Israel, has this come about in Is-*
rael, that one tribe has today been eliminated from Israel?"

4 *The following day the people rose early and built an altar there, and*
offered burnt offerings and peace offerings.

1-4 There has been no previous mention of the *oath* referred to in verse 1.
But the omission is hardly accidental. Withholding mention of it until now
causes us to experience something of the same surprise the Israelites themselves feel as the full consequences of what they have done dawns upon them.
So intent have they been on pressing home their victory against Benjamin that
they have entirely forgotten the oath. The recollection of it now strikes them
with the force of something new — and profoundly alarming.

The problem is that the six hundred men still hiding at Rimmon Rock
(20:47) are all that remains of the tribe of Benjamin, but the Israelites have
sworn not to give them their daughters as wives. So one whole tribe has effectively been doomed to extinction (v. 3).[133] The realization of this at first
evokes the same response from the Israelites that their own defeat at the
hands of Benjamin had done in the previous episode: they assemble at
Bethel, weep before Yahweh (this time *a great deal*), inquire of him, and offer sacrifices (cf. 20:23, 26-28).[134] It is evidence of the radical "repentance"
they have undergone in relation to the Benjaminites (as confirmed in vv. 6
and 15), and their desire for their rehabilitation. But the wording of the inquiry they direct to Yahweh in verse 3 is noteworthy:

> *"Why, Yahweh, God of Israel,*
> *has this come about in Israel,*
> *that one tribe has today been eliminated from Israel?"*

The threefold reference to *Israel,* after addressing Yahweh as *God of Israel,*
implies that the situation is essentially his responsibility. The inquiry is less a
request for information than an oblique form of protest, and an attempt by the
inquirers (consciously or otherwise) to absolve themselves of responsibility.
But Yahweh will not be drawn. Once, at Bethel, he had chastised Israel by
speaking (2:1-4). Here he does so by remaining silent. He does not accept the
implied accusation, and offers them no solution to their predicament. They

133. Intermarriage with Canaanites seems not to be an option they consider, even
though it clearly happened in the judges period (3:6). The difference in this case is that it
would involve all remaining Benjaminites and therefore result in no true Benjaminites being left. This option, too, would effectively mean the end of Benjamin as an Israelite tribe
(v. 3).

134. Cf. also 2:1-4. In a sense this final weeping at Bethel brings the book full circle to where Israel's distress began.

will have to deal with it as best they can; Yahweh is unmoved by their weeping and offerings; he will not be used by them.[135]

But now an apparent solution presents itself in the form of a fortuitous combination of circumstances.

b. An Apparent Solution (21:5-12)

> 5 *The Israelites said, "Which of all the tribes of Israel did not go up to Yahweh in the assembly?" For the great oath had been taken regarding anyone who did not go up to Yahweh at Mizpah: "He will surely die."*
>
> 6 *The Israelites had compassion on Benjamin their brother and said, "Today one tribe has been cut off from Israel.*
>
> 7 *What will we do about wives for those who are left, since we have sworn an oath to Yahweh that we will not give any of our daughters to them as wives?"*
>
> 8 *They said, "Which one of the tribes of Israel did not up to Yahweh at Mizpah?" And it occurred to them that no one had gone up to the camp (that is, the assembly) from Jabesh-gilead.*
>
> 9 *So the people were mustered, and, sure enough, none of the inhabitants of Jabesh-gilead were there.*
>
> 10 *So the assembly[136] sent twelve thousand of their warriors there[137] and commanded them, "Go and strike down the inhabitants of Jabesh-gilead with the sword, including the women and children."*
>
> 11 *This is what you are to do: every male and every woman who has had sex with a man you shall exterminate."[138]*
>
> 12 *They found among the inhabitants of Jabesh-gilead four hundred young virgins who had not had sex with a man, and they brought them to the camp at Shiloh, which is in the land of Canaan.*

5 The *great oath* said here to have been sworn *at Mizpah* must refer to the decision taken at Mizpah to go to war against Gibeah to punish those respon-

---

135. Cf. 10:11-14.

136. The term used here is *'ēḏâ* instead of the *qāhāl* of vv. 5 and 8. But the two are synonymous, as shown, e.g., by the *wattiqqāhēl hā'ēḏâ* of 20:1.

137. Literally, "men of strength/substance/means" *(bᵉnê hehāyil)*. Cf. 20:46, where I have translated the same expression "substantial men" because of the particular nuances it has in that context.

138. The verb is *taḥᵃrîmû (ḥrm,* "utterly destroy, devote to destruction"), as in the holy war material of Deut. 7:2, 26, etc. LXX[B] adds here, *tas de parthenous peripoiēsesthe kai epoiēsan houtōs* ("but the virgins you shall keep alive, which is what they did"). *BHS* recommends emending the MT to include these two clauses. But LXX[B] has probably just made explicit what is implied in the MT.

sible for the outrage that had been committed there (20:8-11). Although the language of oath-taking was not used there, the seriousness of the decision and the fact that it was taken "before Yahweh" (20:1) make it entirely appropriate to see it retrospectively as one. It was a *great* oath in the sense that it was taken in a solemn assembly of the Israelite tribes, and involved the death penalty (20:13; 21:5).[139] The use of the article, "*the* great oath," implies that it was well known to all concerned.

In the present passage the Israelites conceive the idea of invoking this oath as a way of solving their problem of finding wives for the remaining Benjaminites. The problem had arisen not from the oath itself, but from the way it was interpreted and applied in the subsequent war. It was not only the culprits themselves who were put to death, but also all who aligned themselves with them. The rulers of Gibeah did this by refusing to hand the culprits over (20:13), and other Benjaminites did so by sending men to help defend Gibeah (20:14-16). The point is that the death penalty pronounced in the oath was extended, in practice, to all who took Gibeah's side. Furthermore, the first indication of siding with Benjamin had been the decision of the Benjaminites in general to boycott the assembly at Mizpah. They heard that the other tribes had "gone up to Mizpah," but did not go themselves (20:3). This is what the Israelites now seize upon as providing a possible way out of their dilemma. What if some other part of the Israelite federation (a city, perhaps, or clan) did not go up to the assembly? Wouldn't the Israelites be justified in punishing them, too, in the same way the Benjaminites had been punished? And if so, might they not prove to be a handy source of wives for the six hundred men still in hiding at Rimmon Rock?

6-9 These verses repeat in summary form the content of verses 1-3, before moving on to the identification of *Jabesh-gilead* as a target for the proposed action. The effect is to halt the forward progress of the narrative while three things are emphasized: the *compassion* for the Benjaminites that motivates the Israelites (v. 6), the dilemma they face (they restate the problem, v. 7), and the care they take to make sure that what they think about Jabesh-gilead is actually so before taking action against it (vv. 8-9). In other words, the action that follows is not undertaken lightly; after all, it will involve shedding even more Israelite blood. The narrator is fully aware of the casuistry and moral blindness of the Israelites, and they will go from bad to worse as the story continues to unfold. But these verses show that the narrator is not entirely hostile to them either. He recognizes that their change of attitude toward Benjamin is genuine, that they face a real dilemma, and that they do not act without deliberation. Like the old man in Gibeah, they are doing the best they can.

---

139. It has the same form as the solemn pronouncement of Yahweh in Gen. 2:17: *môt tāmût* ("you will surely die").

498

Jabesh-gilead was about 22 miles (36 km.) south of the Sea of Galilee, and one mile (1.6 km.) east of the Jordan River.[140] Its pro-Benjaminite stance was subsequently confirmed when it rescued Saul's body from desecration by the Philistines after the battle of Gilboa (1 Sam. 31:1-13). Some of its population at that time may well have been descendants of the surviving men of Benjamin and women of Jabesh-gilead in the present narrative. The finding that none of its people had gone up to the assembly (v. 9) does not necessarily conflict with the statement in 20:1 that people from all Israel, "including the land of Gilead," had done so. It was not literally everyone who attended, but representatives of all parts of Israel. The puzzling issue is why Jabesh-gilead was singled out for retribution, since representation at the assembly was on the basis of tribes and regions, such as Gilead, rather than individual towns and cities (20:2). The latter seem to have featured only at the subsequent stage of recruiting fighters (20:14, 17). The point is that at the time the Israelites made their investigation (21:9) no men from Jabesh-gilead were found (21:9), and this was taken, for all intents and purposes, as equivalent to nonattendance at the assembly itself. It indicated tacit support for Gibeah and the Benjaminites.[141] The reasoning (if it existed) was dubious, but the Israelites were probably more concerned with finding a justifiable target than with practicing complete rigor in the way they did so.

10-12 The *assembly* (v. 10)[142] now formally commissions men to put into effect its decision to attack Jabesh-gilead. The size of the force dispatched, *twelve thousand warriors (bᵉnê heḥāyil)*,[143] is small compared with the 400,000 mustered at the beginning of the war (20:17). But it was a formidable fighting force nonetheless. Jabesh-gilead overlooked the Jordan Valley, and was a fortified city in biblical times. It could be expected to offer resistance,[144] though there is no indication that it did so. It was probably taken by surprise by such an unlikely attack from fellow Israelites. At any rate, there is

---

140. The probable site is Tell Maqlub, on the northern side of the Wadi Yabis. D. V. Edelman, "Jabesh-Gilead," *ABD* 3:594-95. Edelman herself, however, denies the historicity of its portrayal as Israelite in Judg. 21.

141. This is more likely than Matthews' suggestion that the elders made their decision "after reviewing the records of the assembly." Matthews, *Judges and Ruth,* p. 199. Even allowing that records may have been kept (which is unlikely in the circumstances), the finding against Jabesh-gilead was arrived at by mustering the people (v. 9) rather than reviewing records.

142. See the note to the translation. This assembly at Bethel (v. 2) is the postwar counterpart of the prewar assembly at Mizpah (20:1-11).

143. See the note to the translation.

144. According to 1 Sam. 11:1, the Ammonites later had to lay siege to it to try to take it.

no mention of a fight, or even (in the MT)[145] any explicit reference to the slaughter of the city's inhabitants. The text moves directly from the orders the attackers were given (vv. 10b-11) to the positive outcome of the operation (v. 12). The difference from the earlier campaign against the Benjaminite towns (20:48) is that only women who had already had sex with a man were to be killed. The rest (by implication) were to be spared. And it is this positive aspect of the operation that is emphasized: *They found . . . four hundred young virgins . . . and brought them to the camp at Shiloh* (v. 12). But of course, this raises some very awkward issues for the Israelites. If the *great oath* they appealed to in verse 5 entails putting to death all who had aligned themselves with Gibeah, shouldn't all have been treated alike? On what grounds had this been applied selectively rather than absolutely to Jabesh-gilead?[146] Shouldn't it have been treated in exactly the same way as the towns of Benjamin?[147] And in any case, on what grounds can the forcible acquisition of women for marriage be viewed as positive, except on the grounds of expediency? In other words, this episode exposes the Israelites' justification for their actions as morally vacuous. The real principle they are operating on is that the survival of Benjamin must be secured by whatever means are necessary. In what follows even the pretext of morality is abandoned.

The reference to *Shiloh* in verse 12 anticipates the way it will feature in the remainder of this narrative (vv. 19-21) and the opening chapters of 1 Samuel. It was 13 miles (21 km.) north of Bethel, and the Israelite base *camp* had apparently been relocated there[148] during the raid on Ramoth-gilead in preparation for the formal handing over of the *young virgins* to the Benjaminites when the operation was completed. The reason they were brought there rather than to Mizpah or Bethel is probably the way these places had featured in the war itself. Shiloh was a neutral location, more suitable for postwar reconciliation. But its significance extended well beyond this, as we will see in verses 19-21, where its precise location is given. Here in verse 12 all that is said about it is that it was *in the land of Canaan,* which as a simple statement of fact is curiously redundant (where else could Shiloh be?). Its function must

145. See the notes to the translation.

146. The Mosaic precedent in Num. 31:17-18 is more apparent than real. The implied reason why some women were exempted from the ban there was that, as virgins, they had not been involved in the immorality associated with the Baal of Peor (Num. 25:5-9; 31:15-18).

147. The sparing of the six hundred men who fled to Rimmon Rock can hardly serve as a precedent since it had only been their inaccessibility that had saved them. Only later did the Israelites have the change of heart they are now seeking to justify.

148. It is not clear from the Hebrew text whether the camp was *at* Shiloh, or just somewhere near it. The word *šilōh* does not have any preposition to indicate how it is related to the previous word, *hammaḥᵃneh* (the camp).

therefore be rhetorical rather than informative. It is a subtle reminder that, after all that has taken place in Judges, Israel still lives in an alien land. Even Shiloh, where the tabernacle was erected in Joshua's day, still lies in *'ereṣ kᵉnā'an* (the land of Canaan) rather than *'ereṣ yiśrā'ēl* (the land of Israel). It will not begin to be called *'ereṣ yiśrā'ēl* until the time of Saul. The first occurrence is in 1 Samuel 13:19, and in view of what follows, even that is premature. Israel still has a long way to go to enter fully into its inheritance. In the present passage it is teetering on the brink of complete disintegration.

c. A Further Problem (21:13-18)

This unit is transitional in two ways. It advances the narrative chronologically from one effort to acquire wives for the Benjaminites to the next, and by drawing attention to the inadequacy of the first attempt it shows the necessity for the second.

13 *Then the whole assembly sent word to the Benjaminites who were at the rock of Rimmon, and proclaimed peace to them.*

14 *So the Benjaminites returned at that time, and they gave them the women from Jabesh-gilead that they had let live, but they had not found enough for them.*

15 *The people had compassion on Benjamin, for Yahweh had made a breach in the tribes of Israel.*

16 *The elders of the assembly said, "How can we provide wives for the remainder, for the women have been wiped out from Benjamin?"*

17 *And they said, "Is there an inheritance of the escapees for Benjamin? Won't a tribe be wiped out from Israel?*[149]

18 *As for us, we can't give them our daughters as wives." For the Israelites had sworn an oath, "Cursed is the one who gives a wife to Benjamin."*

13-14   It is clear from these two verses that securing wives for the remaining Benjaminites was intended to do more than just ensure the survival of the tribe of Benjamin; it was meant to be the means of concluding a formal peace settlement between Benjamin and the rest of Israel. *Peace (šālôm) is pro-*

---

149. The MT of this verse is obscure and may be corrupt. Neither part of the verse is formally marked as a question, but the context seems to require them to be taken as such. LXX^L adds *pōs estai* (= *'ēk tiššā'ēr*, "How will there be?") at the beginning of the direct speech, but it is difficult to see how the present text could have been derived from this. I have let the obscurity of the text as its stands show in the translation rather than emend it by guesswork. See the exegetical comments.

claimed (wayyiqrᵉʾû) in verse 13, and then enacted in verse 14 by the handing over (and implied receiving) of the prospective brides. Making peace by such means was a practice well known in the ancient Near East, and later made famous in Israel by Solomon's taking of many wives, and Ahab's marriage to Jezebel.[150] Israel was forbidden to make peace with the Canaanites in this way[151] — a prohibition they had ignored according to Judges 3:6. The irony of the present situation is that the only occasion on which Israel's leaders solemnly undertook to observe such a ban was when it was against their fellow Israelites. In their zeal to punish the outrage committed in Gibeah they had treated the Benjaminites as Canaanites, totally destroying their cities (20:48) and vowing never to intermarry with them. Against this background the present peace settlement with the Benjaminites has special significance. It effectively releases them from their status as "Canaanites" and formally reinstates them as covenant "brothers" (20:23). It brings Israel as a twelve-tribe confederacy back into existence again. There is a problem, however. The four hundred women are insufficient for the six hundred Benjaminite men: the Israelites *had not found enough for them* (v. 14). Two hundred more are needed to complete the healing process.

15-18   In the main these verses go over old ground: the Israelites' *compassion* for Benjamin (v. 15); the issue of how wives can be provided for the survivors, given that the Benjaminite women have all been wiped out (v. 16) and the Israelites have sworn not to give them their own daughters as wives (v. 18). The effect is to arrest the forward movement of the narrative while the various aspects of the problem are surveyed again. The most senior and responsible members of the assembly — the *elders (ziqnê)*[152] — bring their minds to bear on the situation (v. 16), but all they can do is restate the problem as though searching for a solution that for the moment eludes them. They appear to have run out of ideas, and the complexity of the problem makes it appear even more unsolvable than ever. The Hebrew of verse 17 is obscure, and has been left so in the translation since there is no obvious solution to that problem either.[153] The two problems mirror one another and add to the general impression of stalemate.

Some things are noteworthy, however. In verse 15 the narrator comments that *Yahweh had made a breach (pereṣ) in the tribes of Israel*. In other words, the implied accusation of the Israelites back in verse 3 was not entirely unjustified. The sad state of affairs they now find themselves in is not purely of their own making. Yahweh has had a hand in it, too. After all, it was

150. 1 Kgs. 11:1-2; 16:31.
151. Deut. 7:1-4.
152. Cf. 11:5.
153. See the notes to the translation.

he who commanded them to go on fighting Benjamin when they were more inclined to stop (20:28). Clearly the narrative as a whole is about retribution, but it is not simply about eleven of Israel's tribes punishing one. It is also about Yahweh punishing them all. That is why they weep before Yahweh here at the end of the book as they did at its beginning (21:2; 2:4-5).

Second, in spite of its obscurity, it is clear from verse 17 that what is at stake in the present crisis is not simply survival, but *inheritance (yᵉruššâ).* Every previous reference to inheritance through Deuteronomy and Joshua is about land that had been given to people by Yahweh as their inalienable possession.[154] The terminology varies, but the importance of the issue in the present context is shown by the search of the Danites for an alternative allotment *(naḥᵃlâ)* in 18:1, and the eventual return of each clan and tribe to its allotment *(naḥᵃlâ)* in 21:24. A major concern of the Israelites in verse 17 is that such a small remnant of Benjamin might not be able to maintain its hold on its *inheritance* (tribal allotment), and without this its mere survival will be meaningless, so deeply are land and identity connected.[155] If wives can be found for all six hundred survivors, there is a chance that Benjamin will be able to maintain its inheritance. With only four hundred there is little or no chance, so it is imperative that the additional two hundred be found. But how?

d. The Final Outcome (21:19-24)

19 Then they thought,[156] "Ah! There is the yearly Yahweh festival at Shiloh, which is north of Bethel, to the east of the road that goes up from Bethel to Shechem, and south of Lebonah.
20 They commanded the Benjaminites, "Go and lie in ambush in the vineyards,
21 and watch.[157] When you catch sight of[158] the daughters of Shiloh coming out to do the dancing, come out from the vineyards and let each man catch for himself a wife[159] from the daughters of Shiloh. Then go to the land of Benjamin.

---

154. Deut. 2:5, 9, 12, 19; 3:20; Josh. 1:15; 12:6, 7.

155. Cf. Block, *Judges, Ruth,* p. 579.

156. Taking *wayyōʾmrû* metaphorically, in view of the following exclamation ("Ah!"). See the exegetical comments on this verse.

157. Ignoring the verse division, and taking the imperative *lᵉkû* of v. 20 as governing both the *wᵉqatal* verbs *(waʾᵃrabtem* and *ûrᵉʾîtem)* which follow it. Cf. ESV, NIV, NRSV, and TNIV.

158. This is implied by the particle *wᵉhinnê* after the preceding imperatival sequence, "Go . . . watch" (v. 20).

159. Literally, "*his* wife" *(ʾištô).*

22 *When their*[160] *fathers or brothers come to complain*[161] *to us, we will say to them, 'Have compassion on them,*[162] *for we have not taken*[163] *each man's wife in battle, and you yourselves have not given [your daughters] to them, that you should be guilty.' "*[164]

23 *So that is what the Benjaminites did. They took as many women as they needed from the dancers they had seized, and went off, returned to their inheritance, and rebuilt the cities and lived in them.*

24 *The Israelites went their various ways from there at that time, each to his tribe and clan; each went out from there to his inheritance.*

19-21 The elders at last hit on a plan: the exclamation *"Ah!" (hinnê)* indicates a sudden burst of inspiration! They remember that there is a *Yahweh festival* in Shiloh each year (v. 19). It is not clear what this festival was. The only detail we are given about it (dancing in the vineyards, v. 21) does not provide any link with the three annual festivals (Passover, Weeks, and Tabernacles) prescribed in the law of Moses.[165] If anything it suggests some similarity to the vintage festival associated with Baal-berith at Shechem, 12 miles (19 km.) further north (9:26-27). The *daughters of Shiloh* who did the dancing may have simply been local girls, or something more sinister, like the women that Eli's sons slept with at the entrance to the Shiloh sanctuary.[166] If it was the same festival that Elkanah used to go to each year (1 Sam. 1:3), it appears to have been basically orthodox, but still not easily identified with any of the three prescribed festivals, and compromised by the practices of a

---

160. The suffixes are masculine but clearly refer to the abducted women. Boling suggests that they "probably originated in misunderstood dual forms, as in 19:24" (*Judges*, p. 293). But in 19:24 only two women are on view; here there are two hundred. So why dual forms in the first place? Such confusion of gender in suffixes is not uncommon, and is best understood as reflecting a general tendency in biblical Hebrew for the relatively rare feminine plural suffixes to be displaced by masculine counterparts.

161. Reading the Qere, *lārîb*, "to complain, contend."

162. Reading *honnû*, as recommended in the *BHS* apparatus. The MT's *honnûnû* (have compassion on us), which leaves the following object (*'ôtām*) stranded, has probably arisen by dittography. Cf. LXX[A]. JB tries to render the MT as it stands, but has to treat the suffix on *honnûnû* as an indirect rather than a direct object: "Be gracious to them [the Benjaminites] *for our sake.*" LXX[B] takes even more liberties, treating the direct object (*'ôtām*) as feminine: "Grant *them* [*autas,* the young women] freely *to us (hēmin).*"

163. *BHS* recommends following LXX[A], which has *ouk elabon* (= *lō' lāqᵉhû*, they did not take). This is suspect as the easier reading, and the MT has the support of LXX[B].

164. Following the *BHS* apparatus, and reading *kî'attâ* instead of MT's *kā'ēt*. The LXX's "according to the occasion you transgressed," which tries to render the MT as it stands, is unintelligible.

165. Deut. 16:1-17; cf. Exod. 23:14-17; 34:18-23; and Num. 28:26.

166. 1 Sam. 2:22.

504

corrupt priesthood. The elders suddenly realize that this festival holds the possible answer to their problem of finding the two hundred additional wives for the Benjaminites.

The festival may have come to mind because the Israelite camp, where they were meeting, was in the vicinity of Shiloh (v. 12).[167] But if so, why the detailed description of Shiloh's location in verse 19b? And why here rather than in verse 12, where Shiloh was mentioned for the first time? Most scholars take it to be a parenthesis for the sake of later readers who no longer knew where Shiloh was.[168] However, this doesn't explain why it is in verse 19 rather than in verse 12. Kimchi, apparently sensitive to this issue, held that it referred not to the location of Shiloh itself, but to the place where the dancing was to take place.[169] But this does violence to the syntax, since the clause in question clearly qualifies *Shiloh*. Kimchi's general line of thought is correct, however: the description of Shiloh's location occurs in the context of the elders' ruminations about how to find more wives for the Benjaminites. They don't address the Benjaminites until verse 20; here in verse 19 they are just thinking out loud,[170] and it suddenly occurs to them *("Ah!")* that Shiloh is an ideal place for an ambush, not just because of the festival that is held there, but because of its location — in a wine-producing area, where there are vineyards! This thought is then expressed by the command they give in verse 20: *"Go and lie in ambush in the vineyards!"* Shiloh is generally identified with Khirbet Seilun (the modern Seilun), and *Lebonah* with El-Lubban, though the latter, especially, is uncertain.[171]

The plan the elders have come up with is both crude and ingenious. The crude bit comes first: they tell the Benjaminites to *lie in ambush* in the vineyards until the young women[172] come out to dance, then break cover and each *catch* one and carry her off as his wife (v. 21). There is irony in the fact that the Benjaminites, who had been undone by one ambush plan (*'rb*, 20:29), are now told to use another to secure their tribe's survival (*'rb*, 21:20). It is one indication that the narrative is coming full circle, with the end ironically echoing the beginning. Another is the way the narrative begins with the abuse of one woman, and ends with the abuse of many.

---

167. See the comments above on the ambiguity of the bare *šilōh* (without preposition) in v. 12.

168. For example, Soggin, *Judges,* p. 299; Gray, *Joshua, Judges, and Ruth,* p. 395; C. Pressler, *Joshua, Judges, and Ruth,* Westminster Bible Companion (Louisville: Westminster John Knox, 2002), p. 256.

169. A. Cohen, ed., *Joshua and Judges,* Soncino Books of the Bible (London: Soncino, 1950), p. 317.

170. See the note to the translation.

171. Soggin, *Judges,* p. 299; Block, *Judges, Ruth,* p. 401.

172. See the comments above on *daughters of Shiloh* (*bᵉnôt-šîlô*).

The final command in verse 21, *"Then go to the land of Benjamin,"* shows that the elders are confident their plan will succeed: there will be no need to return to Shiloh to see if any further action is needed. It also confirms that they are concerned with more than Benjamin's mere survival. Only when Benjamin again has secure possession of its inheritance (v. 23) will the breach that Yahweh has made in Israel be healed. But there is more to their plan than this, and the rest of it, which follows, is where its ingenuity is most apparent.

22-24 Since the Benjaminites have been told to go back to their own tribal territory (v. 21), they will not face the *fathers* or *brothers* of the abducted women. As their guardians, the fathers and brothers will be incensed at what had been done to their women.[173] The elders are fully aware of this and tell the Benjaminites that they will accept full responsibility for the raid, and have already prepared the answer they will give to the girls' relatives when the time comes.

There are a number of textual uncertainties in verse 22,[174] but the gist of it is as follows:

a. The women were not captured *in battle (bammilḥāmâ)* (v. 22a). That is, there has been no act of war, so there is no justification for going to war in retaliation.

b. The women's relatives, for their part, have not *given* (v. 22b) their daughters to the Benjaminites, so they are not guilty of breaking the oath referred to in verses 1, 7, and 18. So there are no grounds for the rest of Israel to take punitive action against them either.

c. Since there are no grounds for violence on either side, the relatives of the young women should *have compassion* on the Benjaminites, and accept the abduction of the young women as a fait accompli.

While there is no reference to it, some law or custom applying to such cases and known to both parties must lie in the background. Victor Matthews cites the capture of a bride by the Ugaritic hero Keret as evidence of the practice of bride-capture in Israel's ancient Near Eastern environment.[175] Within Israel itself, Deuteronomy 22:28-29 provides the nearest parallel to the present situation. It does not condone the practice, but seeks to protect, as far as possible, the conflicting interests of the parties involved:

---

173. Cf. the fury of Simeon and Levi at the Shechemites for violating their sister (Gen. 34:31), and Absalom's deadly hatred of Amnon for the same reason (2 Sam. 13:22).

174. See the notes to the translation.

175. *KTU* 1:14-16. Matthews, *Judges and Ruth,* p. 200.

If a man happens to meet a virgin who is not pledged to be married and rapes her and they are discovered, he shall pay the girl's father fifty shekels of silver. He must marry the girl, for he has violated her. He can never divorce her as long as he lives. (NIV)

Matthews notes that, according to this law, "there are no circumstances in which the father could deny giving his daughter to her 'captor,'[176] and the stipulation against divorce provides her with legal protections that could balance the father's ire at the loss of his child."[177] However, given the general confusion of the judges period, it is unlikely that the elders had a detailed knowledge of such a law or genuinely thought that their actions could be justified by appeal to it. What the law of Deuteronomy 22 had in mind were isolated acts of passion in which a man "happened to meet" (literally, "found," *yimṣāʾ*) an unbetrothed virgin, not a planned act of large-scale abduction like that in Judges 21. Furthermore, the elders do not offer monetary compensation as required in the Deuteronomic law, but simply urge the relatives to acquiesce as an act of *compassion* (v. 22). The reality is that the women's relatives, like Micah back in 18:25-26, have no option but to accept the situation. They have been outwitted and plundered by opponents too strong for them. All they can do is go home. In fact, that is all that anyone can do: *The Israelites went their various ways from there at that time, each to his tribe and clan; each went out from there to his inheritance.* The good news is that there are still *Israelites,* and still twelve *tribes,* each with its *inheritance* to go to (v. 24).[178]

So, with consummate irony this episode reaches its climax with the *elders (zᵉqēnîm)* doing, in principle, the same thing that the old man (*zāqēn,* the Levite's host), had done in Gibeah (19:16, 24). The rape of the daughters of Shiloh is the ironic counterpoint to the rape of the Levite's concubine,[179] as the campaign against Jabesh-gilead is the counterpoint to the war against Benjamin:

> The rape of the Levite's concubine
>   "Holy" war against Benjamin
>   <u>Problem</u>: The oath — Benjamin threatened with extinction
>   "Holy" war against Jabesh-gilead
> The rape of the daughters of Shiloh

---

176. Contrast Exod. 22:16-17, which deals with seduction in which there is consent rather than capture. In this case the father does have the right of veto.

177. Matthews, *Judges and Ruth,* p. 200, who refers to the work of Carolyn Pressler, *The View of Women Found in the Deuteronomic Family Laws,* Beihefte zur Zeitschrift für die alttestamentliche Wissenschaft 216 (Berlin: de Gruyter, 1993), p. 39.

178. See the comments above on v. 17.

179. The "daughter" motif is a further link between the two incidents (19:24; 21:21).

The conclusion of the story (21:1-24) turns out to be a highly satirical narrative episode in which the assembly, headed by the elders, resorts to a mixture of force, casuistry, and guile to circumvent an oath sworn at Mizpah without actually breaking it. The behavior of the assembly, like that of the host in Gibeah, is a comedy of correctness. The narrative finally moves to a point of fragile equilibrium, with calm restored in 21:23-24. Israel has miraculously survived intact!

e. Epilogue: No King in Israel (21:25)

> 25 *In those days there was no king in Israel; everyone did what was right in his own eyes.*

25 This last occurrence of the refrain rings down the curtain on the story of the Levite and his concubine and on the book's presentation of the judges period as a whole. It attributes the troubles that have threatened Israel's continued existence to two things: extreme individualism expressed in religious and moral anarchy (everyone doing *what was right in his own eyes*), and the absence of a stable, central authority (a *king*) capable of maintaining order. It also foreshadows what is to come (the institution of the monarchy), but leaves us wondering, in view of the disasters that have attended kingship in the body of the book,[180] whether, in the end, kingship will fare any better than judgeship has done.

Summary Reflections on 19:1–21:25

The story of the Levite and his concubine has turned out to be a long and complex narrative, with many twists and turns in which a great many things have happened. But what has it all been about? Is there a unifying theme? In the story of Micah and the Danites in chapters 17–18 the theme was realized principally through the character of Micah and the reversal of his fortunes in the course of the narrative. He figured in all three episodes, and even after he was no longer present his name continued to be mentioned, so that he served as a kind of reference point to shed light on the subsequent behavior of the Danites. No character has such a central significance for the theme of chapters 19–21. The Levite at first appears to be destined to fulfill such a role but disappears without a trace after his speech to the assembly. We never hear what happens to him. The interest lies not so much in the Levite as a person but as the convenor of the assembly. The main function of the Levite is to contribute to the critique of the assembly as an institution; once he has ful-

---

180. Especially in the Gideon-Abimelech narrative.

filled this purpose, he is simply dropped from the story. The same is true of the old man of Gibeah. His function is to contribute to a critique of Israelite hospitality in the period; his personal fortunes are of no intrinsic interest. The same is true of the rapists of Gibeah; for all we know they could have been among the six hundred survivors. The story of the Levite and his concubine is essentially a piece of social criticism of a moral nature. It shows how Israel's hospitality, warfare, justice, and politics were all debased because of the moral blindness and/or perversity of its citizens (including Levites and elders). The institutions that should have given Israel social cohesion and stability were so compromised that they could no longer do so. Yahweh's displeasure is expressed in the chastisement he brings to bear on the whole Israelite community. The outcome (Israel chastened but preserved) testifies to his commitment to Israel's continued existence and his capacity to rule in the midst of chaos.[181]

Chapters 17–21 as the Conclusion to the Book

Chapters 17-21 complete the book, first of all, in the purely aesthetic sense of giving it a balanced, symmetrical shape: the "variations" of 3:7–16:31 are preceded by an "overture" in two parts (1:1–2:6; 2:7–3:6), and followed by a "coda" in two parts (17:1–18:31; 19:1–21:25).

These chapters also complete the book in a rhetorical-literary sense. An effect of literary bracketing or closure is produced by the way these closing chapters of the book pick up and complement elements from the introduction. The frequent reference to Judah here (17:7, 8, 9; 18:12; 19:1, 2, 18) recalls the prominence given to Judah in 1:1-19; the reference to Jebus/Jerusalem as a "city of foreigners" in 19:10-12 recalls the note in 1:21 about the failure of the Benjaminites to expel the Jebusites from it; the weeping at Bethel in 20:18, 26 recalls the weeping at Bochim/Bethel in 2:1-5; and the account of the forced migration of the Danites in chapter 19 recalls the failure of the Danites to gain a secure foothold in their allotted territory in 1:34. The most striking instance of such back-reference is the almost word-for-word repetition of 1:1-2 in 20:18:

> 1:1-2   The Israelites asked Yahweh, "Who will go up to the Canaanites for us first, to fight them?" Yahweh replied, "Judah will go up."

> 20:18   The Israelites asked God, "Who will go up for us first to the battle with the Benjaminites?" Yahweh replied, "Judah first."

---

181. Cf. Boling, "No King in Israel," p. 5.

A similar principle of composition is evident here as in the return to Ophrah at the end of the Gideon story, or the return to Zorah at the end of the Samson story. The bracketing signals the completion of the literary unit and invites us to compare the circumstances the characters find themselves in at the close with those they were in at the beginning.

In terms of thematic development, these chapters come after the climax that is reached in the Samson episode and resonate with the rest of the book and with the Samson episode in particular. The refrain that sums up the religious and moral chaos depicted in these closing chapters as "everyone doing what was right in their own eyes" (17:6; 21:25) uses the same language as was used in chapter 14 to describe Samson's behavior, first by Samson himself, then by the narrator:

"Get her for me, for she is right in my eyes" (14:3).

She was right in Samson's eyes (14:7).

So, in retrospect, Samson appears as the typical Israelite of the period, a perspective on him that echoes the implicit identification of Samson with Israel that we found in the Samson story itself.

Other ways in which chapters 17–21 echo elements in the body of the book include the following:

a. After featuring prominently in the Samson episode, the theme of "knowing and not knowing" resurfaces at a key moment in the story of Micah and the Danites ("Now I know that Yahweh will treat me well" [17:13]), and occurs in a more marginal role in the account of the war against Benjamin. In 20:31-32 the Benjaminites go to confront their enemies again as Samson did in 16:20, unaware, like him, that an ambush has been set for them.

b. The way Yahweh responds to Israel's inquiries in 20:18-25 but not in 21:3 makes the same point that was made by the "calling on Yahweh" theme in 3:7–16:31: while Yahweh is the God of Israel, he is not at their beck and call, and cannot be manipulated by them.

c. The oath that leads to the rape of the virgins in 21:1 recalls Jephthah's vow in 11:30 that led to the sacrifice of his virgin daughter. The daughters of Shiloh, like Jephthah's daughter, "come out with dances," unaware of the fate that is about to overtake them (21:21; 11:34).

d. Micah's manufacture of an ephod (17:5) reminds us of the similar action of Gideon (8:27).

And so we could go on; there are other echoes of the body of the book in these final chapters,[182] though most are of only minor significance.

But chapters 17-21 do more than echo things that have featured in the body of the book. They also bring to a head one issue that has been only a subtheme there, namely, the danger that Israel's internal situation may become so chaotic that it might implode and destroy itself. There is already potential for that in the curse pronounced on Meroz in 5:23 because its inhabitants "did not come to the help of Yahweh." The civil war motif enters explicitly with Gideon and Abimelech, and appears again in the Jephthah narrative (8:1; 9:1-57; 12:1-6). In the Samson story Judahite and Danite are at loggerheads with one another (15:11-13) and Israel as such seems incapable of any action all. But the climactic treatment of this theme is clearly the outright war against the Benjaminites in chapter 20. Paradoxically it is civil war that finally produces a unified Israel again — a tragicomic conclusion, as Boling has rightly described it.[183]

The forced migration of the Danites in chapter 18 is a pointed reminder that the program of conquest and settlement envisaged at the outset of the book was never fully realized. The reference to Jebus as a city of foreigners is another reminder of this (19:12). So, too, is the rather curious note in 21:12 that Shiloh, where the Israelites were camped, was "in the land of Canaan," a phrase that recalls the frequent mention of Canaan and Canaanites in the introduction (17 times in 1:1–3:6). Elsewhere in the book Canaan is mentioned only in the Deborah-Barak episode, where the enemies are specifically the "kings of Canaan" (5:19; cf. 4:2, 23, 24). Kiriath-arba has become Hebron (1:10), Kiriath-sepher has become Debir (1:11), Zephath has become Hormah (1:17), Luz has become Bethel (1:23), and Laish has become Dan (18:29), but at the end of the book *'ereṣ kᵉnāʿan* (the land of Canaan) has still not become *'ereṣ yiśrāēl* (the land of Israel).[184] Israel continues to live in a land it has not fully conquered and occupied. This is precisely the state of affairs the introduction indicated would be the result of Israel's persistent apostasy throughout the judges period (2:20-21). In these closing chapters the situation foreshadowed in 2:20-21 becomes a settled state of affairs. The Danites find a solution to their particular problem (ch. 18), and Israel as a whole occupies itself with more pressing matters (chs. 19–21), but the omi-

182. For example, the left-handed Benjaminites of 20:16 are reminiscent of Ehud (3:15). Zorah and Eshtaol figure in both the Samson and Micah stories (13:25; 16:31; 18:2, 11), as does the motif of "eleven hundred [pieces] of silver" (16:5; 17:2, 3). The Levite's attempt at reconciliation in 19:3 recalls that of Samson in 15:1. Micah's *pesel* (idol) of 17:3-4 recalls the *pᵉsîlîm* (idols) of 3:19, 26.

183. "No King in Israel," p. 44; *Judges*, pp. 37-38.

184. Cf. Malamat's comments in "The Danite Migration," pp. 14-16, on the renamimg of conquered cities — a phenomenon found throughout the conquest traditions.

nous note sounded in 18:30 — "until the day of the captivity of the land" — indicates that the unresolved problem of apostasy is destined to have serious, long-term consequences for Israel's tenure in Canaan. A further indication of what lies ahead is contained in the setting given to the events narrated here by the refrain of 17:6, 18:1, 19:1, and 21:25: "In those days there was no king in Israel." The primary function of this refrain, though, is closure. It cuts off the narrative flow of the book by assigning all the events in these closing chapters to the same, broadly defined period. The effect is heightened by the fact that the last occurrence of the refrain falls at the very end of the book.

The second element of the refrain draws attention to the way the material in these final chapters complements that in the main body of the book. The negative refrain of chapters 3–16, "the Israelites did what was *evil* in the eyes of Yahweh," finds its positive counterpart here in "everyone doing what is *right* in their own eyes" (17:6 and 21:25), with the Samson story providing the link between them:

> Israel does what is evil in the eyes of Yahweh (chs. 3–16).
> Samson does what is right in his own eyes.
> Everyone does what is right in their own eyes (chs. 17–21).

The shift in focus from the sin of Israel to the sins of the individuals and communities that comprise Israel is mediated through the figure of Samson, who is both Samson himself and a symbol of Israel. The expression "*right* in their own eyes" nicely reflects the comedy of correctness that emerges in these final chapters. In all these ways the two narratives of chapters 17–21 complement those in the rest of the book and bring to an end its account of Israel's turbulent history in the judges period — the complete literary and theological treatment of an era.

INDEX OF AUTHORS

513

INDEX OF SUBJECTS

INDEX OF SCRIPTURE REFERENCES